Francis Drake

The Indian Tribes of the United States

Their History, Antiquities, Customs, Religion, Arts, Language....: Vol. II.

Francis Drake

The Indian Tribes of the United States
Their History, Antiquities, Customs, Religion, Arts, Language....: Vol. II.

ISBN/EAN: 9783337182854

Printed in Europe, USA, Canada, Australia, Japan

Cover: Foto ©ninafisch / pixelio.de

More available books at **www.hansebooks.com**

SOI-EN-GA-RAH-TA
OR
KING HENDRICK.

THE
INDIAN TRIBES

OF THE

UNITED STATES:

THEIR

HISTORY, ANTIQUITIES, CUSTOMS, RELIGION, ARTS, LANGUAGE,
TRADITIONS, ORAL LEGENDS, AND MYTHS.

EDITED BY

FRANCIS S. DRAKE.

ILLUSTRATED WITH ONE HUNDRED FINE ENGRAVINGS ON STEEL.

IN TWO VOLUMES.
VOL. II.

PHILADELPHIA:
J. B. LIPPINCOTT & CO.
LONDON: 16 SOUTHAMPTON STREET, COVENT GARDEN.
1884.

CONTENTS OF VOLUME II.

PERIOD I.

EUROPEAN DISCOVERY AND EXPLORATION.

CHAPTER	PAGE
I.—The Landing of Juan Ponce de Leon in Florida, and of Lucas Vasquez de Ayllon in South Carolina—The Ancient Chicora	9
II.—Verazzani explores the Atlantic Coast	13
III.—Narvaez explores Florida and discovers the Appalachian or Floridian Group of Tribes . .	16
IV.—Cartier sails up the St. Lawrence	21
V.—Expedition of De Soto to Florida—Appalachian Tribes—The Dakotas—Discovery of the Mississippi	30
VI.—Coronado's Expedition into New Mexico—The Zuñi, Moqui, Navajoe, and Cognate Tribes .	48
VII.—Voyages of Ribault and Laudonnière—Menendez—Retaliatory Expedition of De Gourgues—Founding of St. Augustine	57

PERIOD II.

EARLY EUROPEAN SETTLEMENTS.

I.—Discovery of Virginia—Efforts for its Colonization—Sir Walter Raleigh—Sir Richard Greenville—Settlement on Roanoke Island abandoned—The Aborigines—Jamestown settled—Captain John Smith—Opechancanough—Massacre of the Colonists—Indian Population	64
II.—The Hudson River explored—The Dutch settle Manhattan—Indian War—Manhattan becomes the English Colony of New York—Indians of New York	80
III.—Champlain founds Quebec and the Canadian Settlements	86
IV.—Settlement of the New England Colonies—Massasoit—Efforts to Christianize the Indians—Their Manners and Customs—The Pequots	87
V.—Maryland settled—Aboriginal Population on the Shores of the Chesapeake—The Susquehannocks—The Andastes	95
VI.—Pennsylvania colonized—The Lenni Lenape	108
VII.—Settlement of the Carolinas	111

PERIOD III.

WAR OF RACES—EARLY COLONIAL HISTORY.

CHAPTER	PAGE
I.—The Pequot Tribe and the Pequot War—Destruction of Fort Mystic—Flight and Extinction of the Tribe	115
II.—The Narragansetts—War between Uncas and Miantonomo	122
III.—The Pokanoket Tribe and Philip's War—The Narragansetts join Philip and are defeated and humbled—Overthrow and Death of Philip	125
IV.—The Merrimac Valley and Abenaki Tribes—King William's War—Governor Dudley's War—Sebastian Rale—Lovewell's Fight	146
V.—The Southern Indians—Massacre of White Settlers—Wars with the Tuscaroras, Yamassoes, Natchez, and Chickasaws—Settlement of Georgia	152
VI.—The Aquinoshioni, or Iroquois—Governor Shirley's War—Capture of Louisburg—Treaty of Aix-la-Chapelle—The Outagamies, or Foxes	159

PERIOD IV.

FRANCE AND ENGLAND CONTEND FOR THE POSSESSION OF THE OHIO VALLEY.

I.—Policy of France—Her Indian Allies—Policy of England—The Iroquois—Sir William Johnson—The Ohio Company—Washington	166
II.—Braddock's Defeat	182
III.—Kittanning destroyed—Battle of Lake George—Capture of Oswego and Fort William Henry	187
IV.—Campaigns of 1758-59—Grant's Defeat—Bouquet's Battle—Reduction of Fort Du Quesne—Conference with the Iroquois—Conquest of Canada—Its Influence upon the Hostile Tribes	192
V.—War with the Cherokees	205
VI.—Conspiracy of Pontiac—Detroit besieged—Frontier Posts captured—Dalzell's Defeat—Battle of Bushy Run—Relief of Fort Pitt—Siege of Detroit raised	210
VII.—Expeditions of Bouquet and Bradstreet—Pacification of the Tribes—Death of Pontiac	220
VIII.—Logan—Dunmore's Expedition—Battle of Point Pleasant—Peace concluded—Indian Trade—Captain Jonathan Carver—Census of the Tribes	230

PERIOD V.

THE AMERICAN REVOLUTION.

I.—State of the Indian Tribes—Brant—Action of Congress—Invasion of Canada, and Defeat at the Cedars	240
II.—The Johnsons—St. Leger invades New York—Fort Stanwix—Battle of Oriskany	248
III.—Employment of Indians in War—Address of Congress to the Tribes—Massacres of Wyoming, Cherry Valley, and Ulster	256

CONTENTS OF VOLUME II. 5

| CHAPTER | PAGE |

IV.—Hostilities with the Western Indians—The Shawnees—Cornstalk—Fort Henry—Conquest of Southern Illinois—Fort Laurens 264
V.—Battle of Minnisink—Sullivan ravages the Iroquois Territory—Indian and Tory Raids in Western New York—Cherokee Hostilities—Massacre of the Moravian Delawares . . 271
VI.—Border Wars of Kentucky—Boonesborough attacked—Bowman's Expedition—Estill's Defeat—Battle of the Blue Licks—The Creeks attack General Wayne 282

PERIOD VI.

POST-REVOLUTIONARY.

I.—Indian Policy of the United States—Treaties with the Tribes 287
II.—Establishment of the Northwestern Territory—War with the Western Tribes—Harmar's Defeat—Scott's Expedition—St. Clair's Defeat—Conference with Brant—Wayne's Campaign—Victory of the Maumee Rapids—Pacification of Greenville 295
III.—Explorations of Lewis and Clarke—Lieutenant Pike—Elements of Discord—Tecumseh and the Prophet organize the Tribes for a Conflict with the United States—Battle of Tippecanoe 308
IV.—War of 1812—Disasters on the Canadian Frontier—Detroit surrendered—Defeat at the River Raisin—Dudley's Defeat—Victory of the Thames, and Death of Tecumseh . . 317
V.—Hostilities with the Creeks—Massacre at Fort Mims—Battles of Tullushatches, Talladega, Hillabee, Attasee, Emuckfau, Enotochopco, and Tohopeka—Surrender of Weatherford—Capture of Pensacola—The War ended 324
VI.—Treaties with the Northwestern Tribes, and Explorations of their Territories—The Chippewas—The Sioux—Cession of Indian Lands—Chippewa Agency established at Sault Ste. Marie 336
VII.—Emigration of the Eastern Cherokees sanctioned—Treaties with the Southern Tribes—Indian Bureau organized 349

PERIOD VII.

REMOVAL OF THE TRIBES WEST OF THE MISSISSIPPI.

I.—Plan of Removal—Statistics of the Tribes 353
II.—Removal begun—Creek Difficulties—Death of the Chief McIntosh—Treaty for the Final Settlement—Boundary Treaties with the Northwestern Tribes 361
III.—Congress authorizes the Colonizing of the Indians in the West—The Tribes generally concur in the Plan 369
IV.—The Black-Hawk War 374
V.—Subdivision of the Indian Territory among the Emigrant Tribes—Important Treaties . 380
VI.—War with the Seminoles of Florida—Massacre of Dade's Command—Battle of the Withlacoochee—Battle of Okeechobee—Osceola—General Worth brings the War to a Close . 387
VII.—Removal of the Cherokees—Opposed by the Ross Party—Effected peaceably by General Scott 394
VIII.—Emigration of the Tribes, continued—Their Condition—Ravages of the Smallpox—Discords between the Eastern and Western Cherokees—Boudinot and the Ridges assassinated—Close of the First Decade of Colonization 399

CONTENTS OF VOLUME II.

PERIOD VIII.

INDIAN AFFAIRS SINCE THE ACQUISITION OF NEW MEXICO AND CALIFORNIA.

CHAPTER	PAGE
I.—Organization of the Territories of Kansas and Nebraska—Hostilities in California and Oregon—Sioux War of 1862-63 in Minnesota—The Cherokees in the Rebellion	413
II.—Operations against the Indians of New Mexico and Arizona in 1862-63-64, in 1869-72, and in 1880—Massacre of Friendly Apaches at Camp Grant—Comanches defeated by Colonel Mackenzie—Victoria's Band of Apaches destroyed	420
III.—Hostilities with the Cheyennes, Arapahoes, and Sioux—Sand Creek Massacre—Powder River War—Massacre of Colonel Fetterman's Command—Hancock's Expedition—Powell's Engagement	423
IV.—Indian Peace Commission of 1867-68—Treaties with the Hostile Tribes—Report of the Commissioners—General Sheridan—Renewal of Hostilities—Forsyth's Battle—Surprise and Slaughter of Black Kettle and his Band—Cessation of the War	428
V.—Troubles in Montana—Piegan Massacre—Red Cloud visits Washington—Cheyenne, Arapahoe, and Wichita Chiefs visit New York and Boston—Modoc War—Black Hills Expedition—Unlawful Order of General Sheridan—Sioux and Cheyenne War of 1876—Destruction of Crazy Horse's Village—Battle of the Rosebud—Massacre of General Custer's Command—Agency Indians disarmed and dismounted—Sitting Bull surrenders—General McKenzie destroys a Large Cheyenne Village—Bannock War—Flight of Dull Knife's Band of Northern Cheyennes	435
VI.—Attempt to remove Joseph's Band of Nez Percés resisted—Battles of White Bird Cañon and the Clearwater—Pursuit of Joseph's Band by General Howard—Repulse of General Gibbon—Stampede of Howard's Pack-Train—Battle of Bear-Paw Mountain, and Surrender of the Indians to General Miles—Troubles with the Utes—Cession of their Lands, September 13, 1873—Murder of Agent Meeker at the White River Agency—Attack on Major Thornburgh's Command—Utes agree to leave Colorado and settle on a Reservation	442

LIST OF PLATES.

		PAGE
83.	FRONTISPIECE.—Soi-en-ga-rah-ta, or King Hendrick.	
84.	De Ayllon attacked by the Indians	10
85.	De Soto at Tampa Bay	32
86.	Landing of Amidas and Barlow in Virginia	65
87.	Esopus Landing, Hudson River	82
88.	The Ohio River from the Summit of Grave Creek Mound	130
89.	Pittsburg in 1790	196
90.	Falls of Montreal River	202
91.	Ruins of Old Fort Mackinac, 1763	212
92.	Michilimackinac	224
93.	Red Jacket	291
94.	Falls of St. Anthony	309
95.	Valley of the Minnesota (St. Peter's) River	342
96.	Itasca Lake, Source of the Mississippi	377
97.	Humboldt, California	414
98.	Dakota Encampment	417
99.	Emigrants attacked by the Comanches	420
100.	Dakota Village	426

THE INDIAN TRIBES
OF THE
UNITED STATES.

PERIOD I.

EUROPEAN DISCOVERY AND EXPLORATION.

CHAPTER I.

THE LANDING OF JUAN PONCE DE LEON IN FLORIDA, AND OF LUCAS VASQUEZ DE AYLLON IN SOUTH CAROLINA—THE ANCIENT CHICORA.

It had required but twenty years from the period of the discovery of America by Columbus to spread the Spanish power from San Domingo through the Caribbean Islands and around the Cuban shores to the Straits of Florida. Juan Ponce de Leon, Governor of Porto Rico, whose youth had been passed in military service in Spain, landed in 1512 on the peninsula of Florida, as if he was about to realize the long-taught fable of the garden of the Hesperides. To his imagination its crystal fountains appeared, as the natives had depicted them, as the fountains of youth. It is known that the cretaceous deposits of this peninsula yield copious springs of the most transparent water. That these pure springs should excite the admiration and superstition of the Indians, and that the natives should form extravagant notions of their sanative qualities, is not strange, nor that reports of their extraordinary virtues should be carried to the neighboring coasts of Cuba. But it is amazing that such stories should have gained belief, even in the low state of knowledge which characterized the opening of the sixteenth century.

Entertaining such a belief, however, Ponce de Leon, the discoverer of the Florida shore, landed near the mouth of the St. John's River. The balmy airs of a tropical spring, redolent with the aroma of flowers, such as saluted his senses on landing, were not calculated to dispel his prior notions of an elysium. From the fact of the day of his discovery being Easter Sunday, and from the luxuriance of the vegetation, he named the country Florida. He was informed that some of the limpid springs were of such wonderful virtue that they would restore the vigor of youth to the person who bathed in them. In search of these fountains of youth he roved over the country. During these excursions the suspicions and animosity of the Indians were excited, and he at last paid the forfeit of his life for his credulity, dying in Cuba in 1521 from wounds received at their hands.

The first attempt to found a government and plant a colony in North America, within the present territorial area of the United States, was in South Carolina. This was about six years before Cortez set sail for Mexico, some fifteen years prior to the descent of Narvaez on the Gulf coasts of Florida, and just a quarter of a century before the celebrated expedition of De Soto.

The knowledge of geographical truth is of slow growth. Florida appears to have been looked upon very generally at this time as a garden of the Hesperides. It chanced soon after that a Spanish mariner, named Miruela, visited the coasts of Georgia and Carolina in quest of traffic with the natives. In this traffic he received a small quantity of gold. The incident created a sensation on his return to San Domingo, where a commercial company was formed to prosecute the discovery thus made. Several men in official positions engaged in this enterprise, the principal of whom was Lucas Vasquez de Ayllon. Two vessels were, in 1520, despatched to the coast prepared for the trade. These reached the mouth of the river Combahee, in South Carolina, where a profitable traffic ensued. The coast was called Chicora, and the Indians Chicoreans. When the trade was finished, the natives were invited to gratify their curiosity to go below-decks, but they were no sooner there than the hatches were closed, and the vessels immediately hoisted sail for San Domingo. One of them foundered on the way, and all on board were lost. The other reached San Domingo, and the Indians were sold as slaves.

In the mean time, Vasquez de Ayllon, who exercised the functions of an auditor and judge at San Domingo, filled with the idea that the newly-discovered province of Chicora abounded in the precious metals, had visited the court of Spain, and made such representations of the region and its natives that he returned with the commission of Adelantado of the newly-discovered country, with authority to found a colony. At San Domingo a squadron of three ships, with Miruela for chief pilot, was fitted out in 1526. Entering by the Straits of St. Helena, Vasquez proceeded to the mouth of the Combahee, the scene of their prior traffic and perfidy, where the largest of the three vessels was stranded. Here he resumed the traffic with the Indians. During this time nothing was revealed on the part of the natives to indicate that they had any remembrance of the carrying off of their countrymen. Having finished his trade, Vasquez went to seek a suitable site for his colony, and pitched on a spot on the waters of Port Royal Sound, at, or perhaps a little south of, the present town of Beaufort, South Carolina. A part of his crews had landed to prepare for the new town, a small number still remaining on board the vessels at anchor in the

roadstead. They had hardly commenced their labors when a deputation of the Combahee Indians arrived to invite the men to attend a great feast at the village at the mouth of the Combahee. Two hundred persons accepted this invitation, and were received and treated with the utmost hospitality. They were feasted for three days. When the feast was over, and while the men were wrapped in profound slumber, the Indians arose near the break of day and massacred the whole party. Not a man was spared. The Indians then proceeded in hot haste to the selected site of the new town of Vasquez, where they knew there was lax discipline. They fell on the parties of men in their disorganized state and put many to death. A sanguinary contest ensued. Indian clubs, spears, and arrows were arrayed against swords and matchlocks. Vasquez escaped, wounded, to his vessels, and died there, in October, 1526. Thus failed the first attempt to found a colony in the area of the United States. This incident presents a dark spot in Spanish colonial history that has been but little dwelt on by historians.

The perfidious treatment of the Indians on the seaboard of Carolina was doubtless one cause of the determined hostility with which the Spaniards were afterwards received on the Florida coasts. Verbal information was communicated by their nimble runners to other Indians with great celerity; and when people of the hated nation reappeared at subsequent periods, under the banners of Narvaez and De Soto, they encountered the most unflinching hostility.

The Chicorean Indians, who thus defended their coasts from invasion, appear to have been the ancient Uchees, who are now merged as an inconsiderable element in the great Muskoki family, but still preserve proud memories of their ancient courage, fame, and glory. We are informed by Colonel Benjamin Hawkins[1] that the Uchees formerly dwelt at Ponpon, Salkehatchie, and Silver Bluffs, in a belt of country which now forms part of Georgia and part of South Carolina, and that they were continually at war with the Muskokis, Cherokees, and Catawbas. By the first-named nation they were vanquished and nearly annihilated; but a few were carried away and incorporated with the conquering tribe, among whom the name and a few of the people still remain. The opinion that the Muskokis prevailed over the Uchees is confirmed by the Muskoki words which are found in the names of streams and places along the southern part of the sea-coast of South Carolina.[2] When De Soto, in 1539, reached Silver Bluff, on the Savannah, the ancient Cofachique, the Indians of that place exhibited to him pieces of armor and arms, which the Spaniards supposed to have belonged to De Ayllon.

The defeat of Vasquez de Ayllon operated to discourage the Spanish from attempting further conquests in that quarter for many years; but it appears from a map in the third volume of Navarrete that the limits of the discoveries of De Soto extended much farther to the north than other writers have supposed him to have reached. Peter Martyr observes that the northern shores of the Gulf of Mexico

---

[1] Sketch of the Creek Country in 1798–1799.
[2] Such is Coosawhatchie, from *Coosa*, the name of a band of Creeks, and *Hatchee*, a creek or river.

had been explored in the year 1516. In 1521, the year of the final fall of Mexico, Francisco Garay received a royal patent to colonize a region which appears to have stretched north of the Panuco or Rio Grande on the Gulf. But it was not till six years afterwards that anything of note was done in the conquest of Florida proper. It is evident from several sources that the Gulf coasts of Mexico at this time had been pretty well ranged by mariners, and that this region had begun to furnish adventurers with a theme of intense excitement. In 1517, Francisco Hernandez de Cordova discovered Yucatan, and the next year Juan de Grijalva made the discovery of the Indian-Mexican empire, the conquest of which was undertaken by Cortez in 1519 and finished with such fame and glory to himself in 1521. The spirit of chivalry seemed to have revived; but the new enterprises were not undertaken for the righting of wrongs, after the manner which Cervantes has so happily satirized, nor were the Spaniards inspired by the example of the Crusaders, who aimed at wresting Palestine from the hands of the infidels. All the new conquests had for their chief object the filling of the pockets of the conquerors with gold. In 1525 and 1526, Pizarro, fired by the successes of Cortez, began those discoveries which led to the conquest of Peru, an enterprise which he completed with excessive perfidy and cruelty in 1535.

These facts may serve to show the furor for the glory of discovery which filled the Spanish court and nation at this era, and may also explain the motives which actuated the chivalric discoverers who landed among the athletic Appalachian tribes of the northern coasts of the Gulf of Mexico. These tribes had no mines, no cities, no aqueducts, no palaces, no emperors; scarcely was there a road or path in their territory that could be traversed without the cunning of a fox. But they were brave and proud. They were democrats, having a simple government of chiefs and councils. Each warrior had a voice in public affairs. They had a high sense of natural right and tribal independence. They not only considered the lands their own, but believed that they had been given to them by the Great Spirit,—thus creating a right that could not, they deemed, be disputed. And when they were recklessly invaded and treated with the harshness and inhumanity which marked the course of De Leon and Vasquez de Ayllon on their eastern borders, they stood manfully by their rights. That the Spanish atrocities were known, and the details circulated among other tribes, prior to the expeditions of Narvaez and De Soto, cannot be doubted. For fifteen years before this event the waters of the Gulf and the Caribbean Sea had been traversed by the vessels of Spain; and wherever they landed the Spaniards created the impression among the natives that white men were freebooters and pirates.

CHAPTER II.

VERAZZANI EXPLORES THE ATLANTIC COAST.

The next reconnoissance of the Atlantic coast tribes was made by Jean de Verazzani. France was not unobservant of the events passing in the West Indies and Florida, and determined to share North America with Spain. The name Florida at that time was applied to all of North America north of the Gulf of Mexico.[1] Verazzani was a noted Italian mariner, a native of Florence, who had been employed by France for some time, with four public vessels, in cruising against the Spanish commerce. Separated from his consorts in a tempest, he resolved to undertake a voyage of discovery and make a reconnoissance of the then indefinitely extended region of Florida. He left the outer isle of the Madeira group, one of the barren islands called the Desertas, on the 17th of January, 1524. About the middle of March he made the American coast, in latitude 34°, at a point somewhere near the present position of Wilmington, North Carolina.[2] Thence he sailed south in search of a harbor, until he noticed the appearance of "palm-trees," or palmettoes, characteristic trees of the coast-region of South Carolina and Georgia. He then changed his course, holding towards the north, and ran down the coast, with occasional landings, till he reached his former landfall, and found himself near a flat diluvial shore of sand-hills and islets, peopled with Indians, but without a harbor. He anchored off the coast and landed. The Indians were in the greatest excitement, running to and fro in wonder and fear. Having by signs of friendship induced some of them to approach, he gradually quieted them, and they brought him some provisions. They were naked, save an *azian*, or small apron of furs. They ornamented their heads with bunches of feathers. They were well shaped, with black eyes, and straight black hair, and were very swift of foot.

It is impossible, from so general a description, to tell what group of tribes he was among, or what region he was in. If he saw at this landing "cypress, laurels, and palm-trees," he had probably retraced his steps to latitude 34°; and, judging from the description he gives of the shore, he was, we believe, off the coast of North Carolina. Still sailing on, he came to a part of the coast which trended east, when, seeing many fires and the natives appearing friendly, he ordered his boat ashore, but the surf was too violent to permit landing. One of the sailors here offered

---

[1] This fact must be borne in mind by naturalists in investigating the history and spread of quadrupeds and other species stated to inhabit Florida in 1600.

[2] New York Historical Collections, vol. i. p. 23. Forster is greatly mistaken in supposing this place to have been in "New Jersey, or Staten Island, or Long Island." (Voyages, p. 434.)

to swim ashore with some presents, but when he came near his fears prevailed, and, throwing out his presents, he attempted to return to the ship, but the waves cast him on the strand half dead and quite senseless. The Indians immediately ran to his assistance, dried his clothes before a fire, and did everything to restore him. His alarm, however, was excessive. When they pulled off his clothes to dry them, he thought they were going to sacrifice him to the sun, which then shone prominent over the hills. As soon as he was restored, the natives gently led him to the shore, and then retired to a distance, until the ship's boat had been sent for him, and they saw him safely get on board.

Verazzani now went on, and observed the coast still trending northward. After a run of fifty leagues, he anchored off a fine forest country, where twenty of his men landed and went two leagues into the interior. The Indians fled into the forest. The sailors caught an old woman and a young woman hidden in the grass. The old woman carried a child on her back, and had, besides, two little boys. The young woman had charge of three young girls. Both women shrieked vociferously as soon as they were discovered. The elder gave them to understand that the men had fled to the woods. She accepted something to eat at their hands, but the young woman refused it with scorn. The latter was a tall and well-shaped person, and they tried to take her with them, but she made such outcries and struggled so desperately that it was impossible. They took one of the boys.

These coast Indians had nets. Their canoes were made from solid trees, burned out with fire. Their arrows were pointed with bone. They were partly clothed with a vegetable tissue. No houses were seen. The trees denoted a more northerly climate than was suited to the palmettoes they had before observed; but the trees had vines climbing to their very tops. Three days were spent in the reconnoissance of these fish-eating Indians. Verazzani was now evidently on the coasts north of the capes of the Chesapeake or of the Delaware, a region then inhabited by numerous small tribes of the Algonkin family, who were without forest meats, subsisting chiefly on the productions of the sea-coasts, navigating the inlets and shores with log canoes, and using bone, and not flint, or hornstone, or jasper, as material for arrows and fish-hooks. These bands stretched apparently along the entire Maryland and New Jersey coasts to the Navasink Highlands and the land of the Metoacs.

Verazzani continued his voyage along these coasts until he came to the outflow of a "large river," and, entering it, found a good harbor, in north latitude 41°. This some historians suppose to have been the Bay of New York.[1] It was thus an Italian footstep that was first planted on these shores.[2] The surrounding country is described as being very pleasant. The Indians, who are pronounced a very fine race, showed

---

[1] Bancroft says Newport.
[2] Forster says, "The three great empires of those times, Spain, England, and France, made, each of them, use of an Italian to conduct the voyages of discovery set on foot by them. Spain employed Christopher Colon, a Genoese; England, Sebastian Cabot, a Venetian; and France, Jean de Verazzani, a Florentine."—*History of Northern Voyages and Discoveries*, p. 436.

him where the deep water was. A storm coming up, they landed on a well-cultivated island (probably Staten Island), beyond which spread the harbor, where they observed numerous canoes. We are indebted to Hakluyt for preserving Verazzani's description of this harbor:

"This land is situated in the parallel of Rome, in forty-one degrees, two tierces, but somewhat more cold by accidental causes. The mouth of the haven lieth open to the south, half a league broad, and, being entered within it, between the east and the north, it stretcheth twelve leagues, when it weareth broader and broader, and maketh a gulf about twenty leagues in compass, wherein are five small islands, very fruitful and pleasant, full of high and broad trees, among the which islands any great navy may ride safe, without any fear of tempest or other danger."

In this ample harbor he remained fifteen days, during which he frequently sent his boat and men, and went ashore himself, to obtain supplies and examine the country. Some of the men stayed two or three days on one of the islands. Their excursions extended five or six leagues into the interior, which was found to be "pleasant, and well adapted to the purposes of agriculture."

With the natives, who were, as we now know, of the Mohican family of the Algonkins, he had frequent intercourse, and he speaks of them with kindness. They were uniformly friendly,[1] and always accompanied his parties, in greater or less numbers, ashore. He describes them as of a russet color, with large black eyes, black hair, of good stature, well-favored, of a cheerful look, quick-witted, nimble, and athletic. He compares them to Saracens and Chinese. The women wore ornaments of wrought copper. Wood only was used in the construction of their wigwams, which were covered with coarse matting, called by him "straw."

This is the first description we have of members of the great Algonkin family of the shores of the North Atlantic. Verazzani appears to have had an aptitude for observing the character and condition of the natives and the geographical features of the country. The marked physical traits of land and people thus noticed by him were also observed and recorded a hundred years later, at the time of the landings in Virginia, under Raleigh, as well as those made by Hudson in New York, and by the English in Massachusetts.

Having refreshed himself and recruited his provisions at this point, on the 5th of May he continued his voyage northward, and after a run of one hundred and fifty leagues[2] he discovered high lands overgrown with forests. The Indians were found to be of savage habits. They lived on roots and other spontaneous products. A large party of the crew who landed here were received with a volley of arrows. He continued his voyage north to a point on the coast of Labrador, and, having given the name of New France to the region of his discoveries, returned to Dieppe, whence he writes his letter to Francis I., bearing date 8th July, 1524.

---

[1] Verazzani's Letter to Francis I.
[2] The leagues of the early voyagers must be computed at two miles.

CHAPTER III.

NARVAEZ EXPLORES FLORIDA AND DISCOVERS THE APPALACHIAN OR FLO-
RIDIAN GROUP OF TRIBES.

PANFILO DE NARVAEZ had been defeated in 1520 by Cortez at Cempoalla, during an attempt to arrest the conqueror of Mexico in his unauthorized career. After seven years' attendance at the court of Spain, expended in vain efforts to obtain redress for a gross civil and military wrong, he returned to Cuba with the appointment of Adelantado of Florida and the grant of full powers to conquer and govern the country. It is affirmed by De Vaca that he left Spain in July, 1527, with six hundred men, well officered by cavaliers and gentlemen. Owing to incidental delays at San Domingo, and to storms and shipwrecks on the coasts of Cuba, it was not until the 13th of April, 1528, that he landed near Tampa Bay, in Florida. His force had then been reduced by desertion to four hundred men and forty-two horses. With this small army he entered a country the geographical features of which opposed great obstacles to a direct march, and the region was soon found to be unable to yield an adequate subsistence for either the men or the horses. Besides this, Narvaez had no interpreter through whom he could communicate with the Indians. To drive the natives out of their impenetrable jungles and fastnesses, he carried bloodhounds along with him.

The Indians who had been descried from the ships' decks the day before he landed had fled, and left their wigwams in haste. As soon as his followers came ashore, he raised the ensigns of Spain, and took possession of the country in the name of the emperor, Charles V. His officers then presented him their commissions and had them recognized, and thus offered a sort of fealty to their civil and military governor. The next day the Indians who had fled came in, and made many signs, but, as there was no interpreter, there could be but little communication. The coast where he landed is a low alluvial tract, intersected with large indentations, bays, ponds, thickets, and streams, which offered the greatest impediments to the march of the troops. To avoid these, Narvaez kept inland, directing his naval forces to continue their explorations by water and to meet him at a more westerly point. He was employed from the 1st of May to the 17th of June in reaching the main channel of the Suwanee River, which he crossed high up.[1] He found its current very strong and deep, and lost a horse and horseman in crossing it, who were carried down the

---

[1] Suwanee is derived probably either from San Juan or from Shawnee. The term "Mucoso," in the narrative of Garcilasso de la Vega (preserved in Theodore Irving's Translation, p. 60, etc.), is nearly the accusative of the name "Little Bear" in the Chippewa dialect of the Algonkin.

stream and drowned. Narvaez was now among the Appalachians, an important group of tribes, who occupied the present area of Georgia, Florida, and the southern part of South Carolina, extending thence to the banks of the Mississippi. Its chief members were the Muskokis or Creeks, Choctaws[1] or Alabamas, and Chickasaws.[2] It is clear from tradition and philology that Florida at that time also contained a member of the Algonkin group, in the tribe of the Shawnees, who lived on friendly terms with the Creeks. These were all expert bowmen; and, although they would not stand their ground in bodies, they kept up a harassing war of details, wounding and killing men and horses at every opportunity.

Narvaez appears to have been deficient in knowledge of the Indian character, and he wholly underrated the effects of kindness and a sense of justice on their minds. His barbarous mutilation of the chief Hirrihigua, and his shocking cruelty to that chieftain's mother, soon after entering the country, produced a feeling of deep-rooted hostility, and was well calculated to make him and his nation abhorred wherever the story spread. It is related that Hirrihigua had offered a determined resistance to Narvaez, but afterwards formed a treaty of friendship with him. Becoming enraged at some subsequent conduct of the chief, which is unexplained, Narvaez directed his nose to be cut off, and caused his mother to be torn to pieces by dogs. Eleven years afterwards De Soto encountered the deepest hostility from this same chief, whom he used every means to conciliate, but without success.

The march of Narvaez from the scene of these atrocities was one unbroken series of hostilities on the part of the Indians. Some captives whom he took west of the Suwanee were compelled to act as guides. They led him through vast forests encumbered with fallen timber, which imposed the greatest toils. Through these his army struggled heroically. Not only were they wandering they knew not whither among solitudes and morasses, but they suffered from want of food and forage. To such a degree was this pressure felt that they were often, when a horse gave out, compelled to kill him and feast on his carcass. Narvaez, on leaving Cuba, was provisioned only to reach the coasts. He supposed he was about to enter a country ample in resources, and promised himself to quarter on the enemy, as Cortez had done. He had but two days' provision when he left the waters of Tampa. He and his followers had landed with their imaginations highly excited by visions of the golden provinces they supposed they were about to enter. Cities and towns flitted before their minds sparkling with the wealth of Mexico and Peru, and they expected to conquer lords and caciques who would supply them with food and auxiliaries. Disappointed at every step, hope still led them on. Their horses were mere skeletons when they landed, and became still more jaded by the long and harassing marches during which they had no time to recruit. The men fared little better. They marched fifteen days at the start with "two pounds of biscuit and half a pound

---

[1] Called Mobilians by Du Pratz.
[2] The fierceness of the attacks of the Chickasaws, their firing a village of which he had possessed himself, and then repeating the successful stratagem of Mauvila, may be said to have driven De Soto across the Mississippi.

of bacon" to a man; and there was no regular commissariat afterwards. They ate the soft crown or cabbage of the palmetto, and were relieved at several points by fields of corn, a grain which was mature about the middle of June. The magic word which led them on was "Apalache," the name of an Indian town. Here they expected to find a solace for all their toils, and a reward for all their losses, struggles, and afflictions. It was to their heated imaginations the town of "food and gold."

In sight of Apalache at last they came, but it proved a damper to all their sanguine hopes. There were forty[1] small Indian abodes of humble dimensions, in sheltered situations, and covered with thatch. The Spaniards were surrounded by dense woods and groves of tall trees, and by large bodies of fresh water, the country being without roads, bridges, or any other signs of civilization. They found, indeed, fields of maize fit for plucking, as well as some dried or ripe maize, and mortars of stone for pounding it. The houses contained also dressed deer-skins, and coarse "mantalets of thread." The men had all precipitately fled, but they soon returned in peace, asking for their women and children. This request was granted, but Narvaez detained a cacique, intending to make use of his authority as another Montezuma for swaying the Indians. This measure, however, had a contrary effect. The natives of Apalache were a more spirited people than the Aztecs. They became much incensed, and, returning the next day, attacked the Spaniards with great fury, and, after firing the houses, fled to the lakes and corn-fields with the loss of but one man.

Having beaten them off, Narvaez and his army remained in the town twenty-five days in order to recruit themselves. He was now evidently on the waters of the Appalachicola. The detained chief of the Apalaches, and the captives before made, were inquired of respecting the country and its resources. They replied that the surrounding country was full of great lakes and solitudes, that the land was little occupied, the people few and scattered, and that there was no place at all equal in population and resources to Apalache itself, but that south of them it was only nine days' journey to the sea, and that there was a town in that direction called Aute, and the Indians there had "much maize, beans, pumpkins, and fish."

To Aute, therefore, Narvaez directed his march. His course was obstructed by large bodies of water, through which the Spaniards had to wade. The Indians attacked them, captured their guide, and shot at them with their arrows from behind logs and trees, sorely wounding the men and horses. The Indians are spoken of as men of fine stature, great activity, very expert and determined bowmen, and most excellent and unerring marksmen, who could hit their mark at the distance of two hundred yards. One of these difficult defiles of water and woods followed another. For nine days the Indians hung around their skirts and harassed them, killing some of their men, wounding many more, and losing but two themselves. At the end of this time they reached Aute, from which all the inhabitants had fled, but they found an abundance of maize, pumpkins, and beans, ready for picking. By this time all

---

[1] Theodore Irving says "two hundred and forty." (Conquest of Florida, p. 30.)

hopes of gold and dominion had fled. To add to their distress, disease attacked the men, and their adventure was changed into a struggle for existence.

Narvaez now determined to search for the sea, which was near at hand; and, having discovered it, without finding his fleet or hearing any tidings of it, he resolved to build boats and continue his explorations along the shore. He was now at the extremity of his affairs. Unwell himself, and his men and animals wounded and exhausted, in an impassable country, with fierce enemies all around him, deserted by his fleet, and finding a conspiracy forming among his men, he was called speedily to decide upon a course of action. To build boats and embark with his miserable followers seemed the best course. But he was wholly without means for such a work. He had neither mechanics, tools, iron, pitch, nor rigging. The next day, while he pondered in perplexity, one of his men came and said he could make pipes out of wood, which could be converted into bellows by means of deer-skins. This idea was at once caught at. Stirrups, spurs, cross-bows, etc., were converted into nails, saws, axes, and other tools. Pitch was obtained from the pine; a kind of oakum was made from the bark or fibre of the palmetto; the tails and manes of the horses served as material for ropes, and the soldiers' shirts were made into sails. They killed their horses for food. Such heroic devotion, and such ingenious adaptation of means to ends, may possibly redeem Narvaez and his misguided followers from some measure of the reproach to which their previous cruel conduct and their complete failure in their enterprise have condemned them. In sixteen days, by hard work, they had five boats ready, each of twenty cubits' length. They were provisioned with oysters and maize, for which the men searched daily; and, as the Indians lay constantly in wait, ten of the Spaniards lost their lives in this hazardous search. Water was provided by filling the skins of horses, flayed entire and partly tanned.

They had now marched about two hundred and eighty leagues.[1] They had lost on the march forty men, and all of their horses but one. With the two hundred and eighty-one men, the remains of that army which had landed at La Cruz, Narvaez embarked on the Bay of Cavallos, at the mouth of a large river, which he had called Magdalena, and which is believed to be the Appalachicola. When all the men and lading were on board the boats, the gunwales were but "a span" above the water. For seven days the men conducted these fragile vessels through sounds and shallow bays, where there was no surf, before they put out in the open sea.

They also captured five canoes from the Indians, which enabled them to lighten the boats; and they made "waist-boards" to the boats, which raised the gunwales. Often they entered and traversed shallow bays. Provisions and water having failed, they suffered incredible hardships. For thirty days they proceeded westward towards the Mississippi,[2] but their only safety lay in creeping along the coast near the land.

---

[1] Buckingham Smith, the translator of De Vaca, thinks it was only two hundred and eighty *miles* (p. 32). This would give a fraction over four miles per day from Tampa Bay.

[2] It has been stated by Mr. Gallatin (*vide* Amer. Ethnol. Trans., vol. ii.) that Narvaez discovered the mouth of the Mississippi; but this is not sustained by De Vaca, and there is no other authority.

The frailty and inadequacy of their boats would not permit them to stand out boldly. If they landed unwarily, they were in danger of being massacred by the Indians, who skirted all this coast and manifested the most determined hostility. No intelligence was received by Narvaez of his fleet, nor was any trace of it found. Some of the men became delirious from drinking sea-water, and four of them died from this cause. One night they were attacked on an island where there was an Indian village in which they had been entertained, and Narvaez received a blow in the face from a stone. The Indians had but few arrows, and the Spaniards beat them off. Their miseries were every day accumulating. Stormy weather succeeded, and they experienced hunger and thirst in their worst forms. They kept on in company till the 1st of November, when the boats parted company. One of them foundered, it is believed, at Pensacola. It appears to have been near the Bay of Perdido that Narvaez was last seen. A storm was blowing off the land, and he told his officers and men that the time had arrived when each one must take care of himself. Many of the men were too weak to lift an oar. The wind increased as night came on. The commander was not afterwards seen by any person who survived to tell the story. The boat of Cabeça de Vaca was cast by the waves on an island a little to the west of this bay, where, famished and nearly lifeless, the Spaniards were kindly received by the Indians; for the latter were no longer hostile when their enemies were overthrown and their sense of humanity was appealed to. Thus terminated the expedition of Panfilo de Narvaez.[1]

Concerning the fate of this twice unsuccessful commander, we may observe that the geography of Florida fought against him; but his expedition was important, inasmuch as it gives us our first view of the Appalachian group of tribes.

Cortez, even in the worst state of his affairs, after the *noche triste*, when he was without food, defeated, and surrounded on all sides by fierce enemies, was marching over lands elevated seven thousand feet above the sea; Pizarro had the Andes beneath him; but Narvaez while in Florida was never a hundred feet above tidewater, and most of the time was wading through swamps and morasses not much raised above the level of the sea. We derive these details from the narrative of De Vaca, the treasurer and high sheriff of the contemplated government of Florida, and the only surviving officer of the expedition, who, after eight years of captivity among the Indians, with three companions, crossed the Mississippi and the Rio Grande del Norte, and, having traversed the breadth of the continent, arrived at Compostella, on the Gulf of California, finally returning to Spain in 1537.[2]

---

[1] From the bones and cooking-utensils found on Massacre Island, at the mouth of Mobile Bay, by D'Iberville, in 1699, a part of Narvaez's men appear to have met their fate at this spot.

[2] Narrative of Alva Cabeça de Vaca, translated by Buckingham Smith, Washington, 1851.

CHAPTER IV.

CARTIER SAILS UP THE ST. LAWRENCE.

The voyage of Verazzani, under the French flag, promised little or no advantage to the revenues of France, and consequently it attracted little attention, and was for some time even forgotten. In 1534, Admiral Philip Chabot represented to the king the advantages to be derived from sharing with Spain the rich prize of North America by establishing a colony. In accordance with this suggestion, Jacques Cartier, a mariner of St. Malo, in Normandy, was presented to the king, and was by him approved as a person suitable for the undertaking.

Cartier sailed from the port of St. Malo on the 20th of April, 1534, with two ships and one hundred and twenty-two men. His crew took a solemn oath before sailing "to behave themselves truly and faithfully in the service of the most Christian king, Francis I." The excitement concerning American discoveries was still unabated in the European courts. The conquest of Mexico had been completed only thirteen years before, and Pizarro was now in the height of his later triumphs at Truxillo, Guanuco, and Caxamarca.

After an unusually prosperous voyage of twenty days, Cartier made Cape "Buona Vista," in Newfoundland, which he states to be in north latitude 48° 30'. Here, meeting with ice, he made the haven to which he gave the name of St. Catherine, where he was detained ten days. This coast had been known since the voyage of John and Sebastian Cabot, in 1497, and had been frequently resorted to by fishing-vessels. Jean Denis, a native of Rouen, one of these fishermen, is said to have published a chart of it in 1506. Two years afterwards, Thomas Aubert brought the first natives from Newfoundland to Paris; and this is the date—1508—commonly assigned to the discovery of Canada. The St. Lawrence remained, however, undiscovered; nor does it appear that anything beyond a vague general knowledge of the coast and of its islands had then been ascertained. The idea was still entertained that America was an island, and that a passage to the Asiatic continent existed in those latitudes.

On the 21st of May, 1534, Cartier continued his voyage, sailing "north and by east" from Cape Buona Vista, and arrived at the Isle of Birds, so named on account of the unusual abundance of sea-fowl found upon it, with the young of which the men filled two boats; "so that," in the quaint language of the journal, "besides them which we did eat fresh, every ship did powder and salt five or six barrels." He also observed the godwit, and a larger but vicious bird, which received the name of margaulx. While at this island they descried a polar bear, which, in their presence, leaped into the sea and thus escaped. Subsequently, while crossing to the mainland, they encountered, as they supposed, the same animal swimming towards land, and "by main strength overtook her, whose flesh was as good to be eaten as the flesh of a calf two years old." This bear is described to have been "as large as a cow, and as white as a swan."

On the 27th, Cartier reached the harbor of "Carpunt," in the Bay of "Les Chasteaux," latitude 51°, where, on account of the accumulation of ice, he was constrained to remain until the 9th of June. The narrator of the voyage describes certain parts of the coast of Newfoundland and adjoining seas, the islands of St. Catherine, Blanc Sablon, Brest, the Isle of Birds, and a numerous group of islands called The Islets; but these memoranda are unconnected with any important observations or discoveries. Speaking of the Island of Brest and the Isle of Birds, he says they afford "great store of godwits, and crows with red beaks and red feet," which "make their nests in holes under ground, even as conies." Near this locality "there is great fishing."

On the 10th of June he entered a port in the newly-discovered island of Brest, to procure wood and water. Meantime boats were despatched to explore the islands, which were found to be so numerous "that it was not possible they might be told, for they continued about ten leagues beyond the said port." The explorers slept on an island, and the following day continued their discoveries along the coast. Having passed the islands, they found a haven, which was named St. Anthony, and one or two leagues beyond discovered a small river, named by them St. Servansport, where they reared a cross. Distant about three leagues from the last mentioned, another river of larger size was discovered, in which salmon were found. Upon this stream they bestowed the name of St. Jacques.

While at St. Jacques River they descried a ship from Rochelle on a fishing-cruise, and, rowing out in their boats, directed it to a port near at hand, in what is called "Jacques Cartier's Sound," "which," adds the narrator, "I take to be one of the best in all the world." The face of the country examined by the explorers was, however, of the most sterile and forbidding character, being little else than "stones and wild crags, and a place fit for wild beasts; for in all the north island," he continues, "I did not see a cart-load of good earth. Yet went I on shore in many places, and in the island of White Sand (Blanc Sablon) there is nothing else but moss and small thorns scattered here and there, withered and dry. To be short, I believe that this was the land that God allotted to Cain."

Immediately following this we have the first account of the natives. The men are described as being "of an indifferent good stature and bigness, but wild and unruly. They wear their hair tied on the top, like a wreath of hay, and put a wooden pin within it, or any other such thing, instead of a nail, and with them they bind certain birds' feathers. They are clothed with beast skins, as well the men as women, but that the women go somewhat straiter and closer in their garments than the men do, with their waists girded. They paint themselves with certain roan colors; their boats are made of the bark of birch-trees, with which they fish, and take great store of seals. And, as far as we could understand since our coming thither, that is not their habitation, but they came from the main land, out of *hotter*[1] countries, to catch the said seals and other necessaries for their living."

From this exploratory trip the boats returned, on the 13th, to the newly-styled harbor of Brest. On the 14th, it being Sunday, divine service was read, and the following day Cartier continued his voyage, steering southerly along the coast, which still wore a most barren and cheerless aspect. Much of this part of the narrative is occupied with the details of distances and soundings, as well as the names of capes and islands, of very little interest at the present day. On the 18th the voyagers saw a few huts upon the cliffs, and named this part of the coast "Les Granges," but they did not stop to form any acquaintance with the tenants. Cape Royal was passed, and duly named, on the 17th, and is described as "the greatest fishery of cods there possibly may be, for in less than an hour we took an hundred of them." On the 24th the island of St. John was discovered. Myriads of birds were seen upon the group of islands named "Margaulx," five leagues westward of which they discovered a large, fertile, and well-timbered island, to which the name of "Brion" was given. The contrast presented by the soil and productions of this island, compared with the bleak and waste shores they had previously visited, aroused their warm admiration; and, under the influence of this excitement, they here saw "wild corn," pease, gooseberries, strawberries, damask roses, and parsley, "with other sweet and pleasant herbs." Here, also, they observed the walrus, bear, and wolf.

Very little can be gleaned from the subsequent details of the voyage, until the arrival of the expedition in the Gulf of St. Lawrence. Mists, head-winds, barren rocks, sandy shores, storms, and sunshine alternate in the landscape presented to view. Much caution was requisite in tacking back and forth on an iron-bound coast, and the boats were frequently made use of in exploring the shores of the mainland. While thus employed near a shallow stream called the "River of Boats," they saw natives crossing it in their canoes, but, the wind beginning to blow towards the land, they were compelled to retire to their vessels without opening any communication with them. On the following day, while the boats were traversing the coasts, they saw a native running after them along the beach, who made signs directing them, as they supposed, to return towards the cape they had left. As soon as the boats turned, however, he fled: nevertheless they landed, and, fastening a knife and a woollen girdle to an upright staff as a good-will offering, returned to their vessels.

This part of the Newfoundland coast impressed them as being greatly superior, both in soil and in temperature, to the portions which they had before seen. In addition to the productions previously found at Brion Island, they noticed cedars, pines, white elm, ash, willow, and what are denominated "ewe-trees." Among the feathered tribes, the "thrush and stockdove" are mentioned; the latter, without doubt, being the passenger pigeon. The "wild corn," here again mentioned, is said to be "like

---

[1] I italicize the word "hotter" to denote the prevalent theory. They were searching for China or the East Indies.

unto rye," from which it may be inferred that it was the zizania, or wild rice, although the circumstance of its being an aquatic plant is not mentioned.

While running along this coast, Cartier appears to have been engrossed with the idea, so prevalent among the mariners of that era, of finding a passage to India; and it was probably on this account that he made so minute an examination of every inlet and bay, as well as of the productions of the soil. Whenever the latter afforded anything favorable, there appears to have been a strong predisposition to admiration, and to derive inferences therefrom correspondent with the pre-existing theory. It must be recollected that seventy-five years later Hudson entertained similar notions while sailing up the North River. Hence the application of several improper names to the animals as well as to the plants of these latitudes, and the apparently constant expectation of beholding trees laden with fruits and spices, "goodly trees," and "very sweet and pleasant herbs." That the barren and frigid shores of Labrador and the northern parts of Newfoundland should have been characterized as a region subject to the divine curse, is not calculated to excite so much surprise as is the disposition evinced with every discovery of fertile soil and verdure to convert the favored region into a land of Oriental fruitfulness. It does not appear to have been sufficiently understood that the increased verdure and elevation of temperature were in a great measure owing to the advancing stage of the season. Cartier arrived off the coast on the 10th of May, and prolonged his stay through July. Now, however, it is very generally known that the summers in high northern latitudes, although short, are attended with a great degree of heat.

On the 3d of July, Cartier entered the gulf, to which, during a subsequent voyage, he gave the name St. Lawrence, and the centre of which he states to be in latitude 47° 30'. On the 4th he proceeded up the bay to a creek called St. Martin, near the Bay of Chaleurs, where he was detained eight days by stress of weather. While at anchor there, one of the ship's boats, being sent off to make explorations in advance, proceeded seven or eight leagues to a cape of the bay, where two parties of Indians, "in about forty or fifty canoes," were observed crossing the channel. One of the parties landed, and beckoned to the explorers to follow their example, "making a great noise," and showing "certain skins upon pieces of wood,"—*i.e.*, fresh-stretched skins; but, fearing their numbers, the seamen kept aloof. The Indians in two canoes prepared to follow them, in which movement they were joined by five canoes of the other party, "who were coming from the sea-side." They approached in a friendly manner, "dancing and making many manifestations of joy, saying, in their tongue, 'Napew tondamen assnatah.'"[1] The seamen, however, suspecting their intentions, and finding it impossible to elude them by flight, discharged two shots among them, by which they were so terrified that they fled precipitately to the shore, "making a great noise." After pausing some time, the "wild men" re-embarked and renewed

---

[1] "Napew" means man in the Sheshatapoosh, or Labrador, language. "Naba" is a male in the Algonkin. It is therefore reasonable to conclude that these were a party of Sheshatapoosh Indians, whose language proves them to be kindred with the great Algonkin family.

the pursuit, but after coming alongside they were so terrified by the thrusts of two lances that they again fled in haste, and made no further attempt to follow.

This appears to have been the first encounter of the ships' crews with the natives. On the following day, on the approach of the "wild men" in nine canoes, an interview was brought about, which is thus described: "We being advertised of their coming, went to the point where they were with our boats; but so soon as they saw us they began to flee, making signs that they came to traffic with us, showing us such skins as they clothed themselves withal, which are of small value. We likewise made signs unto them that we wished them no evil, and, in sign thereof, two of our men ventured to go on land to them and carry them knives, with other iron wares, and a red hat to give unto their captain. Which when they saw, they also came on land, and brought some of their skins, and so began to deal with us, seeming to be very glad to have our iron wares and other things, still dancing, with many other ceremonies, as with their hands to cast sea-water on their heads. They gave us whatever they had, not keeping anything, so that they were constrained to go back again naked, and made signs that the next day they would come again, and bring more skins with them."

Observing a spacious bay extending beyond the cape where this interview had been had, and the wind proving adverse to the vessels' quitting the harbor, Cartier despatched his boats to examine it, for the purpose of ascertaining whether it might not afford the desired passage; for it must be kept in mind that he was diligently seeking the long-sought passage to the Indian Ocean. While engaged in this examination, his men discovered the smokes and fires of "wild men" (the term constantly used in the narrative to designate the natives). These signs were observed upon the shores of a small lake communicating with the bay. An amicable interview resulted, the natives presenting to the navigators cooked seal, and the French making a suitable return "in hatchets, knives, and beads." After these preliminaries, which were conducted with considerable caution by deputies from both sides, the male natives approached in their canoes for the purpose of trafficking, leaving most of their families behind. About three hundred Indian men, women, and children were estimated to have been congregated at this place. They evinced their friendship by singing and dancing, as also by rubbing their hands upon the arms of their European visitors and then lifting them up towards the heavens. An opinion is expressed that these people (who were in the position assigned to the Micmacs, in 1600, in Mr. Gallatin's ethnological map) might very easily be converted to Christianity. "They go," says the narrator, "from place to place. They live only by fishing. They have an ordinary time to fish for their provisions. The country is hotter than the country of Spain, and the fairest that can possibly be found; altogether smooth and level." In addition to the productions before noticed as indigenous on Brion's Island, etc., and which were likewise found here, he enumerates "white and red roses, with many other flowers of very sweet and pleasant smell." "There be also," says the journalist, "many goodly meadows full of grass, and lakes wherein plenty of salmon be." The natives called a hatchet *cochi*, and a knife bacon.[1] It was at this time near the middle of July, and the degree of heat experienced on the excursion led Cartier to name the inlet Baie des Chaleurs, a name which it still retains.

On the 12th of July, Cartier left his moorings at St. Martin's Creek, and proceeded up the gulf, but, encountering bad weather, he put into a bay, which appears to have been Gaspé, where one of the vessels lost her anchor. They were forced to take shelter in a river of that bay, and were there detained thirteen days. Meanwhile they opened an intercourse with the natives, who were found in great numbers engaged in fishing for mackerel. Forty canoes and two hundred men, women, and children were estimated to have been seen during their detention at this place. Presents of "knives, combs, beads of glass, and other trifles of small value" were made to the Indians, for which they expressed great thankfulness, lifting up their hands, and dancing and singing.

These Gaspé Indians are represented as differing, both "in nature and language," from those before mentioned, being abjectly poor, but partly clothed in "old skins," and possessed of no tents to protect them from the weather. "They may," says the journalist, "very well and truly be called *wild*, because there is no poorer people in the world; for I think all they had together, besides their boats and nets, was not worth five sous." They shaved their heads, with the exception of a tuft on the crown, sheltered themselves at night under their canoes on the bare ground, and ate their provisions but partly cooked. They were unacquainted with the use of salt, and "ate nothing that had any taste of salt." On Cartier's first landing among them, the men expressed their joy, as those at the Bay of Chaleurs had done, by singing and dancing; but they had sent all their women, except two or three, into the woods. A comb and a bell, given to each of the women who had ventured to remain, excited the avarice of the men, who quickly brought the other women, to the number of about twenty, from the woods, to each of whom the same present was made. They caressed Cartier by touching and rubbing him with their hands, and also sung and danced. Their nets were made of a kind of indigenous hemp; and they possessed a species of "millet" called "kapaige," beans called "sȧhu," and nuts called "cahehya." If anything was exhibited with which they were unacquainted, they shook their heads, saying, "Nohda." It is added that they never come to the sea except in fishing-time, which, we may remark, was probably the reason why they had no lodges, or much other property about them. They would naturally desire to disencumber their canoes as much as possible in these summer excursions, that they might carry a large return freight of dried fish. The language spoken by these Gaspé Indians was apparently of the Iroquois type, for "cahehya" is, with a slight difference, the term for "fruit" in the Oneida.

On the 24th of July, Cartier erected a cross thirty feet high, bearing the inscription, "*Vive le Roy de France.*" The natives who were present at the ceremony

---

[1] *Koshee* and *bahkoñ*. These are not the terms used to designate a hatchet and a knife either in the Micmac, the old Algonkin, or the Wyandot.

seem, on a little reflection, to have conceived the true intent of it, and their chief complained of it in a "long oration," saying, in effect, "that the country was his, and that he should not set up any cross without his leave." Having quieted the old chief's fears, and used a little duplicity to induce him to come alongside, Cartier seized two of the natives, named Domaigaia and Taignoagny (Iroquois), with the view of conveying them to France, and on the following day set sail up the gulf. After making some further explorations, and being foiled in an attempt to enter the mouth of a river, Cartier began to think of returning. Being alarmed by the rapidity of the tide setting out of the St. Lawrence River, and the weather becoming remarkably tempestuous, he assembled his captains and principal men in council, "to put the question as to the expediency of continuing the voyage." The result of their deliberations was as follows. Considering that easterly winds began to prevail, "that there was nothing to be gotten," the impetuosity of the tides being such "that they did but fall," and storms and tempests beginning to reign, it was evident that they must either promptly return home or else remain where they were until spring. Under these circumstances it was decided to be expedient to return; and with this counsel Cartier complied. No time was lost in retracing their route along the Newfoundland coast, and they arrived at the port of "White Sands" on the 9th of August. On the 15th, being "the feast of the Assumption of our Lady," after the religious services of the day were concluded, Cartier set sail for France. "About the middle of the sea" he encountered a heavy storm of three days' continuance, and on the 5th of September, after an absence of four months and sixteen days, he arrived at the port of St. Malo.[1]

The account which Cartier gave of his discoveries, and the benefits thereby promised to the future commerce of France, verified as the narrative was by the presence of Domaigaia and Taignoagny, the two Iroquois captives, induced Vice-Admiral Meilleraye to recommend him to the king for further employment. Accordingly, early in the spring of 1535, Cartier was placed in command of another squadron, consisting of three ships, well provisioned and manned, for the purpose of still further prosecuting his researches in those latitudes. On the 6th of May, he, together with the crews of his vessels, attended divine service at the cathedral of St. Malo, where they received the ecclesiastical benediction. He sailed from St. Malo on the 19th of May, taking with him a number of young gentlemen who were ambitious to seek their fortunes under his auspices. On the outward passage a severe tempest was encountered, during the continuance of which the vessels parted company. Cartier arrived at Newfoundland on the 7th of July, where, after waiting until the 26th, he was rejoined by the rest of his squadron. The succeeding day he carefully continued his voyage along the coast, taking soundings, with the view of finding good anchor-ground, and tracing out the bays and harbors of this dangerous locality. On the 8th of August he entered the gulf visited by him the previous year, and now named it the St. Lawrence. After some preliminary reconnoissances

[1] Hakluyt.

of the capes, as also of the mainland, and obtaining more definite information concerning the geography of the country from Domaigaia and Taignoagny, who accompanied him, he sailed up the river, and on the 1st of September anchored at the mouth of the Saguenay River, which locality appeared to be familiar to the two captives. At this point the explorers met four canoes containing Indians, who evinced their usual caution and shyness; but, being hailed by the captive Iroquois, they came freely alongside of the ships, and a friendly interview took place.

As Cartier continued to advance up the river, the tides attracted his notice as being very swift and dangerous. Tortoises were found in this vicinity, and for the first time they here observed the sturgeon, which is pronounced "savory and good to be eaten." After ascending for seven days, the vessels reached the island which he named Bacchus, but which is now called Orleans, where, having cast anchor, he ordered the boats to be manned, and went ashore, taking with him Domaigaia and Taignoagny as interpreters, through whose influence the fears of the Indians were appeased and a friendly feeling established. The natives evinced their joy by dancing, and loaded him with presents, comprising several sorts of fish, and a large quantity of the maize, called by Cartier "great millet." On the following day the chief Donnaconna, accompanied by his entire band, arrived in twelve canoes, ten of which he directed to stop at a distance, and with the other two he pulled towards Cartier's ship. Donnaconna stood up as he approached, and, with violent gesticulations, addressed Cartier in a long speech. The captives related to the chief what they had seen abroad, and how kindly they had been treated, with which Donnaconna was so much pleased that he desired Cartier to extend his arm over the side of the vessel that he might kiss his hand. He then laid Cartier's arm fondlingly about his neck, whereupon the latter descended into the chief's canoe, and, having ordered bread and wine to be brought, they ate and drank together, and parted mutually gratified with the interview. Thus happily commenced the intercourse of the French with the Iroquois.

Having determined to ascend the river to Hochelaga, the present site of Montreal, Cartier anchored his larger vessels in the entrance of a small river on the north shore, opposite the head of the island called by him Santa Cruz, and on the 19th of September, in his smallest vessel, accompanied by two boats and fifty men, he commenced the undertaking. To prevent this movement the Indians had in vain employed all their arts and resorted to the most extravagant demoniacal dances, but all this served no other purpose than to encourage him in his design. A voyage of ten days' continuance brought him to an expansion of the river, now called St. Peter's Lake. Finding the river was becoming shallow, he left his vessel at anchor, and proceeded forward with the two boats and twenty-eight armed men. He was charmed with the scenery, the fertility of the soil, and the luxuriant productions of the new country. Everywhere above this point the Indians received him with friendship, and brought him presents of fish, corn, and game. When he anchored for the night the natives assembled on shore, built fires, danced, and uttered shouts of joy, in this manner making his voyage resemble a triumphal journey. He arrived at Hochelaga (now Montreal) on the 2d of October, where a multitude of the natives of both sexes, old and young, awaited his arrival, and expressed their joy by dancing. Cartier, having arrayed himself in gorgeous clothing, landed on the following morning, accompanied by a band of twenty mariners. Following for four or five miles a well-beaten path through the forest, he came to an open spot where a bright fire was burning. Here he was received by a deputation from the town, and requested to rest himself. A speech of welcome was then addressed to him, after which the procession advanced without further interruption to the town of Hochelaga, which was situated amidst cultivated fields, and surrounded with rude ramparts constructed for defence. Mats having been spread for him, he was ceremoniously seated, and was soon joined by the chief, Agouhanna, an old man afflicted with palsy, who, sitting on a stag-skin, was borne on the shoulders of men. Around his forehead he wore a band, or frontlet, of red-colored hedgehog-skins, but in other respects he was not dressed better than his people. As neither Domaigaia nor Taignoagny would accompany Cartier, he had no interpreter, and during the interview communication was carried on principally by signs. After the close of the conference he ascended to the top of the neighboring mountain, accompanied by several natives. It afforded an extensive view of all the surrounding rivers, rapids, plains, and mountains. Transported by the scene, he bestowed on this elevation the name of Mount Royal. Having asked the Indians the name of the adjacent country, they replied, "Canada," having without doubt understood him as referring to the town.

Thus having, on the 3d of October, 1535, terminated this eventful interview, Cartier hastened to return. Favored by both wind and tide, he reached his vessel in Lake St. Peter's on the following day, and the post of the Holy Cross on the 11th. At this place he endured a cold winter, from the middle of November to the middle of March: the ice in the St. Lawrence is said to have been "two fathoms thick," and the snow four feet deep. Twenty-five of his men died of scurvy. He was detained in the river of the Holy Cross until the 6th of May, when he sailed for France, carrying with him the chief Donnaconna, and his two former captives, Domaigaia and Taignoagny. He reached the French coast, and cast anchor in the harbor of St. Malo, on the 6th of July, 1536.

Speaking of the Iroquois, he says, "They possess all property in common, and are clothed in skins during the winter. The men perform but trifling labor, and are addicted to smoking. The condition of the women is one of servitude and drudgery. Polygamy is tolerated; the young women are dissolute, and married women are condemned to remain widows after the death of their husbands. Both sexes are very hardy."[1]

---

[1] The journals of these two voyages are contained in the third volume of Ramusio's Italian Collection (Venice, 1565); also in Lescarbot's "Histoire de la Nouvelle-France."

CHAPTER V.

EXPEDITION OF DE SOTO TO FLORIDA—APPALACHIAN TRIBES—THE DAKOTAS—DISCOVERY OF THE MISSISSIPPI.

Up to this period all attempts to found colonies in continental America had proved complete failures. Ponce de Leon, De Ayllon, Narvaez, and Cartier had each added his quota to geographical knowledge and recorded details of the manners and customs of the Indians, but no one of them had established even the first outlines of a colony. Nine years after the disastrous termination of the expedition of Narvaez, Hernando de Soto determined to effect the conquest and colonization of Florida. As the origin of this expedition cannot be well understood without reference to events which occurred on the northwestern confines of Mexico, it becomes necessary to enter into some details respecting them.

In 1530 an Indian named Tezon, a native of New Galicia, told the governor of that province a wonderful tale about the existence of seven cities in the *terra incognita* north and east of the river Gila, each of which cities was as large as Mexico. He stated that the country so abounded in the precious metals that entire streets in those cities were occupied by goldsmiths. In confirmation of what he asserted, he said that his father, then dead, had been a trader in ornamental feathers, and in return for his goods had brought from that quarter large quantities of gold and silver. This was the germ of the long-prevailing myth of the seven golden cities of Cibola.

It so happened that, while this story was yet credited, Cabeça de Vaca, with three companions, one of whom was an African, arrived at Compostella, the capital of New Galicia, after having been nine years traversing the continent. De Vaca had been the treasurer of Narvaez, and was the only officer of his army who had escaped the fury of the waves and the vengeance of the Indians on the Florida coast. The very fact of his safe passage over vast territories occupied by hostile tribes was of itself a wonder, but yet not more so than the extraordinary tales he related of the state of semi-civilization in which he had found some of the tribes whom he had encountered, and of the arts and wealth they possessed. These disclosures rekindled the latent cupidity in the imaginations of the Spanish adventurers who were seeking their fortune in Mexico. All classes believed in the new land of golden promise, and fresh vitality was imparted to the stories of Tezon. De Vaca was summoned to the viceregal court of Mexico, where his presence created a great excitement. The viceroy, Mendoza, questioned him respecting the strange incidents of his escape, and as to the state of arts and civilization among the Indians. De Vaca represented the tribes on the Rio Grande and Gila as wearing woven stuffs, living in large houses built of stone, and possessing rich mines. From Mexico his fame preceded him to the court of Charles V., where he arrived in 1537, and where he was lionized on account of his adventures and sufferings, and the tales of golden wealth to be found in America. Nothing was too extravagant for the credulity of his audiences. Sufferings and perils he had indeed encountered, but, instead of plainly telling the Spaniards that Florida was a country containing no gold-mines, destitute of cities, possessing no agriculture, roads, bridges, or any traces either of art or of semi-civilization, and that it was solely inhabited by savages who cherished determined hostility to the Spanish race, he conformed to the preconceived notions of the court, the nobility, and the people, and represented, if he did not himself believe, that it was another Mexico or Peru. The public mind was engrossed with the idea. Prominent among the believers of this tale was De Soto, who had been a most valuable assistant of Pizarro in Peru, and had shared largely in the plunder of the Inca, Atahualpa.

De Soto determined to organize a new expedition for the conquest of Florida, one which should exceed in means and splendor anything of the kind that had ever visited the New World. Gentlemen and noblemen of rank and fortune vied with one another for the honor of participating in the scheme. The finest horses of Andalusia and Estremadura, the most chivalric and enthusiastic cavaliers, and the bravest footmen, all armed and equipped in the most glittering style, and well provided with drums, trumpets, and banners, formed the material of the army of De Soto.

De Soto was one of the wealthiest men in Spain, an hidalgo by birth, a man of pre-eminent courage and conduct, an elegant horseman, a soldier without peer. He had passed several years in Spain after the conquest of Peru in ease and elegant hospitality and refinement; and he was celebrated and envied for his wealth both in court and out of court. There was none equal to him in reputation for gallant achievements, for the heroes and conquerors in the New World had mostly risen from low stations, but De Soto, it was affirmed, was doubly entitled to his honors by reason of the claims of gentle birth.

He offered to conquer the country at his own cost. The emperor readily granted his request, and conferred on him the title of Adelantado, with the usual powers and immunities. His standard at Seville was flocked to by the brave and ambitious from all quarters. Portugal as well as Spain sent her volunteers. In little more than a twelve-month his forces amounted to nine hundred and fifty men, many of whom were mounted, including some of the choicest cavaliers, with twelve priests, eight inferior clergymen, and four monks, all of whom embarked in seven large and three small vessels at San Lucar de Barrameda on the 6th of April, 1538. A little less than eleven years before this date, Narvaez had embarked on his ill-starred expedition, sailing from the same port, and against the same people.

Everything favored De Soto during his voyage to Cuba and his sojourn in that island. Here he received a new accession of followers and procured an ample recruit of horses. More than a year elapsed before he was ready to proceed on his conquest. In the mean while he passed his time in entertainments, tournaments, and rejoicings, more like some grand triumphal display of a conqueror than the prologue to a descent among the hammocks and lagoons of Florida, where every thicket concealed vengeful bowmen, and the whole body of the irritated tribes were prepared to assail an invader with the direst hostility. Four Indians had been kidnapped on the coasts and brought to Cuba to serve as guides and interpreters, a point of great importance certainly, but the manner of obtaining these guides served further to irritate the Indians and offend their natural sense of justice and fair dealing. De Soto embarked all his forces about the middle of May, and, after twelve or thirteen days spent on the transit, entered the waters of Tampa Bay,—being the same body of water that Narvaez[1] had entered and named La Cruz, but which De Soto now called Espiritu Santo. He remained in his vessels six days. Everything betokened a hostile reception from the Indians. They had abandoned the coast, along which bale-fires were sending up their columns of smoke to advise the distant bands of the arrival of their old enemy. On the last day of May, 1539, three hundred men were landed on arid ground to take possession of the country for the crown in the customary form. Not an Indian was in sight. But near dawn of the following day, while the men were bivouacked, the Indians rushed upon them with horrid yells, armed with bows and clubs. Several of the Spaniards were wounded, notwithstanding their armor, and the whole body rushed in the utmost confusion to the shore, where they were reinforced from the ships. The enemy were then dispersed with the loss of a single horse, which was shot with an arrow that had been driven with such force as to pass through the saddle and housings and pierce one-third of its length into the body. The whole army now debarked, and during several days while they reposed here after their sea-voyage nothing more was seen of the Indians.

An army of more splendid equipments and appointments had never before landed in America. It was led by the most brilliant and chivalrous cavaliers. It glittered in the splendor of fresh-burnished armor. Its trumpets and drums wakened new echoes in the solitudes of Florida. Its horses, of Arabian blood, were decorated with gaudy housings, and presented an object of terror to the natives. The spear, or lance, was a dreaded weapon in the hands of the horsemen, and the natives quailed before the deadly aim of the matchlock. But the Spaniards were inferior to the Indians in the use of the bow. The Indians were also free from the encumbrance of baggage. They were superior as woodsmen, and superior also in minute knowledge of the land and of its natural resources. They were better inured to the fatigues and hardships of forest-life. They imitated the sagacity of a fox in threading a forest, and the ferocity of a panther in pouncing on their prey. It was their policy not to meet their invaders in battle in concentrated bodies, but to fall on them unawares at night or in difficult defiles. They sought to conquer by delay, and to enfeeble by a strict war of details. When consulted, they often gave vague answers. They were adepts at concealment. It is believed that they often led De Soto from place to place to entangle him deeper in the forest. They perceived that he sought, above all other

---

[1] Narvaez had landed on the west shore of the bay, according to the map of Smith's De Vaca.

objects, gold and gold-mines. Of these they had none, but, ignorant themselves of metallic minerals, they might often deceive and mislead when they did not intend it. To ignorant men, silvery and yellow mica and iron pyrites have often appeared to be gold and silver. The attention of the Indians was so perpetually called to these subjects that they could not mistake the object of the invasion. Besides, it was never concealed by De Soto that he came as a conqueror.

It was not possible in so extended a line for De Soto to keep communications open with his initial point of landing; and the Indians, acting with sound policy and just judgment of the Spanish mode of warfare, parted before their enemy and immediately closed up behind him. The particular districts he traversed were conquered no longer than during the time he actually remained in them. De Soto at first marched towards the northeast and north, then to the west, southwest, and south, and finally towards the north, till he reached the indomitable Chickasaws and crossed the Mississippi. By marching so far inland from his starting-point at Tampa Bay, and crossing the Withlacoochee and the lakes and lagoons near the sources of the St. John's (where we must locate his Vitachucco), he avoided the difficulties that continually beset Narvaez on the Gulf coasts. The movements of his cavalry were irresistible, but it is evident that his infantry lacked drill, discipline, and order. De Soto was a man as noted for his resource and policy as for his bravery and personal presence in the field and the council. He took great pains, on reaching the village of Hirrihigua, but two leagues from his point of debarkation, to appease the feelings of that chief for the outrages perpetrated by Narvaez,—cruel and foolish acts, which, if there were no other proofs, would show Narvaez to have been unfit for command. While negotiating with this chief, De Soto heard of a Spaniard who was held in captivity by a neighboring chief called Mucoso. This was Juan Ortez, a man who had been secretly landed from one of the ships of Narvaez. Ortez, who had learned the language of the natives, was from his influence with the tribes a person of the greatest use to De Soto in all his future negotiations. These two steps were auspicious, and denoted capacity for command. The Spaniard's first line of march, from Tampa Bay to Cofachique, on the Savannah River (a place now in the State of South Carolina), was a military and exploratory achievement of unique character. He was now near the northern limits of the Creeks, or Muskokis, as the place-names sufficiently denote. While at Cofachique, he identified, as we have before intimated, a dagger and certain articles of armor which had been captured about twenty-five years previously from the ill-fated Vasquez de Ayllon. Struck with the obedience yielded to a female ruler of that place, whom he is pleased to call "queen," he thought he could facilitate his march westward by carrying her along in a sort of state captivity. The idea was a repetition of that of Cortez when he carried Montezuma a captive to his quarters, and of Pizarro when he seized Atahualpa. This device seems to have answered very well till the queen found herself getting beyond her proper territorial bounds, when she managed to escape.

De Soto's previous experience of the Indian character had been gained altogether among the South and Central American tribes. He had during the conquest of Peru witnessed their implicit obedience to Incas, by whom they had been subjected, and to whom they yielded both a feudal and a religious submission. It was impossible for him to conceive of the spirit of independence possessed by the free and bold Appalachian tribes whose territories he had now invaded. But, if he mistook their true character on landing in Florida, he was not long permitted to remain ignorant of their determined hostility and intense hatred. The Indians having, as they supposed, received their lands from the Great Spirit, of whom the sun and the moon were only symbols, they could not conceive how their title could be bettered by acknowledging the gift as coming from Charles V. Not only did Hirrihigua, who was still smarting under the atrocities committed by Narvaez, reject every overture of peace, but the same spirit, although often concealed under deep guises, animated every tribe from the Gulf to the Mississippi. Witness what Acuera, a Muskoki chief, said in reply to the messengers of De Soto, who had invited him to a friendly interview:

"Others of your accursed race have, in years past, poisoned our peaceful shores. They have taught me what you are. What is your employment? To wander about like vagabonds from land to land, to rob the poor, to betray the confiding, to murder in cold blood the defenceless. No! with such a people I want no peace,—no friendship. War, never-ending war, exterminating war, is all the boon I ask.

"You boast yourselves valiant, and so you may be; but my faithful warriors are not less brave, and this too you shall one day prove; for I have sworn to maintain an unsparing conflict while one white man remains in my borders,—not only in battle, though even thus we fear not to meet you, but by stratagem, ambush, and midnight surprisal.

"I am king in my own land, and will never become the vassal of a mortal like myself. Vile and pusillanimous is he who will submit to the yoke of another when he may be free. As for me and my people, we choose death—yes! a hundred deaths —before the loss of our liberty and the subjugation of our country.

"Keep on, robbers and traitors: in Acuera and Apalachee we will treat you as you deserve. Every captive will we quarter and hang up to the highest tree along the road."[1]

This was the spirit in which De Soto was met by all the natives, with the single exception of Mucoso, the protector of Juan Ortez. This spirit was sometimes suppressed for the moment, but was openly manifested wherever the invaders could be attacked at a disadvantage. During the twenty days that De Soto's army abode in Acuera to refresh themselves, fourteen Spaniards were picked off and slain as they ventured from camp, and a great many wounded, without the possibility of the Spanish seeing or finding an enemy. Every close thicket and impenetrable hammock seemed armed with Indian vengeance, which it was impossible to retaliate. The bodies of the slain Spaniards, who were almost daily buried, were dug up the following night, cut to pieces, and hung upon trees. The Indians lay in wait in their

---

[1] Irving's Conquest of Florida, pp. 96, 97.

canoes in every deep and winding stream, and let fly their deadly arrows whenever the invader attempted to cross.

Such determined resistance the Spaniards had not met in Mexico or Peru; and the noble sentiments uttered by Acuera should have taught them that here was a class of Indians, hardy, athletic, and free, who had never yet been brought into subjection to any yoke, native or foreign.

De Soto was not insensible to the noble fire of these sentiments, but was not for a moment to be diverted from his task; and he determined to strike terror into the hearts of the natives by adopting the policy of "an eye for an eye, and a tooth for a tooth." Enraged by the peculiar kind of petty opposition he found at crossing the streams and around his encampments, he let loose a noted blood-hound as the minister of his vengeance, who in a few days tore to pieces four of the offending Indians. This act of cruelty was inconsistent with the notions of warfare held by the Indians, and inflamed their rage to desperation. It was a similar cruelty that had rendered Narvaez odious, and by adopting this procedure De Soto made himself and his nation still further hated and abhorred.

What the twelve priests and four monks were doing at this time we are not informed; but it was hard to teach the doctrines of Christianity, which are so full of merciful teachings, while its principles were daily contradicted by such inhuman practices. We may here adduce what Vitachucco, another Creek Indian, at a more advanced point of this march, said to his two brothers, who had been taken captive by De Soto and had sent messages to him advising submission. He was their elder brother, and the ruling chief.

"It is evident enough," he replies, "that you are young, and have neither judgment nor experience, or you would never have spoken as you have done of these hated white men. You extol them greatly as virtuous men who injure no one. You say that they are valiant,—that they are children of the sun, and merit all our reverence and service. The vile chains which they have hung upon you, and the mean and dastardly spirit which you have acquired during the short period you have been their slaves, have caused you to speak like women, lauding what you should censure and abhor.

"You remember not that these strangers can be no better than those who formerly committed so many cruelties in our country. Are they not the same nation, and subject to the same laws? Do not their manner of life and their actions prove them to be children of the Evil Spirit, and not of the sun and moon, our gods? Go they not from land to land plundering and destroying, taking the wives and daughters of others instead of bringing their own with them, and, like mere vagabonds, maintaining themselves by the labors of others? Were they virtuous as you represent, they would never have left their own country, since there they might have practised their virtues, instead of roving about the world committing robberies and murders, having neither the shame of men nor the fear of God before them.

"Warn them not to enter my lines; for I vow that, as valiant as they may be, if they dare to put foot upon my soil they shall never go out of my land alive; the whole race will I exterminate."[1]

"If you want to add to your favors," said four Muskoki captives taken south of the Suwanee, "take our lives: after surviving the defeat and capture of our chieftain, we are not worthy to appear before him, nor to live in the world."

Such were the feelings and temper of the whole body of the Indian tribes who, in 1540, occupied the wide area from the Atlantic shores of Florida and Georgia to the banks of the Mississippi. Separated as their tribes were into different communities, they sank all tribal differences and united in a general opposition to the invaders. Fear of the common enemy drove them into a virtual union. They never omitted a good opportunity to strike, but they often concealed their hatred under the deepest secrecy, and received the Spaniards with an apparent hospitality which lulled the invaders into partial security. The geographical terms which are employed, though obscured in imperfect forms of notation, show that there were seven different tongues spoken by the tribes met by the Spaniards in their circuitous line of march from Tampa Bay to the banks of the Mississippi, at the lower Chickasaw Bluffs, where the army crossed.

The ancient Creeks, or Muskokis, appear at that time to have occupied the entire territory of East Florida and Georgia from the Appalachicola to the Coosawhatchee River in South Carolina.

De Soto passed his first winter in the vicinity of Tallahassee. The next year he reached Cofaqui, which is believed to have been near the present site of Macon. The Creeks, who found him pushing on under false expectations towards the northeast, where they had bitter enemies, gladly facilitated his movements, furnished him with provisions, and took advantage of his marching across the elevated grounds at the extreme sources of the Altamaha, Oconee, and Savannah Rivers, to send the war-chief Patofa, with a large body of warriors, under the pretence of escorting him, but really to fall upon their enemies. These enemies were the ancient, proud, and high-spirited Uchees, who had defeated the Spaniards on the Georgia and South Carolina coasts. As soon as they reached the waters of the Savannah River, the Muskokis secretly left De Soto's camp at night, and fell with the utmost fury on their unsuspecting enemies. The responsibility of this act was of course charged upon the Spaniards. De Soto, finding himself compromitted by this act of perfidy, sent Patofa and his followers back to Cofaqui. They returned with their rich trophy of scalps. The Spaniard then continued his march down the south bank of the river, and crossed over to what had been the will-o'-the-wisp of his hopes ever since quitting Apalache,—namely, the long-anticipated Cofachique,[2] where he expected to find mines of gold and silver. This is a Creek name, which was mentioned to the whites the year before at their winter-quarters near Tallahassee by an Indian boy named Pedro, who, the narrator reports, De Soto had "proved to be a most elaborate liar on various occasions." That the Creeks followed up the blow when De Soto had left the

---

[1] Irving's Conquest of Florida.   [2] Silver Bluffs, Barnwell County, South Carolina.

country, and finally conquered the Uchees and brought off the remnant, whom they incorporated into their confederacy, is denoted by their traditions.

Disappointed in his hopes of finding the precious metals at Cofachique, and of opening a communication with the "Queen-mother" of the Uchee tribe,[1] he carried a young woman, who then ruled the village, captive with him on his march from this point towards the Appalachian Mountains. But she managed to escape on the way towards the country of her enemies. The Spanish and Portuguese narrators of this expedition are constantly on stilts. The words "king, queen, prince," and the like, are continually misapplied to the chiefs of bold and free hunter-tribes, which were ruled by simple democratic councils of chiefs and warriors, who lived in bark wigwams more or less substantial, and had no exact boundaries to their territories, but generally left a strip of hunting- and war-ground undisturbed between the tribes, as at this day.

Reports of gold and silver carried De Soto north and northwest towards the Appalachian Mountains, where he passed through a part of the territory occupied by a tribe who are called "Achalaques," the modern Cherokees. This is the first notice we have of this tribe. While encamped among the barren eminences at Ichiaha, the Cherokees told him that about thirty miles north there was gold. He sent two men into the spurs of the mountain to search for this metal, who, after an absence of ten days, reported the discovery of a country of grain and pasturage: "the appearance of the soil indicated the probable presence of gold and silver in the neighborhood."

It is remarkable that in this part of his march De Soto should have passed over the region of Dahlonega, where gold has been found in such quantities in the detritus of the mountains that the United States government for a time had a mint at that place. This proves that the reports of the Indians, though often vague, were sometimes reliable.

He now marched south and re-entered the country of the Creeks, following down the fertile and beautiful banks of the Coosa. The spirit of Hirrihigua, Acuera, and Vitachucco appeared to have died away; and, notwithstanding some difficulties, the Europeans were received with general friendliness, being heralded from one Indian village to another, as far at least as Coosa, their principal town. De Soto now approached the borders of the Choctaws and Chickasaws. In his triumphal march down the banks of the Coosa, the Creeks accompanied him, with hidden motives. They carefully concealed a plot which was afterwards revealed at Mauvila. The practice of making the ruling chief captive, and taking him along to secure the obedience of his warriors, who were compelled to carry the baggage of the army, was always grating to the natural feeling of independence of the aborigines. Yet no outbreaking opposition was made. The Spaniards regarded the tribes as conquered, and therefore relaxed their military diligence and discipline. They marched along, spreading out over large spaces. Their encampments were loosely guarded. It is

---

[1] The Muskokis had a Salic law.

evident that they often neglected even to post sentinels. The "camp-master" was very remiss,—so much so that he was finally displaced.

There was at that time a noted chief living on the Coosa, of gigantic frame and great courage and vigor of intellect, called Tuscaloosa, or the Black Warrior. He had been carried along by De Soto a captive like the preceding chiefs, on the march down this magnificent valley. But he bore the indignity with a degree of impatience that nothing short of his Indian stoicism could control. As De Soto marched down the river towards the village of Mauvila, he had some suspicions of the Black Warrior's intentions from the frequent Indian messengers he noticed, but there were no additional warriors to his train. The Spaniards entered the town in a straggling manner and at intervals, a fact which shows that no direct hostility was anticipated, and certainly no additional precautions were taken against such hostility. Tuscaloosa was brought a virtual captive to his own capital. But the hour foretold by Acuera had arrived. The day of Indian vengeance was at hand. Mauvila was a strongly-fortified village, situated on a peninsula or plain made by the windings of the Coosa. It was surrounded by stout palisades, with inner cross-ties and loop-holes for arrows, having an east and a west gate. Eighty large and single-roomed houses, thatched in the Indian manner, stood around a square. Some of the trees about this enclosure retained their natural positions, and were covered with a dense foliage, which threw a pleasing shade over the square. It was an Indian stronghold. De la Vega's description is drawn in a manner to enhance our notions of its means of defence; and he certainly much overrates the number of its Indian defenders, all of which is done with the view of magnifying the glory of the hard struggle which awaited De Soto here.

That one hundred foot and one hundred horse, not one of the latter of which could enter the town, should have sustained a conflict with "ten thousand" Indian warriors, would be sufficiently wonderful in itself; yet that number is only half of the Indian force, if we admit La Vega's estimate; but the Spanish author has doubtless greatly exaggerated the strength of the Creeks. For it is perceived that even the small force with De Soto were, by the direction of Tuscaloosa, encamped "a bow-shot" outside of the walls, while his attendants and personal cortège were assigned quarters inside. Within the walls were also stowed all his baggage, provisions, and equipage, which had been brought in advance by the Indian burden-carriers. The rest of the army, consisting of some seven or eight hundred men, was left to come on by an easy and, it seems, very careless march under Moscoso, the camp-master.

It was on the 18th of October (1540), at an early hour in the morning, and while the troops were thus separated and were in the act of adjusting their encampment, that the war-cry of Tuscaloosa broke forth. In an instant hosts of Indians sallied from the houses where they had been concealed. The place had previously been emptied of the matrons and children, and the ground about the town cleared as though for battle. De Soto and his attendants were suddenly expelled from the fort, and its gates shut, leaving five dead. They were pressed so closely that many of the horsemen could not get to their horses, which were unsaddled and tied to trees without, and some of these animals were immediately pierced with arrows and fell dead. The Indians were divided into two columns, one of which attacked the cavalry, and the other the footmen. With the usual Spanish gallantry, De Soto led the remaining sixty horsemen and a party of foot to storm the fort. He was soon joined by some few of Moscoso's horse, and drove back the assailants. They found the gate closed, very narrow, and well defended, and were dreadfully annoyed while before it by the arrows which were shot from the walls and loop-holes with amazing force and accuracy. Some of De Soto's most gallant cavaliers were fatally pierced between the joints of their armor, and numbers of their horses were killed. In the mean time, the yells of the Indians were deafening; they beat their drums in loud defiance, and shook the spoils they had taken from the Spaniards in triumph from the walls; and they were provided with stones to cast on such as came too near. De Soto could not maintain his position beneath the walls, and was compelled to retreat.

Seeing this, the courage of the Indians rose to the highest pitch of fury. Their yells and wild music were deafening; some of them sallied from the gates, others let themselves down from the walls and rushed upon the Spaniards. The latter kept in close and compact bodies, and returned their charges. For three hours they fought in this manner, charging backward and forward over the plain; but the advantage in point of numbers killed was with the Spaniards, who, although suffering severely, were cased in armor, while every blow was effective on their foes. At length the Indians withdrew from the plain and shut themselves up in their fortress.

De Soto now ordered his cavalry, being arrow-proof, to dismount, and, taking battle-axes, to break open the gate. By this time the remaining horsemen had reached the field, and two hundred cavaliers dashed forward to his support. The gate was soon broken, though furiously defended by darts and stones, but was found too narrow to admit all. Some rushed in pell-mell, others battered the rude plastering from the walls and climbed over. The fight was furious. The Indians fought from the tops of their houses. They thronged the square. Lance, club, and missile were wielded from every quarter. The struggle was so fierce, particularly from the roofs of the houses, that the Spanish soldiers, fearful lest the Indians should regain some houses that had been taken, set fire to them. As the houses were constructed of canes and other combustible materials, smoke and flame soon spread through the place, and this added tenfold to the horrors of the scene. Those of the Indians whom the lance and battle-axe spared were suffocated in the smoke or leaped over the walls. The Indians fought with desperation; even their young women snatched up the swords of the slaughtered Spaniards and mingled in the fight, showing more reckless desperation than even the men. The battle, in all its phases, lasted for nine hours. At length the Indians gave way. Those who left the fort fled in all directions, pursued by the cavalry. Those who were encountered within the walls would neither give nor take quarter. They preferred to die on the spot, and to fight till the last gasp. Not a man surrendered. The slaughter was immense. The Spaniards acknowledge a loss of eighty-two men, eighteen of whom were shot in the eye or mouth with arrows, so unerring was the aim. They lost forty-two horses. They claim to have killed twenty-five hundred natives. This battle appears to have been fought by the combined forces of the Creeks, Choctaws, and Chickasaws. Tuscaloosa fell, but his name has been perpetuated to the present day, though the traditions of his people do not reach back to the time of De Soto. So determined a resistance De Soto had never met with before. The feebler Peruvians had shown him no such opposition. It was a victory dearly purchased, as in its practical effects it had all the evil consequences of a defeat. The worst calamity that had befallen him was the loss of all his baggage, stores, and supplies. He had not even a scrap of lint left to dress a wound. Clothing, extra equipage, goods which had been taken along as presents to the Indians or to repay their services, were all consumed. Destitution made the general moody and taciturn, and from this moment his whole plan of operations was changed. He had vested his ample fortune, acquired by the plunder of Atahualpa, in an adventure which had signally failed; visions of golden empire no longer flitted before his mind. He had been pushing on to reach the sea-coast at the splendid harbor discovered by Maldonado, and now named Pensacola, near Perdido Bay, where he supposed that commander to be awaiting his arrival with new supplies from Spain. He had fixed on this as the capital of his projected settlement. He was now within less than a hundred miles of that point. But the battle of Mauvila had thrown a dark cloud over his prospects. There were murmurs in his army; the men had lost everything, even their clothes. He overheard some of his officers expressing the intention of embarking as soon as they reached the sea, and returning to Spain. He determined at once to balk this plan, and, as soon as the wounds of his men would permit, to change his course and march towards the north. To the north he therefore wheeled with all his forces, horse and foot. But an evil rumor went before him. The stand made by the Indians was heralded among them as a triumph. It had broken the charm of invincibility, and taught them the possibility of a victory even over the dreaded horse. And from this point, wherever he went, De Soto encountered nothing but hostility of the deepest kind. "War is what we want," said the natives; "a war of fire and blood." Such was his reception at all the various points at which he encamped before reaching the Mississippi. But from none of the tribes did he encounter so determined a resistance as from the Chickasaws. This tribe, who are closely allied to the Choctaws, have maintained a high character for bravery and independence ever since they have been known to history.

From Mauvila De Soto took up the line of march across the Tuscaloosa and Tombigbee, northwestwardly, till he came to the waters of the Yazoo. A village on the Tuscaloosa, at the site of the present city of that name in Alabama, was abandoned before him. Little opposition, indeed, was encountered till he reached the Tombigbee, where the Indians were drawn up in force on its northern banks to oppose his crossing. A messenger who was despatched with offers of peace was massacred in De Soto's sight, the Indians then fleeing with loud shouts of triumph. Boats were constructed in two days to cross the wide stream, after which the army marched on, still northwestwardly, crossing the fertile uplands of Mississippi, till they reached a village called "Chicaza." This stood, apparently, on the banks of the Yazoo. It was now the 18th of December, an entire month after the army had left the smoking ruins of Mauvila. The bleakness of autumn characterized the forest, and the season began to exhibit a degree of cold before which the men shrunk. De Soto had not many days left the country of the Choctaws, and now entered on that of the Chickasaws. The enemy vanished before him, and when pressed by the cavalry retired into reedy thickets and positions where they could not be followed. On entering the Chickasaw village it was found completely deserted. There were some two hundred wigwams, occupying a gentle hill covered with oaks and walnuts, having a stream on each side. It was a favorable position for an encampment, and De Soto determined to occupy it for his winter quarters. For this purpose he caused other and larger buildings to be erected with wood and straw brought from neighboring hamlets. For two months he reposed in these quarters, sending out, however, almost daily, foraging and scouting parties into the adjacent forests.

At length the thought to burn the encampment appears to have entered the minds of the Chickasaws, and well did they conceal their plan till they could carry it into effect. For several nights previously they had made feigned night-attacks on the camp, as if, by the frequency of these alarms, to throw the Spaniards off their guard; in the course of which time, however, the rapacity and lawlessness of the soldiers brought the commander into serious difficulties. A dark and wild night was chosen by the Indians for the attack, when the wind was blowing strongly from the north. They came on in three parties, moving cautiously, and choosing the intervening spaces between the sentinels to penetrate the camp. They carried live embers in covered clay jars, and in separate places set fire to the light combustible materials of which the wigwams and barracks were made. The wind soon blew up a flame, which, being fed by the dry straw mats, raged with fierceness. It was in the darkest part of the night, and the soldiers, suddenly aroused from their slumbers by a terrible outcry, were half bewildered. Some of them at first took to the woods, but, being recalled, joined in the fight, and as day broke the assailants were chased into the woods, and the army kept its ground.

De Soto, who always slept on his arms, at least "in doublet and hose," fought valiantly, and was well sustained by his principal officers and men. But this midnight attack turned out to be more disastrous than even the terrible battle of Mauvila. On account of the suddenness of the flames, some of the men had barely time to leap out with their lives, leaving a part of their arms and equipments. Swords and lances required to be retempered, for which purpose a forge was built. Many of the saddles were burnt, and much of the furniture of the houses consumed. Forty Spaniards had fallen in the combat. The only Spanish woman in the army—a soldier's wife—was burned to death. Fifty horses had perished, either by the dart or by the fire, as it was impossible in the *mêlée* to untie them from the pickets, and many more were wounded. Another grievous loss was that of the swine that had been brought as an element in the contemplated agricultural settlement. They had been penned, and nearly all of them perished in the fire.

This disastrous battle, following so soon after the conflict at Mauvila, was enough to appall the stoutest heart. Yet it was amazing with what energy the Spaniards set to work to repair their losses. In three days they had established a new camp within a league of the old site, to which De Soto gave the name of Chicacilla, or Little Chickasaw. Not only were their armorers put to work in repairing their arms, but while they remained in this position, which was during the rest of the winter, they made saddles, shields, and lances. Here they suffered greatly from cold and the want of suitable clothing and bedding; for the conflagration had left them nothing but what they had on their backs. It was the 1st of April (1541) before De Soto was ready to quit his encampment. But it was only to encounter new opposition. The hostile spirit of the Indians seemed to be deeply and generally aroused in every direction. An easy march of four leagues, through open plains with deserted hamlets, brought them in sight of a strongly-stockaded fort, called Alabama (situated on the banks of a stream), which was carried by assault after a desperate resistance. In this contest the Spaniards had many men wounded, of whom fifteen died; and although they killed great numbers of the Indians, those who remained were in no wise humbled, and never omitted an opportunity to fall upon their enemies when they could do so to advantage. They seemed to be very accurate and powerful marksmen with the arrow, this deadly weapon being sometimes driven with such force as to pass entirely through the body of a horse. After a halt of four days to attend to their wounded and dead, the Spaniards again set forward, marching through tangled and dense forests and waters, till they came to the banks of the Mississippi, which they appear to have struck at the lower Chickasaw Bluffs, in north latitude about 32°. This discovery was the grand and crowning event of De Soto's expedition, and this alone is destined to carry his name to the latest times. Mines of gold and silver had indeed eluded his grasp, but by the discovery of this great artery of the North American continent he had found the highway that was destined, in after-years, to carry down agricultural products of far greater value to the commerce of the world than the wealth borne by the proudest streams of antiquity. In comparison with this wealth, the rich product of the mines of Mexico and Potosi shines with diminished lustre. Already twenty States of the American Union cluster on that mighty stream and its innumerable branches,—States containing many times the population of the dominions of old Spain, the nation whose proud banners were the first to be displayed on its banks.

The village that was seated here was called Chisca. Its chief had his lodgment on a high artificial mound. The army, impatient of the continual attacks they had encountered, immediately rushed into the village and carried it by assault, making prisoners of the women and children. By this means the Spanish leader held in his hands hostages for good conduct, and he succeeded, after full negotiation, in concluding a peace.

On this elevated and eligible spot, De Soto rested for twenty days, while engaged in making preparations to cross that magnificent stream and pursue his explorations to the west of it in the direction of the Pacific Ocean. By a very devious line of march he had traversed the area of the present States of Florida, Georgia, South Carolina, Alabama, Mississippi, Louisiana, and Tennessee, and at every point had encountered either an open or secret enmity from the Indians, especially from the Muskokis, Choctaws, and Chickasaws, who had fought with unexampled ferocity. Tribes which had formerly been at variance united to repel this formidable invasion. They were, ethnologically speaking, branches of one great stock. During the previous twenty-five years they had acquired bitter experience of Spanish invasion, and hence hated the race with such intensity that they determined to die rather than surrender the country.

The Spaniard had learned from hard experience that his incessant conflicts with the Indians, though he might kill double or treble his numbers, had an inevitable tendency to weaken his forces, exhaust his means, and dispirit his men. He had lost some of his best troops, nearly half of his noblest horses, and all his baggage; and after his most chivalric battles victory only gave him empty towns or unbroken forests. The natural magnificence of the country kept up his hopes while marching from encampment to encampment, but it was only the magnificence of woods, forests, and waters. The land was occupied by a poor, brave, and hardy race, who were determined to sell their lives at the dearest rate, since they had never submitted to the yoke of a conqueror. Thus he had found that every victory tended to exhaust him, and that his army must at last melt away and be subdued by a continuation of such victories.

While De Soto recruited his army on the high and beautiful elevation of the Chickasaw Bluffs, and restored to some extent its failing strength, every means which an able commander could adopt was resorted to for further repairing his losses. Forges were erected, where the swords and spears of his soldiers were retempered. Buckskin was employed in repairing the burnt saddles and accoutrements. The horses regained their strength when pastured on the rich prairie grass, and all the arms were reburnished. Once more the squadrons of De Soto were able to assume a martial bearing. Plumes nodded and glittering steel again flashed before the eyes of the wondering natives. The gallant men and fine horses lost at Mauvila, at Fort Alabama, on the Yazoo, and at Chickaza were for the moment forgotten, and the chivalric character of the Spaniard shone forth with renewed lustre as he marched down to the margin of the Mississippi and prepared to pass that boundary which he was destined never again to recross, but, like another Alaric, to make its bed his mausoleum. The month of May had but just manifested its arrival by its mild airs, and the expanding vegetation, combined with the increased flow of the waters, served to give life and animation to the scene. The river was judged to be half a league in width, but deep and swift, carrying down on its surface uprooted trees and floodwood. He effected a passage without molestation, and two hours before sunset his whole force was safely across, and he thus turned his back on the fierce Appalachian tribes who had so stoutly opposed him. Here, then, was the first expedition to penetrate that mighty and unconquerable West, which has for three centuries continued to be the theatre of geographical explorations conducted by the Spanish, French, and

Americans. It was not, indeed, till 1806, under the conduct of Lewis and Clarke, that De Soto's object was finally attained, the Cordilleras of the Rocky Mountains scaled, and the Pacific shores reached. He immediately made arrangements to put his columns in motion for the high grounds. But his position was one of embarrassment. He had rid himself of the Chickasaws and their affiliated tribes on the east banks of the river, but was surrounded by other Indians of even more savage character and actuated by a still fiercer spirit of enmity. Their language, also, being entirely different, Ortez could no longer make himself understood, and the tediousness and difficulty of communicating with the Indians may be imagined when we learn that at times four different interpreters had to be employed at once in the business of translating a single communication. These tribes were of the Issati or Dakota lineage. Dense forests, rearing their towering growth on swampy lands, surrounded him, but onward he marched, following the Indian footpath.

De Soto was a man not to be daunted by ordinary obstacles. After five days' march, partly through lagoons, he reached the highlands of Missouri; and here he found himself surrounded by the Casque, who are supposed to have been the Kaskaskias of the Algonkin group,—a people who, on the settlement of Illinois by the French, were found entirely east of the Mississippi. He here fell into a mistake similar to that which he had made in his march to Cofachique in relation to the Uchees. The Kaskaskias received him with friendship, glad to find an ally who might sustain them in a war with a neighboring tribe. They accompanied him in great force against their enemies the Capaha (Quappaws or Arkansas), under the pretext of aiding in carrying the baggage and acting as scouts and pioneers; but they had no sooner reached the vicinity of their enemies than they pushed ahead of the Spaniards and fell without mercy on the hostile tribe, killing and scalping all they met with, and plundering the previously deserted village.

This action cost De Soto a war. He attacked the Quappaw tribe in a stronghold on an island to which they fled in the Mississippi, where he was deserted by his allies. His new enemies belonged to a different group of the aborigines, who are known to us, ethnologically, as the Dakotas,—the nomades of the Western prairies. From this attack he withdrew with difficulty. While at the Capaha village, he sent messengers westward to inquire into the truth of rumors of mineral wealth, but the messengers found nothing but copper. They, however, penetrated into the Western plains, and discovered the buffalo. He then returned to Casque, on the St. Francis, a large village with abundance of food, where he remained many days to recruit his army. He then marched south, but soon, hearing reports of mineral wealth at the north, countermarched to the wild granitic regions on the sources of the St. Francis. He was at this time in the granite tract of St. Michael's, Missouri, celebrated for its volcanic upheavals and pinnacles of azoic rocks, its iron mountains, its lead-mines, and its ores of cobalt. This was the highest northern point west of the Mississippi River reached by him. He sent out runners to the salt country and to the buffalo country. He ranged through the Ozark Mountains and the defiles of White River.

Reports of new and tempting mineral regions in the south soon led him in search of a country called Cayas. He crossed the Unica or White River at Tanico, and allowed his troops to rest for twenty days in a fine valley at a place called Tula. The Indian residents of this place were "ill-favored, tattooed, and ferocious." The army then marched five days towards the west, over an elevated, uninhabited region, comprising the broad and rugged district of the modern Ozark Mountains. Beyond this broken chain De Soto entered the country of the Quipano (Pani, or Pawnee), which has a comparatively level surface. A few days' farther march westward, and he found himself in a territory abounding in game, well supplied with grass, and dotted over with prairies. Having discovered the Arkansas River, he determined to establish his winter-quarters near that stream. Ordering stalls to be constructed for his horses, and a regular encampment to be formed, on this spot he passed the winter of 1541-42. The site of this camp appears to have been on the banks of the Neosho, and was in the midst of beautiful natural meadows.

When spring had opened sufficiently to warrant him in moving forward, he proceeded down the Arkansas, crossing that stream near the present site of Van Buren, or Fort Smith, and following its southern plains down to Little Rock, where he again crossed to the north, and directed his course along the banks of the stream till he reached its mouth. He was greatly embarrassed in this march by a deep inlet of White River.

He selected a site on the eastern banks of the Mississippi for the capital of a Spanish colony, in the territory of a people who were sun-worshippers, and who were, judging by their language and religion, the Natchez. This tribe, who appear to have occupied a higher position on the Mississippi than they were found to possess at the period of the settlement of Louisiana, were called Quignaltangui. They manifested the deepest hostility, and ridiculed the idea of De Soto's being a child of the sun,—an idea which he had thrown out in his message to them requiring submission to his arms. "If you are a child of the sun," was the haughty reply, "return to him, dry up the Mississippi, and we will submit to you."

Being in a feeble state of health, and a fever beginning to prostrate him, De Soto encamped, and calmly prepared for his approaching end. After having appointed Moscoso, his camp-master, to succeed him, De Soto died, surrounded by his officers, who had followed him through scenes of danger and trial over nearly half the continent of North America. On the last day of May, 1542, he calmly yielded up his spirit. At first his body was interred in the vicinity, great precautions being taken to conceal the spot, lest the Indians should exhume and mutilate his remains. Finally his followers placed the corpse in the hollowed trunk of a tree, which they conveyed in a boat at midnight to the centre of the Mississippi River and sunk beneath its turbid waters.

With the death of De Soto the intrepid daring and noble emulation which had been called into action by his master mind began to flag; but, though the enterprise was in reality crushed, the fact did not immediately appear.

As soon as the funeral rites were finished, Moscoso prepared to lead a new expedition towards the west. He ascended the southern banks of the Arkansas, directing his course in a southwesterly direction across the Washita and the smaller affluents of the Arkansas and Red Rivers. He encountered the most determined opposition from all the tribes he met. They fought with a desperation which was extraordinary, and were repulsed with that chivalrous and dashing bravery which characterized the entire operations of the expedition. He eventually reached the buffalo plains which stretch from the Canadian River to the sources of the Red River. It had been expected that they should somewhere in this vicinity meet parties of Spanish military explorers from the south; but this hope was at last relinquished, and the army retraced its steps to the mouth of the Arkansas amid great perils and with unparalleled toil.

To found a colony at a point so remote from the sea, with the crippled and inadequate means in their possession, and in the face of the active hostility of all the Indian tribes both east and west of that stream, appeared to be a project so impracticable that Moscoso resolved to build boats and descend the Mississippi to its mouth. As soon as they were completed, the whole force embarked, the horses being placed in long narrow boats, with their fore feet in one and their hind feet in another. The Indians exulted on seeing the Spaniards making preparations to leave their country, and, embarking in their canoes, pursued the retiring troops with the utmost boldness and energy. The retreating forces were often obliged to deploy and defend themselves, and in these skirmishes the Spaniards suffered severely. The armor of the soldiers was proof against the arrows of the foe, but the flanks of the horses were exposed, so that these noble animals were thinned off day by day, until, on arriving at the mouth of the river, there was not a single horse left alive.

As soon as Moscoso entered the gulf, he steered for the coast of Panuca, where he finally arrived, after encountering great perils both from the warring elements and from the disagreement of the pilots. Thus terminated an expedition which had been organized with extraordinary splendor, and the members of which comprised some of the ablest and most chivalrous officers of the age. Nearly three years had been spent in traversing the immense tract of wilderness intervening between the peninsula of Florida and the plains of Arkansas. Everywhere the Indians had been found to be inimical to the Spanish race, and had manifested the most heroic spirit in repelling the invaders.

The track of De Soto west of the Mississippi is outlined more fully by Mr. Schoolcraft as follows:

After crossing at the lower Chickasaw Bluffs, he marched five days on an Indian trail over the alluvions of the Mississippi, west to the hill-country of the St. Francis, and reached the site of Casque, very probably a location of the Illinois Indians (Kaskaskias). He followed the wily chief of this village northeastwardly against his enemies the Capahas (Quappaws), on a bayou of the Mississippi, difficult to approach from that quarter. This was probably some seventy miles above his original crossing-point. He then returned southwest to Casque, and thence marched south to Quiguate, probably near Black River. Hearing fresh reports of mineral wealth, he now marched northwest to Coligoa, near the source of the St. Francis, in latitude about 35° 30′ or 36°. This was his utmost northern point. He was now at the foot of the high granitic peaks of St. Francis County, Missouri, celebrated in modern days for its Iron Mountains and the lead and cobalt mines of Mine La Motte. He then marched south in search of a rich province called Cayas (Kansas), and probably crossed the White River Valley at Tanico. He thence crossed a hill country to Tula, in the fine valley of Buffalo Creek. Recruiting at this place for twenty days, he passed an uninhabited region for five days, going west over elevations of the Ozark chain, and came to fertile prairies beyond, inhabited by Indians called Quipano (Pani, or Pawnee). A few days' farther march brought him to the banks of the Arkansas, near the Neosho, very likely at a point about the present site of Fort Gibson. Here, in a fruitful country of meadows, he wintered. Next spring he marched down the north banks of the Arkansas to a point opposite the present Fort Smith, where he crossed in a boat. He then descended the south bank of the river to Anilco (Little Rock), where the army crossed to the north bank, partly on rafts, and reached the mouth of the Arkansas, where he died.

CHAPTER VI.

CORONADO'S EXPEDITION INTO NEW MEXICO—THE ZUÑI, MOQUI, NAVAJOE, AND COGNATE TRIBES.

THE year 1519 was one of deep interest in the fortunes of the Gila, Rio del Norte, and Colorado Indians. Florida had been known nine years, when an event occurred of the greatest interest in the history of the continent. This was no other than the discovery of Mexico. The empire of Montezuma, which had been founded (according to tradition) on that of the Toltecs, had that year reached its culminating point. When Cortez landed on the Mexican shores, judging from the ordinary course of things, he appeared more likely to serve, with his few followers, as an offering to Huitzilopochtli, the war-god of the country, than to conquer it and bring it into subjection to Charles V. Yet in two years he was master of the empire. He had during that period entered Mexico the first time, turned upon Narvaez and defeated him, founded the city of Vera Cruz, and re-entered Mexico with the conquered troops, levelling its walls as he advanced; and he was soon heralded in Spain as a hero, and urged his claims at the Spanish court for rewards, as if he had performed feats worthy of a Hannibal or a Scipio.

Of the conquest we have only to remark that it exposed the tribes of the present enlarged area of the United States north of the line of the Gila and west of the Rio Grande del Norte to invasion. This result followed the taking of Mexico within the period of twenty years. It was resolved in 1530 to make New Spain a viceroyalty, and, after some delay in finding a suitable person, Mendoza was appointed to the chief office by the Spanish court. He reached the city of Mexico in 1535, bringing a printing-press,—the first, it is believed, ever brought to the American continent. Under his wise, energetic, yet calm and beneficent rule, the disorders of the country were remedied, various insurrections were quelled, and the reign of law was fully established.

It so happened that in the course of a few years a Franciscan missionary named Marcos de Niza, who had visited the country north of Sonora, reported that he had discovered a populous and rich kingdom called Quivera, or the Seven Cities, abounding in gold, the capital of which was named Cibola. Towards Cibola, therefore, all eyes were directed.

The enthusiasm of all who credited the story of De Niza received a new impulse, and large accessions were made to the number of believers, from the accounts given by Cabeça de Vaca of the Indian tribes he had seen during his extraordinary peregrinations, extended through a term of eight or nine years, between the point where he was wrecked on the Florida coast and New Galicia on the Pacific. Not only did his presence in Spain give origin to the expedition of De Soto, but also at the same time to the almost equally renowned one organized by Mendoza, the viceroy of Mexico, and placed under the command of Coronado. This expedition had been preceded by one sent out by Guzman, the governor of New Galicia, in search of the seven cities of Cibola; but this party penetrated no farther than Culiacan, whence it returned on account of the difficulties attending the enterprise. This effort only tended to stimulate the equipment of a more formidable organization by the viceroy.

As a preliminary step, Mendoza despatched De Niza, with two other friars and a competent military escort, into the region, taking Estevan, a negro who had accompanied Cabeça de Vaca, as a guide. On reaching Culiacan, on the borders of the country, they rested a few days, and prepared themselves with further information. Estevan, evincing the impatience natural to his African blood to participate in the first advantages of the anticipated discoveries, in his great eagerness to reach the place, preceded the three friars with a few Indians. He crossed the Gila, and, hurrying over the desert, which was without an inhabitant, reached the valley of Cibola, where they found the first town, while De Niza and his two companions were still sixty leagues in the rear. He made haste to present himself before the caciques of the town, of whom he insolently demanded their gold and their wives. On hearing this audacious demand, unsupported as it was by any power to enforce it, the chiefs questioned him closely as to his authority for making it. Judging from his replies that he was a spy from a party on its march to invade their country, they decided, after a short consultation, to put him to death, and immediately carried this decision into effect. When De Niza and his companions heard of this, they at once returned to Compostella; and thus ended the second attempt to reach the kingdom of the seven cities.

But a golden lie is not easily put down. It was an age in which nothing but wonders would be believed. Golden Indian provinces were constantly in the Spanish mind, and the friar De Niza, when he had reached Compostella, determined not to be behindhand in fanning the fires of expectation. He went to Mexico, and in an interview with Mendoza not only confirmed him in his ideas of golden regions north of the Gila, but published a description of his tour, in which, according to Castefiada, he gave the most alluring account of a country respecting which he found the popular impression so high.

Mendoza thereupon determined to hasten an expedition to explore and conquer the country and thus add it to the already large acquisitions made under the banners of Charles V. This was the beginning of the history of the intendency of New Mexico. To lead this expedition he finally named Francisco Vasquez Coronado, the successor of De Guzman as governor of New Galicia.

It was only necessary to announce such a design from the viceregal court at Mexico to attract adventurers from every quarter. Indeed, such was the enthusiasm evinced on this occasion that men of the highest rank sought eagerly for even subordinate places in the expedition. Of a force of three hundred men, it is said by

Casteñada that there never was an expedition organized in America which had such a proportion of gentry.

Mendoza himself repaired to Compostella to review the troops, and accompanied them two days' march on their way. Eight hundred Indians (doubtless glad to be fed) immediately joined this little army of cavaliers. It is worthy of note that this expedition set out at the same time that De Soto was traversing Florida, and that it had actually reached the Gila when he crossed the Mississippi. At Chiametta, Coronado met De Niza, who had been appointed guide to the expedition, and who, with a dozen men, had been despatched in advance. These men had penetrated to Chichiticale, two hundred leagues from Culiacan. De Niza's companions reported secretly that the country was nearly a desert. This was soon whispered about, and greatly dispirited many; but Fray de Niza endeavored to reanimate the desponding by telling them that the country seen by the officers was "good," and that he would guide them to rich provinces.

On reaching Chichiticale, of which so much had been boasted, Coronado found a single roofless and ruinous house, which had been built of "red earth," surrounded by the remains of a population which had evident claims to be regarded as belonging to a higher type of civilization than any of the existing tribes. The army soon entered the desert north of the Gila, and spent a fortnight in traversing it. After eight leagues' farther march, they came to a river, on the banks of which they soon after reached the long-sought Cibola. It was a small town, built on a high rock, and containing not over two hundred warriors. The houses were terraced in three or four stories, with a narrow and steep ascent. They were now probably at the old town of Zuñi. They immediately assaulted it, sword in hand, but were opposed by the casting down of stones, one of which knocked down Coronado. An hour's struggle, however, gave them the place. The country was one of those picturesque regions of remarkable geologic formation so common in that part of New Mexico. It gave them provisions, but no gold. There was such an utter disappointment in this respect that it was not without a strong effort that Fray de Niza could be protected from the rage of the disappointed soldiery, and he was soon sent off secretly for his own security.

Coronado made his head-quarters at Cibola, and sent out various expeditions into the adjacent regions: he also despatched invitations to the Indians to come in and establish friendly relations with him. These told him, apparently to rid themselves of such a guest, of a province of seven towns, called Tusayan, twenty-five leagues distant, the people of which were represented as living in high houses and being very valiant. The course is not mentioned, but, judging from subsequent events, it must have been generally west. He despatched Don Pedro de Tobar, with seventeen horsemen, four foot-soldiers, and a friar, to explore it. On reaching it, they found the Indians in possession of cultivated fields. As soon as they were aware of the presence of an enemy, they assembled in a body, armed with arrows, clubs, and bucklers. They drew a mark on the ground and forbade the Spaniards to pass it; but this only served as a signal for Tobar to advance, and he and his followers slew "great numbers of them." After this the Tusayans submitted, and presented their invaders with "cotton stuffs, tanned hides, flour, pine-apples, native fowls, maize, and turquoises." Such is, in part, the exaggerated language of the narrative of Casteñada. Tobar was now, doubtless, at the seven villages of the modern Moqui. They told him of a great river at twenty days' distance, which he would reach after crossing a desert inhabited by a gigantic people.

Coronado, on the return of this party, ordered Don Garcia Lopez de Cardenas, with twelve men, to explore this great river. They were well received by the Indians of Tusayan, who supplied them with food and guides, and after twenty days' march over an entirely uninhabited country the Spaniards stood gazing on the banks of the great cañon of the river "Tizou," now called Colorado. They were surprised at the elevation of its banks, which they thought "three or four leagues in the air." For three days they tried to find some depression to get down to the river, but, failing in this, and being threatened with a want of water, they retraced their steps to Cibola, passing in their way a high cataract, near which there were crystals of salt.

The information collected by Coronado at least made him better acquainted with his geographical position. After passing north of the Gila from Chichiticale he had found nothing but a desert. The first watercourse met with was a stream to which he gave the name of Vermejo, on ascending the banks of which he had indeed reached the long-sought Cibola, a name which had been long bandied about vaguely by rumor, but which there is no reason to believe that the Indians had ever bestowed upon it. The reports of De Niza and of De Vaca had proved alike fallacious; but the Spaniards were not to be thus discouraged. Coronado looked stoutly about him. By the expeditions of Don Pedro de Tobar and of Don Garcia Lopez de Cardenas he had evidently fixed the location of the town of the Moqui and the Colorado or Tizou River, and had clearly determined the existence of large desert tracts west of him.

In the mean time, information from the east and northeast poured in upon him, and denoted that to be the quarter from which he had most to expect. A chief of considerable presence and plausibility, called Bigotes, came to him from a town called Cicuyé, four days' march east of the Rio Grande del Norte. It was seventy miles east of Cibola, which, in the longitude of 35°, would denote the place to have been on the Pecos. Bigotes was well received, and was the first person to inform the invading army of the existence of the bison in that vicinity. One of the military parties had, on crossing the desert north of the Gila, found an enormous pair of horns, doubtless those of some animal of the deer tribe; another had encountered a flock of large-horned sheep; but they had witnessed nothing of the animal spoken of by this chief, and the intelligence created much excitement. The visit of Bigotes appears to have had the object of opening trade in that quarter. But, whatever his motives, he spoke far too favorably of the country and its resources. In effect, a most friendly alliance ensued.

Hernando de Alvarado, taking twenty men, with Bigotes as his guide, was first sent in that direction, having permission to be absent eighty days. He departed with alacrity. After five days' march, they arrived at a rock-castled town, called Accuco,—the modern Acoma in New Mexico. It was so high above the plain that the narrator quaintly says that the shot from an arquebuse could scarcely reach its summit. It had a stairway of steps cut in the rock, which were plain and convenient at the bottom, but which became faintly scraped in the rock and dangerous at the top, so that it was necessary to scramble in ascending. Provision was made for its defence by piles of stones which could be rolled down on the assailants. There was on this elevated area space to cultivate and to store maize, and the town had tanks of water.

No hostility was offered here, and, after viewing the place, Alvarado continued on his way. After three days' farther march, he came to another town, called Tigouex, on the Rio Grande, where the natives, seeing that he was accompanied by Bigotes, also received the party well. His next march occupied five days, which brought him to Cicuyé, the object of his expedition. This place was strongly fortified, but its inhabitants received them as those of the other towns had done,—as messengers on a friendly visit,—and they were courteously entertained.

While at this place, Alvarado was introduced to an Indian of striking appearance and demeanor, called El Turco. He wore a noted beard (whence the name), and spoke with great fluency. He had been taken prisoner by the Cicuyan Indians on the east of the Rio Grande; and, probably observing the eagerness which the Spaniards manifested for gold and silver, he spoke of these metals as being plentiful in the region in which he had been captured. It is likely, judging from subsequent events, that he thought only of his liberation through the march of the Spaniards into that region. However this may be, he was very lavish in his descriptions of the country, and said many things which were mere exaggerations. Under this new cause of excitement, the bison, which they had so eagerly wished to see, lost interest; and when Alvarado had accomplished his mission, he hurried with El Turco back to his starting-point, that he might communicate the intelligence in person to Coronado. The latter had in the mean time moved the position of the invading army from Cibola to Tigouex, on the Rio Grande. El Turco repeated his florid descriptions. He added that there was in that quarter a river two leagues wide, which contained fishes as large as horses, and was navigated by great lords, in canoes propelled by twenty oarsmen, having flags with golden eagles flying over their heads. This lying story was partly believed. The general sent Alvarado, with El Turco for his guide, back to Cicuyé, to reclaim certain golden bracelets of which he said he had been despoiled when he had been made a captive by the Indians of that village. But the cacique of Cicuyé assured Alvarado, on his arrival, that he had taken no bracelets from the prisoner, and that El Turco was "a great liar." Hereupon Alvarado lured Bigotes and the cacique of Cicuyé into his tent, and put them both in chains. In this condition they were marched back five leagues to Coronado, at Tigouex, who kept them imprisoned for six months. Affairs began thus to be involved by the bad judgment of Alvarado, who served the truth-teller and the liar alike.

Tigouex was now made head-quarters. At this place there were some houses of "seven stories," which rose above the rest like towers, and had "embrasures and loop-holes." This is called the "handsomest, best, and largest village in the province." The whole army was finally concentrated here, and passed the winter (1540–41[1]) at this place. Snow fell in December nearly two feet deep, it became cold, and the soldiers suffered from want of suitable clothing. To supply this, Coronado called for three hundred garments from the Indians; and when they interposed objections, saying that there were twelve villages to contribute their share, and that the chiefs must be consulted, he would brook no delay. The cavaliers sent by him stripped the poor natives on the spot, leaving them exposed to the inclemency of the weather; and when the dresses did not suit in quality, they stripped the next Indian they met, chief or commoner, and carried away his garments.

Coronado was not only inhuman in his exactions, but impolitic in his dealings with the red men. He had early in the autumn offended the sense of justice of the people of Cicuyé by imprisoning their chief, an aged man, instead of El Turco, who amused him with falsehoods. To the stripping the Indians of their garments were added, in the course of two months' wintering there by the Spaniards, acts of licentiousness and perfidy that roused the natives to a keen sense of wrong, and when the next campaign opened there was a general state of hostility. It appears that Coronado did not occupy the town of Tigouex, but camped in the open plain near it. In the course of the hostilities brought on by the folly and wickedness of some of his subordinates, orders were given to assault the rock-town. It sustained with firmness a long siege, and was finally abandoned by its inhabitants only from the want of water.

Coronado was now among the Indian rock-towns, with terraced houses, which compose a line of native "pueblos" connecting the Rio Pecos with the upper waters of the Little Colorado, up which latter he had marched by way of the fork of the Vermejo till he reached Cibola. This latter had been the talismanic word since first leaving Compostella and Culiacan. The disappointment when on reaching it they found it neither populous nor wealthy, the several fruitless expeditions of De Tobar and De Cardenas towards the west, and the experience and observations of the winter while the army was at Tigouex, had completely dissipated Coronado's sanguine hopes. The reports of Bigotes and El Turco from the east had, however, rekindled the Spanish enthusiasm, and fresh hopes were inspired by the word "Quivera," now on every soldier's tongue. The siege of Tigouex had not been completed when Coronado pushed on to Cicuyé (on the Pecos), with a view to leading an expedition to Quivera, and as soon as the spring opened the rest of his force followed. Unlike the previous experience of Alvarado, who, with only twenty men, had been everywhere received with friendship, the army was now compelled to fight its way. No longer received as a friend who desired only to open intercourse and commerce with the Indians, Coronado was regarded as an enemy, with the reputation of being both

---

[1] There is a discrepancy of a year in the statement of this writer.

cruel and treacherous,—a man who did not respect alliances, or regard truth and virtue.

When Coronado came to the Pecos it was still frozen so solid that horses could cross. On reaching Cicuyé he camped near the town, to which he restored its chief, so long and unjustly retained in captivity. This act was followed by the liberation of Bigotes, and friendly relations were apparently restored. Parties were sent out to establish intercourse with the neighboring towns, particularly with Chia and Quirix; but the more westerly towns, where he had sojourned, remained implacable, nor would the expelled natives return to the towns from which they had once deliberately fled. A belief in the ill-luck of certain localities, a trait of the Indian mind, accounts for the abandonment of towns, the ruins of which still exist in New Mexico.

The statements of El Turco respecting the wealth of Quivera were still believed, although denied by an Indian named Xabe, a native of Quivera itself. It was the 5th of May before the army left its camp at Tiguex, after a hard winter, to rejoin its general at Cicuyé, and as soon as the river was free from ice he began his march for Quivera, with El Turco and Xabe as guides. Here commences an extraordinary series of adventures, which, for reckless daring, are unparalleled by anything of the kind except those of De Soto, who had died the year before at the mouth of the Arkansas, but whose successor, Moscoso, was at this time pursuing his wild adventures west of the Mississippi. Coronado at once set out from Cicuyé. Four days' march towards the north-northwest, over a mountainous country, brought the army to the banks of a large and very deep river. It was necessary to bridge it, and after thus crossing it they continued to advance in the same course for ten days, when they reached the buffalo country, and found a nomadic people called Querechos, who lived in buffalo-skin tents and subsisted entirely on buffalo meat. Having communicated with El Turco, these Querechos confirmed his statements. Coronado was now marching in a northeastern direction, and every step carried him farther from the true position of Quivera.[1] These nomadic Querechos directed him to march eastwardly, where he would find a large river, which he could follow ninety days without leaving a populous country, and which was more than a league in breadth. Continuing their march in the same course, the Spaniards reached extensive plains, and came into the midst of incredible multitudes of the bison. The flying natives were again encountered in their march towards the east, and El Turco asserted that they were now but two days' march from a town called Haxa. There was an Indian in the army named Sopete, a native of Quivera, who is called "a painted Indian," who constantly affirmed that El Turco was a liar. Still, Sopete was not believed, because the nomads, in whom we may probably recognize the modern Comanches, concurred with El Turco. But the warnings of Xabe and Sopete were disregarded. On Coronado went, traversing immense plains, seeing nothing for miles together but

---

[1] It is noticeable that Grand Quivera, on the modern maps, is in another direction, being nearly due east of Don Pedro.

skies and herds of bison; hundreds of these they killed. Gulfs and valleys, which were occasionally encountered, formed no impediment to the indomitable zeal and courage of his followers. Literally they overcame every physical obstacle. For seven-and-thirty days they pushed on, horse and foot. It was said, on the authority of an Indian woman captured, that they had reached to within nine days' journey of the advance party of De Soto. From the accounts given, Coronado must have marched seven or eight hundred miles east of the point at which he crossed the Rio Grande. He was forty days with a light party in retracing his steps to Cicuyé; and he had penetrated, without doubt, through portions of Texas and far into the present area of Arkansas, the supposed "Arache" of Castefiada.

The ardently-sought Quivera still eluded discovery. It was the golden town of this talismanic name that was to reward the toils of these arduous and harassing journeys through immense solitudes inhabited only by countless herds of bison and by their flying enemies, the Indian nomads of the prairies. At length Coronado, when he had probably reached the great south branch of the Arkansas, determined to send his army back, and at the same time, taking a light party of cavalry, to continue the search a little farther. As a preliminary step to these movements, El Turco was closely examined as to the cause of his numerous and persevering falsehoods. The Indian, if not taken entirely aback by these examinations, was put to extremities, and, from whatever cause, confessed that his design had been to entangle and mislead the army and cause its destruction on these bleak wastes and level plains of grass. On this discovery of his bad motives, Coronado ordered him to be strangled. This was done with military promptitude, and thus perished a man who had exercised a leading influence for a long time in determining the movements of this army,—who seemed, indeed, reckless of truth in his assertions, but who, if the secret workings of his mind could be unfolded, perhaps thought himself to be doing the general cause of the Indian a service by leading its direst enemies to destruction.

After this act the army marched back under trusty Teyas guides, who led them in twenty-five days a distance which they had by involved courses been thirty-seven in originally traversing. Coronado spent a few days more in his search, and then returned and rejoined his forces west of the Rio Grande, bringing the report that he had visited Quivera, which is said to exist "at the foot of the mountains bordering the sea,"—an expression that would puzzle the wits of any geographer. The description given of its position, resources, and population is at best so vague that the term appears to be used by Castefiada rather as something to salve disappointed hopes, or garnish over ill-formed or ill-executed plans of discovery.

Every practical object of the expedition had indeed failed. There was not only no new Mexico or new Peru, as it was fondly hoped there would be, to serve as the basis of conquest and discovery, but not even a particle of gold or silver was found. Instead of it they had found rough mountain-tracts, or vast deserts of sand, covered with grass, generally without forests and without water, and occupied by tribes devoid of civilization. The valleys susceptible of cultivation constituted but an inconsiderable portion of the whole country, and could be made productive only by irrigation. The Indians who occupied these often lived on high castellated pinnacles of sandstone rock, of which they had taken possession, and which they had rudely fortified against the wild roving tribes. They cultivated maize in isolated valleys, far separated from one another by wide deserts. There were some slight traces of a fixed industry and incipient art, but there were few and very detached elements out of which to construct a civil government.

Coronado, when he had reached his head-quarters at Tigouex, turned his thoughts towards a return to New Galicia. This design was not, however, it would seem from Casteñada, in accordance with the wishes of the body of his army, who desired to explore farther; but in April, 1643, the army took up its line of march for Mexico. Thus terminated the expedition of Coronado, which was the first to give to Europeans a knowledge of the manners, customs, arts, and character of the Indians of New Mexico.

CHAPTER VII.

VOYAGES OF RIBAULT AND LAUDONNIÈRE—MENENDEZ—RETALIATORY EXPEDITION OF DE GOURGUES—FOUNDING OF ST. AUGUSTINE.

UP to this point our information regarding the Indian tribes has been derived in direct sequence from incidental notices of the operations of De Leon and De Ayllon in the south, of Cartier and Roberval in the north, of Verazzani in the region of the central littoral tribes, of Narvaez and De Soto among the Appalachian and the Issati, or Great Western family, and of Cabeça de Vaca and Coronado among the buffalo-hunters and the house-building tribes of the high plains of New Mexico. The year 1542 witnessed the failure of three principal attempts at colonization,—those of Cartier, De Soto, and Coronado.

Twenty years of comparative inaction and quiet succeeded these energetic efforts to found territorial sovereignties in the extensive country possessed by the Indians. In the mean time the Reformation had made such progress in Europe as to engender a new and bitter source of discord between the subjects of the colonizing powers. Xavier had taught the ancient Christian faith to the natives of India, and Las Casas was selected to perform the same service for the benighted and ill-used aborigines of America. Religious instruction was considered to be an essential adjunct of every attempt to explore, conquer, and colonize, an ecclesiastical force always accompanying each expedition, whose duty it was to turn the native tribes from their gross demonology and idolatry to the service of God.

Prominent among the converts in France to the new doctrines promulgated by Luther and Calvin was Admiral Coligny, a man of much influence, one of the nobility, and holding a high rank. The narrow-minded Charles IX., then a mere boy, and his bigoted mother, Catherine de Medicis, were then in power in France. Coligny, being desirous of providing an asylum for his persecuted countrymen professing the Protestant faith, turned his attention to the New World. He first made an experiment in Brazil, which failed through the treachery of Villegagnon, his agent, who renounced his faith. Coligny next directed his thoughts to Florida, which was a part of the region which, in 1524, had been named New France by Verazzani. He received a patent from the king for founding a colony in this quarter, and provided two ships, which were placed under the command of Jean Ribault, a skilful and resolute Huguenot, who set sail from Havre on the 18th of February, 1562. Steering a nearly direct course across the Atlantic, without touching at any of the West India islands, he made the coast of Florida on the last day of April, the voyage, owing to tempestuous weather, having occupied a little over two months. The following day he cast anchor off the mouth of the St. John's River, naming it the river of May; then, entering it with his boats, he ascertained that there was a good depth of water in the channel.

Ribault took possession of the country in the name of the king, and erected a stone monument which he had brought with him from France for that purpose. Having established a friendly and pleasant intercourse with the natives, after spending a few days with them he re-embarked, and during four weeks continued his voyage along the coast until he arrived at Port Royal, within the present limits of South Carolina. Finding, on exploring it by means of his boats, that the harbor was spacious, the water deep, and the anchorage excellent, he entered it with his largest ships and dropped his anchors. The territory in which he then was had been named Chicora by the natives, as also by the early Spanish adventurers. Magnificent scenery, both land and water, was spread before him in every direction. Delighted with the prospect, he took formal possession of the surrounding territory by erecting an engraved monumental stone bearing the king's arms. Having determined to found a settlement at this place, a suitable spot was selected, which is supposed to have been near to or on the site of the present town of Beaufort, where he erected a fortification, called, in honor of the king, Fort Charles. Leaving thirty men, well provided with arms, tools, and supplies, to begin operations, he placed them under the command of Albert de Peirria, and then returned to France. Being a strictly conscientious man, Ribault did not follow the example of the Spanish mariners and abduct the natives of the country that he might exhibit them in Europe as specimens of the Indian race.

The Chicora Indians, having naturally very gentle manners, very kindly supplied the colonists with maize, besides rendering them other services. In these offices of kindness the local chief, Andasta, took a prominent part, and was seconded by other chiefs at more southerly points, who were respectively entitled Ouade, Couexes, Maccoa, Outina, Satouriona, Wosta, Oleteraca, Timagoon, and Potanou, the orthographical elements of which names do not coincide with the Muscogee, Cherokee, or any known member of the Floridian stock.

The colonists themselves, however, being idle and factious, planted nothing, and had no idea of directing their attention to the real business before them. Peirria, having no proper conception of the authority delegated to him, became an inflated tyrant, hanged one of the men as a measure of discipline, and performed other arbitrary acts. Eventually the colonists rebelled against his authority and put him to death, after which, having appointed another leader in his stead, they determined to build a vessel and return in it to France. This plan was carried out, and the entire party embarked, abandoning the fort. The voyage was long and tempestuous, and, the vessel proving unseaworthy, they suffered horribly. Most of them died of starvation and exposure. At length, when near the coast of France, an English vessel hove in sight, and the few survivors were saved.

When Ribault returned to France, after establishing his little colony at Fort Charles, he found the contest between the Catholics and the Reformers raging with greater violence than ever; and Coligny was so deeply involved in this struggle that he applied to the king in vain for succor for the colony. As soon, however, as the warfare against the Huguenots had subsided, three ships were fitted out to convey assistance to the colony in Chicora, and placed under the orders of René de Laudonnière, who, in addition to the ordinary outfit of men and supplies, was provided with an artist, who had orders to sketch the features of the natives, as also their costumes and other curiosities.[1]

Laudonnière sailed from Havre on the 22d of April, 1564, one year and nine months subsequent to the first departure of Ribault from the same port. Intelligence of the sad fate of those left at Fort Charles had probably been received in France prior to this time, although the fact is not distinctly stated. At all events, Laudonnière did not proceed to Fort Charles, but on the 25th of June cast anchor off the mouth of the river of May (St. John's), in Florida. On entering the river he was received by Satouriona and his tribe, who shouted in French *ami, ami*. By them he was guided to the monument of possession erected by Ribault, which he found crowned with garlands and surrounded by little baskets of maize. There was, indeed, a cordiality in the reception of the French by these aborigines, which, whatever may have occasioned it, has always marked the intercourse of the French with the Indians from that day to the present, and which has not been manifested by them towards any other nation.

Laudonnière was entranced, not only with the picturesque beauty of the country, but also with its fertility, and its fragrant flowers and luxuriant vegetation. Quitting the St. John's, he sailed northwardly along the coast until he entered a river, which he named the Somme, where he was also received in a friendly manner by the Indians. A few days subsequently he returned again to the St. John's, and built a fort on its southern bank, about three leagues from its mouth, which he named Caroline, in honor of Charles IX. The events connected with the history of this fort—the mutiny, the improvements, the buccaneering and the executions, the visit to the friendly chief Andasta at Port Royal, Indian negotiations, fights, and other occurrences—would impart a deep interest to this portion of the narrative, but can only be thus incidentally noticed. Their result was the transmission of false reports to France, in consequence of which Laudonnière was recalled.

SECOND VISIT OF RIBAULT TO FLORIDA—TREACHEROUS MASSACRE OF HIMSELF AND HIS MEN.

The intestine dissensions in France having been in a measure allayed, Admiral Coligny renewed his representations to the king in favor of his plan of colonization in Florida. Early in January, 1565, authority was granted him to equip seven vessels for another voyage thither, with all possible despatch. This squadron was placed under the command of Ribault, who found no difficulty in procuring as many vol-

---

[1] The artist was Le Moyne, to whom we are indebted for the first attempts to delineate the ancient Indians of this part of America.

unteers as he deemed necessary for the service, some of whom carried with them their wives and children. Whatever reports may have reached France concerning the untoward events at Fort Charles, they do not appear to have dampened the energy with which this expedition was equipped. Ribault sailed from Dieppe on the 27th of May, and arrived at the river St. John's, Florida, on the 28th of August. Ascending the river to Fort Caroline, he was welcomed by Laudonnière, whose conduct he approved. A few days subsequently, September 4, a Spanish squadron, under the command of Pedro Menendez de Aviles, a narrow-minded and cruel bigot, arrived at the same place with a comparatively large force of men, and more substantial and larger vessels. He held a commission from Philip II. to make discoveries and found a colony, and had explicit instructions to expel the Huguenots and Lutherans who had fled from France under the patronage of Coligny.

On the 8th of September, Menendez landed a few leagues south of the St. John's, at a point where laborers had been set to work a day or two previous to erect a fortification, which he named St. Augustine. This is the oldest town in the United States by more than forty years. Ribault, having determined to put to sea and attack the squadron, assembled his officers to deliberate on the measure. Objections were made to this plan by Laudonnière, but the majority pronounced in its favor. At this time an Indian chief arrived with the news that the Spaniards were digging trenches and erecting breastworks at the place where they had landed. By attacking their shipping, Ribault thought he could frustrate their design. Flushed with this idea, he took nearly all the available force of the fort and set sail to encounter the enemy. At first calms prevented the contest, and subsequently a storm drove the French out to sea. Menendez, learning the defenceless condition of Fort Caroline, determined to march against it with five hundred men. Heavy rains and intervening marshes protracted his movements, but after three days' march across the country under the direction of Indian guides his army reached the environs of the fort. The Spaniards advanced cautiously, and were not seen until they were close to the fort, which, taking advantage of some breaches, they at once assaulted. The contest was short: the works were soon stormed, and the survivors were nearly all immediately put to the sword, bigoted zeal adding its incitement to the perpetration of these horrors. It is stated that on the 20th of September, when it was attacked, Fort Caroline had but eighty-six persons within its walls, a part of whom were women and children. Only nine or ten had ever borne arms, and but seventeen soldiers were fit for service, including some who were still confined from the effects of wounds received in a battle with the Indians. The fort itself was found to be in a dilapidated state, Laudonnière having used the timber of one angle to build a vessel when he had determined to abandon it. Laudonnière escaped into the woods, together with some others. Several of the prisoners were taken to a tree standing near the fort, and were all hanged on its limbs. The following inscription was then affixed to the trunk: "Not as Frenchmen, but as Lutherans."

Meantime, the squadron of Ribault was wrecked on the Florida coast, without, however, the loss of any lives. The commander, after organizing his force, began his march back to Fort Caroline, following the coast-line. Starvation soon reduced the men to mere skeletons. At length, on the banks of a stream, they were confronted by Menendez with superior forces. A parley, negotiations, and a surrender ensued, the French delivering up their arms. They were then conveyed across the river in squads, and as soon as each squad reached the other side their hands were tied behind their backs, after which they were marched off to a distance and shot. When Ribault at last discovered the treachery, he was almost immediately deprived of life by a Spanish soldier, who stabbed him with a poniard; and Ortez, his junior in command, shared the same fate.

Intelligence of the horrid treachery of the Spaniards was received in France with one universal burst of indignation. The relatives of the persons massacred in Florida petitioned the king for redress, alleging that the colonists had gone thither by his authority, and that consequently it was his crown that had been insulted. The nation demanded that the King of Spain should be required to make amends for the atrocities of his subjects. But Charles IX. cared no more for these events than did Philip II. Protestantism being a heresy loathed by both monarchs, nothing was done. The blood of Ribault and of his nine hundred followers vainly appealed to the French government for vengeance.

At length the matter was taken in hand by the Chevalier Dominique de Gourgues, a Gascon gentleman, descended from an ancient family. He possessed an enviable reputation for courage and character, and stood high in public estimation for his military services both in France and in foreign countries. His success and skill in naval affairs were also of a high order.

At his own cost Gourgues equipped three vessels of moderate tonnage, adapted to the navigation of small rivers and shallow bays. In calling for volunteers, both soldiers and sailors, he told no one his precise object, the prestige of his name being sufficient. He mustered one hundred soldiers having fire-arms (among whom were several gentlemen), and eighty mariners armed with cross-bows. He carried with him provisions for one year. It was the 22d of August before he left the coast of France. He appeared to meditate a descent on the shores of Africa, which he really visited, but finally, steering across the Atlantic, he made the shores of Brazil, whence he directed his course to Cape San Antonio, the west extremity of Cuba. At this place he called his men together and revealed to them the object of the expedition. He stated the injuries inflicted upon their country, the insult to their king, the gross violation of all recognized laws of war, and, above all, the outrage upon humanity. Having aroused their feelings and sense of justice, he sailed into the river Somme, or St. Mary's, now a part of the boundary between Florida and Georgia.

Nearly a year had elapsed in the performance of the long and circuitous voyage, and in the delays incident to the landings which had been made. Spring had again clothed the Florida coasts in verdure. It was early in the month of April when Gourgues entered the river St. Mary's. The Indians were assembled in considerable numbers, and evinced signs of hostility until they ascertained that the new-comers were French. The chief, Satouriona, was there to welcome him, and restored to him a young Frenchman (Pierre Delre), who had escaped to the Indians after the massacre of the garrison of Fort Caroline, and who subsequently became very serviceable to the French as an interpreter. Satouriona soon gave Gourgues to understand that the Indians hated the Spaniards, whose domination was irksome, and at once agreed to aid Gourgues in an attack on the three Spanish forts, then located on the St. John's. The movements of Gourgues were very rapid. Finding the Indians ready to second him, he determined to attack the enemy immediately. In three days the Indians, to the number of three hundred, armed with bows and led by experienced warriors, set out by land for a rendezvous on the St. John's. Gourgues, intending to proceed by water, embarked his men in boats, but, the winds being adverse, when half-way thither he landed and marched across the country. When he arrived at the rendezvous all the Indians were there, eager for the fray.

A conference having been held with the Indian chiefs, they marched forward, and just at nightfall reached the river. It was decided to attack the fort on the south bank at daybreak, the Indians being skilful guides, but it happened that the tide in a creek near the fort was up, making it then too deep to ford. This caused a delay, during the continuance of which they lay concealed in the forest. When the tide flowed out, the allies crossed the creek unobserved, and stormed and carried the fort, sword in hand, retaining but few prisoners.

The feelings of Gourgues and his men were much excited by the capture of a culverin having the arms of Henry IV. engraved on it, which had been mounted in Fort Caroline. Ordering his boats around, he determined immediately to assault the north fort. He embarked his men in military order, but the Indians, too impatient to wait for the return of the boats, plunged into the river and swam across. Seeing so great an array, the garrison, sixty in number, made no show of defence, but fled, with the intention of seeking shelter in another fort, situated three miles above. But they were met by another strong party of French, and, being hemmed in by the Indians in the rear, were completely cut to pieces, with the exception of fifteen men, who were detained that they might be hanged.

Fort Mateo, the strongest of the three works which the Spaniards had erected after the capture of Fort Caroline, was still unharmed. While meditating on the best mode of attack, they were informed by one of the Spanish prisoners, a soldier from Fort Mateo, of the exact height of its walls, to scale which ladders were at once prepared. At this time the Indians discovered a Spaniard in camp in the disguise of an Indian, who proved to be a spy. From him Gourgues learned that the garrison consisted of two hundred and sixty men, that the fort was large, and that it was believed that Gourgues had a force of two thousand men. He instantly determined on his plan of attack, and, after two days spent in preparation, he directed the Indians to conceal themselves in the forest, on both sides of the river, near the fort. He then crossed in boats with his whole force, merely leaving behind him fifteen men as a guard. As soon as his army was seen from the fort, the Spaniards opened their culverins on him, to avoid the effects of which he landed and took possession of an eminence, whence he could overlook the fort and the movements of its garrison, while his own troops were concealed and protected. He designed taking the work by escalade the following morning, but the Spaniards precipitated matters by making a sally of sixty men. Gourgues ordered an officer and twenty men to get between the fort and the sallying party by a circuitous route, which being accomplished, he marched rapidly forward, directing his forces to reserve their fire for a close contest, and after the first discharge to rush on sword in hand. Many of the foe fell, and though the rest fought bravely they were at length obliged to retreat, but, encountering the force in their rear, every man was slain, no quarter being given.

Seeing the flower of their force thus cut down, the garrison, crediting the exaggerated reports of the French strength, fled across the river, where the Indians lying in ambush fell upon them with overwhelming fury. Such was the skill of the savages in the use of the arrow that one bolt passed through the buckler of a Spanish officer and entered his body, killing him on the spot. The French, having again crossed the river, assaulted the Spaniards in the rear, killing all who escaped the Indians, and thus the entire garrison perished, with the exception of a few reserved for the gallows as a retaliation for the cruelty of the Spaniards after the surrender of Ribault.

Fort Mateo was entered triumphantly, and was found to contain a large quantity of arms, nine culverins, and eighteen casks of powder. The following day the boats were freighted with the artillery, but the magazine was blown up by a secret train left by the enemy, which was unwittingly fired by an Indian while cooking fish.

The work of retribution was not, however, as yet fully completed. Drawing up his men, and the auxiliary Indians who had taken so active a part in the short campaign, and placing all the Spanish prisoners whom he had taken in the centre, Gourgues addressed the latter, recounting to them the atrocities committed by Menendez, and finished by condemning them to immediate execution in the same manner as that adopted by the Spaniards. They were then taken to the same tree which had served the nefarious Menendez, and upon which the latter had placed the inscription, "Not as Frenchmen, but as Lutherans." The thirty prisoners having been suspended upon its limbs, Gourgues, with a red-hot pointed iron, inscribed a strip of pine board with the words, "Not as Spaniards, but as traitors, robbers, and murderers," and fastened it to the gallows-tree.

Immediately returning with his cavaliers and his native allies to St. Mary's River, where he had left his ships, and having distributed presents to the Indians, who were greatly pleased with his martial exploits, Gourgues, on the 3d of May, set sail for France, arriving at the port of Rochelle on the 6th of June, after a very prosperous voyage.

PERIOD II.

EARLY EUROPEAN SETTLEMENTS.

CHAPTER I.

DISCOVERY OF VIRGINIA—EFFORTS FOR ITS COLONIZATION—SIR WALTER RALEIGH—SIR RICHARD GREENVILLE—SETTLEMENT ON ROANOKE ISLAND ABANDONED—THE ABORIGINES—JAMESTOWN SETTLED—CAPTAIN JOHN SMITH —OPECHANCANOUGH—MASSACRE OF THE COLONISTS—INDIAN POPULATION.

The skill and daring of John and Sebastian Cabot gave to England, in 1497, such possessory right to the North American continent as priority of discovery could confer, but for nearly a century she made no attempt to enforce it. The first energetic effort in this direction was made by Sir Walter Raleigh, than whom no man living during the reign of Elizabeth acquired greater celebrity for military exploits, naval skill, enthusiastic pursuit of transatlantic discoveries, and the furtherance of colonization. He was equally renowned for his wit, learning, eloquence, and accomplishments. Descended from an old family in Devonshire, he was educated at Oxford, and after serving with distinguished credit in France under Coligny and Condé, in the Netherlands under the Prince of Orange, and in Ireland against the rebels, he was received at Elizabeth's court with marked favor. The world is indebted to Raleigh for the discovery of Virginia. His plans for promoting colonization on the Atlantic coast were early developed, and he was, beyond all others, a zealous as well as steadfast advocate of the policy of extending the power and civilization of England to the wild shores of America. He commanded an expedition which explored Guiana, in South America, and ascended the Orinoco to the distance of four hundred miles from its mouth. Subsequently he wrote an account of the countries visited by him, which is celebrated for its truthful, glowing, and graphic descriptions. Having been one of the originators of the expedition of Sir Humphrey Gilbert (his half-brother) to Newfoundland, when that attempt to found a colony failed, he obtained letters patent from Elizabeth authorizing him to renew the effort in a more southerly latitude on the Atlantic. These letters were dated on the 25th of March, 1584, nearly six years after the failure of Gilbert's attempt. The authority to make discoveries and found a colony was plenary, but the government did not undertake to defray any part of the cost. It was, strictly speaking, a private or associate adventure,

the crown conferring upon the projectors the proprietorship of the country discovered, merely stipulating for the usual acknowledgment of sovereignty by the surrender of one-fifth of the proceeds of all mines. Some grants of licenses on wines, and other emoluments, were at the same period bestowed upon Raleigh to enable him to liquidate the charges of his equipment; in addition to which, he associated with him other persons possessing means and influence, among whom were included blood-relations. Two vessels were provided and placed under the respective commands of Philip Amidas and Arthur Barlow, the latter of whom had served under Raleigh in Ireland as an officer of the land-forces. On the 27th of April the ships sailed out of the Thames, and, following the usual circuitous route, via the Canaries and the West Indies, arrived off the coast of Florida on the 2d of July. The Virginia coasts were occupied by clans of Algonkins of the Powhatanic type. The natives were too feeble to inspire terror, clothed in deer-skins, having for weapons bows and arrows, hatchets of stone, and wooden swords, and shields made of bark and sticks woven together. The greatest chief in the country could not muster more than seven hundred or eight hundred fighting-men. Their wars were carried on by sudden surprises at daybreak or by moonlight, ambushes, and other subtle devices. Captain Smith once met a party of seven hundred, and so great was the superiority conferred on the English by their fire-arms that with fifteen men he was able to withstand them all. Their largest town contained but thirty houses, with walls of bark, or of upright poles bent over and fastened at the top. Each clan obeyed the authority of its own chief, but all were associated in a general confederacy, which was ruled by Powhatan, whose council-fire and residence were located on the James River. Those who lived on the coasts relied on fish as one of the means of their subsistence. The hunting-grounds extended west to the general line of the falls of the Virginia rivers, where people of a diverse stock as well as language supervened, extending to the Alleghanies. Whatever occurrence of moment happened on the borders, as the appearance of enemies or strangers, was immediately communicated to the central administration. In this way a sort of inchoate republic was governed.

Amidas and Barlow approached a low shore covered with trees and fringed with an outer line of islands and islets. Having cast anchor, Barlow landed in his yawl at the island of Wocoon, where he admired the handsome trees, indigenous fruits, and vigorous vegetation. But no Indians appeared until the third day, when three of the natives approached in a canoe, and a friendly intercourse ensued. The following day the ships were visited by several canoes, in one of which was Granganameo, Powhatan's brother. His attendants spread a mat on the ground, upon which he fearlessly seated himself, and evinced perfect self-possession, though the Englishmen were completely armed. He made gesticulations of friendship by stroking his head and breast with his hand and repeating this ceremony on his visitors.[1] He then

---

[1] This custom of passing the hand over the face and breast was noticed by Cabeça de Vaca in tribes west of Arkansas about 1536. Jacques Cartier also found this custom, in 1534, in the tribes who visited his ships in the St. Lawrence.

arose and addressed them in a "long speech," all his attendants standing in silence. Presents were now laid before him, and before four other persons who appeared to be officials, which at the close of the interview he directed to be taken away as all belonging to himself. At this interview friendly salutations were exchanged. The Indians are described as "a proper well-proportioned people, very civil in their manners and behavior." After this interview, reciprocal confidence being established, a traffic was commenced.

Amidas then proceeded to enter Pamlico Sound, and the following day, at evening, anchored near the island of Roanoke, which he estimated to be seven leagues distant from Occoquan, the first place of landing.

At Roanoke the English found a small village, comprising nine houses, one of which was occupied by the family of Granganameo. The chief being absent, his wife received Amidas with courtesy and hospitality. She was an energetic woman, and ordered their boat to be drawn ashore and the oars to be carried up to the village to guard them from thieves. The feet of the English having been washed in warm water, she then invited them to partake of hominy, boiled venison, and roasted fish, with a dessert of "melons and other vegetables."

Fearing treachery, Amidas embarked in his boat at evening, and, pushing it out into the sound, anchored off the village, intending thus to pass the night. The wife of Granganameo, divining the reason for this precaution, and evidently regretting his mistrust, sent down the evening meal in pots to the shore. She also ordered mats to be carried to the boat to shelter the English from the night dews, and directed several men and thirty women to remain there all night as a guard.

This constituted the extreme limit of their discoveries. Returning to their anchorage, the explorers spent two months and a half on the coast, when, having finished their traffic, they set sail for England about the middle of September, carrying with them two natives, called Manteo and Wasechoe. The safe return of the ships, and the narration of the discoveries made, created a strong sensation, and Elizabeth was so much pleased with the description of the country, and with the prospect of extending her sovereignty which it presented, that she named it Virginia, in allusion to her own state of single-blessedness.

The desire to found colonies was effectually aroused in England by the results of this discovery, which was the germ of the British colonial establishments. The pioneer ships had scarcely returned from Virginia, when a second voyage was resolved on. Sir Richard Greenville, who had been one of the promoters of the first effort, originated this second adventure, and determined to lead it. For this enterprise seven ships were equipped in the harbor of Plymouth and fully provided with all necessary supplies. Raleigh was deeply interested in this new effort, and to render it successful nothing was omitted which at that era was deemed essential. The presence of Manteo and his companion had excited a lively interest in the public mind respecting the aborigines, and, in order to acquire correct ideas of their features, manners, and customs, Raleigh sent out Mr. With, or Wyth, a skilful writer. A gentleman of his household, Thomas Harriot, a noted mathematician and scholar, also accompanied the expedition for the purpose of describing the Indian character. Thomas Cavendish, who afterwards circumnavigated the globe, was one of the adventurers. Manteo returned to Virginia as guide and interpreter.

The ships sailed from Plymouth on the 9th of April, carrying one hundred and eight colonists, and, after crossing the Atlantic, on the 26th of June anchored off the island of Occoquan. At this time the principal local ruler on the coast was Wingina, who resided on the island of Roanoke. To him a deputation was immediately despatched, under the guidance of Manteo, who is uniformly praised for his fidelity.

Other parties were sent off in different directions to acquire a knowledge of the geography and make inquiry concerning the productions of the country. Sir Richard himself crossed to the mainland and explored the villages on the Chowan River, where he involved himself and attendants in hostilities with the natives. The manner in which this difficulty arose was as follows. The Indians had stolen a silver cup from his mess-furniture, in revenge for which, after his return to the island of Occoquan, he burned their village and destroyed their corn. After this impolitic and cruel act, he suddenly determined to return to England. He left a colony of one hundred and eight persons on the island of Occoquan, over whom he appointed Mr. Ralph Lane governor. On his route home he visited the West Indies, in the expectation of encountering Spanish vessels, and, having captured a large ship, returned with his prize to Plymouth, which he reached on the 18th of September, after an absence of a little more than six months.

Sir Richard Greenville's exploratory trip, and his severity towards the Indians, seconded as it was by the aggressive policy pursued by his successors, had the effect of keeping the settlers in a state of confusion and continual dread of the aborigines. It is not to be wondered at that the colonists soon found that they were regarded by the Indians with suspicion and mistrust. Finesse was retaliated by finesse, deception by deception. About the same time Granganameo, their best friend, died, and his death was followed by that of his aged father, Ensenore. A general state of unfriendly feeling at this time existed towards the English. The colonists planted nothing, and with great reluctance the Indians partly supplied them with corn, game, and fish, which at length they withheld altogether. The result of this non-intercourse policy was that parties of the colonists were necessitated to forage for supplies on the islands, and some on the mainland. Finally they were compelled to subsist on roots and shell-fish, until, at their own request, they were carried back to England in the fleet of Sir Francis Drake.

Of the customs, rites, creed, and opinions of the Indians, Mr. Harriot gives the following account: "They believe in one God, who is self-existent and eternal, and the creator of the world. After this he created an order of inferior gods to carry out his government. That then the sun, moon, and stars were created as instruments of the secondary gods. The waters were then made, becoming the vital principle of all creatures. He next created a woman, who, by the congress of one of the gods, brought forth children, and thence mankind had their beginnings. They thought the gods were all of human shape, and worshipped them, by their images, dancing, singing, and praying, with offerings. They believed in the immortality of the soul, which was destined to future happiness, or to inhabit *Popagussa*, a pit or place of torment, where the sun sets; and this doctrine they based on the assertion of persons who had returned after death." These doctrines are said to have had much weight with the common Indians, but to have made but little impression on their Weroances, or rulers, and priests. How accurately they were reported, and how much they were colored by Christian predilections, may be judged of from the known repugnance of the native sages to give information on such points, from their soon being on ill terms or at open war with the English, and from the probability that some of the more striking characteristics of this alleged Indian creed had been derived from traditions related by Manteo and Granganameo, the first a baptized convert, and the latter a politic friend of the English and an admirer of their manners.

Wingina himself would often be at prayers with the English, it having been their practice to read the service publicly in the presence of the Indians. But it was evident that they deemed the English great necromancers, possessing almost unlimited influence with the gods, firmly believing that they could inflict diseases, insure death, and impart vigor to the growth of or destroy their corn-crops. The use of letters, the burning-glass, mathematical instruments, clocks, and guns seemed to them the work of gods rather than of men, and the terrors of the latter they could neither comprehend nor resist. They even attributed every new sickness which appeared among them to wounds from unseen bullets discharged by invisible agents in the air around them. The Bible, which was read by the English, the Indians considered to be a talisman, whose virtues resided in the material of the book, and not in its spiritual teachings. They deemed it a favor to be allowed to handle, hug, and kiss it, passing it over their faces, and rubbing it over their breasts.

Mr. Harriot also observed that they had great veneration for a certain plant,—a spontaneous growth of the country,—which they called *uppowoc*, but which was even then better known by the name of tobacco. The leaves of this, cured and dried, they smoked in earthen tubes, drawing up the smoke by inhalation. The fumes of this plant were offered to their gods with ceremonial rites and extravagant genuflections. They threw its dust on nets to consecrate them for use, and into the air as a thanksgiving for dangers past. But its most sacred use was casting it into fires kindled for sacrifice, to produce a kind of incense to heaven.

Harriot carefully examined the productions of the country, especially those that would furnish commodities for commerce. The culture of maize, and its extraordinary productiveness, attracted his particular attention, and he found the tuberous roots of the potato, when boiled, to be excellent food. The credit of introducing this important factor in the world's progress into Europe seems to belong to Sir Francis Drake, who was also the first to discover gold in California.[1]

---

[1] A statue of Sir Francis Drake, thus inscribed, "The Introducer of the Potato into Europe, 1586," was noticed by the writer at Offenburg, Germany, a few years since. It is singular that it has been left for an obscure German town to recognize thus publicly an event which has exerted so vast an influence upon social economy.—F. S. D.

The early intercourse of the English with the Virginia tribes was of an entirely friendly character. The interests of both parties were subserved. The Indians were glad to exchange their commodities for European fabrics, of which they stood in need, while this new branch of commerce promised to be very remunerative to the adventurers. The friendship of Powhatan's brother, Granganameo, who resided on the island of Roanoke, was secured by the first voyagers, and, through the means of Manteo and Wasechoe, who accompanied the first ships on their return to England, considerable advance was made in the study of the habits and tribal relations of the Indians, and of the geography of their country. Manteo, having made some progress in English, returned from England with the colonists, and was of great service to them as an interpreter, guide, and adviser. Granganameo, who had welcomed Amidas, continued to be friendly, but this friendship was incited by a motive which did not at first appear. He expected the English to aid him against Wingina, his elder brother, or half-brother,—a powerful and ambitious sachem,—who, unfortunately for the English, appears not to have yielded to the sway of Powhatan, and against whom he was consequently at war. In a short time the colonists began to regard Wingina with great suspicion. They watched his motions, and in the end accused him of concocting a plot to exterminate them. Amidas had been abundantly supplied by Granganameo with venison and fish, and he had been received by his wife at Roanoke during the absence of the chief with great attention and hospitality; but it appeared that he did not consider the island to be a safe permanent residence, for on a subsequent voyage Sir Richard Greenville found him located at Cape Hatteras. One of the first acts of Sir Richard on reaching Occoquan was to send to the island of Roanoke and announce his arrival to Wingina, who is styled "the king." Manteo kept up friendly relations with both chieftains. He accompanied an agent to visit the tribes on the mainland, and proved himself a very trustworthy person. Sir Richard was so much pleased with this reconnoissance that, accompanied by a select body of men, he repeated the visit to the mainland, and discovered several Indian towns. During this excursion occurred the loss of the silver cup, already mentioned, in revenge for which he burned an Indian town and destroyed the cornfields of its inhabitants.

After committing this imprudent action, he with some precipitancy returned to England, consigning the government of the colony to Mr. Ralph Lane, and the charge of the ships to Captain Amidas. Mr. Thomas Harriot was directed to continue his observations on the manners and customs of the Indians. Lane immediately removed the colony to Roanoke, at the entrance to Albemarle Sound, and, employing persons to make a thorough survey of the coast, made himself acquainted with the geography and resources of the country. These researches extended southwardly eighty leagues to the Nense River, and northwardly to the territory of the Chesapeakes, an Indian tribe located on a stream named by the English Elizabeth River.[1]

---

[1] The name Chesapeake Bay is stated by Stith to be derived from this tribe. Others have asserted that in the Indian language it meant "the mother of waters." The word is Algonkin, and appears to be a com-

These explorations were extended towards the northwest, up the Albemarle Sound and Chowan River, a distance of one hundred and thirty miles. Lane personally directed the exploring party, and was accompanied by Manteo. The Chowan is formed by the junction of the Meherrin and Nottoway. At this point Lane entered the country of the Chowanocks.[1] The ruling chief, a lame man, named Menatonon, possessing an excellent understanding, told Mr. Lane a notable story of a copper-mine and a pearl-fishery, the latter of which he located on the coast. He intermingled his narrative with a strange tale that the head of the Maratuc, now called Roanoke River, sprang out of a rock which was so close to the sea that when high winds prevailed the "foam from the waves was driven over into the spring." Presuming this sea to be an arm of the Gulf of Mexico, or the South Sea (Pacific), Lane undertook a voyage to find it. Every hardship was endured while prosecuting this hazardous undertaking with the hope of making golden discoveries. At last the explorers were compelled to subsist on a pint of corn per day, and when this was exhausted they boiled two mastiff dogs with sassafras-leaves. After some days spent in a fruitless search, the adventurers were glad to return to their quarters at Roanoke.

At this time Granganameo died. He had been the tried friend of the English, and was at all times seconded in his good offices by his father Ensenore. Their joint influence had been sufficient to restrain Wingina's malice and perfidy. But after Granganameo's death, being afforded a free scope for the pursuit of his machinations, he at once changed his name from Wingina to Pemissapan, and became the inveterate enemy of the Virginia colonists. By his representations he had been instrumental in entailing much suffering and hardship upon Mr. Lane in his explorations of the Chowan River; but when the governor returned, bringing with him the son of Chowanock as a prisoner, and Manteo and others related the bravery and power of endurance of Lane's company, his haughty aspect was changed, and the bravado speeches made during their absence were heard no more. These reports of the capacity of the colonists to sustain themselves seem to have greatly increased the respect entertained by the Indians for the whites, and to have aroused a strong desire to conciliate the favor of the English. A present of pearl was accordingly sent to Mr. Lane from Menatonon, the king of the Chowanocks, and another present from Okisco, the chief of the Weopemeoka, a powerful coast-tribe. These friendly demonstrations had such an effect upon Wingina that he directed weirs to be constructed for the supply of the colonists with fish, and caused them to be taught how to plant

---

bination of the terms *cheeg*, ashore, and *abeeg*, waters, which compound is at this day familiarly used by these tribes to signify "along shore;" but the evident meaning of the name in its relation to the bay was intended to convey the idea of long, or long-stretching, or magnificent bay. It is probable that the tribe of the Chesapeakes received their name from their position at the foot of the bay.

[1] Mr. Jefferson classifies these Indians with the Iroquois. The name is Algonkin, however, and denotes that (contrary to Cusic, vol. v. p. 682) the Iroquois had immigrated from the south. The meaning is nearly the same as that of Chowan (southerners). The Chowans were a well-known Algonkin tribe, natives of the south.

their fields of corn. But this friendship was speedily interrupted by the death of the venerable and wise chief, Ensenore. The two best friends of the English being now dead, Wingina, under pretence of celebrating his father's funeral, invited a large number of Indians to assemble, with the intention of annihilating the colony at one blow. The plot was revealed by Skico, the son of Menatonon, who had been taken prisoner by the expedition to the head of the Chowan River.

The colonists immediately seized all the Indian canoes on the island, thinking thus to entangle the Indians in their own toils. But the latter took the alarm, and, after a skirmish in which five or six of their number were slain, made good their escape to the forest. Both parties now maintained the closest watch over each other's movements, until, after much manœuvring, Wingina was at length entrapped and slain, together with eight of his principal warriors.

Although the death of Wingina seemed to have prepared the way for a more peaceful occupation of the country, yet a general scarcity of food, combined with a singular concurrence of untoward events, finally led to the abandonment of the island. The stringency of affairs at Roanoke had, despite the efforts of industrious individuals, been greatly increased by the withdrawal and hostility of the Indians, who had been chiefly relied upon for supplies of food. To relieve the colony, Captain Stafford, a prominent and energetic man, was despatched with nineteen men to the friendly Indian village of Croatan, on Cape Lookout, with the twofold purpose of providing subsistence and of keeping a watch for ships expected with relief from England. They had not been there more than seven days when twenty-three sail of ships made their appearance. This fleet was commanded by Sir Francis Drake, who was returning from an expedition against the Spaniards in the West Indies and on the Spanish main. He had taken Carthagena, plundered the capital of Hispaniola, and burnt the towns of St. Anthony and St. Helena on the Florida coast. Having received orders to succor the Virginia colony, he offered them a ship of seventy tons' burden, one hundred men, and four months' provisions, as well as four smaller vessels. But these vessels were all driven to sea in a storm. Drake then tendered them a ship of one hundred and twenty tons, but unfortunately it could not be navigated into the harbor of Roanoke. Under these circumstances, and in view of their having suffered much misery, and their dangerous position, the colonists, after some discussion, determined to solicit Sir Francis to convey them to England in his fleet. This favor was granted, and they arrived at Portsmouth in July, 1586. On this trip Governor Lane carried the first tobacco-plant from Virginia to England. Drake was not more than a few days' sail from Roanoke on his homeward passage, when a ship of one hundred tons' burden arrived from England with the expected supplies. The commander, having made search for the colonists in vain, returned home with his vessel. About a fortnight after the departure of the latter ship, Sir Richard Greenville arrived with three ships and ample supplies. Receiving no intelligence of the colony, he landed fifty men on the island of Roanoke, furnished them with provisions for two years, and then returned. Of these successive arrivals and departures the Indians remained silent spectators, but they could not fail to be impressed with the idea that a nation which could furnish such resources was not only affluent but also in earnest.

During the month of July of the following year (1587) three ships arrived which had been sent out by Raleigh, under the command of Governor John White, with the design of reinforcing the colony and permanently establishing it as the foundation of an agricultural State. Making Cape Hatteras, Governor White proceeded to the island of Roanoke to seek for the fifty men, but he found nothing but the skeleton of one man. The buildings were not destroyed, but the fort was dilapidated, and the ground in its vicinity overgrown with weeds. Governor White refitted the houses, resumed the occupancy of the spot, and established his government, laying there the foundations of a city called Raleigh. Mr. Howe, one of the newly-appointed council, having wandered into the woods, was shot by one of Wingina's men. Captain Stafford, with twenty men, accompanied by Manteo, who had sailed to England with Drake and again returned, was sent to Croatan to make inquiries as to the fate of the fifty colonists. He was told that the colony had been attacked by three hundred Secotan, Aquoscojos, and Dessamopeak Indians, and that after a skirmish, in which but one Englishman was slain, the white men had retreated to their boat and fled to a small island near Hatteras, where they stayed some time, and then departed they knew not whither.

Governor White took immediate steps to renew a good understanding with the Indians, but he found them sullen and revengeful. Determining to evince the national indignation for the loss of the fifty colonists by attacking the Dessamopeaks, who occupied the coast opposite Roanoke, he detailed for this purpose twenty-four men, under Captain Stafford, who, with Manteo for his guide, left the island at twelve o'clock at night. At daybreak they landed on the main shore, beyond the town, and assaulted four Indians sitting at a fire, killing one of them. On examination, these proved to be friendly Croatans, who had come thither to gather their corn, the Dessamopeak Indians having fled, as they then ascertained, after killing Howe.

On the 13th of August, 1587, Manteo, who had, it is believed, made three voyages to England, and had acquitted himself satisfactorily as the Mentor of the colony, was baptized in the Christian faith, receiving, at the request of Sir Walter Raleigh, the title of Lord of Roanoke. Another event signalized this month: the daughter of Governor White, married to Mr. Dare, a member of the council, was, on the 18th, delivered of a female child, which received the name of Virginia, the first child born of English parents on the soil of the United States.

It now became necessary to select a person to visit England and solicit supplies. The Indians being generally hostile, the colonists could not cultivate sufficient ground to sustain themselves. England was at this time convulsed with alarm in expectation of the descent of the Spanish Armada, and it was justly feared that the interests of the distant little colony would be overlooked. White being selected, before leaving the coast he established a colony of one hundred men on an island near Cape Hatteras. Nothing was ever subsequently heard of this party. Whether they perished by the Indian tomahawk or by starvation has never been ascertained.

On arriving in England, White found the nation in such great turmoil that nothing could be done. The company underwent a change, and an abortive attempt was made to send two barques from Bideford in 1588. Renewed efforts were made to succor the colony, but March, 1590, had arrived before relief could be despatched to them. It was the 2d of August when the ships under Governor White reached the latitudes of Croatan and Hatteras. At the latter place a smoke was observed, but, after diligent search where the governor had three years previously left a colony of one hundred men, no traces of them could be found. Cannon were fired, but produced no other response than their own reverberations, and trumpets were sounded in vain. It appeared that the smoke arose from Indian fires hastily or carelessly left. While prosecuting their search, they found the word "Croatan" written on a post, and hence presumed that the Hatteras colony had gone to that place, where friendly Indians lived. No subsequent search developed any further trace of them: their fate had become identified with the mysteries of Indian history. The attempts made to find this colony were, however, of a very puerile character. In the effort first made under Governor White, two boats were despatched with a competent commander, but in passing a bar on the Hatteras coast one of the boats was half filled with water, and the other was upset, the captain and six men being drowned. This accident exercised a depressing influence on the spirits of all concerned, but at length two other boats were fitted out and sent off with nineteen men on the same service. It was by the second expedition that the inscription before mentioned was found, together with the evidences of the hasty abandonment of the place by the colonists. Following the index of this inscription, the commander ordered the ships to weigh anchor and sail for Croatan, on Cape Lookout. While proceeding thither, one of the vessels parted its cable, losing not only the anchor attached, but also another which had in some manner become entangled with it, and before they could drop a third anchor they were in imminent peril of being driven on the strand. Discouraged by these attempts, and influenced by fallacious hopes of profit to be derived from a trip to the West Indies, whence they proposed to return in the spring and resume the search, they bore away for these western islands, an ever-attractive spot to those who coveted the wealth of the Spaniards. But the commander of the ships, after he had finished his cruise in the West Indies, would not again visit the Virginia coast, announcing his intention to return to England, which he did despite all remonstrances. Nothing was ever heard of the colony supposed to have gone to Croatan, and the return of Governor White to England was a virtual abandonment of Virginia, after six years' fruitless toil, to the possession of the aborigines.

During the same year which witnessed the death of Queen Elizabeth and the accession of James I., Raleigh, a true friend of Virginia and of American colonization, was tried for the crime of high treason, and unjustly condemned to death, though his execution did not take place until fifteen years afterwards. In 1590 Virginia had been abandoned; and, although the colonists left at Hatteras were not entirely forgotten, the attempts made to ascertain their fate were feeble, and proved to be altogether futile. The Indian tribes may be supposed to have achieved a triumph in driving the English from their shores, but the state of discord and anarchy in which they lived, the feeble nature of the ties existing between them as tribes, and their absolute want of any stable government, were not calculated to fit them for successful resistance to the power of a civilized nation. More than twelve years elapsed before the project of establishing a colony on the shores which had been the scene of the former ineffectual struggles for colonial existence was again broached. The most important efforts made by the proprietors of the Virginia company were the voyage of Bartholomew Gosnold, in 1602, in which he discovered Cape Cod, Martha's Vineyard, and the Elizabeth Islands, and that of Captain Pring and Mr. Saltern, in 1603, who followed nearly the same track as that pursued by Gosnold. Two years subsequently, George Weymouth visited a part of the eastern coast, in latitude 41° 20', and it is conjectured from his descriptions that he entered either Narragansett Bay or the Connecticut River. On every side were found tribes of the Algonkin lineage, speaking the same language, and having identical manners and customs. The natives were mild, affable, and fond of traffic, but hostile to white men, and very treacherous. Nothing more conclusively settles the question of their nationality than their language. They obeyed chiefs who were called sagamores, and they had also a higher class of rulers, denominated bashabas.

Captain Gosnold made such favorable reports of the beauty and fertility of the country he had visited, and of its many advantages, that renewed interest was imparted to the subject of colonization. After some years spent in advocating the plan of a colony, Gosnold induced several gentlemen to engage in it, among whom were John Smith, Edward Maria Wingfield, and the Rev. Robert Hunt. A charter was procured from King James, bearing date the 10th of April, 1606, in which Sir Thomas Gates, Sir George Somers, and Richard Hakluyt were vested with the necessary authority. Three ships were provided, and placed under the command of Christopher Newport, who sailed from England on the 19th of December. After a long and tedious voyage, which was rendered more disagreeable by violent dissensions among those on board, the ships arrived off the coast on the 26th of April, 1607, at the entrance to Chesapeake Bay, the right cape of which was named Henry, and the left Charles.

How the Indian tribes would receive the new colony, then a point of deep interest, was not long involved in doubt, for thirty men who landed on Cape Henry to recreate themselves were attacked by Indians of the Chesapeake tribe, who wounded two of them. This might have been regarded as an indication that the colony was destined to be founded by the aid of the sword; and such literally was its history, notwithstanding the fact that its charter enjoined kindness to the savages, with the use of all proper means for their conversion. After passing the capes of the Chesapeake, the magnificent beauty of the surrounding country, the great fertility of its soil, and its numerous fruits and productions, were found to surpass every anticipation. Stith, a contemporary historian, in speaking of it, says, "Heaven and earth seem never to have agreed better to frame a place for man's accommodation and delightful habitation, were it fully cultivated and inhabited by an industrious people." The vessels entered the waters of the noble Powhatan River, to which the name of James was given, and the voyagers, after making diligent search for a location for the colony, at length selected a small peninsula on the north shore of the river, about forty miles from the ocean. The town which was here founded, one hundred and nine years after the discovery of the American continent by Cabot, was called Jamestown.

The English were now surrounded by a host of wild men, who implicitly obeyed the behest of their forest monarch. The Indians were the proprietors of a country abounding in game, fish, fowl, and every provision of nature for the sustenance of man, and cultivated a fertile soil, from which they gathered abundant crops of corn. No part of America abounds in more magnificent scenery than may be here found along the rivers, or in the beautiful grouping of mountains, forests, and plains. Powhatan had raised himself to a kind of kingly eminence by his bravery, energy, and wisdom in council. In addition to his claim to the dignity by hereditary right, he derived a title by the conquest of the surrounding tribes, and his position had been greatly strengthened by the practice of polygamy, which surrounded the chief with a numerous kindred, both lineal and collateral. At the time of the settlement of Virginia, Powhatan was about sixty years of age, and, though the era of his personal prowess had passed away, he wielded undiminished sway as the reigning chief, both in his lodge and at the council-fire. His head was then somewhat hoary, and this fact, together with his stature, carriage, and countenance, gave him an air of savage majesty. The confederacy of which he was the ruler comprised thirty tribes, numbering about twenty-four thousand souls. It was estimated that there were five thousand persons then residing within sixty miles of Jamestown, of whom fifteen hundred were warriors. The people of these tribes detested civilization in all its forms, and despised labor, arts, letters, and Christianity. The conduct of Powhatan, as well as that of his stalwart chiefs and followers, presents an instance of that Indian duplicity which conceals hatred under the most mild, docile, dignified, and respectful bearing. It soon, however, became evident that the calmness of the Indians too much resembled a lull of the tempest. The policy of Wingina, on the sandy coast of Albemarle Sound, which developed itself a few years earlier, was the same as that which governed Powhatan. Surrounded by thirty tribes and five thousand warriors, how long could the colonists have reasonably expected to remain unmolested? When the first ship returned to England it left but one hundred white men in Virginia. The dissensions which soon originated among them were aggravated by sickness, improvidence, and the exhaustion of their supply of provisions. The Indians, who at first appeared to be friendly, now assumed a hostile attitude and attacked the town. No more corn being delivered, speedy ruin impended, and had it not been for John Smith, who stepped forward in this emergency, utter destruction to the colony must have resulted.

Captain John Smith was the true founder of Virginia. He was born in Willoughby, Lincolnshire, England, in 1579, and after many adventures, and having acquired a high reputation for courage and sound judgment, embarked, at the age of twenty-six, for Virginia. Named one of the council, he, with Captain Newport, headed an expedition to discover the source of the James River. He became the real head of the colony, and to his almost unaided efforts the salvation of the infant settlement was owing. September 10, 1608, he was inaugurated president of the colony. Having been severely burned by the explosion of a bag of gunpowder, and feeling the want of surgical skill, and tired also of the struggle with malicious enemies, he returned to England in the autumn of 1609. In subsequent voyages he made important explorations of the New England coast, and spared neither time nor labor to advance the colonization of America. He was of an enthusiastic, determined, and uncompromising spirit, and this made him many enemies. His "Generall Historie of Virginia," and his "True Travels, Adventures, and Observations," are important contributions to the early history of the country. He died in London in 1631.

We do not propose to enter here into a detail of that remarkable instance of heroism displayed by Pocahontas when she offered her life as a ransom for that of the intrepid captive and thus unwittingly placed herself in the position of guardian angel of the colony. The narrative is familiar to all, and history nowhere records a stronger case of spontaneous sympathy elicited under parallel circumstances. But the redemption of the life of Smith was the salvation of the colony, and from this period we may date the exercise of that influence which induced Powhatan to assume at first a neutral position, and then a friendly one. This influence, however, although it enabled the colony to pass through its incipient trials, was soon withdrawn. Pocahontas lived only eight years (1616) after the foundation of Jamestown, and Powhatan but ten (1618). At the age of seventy his mortal remains were laid beside those of his fathers, and nothing remained of the chief who was once the terror of the coast-tribes and the colonists but his name. Properly estimated, Powhatan was not a great man. Bravery, energy, and prudence he evidently possessed, and among the tribes he had enjoyed a high reputation and was obeyed as a prince.

But there was one of his brothers who possessed a more comprehensive mind, more firmness of character, and greater power of intellect, and was equally courageous and active. This was Opechancanough, who captured Smith near the hill-sources of the Chickahominy. Opechancanough was six feet high, had a large frame, and possessed great physical power and activity. He had a head of grand and noble outlines, with a countenance grave, severe, and inflexible. While Powhatan lived, Opechancanough was under his influence, but the former was no sooner dead than he plotted the destruction of the colony. His plans were carefully concealed for several years after the decease of his distinguished brother; nor were they ever revealed until the night preceding the very day on which the massacre took place,—on the 22d of March, 1622. Four years had elapsed after the death of Powhatan before Opechancanough could consummate the plot. Its realization was preceded by a striking incident. Among the warriors who had attracted the notice of their brethren was Nemattanow, who deemed himself invulnerable. He had been engaged in many battles, but, having escaped without a wound, his vanity was much inflated, and the Indians regarded him as a person who could not be killed. Owing to some peculiarity of his head-dress, he was known as Jack of the Feather. This man called on a trader named Morgan, and, coveting some of the goods belonging to the latter, requested his company to a place where he stated that a good traffic could be conducted. While journeying together through the woods, the Indian murdered Morgan, and within a few days thereafter he reappeared at Morgan's store, wearing the cap of the deceased. Two stout and fearless lads who had charge of the store asking him for tidings of their master, Jack replied that he was dead. Thereupon they seized the Indian, with the intention of conveying him before a magistrate, but the captive made such resistance after being placed in the boat which was used as the means of conveyance that the boys shot him. He was not immediately killed, but, knowing the close of his career to be near at hand, he begged they would not tell his tribesmen that he had been killed by an English bullet, and desired them to conceal his body by interring it in an English burial-ground.

Opechancanough affected to be much grieved at the death of this man, but he was really gratified that he was out of the way, and made use of the circumstance as a cloak to cover his own deception. He had previously attempted to convene a large assemblage of Indians under the pretence of doing honor to the remains of Powhatan; but his design had been frustrated. In order the more effectually to accomplish his object, he resolved to enforce strict secrecy among his followers, and to make no manifestation of hostility until the time chosen for a general attack. He counselled the Indians in every part of the country to fly to arms on an appointed day and at the same hour, when they were to spare no one with an English face, whether man, woman, or child. At the time designated (March 22, 1622) the Indians suddenly rose, and perpetrated the most cruel and sanguinary massacre. Three hundred and forty-seven men, women, and children, scattered through distant villages extending one hundred and forty miles on both sides of the river, fell during one morning, and six of the colonial council were numbered with the slain. One of the first victims was Mr. George Thorp, the benefactor, teacher, counsellor, and friend of the natives. He had left England with the hope of effecting their conversion to Christianity, and had on all occasions been their most kind, undeviating friend. He had built a house for the chief, and was about to found a college for the instruction of Indian youth. The slaughter would have been still greater had not an Indian convert, named Chanco, chanced to sleep the previous night with a friend, and revealed to him the plot, by which incident the people of Jamestown and its environs, being immediately apprised of it, were enabled to take the necessary precautions for their own security, and thus the larger part of the colony was saved.

A war of extermination ensued. In July of the following year the inhabitants of several settlements, in parties, fell upon the neighboring tribes, and a law of the General Assembly commanded that in July, 1624, the attack should be repeated. Six years later the colonial statutes insisted that no peace should be concluded with the Indians, a law that remained in force till a treaty was made during the administration of Harvey. One more attempt at a general massacre occurred on the 18th of April, 1644, when three hundred victims fell. Prompt measures for security were taken by the English, and the aged Opechancanough was made a prisoner, and died in captivity of wounds inflicted by a brutal soldier. A border warfare was finally ended in October, 1646, by submission and a cession of lands by Necotowanec, his successor, and the original owners of the soil gradually receded from the settlements, leaving in the names of the rivers and mountains the only remaining memorials of their former existence.

The earliest accounts of the Indian population begin in conjecture and uncertainty. Mr. Jefferson informs us that when the first effectual settlement of Virginia was made, in 1607, the littoral and forest regions between the Potomac and James Rivers, extending to the mountains, contained upwards of forty different tribes, including the Monacans or upper tribes.[1] He represents the territories lying south of the Potomac, comprehending the Powhatanic confederacy, as containing about eight thousand inhabitants, of whom three in ten were warriors. There were probably about two thousand four hundred fighting-men. It appears that when the Virginia Legislature turned its attention to the number of the Indian tribes within its bounds, in 1669, they were reduced to five hundred and eighteen warriors, or two thousand six hundred persons, denoting a decline of over two-thirds of the entire population in sixty-two years. Regarding the forty coast and midland tribes, nothing further was ever published in an official form, and they seem to have reached the lowest point of their depression at the date of Mr. Jefferson's Notes, in 1781.[2] The account he gives of the Virginia tribes is the most authentic extant. "Very little can now be discovered of the subsequent history of these tribes severally. The Chickahominoes removed, about the year 1661, to Mattapony River. Their chief, with one from each of the Pamunkies and Mattaponies, attended the treaty of Albany, in 1685. This seems to have been the last chapter in their history. They retained, however, their separate name so late as 1705, and were at length blended with the Pamunkies and Mattaponies, and exist at present only under their names. There remain of the Mattaponies three or four men only, and they have more negro than Indian blood in them. They have lost their language, have reduced themselves by voluntary sales to

---

[1] These tribes were of Iroquois lineage. They were located entirely above the falls of the leading Virginia rivers. Their language was so diverse from the Powhatanic dialects, which were of the Algonkin group, that not a word could be understood without interpreters. They were called also Tuscaroras in the early period of Virginia. Mr. Jefferson reveals the fact (Notes, p. 155) that the Eries, called by him Erigas, who had formerly occupied the Ohio Valley (and were then by inference in Virginia and North Carolina, east of the Alleghanies), were of kindred lineage, and had belonged to the stock of the Five Nations, or, as they were called by the Virginia Indians, *Massawcomack*.

[2] Verbal information on which we may rely describes the existence of a remnant of the Accomacs of Virginia in the county of Northampton. Of their numbers and condition nothing is known. It is also stated that there are a few descendants of the Nottoways residing in that State in amalgamation with the African race. Hon. Henry A. Wise, of Virginia, informed Mr. Schoolcraft that the Gingaskins, a part of the Accomac tribe, had their lands in common as late as 1812. The principal seat of the Accomac tribe was the upper part of Accomac,—the Gingaskins living near Eastville, in Northampton County. In 1812 an act was passed dividing their lands, which were held by them till the Nat Turner insurrection, say 1833, when they were treated as free negroes and driven off.

about fifty acres of land, which lie on the river of their own name, and have from time to time been joining the Pamunkies, from whom they are distant but ten miles. The Pamunkies are reduced to about ten or twelve men, tolerably pure from mixture with other colors. The older ones among them preserve their language in a small degree, which are the last vestiges on earth, so far as we know, of the Powhatan language. They have about three hundred acres of very fertile land on Pamunky River, so encompassed by water that a gate shuts in the whole. Of the Nottoways[1] not a male is left. A few women constitute the remains of that tribe. They are seated on Southampton River, on very fertile land. At a very early period certain lands were marked out and appropriated to these tribes, and were kept from encroachment by the authority of the laws. They have usually had trustees appointed, whose duty it was to watch over their interests and guard them from insult and injury." It has been the generous design of Virginia's statesmen and legislators to stay the decline of a people who were hastening to extinction by reason of their contact with a civilization to which they as a race seem very ill adapted. It was the littoral tribes of that State which in early days suffered most severely from contact with Europeans. The upper tribes, who were of Iroquois lineage, were less exposed to deteriorating influences. "The Monacans and their friends," says Jefferson, "better known latterly as Tuscaroras, were probably connected with the Massawomacks, or Five Nations. For though we are told their languages were so different that the intervention of interpreters was necessary between them, yet do we also learn that the Erigas, a nation formerly inhabiting on the Ohio, were of the same original stock with the Five Nations, and that they partook also of the Tuscarora language. Their dialects might by long separation have become so unlike as to be unintelligible to one another. We know that in 1712 the Five Nations received the Tuscaroras into their confederacy, making them the sixth nation. They received the Meherrins, or Tutelos, also into their protection, and it is most probable that many other of the kindred tribes, of whom we find no particular account, retired westwardly in like manner, and were incorporated into one or other of the western tribes."[2]

In 1880 the United States Census reported the total number of Indians in Virginia at eighty-five.

---

[1] This word appears to be of Algonkin origin. Nadoway in the dialects of the Western and Lake Algonkins—as the Chippewas, Ottawas, Pottawatomies, etc.—is the term for an Iroquois. It is a derogatory term in those languages,—equivalent to that of viper or beast, from their striking in secret. It is a compound word, having its apparent origin in *nado*, an adder, and *awasie*, a beast. According to Mr. Jefferson, the Nottoways, with the Tutelos, or Meherrins, were Monacans, who used the generic language of the Iroquois. It was not, therefore, a name of their own choosing, but was probably a nickname given by Indians of the Powhatanic tribes.

[2] This view of the decline of the Monacan stock of Virginia is confirmed by all that we know of their history. The Monacans, who occupied the country at the foot of the Alleghanies and above the falls of the Virginia rivers, were the natural enemies of the colonists during the whole early history of Virginia, and when difficulties occurred with the aborigines they naturally sided with the Powhatanic tribes.

CHAPTER II.

THE HUDSON RIVER EXPLORED—THE DUTCH SETTLE MANHATTAN—INDIAN WAR—MANHATTAN BECOMES THE ENGLISH COLONY OF NEW YORK—INDIANS OF NEW YORK.

THE colonization of New York followed soon after the discovery of the Cohahatea, or Hudson River. While Virginia was strengthening her foundations among the powerful and hostile Powhatanic tribes of the Algonkin stock, another settlement of whites sprang into existence among the more northerly sea-coast families. Only two years subsequent to the founding of Jamestown, Hendrick Hudson entered the Bay of New York, which was first discovered by Verazzani in 1524, although the large river of which it is the recipient still continued unexplored. Hudson appears to have passed the point now called Sandy Hook on the 3d day of September, 1609. He remained in the bay several days, making surveys and trafficking with the Indians. From the notes of his surveys, he seems to have kept close along the southern parts of the bay, the natives of which appeared to be friendly. These shores were occupied by the Navisinks, Sanhikins, and other bands of the Mississa totem of the Lenni Lenape (Algonkin) family. The northern shores of the bay and Manhattan Island were occupied by the Mohicans, or Wolf totem of the same subgenus of the original stock. The Metoacs of Long Island were of the same type. Between these two totemic types there existed either smothered hostility or open war. They kept Hudson in a state of constant perplexity, and, regarding all red men with equal mistrust, he was ever on his guard against treachery. Of all the bands, however, he found that of Hell Gate, or the Manhattans, to be the fiercest. On the third day after sailing up the bay he sent out a boat in charge of his mate, Colman, to examine the East River. An open sea was found beyond. While the exploring party were returning to the vessel, the Manhattans attacked them and killed the mate, who received an arrow in his throat. These Indians possessed implements of copper, and earthen cooking-utensils, the art of making which was at this period common to all the coast-tribes, but, the use of the brass kettle having been introduced among them by Europeans, they very soon ceased to manufacture earthen-ware. They offered Hudson green tobacco as a most valuable present, and had an abundance of maize, which he called Indian wheat. They also brought him oysters, beans, and some dried fruits. These Indians dressed in deer-skin robes, and possessed mantles made of feathers and also of furs. There is no evidence to prove that they did not live in a state of anarchy, without any government save that of petty independent chieftainships, the curse of all savage and barbarous tribes. On the afternoon of the

EARLY EUROPEAN SETTLEMENTS.

7th of September, Hudson began to ascend the river, but progressed only two leagues the first day, sailing with extreme caution during the day, sounding frequently, and casting anchor at night. Twelve days elapsed before he reached a point opposite to or above the present city of Hudson. The general features of the country in that part of the valley are mentioned by him. Having arrived, on the 22d, at a place where the soundings denoted shoal water, Hudson despatched his boat to make further explorations. It returned the following night at ten o'clock, having progressed only eight or nine leagues, and the crew reported finding but seven feet seven inches soundings, which would seem to indicate that they had reached the present site of Albany. The Indians, as high as they had proceeded, were, by the names, apparently of the Algonkin family. If the explorers really ascended in their boat as far as the present position of Albany, they entered the country of the Mohawk tribe of the Iroquois nation, whose summer residence was on the island. The tribes maintained a hostile attitude until Hudson had passed the Highlands, but those he subsequently encountered evinced great friendliness, as well as mildness of manners, and hence are called by him "a loving people." The Indians visited the strangers on board their ship, and several excursions were made by the crew on the shore. On one occasion two venerable chiefs, accompanied by their sons and daughters, were entertained by Hudson in his cabin. These interchanges of civility characterize this part of the voyage, and furnish striking evidence of the beneficial effects of kindness in dealing with the red man. On the 20th of the month, while the ship lay at anchor at one of the highest points attained, Hudson tried the experiment of giving his aboriginal guests a taste of alcoholic drinks. The description of this event may be entertaining for its quaintness: "Our master and his mate determined to try some of the chiefest men of the country, whether they had any treachery in them, so they took them into the cabin, and gave them so much wine and aqua vitæ, that they were all merrie, and one of them had his wife with him, which sat as modestly as any of our country women could do in a strange place. In the end one of them was drunk,[1] which had been on board of our ship all the time that we had been there, and that was strange to them, for they could not tell how to take it. The canoes and folks all went on shore, but some of them came again, and brought strings of beads (wampum), some had six, seven, eight, nine, ten, which they gave the inebriate. The drunken man slept all night quietly."

The Indians below the Highlands who were found to be hostile on the ascent proved doubly so during the descent. The narrowness of the channel in some places gave them the opportunity of using their arrows with effect, and they assembled on several of the most prominent headlands in great force. But the intrepidity of Hudson foiled every effort. By his musketry, and by the discharges from a culverin,

---

[1] This scene of intoxication is erroneously placed by Mr. Heckewelder on Manhattan Island, and the island itself is stated to have been named, from the circumstance, "the place where we all got drunk." Doubtless some old Indian had imposed on his credulity in this, as in other cases named in his historical account of the Delaware tribes. Stone has been misled by this.

he killed several of them and dispersed the rest. He got through the mountains on the 1st of October. Below this one of their canoes, containing one man, pertinaciously followed the ship. This individual, having climbed up the rudder, crept into the cabin-window, and stole two bandoleers, a pillow, and two shirts, for which theft the mate shot him dead. The Indians followed the vessel, and a running skirmish ensued, in which several of the pursuers were killed. On the 4th, Hudson reached the bay, where, being favored by the wind, he made no attempt to land, but put out to sea, arriving at Dartmouth, England, on the 7th of November.

The only name bestowed by him on the stream appears to have been that of The Great River.

About the year 1614 the first rude fort was erected by the Dutch, probably on the southern part of Manhattan Island. In 1623 the country from the southern shore of Delaware Bay to New Holland, or Cape Cod, became known as New Netherlands. The new block-house on Manhattan became the nucleus of a colony, and Peter Minuit, agent of the West India Company, held for the ensuing six years the office of governor.

In February, 1643, a small party of Mohawks from the vicinity of Fort Orange, armed with muskets, emerged from their fastnesses, and claimed tribute of the Algonkins around Manhattan. These more numerous but less warlike tribes, upon the approach of the formidable Mohawks, terror-struck, begged the assistance of the Dutch, between whom and themselves petty injuries had caused bad blood. Kieft, the Dutch governor, seized the opportunity for an exterminating massacre. On the night of February 25 the soldiers from the fort, joined by some privateersmen, crossed the Hudson, and, falling upon the unsuspecting natives, massacred nearly one hundred of them. This cruel and impolitic act was terribly avenged: villages were laid waste from New Jersey to Connecticut, settlers were slain in the fields, and children carried into captivity. Among the victims was Anne Hutchinson, one of the remarkable women of the time, who perished with her family. In March the Dutch sought peace, which was effected through the aid of Roger Williams, then about to visit England. The war was, however, renewed in September, and on the part of the Dutch was conducted by the veteran Captain John Underhill, a fugitive from New England, at the head of a force of one hundred and twenty men. After two years of savage warfare, peace was concluded on the beautiful spot in front of Fort Amsterdam, now known as the Battery, in the presence of the sachems of New Jersey, of the River Indians, of the Mohicans, and those from Long Island, acknowledging the chiefs of the Five Nations as arbiters, and having around them the Director and Council of New Netherlands, with the entire Dutch population. Ten years later (September, 1655), in the absence of Governor Stuyvesant, the neighboring Algonkins, never friendly to the Dutch, made a desperate attack on Manhattan. They appeared before the town in sixty-four canoes, and ravaged the adjacent country. The captives were subsequently ransomed, and the attack was not renewed. Confidence was restored, and industry soon repaired the losses of the colonists.

King Charles II. having in 1664 granted to his brother, the Duke of York, the

whole territory from the Connecticut River to the shores of the Delaware, the Dutch colony, left to itself, and incapable of defence, was formally surrendered, September 8, to an English squadron, and received the name of New York.

Whilst a foreign power held sway over the entire territory bordering New England on the west and south, facilities were offered for the escape of Indian marauders into that province, and the impression prevailed, whether well or ill founded, that such fugitives received countenance from the Dutch authorities, or at least that the Indians under their jurisdiction sheltered the runaways. But this state of affairs ceased after the province was taken by the English. The British flag then waved from the utmost boundaries of New England to the borders of Florida. It is an unquestionable fact that when the Pequot war terminated, in 1644, many of this indomitable tribe, after escaping from the massacre at Fairfield, sought shelter in the territory of the Mohawks. Some individuals of it, also, as well as of the Nanticokes, appear to have been incorporated with the Schoharie band of the Mohawks, but by far the greater number located themselves on a branch of the North River, called Schaghticoke, in a valley as fertile as it was beautiful, which was granted to them by the authorities of Albany. These fugitives, among whom were some other fragments of the sea-coast Algonkins, never resumed their original tribal appellation, but settled down under the government of the Iroquois cantons, who sheltered the remnants of the despoiled and conquered tribes. Delegates from these Indians attended some of the Mohawk councils, but they retained none of their former independent character, and were not much respected. Some years after the establishment of the English supremacy in New York, the entire Schaghticoke band precipitately fled, and located themselves under the protection of the French at Missisquoi Bay, on the northern waters of Lake Champlain. To this course they were impelled by several reasons: because small countenance was shown them by the New York authorities, on account of the repeated complaints of the Connecticut colonists; the whites infringed too much on the land assigned them; the Canadian authorities, who were in communication and sympathy with them, exercised a persuasive influence; and it is probable that the Indians feared the New Yorkers were about to avenge the wrongs inflicted on the Connecticut settlers.

At the period when the English and Celtic elements of population were introduced into New York, there were, as there had been previously, two Indian powers contending for the sovereignty in this colony,—the Algonkin and the Iroquois. The Algonkins, divided into numerous bands under local names, had from an early date occupied the valley of the Hudson below the site of Albany, and the right bank of that river as high up at least as the influx of the Wallkill was occupied by the second totemic class of the Lenni Lenapes,[1] who bore the name of Munsees, the various tribes of which, known as the Raritans, Sanhikans, etc., covered the entire surface of New Jersey. On the right banks of the Hudson were the Mohicans proper, known under the tribal appellations of Wappengers, Tappensees, and Wequa-

---

[1] Manly men, from *lenno*, a man, and *inape*, a male.

esgecks, and other bands of the Westchester Algonkins. These latter extended their possessions into the boundaries of Connecticut. The Manhattans were the band residing on the island of the same name, and the Long Island tribes, descriptively called Sewanakies,[1] or shell-land bands, were known by the generic name of Metoacs. Nearly every prominent bay, island, or channel near the great bay of New York possessed its local name, derived often from that of a tribe.

In the middle and western parts of the State, between the Tawasentha Valley of Albany County and the Niagara River, resided the Iroquois, consisting of the five tribes of the Mohawks, Oneidas, Onondagas, Cayugas, and Senecas, who, after the formation of their confederacy, filled by far the most important position in the history of the North American Indians. According to some authorities, this league had been formed but a short time anterior to the discovery of the Hudson River. Others, among whom is the Indian annalist, Cusic, whose chronology is not, however, reliable, aver that the date of the confederacy is far more ancient. From all accounts, during the first half-century after the settlement of Virginia the Algonkins were the most numerous in population along the sea-coasts, and for more than a century and a half in the interior. This numerical supremacy continued until the European population, crossing the Alleghanies, passed the great lake basins and scattered freely over the Mississippi Valley. Colden says that the supremacy of the Algonkins had in more ancient times been acknowledged by the Iroquois. This early development of Algonkin power had, however, declined before the foot of the white man trod these shores, and it is certain that so far as related to policy and warlike achievements it had passed away before the era of the Dutch, and long before the English became identified with New York history. The Algonkins of both the Hudson and Delaware Valleys had been conquered by the Iroquois, and were then in a state of vassalage to that confederacy, either paying tribute or being deprived of the sovereign right of ceding lands. When the latter power was attempted to be exercised by the Lenni Lenape, some forty years after the advent of Penn, the contemptuous rebuke of Canassatego, which we have elsewhere cited, showed that the power of the club and tomahawk was ready to enforce the claim of the Iroquois to the hegemony.

About ten years previous to the conquest of New York by the English, say in 1653, the Seneca Iroquois, with the aid of the other tribes of the league, began a war against the Eries, as well as against the neuter nation of the Niagara River and their allies, the Andastes of the Erie shore. When Le Moyne first visited Onondaga, in 1655, this war against the Eries was in progress. Cusic denominates them the Cat Nation,—meaning the wild-cat, for the domestic animal was to them unknown. They were evidently affiliated in language with the Iroquois. No one can peruse the writings of the missionary fathers and not perceive this. A full account of the origin of this war against the Neuter Nation is furnished in our first volume.

The early French writers call this tribe the Neuter Nation, owing to their apparently pacific character. This name, however, is not derived from the Indian, and

---

[1] A compound from *sewan*, wampum shell, and *aukie*, land.

has only served to mystify modern inquirers, as no such nation of neuters can be found in any position except in the area occupied by the Eries, on the Niagara. The name by which the Senecas designate the Eries is Kahqua. The Andastes occupied the shores of Lake Erie. As previously denoted, they were Susquehannocks.

The war, fiery, short, and bloody, resulted in the overthrow of the Eries and their allies, and led to their subsequent incorporation into other tribes or their expulsion from the country. From this time the tribal name of Erie (as in a prior case that of the Pequots) disappears from history. Mr. Evans, in his map and memoir published at Philadelphia in 1755, avers that the refugee Eries took shelter in the Ohio Valley, whence they eventually crossed the Onosiota, or Alleghany chain, to rejoin kindred tribes. Mr. Jefferson repeats this fact in his Notes on Virginia, in 1780. Evidence that these fugitive Eries are the brave and indomitable people known to us as Catawbas has been elsewhere given in the present work.

To conciliate the Iroquois, who were thus rapidly raising themselves to a position of power and influence among the Indians of the colonies, became immediately a measure of English policy, and to secure this result the most wise and prudent steps were taken. The fur-trade, which had been established upon a satisfactory basis by the Dutch, was continued, and the bonds of friendship with the Iroquois were cemented by an offensive and defensive alliance. Their enemies became the enemies of the English, and the friends of the former the friends of the latter. Thus the Iroquois were constituted the defenders of the territory of Western New York against the French. If the latter could succeed in driving them from their forests, Western New York would be added to New France; if they failed, it was a gem in the British crown. Who can read the details of a hundred years' sanguinary contests without perceiving that it was the undying vigilance, the unerring accuracy of their geographical knowledge of the wilderness, and the manly bravery of the Iroquois which, up to the year 1775, preserved Western New York to the English crown?

CHAPTER III.

CHAMPLAIN FOUNDS QUEBEC AND THE CANADIAN SETTLEMENTS.

NEARLY seventy years had elapsed before France, desolated by civil war and torn by religious dissensions, could renew her purpose of founding a French empire in America. In the mean time, however, her fisheries had largely increased, one hundred and fifty French vessels being at Newfoundland in 1573, at which time voyages for traffic with the natives were regularly and successfully made. In 1603 the merchants of Rouen formed a company, which was placed under Samuel de Champlain, an able marine officer and man of science, the father of the French settlements in Canada. Active and fearless, and at the same time cool and persevering, Champlain's account of his first expedition proves his sound judgment and accurate observation, and abounds in exact details of the manners of the savage tribes. Selecting Quebec as the site for a fort, he returned to France just before the issue to De Monts of the patent of Acadia, a region which, as then defined, extended from Philadelphia to beyond Montreal. The expedition, which left France March 7, 1604, after attempting a settlement on the island of St. Croix, at the mouth of the river of that name, planted, in the spring of 1605, a colony at Port Royal, called Annapolis, after the conquest of Acadia (Nova Scotia) by Queen Anne. Thus the first French settlement on the continent preceded by two years the colonization of Virginia. With a view to future settlements, De Monts then explored and claimed for France the rivers, coasts, and bays of New England as far as Cape Cod; Jesuit priests began the conversion of the natives, who were already hostile towards the English, who had visited their coasts; and a French colony was, in 1613, planted on Mount Desert, within the present limits of the United States. In 1608 the city of Quebec was begun by Champlain, who in the next year joined a party of Hurons and Algonkins in an expedition against the Iroquois, and explored the lake which perpetuates his name. The monopoly of De Monts having been revoked, and a new colonial patent having, in 1615, been obtained by merchants of St. Malo, Rouen, and Rochelle, Champlain embarked once more for the New World. In a subsequent invasion of the Iroquois territory, he was wounded and repulsed, spending the first winter after his return in the country of the Hurons. In 1524 he built the castle of St. Louis, so long the place of council against the Iroquois and against New England, and, in spite of obstacles, in a few years established the authority of the French on the banks of the St. Lawrence. He died here in 1635.

CHAPTER IV.

SETTLEMENT OF THE NEW ENGLAND COLONIES—MASSASOIT—EFFORTS TO CHRISTIANIZE THE INDIANS—THEIR MANNERS AND CUSTOMS—THE PEQUOTS.

THE idea of migrating to America to escape the intolerance of the house of Stuart had been for a long time entertained by the English exiles in the Low Countries. Intelligence of the discoveries in Virginia and in the region of New York probably had the effect of reviving the agitation of the project, as well as of demonstrating its practicability, and in effect the exiles were in a short time thereafter on their way to the New World. The first colony which landed in Massachusetts Bay, December 21, 1620, was surrounded by small tribes and bands of the Algonkins, the principal of which were the Pequots, Narragansetts, Pokanokets, Massachusetts, and Pawtuckets, each of which was subdivided into numerous clans. There were also the Mohicans and Nipmucks. During the years immediately preceding European settlement fatal epidemics had greatly thinned the coast-tribes, and in some instances nearly annihilated them. Whole villages appeared to have been depopulated, and deserted fields everywhere met the view. This decadence of the race was a favorable circumstance for the colonists, whose utmost efforts were required to combat the difficulties of their position.

The principal personage among the aboriginal chieftains was Massasoit, the ruler of the Pokanokets, or Wampanoags, living at Mount Hope, on the waters of Narragansett Bay. He had been a noted warrior, but was at that time a man far advanced in life. He was of good stature, full and fleshy; and, possessing a manly mien, mild manners, a moderate temper, and a noble spirit, amicable relations with him were soon established. The jurisdiction of the Massachusetts coast appears to have belonged to him in quality of his office of bashaba, or presiding chief-holder, as is more certainly evinced by the authority assumed after his death by his sons, Alexander and Pometacom.[1] The first interview with this potentate was conducted with equal ceremony by the colonists and by the semi-imperial chief. He was received by Governor Carver and his retinue with every attention. There was military music and a salute of musketry; mutual embraces followed. They then sat down side by side; "a pot of strong water" was brought forward, from which both drank. The chief, not knowing how to graduate his draught, from ignorance of its strength, was thrown into a violent perspiration, which lasted during the interview. A pacific course of policy was established by a treaty which was sacredly kept for more than half a century, and from this era the aboriginal words Manito, wigwam, powwow,

---

[1] Drake, p. 13.

samp, moose, and others from their vocabulary, began to be incorporated into the English language. Soon after their landing, Samoset, who had acquired a little English of the fishermen at Penobscot, came into Plymouth, exclaiming, "Welcome Englishmen," and in the name of his nation invited them to take possession of the soil, the old occupants of which were no longer living.

The country had been first explored by the English in 1583, when Sir Humphrey Gilbert visited the coast. In 1602 Gosnold bestowed names on Cape Cod, Elizabeth Islands, and Martha's Vineyard; and in 1614 Captain Smith, of Virginia fame, gave the name of New England to this part of the continent. The coast had been explored by Dutch navigators subsequent to the discoveries made by Hudson, and is designated in an ancient map by the name of Almochico. The Indians, being deficient in generalization, had no generic name for it, unless it were that of Abenakee which they subsequently made use of. The first colony landed on the banks of a river, which we are informed the natives called Accomac, but which the English named Plymouth.[1] One hundred and one persons debarked on the confines of twenty tribes, whose exact numbers were unknown, but whose hostility to the colony was undoubted. Prince says these "hundred and one" were the persons "who, for an undefiled conscience, and the love of pure Christianity, first left their native and pleasant land, and encountered all the toils and hazards of the tumultuous ocean, in search of some uncultivated region in North Virginia, where they might quietly enjoy their religious liberties, and transmit them to posterity, in hopes that none would follow to disturb or vex them."

Canonicus, sachem of the Narragansetts, a chief of extraordinary capacity, and the enemy of Massasoit, and whose territory had escaped the terrible ravages of the pestilence, at first desired to treat for peace, but in 1622 he sent to the English settlement a bundle of arrows wrapped in the skin of a rattlesnake in token of hostility. The skin was promptly returned by Governor Bradford stuffed with powder and shot, and the frightened savage sought to be on terms of amity with his formidable neighbors.

Winthrop's company, which in the summer of 1630 settled in and around Boston, in Massachusetts Bay, at once established friendly relations with the natives. The sagamore of the Mohicans came to solicit an English plantation as a bulwark against the terrible Pequots, and the nearer Nipmucks asked aid against the Mohawks. The son of the aged Canonicus exchanged presents with the governor, and Miantonomo himself, the great Narragansett warrior, became the guest of Governor Winthrop. Even a Pequot sachem, with wampumpeag and promises of skins, came to obtain the alliance of the English.

Within a few years thereafter, Maine, New Hampshire, Connecticut, and Rhode Island were successfully colonized. To endure patiently and to hope amidst every ill were primary principles with the colonists, and as soon as they came into contact

---

[1] Smith, vol. ii. p. 177. Accomac is also the name of a location in Eastern Virginia, probably signifying the line where the wilderness meets an eligible and cultivated country.

with the Indians they aimed, both by precept and by example, to teach them the advantages of thrift over the precarious pursuit of the chase. Among a people characteristically idle, listless, and prone to regard with favor the rites of demonology and the practice of magic, nothing coul l be more unpalatable or more certainly productive of hostilities, for the priests and sages, powwows and necromancers, clung to their ceremonies and orgies with a desperate tenacity. To live on the products of the bow and arrow had been the practice of the people for untold centuries, and they regarded the new-comers with a feeling of distrust and hatred which grew stronger and more intense with every succeeding decade of colonial existence.

The attempt to introduce the principles of civilization among the New England tribes, who were half hunters and half ichthyophagi, gives us a stand-point from which we may contemplate the Indian character in a new and instructive phase. When, in 1586, the scholar Harriot showed the Virginia Indians the Bible, and explained to them its contents, they imagined it to be some great talisman, and handled, hugged, and kissed it with great reverence, rubbing it against their heads and breasts. They were strongly impressed with the belief that it was the material of the book, and not its doctrines, which embodied its virtues. In 1608, when the shores of the Chesapeake were explored by Smith, the English were accustomed to have prayers recited daily, and a psalm sung, at which the Susquehannocks, who were spectators, greatly wondered, regarding the rites and ceremonies with deep interest,—feeling animated by the vocal sounds, but profoundly ignorant of the language and of its true import. Being themselves ceremonialists to an almost unlimited extent, in the worship they offered to the gods of the air, hills, and valleys, and also ready interpreters of symbols, the ritual was to them an object of wonder.

Harriot informs us that the Virginia Indians believed in the existence of one God; yet in the same sentence he also says that the sun, moon, and stars were subordinate gods, that the gods were all of human shape, and that offerings were presented to their images. Very similar to this were the declarations of the Northern Indians; but yet, while they acknowledged God as riding on the clouds, the images they worshipped in secret and in their assemblies were, in fact, demons and devils. To disseminate the doctrines of the gospel amid such an embodiment of dark superstition was not an easy task, yet it was zealously and firmly pursued. Cotton Mather informs us that within thirty years from the time when the first formal efforts were made to preach the gospel to the Indians, there were six churches and eighteen assemblies of catechumens, or converted natives, within the boundaries of Massachusetts, and in 1682 the entire Bible was made accessible to them by means of the translation of Eliot.

Within the space of a few years the English population spread themselves over the entire country, enterprise having been a marked characteristic of all the early settlements. The Indians, divided into innumerable small tribes and bands, occupied the interior territory and a great part of the immediate coast-line. Wherever the colonists located themselves the natives watched their movements with jealous interest. The colonists being uniformly industrious, thrifty, cautious, courageous, and temperate, the more reflecting sagamores could hardly fail to be impressed with the idea that the settlers were the mere heralds of a people destined to increase rapidly both in number and in power, and to occupy the whole country, to the detriment of the red man, whose dominion must decline as the influence of the white man increased.

It would be erroneous to suppose that such a deep sense of danger could have been produced without exciting the strong antipathy of the Indian. On the contrary, a virulent, secret, deep-seated, and almost universal opposition was developed among the native powwows from the waters of the Connecticut to those of the Penobscot. Bitter, indeed, was this sense of the inevitable decay of their own race to the Indians, and equally bitter to them in every phase was their experience of civilization. They detested a life of labor, and had no relish for the Puritan standard of stern virtue and personal responsibility. The idea that such members of the wandering tribes as were guilty of theft, murder, prevarication, and covetousness would be brought to judgment therefor was utterly repugnant to them; but when to this doctrine was joined the requirement that they should relinquish their system of worship, their necromancy, their magic ceremonies, and all their forest rites, their deepest ire was aroused.

In missionary labor among the red men, Eliot, commonly called the Apostle to the Indians, greatly distinguished himself. He emigrated from England in 1631, and was chosen minister at Roxbury, where in the exercise of his pastoral duties his attention was directed to the Indian tribes, of whom numerous clans and villages then overspread the territory and were interspersed among the settlements of the whites. Being a graduate of the university of Cambridge, England, and a person of considerable learning, Eliot began the study of the Indian languages, under the no small stimulus, it is inferred, of finding therein some elements of the Hebrew. In this important inquiry into the affinities of nations, a research far in advance of the age in which he lived, Eliot's principal aid and pundit was Nesutan, a descendant of the Massachusetts stock, who had learned to speak the English language, and who was pronounced by a divine of that period "a pregnant-witted young man."

In 1646 the subject of the conversion of the Indians was discussed by the Association of Colonial Ministers, who adopted a resolution strongly urging the expediency and necessity of immediate action. In accordance with this view, Mr. Eliot appointed a time and place for an assemblage of the Indians, which was convened on the 28th of October of the same year. His text was, "Prophesy unto the wind, prophesy, son of man, and say to the wind, Thus saith the Lord God; Come from the four winds, O breath, and breathe upon these slain, that they may live."[1] The place was called Nonantum (God's word displayed), and a strong impression was made upon the Indian mind by this appeal.

Another convocation of the Indians took place a fortnight subsequently, at the same place, where Eliot addressed them in their own language. Other meetings followed thereafter. The Indians who attended agreed to settle at that place, as also

---

[1] Ezekiel xxxvii. 9.

to adopt the rules and observe the practices of civilization, and faithfully to adhere to the precepts of Christianity. Thus was established the first settlement of praying Indians. They received instruction gladly, labored diligently at husbandry, and became very expert in the use of farming-tools. Being regularly catechised and instructed, a congregation of converts was in the end established. The Indians being carefully watched over, with the aid of native helps the new principles spread rapidly among them. A second meeting was held at Neponset, in Mr. Eliot's parish, and others at Pawtucket, at Concord, and on the peninsula of Cape Cod, which were all equally successful. These proceedings elicited strong opposition among the native priests and powwows, who, seeing their ancient power over the Indians about to depart, beat their necromantic drums at their secret meetings with greater energy.

Accounts of the successful propagation of the gospel in America were published and circulated throughout England, where they excited so much interest during the two following years (1647 and 1648) that when an appeal was made to Parliament to second their efforts that body passed an act to incorporate a Society for the Propagation of the Gospel in New England. In 1661, Eliot published a translation of the Old Testament in the Indian dialect of Massachusetts, which was called by him the Natick, manifestly because he deemed that to be the generic language. This volume was a work of great labor, and had received the most careful attention. After a long interval it was followed by a translation of the Gospels, and in 1684 the two parts were reproduced together, in one volume, at Cambridge, Massachusetts. This was in every way a gigantic work, and could not have been accomplished without the aid of the London Society for Propagating the Gospel, under whose auspices it was executed. Eliot and Nesutan had spent many long years upon it; and, as it progressed, the several parts of each book were practically employed in the dissemination of the truths they contained. It still retains its position as the most considerable and important monument of our Indian philology.

The New England settlers made no attempts to impose a ritual on the aborigines. It was noticed that these tribes were under the religious rule of self-constituted priests, powwows, and ecclesiastical sagamores, who directed them in the appalling worship of evil spirits, and of elementary gods, whose names were emphatically "legion." In the words of a quaint historian of that period, "the whole body of the multiplied tribes and septs who cover the land are the veriest ruins of mankind."[1] This writer observes, "Their wigwams consist of poles, lined with mats, where a good fire supplies the warmth of bed-clothes in cold seasons. The skins of animals furnish exclusively their clothing. Sharp stones are used for knives and tools. Wampum, a kind of bead made from sea-shells, is a substitute for money. Indian corn constitutes their staple of vegetable food; the forest supplies them precariously with meat. Fish are taken in their streams. The hot-house is their catholicon for a large class of their diseases. Their religion is a confused and contradictory theism, under the rule of a class of priests called powwows, who offer incense by the fumes of

---

[1] Cotton Mather.

tobacco." There was absolutely nothing in their plan of dwelling that deserved the name of architecture, but they had considerable skill in manufacturing arrows, bows, war-clubs, bowls, pipes, fishing-rods, and nets. The women made clay pots, which, when used for the purpose of cooking, were suspended from a tripod formed of three poles tied together at top and spread over the fire. They wove mats of flags, baskets of the split cortical layers of wood, and nets from a native fibre. The clam-shell was frequently used as a spoon, but spoons were also carved out of wood, as also were onagons, or bowls. Darts were chipped from horn-stone, as well as from other species of silicious rock, and frontlets ornamented with birds' feathers were employed for head-dresses. The cawheek and succotash, or pounded corn, were their favorite dishes: when the hunter was successful he had deer or other meat. Fish was abundant, even in the interior streams, as were also oysters and other shell-fish on the sea-coasts. Canoes were made from solid trees, hollowed by the aid of fire, and a peculiar axe, which is frequently found among Indian relics. The red man was ingenious in setting snares for birds and beasts, and sometimes large animals were entrapped by bending down saplings, which would rebound when any beast trod on the string which held them in place. The Indian buried his dead in outer wrappings of bark, placing at the head of the corpse a wooden post, on which were carved the totem of the clan and some other hieroglyphics. His success in war and in hunting was also sometimes rudely sculptured on the face of rocks or boulders, some of these *muzzinabiks* remaining to this day.

With manners and customs thus entirely opposed to everything like civilization, it needed but slight incitement to arouse the deadliest feelings of hostility. Very little difference existed, either in dress or in manners, between individual Indians, or between the various tribes, all looking and acting very much alike, and the innocent were frequently mistaken for the guilty.

The spirit of opposition to the entire constitution and system of civil society and of Christianity originated early, and led to repeated combinations of the Indians to exterminate the white race. The first general and alarming effort of this kind against the peace and welfare of the New England colonists developed itself in the area of Connecticut, among the Pequots. The primary settlements in the Connecticut Valley were made in 1633. Within four years from that time the Pequots evinced their hostility, for which there was an additional and highly irritating cause.

Prior to the settlement of New England, feuds had existed in the Pequot tribe. This was a numerous organization, extending from the western boundary of the Narragansetts, on the Pawcatuck River, to the banks of the Pequot or Thames River. It is evident that their extreme western boundary originally extended to the Connecticut. They were under the rule of the powerful, brave, and ambitious Sassacus, there being no evidence that Uncas occupied the valley by right of conquest. But at the era of the founding of the Connecticut colony this valley was occupied by the Mohicans, who were ruled by the sachem Uncas. The Pequots and the Mohicans spoke the same language, which was a secondary form of the generic Algonkin. Uncas had married a daughter of Tatobam, a Pequot, of the blood of the chief, and was, according to the general principles of descent, regarded as one of the hereditary line. Uncas was himself a wise, brave, and politic chieftain. Whatever the causes of tribal discord were, his separation from the parent tribe, and removal westwardly, had occurred prior to the settlement of either Windsor or Hartford, the oldest Connecticut towns, for the enmity between these two rival native chiefs became at once apparent to the English. Uncas, with the view of strengthening his position against Sassacus and the larger body of the tribe, hailed the arrival of the colonists with joy, became their protector against the inroads of the Pequots, and remained their firm and consistent friend. This line of policy served rather to irritate than to allay the Pequot enmity to the English. At length, after the lapse of a few years marked by bitter hostilities, murders, and cruelties, from which outrages the English and their Mohican allies were alike sufferers, a formidable expedition was organized against Sassacus and his two forts. The murder of John Oldham while on a trading expedition near Block Island, in July, 1636, was its immediate occasion. It is not necessary here to speak of the cruel murders, of the breaches of treaty stipulations, or of the depredations and other outrages committed: suffice it to say that, excitement being at its height, forbearance had ceased to be a virtue, and all were compelled either to fight or die. Four years of agonizing strife thus passed away, during which at least thirty English had been put to death, some with the addition of cruel tortures. The existence of the colonies was at stake; it was a contest between civilization and barbarism. If Connecticut succumbed, Massachusetts and Rhode Island must necessarily follow. Sassacus at that period being on the best terms with the Narragansetts, who then acknowledged the dominion of the aged Canonicus, and of his more efficient son, Miontonomo, he aimed in vain by negotiations to obtain their aid against the Mohicans and the English. A general rising was only prevented by the influence of Roger Williams, who at the imminent hazard of his life succeeded in dissolving this formidable coalition. As a ruler Sassacus was greatly feared and respected by his people, as well as by the Narragansetts. He was a brave warrior and an eloquent speaker. Mason tells us of an Indian saying that "Sassacus is all one god; no man can kill him." The views he expressed with respect to the English settlements in New England prove the expansion and forecast of his mind. He regarded the white men as destined to supersede the Indian race, and said that when they had exterminated the Pequots they would then turn their attention to the Narragansetts. He urged an alliance for general purposes, and argued that it would not be necessary to fight great battles, as the whites could be destroyed one by one. The Indians could lie in ambush for the colonists, could burn their dwellings, could kill their cattle. Every view we take of the character of Sassacus only serves to confirm the impression that he was a man of uncommon energy as well as forecast, and he occupies a prominent position among the bold aboriginal chiefs who so resolutely resisted the occupancy of their country by Europeans. He clearly foresaw and pointed out to his countrymen that with arts and energies such as their invaders had already demonstrated the possession of, they must extinguish the light of their council- and altar-fires; one after another the tribes must succumb. The history of the great internal conflicts of ante-historical periods by which the Pequot nation had been divided and Uncas expelled being involved in obscurity, we are unable to furnish any accurate details. We know, however, that the feud was existing in all its original intensity when the colonists first entered the country, and, unfortunately for the perpetuation of his power, Sassacus, like many others of the aboriginal chiefs and leaders, lacked the spirit of conciliation, aiming to achieve by force what he might have attained by delay and negotiation, placing too low an estimate on the value of union and co-operation with the surrounding tribes. He was feared and suspected by the numerous tribe of the Narragansetts on the east, while the unfriendly Mohicans lined the boundary of his dominion on the west. The small bands of the Niantics and Ninigret's men he evidently controlled, and the interior country to the north was open to him. Two of his strongest positions were stockaded villages which assumed the character of forts, and had the English been less prompt or bold in their movements, and given him more time to consummate his arrangements, the result might have been protracted, although it certainly could not have been averted.

CHAPTER V.

MARYLAND SETTLED—ABORIGINAL POPULATION ON THE SHORES OF THE CHESAPEAKE—THE SUSQUEHANNOCKS—THE ANDASTES.

DURING the year immediately following the establishment of the settlements in the Connecticut Valley, the tribes of Maryland proper, as distinguished from those of Virginia, were particularly introduced to historical notice. On the 27th of March, 1634, Leonard Calvert landed on the banks of a river, to which he gave the name of St. Mary, situated on the western shores of Chesapeake Bay. Captain John Smith, who visited and circumnavigated the bay in 1608, furnishes the first account of the Susquehannocks,—a bold, stalwart, and athletic tribe, who spoke in a hollow tone, with a full enunciation. The Indians living near the St. Mary's River, and in whose vicinity Calvert landed, were called Wicomocos. Friendly relations were cultivated with the natives, who sold him a tract of land thirty miles in extent, for which they received axes and other useful articles.

In their manners, customs, and general character these Indians closely resembled the Virginia tribes. They built their lodges in the same manner, as well as of the same materials, in all respects practised the same arts, and observed the same religious ceremonies. Like them, they acknowledged a great God, but also offered sacrifices to local *Okees*. They smoked tobacco, holding it in the highest estimation, cultivated maize, hunted the deer, and snared water-fowl. Ethnologically they were descendants of the same race with the Powhatanic tribes, and spoke dialects of the great Algonkin language. Indeed, Powhatan claimed jurisdiction over the Patuxent, though it is doubtful whether his claims were much respected.

This colony was founded under a charter granted by Charles I., through the influence of his consort, Mary, and appears to have been intended as a refuge for persons professing the same religion with the queen, who was a Roman Catholic. Under the protectorate of Cromwell, who soon after gained the ascendency in England, Maryland became the resort of men holding various creeds, and the country obtained a wide-spread fame as the land of tolerance. But, however the white men differed in their religious faith, they agreed generally in their mode of treatment of the Indians. Barbarism and Christianity could not exist in close proximity.

A good understanding, however, was maintained with this people, in the hope that their eyes might be so far morally and intellectually opened that they might be brought under the influence of the gospel. The accounts of the Maryland Indians state that "they were a simple race, open, affectionate, and confiding, filled with wonder and admiration of their new visitants, and disposed to live with them as neighbors and friends on terms of intimacy and cordiality. To the Europeans they seem to have been quite as much objects of curiosity as the Europeans were to them. To Englishmen coming from the midst of a civilization which had been steadily progressive for a thousand years, the persons, manners, habits, and sentiments of the savages of North America must have been objects of lasting astonishment."

The following testimony respecting the Chesapeake Bay Indians is from the pen of Father White, who accompanied Calvert: "This race is endowed with an ingenious and liberal disposition, and, what may surprise you when stated, an acuteness of taste, smell, and sight that even surpasses Europeans'. They live mostly on a pap, which they call *pone*, or *omini* [hominy]. They add sometimes a fish, or what they have taken, either beast or bird, in hunting. They keep themselves as much as possible from wine and warm drinks, nor are they easily induced to taste them, except in cases where the English have infected them.

"Ignorance of their language makes it as yet impossible for me to assert what are their religious opinions, for we have not full confidence in Protestant interpreters. These few things we have learned at different times: they recognize one God of heaven, whom they call our God; they pay to him no external worship, but endeavor to propitiate by every means in their power a certain evil spirit which they call *Okee*. They worship corn and fire, as I am informed, as gods wonderfully beneficent to the human race.

"Some of our people relate that they have seen the ceremony at Barcluxor. On an appointed day all the men and women from many villages assembled around a great fire. Next to the fire stood the younger people, behind them the men advanced in life. A piece of deer's fat being then thrown into the fire, the hands and voices being lifted towards heaven, they cried out, Taho! Taho! They then cleared a small space, and some one produced a large bag; in the bag was a pipe, and a kind of powder which they called potu. The pipe was such as our countrymen use, but larger. Then the bag was carried around the fire, the boys and girls singing with an agreeable voice, Taho! Taho! The circle being ended, the pipe and powder were taken from the pouch. The potu was distributed to each of those standing round, which he put into the pipe and smoked, breathing the smoke over his limbs, and sanctifying them as the smoker supposes. I have not been able to learn more than that they appear to have some knowledge of the flood by which the world perished because of the sins of men."

There is nothing either in these ceremonial rites of Taho and offerings of the fumes of the fat of animals and of tobacco to the god of fire, or in the traditions of a flood, or in the language employed, to denote that the Maryland tribes differed essentially from others of the great Algonkin stock.

When Calvert landed, he was imbued with the most friendly feelings towards the Indians, for they were regarded with much interest in Europe. As with the rulers of all the new colonies, a knowledge of the policy which controlled the Indian tribes was with him a subject of primary importance. It soon became evident that a great aboriginal nation in the interior was alike the terror and the aversion of all the midland and coast tribes. This governing power was the Iroquois, the dreaded

Massawomacks of the native Virginia tribes, before the crushing force of whose prowess the Susquehannocks and their feeble allies were eventually compelled to succumb.

The Chesapeake Bay may have derived its name from a tribe called Chesapeake, which occupied Cape Henry and the surrounding country, now included in Princess Anne County, Virginia, but we have hitherto shown that the tribe more probably took its name from that of the bay. It appears from the geographical position of the bay within the limits of the Powhatanic territory, as well as from the etymology of the word, which we have elsewhere given, that the name is of Algonkin derivation.

When in 1608 Captain Smith made a voyage to the head of this bay, and entered the magnificent river which debouches into it, he found that the Susquehannocks, who were located on its western shores, comprised six hundred warriors, which would denote a population of three thousand souls, and he was struck with admiration of their fine physical proportions and manly voices. At that time twenty-three years had elapsed from the date of the first voyage to Virginia. Whether a change had taken place in their location, or whether the Virginia band had been but an outlying branch, cannot now be determined, but it is more than probable that the Susquehanna Valley was their original residence.

Along the eastern shores of the bay from Cape Charles up, Smith mentions the location of the Accomacs and the Accohanocs, tribes who retained this general position during the greater part of colonial history, and who certainly existed down to the period of the Northampton massacre, when they became mingled with the negroes. Next in position north he places the Nanticokes, under the name of Tockwaghs, a name which may readily be inferred to apply to that tribe when we learn that they were called Tawackguáno by the Delawares.[1] Thence in succession came the Ozimies, the Huokarawaocks, and the Wighcomocos, the latter of whom are called Wicomocos by Calvert.

The entire eastern shore above Virginia has in latter days been regarded as the country of the Nanticos or Conoy, for these are synonymous names for the same people. An adverse fate befell that scattered tribe. From the earliest dates they were at variance with the Iroquois, whose war-canoes swept down the Susquehanna from their fastnesses in Western New York. We learn from a competent authority[2] that the Nanticos were forced into a league with the Iroquois, who finally adopted them, holding out the flattering prospect of the tribe being received into their confederacy; but if this plan was ever carried out (and there is evidence of it in a declaration made in 1758 by Tokais, a Cayuga chief), their fate was not unlike that of the stag which falls into the power of the anaconda. They helped to minister to the pride of the Iroquois, as did also the Tutelos from Virginia.

The Nanticokes and Conoys (different bands of the same people), wearied with strife, abandoned their residences in Lower Maryland, and moved up the Susquehanna,

---

[1] Gallatin's Synopsis, p. 52. [2] Charles Thomson.

pursuing its western branches into the territories of their conquerors, the Iroquois. Eventually they settled down beside fragmentary bands of Shawnees and Mohickanders, at Otsiningo, the present site of Binghamton, New York, with whom they formed a league, in the hope of recovering their former position by this policy. This league was called the "Three Nations." During the month of April, 1757, Owiligascho, or Peter Spelman, a German, who had resided seven years among the Shawnees on one of the western branches of the Susquehanna and married a Shawnee wife, arrived at Fort Johnson, where resided the Indian superintendent for the northern colonies, and reported that this new confederacy would visit him in a short time with a body of nearly two hundred men, and that they were now on the road. Their object was to smoke a friendly pipe with Sir William Johnson, after the manner of their fathers, and to offer him assistance in the war against the French. He presented two strings of wampum from the chiefs as the credentials of his authority. On the 19th of the same month these Indians arrived on the opposite bank of the river, which was then swelled by the spring flood. The chiefs, having crossed in canoes, were admitted to a council. The Shawnees were represented by Paxinosa and fifty-two of his warriors; the Mohickanders by Mammatsican, their king, with one hundred and forty-seven of his nation; and the Nanticokes by Hamightaghlawatawa, with eight of his people. Having been addressed in favorable and congratulatory terms by Sir William, who explained to them the true position of the English, as contrasted with that of the French, respecting the Indians, two days subsequently the chiefs replied, accepting the offer of the chain of friendship, and promising to keep "fast hold of it, and not quit it, so long as the world endured." In this address allusion is incidentally made to a belt sent the previous year to the unfriendly Delaware and Ohio Indians in the vicinity of Fort Du Quesne, and also to a similar belt sent to the Delaware chief, Tediscund, residing at Tioga.[1] They formally apprise Johnson of the league between the Nanticokes, Mohickanders, and Shawnees, of which he had been previously informed by Owiligascho, and also that they have concentrated at Otsiningo, on the Susquehanna, where messages are directed to be sent to them in future.

There is a trait of Indian shrewdness observable at the conclusion of their reply to Sir William Johnson, in a curious allusion to an event which occurred while the Mohickanders still resided on the Hudson. "'Tis now nine years ago,"[2] said the speaker, "that a misfortune happened near Reinbeck, in this province; a white man there shot a young man, an Indian. There was a meeting held thereon, and Martinus Hoffman said, 'Brothers, there are two methods of settling this accident; one according to the white people's customs, the other according to the Indians'. Which of them will you choose? If you will go according to the Indian manner, the man who shot the Indian may yet live. If this man's life is spared, and at any time hereafter an Indian should kill a white man, and you desire it, his life shall also be

---

[1] Spelled "Tiaogo" in Col. Doc., vol. vii. p. 249.
[2] This settles the final withdrawal of the Mohickanders from the Hudson after 1748.

spared.' You told us, two days ago, that when a man is dead there is no bringing him to life again. We understand there are two Indians in jail at Albany accused of killing a white man. They are alive, and may live to be of service, and we beg you, as the chief of the Great King, our Father, that they may be released."

The alliance thus formed with the British government in 1757 was carefully fostered, and remained unbroken during the progress of the Revolution. The larger part of these Indians probably afterwards went to Canada with the Munsees and Delawares, where numbers of the latter tribe were located. A few of them, however, who lingered within the precincts of New York, probably became absorbed in the Brothertons, a band comprising fragments of various Algonkin tribes who had dropped their own dialects and adopted the English language.

At the time of the settlement of Jamestown, the Susquehannocks claimed the country lying between the Potomac and Susquehanna Rivers,—an area comprising the entire western half of Maryland. This was their hunting-ground, and marked the boundary-line between their jurisdiction and that of the Powhatanic forest kingdom. Whatever were the local names of the bands occupying the banks of the several intermediate rivers, they were merely subordinate to the reigning tribe primarily located on the shores of the Susquehanna. Subsequently the tribe transferred their council-fire to a point on the Patuxent, in a position less exposed to the incessant inroads of the Iroquois.

The lower class of adventurers and settlers who emigrated to Virginia and Maryland at this early period was composed of persons who were liable to become embroiled with the Indians, whose character they invariably misjudged and whose lives they held to be valueless. By these persons the natives were regarded only as the medium through which they could pursue a profitable traffic in skins and furs, which was free to every one who chose to engage in it or possessed the requisite capital. Unfortunately for the Indians, they could not restrain their appetite for ardent spirits, and consequently it should excite no surprise that a tribe thus pressed on one hand by a powerful and infuriated enemy and on the other enticed by temptation to indulgence should rapidly decline.

The effects of commerce with the whites on the condition of the aboriginal tribes of Maryland, located on the shores skirting the open waters of the Chesapeake, were of so baneful a character as to destroy their power and importance within fifty years after the landing of Calvert. Without any strong political organization, or any permanent union among themselves, ever anxious to obtain the benefits of commerce and trade, and lacking the firm moral purpose to resist the evil influences to which they were exposed, the Indians were placed in precisely the same position as were the coast-tribes of Virginia, who wasted away with a degree of rapidity which surprised her statesmen. They exchanged their furs and fish, the only available products of their forests and streams, for the means of indulgence, and when this resource failed they sold their lands to obtain the same destructive stimulants. Whether gunpowder, which annihilated the animals, performed its work more effectually than alcohol, which thinned the ranks of the Indians, may well be doubted.

Jealous of their tribal sovereignty, the Susquehannocks by intestine wars increased the work of self-destruction begun by intemperance, and when, like the other tribes, they began to assert their rights and resist the encroachments of Europeans, they had already diminished so much in population that they lacked the ability to maintain their ground. They were outwitted in diplomacy by a civilized nation, and if they did not disappear before the steady progress of arts and industry, they were enervated during peace and conquered in war.

One cause operated powerfully to hasten the downfall of the Susquehannocks,— the mismanagement of their relations with the settlers of Virginia. The Virginians on the southern banks of the Potomac, for some reason, believed the Susquehannocks to have been guilty of committing depredations and foul murders on their frontiers. In 1675 some of the inhabitants of the most northerly portion of Virginia, while on their way to attend church, found the nearly lifeless body of a settler lying across the threshold of his own door, and an Indian lying dead on the ground near him. The white man was mortally wounded, but lived long enough to inform them that the Indians came from the Maryland shore.

The sensation produced by this outrage was extreme. Two spirited officers of the militia, Mason and Brent, accompanied by thirty men, promptly pursued the murderers. Ascending the valley of the Potomac some twenty miles, they crossed its channel to the Maryland shore, where they found two Indian paths. Dividing their force, Mason took one trail and Brent the other. A short pursuit by each party terminated in the discovery of two Indian wigwams. Brent having accused one of the occupants of the lodge which he found as the murderer, the Indian denied the accusation, and attempted to escape, but was shot down by a pistol-ball which lodged in his back. The other inmates then fired and made a spring for the door of the wigwam, but the rifle laid ten of the number dead on the spot. Meantime, Mason had arrived at the other lodge, the Indians in which, hearing the firing at the first lodge, hastened to effect their escape. Fourteen of them were shot, when one of the survivors having rushed up to Mason and declared that they were Susquehannocks and friends, the firing was instantly stopped.

The Susquehannocks subsequently accused the Senecas of having committed the murders in Virginia. Who the perpetrators really were is unknown, but other massacres immediately followed on those borders, which so excited the people of Maryland, as well as of Virginia, that they united in mustering one thousand men to march against the Susquehannocks. This force was placed under the command of Colonel John Washington.[1] Meanwhile, the Susquehannocks had taken possession of an old abandoned fort, which, having been used by the whites in previous wars, was singularly well calculated for defence. It was encompassed by ample earthen walls, containing a gate and surrounded by a ditch, the counterscarp of the latter being planted with trees, closely wattled, which presented an impenetrable curtain.

The Maryland and Virginia forces appeared before this fort on the 23d of Sep-

---

[1] Great-grandfather of General George Washington.

tember. Conferences were held, in which the Indians, although boldly accused of the murders, strongly denied their complicity, notwithstanding three of the bloody deeds had been identified as their acts. They agreed to deliver Harignera and five others of their principal chiefs to the English as hostages for the security of their frontiers. The morning after the consummation of this treaty, one Captain John Allen, a leader of the Maryland Rangers, having reported the circumstance of the murder of Randolph Hanson among the recent outrages, was sent with a guard to ascertain whether it had been the work of Indians. It so occurred that during the final conference for the conclusion of the treaty by the terms of which the six chiefs had been delivered over to the custody of the military, Allen returned from this examination, bringing with him the mangled remains of the victims, the appearance of which left no doubt that they had been foully murdered by the Indians. The whole camp was instantly a scene of excitement, every one imagining he saw his nearest friend, or some loved one, in the cruel grip of savages. Five of the hostages, comprising the leading sachems and wise men of the Susquehannocks, were immediately condemned to death, and were accordingly executed. During the night the Indians dexterously and silently evacuated the fort and fled, taking with them all their women and children. The warriors of this party attacked with savage fury the white residents on the frontiers of Virginia, killing many, and committing numerous depredations, finally either being exterminated in these forays or becoming scattered among other bands.

This was not, however, the severest blow that the Susquehannocks received. It appears from the relation of Evans that a body of troops led by a Marylander attacked them at a position east of the Susquehanna, about three miles below Wright's Ferry, now known as Columbia, killing several hundred men. It is proved by Colden (from data produced at the treaty of Lancaster, negotiated in 1744) that the Susquehannocks formed a part of the Conestogas, an original Oneida tribe, and that they were finally settled in the territory of that nation in Western New York. Oneida tradition places the birth and origin of the celebrated chief Skenandoah at Conestoga, whence in early life he came to Oneida Castle.

The synonymous names of the Indian tribes in the United States have operated greatly to complicate or retard the development of their true history. This subject has been a stumbling-block to writers, as well at home as abroad, where some of the ablest historians have been misled by it, mistaking the several names of the same tribe for those of different tribes. The Indian history of Maryland, and of its leading tribe, the Susquehannocks, has been obscured in this way. The early French writers in Canada, and those who on their authority have since written of that country, constantly mention a tribe whose name in the softest form is given as Andastes. Although residing in well-known limits of the United States, their name is not to be found in the works of any of our historians. Fortunately, however, there existed between them and the Indian allies of the French sufficient intercourse to give us data whereby to determine their location, language, numbers, and power.

Friends of the Swedish colony on the Delaware, friends of the Hurons in Upper

Canada, friends at a later date of Maryland and Pennsylvania, they were repeatedly at war with the powerful Iroquois. Like the latter and the Neuters, they were a branch of the great Huron-Iroquois family. According to Bressani, they were located five hundred miles—or, as the "Relation" of 1647-48 has it, one hundred and fifty leagues—southwest by south of the Hurons, inclining a little eastward. This measurement was in a direct line, the road usually taken being somewhat longer, and at least two hundred leagues. A large river, rising near Lake Ontario, led to the town. They resided near the Swedish settlement, and were on friendly terms with the Scandinavian colonists.

Quite naturally we turn to Swedish accounts to find some traces of this people. Proud, in his "History of Pennsylvania" and the "Historical Collections," actually locates a tribe called Andastakas on Christiana Creek, but does not indicate on what authority. The name does not appear in Swedish accounts, and this is natural, as the surrounding tribes were Algonkin, and the Swedish name would of course be Algic. A band of the Akwinoshioni existed near the Swedes, whom they called Mengwe, a term that Heckewelder tells us is the same as Mingo. Campanius has preserved a vocabulary of their language, which is a dialect of the Huron-Iroquois, as Duponceau long since observed. This word is not to be confounded with Minqua. Minqua was the Dutch and Swedish name for the Susquehannocks. A creek running into the Delaware bore the name of Minquakill, not that the Minqua lived on it, but because it led to their country. This would place them on the Susquehanna, where the French locate the Andastes. Their town is thus described by Campanius: "The Minques, or Minckus, lived at the distance of twelve [fifty-four English] miles from New Sweden, where they daily came to trade with us. The way to their land was very bad, being rocky, full of sharp gray stones, with hills and morasses, so that the Swedes when they went to them, which happened once or twice a year, had to walk in the water up to their armpits. . . . They live on a high mountain, very steep and difficult to climb; there they have a fort or square building in which they reside. They have guns and small iron cannon, with which they shoot and defend themselves, and take with them when they go to war. They are strong and vigorous, both old and young; they are a tall people, and not frightful in their appearance."

There can be little doubt as to the identity of these Swedish Minqua and the Andastoe, or Gandastogué, of the French. Let us now see what we can elicit from European annals regarding their history. Towards the close of the seventeenth century, they had in a ten years' war almost exterminated the Mohawks. The Minquas were a warlike people, and, as usual with the Huron-Iroquois, were a superior race to their Algic neighbors. "They made the other Indians," says Campanius, "subject to them, so that they dared not stir, much less go to war against them." In 1633, De Vries found them at war with the Timber Creek Indians. A short time thereafter the Swedes purchased a portion of their territory, and in 1645, under the name of Susquehanna or Conestoga Indians, they ceded to Maryland a tract beginning at the Patuxent River on the west and terminating at the Choptank

River on the east. The Andastes, or Gandastogués, who are evidently these Conestogas, were from time immemorial friends and allies of the Hurons, and not overfriendly to the Iroquois. In 1647, when the former were on the brink of ruin, the Andastes, then able to send from their single town thirteen hundred warriors, "who, when fighting, never fled, but stood like a wall as long as there was one remaining," despatched an embassy to Lake Huron with an offer to espouse their quarrel.

An embassy, headed by the Christian, Charles Ondaaiondiont, soon after set out from the villages of the Wyandots or Hurons. In ten days they reached the Andaste town, and on their appeal the Andastes resolved to interfere. An embassy, loaded with rich presents, was sent to Onondaga to demand why the Iroquois struck the Wyandots, and to ask them to be wise and bury the hatchet. Charles, meanwhile, leaving a person to await the return of the deputies, set out for the Huron country, which he reached only after a long and tedious march of forty days, made necessary by the war-parties which the Senecas sent out to intercept him. His journey to Andaste had occupied but ten days. While at Andaste, he visited the churchless settlement of the Swedes, where was lying a Dutch ship from Manhattan, by which he received tidings of the murder of his old friend Ondessonk, the Jesuit Father Jogues, whom the Mohawks had mercilessly butchered near Albany.

The Iroquois accepted the presents of the Andastes, but nevertheless continued the war. The Hurons, however, never required the Andastes to enter the field, and the latter seem to have taken no further part in the war.

Yet, in 1652, the Journal of the Superior of the Jesuits at Montreal, which gives as synonymous the names Andastoe and Atrakwer, mentions a report that six hundred of the Andastes had been taken by the Iroquois. This report was probably unfounded. They were at peace in 1656, although we learn that in that year some Andastoe hunters were robbed by the Onondagas on Lake Ontario, and war was expected in consequence.

In 1660 the successors of the Swedes still continued their friendly intercourse with the Andastes, or Minquas. In the following year we find their town ravaged by the smallpox; and, as Campanius tells us, their loss by that scourge of the Indians was such as to weaken them greatly as a nation. Yet under this affliction their spirit remained unbroken. In 1661 some of their tribe were cut off by the Senecas, and they in return killed three Cayugas in the same year. In the following year they defeated the western cantons, who then supplicated the French for aid. The Senecas soon after renewed their request, and we find that in May, 1663, an army of sixteen hundred Senecas marched against the Minquas and laid siege to a little fort defended by one hundred warriors of that tribe, who, confident in their own bravery, and assured of receiving assistance from their countrymen, as well as from their white friends in Maryland, held out manfully. At last, sallying out, they routed the Senecas, killing ten, and recovering as many of their own countrymen. For a time this victory gave them a preponderance, and such was the terror of their arms that a portion of the Cayugas, being hard pressed and harassed by their inroads, removed to Quinté, north of Lake Ontario.

The war was continued in a desultory manner. In 1668 the missionary resident at Onondaga beheld a Gandastogué girl tied to the stake, and in 1669 the Oneidas sent out parties against them. In 1670 prisoners were again brought to Seneca and Oneida, where they were tortured. During the previous autumn the Gandastogués had again attacked the Cayugas, but at last they sent an ambassador to the latter, who, contrary to usage, was imprisoned, and in the spring put to death, together with his nephew.

About this time an Iroquois medicine-man, when dying, ordered his body to be interred on the road to the country of the Andastes, promising to prevent, even in death, the inroads of that waning yet terrible tribe. He also promised that Hochitagete, the great chief of the Andastes, should fall into their hands. Notwithstanding his prophecy, despite the potency of his bones, the Andastes carried off three Cayuga women, and when a party of Senecas took the field, with promises of support from a reserve of Cayugas, they were met, attacked, and defeated by a party of sixty Andaste youth, or rather boys, who, having killed several and routed the rest, started in pursuit of the Cayugas, whom, however, they failed to overtake.

This victory was needed; for the Andastes had suffered greatly in point of numbers. "God help them!" says the missionary who relates the preceding victory: "they have only three hundred warriors!"

The war continued, but the Marylanders became the enemies of the Andastes or Conestogas, and by the year 1675 they had at length yielded to the Iroquois, who removed a portion of them, at least, from their old position to one higher up, perhaps to Onoghquage.

Some of the Conestogas, however, remained at the place which still bears their name. They made a treaty with Penn in 1683, but when that proprietor became aware of their dependent state he applied to the Iroquois through Dongan. When a subsequent treaty was concluded with them, in 1701, a deputy from Onondaga was present, and ratified the acts of Conoodagtoh, "the king of the Susquehanna[1] Menquays, or Conestoga Indians." At this period other Indians had joined the survivors, and Shawnese, as well as Ganawese, also appear among them. Subsequently, when a treaty was negotiated with Lieutenant-Governor Patrick Gordon, four chiefs of the Conestogas (one the somewhat celebrated interpreter, Civility) were present, and also the same number of Algonkin chiefs, headed by Tiorhaasery. Colden represents them as speaking Oneida, and in fact their dialect approximates it greatly.[2] Besides the Algonkins, there were some kindred Nanticokes at Conestoga; but they formed only a small village, destined soon to perish.

---

[1] It will be seen that the term Susquehannas is used as if it were a synonyme of Conestogas. Smith (p. 182) speaks of the Susquehannocks as using a different language from the Virginian—that is, from the Algonkin—tribes. Unfortunately, no trace of their language remains, as Gallatin assures us, unless, indeed, the unpublished grammar, dictionary, and catechism of the Jesuit Father White, one of the first settlers of Maryland, which are still preserved at Rome, should prove to be in that language.

[2] Colden, ii. 58. The name Tiorhaasery is that borne by the celebrated missionary Lamberville, and means "dawning of the day."

In 1763 they numbered only twenty souls, living in a cluster of squalid cabins, and all dependent on the industry of the female portion. The men were wild, gypsy-like beings, and, in the troubled state of the country, while Pontiac was encircling the colony with an ever-narrowing hedge of burning dwellings, excited suspicion by their careless if not threatening language. In their vicinity was the town of Paxton, settled by Irish Presbyterians, who had imbibed a fanatical hatred of pagan institutions. These men, having suddenly resolved to destroy the last distinct remnant of the Andastes, Minquas, or Conestogas, armed themselves, and in mid-winter attacked the little village, in which they found only six persons, whom they butchered, and then fired their log huts. The sheriff of Lancaster, upon learning of the outrage, hurried the survivors to the jail of that town as a place of security; but even here they could not escape the fury of the Paxton boys. On the 27th of December, while the townsfolk were in church, they entered the town, broke open the jail, and massacred the survivors, who fought desperately with billets of wood, thus maintaining to the last their ancient renown.[1]

Such was the close of the history of the Andastes. The remnant of a nation which had during fourteen years engaged the victorious Iroquois hand to hand were massacred by a band of lawless whites.

It will not be deemed improper before closing the history of one of the most prominent and characteristic tribes existing during the early days of the central colonies of the United States, a brave and high-spirited race, to collate, in a brief form, the principal events of the times which constitute the basis of their history. In this *résumé* it will be found necessary to repeat some statements which we have already made.

According to a tradition narrated in the Jesuit "Relation" for 1659-60, the Andastes had, prior to 1600, during a ten years' war, almost exterminated the Mohawks, and so completely humbled that bold and warlike tribe that after the period mentioned they seldom dared to provoke them.

However, in 1608, Smith found the tribes still contending with one another, equally resolute and warlike,—the Susquehannas, or Andastes, being impregnable in their palisaded town, and ruling over all the Algonkin tribes.

Soon after the Dutch settled New York they visited the Delaware River, and became acquainted with the dominant tribe, the Minquas, who came from the Susquehanna, by Minquaskill, to trade with them. In 1633, De Vries found them ruling with an iron hand the tribes located on the banks of the Delaware. Five years subsequently, Minuit, at the head of a colony of Swedes, founded New Sweden, purchasing the land from the Minquas. A strong friendship grew up between the settlers and this tribe, and a lucrative trade was carried on, which excited the jealousy of the Dutch, who made repeated endeavors to obtain a share of it.

Of the trade of the Swedes with the Susquehannas, and especially of their supplying the latter with fire-arms, we have a proof in Plowden's "New Albion:" "The

[1] Parkman's Conspiracy of Pontiac.

Swedes hired out three of their soldiers to the Susquehannocks, and have taught them the use of our arms and fights.'

In 1647 the Hurons were on the brink of ruin. The Iroquois had pursued them, after their alliance with the French, with the utmost fury. By stratagem the whole district of country from the Oswego, G nesee, and Niagara Rivers to the very skirts of Montreal was covered by war-parties, who waylaid every path. Themselves of the Iroquois lineage, the war was waged with the desperation of a family quarrel. There was no pity and no mercy in the Iroquois mode of warfare. They have been known to travel a thousand miles and then conceal themselves near the cabin of some unsuspecting foe that they might deprive him of his scalp. During the war with the Iroquois, the Susquehannas, then able to send thirteen hundred warriors from their single town, despatched an embassy to the shores of Lake Huron to offer their aid to their ancient allies, promising to take up arms whenever called upon. The infatuated Hurons relied on their own strength, and seem to have slighted the proffered assistance till it was too late.

The Dutch still continued to struggle for the Minqua or Susquehanna trade, from which the Swedes no less zealously endeavored to exclude them; but in 1651 the Dutch purchased of the Minquas all the land between the Minquaskill and Bomties Hook, in the name of the States-General and the West India Company.

At the period of Calvert's colonization, the Susquehannas had been at war with the Piscataways, as well as with other Maryland tribes, and seem to have cut off a missionary settlement. In 1642 they were declared enemies of the colony, and, as they still continued their ravages with the Wycomeses, and apparently with the Senecas, Captain Cornwallis was sent against them, and a fort was erected on Palmer's Island to check their inroads. The war continued, however, and an effort made to bring about a conference in May, 1644, with a view to establishing peace, failed. The new settlements of the Puritans on the Severn, in the very territories of the Susquehannas, having given fresh umbrage, the frontier was ravaged by predatory bands. In 1652, however, peace was firmly established by a treaty signed at the river Severn, on the 5th of July, by Richard Bennett, Edward Lloyd, William Fuller, Leonard Strong, and Thomas Marsh, on behalf of the colony, and Sawahegeh, Auroghtaregh, Scarhuhadigh, Rutchogah, and Natheldianeh, Susquehanna "war-captains and councillors," in the presence of "Jafer Peter for the Swedes Governor."

By this treaty all past grievances were forgiven on both sides, peace was established, and provision made to prevent future hostilities. The Susquehannas thereby ceded to the colony all the territory between Patuxent River and Palmer's Island, on the west, and from Choptank River to the branch above Elk River, excepting Palmer's Island, on which both parties were at liberty to have trading-houses.

In 1652 a war broke out between the Andastes and the Senecas, which continued as late as 1673, for in the Jesuit "Relation" for 1672–73 we find the following remark of Father Lamberville: "Two Andastogues taken by the Iroquois were more fortunate: they received baptism immediately before the hot irons were applied. One of them, having been burnt in a cabin during the night from the feet up to the knees, prayed with me the next day, when bound to a stake in the square of the castle. I need not repeat here, what is already known, that the tortures inflicted on these prisoners of war are horrible. The patience of these poor victims is admirable; but it is impossible to behold without horror their flesh roasted and devoured by men who act like famished dogs.

"Passing one day by a place where they were cutting up the body of one of these victims, I could not refrain from going up to inveigh against this brutality. One of these cannibals was calling for a knife to cut off an arm; I opposed it, and threatened, if he would not desist, that God would sooner or later punish his cruelty. He persisted, however, giving as his reason that he was invited to a dream-feast, where nothing was to be eaten but human flesh, brought by the guests themselves. Two days after, God permitted his wife to fall into the hands of the Andastogues, who avenged on her the cruelty of her husband."

Of the two following years we have no definite account, but in 1675 the "État Présent" of Monseigneur de St. Valier, Bishop of Quebec, speaks of the pride of the Iroquois since the defeat of the Andastes. When or where the decisive battle was fought, I have been utterly unable to trace: from what can be gleaned from the annals of Maryland and Virginia, it seems probable that their stronghold was taken, and that the survivors fled south.

According to the historians of Maryland and Virginia, the Senecas had, in 1674, conquered the Susquehannas, and driven them from their abode at the head of the Chesapeake to the vicinity of the Piscataways. The fugitives had taken refuge in an old fort which had belonged to their former antagonists, and there resolutely defended themselves against the Senecas, who still pursued them, ravaging without much concern the lands of the whites. Some of the colonists were actually cut off, and, as the Susquehannas had in the olden time been enemies, and were now apparently invading the colonies, it was agreed to send a joint Maryland and Virginia force against them. On the 25th of September, 1675, the Maryland troops, under Major Trueman, appeared before their fort. He was apparently satisfied with their protestations of innocence, but being joined on the following day by the Virginians, under Colonels Washington and Mason, under the strong provocations before stated, he caused five of the chiefs, who came out to treat with them, to be seized and bound. To prove their friendship they showed a silver medal and papers given them by governors of Maryland, but in spite of all they were put to death. Many fell in the fight; the rest evacuated the fort, and commenced a retreat and a war of revenge; and soon, these being joined by other tribes, the whole border was deluged in blood. Bacon's rebellion in Virginia grew out of this act of treachery, and the war was finally ended, it would seem, by the aid of the Iroquois, who, joining the Maryland and Virginia army, forced the surviving Susquehannas to return to their former post, where a number of Iroquois were incorporated with them.

The Susquehannas were finally exterminated as a nation, but their name will be perpetuated by their noble river, which is a more enduring memorial than the perishable monuments erected by man.

CHAPTER VI.

PENNSYLVANIA COLONIZED—THE LENNI LENAPE.

TRADITION assigns to the Lenni Lenape an organization anterior to that of most of the other Indian tribes. Heckewelder informs us that they came from the West, and that from their ancient traditions it is gathered that they crossed the Mississippi River in their migration to the East. Authors have attempted to prove that their *ola walum* have reference to a very ancient migration from foreign countries. But these are merely ordinary pictographs, denoting a simple mode of ideographic communication which is common among the entire Algonkin family, of which the Lenni Lenape assert that they were the head.

It is mentioned that after crossing the Mississippi River they were opposed by the Allegans, or Allegewi, who occupied the principal ranges of the Alleghany Mountains. At this epoch, the tradition adds, they discovered the Iroquois, their apparent precursors, towards the north, who became their allies and aided them in driving the Allegans out of the Ohio Valley towards the south. The vestiges of tribal strife still extant in that valley are the evidences of this ancient war. If the term *any* in the word Alleghany denotes a stream or river, as it appears to do, and if the river has prior right to the name over the mountains, then it may be said that the Youghiogha*ny*, in which the same word for stream is employed, is also a term of Allegewi origin. These appear to be the only words of that language which have survived the lapse of time.[1]

The name of this tribe has been said to imply "original men," but the orthography does not sustain this assertion. Lenni is the same as *illini* in the Illinois, and *innini* in the Chippewa, the consonants *l* and *n* and the vowels *o* and *i* being interchangeable in the Algonkin. Lenape (ee) is in the same language, and, under the same rule, the equivalent of *inabi* and *iabi*, a male. The true meaning is "manly men," —a name involving a harmless boast. There is no tribal name in the Vesperic group of tribes which has the least reference to their origin. The Iroquois, by the term *ongwe honwe*, also declared themselves to be superior men. To be men was, symbolically, to be brave, and bravery was the glory to which the red men all aspired.

We must rest satisfied with the Indian traditions, bare as they are of details.

---

[1] The philologist, however, will perceive the analogy which exists between the term *any* and the inflections *anock* and *hannock*, meaning river, in the compound words Susque*hannock* and Rappa*hannock*. If, therefore, part of the Allegans crossed to the waters of the Chesapeake, and were driven thence towards the south by the Lenni Lenape and Iroquois, these words, originally in the tribal list, would seem to belong, as a point of Indian history of suggestive importance, to the Susquehannocks and to the Powhatanic family, both offshoots from the mother Algonkin.

Even this much is an important contribution to their ancient history, which we should carefully cherish, and for which we are indebted to the meritorious labors of a pious follower of Zinzendorf, who thought far more of saving the souls of this people than of recording their history.

But wherever the Lenape originated, and whatever were the details of the history of their migration from the Mississippi eastward, they were found at the earliest dates to be located in the Valley of the Delaware. In a revised map published at Amsterdam in 1659 they are represented as occupying that valley from its source to its mouth, their lands extending westward to the Minqua, or Susquehannocks, and to the sources of the rivers flowing into the Delaware, which separate them from the latter tribe; and eastward, under the names of various local and totemic clans, across the entire area of New Jersey to the Hudson. The Dutch, who entered the Hudson in 1609, found affiliated tribes of their stock along both banks of that river to near the point of influx of the Tawasentha. When they extended their settlements to the waters of the Delaware, they discovered themselves to be in the central position of the original stock. The fact of their aboriginal occupancy was known to the Swedes, who first entered the Delaware River in 1643. The events attending these colonial extensions into the domains of the Delawares furnish no incidents of history warranting any lengthy detail in this place. European colonization opened to them a commerce in the skins of animals, stimulating them to unusual exertions, which, however, exposed them to the perils of luxury and indulgence. It furnished them with the new and superior products of arts and manufactures, which at once took the place of their former imperfect implements and utensils of wood, bone, clay, and flint. It taught them the use of gunpowder, the firelock, and the steel-trap, by which the prowess of their young men on the war-path was made more severe and destructive, and the species of fur-bearing animals were more speedily annihilated. Depopulation, which had long previously begun to undermine the prosperity of the Indian tribes, was greatly accelerated by the advent of the Europeans. This was the position of affairs when William Penn landed on the shores of the Delaware in 1682. The idea of forming a colony of refuge in America for the poor, suffering, and oppressed people of some parts of Europe had been broached at an early day. The Puritan refugees were the first, in 1620, to develop a project of this kind. A similar necessity for a land of refuge was felt by the Catholics, who emigrated to Maryland under the guidance of Lord Baltimore in 1634. In 1682, Penn provided a like haven of safety for the Quakers, who came thither professing principles of peace and love towards men of every hue. He was especially desirous to protect the Indian race and to treat them with the most enlarged philanthropy and charity. In his hands civilization was rendered mild and enticing. Christianity, as taught by those who understand its precepts, has ever been a law of good will towards all mankind. Penn did not attempt any rude interference with the principles and practices of the natives. Persuasion and example were his only weapons, and strict justice in all transactions with them was his cardinal rule. Time was deemed to be necessary to enable the principles of the new system to take root in such dark and bewildered minds. Penn approached the natives in their councils, as at their lodge-fires, in an open, simple, straightforward manner, which gained him their confidence and made them receive him as a Friend indeed.

Penn's famous treaty with the Indians at Shackamaxon, on the northern edge of Philadelphia, was not for the purchase of lands, but to the effect that the Englishman and the Indian should respect the same moral law and be alike secure in their pursuits and their possessions, and provided that every difference should be adjusted by a tribunal composed of an equal number from each race. Neither oaths, signatures, nor seals were made use of in this treaty, and no written record of it exists; but it was sacredly kept, and it is said that not a drop of Quaker blood was ever shed by an Indian. This was in some measure owing to the fact that the Delawares had been disarmed and conquered by the Iroquois, whose vengeance would have been visited upon them had they dared to lift the hatchet against their English allies. By a series of unjust measures Penn's sons gradually alienated the Indians, and, after a peace of seventy years' duration, produced a disastrous rupture.

At the period of settlement there were three principal totemic divisions of the Lenni Lenapes, known as the Turtle, the Turkey, and the Wolf tribes. The Monseys or Wolf tribes, the most active and warlike of them all, occupied the mountainous country between the Kittatinny Mountains and the sources of the Susquehanna and Delaware Rivers, kindling their council-fire at the Minisink Flats on the Delaware, above the Water Gap. The tribes included the Assanpink or Stony Creek Indians; the Rankokas; the Andastes, at Christiana Creek, near Wilmington; the Neshaminies, in Bucks County; the Shackamaxons, at Kensington; the Mantas, or Frogs, near Burlington; the Tutcloes and Nauticokes, in Maryland and Virginia (the latter afterwards moved up the Susquehanna); the Monseys, near the Forks of the Delaware; the Mandes and Narriticongs, near the Raritan; the Capitanasses and Gacheos, the Monseys, and the Pomptons, in New Jersey. A few Mingoes were scattered among these. The Shawnees had a village at the Shawnee Flats, below Wilkesbarre, on the west side of the Susquehanna.

CHAPTER VII.

SETTLEMENT OF THE CAROLINAS.

SOUTH CAROLINA was occupied in 1670, ten years before Pennsylvania. The settlement of North Carolina dates from the year 1664. Before bringing to a close our narrative of the events of the seventeenth century, it will be important to take a cursory glance at the families of Indian tribes located along the sea-coast and in the interior of the Carolinas. The Indians informed the Spaniards who visited their shores early in the sixteenth century that the name of the country was Chicora, whence their visitors called them Chicoreans, and the race is supposed to be identical with the people now known as Corees, Catawbas, etc. Of the ancient existence of the elements of such a group we have, however, but little evidence beyond their geographical names. We have already presented evidence tending to show that the Catawbas proper were of the Iroquois-Huron stock, and that they sprang from the relics of the once famous Neuter Nation (Eries) of Canada. The most important of the tribes who resided in South Carolina at the time of its settlement were the Catawbas and the Cherokees. The Catawbas could muster nearly fifteen hundred warriors, indicating a population of about seven thousand five hundred souls. They were a fierce, subtle, warlike, and brave people, and at one time either comprised or ruled over twenty-eight subordinate tribes,—the Westoes, Stonoes, Coosaws, Sewees, Yamassees, Santees, Congarees, etc. The Cherokees occupied the upper parts of the State, extending their possessions to the head-waters of the Savannah, Coosawhatchie, Alabama, Tennessee, and Cumberland.

North Carolina was included in the general but undefined area of Virginia, which was first discovered by the parties sent out under the grant made to Raleigh in 1586, and may at an earlier period have contained some portions of the adventurous population of Southern Virginia, who, it is conjectured, might have retired thither after its successful colonization. But the Indian residents of the Carolinas appear to have been regarded as little more than encumbrances upon the land, to be evicted as easily and as speedily as possible. The earliest accounts make scarcely any mention of them, a fact which may be in some measure attributed to the circumstance that in those historical sketches published in London with the view of directing attention to emigration, the inducements for it would not have been enhanced by the introduction of such a topic. The age of philanthropy and of interest in aboriginal or savage tribes in any part of the globe had hardly yet arrived. At any rate, very little can be gleaned from the details of the political and commercial plans of colonization of the period.

The Carolina tribes eagerly availed themselves of the conveniences, luxuries, and indulgences introduced from Europe, and in an almost incredibly short time the little clans and chieftainships which stretched along the shores became extinct.

Dr. Hewit, an early historian, remarks that attempts were made to shield them against unjust encroachments and to protect their rights.[1] He thus writes: "Plans of lenity were, with respect to those Indian tribes, likewise adopted by government, and every possible precaution was taken to guard them against oppression and prevent any rupture with them. Experience has shown that rigorous measures, such as humbling them by force of arms, were not only very expensive and bloody, but disagreeable to a humane and generous nation, and seldom accompanied with any good effects. Such ill treatment rendered the savages cruel, suspicious, and distrustful, and prepared them for renewing hostilities by keeping alive their ferocious and warlike spirit. Their extirpation, even though it could easily be completed, would be a cruel act, and all the while the growth and prosperity of the settlements would be much retarded by the attempt. Whereas, by treating Indians with gentleness and humanity, it was thought they would by degrees lose their savage spirit and become more harmless and civilized. It was hoped that by establishing a fair and free trade with them their rude temper would in time be softened, their manners altered, and their wants increased, and instead of implacable enemies, ever bent on destruction, they might be rendered good allies, both useful and beneficial to the trade of the nation.

"It has been remarked that those Indians on the continent of America, who were, at the time of its discovery, a numerous and formidable people, have since that period been constantly decreasing and melting away like snow upon the mountains. For this rapid depopulation many reasons have been assigned. It is well known that population everywhere keeps pace with the means of subsistence. Even vegetables spring and grow in proportion to the richness of the soil in which they are planted, and to the supplies they receive from the nourishing rains and dews of heaven; animals flourish or decay according as the means of subsistence abound or fail; and, as all mankind partake of the nature of both, they also multiply or decrease as they are fed, or have provision in plenty, luxury excluded. The Indians, being driven from their possessions near the sea, as the settlements multiplied, were robbed of many necessaries of life, particularly of oysters, crabs, and fish, with which the maritime parts furnished them in great abundance, and on which they must have considerably subsisted, as is apparent from a view of their camps still remaining near the sea-shore. The women are not only much disregarded and despised, but also naturally less prolific among rude than polished nations. The men being often abroad, at hunting or war, agriculture, which is the chief means of subsistence among a civilized people, is entirely neglected by them, and looked upon as an occupation worthy only of women or slaves. That abstinence and fatigue which the men endure in their distant excursions, and that gluttony and voraciousness in which

---

[1] "Historical Account of the Rise and Progress of the Colonies of South Carolina and Georgia." London, 1776.—Carroll's "South Carolina Collections," 1836.

they indulge themselves in the times of plenty, are equally hurtful to the constitution, and productive of diseases of different kinds. Now that their territories are circumscribed by narrower bounds, the means of subsistence, derived even from game, is less plentiful. Indeed, scanty and limited are the provisions they raise by planting, even in the best seasons; but in case of a failure of their crops, or of their fields being destroyed by enemies, they perish in numbers by famine. Their natural passion for war the first European settlers soon discovered, and therefore turned the fury of one tribe against another with a view to save themselves. When engaged in hostilities, they always fought not so much to humble and conquer as to exterminate and destroy. The British, French, and Spanish nations having planted colonies in their neighborhood, a rivalship for power over them took place, and each nation, having its allies among the savages, was zealous and indefatigable in instigating them against the allies of its neighbor. Hence a series of bloody and destructive wars has been carried on among these rude tribes with all the rage and rancor of implacable enemies.

"But famine and war, however destructive, were not the only causes of their rapid decay. The smallpox, having broken out among them, proved exceedingly fatal, both on account of the contagious nature of the distemper, and their harsh and injudicious attempts to cure it by plunging themselves into cold rivers during the most violent stages of the disorder. The pestilence broke out among some nations, particularly among the Pemblicos in North Carolina, and almost swept away the whole tribe. The practice of entrapping them, which was encouraged by the first settlers in Carolina, and selling them for slaves to the West India planters, helped greatly to thin their nations. But of all other causes, the introduction of spirituous liquors among them, for which they discovered an amazing fondness, has proved the most destructive. Excess and intemperance not only undermined their constitutions, but also created many quarrels, and subjected them to a numerous list of fatal diseases to which in former times they were perfect strangers. Besides, those Europeans engaged in commercial business with them, generally speaking, have been so far from reforming them by examples of virtue and purity of manners, that they rather served to corrupt their morals and render them more treacherous, distrustful, base, and debauched than they were before this intercourse commenced. In short, European avarice and ambition have not only debased the original nature and stern virtue of that savage race, so that those few Indians that now remain have lost in a great measure their primitive character, but European vice and European diseases, the consequences of vice, have exterminated this people, insomuch that many nations formerly populous are totally extinct, and their names entirely forgotten."

The South Carolina tribes have left but few traces or monuments of their existence except the heaps of oyster-shells which are still observable along the alluvial margins of the rivers. From their ancient places of sepulture the remains of stone pipes, amulets, and other relics of the arts peculiar to a hunter age are from time to time disinterred. There are some mounds still existing on the waters of the Coosawhatchie, as at Pocotaligo, and on some other streams, which have been but little examined, and in some instances where the mounds and shell-heaps have been properly explored the researches have developed nothing of a new character. On the alluvial banks of the Congaree, Mr. Howe has discovered some curious evidences of ancient metallurgic operations which were apparently carried on by the ancient Indians, who also appear to have deposited the bones and ashes of their dead in vases. Mr. Lawson, in his "Travels" (1700), notices some of the rites, manners, and opinions common to the Santees and other bands which convince us that their beliefs and superstitions were similar to those of the more advanced tribes. We are indebted to the same gentleman, also, for our most complete vocabulary of their languages. Their history, however, gives no evidence that they differed from the leading Vesperic groups, except in their names, and in some peculiarities of their dialect, which may be more readily observed in the geographical terminology.

When North Carolina was first settled by the whites there were many small tribes located along the coasts, who numbered collectively ten thousand souls. The Tuscaroras principally occupied the valley of the Neuse, extending from the sea to the mountains. The unfortunate attempt they made at a subsequent period to annihilate the colony by a simultaneous rising forms one of the most thrilling chapters in North Carolina history. This bold, cruel, and partly unsuccessful movement appears to have been a renewal of the project originated by Opechancanough, of Virginia, in 1622; and one cannot help feeling that it was but a rehearsal of the tragedy enacted in 1590, of which the unfortunate colonists left at Cape Hatteras were the victims,—the proximity of the Tuscaroras to that location giving additional countenance to the suggestion. Cusic, in his traditional sketches of the Iroquois, which indicate his profound ignorance of chronology, appears to allude to this, or possibly to some prior event, which occurred in the ante-historical period of America, wherein a Manteo and his English companions, or a Madoc and his Cambrian followers, may be symbolized.

The archæological remains on the late Mr. Calhoun's plantation, at Fort Hill, in Pendleton County, and also those of Fort Kienuka, attest the power of the ancient Iroquois in this quarter, and are yet probably in a condition to admit of satisfactory examination.

PERIOD III.

WAR OF RACES—EARLY COLONIAL HISTORY.

CHAPTER I.

THE PEQUOT TRIBE AND THE PEQUOT WAR—DESTRUCTION OF FORT MYSTIC—FLIGHT AND EXTINCTION OF THE TRIBE.

VIRGINIA, the mother of the English colonies in the United States, was the first to suffer from the efforts of the natives to root out and destroy the infant European settlements. The tragic fate of the first colony planted within her borders, and the wholesale massacre carried into such terrible effect by Opechancanough on the 22d of March, 1622, have been already related. While the immediate causes of the almost constant wars between the red and the white race, from the earliest down to that of Tecumseh, were varied in their character, yet their underlying motive has undoubtedly been the antagonism natural to people differing so radically in character and civilization, and the not unreasonable fear of the Indian of the disastrous result to him and his race likely to flow from the superiority of the white man.

The name of the Pequot tribe, which appears to mean a wooden arrow, reveals its Algonkin origin. In a map published at Amsterdam in 1659 these Indians are called Pequatoas, but on what account, or when the title was conferred upon them, is unknown. Most of the subdivisions of our aboriginal tribes have trivial names assigned them, on account of some event, important or otherwise, the history of which has not been transmitted to us by tradition. It is certain, from both their language and traditions, that the Lenape Algonkins, after crossing the Hudson towards the northeast, divided into a multiplicity of clans and tribes. In this ancient migration the Wolf totem, or Mohicans, were the first to cross the Hudson, and they appear to have regarded its valley, from the sea to the present site of Albany, as their rightful domain. The Iroquois penetrated into it from the north, and subsequently continued their conquests down the river.

The Mohican language and blood still constituted a tie of affiliation, but each class and sept either adopted some distinctive appellation themselves or received one from their neighbors. Thus, the tribe whose totem included the whirlpool of Hell-Gate called themselves Manhattans; the Long Island Indians, whose shores abounded in the prized sea-shells of which wampum is made, styled themselves, or were named by others, Metoacs; those living near the stone cliffs of Westchester were called Singsings, or Ossining; and those residing on the wide expanse of the Hudson below the Highlands, Tappensees. The early colonists, finding the tribes of this valley to be of one species and lineage, called them Mohikander, a compound formed from the Mohican and Belgic languages. The clans located nearest to Albany retained the name of Mohicans, and when they were eventually driven over the Hoosic and Taconic ranges into the valley of the Housatonic they carried with them their primitive appellation. That the Pequots, who once held possession of the territory along the East River and on the Connecticut shores, also bore the Mohican name is very probable, from the recurrence of Uncas to the parent term when he became involved in a political feud with Sassacus. At what time this dissension commenced is unknown. The first intimation of it dates from the era of the primary settlement of Connecticut in 1633. The colonists were dispersed over a wide surface, unprotected, and exposed to the caprices as well as to the incursions of the Indians. The oldest settlement had been located but a few years when the inhabitants found that a contest was being waged for the Indian sovereignty between Uncas and Sassacus.

Uncas held possession of a beautiful point of land, now called Norwich, at the head of the river Pequot (now the Thames), and it is probable that he had but recently segregated his tribe from the Pequots. His comprehensive mind immediately discerned the advantages that would result to his cause from an alliance with the Connecticut settlers, and it was as clearly the policy of the latter to form such an alliance. Their very safety depended on it, and wisdom was evinced in their choice. Uncas became the protector of the colonists; his scouts watched over the infant settlement, and not only reported the advance of hostile parties, but hastened to repel them. This alliance was never broken by either white or red man, and affords one of the most complete and satisfactory evidences to be found in history of the beneficial effects produced on Indian character by unwavering justice and uniform kindness and good will. Half a century later it was not in the power of Penn, with equally benevolent views, to maintain the Delawares in their position; yet through every change in their affairs the tribe of Uncas was protected and cherished by the people and by the authority of the State of Connecticut. Even after the venerated chief had passed from the stage of life, his successor and family were regarded with kind interest, and a monument has been erected to mark the resting-place of the great aboriginal sage of Norwich.

At the time we have indicated, 1637, the Pequots had the prestige of being a powerful and warlike people. They had escaped the great pestilence which had desolated the Massachusetts coast about the year 1617, could bring six hundred fighting-men into the field, and probably numbered a population of about three thousand souls. They were expert bowmen, and possessed sixteen guns purchased from the traders. The military strength of Connecticut was then estimated at two hundred men. If the Pequots had obtained the ascendency, the question of the very existence of the colony would have been settled forever.

John Mason, the man selected to conduct this war, was a veteran soldier, who, with Miles Standish and Underhill, had learned the art of war in the Low Countries under that renowned military tactician, William, Prince of Orange. The infant colonies required men possessing his decision of character and unflinching nerve to baffle the wiles of their savage enemies. It was evident that the Pequots meant to annihilate the colonists. Recent and most shocking murders having been perpetrated in the settlements, energetic and prompt action was necessary to enable the colony to maintain its ground. To begin the war Mason could muster but ninety men, which force is stated to have been half the militia of the colony. Uncas joined him with seventy Mohicans, who were chiefly useful as guides and scouts. The auxiliaries promised by the Plymouth colony and from other quarters were slow in making their appearance.

Mason, however, pushed forward with energy, as in his opinion their operations must be conducted with vigor, delay only furnishing Sassacus an opportunity to mature his plans. With the hope that the expected reinforcements would arrive in season to be of service, on the 10th of May he embarked his force at Hartford in three small vessels, and, dropping down the Connecticut River to Fort Saybrook, was there joined by Underhill, his second in command. After coasting along the shore to the entrance of Narragansett Bay, he landed in the vicinity of the village ruled by Canonicus, whose permission he obtained to march across his territory and attack the Pequots. The old chief thought his force too small for such a purpose, but, though he evidently did not expect much from the auxiliary Mohicans, he yet allowed two hundred of his men, under his son Miantonomo, to accompany them, without, however, engaging to take an active part. The Pequots had two forts, the principal of which, located on the Mystic River, was occupied by Sassacus in person. A march of eighteen or twenty miles through the forest brought Mason to a fort of the Niantics, on the borders of the Pequot territory. These people were tributaries and covert allies of the Pequots. The chief treated Mason haughtily, and would not allow him to enter the fort. Fearing that intelligence of his arrival might be transmitted by runners during the night, Mason encamped his men around the fort, giving them strict orders to intercept every person who attempted to leave it.

The following morning several of Miantonomo's men tendered their services as auxiliaries, making many professions of their anxiety to aid in carrying on the war. The number of Indians who now accompanied Mason being five hundred, they made a great display, but not much dependence could be placed upon their conduct on the battle-field, notwithstanding their lavish professions. Although Mason placed no reliance on them, he was willing to avail himself of the effect their appearance would produce on the enemy. Uncas, when questioned as to how many of his Indian allies would run away when the battle commenced, answered, "Every one but myself;" and such proved to be the result.

After a tedious march of twelve miles from the Niantic borders the army arrived at Pawcatuck Ford (now Stonington), weary, hungry, and foot-sore. Resting themselves there for some time, they continued their march with Uncas and Wequa, a recreant Pequot, for their guides, sometimes passing through corn-fields. Warm weather having set in unusually early, these marches, conjoined with the scarcity of food, were very irksome to men unaccustomed to the toil. Yet they pressed on energetically, and one hour after midnight encamped on the head-waters of the Mystic River. They had now been two days on the march. Their guides informed them that the Pequots held two strong forts in the vicinity, but four or five miles asunder. Although Mason had resolved to make simultaneous attacks on both forts, the fatigues and sufferings endured by the men while threading the mazes of the forest without provisions or tents, and exposed to every inconvenience, induced him to concentrate his efforts on the nearest position, within the present bounds of Groton. They reposed but a short time, and then took up their line of march, arriving before the fort, which was distant two miles, about two hours before daybreak (May 26, 1637). The moon was shining brightly when they reached the foot of the eminence on which the fort was situated, and by this time their boastful red allies had fallen in the rear, quaking at the very name of Pequot.

The walls of the fortification enclosed one or two acres of ground, and consisted of trunks of trees, cut in lengths of twelve feet, sunk three feet deep in the ground, and embanked with earth. These palisades were placed so far apart that missiles could be discharged through the interstices, yet not so much so as to admit a man. Twelve small gates or sally-ports, placed at opposite ends, were closed with trees and brush. The tops of the palisades were bound together with withes, and within, on a level esplanade, were about seventy lodges, constructed of thick matting covering a light frame-work. These lodges, arranged in parallel rows, were surrounded by a circular line of lodges next to the palisades. Mason had approached within a rod of the northeast sally-port without arousing suspicion, when he heard a dog bark within the fort. Instantly an Indian cried out, "Owanux! Owanux!" (Englishmen! Englishmen!) which brought the Pequots to their feet, some of whom were thought to be laboring under the effects of a recent revel. Mason, removing the obstacles, entered the fort at one end with sixteen followers, while Underhill did the same at the opposite sally-port, before the Pequots had time to oppose them. Surprised and confused, they ran about foaming with rage. The fight became desperate, the superiority of fire-arms and swords over arrows and clubs being signally demonstrated. Many of the Indians took shelter in the wigwams, covering themselves with the thick mats, from which it was impossible to dislodge them. Wearied with pursuing them, Mason at length exclaimed, "We must burn them." Suiting the action to the word, he applied a brand to the windward side of the lodges, and Underhill immediately followed his example. The fire spread with great rapidity through the combustible materials, soon filling the whole area with roaring flames. The living and the dead together were roasted in heaps. The English, being themselves expelled by the furious flames, formed a circle outside the palisades to prevent any of the enemy from effecting their escape. Their Indian auxiliaries, having recovered their courage, now came up and completed the work. Forty of the Pequots, who attempted to scale the palisades, were shot as they emerged from their flaming prison. In one hour about six hundred men, women, and children perished.

Though the Pequots had with dreadful cruelty massacred the unsuspecting Oldham, and Sleeping-Stone and his companions, though they had invaded the sanctity of dearly-loved homes with the fury of the tiger and the hyena, yet this was a dreadful retribution, the severity of which could not have been premeditated. Having inflicted this terrible blow upon the Pequots, Mason deemed his position to be a perilous one. He anticipated the speedy vengeance of Sassacus, who was but a few miles distant, at the upper fort, and many of his men were wounded, although but two had been killed in the conflict. It was necessary to carry the wounded on litters, and the soldiers were unprovided with either food or ammunition. In this emergency not a moment was lost in returning to the vessels, which had sailed round to the neighboring port of Pequot Harbor, and all speed was made towards the Connecticut.

The capture and burning of the Pequot fort on the Mystic exercised a controlling influence on the future prosecution of the war. It was a blow more terrible even than at first appeared. The night previous to the attack the post had been reinforced by one hundred and fifty warriors from the upper fort, as Sassacus was conscious of the perils of this position. More than half of his available force had certainly been destroyed, and the warriors he had despatched from his own fortification to reinforce the other had so diminished his strength that he did not deem himself able to sustain another attack. The war had now assumed the acme of bitterness on both sides. Spring, the season of planting, was passing away, and, though food was as scarce with the Indians as with the English, not a grain of corn could be planted in the Connecticut Valley, so great was the danger of being pierced by a Pequot arrow. With the English it was a struggle for existence, and the name of Pequot was to them identified with that of fiend. Delay would only enhance the danger of the whites, while the situation of the Pequots was equally perilous.

Sassacus, realizing his hazardous position, determined to abandon his country and fly westward. Although the Mohawks had been his most dreaded enemies for untold years, he hoped to find some friendly shelter in the small unoccupied valleys of the tributaries to the Hudson, or among the western affluents of the Mohawk. With the energy of a man whose necessities are pressing, he resolved to throw himself on the mercy of his Indian foes, and fly immediately. Collecting his people, he crossed the Connecticut, on his passage killing three Englishmen who were found descending the river on their way to Fort Saybrook.

The capture of Fort Mystic occurred on the 26th of May, and the 15th of the following June was observed by the colonists as a day of thanksgiving for the victory. About a fortnight after the return of the victors to their homes, one hundred and twenty men, under Captain Stoughton, landed at Pequot Harbor to prosecute the war, and on the 26th of June Mason descended the river with forty men to join him. The allies having resolved to pursue Sassacus, Uncas accompanied them with an effective force of Mohicans, this species of warfare requiring the exercise of that peculiar skill in following a trail, for which the minute observation and knowledge of Indian habits have so admirably adapted the aborigines.

Sassacus, being encumbered with a large body of women, children, and invalids, marched slowly, and kept near the open coast, in order to avail himself of the abundant supply of shell-fish to be found on these shores. The allies, while pursuing the fugitives, sometimes came to localities where clams had been dug up. The duty of scouting along these shores being committed to Uncas and his men, they captured a Pequot sachem, who was beheaded at a place now called Guilford Harbor, and his head placed in the forks of an oak-tree. From this circumstance a promontory in the vicinity received the name of Sachem's Head.

After passing the Quinnipiak River, now the site of New Haven, they espied a large body of Pequots, and pursued them. From an eminence they beheld in the distance a cluster of wigwams, situated between the foot of a hill and a swamp, within the present boundaries of the township of Fairfield. A straggling Pequot, who had been captured, guided them to this retreat. But Sassacus, and Mononotto, his principal war-captain, suspecting the design of the English, fled towards the Mohawk country, taking with them most of their active warriors. About eighty of the Pequots, with a few Indian residents of the place, who were vassals of the latter, and nearly two hundred old men, women, and children, took refuge in this swamp, which occupied the area of a mile. Portions of it were impassable quagmires and tangled bushes; but running into it, and nearly subdividing it, was a dry passage. Being doubtful how to approach it, some of the men waded in, stuck fast in the mud, were wounded severely, and were with difficulty extricated. The assailants then formed a circle around the margin of the swamp. Not wishing to punish the feeble and innocent alike with the guilty, a negotiation was opened which resulted in the surrender of one hundred and eighty old men, women, and children to the English. The warriors, however, refusing to capitulate, were still closely besieged.

A night thus passed away, and was followed by a foggy morning. As the besiegers stood nearly a rod apart, about three o'clock in the morning the Pequots made a sally to pass the circle, which proved unsuccessful. Another attempt at a different point resulted in the same manner. Shifting their ground, a third and desperate dash was attended with such success that about seventy of the enemy escaped. The number of Pequots killed on this occasion, and in the other struggles immediately preceding, was twenty.

But the stern foe of the English, he who had been dignified by the title of the Tyrant of Connecticut, was yet at liberty. Sassacus approached the upper Hudson by a point in possession of Indians linked in the ancient ties of affinity with the Mohicans, dwelling beyond the mountain-range of the Taconic. Sassacus having been at variance with the race residing in New England, it is not improbable that the sympathies of the Mohicans of the Hudson leaned towards Uncas. However this may be, the Mohicans of the Hudson, from its head-waters to its mouth, were the vassals of the Mohawks. In throwing himself upon the mercy of his enemies the Mohawks, as a defeated and ruined sachem who was obliged to forsake his country, Sassacus adopted a course sanctioned by the previous example of wiser and greater men. But the Mohawks were merciless, at least in this instance, for the fugitive chief was no sooner recognized by them than an arrow was driven through his heart. With him fell the Pequots; the power which had once been the terror of the New England colonies was destroyed, and from this time forth they ceased to be known as a tribe.

With Sassacus fell his brother, and Mononotto, his second in command, who, at first only wounded, was finally killed, together with five other sachems, all of whom were scalped, and the reeking trophies sent to the English in the hope of receiving a reward. It being apparent from the statement of the Indians that there were nearly two hundred Pequots dispersed among the various tribes, a price was set upon their heads. They were hunted throughout the country in all directions, any one being not only permitted but even encouraged to shoot them down at sight. This remnant of the tribe at last having offered to surrender themselves as vassals to the English, the proposition was considered and accepted. A council convened for this purpose at Hartford, September 21, 1638, at which Uncas and Miantonomo were present. It was decided that eighty of the captives should be assigned to Uncas, eighty to Miantonomo, and twenty to Ninigret, chief of the Niantics.

Some members of the non-combatant families who surrendered at the swamp were dispersed as domestics over the country which had been the scene of the conflicts. Forty-eight women and children came to Boston. A portion of those distributed as domestics fled from servitude, but, being retaken by the Indians, they were branded on the shoulder. The best authorities state that they were very restive under the yoke of slavery, and were valueless to their masters. One of the males was given to a gentleman to take to England; fifteen boys and two girls were sold as slaves to a resident of the Bermudas. The superannuated old men, mournful witnesses of the terrible retribution visited on their country, were allowed to descend into the grave unmolested.

Those of the tribe who accompanied Sassacus to the Hudson, or followed the seventy warriors who broke through the English line at the swamp, after reaching the valley of the Hudson, sent a messenger to the Mohawks requesting their permission to settle on this unclaimed territory. They were assigned the position of Schaghticoke, whence they eventually fled to Missisquoi Bay, near the foot of Lake Champlain, in Lower Canada.

For a long time the name of Pequot was a hated epithet, and twenty years after the occurrence of these events, viz., in March, 1658, the Connecticut court passed an act changing the name of the Pequot River to the Thames, and that of Pequot Point, or Harbor, to New London.

CHAPTER II.

THE NARRAGANSETTS—WAR BETWEEN UNCAS AND MIANTONOMO.

During the greater part of the seventeenth century the three most potent tribes of Southern and Western New England were the Pokanokets or Wampanoags, the Pequots, and the Narragansetts. The bands who claimed the name of Massachusetts Indians may be deemed to have been represented at that period by the Naticks. These were the bands to whom the gospel was especially preached, and over whom all the elements of civilization had obtained more or less influence, and the natural result of their progress in civilization was non-participation in the Indian wars. The Pennacooks and Abenakis, powerful tribes on the northern borders of the colony, did not come into collision with it, and their history more properly belongs to that of New Hampshire and Maine.

By the displacement of the Pequots, the Mohicans, a minor branch of that tribe, under the government of Uncas, were placed in antagonism to the Narragansetts. After the death of the Narragansett chief Canonicus the power devolved on his son Miantonomo, a talented, energetic, intrepid, and wily savage. Uncas, having sustained the English with all his power in their contest with the Pequots, under Sassacus, against whose domination he had rebelled, was henceforth regarded as the guardian spirit of Connecticut. His bravery in war, his decision of character, his wisdom, and his amenity of manners won praises from every lip. But in the field, as well as in the council, Uncas found a rival in Miantonomo, who ruled the more numerous and powerful nation of the Narragansetts. At that period this tribe possessed probably a greater numerical strength than any other of the New England tribes. They were located on the large islands in and along the fertile shores of Narragansett Bay, having a few years earlier sold Aquidneck, now Rhode Island, to Roger Williams. Their principal position was on the large island of Canonicut, which afforded all the requisites for a people who, being expert in the use of the canoe, levied contribution alike upon the game of the neighboring forests and the fish in the surrounding waters.

The Narragansetts had never been hearty friends of the English, and, although they seemed to be amicably inclined, they pursued a devious line of policy, holding an apparently neutral position between the colonists, the Pequots, the Mohicans, and the Pokanokets. The pacific influence exercised by Williams, who had located himself at an Indian village on the head-waters of the west fork of the bay, called by him Providence, kept them in check. But no sooner were the Pequots defeated and the power of Sassacus destroyed than a secret enmity against the Mohicans, under Uncas, developed itself. The details of this feud are too unimportant to be stated at length. A few years passed, characterized only by a surly and suspicious intercourse between the two rival chiefs. The sympathies of the English inhabiting the three central positions of Hartford, Boston, and Plymouth were undoubtedly with Uncas and the Mohicans. They negotiated treaties with the Narragansetts, in the expectation that this powerful Indian tribe would execute their agreements with the precision and under the operation of the same moral principles as those which govern civilized nations. The compact entered into with the English bound the Narragansetts not to engage in hostilities against Uncas without apprising the then united colonies.

In 1644, after six or seven years of mutual distrust had elapsed, the Narragansetts, eluding even the vigilance of Roger Williams, suddenly marched a body of nine hundred warriors into the Mohican territories with the design of attacking Uncas at a disadvantage; but it happened that some of the Mohican hunters discovered them, and with all speed conveyed the intelligence to their chief. The tribal seat of the Mohicans of Connecticut was then located, as it had been from time immemorial, at the head of the Pequot River, now the Thames, on the site of the present city of Norwich.

Collecting a force of five or six hundred warriors, Uncas determined not to await the onset of his adversary, but to advance and attack him. After marching five or six miles, he encountered Miantonomo and his army on a plain stretching along the banks of the Shetucket, whereupon he halted his force. There appeared to be no choice of position on either side, the plain being level and spacious. Uncas, who had become somewhat versed in English strategy, and understood the advantage to be gained by prompt movements, perceived at once that if he could by a sudden attack produce confusion and drive Miantonomo down the banks of the Shetucket he would be able to overcome his foe's superior numbers. This is the only explanation that can be given of the course he adopted. No sooner had he halted within speaking distance than he stepped forward and tendered his adversary the choice of deciding the fate of the day by personal combat. Miantonomo replied that his men had come to fight, and fight they should. On the instant, Uncas, who was a very tall man, threw himself on the ground, that being a preconcerted signal for his troops to advance, which they did with such ardor and fury that they drove the enemy down the escarpment of the river, and pursued them so vigorously that some of the swift Mohican runners, knowing Uncas to be near at hand, caught Miantonomo by some portion of his dress, temporarily impeding his flight, which enabled the former to make the capture himself. Uncas then sounded the whoop of victory to recall his men, and to signify that Miantonomo was a prisoner, as if his capture had been the only object of the Mohicans.

Not a look of the Narragansett sachem, far less a word, evinced any dread of his enemies. He bore himself before his captor with unflinching dignity and pride. "Had you taken me," said Uncas, with some of that suavity of manner derived from his English associations, "I should have asked you to spare me." Not a word, however, was deigned in reply. Notwithstanding, Uncas spared his life, the usual privilege of an Indian victor; but he carried him with him to Norwich, as a trophy of his victory, whence he conducted him to Hartford. The question of his fate was submitted to the English, as one requiring grave deliberation. It had been felt ever since the close of the Pequot war that the Narragansetts exercised an influence adverse to the growth and prosperity of the settlements. The very war in which they had just been engaged was in violation of a solemn agreement made with commissioners formally appointed, and was waged against the worthiest and most trusty sachem who had befriended the colonies. Yet the English considered the case to be beyond their jurisdiction: the territory being Indian, they decided that aboriginal customs and laws must be allowed to take their course.

Miantonomo was, therefore, conducted back to the battle-field, on the banks of the Shetucket, escorted by two Englishmen, to shield him from any attempt at cruelty. The retinue traversed the scene of the late conflict with all the impressive dignity of an official cortège. Uncas, who knew the chief personally, determined to have no hand in the execution, and therefore deputed the duty to one of his war-captains, enjoining him to leave the Narragansett in entire ignorance of his fate. He only knew that he was remanded to the spot of his capture. Before reaching this point, the warrior intrusted with the task, who walked immediately behind him, suddenly drew a tomahawk and with one blow laid him dead at his feet. The scene of this tragedy has since been called Sachem's Plain. Though burning with desire for vengeance, his tribe feared a conflict with the English, and were at length compelled to submit to a peace, the conditions of which were onerous in the extreme. Joining Philip in his war upon the Massachusetts colonists, in 1675, the Narragansetts were almost totally destroyed by the terrible blow inflicted upon them at the "swamp fight" in South Kingstown, Rhode Island, December 8 of that year.

CHAPTER III.

THE POKANOKET TRIBE AND PHILIP'S WAR—THE NARRAGANSETTS JOIN PHILIP AND ARE DEFEATED AND HUMBLED—OVERTHROW AND DEATH OF PHILIP.

When the New England colonies were established, the Pokanoket tribe was in the ascendency. The coast tribes, indeed, if not almost annihilated, had been decimated by a pestilential disease; but there is every reason to believe that the chiefs who sat in the council lodges surrounding the waters of Massachusetts Bay acknowledged fealty to the reigning sachem of Mount Hope. Such was the complexion of political affairs when the Pilgrims landed at Plymouth in 1620.

The Pokanokets were descended from an ancient stock, and it is believed that they established themselves on the peninsula with the aid of their friends and allies the Narragansetts and Pequots, after conquering the tribes which then held possession. Evidences of their ancient triumphs have, it is believed, been found in the rude and simple pictographs of the country,—a few heads and cross-bones or clubs, sculptured on a boulder or on a cliff, as mementos of battle. These simple historical memorials were more common among the hills and valleys of the country when it was first occupied than they are at the present day. It is deeply to be regretted that a wanton spirit of destructiveness should have led in so many instances to the mutilation or alteration of the primitive monuments of the Indian nations. The most noted, as also the largest, of these pictographs yet legible is on the Massachusetts borders of the Taunton or Assonet River. Foreign archæologists have attempted to give this inscription an unmerited historical value as a Scandinavian monument. Having visited the locality and made it a study, with the aid of an Indian interpreter, Mr. Schoolcraft had no hesitation in pronouncing it an Algonkin pictographic record of an Indian battle. This was also the interpretation given by an intelligent Indian jossakeed and Indian pictographist to whom he exhibited a copy of it on the island of Michillimackinac. Being well versed in the Indian creed and practices, he found in the pictograph a record of priestly skill in necromancy, and the success here pictured was, as he said, due partly to the expertness of some priest in the necromantic art. The amazement of the vanquished at the sudden assault of the victors is symbolically depicted by their being deprived of both hands and arms, and hence of the power of making any resistance. The name of the reigning chief of the tribe is likewise described by a symbol as having been Mong, or the Loon, and his totem the sun.

The Pokanokets, who may be considered to have been allied with the Narragansetts in the victory represented in the above pictograph, had preserved friendly relations with that powerful coast-tribe from the earliest dates. It is evident that they were also allied with the Pennacooks of the Merrimac in the north, and with the Pequots, who, under Sassacus, were so unfortunate as to wage war against Uncas and his Mohicans, protected as the latter were by the ægis of the infant Connecticut colony.

The name of Wampanoag, by which the Pokanokets were also designated, appears to denote the fact that they were, from early times, the custodians of the imperial shell or medal. They were so brave and warlike that the surrounding tribes regarded them as the most powerful organization on the coast from Narragansett Bay to Massachusetts Bay.

When the Plymouth colony was founded, the Pokanoket tribe was governed by Massasoit. We have seen that the colonists found the vicinity of their location unoccupied,—old corn-fields, deserted lodges, and graves hastily covered denoting the ravages of the pestilence which had depopulated this region. They made it their early endeavor to seek an interview with Massasoit and establish friendly relations with him, the conference being managed carefully with a view to effect. Musicians and soldiers, armed with muskets, accompanied the English governor, and the negotiations afforded a fair specimen of both Indian and colonial diplomacy. It was characterized, also, by the introduction to the Indians of that element which has since proved a source of so much injury to the race. Here the Indians first learned to drink alcoholic liquors.

Political power among the Indians of New England was at this time wielded principally by two influential bashabaries,—namely, the Pokanoket and Pennacook tribal leagues. Both confederations comprised a union of the religious and political elements. A simple sagamore appears to have wielded only a local power, while the bashaba also filled the priestly office of chief jossakeed, powwow, or prophet. The Pennacook bashabary was confined almost exclusively to the country north of the Merrimac, extending through New Hampshire into Maine, and gave the early colonists but little trouble. But the Mount Hope (or Montaup) government included the territory immediately around the new homes of the colonists. Every foot of land they added to their possessions was gained by permission of, agreement with, or purchase from, the chiefs and sagamores of this confederacy. The fact that neither the Narragansetts nor the Pequots in the west, nor the Pennacooks in the north, made grants in the territory of Massachusetts, is conclusive proof that the authority of Massasoit was supreme. One of the first objects of the colonists was to secure peace on their frontiers by concluding treaties of amity with the Indians. Considering the influence of this central organization, it is not surprising that for so long a period they kept the storm of open Indian warfare from their continually progressing settlements, Massasoit being in allegiance with the three great powers around him, namely, the Narragansetts, the Pequots, and the Pennacooks. These tribes and their component septs and bands all originally spoke one language, practised one religion, were conversant with precisely the same arts, and were under the influence of identical customs and manners. According to Prince, the news of the massacre in Virginia in March, 1622, perpetrated by Opechancanough, reached

Plymouth in May, and made the colonists more fearful of Indian treachery. By great vigilance and caution in circumventing the schemes and diverting the animosities of the petty chiefs, the colonists succeeded in securing some twenty years of undisturbed peace. It was not until the year 1646, when John Eliot began to preach the gospel to the Indians, and held his religious conference with them under the old oaks at Natick, that the Indian jossakeeds became seriously alarmed.

While the English were making themselves acquainted with the character, positions, and wants of the Indians of New York, the causes of discord between the New England tribes and the colonists still continued, but, like a smouldering fire, they were very much concealed from public view. The severity with which the Pequots were treated secured the peace of the country for some thirty years, though at no time during this period could the colonists relax their vigilance for one moment. The war between the Mohicans and the Narragansetts, under Uncas and Miantonomo, demonstrated to the tribes that, however fiercely discord and war might rage among themselves, the great and vital objects of the colonists were not retarded, but were rather promoted, by the extinction of the petty Indian sovereignties.

At length, in 1675, those smothered burnings burst forth into a flame. Massachusetts having been in truth the mother of the British colonies of the North, she now became the principal object against which the long pent-up wrath of the aborigines was directed. The majority of her sea-coast and inland tribes had, indeed, yielded to the influences of civilization and gospel teachings, and had engaged in the pursuits of agriculture, but in her assemblies of neophytes there were disciples of the native Indian priesthood who sometimes maintained their view of the questions at issue with great boldness. The larger part of the Indian population of the interior, and towards the south, southwest, and west, hated a life of labor, as also the religion of the Puritans, and secretly banded together to make another combined effort for the extinction and expulsion of the English. This combination was headed by the Pokanokets, whose council-fires burned on Mount Hope (now Bristol, Rhode Island).

It has been previously stated that this tribe had very extensive affiliations with the principal Indian families of the country. They were the leading tribe of the Pokanoket alliance, which constituted a kind of aboriginal hereditary presidency.[1] The benevolent Massasoit held the chief office at the period of the founding of the Plymouth colony, and both he and his descendants were, up to the close of the war, deemed the legitimate sovereigns, possessing power to alienate land. Massasoit, who by his equanimity and conservative character had maintained a good understanding with the colonists, died just previous to 1660, and was succeeded at alternate periods by his sons Popquit and Metakom, or, according to the researches of Mr. Drake,[2]

---

[1] This group appears to have consisted principally of the Pawtuckets, Neponsetts, Nonantums, Wichagashas, Nashoways, Nantuckets, Puncapaugs, Nipmucks, Nocanticks, and Wampanoags or Pokanokets, the latter being the reigning tribe. The Pokanokets had been very numerous, but their population had been diminished by the general sickness prior to the year 1620.

[2] Drake's Book of the Indians, p. 14.

more correctly, Pometakom. The colonial court at one of its sittings gave them the names of Alexander and Philip, in compliment to their martial bearing. Alexander, who possessed a high spirit, ruled but a short time, dying of a fever suddenly contracted while on a visit to the Plymouth colony. Pometakom, better known as King Philip, succeeded him. He had a large and finely-developed head, and possessed great resolution, activity, and powers of endurance. John Josselyn, who saw Philip at Boston about 1669, thus describes his dress: "His coat and buckskins were thick-set with beads (wampumpeag) in pleasant wild works, and a broad belt of the same. His accoutrements were valued at twenty pounds sterling." He may be regarded as the true representative of the Indian hunter. He was familiar with every foot of ground between Mount Hope and Massachusetts Bay, had witnessed the foundation and rise of the colonies, was well known to the colonists, and they to him, loved the independence of savage life and rule, took great pride in his ancestry, loved the old Indian rites, and retained in his service a numerous priesthood, or body of prophets, sagamores, and powwows, demonology and idolatry, magic and soothsaying, being cherished by him as the religion of his ancestors. He loved hunting and fishing, and despised the life of labor recommended to him. He may be said to have detested civilization in all its forms, and he abhorred the doctrines of Christianity.

During twelve years Philip had been a silent observer of the growth of New England. Twenty years had elapsed since the close of the war between the Narragansetts and the Mohicans, of which the colonists had been passive though deeply interested spectators, merely employing their influence with the tribes to keep them at peace with the colonies and with one another. For several years prior to the breaking out of the Pokanoket war, Philip had been regarded with suspicion, and a close eye was kept on his movements. It appears that, in addition to his authority among the eight or ten tribes who acknowledged his supremacy, his influence was exerted among the Narragansetts, his immediate neighbors on the south, whose possessions extended northwardly to those of the Pennacooks of the river Merrimac, and the other tribes of the Pawtuckets.

It was a current belief among the colonists as early as 1671 that a rising of the Indians was planned and ready for execution, and that Philip was accountable for any injuries they might receive from the Indians supposed to be under his influence. Summoned on September 29, 1671, before the Commissioners of the United Colonies, he was compelled to sign a paper acknowledging himself subject to the Plymouth government and laws, and to pay one hundred pounds sterling, for which, as he could not at once do it, he was to have three years' time, and was to pay "in such things as he had." Five wolves' heads were to be sent annually as tribute to the governor. These exactions, which he was in no condition to refuse, were extremely galling to his proud and haughty soul.

Philip and the tribes that were under his influence, surrounded by the constantly increasing plantations of the English, crowded by hated neighbors, losing one by one their fields or hunting-grounds, and he himself frequently summoned to Boston or Plymouth to reply to an accusation or to explain his acts, sighed for their old freedom, and nursed a spirit of savage independence. The haughty chief, who had been obliged to give up his "English arms" and to pay an onerous tribute, again fell under suspicion in 1674, and was again summoned for examination.

There is no doubt that Philip was long very averse to the war. This is the constant tradition among the posterity of persons who lived in his immediate vicinity and in familiar intercourse with him, and also with the Indians who survived the war. The spot is still pointed out in Bristol where Philip—who only the day before had rescued and returned safely to his home a captive Englishman—shed tears on receiving the news of the killing of the first Englishman who fell. He was convinced at length that a war could not be avoided, and during its progress he enlisted in his behalf as many allies as possible. Neither Bancroft, Palfrey, nor Drake takes the view that Philip's war was a wide-spread, premeditated effort to expel the English colonists.

A conference to settle the existing difficulties took place April 10, 1675, only a few weeks before the war broke out, at the meeting-house in Taunton, Philip and his warriors, painted, armed, and in war-costume, occupying one side of the house, and the English, also armed, the other. The result of this conference was the delivery of all the guns of the Indians to the colonists, and an increase of hatred on the part of the former for the latter. Philip's principal councillors, all of whom were heads of small clans or tribes of Wampanoags, and all of whom perished in the war, were Watuspaquin, styled the Black Sachem, his son William, Peebe, Uncompoin, Unnathum or Munashum, usually called Nimrod, and Annawan.

Philip's plan for uniting all the border Indians in a general war against the colonies is supposed to have been revealed by a friendly Christian Indian called Sausaman. He, being Philip's scribe or counsellor, was in his confidence and acquainted with his designs. For this act he was made to pay the forfeit of his life. He was murdered by three emissaries of Philip. While fishing on a pond through an orifice in the ice, he was approached without suspicion by his foes, who knocked him on the head and then thrust his body through the opening. In June, 1675, the murderers were identified, tried, and hanged.

It is estimated that in 1673 the entire white population of New England was about fifty thousand souls, of whom eight thousand were capable of bearing arms. About this time Massachusetts alone mustered twelve troops of cavalry, comprising sixty men each, who were armed and stationed at various points to punish any sudden aggressions. The white population had within forty years spread from its original nucleus at Plymouth more than one hundred miles westward, and in some places the same distance to the north. But, owing to this very expansion, it presented on every frontier a broken, unconnected line, continually subject to the depredations of the hostile Indians. At these exposed points in the line of the advancing settlements every man was the daily guardian of his own life, untiring vigilance being the only guarantee of safety. The Indians numbered about thirty thousand.

To qualify himself for his great effort against the New England colonies, and to relieve his men from domestic cares, Philip sent his own family, and all the women and children of his nation, into the country of his friends and neighbors the Narragansetts. The Narragansett chief Canonchet, the son of Miantonomo, who had been the reigning sachem since the death of his father, by this course involved himself deeply with the colonies, and it ultimately cost him his life; for the colonists could now no longer doubt that the Narragansetts not only sympathized deeply with Philip, but had acceded to his plans. They therefore organized a strong force against this tribe, and, after the capture of Canonchet in a conflict which occurred near Seekonk, the tribe succumbed and formed a new treaty with their conquerors. Canonchet himself was sent to the Mohicans, under Uncas, and by them executed.

Philip had kept up his communications with the central powers of the colonies, particularly by two personal visits to Plymouth in 1662 and 1671, during which time he renewed the fealty first pledged by his father Massasoit. After the disclosure made by Sausaman, his intentions could no longer be concealed, and when it became known that he had abandoned his ancestral seat at Mount Hope, and sent the women and children to a place of safety, it was supposed, and with truth, that he was ranging up and down among the tribes, arousing his followers, and exciting in them a desire for war and plunder. The tragedy soon opened along the entire line of the New England frontiers, and the struggle which followed was by far the severest ordeal the New England colonies ever passed through.

Philip's energies appeared to be almost superhuman, for it was either his voice which animated or his hand which directed every attack. The war commenced near Mount Hope on the 24th of June, 1675. A party of Philip's warriors being sent to the English settlement at Mattapoisett (now Swanzey), they plundered the houses, and killed some of the cattle. In this foray an Indian being shot, the others rushed forward and murdered nine of the English. Intelligence of the affray was quickly spread, and the Plymouth and Massachusetts colonies immediately sent troops into the field. Within four days thereafter a company of foot, under Captain Daniel Henchman, and a troop of horse, under Captain Thomas Prentice, were on the march, and were joined on the 27th by Captain Samuel Moseley's company of one hundred and ten men, who had with them a number of dogs to be used in hunting the Indians. Arriving at Swanzey on the 28th, they were there joined by the Plymouth men under Captain James Cudworth, who took command of the united forces. Captain Benjamin Church, afterwards conspicuous as an Indian fighter, was a volunteer in this command. A month later a company of Christian Indians under Captain Isaac Johnson, of Roxbury, joined Major Savage, and acquitted themselves "courageously and faithfully" in the service.

Several skirmishes ensued, and a few Indians as well as English were killed. The forces of the latter being soon recruited, they proceeded, under Captain Thomas Savage, commander-in-chief of the Massachusetts forces, to Mount Hope, which was found to be deserted, the enemy having fled. The dragoons while reconnoitring the vicinity discovered a small party of Indians, and killed four or five of the number. The troops then received orders to march into the country of the Narragansetts and bring them to an account, but were met with many professions of a desire for peace.

Negotiations having been opened, the Narragansetts signed a treaty July 15, binding themselves "as far as was in their power" to oppose Philip. At this time a price was placed on Philip's head delivered "dead or alive."

While the English were concluding with the Narragansetts a worthless treaty, the hostiles were actively occupied in burning houses, destroying property, and killing and mutilating the inhabitants. Taunton, Middleborough, Dartmouth, and Mendon were thus visited, small parties spreading in various directions. One of these attacked the house of John Minot, in Dorchester.

Meantime, Captain Benjamin Church had penetrated Pocasset, into whose extensive swamps Philip had withdrawn his warriors, where he found and engaged some straggling parties, but, not meeting with the success he desired, he soon after returned to the same locality with fifty men. Dividing these for the purpose of more effectually pursuing the search, Fuller led one party towards the open bay, while Church with the other penetrated the interior, where, encountering the enemy in force, he was driven back. Fuller was also attacked by superior numbers, and, after reaching the shore, both parties were saved from destruction only by the fortunate proximity of a Rhode Island sloop. As soon as the English force could be concentrated, another expedition was sent to Pocasset, and several desultory engagements resulted in the killing of fourteen or fifteen Indians. On the arrival of the entire allied force, Philip, after some slight skirmishing, retired to that favorite natural fortress of the Indians,—a swamp. With the approach of night the English retired, but being reinforced the following day by one hundred men, and observing that Philip occupied a narrow peninsula, seven miles in length, having an impenetrable swamp in the interior, they resolved to cut off his communications and starve him out. The chief, seeing his critical position, took advantage of a dark night (August 1), and, constructing rafts of timber, escaped across the Assonet or Taunton River to his allies the Nipmucks, a wandering tribe, whose segregated bands occupied a large area of territory. When, the following morning, it was discovered that Philip had fled, the allies hotly pursued him, and, tracing his trail by the aid of the Mohicans, they overtook him at night on Rehoboth Plain, and killed thirty of his warriors, the wily chief, with the rest of his force, succeeding in making good his escape. Within a week from the commencement of hostilities the savages had been driven from Mount Hope, and in less than a month Philip was a fugitive among the interior tribes of Massachusetts. Philip had fled to the quarter where he had the greatest number of allies. His plan apparently was, if defeated in New England, to retire towards the territory occupied by the Baron de St. Castin, an influential trader, or Indian factor, who resided in Maine, had intermarried with the Penobscots, and sympathized with the effort of Philip, with whom he is said by all the authorities of that period to have been in league. There is no doubt of his friendship for, and alliance with, the Pennacooks and their affiliated bands of the Merrimac, extending northward to the Penobscot, Canada, and Acadia, where an adverse political element existed. France was regarded by the aborigines in all respects as the friend of the Indian race, and the destruction of the English colonies was as much of an object to the French as it ever could have been considered by Philip. The Indians acting under Philip had been, without doubt, supplied with fire-arms and ammunition from the commercial dépôt of the Baron de St. Castin, and this species of aid and sympathy may be considered as having afforded Philip good grounds for hoping for success in what would otherwise have been a desperate undertaking.

In after-years, when the Pennacooks and the other Indians of Southern New Hampshire fled to the north and allied themselves with the Abenakis, it was this very French influence upon which they relied. After a few years spent in various employments in the West, subsequent to the year 1689, Sebastian Rale established himself at Norridgewock, on the Kennebec, when this connection with the New England Indians became more fully apparent. The fugitive Indians were encouraged in their hostility to the English, and became expert in the use of fire-arms, which at that era had entirely superseded bows and arrows. Returning in detached parties, like hyenas in search of prey, they fell upon the people of the new and isolated settlements, from whose precincts they had previously fled, with the exterminating knife and tomahawk, marking their course with scenes of arson and murder which are heart-rending and horrible to contemplate.

St. Castin, it is affirmed, was a French nobleman of distinction, a colonel in the king's body-guard. He was a man noted for his intrigue as well as his enterprise, who had formed an alliance with the Abenakis and other Indians of this part of the country, the object of which was to impede the progress of the colonies of Plymouth, Massachusetts, and other parts of New England. He had married and had living with him at one time six Indian wives. Several Roman Catholic priests also resided with him in his palace, which formed a sort of aboriginal court and was located on the eastern bank of the Penobscot, near its mouth, where the town of Castine, in Maine, now stands. By these means, as well as by his genius and enterprise, he had acquired a vast influence over the natives, not only furnishing them with firearms, but also instructing them in their use. He began his career among the Penobscots in 1661, and followed it up with such success that at the commencement of Philip's war the knowledge of the use of gunpowder and fire-arms was universal among the Indians.

It must not, however, be forgotten that Philip, independently of his expectations from the sympathy of the French, was actuated by his own natural antipathies in his attempt to drive the English out of New England, and that when he abandoned Mount Hope he threw himself among his Indian friends and allies with the purpose of inciting them to make incessant attacks on the settlements. To do this effectually it was necessary to surprise them in detail. Places known to be in the occupancy of the militia were avoided unless when a small force could be suddenly attacked by a larger one. The Indians have seldom been willing to meet a large regular force in the field; they have always preferred the guerilla system.

After Philip's flight from Pocasset the war assumed a fiercer character. No agricultural labor could be pursued; every clump of bushes hid an enemy, and every fence and wall covered an ambuscade. The Nipmucks, who had heretofore occupied a doubtful position, now commenced open hostilities, spreading the alarm westward. At Lancaster a man and his wife were killed on the Lord's day. Non-combatant Indians were arrested and committed for trial; and no Indian was safe from the suspicion of treachery, no matter how good his conduct had previously been, except those of the communities of praying Indians, and even they were closely watched. A short time subsequent to the alarm at Lancaster a detachment of soldiers was sent out to make reconnoissances as far as Hadley.

The authorities at Boston still entertaining the idea that the Nipmucks could be restrained by negotiation, the latter agreed to meet commissioners at Brookfield, but it proved to be a mere ruse on the part of the Indians. The officers sent thither were accompanied by twenty horsemen, and were joined on the route by a considerable number of the citizen soldiery. Finding no Indians there, they marched, on August 2, four or five miles farther, to a narrow defile, flanked by a swamp, where three hundred Indians rose from an ambuscade and poured upon them a heavy fire. Eight of the men were killed by the first discharge, and the commander, Captain Edward Hutchinson, as well as several others, was wounded. They then retreated to Brookfield, whither they were pursued by the Indians, who set the town on fire in several places. The inhabitants retired to a log house, slightly fortified, where they defended themselves. The Indians surrounded it, keeping up an incessant fire, and attempted to burn it by discharging blazing arrows upon it, and by thrusting combustibles against it, placed on the ends of long poles. They then filled a cart with hemp, and, setting it on fire, backed it up to the house. Had this effort succeeded, seventy men, women, and children, who were huddled together within, would have been roasted alive, but fortunately a shower of rain, which fell at this moment, extinguished the flames. The Indians were eventually frightened off by the reported arrival of reinforcements, which they supposed to be very large from their being preceded by a drove of frightened cattle. Only one man was killed and one wounded in this siege.

The affair was scarcely over when four separate bodies of troops, under different commanders, reached Brookfield. But the Indians had fled westward, effecting a union with the Pocumtucks at Deerfield and at Northfield. Being pursued in that direction, a battle was fought on August 25 near Sugar-Loaf Hill, in which nine English and twenty-six Indians fell; the rest of the Indians then joined Philip's forces. Hadley was now occupied by the troops, the natives in the vicinity having begun to show a hostile disposition and to menace the towns above it in the Connecticut Valley. On the 1st of September (1675) they attacked Deerfield, burned most of the houses, and killed one man. Next day nine or ten men were killed by them in the woods at Northfield. On September 3 a reinforcement of thirty-six mounted infantry, with a convoy of provisions for the garrison at Northfield, fell into an Indian ambuscade within two miles of their destination, Beers, the commander, with sixteen men, being killed, and the baggage and wounded captured by the enemy. The place is to this day called Beers's Plain, and the hill where the captain fell, Beers's Mountain.

On the 18th of September a force of eighty men, convoying a train of teams loaded with grain, left Deerfield to proceed to Hadley, but while passing through a dense forest in the vicinity of a place called Bloody Brook (now South Deerfield), some seven hundred Indians, who had been screened from view by the bushes of a morass, rushed furiously upon them. The troops, being thrown into complete confusion, broke ranks, and attempted to fight the enemy from behind trees, in their own customary manner. But it was to no purpose: they suffered an utter and most appalling defeat, Captain Lathrop and seventy-one men, including the teamsters, being slain. The firing being heard at Deerfield, four or five miles distant, reinforcements under Captain Moseley and Major Treat were hurried forward, but did not reach the scene until after the close of the action, when the victors were engaged in stripping the dead and mangling their bodies. Rushing on boldly, without breaking their ranks, the Deerfield men drove the enemy from the field, killing many of them. The loss of the Indians in the several actions fought on this day is reported to have been quite heavy.

It is to be inferred that in these systematic attacks Philip himself was either the leader or the inciting spirit of the Indians. Throughout a large extent of country the Indians were actuated by one motive and one policy; for, like his own fabled Hobbamok, Philip appeared to be ubiquitous, shifting his position with inconceivable rapidity from one point to another. From information subsequently obtained, he is believed to have led the attack at Bloody Brook. The following day he displayed his forces in numbers on the west banks of the Connecticut, near Deerfield, which was garrisoned by only twenty-seven men. This circumstance led to the abandonment of that post, as being too distant to secure proper support, and it was soon after destroyed by the enemy.

Emboldened by these successes, the Indians in the vicinity of Springfield attacked that town on October 5, killed an officer and one man who were out reconnoitring, and burned thirty-two dwelling-houses, including the minister's, with his valuable library, as also twenty-five barns, including their contents,—a loss which reduced the inhabitants to great straits during the winter. Fortunately, the intentions of the enemy had been disclosed by a friendly Indian, so that the people were able to take refuge in their fortified houses and thus save themselves from a general massacre.

Flushed with his triumphs, Philip ascended the valley with the determination of attacking the English head-quarters. On the 19th of October he appeared with seven or eight hundred warriors near the town of Hatfield, and, having cut off several scouting-parties in the woods, made a rapid attack on the town from various quarters. It was defended with great resolution, having been reinforced a short time previous, and after a severe contest Philip was compelled to withdraw his forces. This he effected during the night, not without some confusion, as he was encumbered with his dead and wounded. He also lost some of his guns in the river. He succeeded, however, in firing several dwellings, which were consumed, and in driving off a number of cattle and sheep belonging to the colonists.

Autumn now drawing to a close, it became necessary for the large mass of the

Indians to disperse to places where they could readily obtain their wanted supplies. Philip had determined to pass the winter with the Narragansetts, but in a short time his guerilla parties were kept busy on the waters of the Connecticut. Late in October some unprotected teams near Northampton were attacked, three men were killed in a meadow near that town, and the Indians attempted to burn a mill. Three men were also killed between Springfield and Westfield, and four houses were burned at the latter place. Other depredations were committed at Longmeadow, and likewise at Springfield.

While the knife, club, gun, and incendiary brand were thus actively wielded on the waters of the Connecticut, Philip's warriors were busy in the east and southeast. Two separate companies of militia marched from Boston and Cambridge to repress Indian hostilities at Mendon, Groton, and other places. In effecting this, several encounters occurred, in one of which an officer named Curtis and one soldier fell. A considerable quantity of corn was destroyed, and one captive was released.

Prior to the last-mentioned action an affair occurred at Wrentham. One of the colonists, having one evening discovered a party of Indians on their march, silently followed their trail, and saw them encamp near a precipice. Returning and giving immediate notice of his observations, thirteen men accompanied him to the spot, where they concealed themselves until the Indians arose at daybreak, when they fired upon them, and, driving them over the precipice, killed twenty-four. The rest effected their escape.

Without the details being given, it is impossible to conceive the harassing nature of this war. The English were ever on the alert, ever vigilant, active, brave, and enterprising. They were ready at a moment's warning to pursue the enemy and retaliate his attacks, and whenever they suffered defeat it was owing to their impulsive bravery and a disposition to underrate and despise their enemy. This induced them to make rash movements, in which they frequently neglected the ordinary rules of military caution. Bodies of men were suddenly aroused and marched boldly into the forests and defiles without sending out scouts to ascertain the position of the foe. Besides, it always required a large force to watch a smaller one, when the latter were secreted in the woods, ready to spring upon them when least expected.

Indian history demonstrates that in this guerilla warfare the advantage is generally at first on the side of the natives, who are more intimately acquainted with the local geography as well as with the natural resources of a wilderness country, and also with their own capacity for endurance, which circumstances generally determine their mode of attack and defence. Solid columns of men, encumbered with heavy baggage and a commissariat, when marching through a forest must necessarily progress slowly. They soon become fatigued and harassed by their encumbrances, while the light-footed Indians dart around them and before them, like the hawk toying with its prey, until a suitable opportunity occurs for them to strike. If it be merely a war of skirmishes and surprises, this is their favorite and generally successful mode of attack. Another error committed by the whites in this war was the employment of a multiplicity of separate commanders, frequently exercising discordant powers and lacking unity of action.

The good sense of the commissioners of the New England colonies, now confederated for defence, convinced the country of this. The war had been in progress scarcely three-fourths of a year, during which time many valuable lives had been lost by Indian ambuscades and a large amount of property had been destroyed. Although the settlers were kept in a state of perpetual alarm, no effective blow had been struck; nothing, in fact, had been done to subdue the daring spirit of the Indians, and their entire force was still in motion. In a council held at Boston it was determined, therefore, to adopt more general and effective measures for the prosecution of the ensuing campaign. Agreeably to a scale then established, Massachusetts colony was directed to furnish five hundred and twenty-seven men; Plymouth colony, one hundred and fifty-eight; and Connecticut, which now included the New Haven colony, three hundred and fifteen; making a total force of one thousand men.

It was subsequently determined to fit out a separate expedition against the Narragansetts, whose hostility to the colonies and complicity with Philip could no longer be doubted. They were designated as the first object of attack. One thousand men were also mustered for this service, officered by experienced captains, and placed under the command of Josiah Winslow. Advanced as the season was (December 8), this force was marched in separate bodies through Seekonk and Providence and over the Patuxent River to Wickford, the place of rendezvous. On the route a system of wanton destruction of person and property was carried out, it being their design to make the Indians feel the effects of the war. The latter, being apprised of the movement, burned Pettiquamscott, killing fifteen of the inhabitants, and concentrated their forces on an elevation, several acres in extent, surrounded on all sides by a swamp,—a position located in the present township of South Kingstown, Rhode Island.

At this place they had fortified themselves by a formidable structure of palisades, surrounded by a close hedge curtain, or rude abatis, leaving but one passage to it, which led across a brook and was formed of a single log, elevated four or five feet above the surface of the water. At another point of the fortification was a low gap, closed by logs four or five feet high, which could be scaled. Close by was a blockhouse to defend and enfilade this weak point. The whole work was ingeniously constructed, and well adapted to the Indian mode of defence. The authorities do not mention that Philip was present, but there appears to be no doubt that he had given every aid in his power to his allies. It was a death-struggle for the Narragansetts, and their fate would determine his, for they were far superior to his people in numbers.

By the destruction of Pettiquamscott and its little garrison, the troops composing Winslow's army, who had expected to take up their quarters there, were deprived of all shelter. They had no tents, and were consequently obliged to pass a very uncomfortable night in the open air. It was late in December, and bitter cold, with snow on the ground. The Connecticut forces having joined him on the 18th, on the next day Winslow put his army, now amounting to fifteen hundred men, in motion at an early hour, as they had eighteen miles to march through deep snow. Captains Moseley and Davenport led the van, Gardner and Johnson the centre, and Major Appleton and Captain Oliver the rear of the Massachusetts forces; the Plymouth men, under Major Bradford and Captain Gorham, with whom was General Winslow, marched in the centre; while the Connecticut troops, under Major Treat and Captains Seely, Gallup, Mason, Watts, and Marshall, brought up the rear. At one o'clock in the afternoon, guided by an Indian, they reached the vicinity of the swamp, where a party of the enemy had been stationed as a corps of observation. These were immediately attacked, but fled to their citadel. A detachment, comprising four companies, immediately rushed through the swamp at a venture, and accidentally reached the log gap, which they began to scale, but they were compelled to fall back before the destructive fire from the Indian block-house. They were reinforced by two other companies, when, pressing gallantly forward, they scaled the log sally-port and entered the fort, maintaining themselves in their position under a terrible fire.

While victory thus hung in suspense, the remainder of the army succeeded in crossing the swamp, and entered the works at the same gap, after which the contest was maintained with great obstinacy during three hours. The Indians had constructed coverts in such a manner that the place could be taken only in detail.[1] Driven from one covert after another, the savages kept up a galling fire, resolutely contesting every inch of ground. At length they were compelled to abandon the fort and effect their retreat by the log gate, across the narrow bridge, which, though well adapted to the use of Indians, must have proved a difficult passage to the English. During the contest it was observed that a large body of the Indians had assembled behind a certain part of the fort, whence they kept up a most annoying fire. Captain Church, the aide of General Winslow, having the command of a volunteer company, led them out against these Indian flankers, whom he silenced or dispersed, when, charging again with great gallantry, he re-entered the fort through the oft-contested gap, driving the Indians before him. He encountered them on every side, hunted from their coverts, and falling fast before the English musketry. The Narragansetts finally gave up the struggle and fled into the wilderness.

Six hundred lodges were found in this fortified enclosure. It was in the winter season, and the natives placed great reliance on the strength of their position, as well as on the English custom of suspending war operations during the winter months; therefore the Narragansetts had conveyed their women and children to this place for shelter. It has been stated, and there is no reason to doubt it, that some of the most bold and reckless of the English officers had been formerly sea-captains, and probably buccaneers in the West Indies. Nothing short of the diabolical spirit innate in men of that class could have suggested the cruel scene that followed the flight of the warriors. The wigwams, containing the aged and superannuated, the

---

[1] This reveals the object of pits and ditches inside of our antiquarian remains of fortifications in the West.

wounded who were unable to escape, and about three hundred women and children, were set on fire. The miserable inmates ran shrieking in every direction as the flames advanced, but, there being no chance for flight, they were all consumed in this inhuman holocaust.

The Indians who escaped took shelter in a swamp near by, where they passed the night in the snow, and where many of their number died from exposure and the want of both fire and food. The Narragansetts afterwards asserted that they lost about seven hundred warriors at the fort, besides three hundred who subsequently died of their wounds. The entire number assembled at the fort has been computed at four thousand, and if we allow but five persons to a lodge it would sum up a total of eight hundred families.

The conflagration of the lodges, after the Indian warriors had fled, was not merely unnecessary, cruel, and inhuman, but it was also an unwise measure on the part of General Winslow, for the Indian wigwams might have afforded shelter during the night for the wounded and exhausted soldiery. But the English were themselves driven out by the flames, and were compelled to retrace their way through a severe snow-storm, carrying with them many of their dead and wounded. The intensity of the cold, added to the pangs of hunger, occasioned the death of many of the latter, whom ordinary care might have saved. They reached the desolate site of Pettiquamscott after midnight, and the following day thirty-four of their number were buried at that place in one grave. Many were severely frost-bitten, and four hundred were so much disabled as to be unfit for duty. Had the Indians rallied and attacked them at Pettiquamscott, not over four hundred of the army could have handled a gun or a sword. Eighty-five of the English were killed in the storming of the fort, and one hundred and fifty wounded, including eight captains and several subalterns.

This severe blow crippled the power of the Narragansetts, but did not humble them. On the contrary, the survivors cherished the most intense hatred against the English, from this period becoming the open and fearless allies of Philip; and the majority of them, under Canonchet, a short time subsequently joined the Nipmucks, and Philip's allies, near Deerfield and Northfield. Driven from their villages and their country, they turned their backs on their once happy homes with a feeling akin to that which had at a prior period animated Sassacus. It might naturally be supposed that many of them must have suffered greatly from want of food; but the forests were still filled with game, and they also frequently seized the cattle which were straying about on the borders of the settlements. Early in February, 1676, they made a descent upon Lancaster, which they burned, and captured forty-two persons; and a short time thereafter they killed twenty of the inhabitants of Medfield, at the same time burning half the town. Seven or eight buildings shared the same fate in Weymouth. On the 13th of March, four fortified houses were reduced to ashes in Groton. Five houses were burned and five persons killed at Northampton, whence the Indians were repulsed, losing several of their number. A few days later, Warwick, in Rhode Island, was burned, and before the close of the month the largest portion of the town of Marlborough was likewise consumed, and the town deserted by its inhabitants. On March 27 about forty Sudbury men surprised and attacked in the night three hundred Indians, killing thirty of them.

The Indians had been taught the efficacy of fire by their bitter experience at Kingstown fort, and they soon became expert in using it against the English. The torch was now their most potent weapon. This novel mode of warfare created such a panic that a large force was kept on the alert both day and night. Before the depredations could be checked in one direction, they were duplicated at another and, frequently, distant point. On March 26, Captain Pierce, of Scituate, and fifty men, together with twenty Cape Cod Indians, falling into an ambuscade at Pawtucket, were suddenly attacked and almost entirely annihilated, after having slain a much larger number of the enemy. Two days subsequently, forty dwelling-houses and thirty barns were burned at Rehoboth, and the next day thirty more were destroyed at Providence. Eleven persons were killed and their bodies consumed in the flames of one house at Plymouth. Chelmsford, Andover, and Marlborough suffered by the torch early in April.

The Indian army which committed these depredations numbered some five hundred men. Finding that they were not closely pursued after their attack upon Sudbury, they encamped in the neighboring forest. Meantime, a force of seventy men, under Captain Wadsworth, who were marching to protect other towns, learning that a body of Indians was concealed in the woods near Sudbury, determined to find them. Seeing a small number of the enemy returning, they instantly started in pursuit of them, and were thus led into an ambush, from which the entire force of the Indians issued and commenced a fierce attack. Flight being out of the question, the English fought bravely, and finally gained an eminence. But nothing could withstand such numerical odds, and Wadsworth and above fifty of his command were killed. The same day a provision-train was attacked in Brookfield, and three men killed or captured. This day, April 21, is memorable as the last great success of Philip. The ire of the Indians was next directed against the old Plymouth colony, which they hated on account of its having been the nucleus of the colonists. Nineteen buildings were burned at Scituate, seventeen at Bridgewater, and eleven houses and five barns in Plymouth itself. A short time subsequently, several buildings were consumed at Nemasket (Middleborough). Very few persons were killed in these depredations, but the Indian firebrand was constantly in operation against every isolated house or unguarded village. Marauding parties stealthily traversed miles of territory every night, and no man could step out into his field to look at his farm or stock without incurring the danger of being pierced by the swift-winged arrow or the unerring ball of a savage foe. The hills and valleys of New England resounded anew with the terrible war-whoop.

While the eastern townships thus presented a scene of universal devastation, the English inhabitants on the western borders experienced but little disturbance from the Indians. But when the latter were driven from the eastern section, they commenced a series of attacks by night and by day on the scattered settlements of the west. To repress these outrages, Massachusetts and Plymouth sent a considerable force into that quarter.

After the storming of his principal fort in the swamp of South Kingstown, Canonchet, the reigning chieftain of the Narragansetts, fled to another strong position, but there is no evidence that defeat had humbled him. His grandfather, Canonicus, had been the ruling chief of his tribe, and had sold Aquidneck, now Rhode Island, to the English. Canonicus's son, Miantonomo, equally noted for his politic character and his personal bravery, had acted a distinguished part in the war which followed the overthrow of the Pequots. Canonchet himself could look back to no period of the Narragansett history which did not afford him cause for pride. Whatever course his reflections took, he appears only to have been hardened in feeling, and more than ever incited to hatred of the English, by the contest with Winslow.

As spring advanced, he issued from his place of retreat, and, accompanied by a party, came to Seekonk to procure seed-corn for planting. This movement was revealed by two Indian women who were captured, and who also informed the colonists that his place of refuge was on Black River. Some Connecticut soldiers, under Captain George Denison, who happened to be in the vicinity at the time, proceeded to make search for him, and succeeded in finding some of his party. They then immediately scattered, with the view of intercepting him, each squad taking a different route. Canonchet had adopted a similar policy, dividing his followers into separate parties. Forty-four of his men were killed or taken, Denison not losing a man. The sachem was seen by a person who recognized him, and hotly pursued. In order to expedite his flight, he threw off his laced coat and wampum belt, and would have escaped had he not made a false step and fallen into the water, wetting his gun. A swift-footed Pequot, who was in the English army, immediately seized and held him until some of the soldiers arrived. He was desired to indicate his submission, but refused, maintaining both in his air and in his manner a proud, unconquered aspect, and disdaining to make any answers compromising his honor.

He was taken under a strong guard to Stonington, where he was allowed the formality of a trial. This local tribunal condemned him to be shot, which sentence was executed by the Mohicans and Pequots. "I like it well," said the proud chieftain, when informed what was to be his fate. "I shall die before I speak anything unworthy of myself."

With Canonchet the Narragansett power in reality expired, and his people were all driven out of the country, except those under Ninigret, at what is now known as Westerly, Rhode Island. The Narragansett nation had doubtless produced greater chiefs than Canonchet, but none who had possessed a higher or a firmer sense of his power and authority, or who had entertained a greater repugnance to the influx of the English race. Canonicus dreaded the approach of the foreign race, but he saw some advantages in that commerce which supplied a market for what the natives could most easily procure, and which furnished them with articles of which they stood in need. These circumstances, coupled with the influence of Roger Williams, induced him to adopt a conservative course, and to prevent his tribe from committing hostile acts. His son, Miantonomo, was greatly his superior, both in mental and in personal endowments, but he possessed a fiery, ungovernable spirit. Impatient under the pressure of wrongs that he could not redress, he was too eager to avenge injuries received from his kinsmen, the Mohicans, by a sudden, impulsive movement, the object of which might have been attained by more deliberation. His death on Sachem's Plain is not remarkable as an act of savage cruelty, but it affords a clear proof of the crafty policy of the colonial authorities. An Indian hand was made to strike the executionary blow which Indian clemency or diplomacy had withheld. Canonchet, also, as we have seen, fell by the same questionable system.

Winter is not usually a season of warfare among the forest Indians, who can be traced in the snow, and cannot camp without fires, but where the plunder of barns and cattle is at hand to afford them sustenance the rule is violated. Philip resolved that neither cold nor hunger should stay his onset; he had engaged in a death-struggle with New England, and it may truly be said that she never had to cope with another enemy so energetic and desperate as he.

After the capture of Canonchet, the party which had been led by him fled in the direction of Deerfield and Northfield, in which vicinity Philip's Indians had been for some time collected, committing depredations on the inhabitants. Philip made this part of the country his head-quarters, and, according to accounts then current, he had received countenance from the French in Canada, who had sent, and continued to send, Indian marauding parties into this part of the Connecticut Valley. He had himself visited Canada, and he purposed, in case of final defeat, to retire into that province. A Natick Indian who had been sent out as a spy reported that Philip had visited Albany to obtain assistance from the Mohawks. The Mohawks might have been inclined to aid him, but for a piece of treachery which unexpectedly came to light. Philip's men had killed a few Mohawk hunters on their hunting-grounds in the Connecticut Valley, and the chief had adroitly laid the blame on the English. But one of the men supposed to be dead had recovered, and revealed the true state of the case.

It soon became evident that Philip entertained no idea of giving up the contest, but was preparing to carry on the campaign of 1676 with renewed vigor. As the spring advanced, his central position appeared to be at or about Turner's Falls, on the Connecticut, then a noted locality for the catching of shad and other species of fish abounding in this river. At Longmeadow, on the 26th of March, an armed cavalcade, while proceeding to church, was attacked, and two men killed and a number wounded. On another similar occasion two women and their children became so much frightened that they fell from their horses and were dragged by the Indians into a swamp. These affairs, with many others of a similar character, in which men were killed on both sides, rendered it clear that Philip's main force harbored in this vicinity, and thither, therefore, the English troops were marched, corps after corps, both horse and foot, under approved leaders, until the force swelled to a considerable number. The Indians were camped around the falls on both banks in detached bodies, and were also congregated on its cliffs and on the neighboring islands. As the English force in this quarter was not at the outset very numerous, the Indians were not in much fear, and consequently became careless. Two captives who had escaped reported this supineness and described their position. About one hundred and sixty mounted men marched for the falls, under Captain Turner, whose gallantry was commemorated by giving to the place his name. They were joined by militia from Springfield and Northampton, and then led by skilful guides to within half a mile of the spot, where Turner dismounted his men and fastened his horses, leaving a small guard to protect them. Having been previously joined by parties under the command of Holyoke and Lyman, the whole force proceeded with silence and caution toward the Indian camp. Day had not yet dawned, and the enemy, deeming themselves secure, kept no watch. They were yet asleep, and scattered around at several points, mostly above the falls, where the river poured at one leap over a precipice of forty feet. A well-directed fire gave them the first indication that the detested English, shouting "Mohawks!" were upon them. Seizing their arms, they fought distractedly. A large number of them leaped into their canoes to cross the river, some of which, having no paddles, were soon swept over the falls, and all who were in them, with one exception, drowned. It is estimated that the entire loss of the Indians was three hundred warriors. One hundred and forty were swept over the falls, only one of whom was saved. Those who succeeded in escaping across the river joined the others in their flight. It was a complete surprise and a disastrous defeat. The slaughter was so great that one hundred dead were counted on the field.

After their flight the Indians again rallied, crossed below the falls, and attacked the guard which had been left with the horses. An Indian captive reported that Philip had arrived with a reinforcement of one thousand men. This news produced a panic, and a separation of the English forces. A thickly-wooded morass flanked the left banks of the falls, extending nearly to Green River. Those who retreated by this route were subjected to repeated attacks, and one of the parties which attempted to cross it was entirely cut off, and the men taken prisoners and burnt at the stake. Turner beat back the party which attacked his camp, remounted his horses, and vigorously pursued the enemy, who, dividing as he advanced, closed in behind, and pursued him in turn. He fell, pierced by a bullet, while crossing Green River. Holyoke, who had killed five Indians with his own hand, now assumed the command, and, crossing the plains and Deerfield River, he entered that town, closely pressed by the Indians. In this retreat he lost thirty-eight men.

This action, however, was the turning-point of the war. The Indians, who were thrice the number of their assailants, had been posted in a country where they could obtain ready subsistence and keep the surrounding territory in alarm by their secret attacks. Believing themselves invincible, they had at last become careless, and, when they least expected it, had been surprised by a comparatively small force, a large number killed, and the rest dispersed. They had never before experienced so decided an overthrow, and, though they rallied and fought desperately, the dreaded combination was broken up, and was never afterwards re-formed.

After this affair, Philip, who had during many months made this place his head-quarters, determined, it appears, to retreat towards the north. This chief, the various authorities state, had kept himself somewhat in retirement after a price had been placed upon his head. In the course of a few years he had seen Sassacus, Miantonomo, and Canonchet fall. He had also seen the colonies spread instead of diminish. Whether he meditated striking another blow at the settlements after the action at Turner's Falls, or relinquished the idea of a retreat to Canada through the territory of the great Iroquois nation and across the waters of Lake Champlain, is not known. He never again, however, attained to the power he had once possessed, and his fortune and influence appear to have henceforth deserted him.

The action at Turner's Falls occurred on the 18th of May. On the 30th of the same month six hundred Indians attacked Hatfield with great fury, burned twelve buildings, assaulted several palisaded dwellings, and killed a number of the inhabitants, but the latter, being reinforced from Hadley, succeeded in saving the town from complete destruction and in driving the Indians out of it. The loss of the colonists was five men, and that of the Indians twenty-five. The latter in their retreat drove off a large number of sheep and cattle.

Early on the morning of the 12th of June the Indians assaulted Hadley with their entire force, reported at seven hundred warriors. An ambuscade was formed by them at night at one end of the town, into which they endeavored to decoy the inhabitants the following day. Not succeeding in this, they secured possession of a house, which afforded them shelter during the assault, and also fired a barn. They were at length repulsed with but little loss. The story originally told by Hutchinson, and often since repeated as veritable history, that on this occasion the regicide Goffe suddenly appeared, placed himself at the head of the townspeople, and drove off the Indians, is wholly wanting in authenticity.

Philip next turned his attention to Plymouth, the old thorn which still rankled in his side. To this quarter he repaired personally, in the latter part of June, at the head of a large force, and harassed the surrounding settlements by his marauding attacks, but effected nothing of importance. This move had the effect, however, of inducing the colonists to send fresh troops into the field, who were animated with the warmest zeal against their common enemy. Distinguished among these was the veteran Captain Benjamin Church, who was indefatigable in scouring the country, destroying the lodges of the Indians, capturing their women and children, and killing their warriors. He spread the terror of his name far and wide. The hunted sachem, although he had no longer a fixed point at which to convene his council and could not count upon a place where his person would be safe, still maintained a haughty mien, and evinced no signs of submission, but on the contrary manifested a persevering spirit of hostility and hatred.

Major John Talcott, of Connecticut, on July 2 came upon a large body of Indians in the Narragansett country, at a place called Nipsachooke, in a great spruce swamp, and within three hours slew or captured one hundred and seventy-one, and sixty-seven more on the following day. This was in what is now Smithfield, Rhode Island. Queen Magnus, "that old piece of venom," was among the slain. Two hundred surrendered in Plymouth colony a few days later. One hundred and fifty had been killed or taken by the Massachusetts forces prior to July 22, at which time they returned to Boston. July 27 the sagamore John, a Nipmuck sachem, came in and surrendered at Boston, with one hundred and eighty followers.

While Church was in Rhode Island, Pometakom was driven from his covert like a hunted lion, his wife, children, and others of his household being surprised and killed. The chief himself, however, escaped, and fled from place to place. At length the brother of an Indian whom Philip had unjustly killed brought intelligence that the haughty Pokanoket had taken refuge in a swamp located on Mount Hope Neck. Church proceeded to the peninsula with a number of volunteers and a party of friendly Indians, guided by the informer. They crossed the Taunton River in perfect secrecy, and reached the swamp after nightfall (August 11). Church then formed his men in segments of a circle, in open order, and marched them upon the swamp. Having placed a friendly Indian alternately next to a white man, he issued orders to fire on any person who should attempt to escape through the closing circle. They waited for daybreak in intense anxiety and profound silence. A small select party, under Golding, was detailed to advance and rouse up the Pokanoket chief. While these arrangements were being perfected, and the attacking party was still behind, a shot whistled over Church's head, followed by a volley, fired by a party of Indians sent out by Philip. Daylight had now appeared. The report of guns attracted the attention of the chief, and, seizing his tobacco-pouch, powder-horn, and gun, he started immediately to sustain his advanced party. The Indians followed Philip in files. An Englishman, not knowing the chief, levelled his piece at him on a venture, but it missed fire. An Indian placed next him then discharged his musket at him, sending two balls through his body, and laying him dead on the spot. Ignorant of the fate of the chief, an Indian voice was heard thundering through the swamp, "*Iootosh! Iootosh!*" (Onward! Onward!) which cry proceeded from Annawon, Philip's principal war-captain, who was urging his men to maintain their ground. The result was a bloody conflict, in which the Indians fought like tigers. Church finally made a determined charge with all his force, killing one hundred and thirty men, but Annawon,[1] with about sixty followers, escaped.

During the whole of this terrible war the Mohicans remained faithful to the English, and not a drop of blood reddened the soil of Connecticut. But in the adjacent colonies twelve or thirteen towns were destroyed, and more than six hundred men, chiefly the young, the flower of the country, perished; six hundred houses were burned, and an immense amount of property was destroyed. Of the able-bodied men one in twenty had fallen.

The death of Philip was in effect the termination of a war which had threatened the very existence of the colonies, for, although the Pokanokets had been the prime

---

[1] This chief was the uncle of Philip, and when captured surrendered his war-paints, scarlet blanket, and broad wampum belts. See Drake's "Book of the Indians."

instigators of it, the powerful tribe of the Narragansetts, and other auxiliaries, one after another, had joined the league; and although less than two years had elapsed since the commencement of the war, the entire Indian power of the country was openly or secretly enlisted on the side of the Mount Hope sachem. Notwithstanding his rooted hatred of the whites and of the whole scheme of civilization, it cannot be doubted that he was a man who took a comprehensive view of his position and of the destiny of the New England tribes; much less can it be questioned that he possessed great energy of character, persuasive powers suited to enlisting the sympathy of the Indians, and very considerable skill in planning, as well as daring in carrying his projects into effect. Gookin calls him "a person of good understanding and knowledge in the best things." We may lament that such energies were misapplied, but we cannot withhold our respect for the man who was capable of combining all the military strength and political wisdom of his country, and of placing the colonies in decidedly the greatest peril through which they ever passed.

CHAPTER IV.

THE MERRIMAC VALLEY AND ABENAKI TRIBES—KING WILLIAM'S WAR—GOVERNOR DUDLEY'S WAR—SEBASTIAN RALE—LOVEWELL'S FIGHT.

At the period of the first settlement of New England by the English, the principal Indian powers located in that territory were the Pokanokets, under Massasoit; the Narragansetts, under Canonicus; the Pequot-Algonkins, of Connecticut; and the Merrimacs or Pennacooks, of Amoskeag. Each of these comprised several subordinate tribes bearing separate names, and, although bound by both lingual and tribal affinities to the central tribal government, yielding obedience to it in the ordinary loose manner of local Indian tribes. Each of these tribal circles was ruled by its particular chief, who, although he arrogated to himself the powers and immunities of hereditary descent, exercised no absolute controlling influence beyond what the popular voice allowed him. The colonists were not long in ascertaining who were the principal rulers, or in taking the necessary measures to conciliate them.

Their mode of treating with the Indians was to assert that the sovereignty and fee-simple of the soil were vested in the English crown, but yet to acknowledge the possessory right of the aborigines by presents or by purchase, in order to conciliate the local chiefs. When collisions were occasioned by disputed boundaries, or by questions of trade, they were adjusted in councils of both parties. No difficulties of any general moment occurred until the origination of the Pequot war. The bloody feud between the Mohicans, under Uncas, and the Narragansetts, under Miantonomo, was a consequence of the Pequot outbreak. The colonies endeavored as much as possible to abstain from any participation in this struggle, but in a very short time they became involved in open warfare with the Narragansetts. It could not be supposed that the Pokanokets or Wampanoags, who under the benevolent Massasoit had lived in amity with the English for so long a period, could sit calmly by and see a foreign people, whose manners, customs, and opinions differed so widely from their own, attain the possession of power, and spread over their country, without experiencing feelings of jealousy and animosity. The impatient spirit which Alexander evinced during his short reign, and the more deliberate and crafty policy of Philip, developed this latent Indian feeling. These events have, however, been already related in detail.

The Merrimac tribes, among whom the Pennacooks appear to have held the highest position, had located the seat of their government at the Amoskeag Falls (now Manchester, New Hampshire), a name denoting the abundance of beaver on that stream. The ruling sachem was Passaconnaway, a celebrated magician, a distinguished war-captain, an eloquent speaker, and a wise ruler. Few aboriginal chiefs ever surpassed him in mental or magisterial qualifications. For a long period he prudently maintained friendly relations with the Massachusetts and New Hampshire colonies, and his interviews with John Eliot denote that he possessed a mind capable of grasping the truths of religion. It is manifest that his most earnest desires were to make the vicinity of his beloved Amoskeag his home in old age, and that his bones should be deposited on one of the beautiful islands in the Merrimac. But the spirit of aggression frustrated his wishes. There was a strong prejudice in the English mind against the natives, which brought the colonists and the Merrimacs into collision in many different ways. Injury was retaliated by injury, and blood was avenged by blood. Murders were followed by wars, in which the English were invariably successful, and finally Passaconnaway and his Pennacooks were driven from their homes. New Hampshire and Maine, from the Merrimac to the Penobscot, were drenched with Indian as well as English blood. The time will arrive when the history of these sanguinary strifes will become a fruitful theme for the pen and the pencil, and then the bold and heroic men whose lot it was to act the part of their country's defenders in these perilous scenes will receive their due meed of praise.

The Abenaki tribe also acted an important part in the Indian history of Maine and New Hampshire. This word is too vague for any ethnological purpose, being the mere Indian term for Eastlander.[1] The language of this people designates their Algonkin lineage, the latter being distinguished by some orthographical peculiarities, the principal of which is the use of the letter *r*. The early colonists called them Tarrantines, but among the Iroquois they were known by the name of Onagunga.

The news of the rising of Philip was the signal for the commencement of hostile demonstrations at the eastward, which in the space of a few weeks extended nearly three hundred miles. In Maine a border warfare was waged, unattended, however, by any prominent event. Of the English settlements nearly one-half were destroyed in detail, and the inhabitants driven away, killed, or carried into captivity. The Indians were supplied with arms by the French on the Penobscot. Peace was at length secured by the treaty at Casco Bay in 1678.

In July, 1687, Denonville, Governor of New France, with a force of three thousand, consisting mostly of Indians gathered from all points, set out from Irondequoit Bay to invade the Seneca country. On the way he seized a party of English traders, distributed their goods among the savages, and sent them prisoners to Canada. The Senecas laid an ambuscade for him, into which he fell, but finally they were routed, their village burned, and their corn-fields laid waste. Returning to Montreal, he rebuilt Fort Niagara on his way, and garrisoned it with one hundred men. The campaign enraged without seriously injuring the Senecas, whose chief town, destroyed by Denonville, and named by him Gannagaro, was on Boughton's Hill, near the present village of Victor, New York.

King William's war began in 1689, and was terminated by the peace of Ryswick in 1697. Count Frontenac, Governor of Canada, the ablest of all the French officers

---

[1] From *wabun*, the east, or place of daylight, and *ackee*, earth, or land.

in America, was charged to recover Hudson's Bay, to protect Acadia, and by a descent from Canada to assist a fleet from France in conquering New York. At daybreak on the 25th of August, 1689, fifteen hundred Iroquois reached the Isle of Montreal, at La Chine, burned the houses, and massacred two hundred people. They then made themselves masters of the town, the fort, and the whole island, which they held until the middle of October. In the alarm Fort Frontenac, on Lake Ontario, was evacuated and razed.

In the east, Cocheco (Dover, New Hampshire) was burned by the Pennacooks on the night of June 27, Major Waldron and twenty-two others slain, and twenty-nine captives taken, and the stockade at Pemaquid (Maine) was taken in August by the Penobscots. At midnight on the 8th of February, 1690, Schenectady was attacked and burned by a party of French and Indians under De Mantet and Ste.-Hélène, with D'Iberville as a volunteer, and sixty persons massacred, the remainder of its inhabitants fleeing, some half clad, through the snows to Albany. A party from Three Rivers, led by Rouville, on March 27 surprised the settlement at Salmon Falls, on the Piscataqua, which was burned after a bloody engagement, and fifty-four prisoners were taken, chiefly women and children. On his return, Rouville met a war-party from Quebec under Portneuf, and, with them and a reinforcement from Castine, successfully attacked the fort and village at Casco Bay. Acadia was conquered in the following May by Sir William Phipps, who failed ignominiously in an expedition against Quebec in October. York, Maine, was surprised by French and Indians in February, 1692. An attack on Wells, June 9, was foiled by its resolute defenders. Ninety-four persons were killed or carried into captivity from Oyster River, New Hampshire, in July, 1694, and in March, 1697, an attack on Haverhill made Hannah Dustin famous as the heroine of one of the most daring exploits on record.

Frontenac in the West endeavored by alternate missions and incursions to win over or to terrify the Five Nations into an alliance. In 1693 he captured three of the Mohawk castles, but Schuyler, of Albany, with two hundred men, overtook the party and succeeded in liberating many of the captives. In 1696 the French and their allies renewed their efforts, Frontenac himself, then seventy-four years of age, heading the forces. Two bundles of reeds suspended on a tree, which they encountered on their way, denoted that fourteen hundred and thirty-four warriors (the number of reeds) defied them. The great village of the Onondagas was set on fire and destroyed; the country of the Oneidas was ravaged, their corn cut up, and their villages burnt; and it was proposed to go against the Cayugas, but Frontenac decided to return to Montreal, leaving the Iroquois humbled, indeed, but unsubdued. In the summer of 1700 peace was ratified between the Iroquois on the one side and France and her Indian allies on the other.

The peace that followed the treaty of Ryswick was of brief duration. In the year 1700 Europe was once more in arms over the question of the Spanish succession, and the colonies of France and England were again involved in a bloody strife, which lasted until the peace of Utrecht, in 1713. A congress of Abenaki chiefs, in June, 1703, declared to Governor Dudley that the sun was not more distant from the earth than their thoughts from war, yet within six weeks the whole country from Casco to Wells was in a conflagration. Several parties of Indians and French burst upon every house or garrison in that region on the 10th of August, sparing neither old nor young. A party under Hertel de Rouville attacked Deerfield in the early morning of March 1, 1704, and, entering the palisades, which four feet of snow had rendered useless, set the village on fire, killed forty-seven of the inhabitants, and carried one hundred and twelve into captivity. During all these years the Massachusetts frontiers were desolated, presenting a shocking picture of danger and misery. Children at play, laborers in the fields, mothers employed about their households, all were victims to an enemy who disappeared as soon as a blow was struck, and who was quick to discover and profit by any lack of vigilance in a family or garrison. In 1706, Chelmsford, Groton, Sudbury, Exeter, Dover, and many other places suffered more or less severely. Many New-Englanders were carried into captivity to Canada, and many were killed on the way. In the night of August 29, 1708, Haverhill, on the Merrimac, was attacked by a party of Indians and Canadians under Des Chaillons and Rouville, the destroyer of Deerfield. It contained at that time thirty houses, the new meeting-house standing in the centre of the village. These were all assaulted simultaneously. Benjamin Rolfe, the minister, was beaten to death, and his wife and infant child savagely slaughtered, and many others fell under the rifle and tomahawk. As the destroyers retired, Samuel Ayer, with a few men, hung on their rear, and succeeded, although at the cost of his own life, in rescuing several from captivity.

In 1710, Colonel Nicholson, with a fleet and four New England regiments, captured Port Royal, to which, in honor of Queen Anne, was given the name of Annapolis. An unsuccessful expedition against Quebec, in 1711, under Admiral Walker, was the finale in America of this horrible warfare, instigated by Christian princes, which had occasioned such needless and inhuman butchery. In a single year of this cruel war one-fifth part of all who were capable of bearing arms in Massachusetts were in active service. Some of its fruits, afterwards apparent, were an intense hatred of the French missionaries, and a willingness to exterminate the natives. As these latter could not be reached by the usual methods of warfare, a bounty was offered for every Indian scalp, and men scoured the forests for Indians as they would for wild beasts. By the peace of Utrecht England obtained supremacy in the fisheries, and the possession of Hudson's Bay and its borders, Newfoundland, and Acadia.

About 1692, while the colonies were contending with the refractory tribes on their western borders, Sebastian Rale, a Jesuit missionary from Quebec, who had previously visited some of the Western tribes, made his appearance among the Abenakis. He located himself at Norridgewock, and earnestly devoted his attention to the task of teaching them the truths of Christianity. It must be remembered that the French residents in Canada aimed to construct an empire in America by obtaining influence among the Indian tribes east, west, north, and south, which might be turned to political account in the hour of emergency. To a great extent the new system of instruction introduced by Rale had not only a religious character, but also a powerful political tendency. The people of New England and New York, nay, of all the colonies, regarded the Jesuit teaching and the French influence with equal horror, and numerous and protracted negotiations between the colonists and the tribes, as well as between the respective authorities of the two countries, were the consequence. This position of affairs caused Rale to be regarded by the colonists as a partisan and a leader of the insurgent Indians. Throughout New England his labors were deemed to be directed towards perverting the Indians and implanting in their minds the seeds of error and of hatred to the colonies. He was cited before the authorities of Boston, but the negotiations resulted only in mutual misapprehension and vituperation. Every movement was either in reality or was conceived to be the result of Canadian jealousy of the British colonies, or of British animosity against Canada. If the Indians committed a murder or perpetrated a massacre, it was alleged that the French authorities had incited them to the act, or had countenanced them in its performance. Squadrons of ships sailed from England to avenge these reported injuries, and for a long period the country from the mouth of the St. Lawrence to that of the Mississippi was the battle-ground of the contending nations.

After the peace of Utrecht, Massachusetts, having extended her boundaries and founded new settlements on the east bank of the Kennebec, had protected them by erecting forts. The Abenakis resisted her claims to territory that had always been theirs, and determined to retain it. Several of their chiefs had been seized by stratagem by the government and detained as hostages. The tribe demanded the evacuation of their territory and the release of their imprisoned warriors whose ransom had been paid, and threatened reprisals. The English then seized the young Baron de St. Castin, a half-breed and war-chief, who held a French commission, and after vainly soliciting the savages to surrender Rale, "that incendiary of mischief," Captain Westbrooke, in January, 1722, led a strong force to Norridgewock to surprise him. Rale had timely warning, and escaped into the forest, but his important correspondence with Governor Vaudreuil was found, and with it a vocabulary of the Abenaki language which he had made, and which is still preserved.

The war-chiefs soon assembled at Norridgewock, and, resolving to destroy the English settlements on the Kennebec, began the work of destruction by the burning of Brunswick. Rale, foreseeing the issue, bade his people retire to Canada. Many of them went, but he declined to accompany them.

In July war was declared against the Eastern Indians by Massachusetts, and, to stimulate partisan activity, a bounty of fifteen pounds sterling was offered for each Indian scalp, a sum afterwards increased to one hundred pounds. In March, 1723, Westbrooke, with his party, after five days' march through the woods, came upon the Indian settlement that was probably at Oldtown, above Bangor. Here was a fort seventy yards long and fifty broad, with stockades fourteen feet high, enclosing twenty-three houses. A chapel, handsomely furnished, sixty feet long and thirty wide, stood near it. Arriving in the evening of March 9, the invaders set fire to the village and reduced it to ashes.

After two futile attempts to seize Rale, a party at length succeeded in reaching Norridgewock unperceived August 23, 1724, and discharged their guns at the cabins. The Indian warriors, fifty in number, seized their arms and rushed out to secure the retreat of their wives, children, and old men. Rale heroically endeavored to save his flock by drawing the attention of the assailants upon himself. In this he partly succeeded, many of the Indians swimming the river, the English meanwhile pillaging the cabins and the church and then setting them on fire. After the retreat of the English the mangled body of Rale was buried by some of the natives beneath the spot where he used to stand before the altar.

Thus perished Rale, the last of the Jesuit missionaries in New England, in the sixty-seventh year of his age, and the thirty-seventh year of his service in America, and with him fell the influence of France within the New England borders.

In May, 1725, the brave John Lovewell and his companions, who had twice returned successful from Indian forays, on a third expedition fell into an ambush of a large party of Saco Indians, under Paugus, chief of the Pequawkets, in Fryeburg, Maine, near a sheet of water which has since borne the name of "Lovewell's Pond." Although the Indians outnumbered them more than two to one, and although they lost their leader early in the action, the whites kept up the contest until nightfall, when they withdrew, having lost twenty out of the thirty-four men composing the party. Paugus, the Indian leader, also fell in the action. With the Androscoggins, the Pequawkets soon after retired towards the sources of the Connecticut River, subsequently removing to Canada, where they were known as the St. Francis tribe. The Pequawkets remained upon the Connecticut, and at the period of the Revolution were under a chief named Philip.

Peace was at last concluded with the Eastern Indians, who found themselves excelled by their opponents even in their own modes of warfare. The peace was solemnly ratified by the chiefs as far as the St. John's, August 6, 1726, and was long and faithfully kept, and English trading-houses supplanted French missions.

CHAPTER V.

THE SOUTHERN INDIANS—MASSACRE OF WHITE SETTLERS—WARS WITH THE TUSCARORAS, YAMASSEES, NATCHEZ, AND CHICKASAWS—SETTLEMENT OF GEORGIA.

ENGLAND attained great political and literary fame during the reign of Queen Anne, while her American colonies, within the gloomy shadows of a distant and savage wilderness, were defending themselves from the horrors of impending starvation on the one hand and from aboriginal hostility on the other.

European intercourse with the Indians had during a period of one hundred years produced no appreciable good effects on their general manners, opinions, and modes of life. The tribes located nearest the settlements dressed in blankets and strouds instead of skins; they used metallic cooking-vessels instead of the clumsy clay *akeek*, or cooking-pot, implements of iron and steel instead of stone and bone, and the European fire-lock instead of the flint arrow. The fur-trade was in their view the great benefit which had resulted from the influx of civilized races. They hunted deer and beaver with increased vigor, indulging in luxuries of which their fathers had never even thought, and particularly in the use of intoxicating liquors. They did not, however, in reality appreciate anything else which came from Europe. They still detested and discouraged the introduction of schools, churches, letters, and labor, preferring to live, as their forefathers had done, by the chase, and not by agriculture. Game was still plentiful; their hunting-grounds were so vast that they appeared of almost illimitable extent; and the tribes from Maine to Georgia, and from the Gulf of Mexico to the borders of the Great Lakes, feasted, danced, sung, and rioted, and warred with one another, precisely as their ancestors had done a century before. When more sombre views of their existing condition were forced upon them, when the plough of the white man encroached so rapidly on their hunting-grounds that difficulties resulted, they plotted against the settlers, making sudden attacks upon them, or enticing them into ambuscades. These fitful efforts were succeeded by a relapse into their primitive state of idleness and inaction, without the Indians having derived from their spasmodic outbreaks any permanent advantage to themselves, or having inflicted any permanent injury upon the settlements.

During the establishment of the colonies, the impressions created by this feverish and changeful policy of the natives were alike unfavorable to the Indian and to the colonial character. Wherever attempts had been made to introduce education and the gospel, and to graft civilization, as it were, on the original stock, they had submitted, as if in expectation of deriving therefrom ulterior advantages, with such mildness of manner, accompanied by such deep duplicity, as to deceive the settlers; but in the end their real nature developed itself in the commission of cruel and sanguinary acts. Such were the results of colonial experience in Virginia between the period of the establishment of the settlement at Jamestown and the perpetration, in 1622, of that terrible massacre under Opechancanough, when over four hundred persons were killed in one day, among whom the first victims were those who, with the aid afforded them by the benevolent in England, had labored most zealously and efficiently to teach the Indians and to found a seminary of education for the tuition of their youth. Another terrible example was afforded in Massachusetts in 1675 by Pometacom, after nearly thirty years had been spent by Eliot and his missionary compeers in zealous and effective teaching of the tribes. These repulsive traits in the Indian character did much towards repressing, and for a time may be said to have extinguished, that benevolent and humane spirit with which they had been previously regarded. In Virginia, as in the entire South, these acts may be said to have originated a thorough detestation of the whole Indian race. Indeed, the details of these early deeds of sanguinary treachery, having been widely spread throughout America and Europe by means of newspapers, exercised an adverse influence which is felt even at the present day.

Thus far twelve of the original thirteen colonies had been established: Georgia, the thirteenth, was not founded until some time afterwards. Events which followed one another in rapid succession furnish us with still further knowledge of Indian character. The beginning of the eighteenth century was marked by three events in the history of the colonies which exercised an important influence on the Indian policy. 1. Penn, who had sailed up the Delaware in 1682, selected a site for the capital of his colony in the heart of the Lenni Lenape territories, and in 1701 laid out the city of Philadelphia. 2. Frontenac, the Governor-General of New France, to the chagrin of the Iroquois, directed a post to be established in the country of the Wyandots and their allies, in the vicinity of the lakes. M. de la Motte-Cadillac, who was intrusted with this duty, arrived with a military force at the straits between Lakes Erie and Huron in July of the same year, and founded Detroit, that central point of a French influence whose baleful effects were felt upon the Western frontiers during the long and bloody period of sixty years previous to the fall of Quebec. 3. The founding of Louisiana. The first settlement was made in 1699 at Biloxi, in the country of the Choctaws, but the province was not ceded to Crozat until 1712, nor was New Orleans founded until 1719. It was the policy of the French to establish trading- and missionary-posts first, and subsequently cities. Michilimackinac, the earliest point of fixed occupancy in Michigan, was the central position of the Western Algonkins in 1662, as was also Kaskaskia, Illinois, in the country of the same generic group of families, as early as the first visit of La Salle, in 1683. Vincennes, in Indiana, the Au Poste of early writers, was first occupied in 1710. The primary impulses were thus given to that Franco-Indian power which, like a gigantic serpent, coiled its folds around and for a period threatened to crush the British colonies.

Meantime, the Indians, true to their instincts, did not abandon their system of massacre. The opening of the century was characterized by the South Carolina war with the Creeks or Appalachians; the daring and successful expedition of Colonel Moore against them, within the Spanish territories, in 1705; the wide-spread and startling massacre by the Tuscaroras, in North Carolina, in 1711; and the Yamassee massacre, in 1715.

The Yamassees were one of some twenty-eight small tribes, of the group of Chicoras, who occupied the coasts and islands, as well as the banks of the rivers, of South Carolina, a group of which the Catawbas appear to be the only remaining but now rapidly diminishing tribe. It was the Yamassees, noted for their gentle manners but bitterly revengeful disposition, who had encountered the early Spanish visitors to this coast with such intrepidity, returning treachery for treachery. The Tuscaroras belonged to the Iroquois group, a fact that would clearly appear from philology, were it not also affirmed by their traditions, and by the fact that after their final defeat at Kienuka they fled to their kindred, the Five Nations, and were admitted as the sixth canton.

The war of the Spanish succession (1700–13) involved that part of South Carolina bordering on Spanish Florida, as well as New England, which adjoined Acadia. In September, 1702, Governor James Moore, of South Carolina, led an unsuccessful expedition against the Spaniards at St. Augustine. Late in the year 1705 he headed a mixed force of whites and Indians to attack the Muskokis, on the Bay of Appalache, who had been gathered by the Spaniards into towns and instructed by missions of Franciscan priests. These Indians had learned the use of horses and beeves, which multiplied without care in their favoring climate, and their continuous line of communication from St. Augustine to the settlements in Louisiana had inspired the Carolina traders with alarm. Penetrating regions which none but De Soto had till then invaded, Moore reached the Indian towns near the port of St. Mark's, and on December 14 attacked Ayavalla. Repulsed with loss from this strong place, he succeeded in setting fire to the church adjoining it, and more than fifty warriors and one hundred women and children were captured and kept for the slave-market. Next day the Spanish commander in the bay gave battle to double his number, and was defeated; but the Spanish fort proved too strong for the Carolinians. The chief of Ioitachnea compounded for peace with the plate of his church and ten horses laden with provisions. Five other towns submitted unconditionally. Most of their people abandoned their homes, and were received as free emigrants into Carolina. Thus was the English flag advanced through the wilderness to the Gulf of Mexico, and an additional claim established to the fertile region soon to be known as Georgia. Its boundaries extended far into Spanish territory.

In 1709 one hundred German families,—unhappy fugitives who had been driven by religious persecution from the Neckar and the Rhine,—conducted by De Graffenried, sought a refuge in North Carolina. The Indians along the sea-coast, greatly reduced in number by strong drink and other vices of civilization, had sold their lands or been cheated out of them, and their beautiful country as far as the Yadkin and the Catawba had been opened to the encroachments of the white man. The Tuscaroras of the inland regions and the Corees southward, upon whom their countrymen of the coasts had retreated, resolved to prevent their own extinction by exterminating the intruders. On the 22d of September, 1711, small bands of these Indians, acting in concert, fell upon the scattered German settlements along the Roanoke and Pamlico Sound, and in one night one hundred and thirty persons perished by the hatchet. At Bath the Huguenot refugees and the neighboring planters were slaughtered without mercy. The savages also scoured the country on Albemarle Sound, burning and slaying for three days, until disabled by fatigue and drunkenness.

The Assembly of South Carolina promptly voted relief. Captain Barnwell, with six hundred white men and three hundred and sixty Indians,—Cherokees, Creeks, Catawbas, and Yamassees,—marched through the wilderness against the Tuscaroras, and, driving them back to their fortified town near the Neuse, a little above Edenton, forced them to treat for peace. The South Carolinians themselves violated the treaty on their return, and the massacres on Neuse River were renewed. But Governor Spottswood, of Virginia, succeeded in dividing the Tuscaroras, and in March, 1713, Colonel James Moore, with forty white men and a large Indian force, besieged them in their fort and took eight hundred of them prisoners. The hostile portion of the tribe abandoned their old hunting-grounds, and, migrating to the vicinity of Oneida Lake, were received by their kindred of the Iroquois as the sixth nation of their confederacy. In 1715 peace was concluded with the Corees, who were established as a single settlement in the precincts of Hyde County, and the power of the native races of North Carolina was finally broken.

After the peace of Utrecht the Indian traffic in South Carolina rapidly increased, especially with the Yamassees, who, from impatience at the attempts to Christianize them, had quitted Florida, their old home, and planted themselves from Port Royal Island along the northeast bank of the Savannah River, where the Huguenots first attempted a settlement. This powerful tribe had long been friendly to the Carolinians, engaging with them as allies in their wars against the Spaniards at St. Augustine. The latter finally succeeded in uniting the Cherokees, Choctaws, and other Appalachian nations in a league for the destruction of the colony. On the morning of Good Friday, April 15, 1715, an indiscriminate massacre of the English began. Seaman Burroughs, a strong man and swift runner, broke through the Indian ranks, and, though hotly pursued and twice wounded, by running ten miles and swimming one mile, reached Port Royal and alarmed the town. Its inhabitants fled, some in canoes and some on board a ship that chanced to be in the harbor, to Charleston. Attacking the scattered settlements by night, and hiding in the swamps by day, the Indians drove the planters towards the capital, which was itself in peril, and the ruin of the colony seemed imminent. The Yamassees and their confederates halted at Stono, where the prisoners were sacrificed.

By this time the colony was aroused. On the north the savages received a check, and vanished into the forests. On the south, Governor Craven, acting with the greatest energy, proclaimed martial law, laid an embargo on all ships to prevent men or provisions leaving the colony, and, seizing arms wherever they could be found, placed them in the hands of faithful negroes. With twelve hundred men, white and black, he promptly led the forces of Colleton district to confront the savage horde, now advancing with the knife, hatchet, and torch in dreadful activity. In the first conflicts the Indians were victors, but Craven forced them finally to fall back to their camp on the Salkchatchie. The conflict was bloody, and was often renewed. Savage yells filled the air. Arrows and bullets were directed with fatal aim from every cover, and victory was long doubtful. At last the savages gave way, and were pursued beyond the present limits of Carolina, seeking shelter under the guns of St. Augustine. It is believed that the Yamassees penetrated the Everglades of Florida and became the ancestors of the powerful Seminoles. South Carolina had lost about four hundred of its inhabitants.

In 1730 an attempt was made to secure the friendship of the neighboring tribes. An embassy under Sir Alexander Cumming met the chiefs of the Cherokees at Nequassee, in the valley of the Tennessee. A treaty of alliance was drawn up and signed in England. The seven Indian envoys, astonished and bewildered at the vastness of London and the splendor and discipline of the army, were presented at court, and when the English king claimed their lands as his property, one of them gave the irrevocable answer, "To-yen-hah," it is "a most certain truth," and the delivery of eagles' feathers confirmed his words. The peace was faithfully kept, at least for one generation.

Near the banks of the Mississippi, between the Choctaw and Chickasaw tribes, in a region of great fertility, dwelt the Natchez Indians. The great chief of the tribe was revered as one of the family of the Sun, and his power was almost despotic. The French who came among them coveted their land, and Chopart, the French commander, demanded as a plantation the site of their principal village. In concert with the Cherokees and a part of the Choctaws, a general massacre of the French was determined on. The butchery began on the morning of November 28, 1729, and before noon nearly every Frenchman in the colony was slaughtered. The Jesuit Du Poisson, Du Codère, commander of the Yazoo post, the planter De Koli and his son, together with the Capuchin missionary to the Natchez nation, were all killed, only two white men, mechanics, being saved. Two hundred victims had fallen.

New Orleans was in terror; but the brave Le Sueur, repairing to the Choctaws, won seven hundred of them to his side, while the French forces, under Loubois, gathered on the river. Le Sueur, with his Choctaws, on the morning of January 29, 1730, surprised the Natchez villages, liberated the captives, and brought off sixty scalps and eighteen prisoners, losing but two of his own men. He completed his victory February 8, when the Natchez Indians fled, some taking refuge with the Chickasaws and Muskokis, others crossing the Mississippi to the vicinity of Natchitoches. These were pursued and driven still farther west. The Great Sun and more than four hundred prisoners were shipped to Hispaniola and sold as slaves. The Natchez nation no longer existed.

In 1736 the French government, in order to control the eastern valley of the Mississippi and establish its supremacy throughout Louisiana, determined to subjugate the Chickasaws. This tribe had maintained its savage independence, and, while it welcomed the English traders from Carolina, intercepted the French connections between Kaskaskia and North Carolina. Troops from the south, and from Illinois, under D'Artaguette, were directed to meet in the Chickasaw territory on May 10. Bienville, the French commander at New Orleans, left Fort Condé, at Mobile, April 4, and ascended the river to Tombeckbee, where a fort had been constructed. Here he was joined by twelve hundred Choctaws. At a point twenty-one miles southeast of the Chickasaw village, now Cotton-Gin Port, he left his artillery, and, marching on, encamped a league from the valley on the evening of May 25.

Early next morning they advanced to surprise the Chickasaws. The latter, behind strong intrenchments, over which waved English flags, were on the watch, and, aided by English traders, repulsed two attempts to storm their log fort, killing thirty of the French, four of them officers. The next day skirmishes occurred between parties of Chickasaws and Choctaws, and on the 29th Bienville retreated, throwing his cannon into the Tombeckbee.

Meanwhile, D'Artaguette, with fifty French and one thousand Indians, accompanied by De Vincennes, on the evening before the appointed day encamped near the rendezvous. For ten days he awaited the expected junction; then, to prevent the desertion of his allies, he decided to make the attack. On May 20, after carrying by storm two of the forts, he attacked the third. Disabled in the moment of victory, his red allies fled in dismay, and the French retreated, leaving D'Artaguette and Vincennes in the enemy's hands. After the retreat of Bienville the captives were burned at the stake.

Ill success only roused the French to still greater efforts. On the 30th of June, 1739, an expedition made up of twelve hundred whites and twenty-four hundred red and black men reached Fort Assumption, on the bluff of Memphis. Here they remained until the next spring, the French and Canadians falling victims to the climate. In March a small detachment on its way to the Chickasaws was met by messengers who supplicated for peace, and Bienville gladly accepted overtures that saved him from utter failure. The fort at Memphis was razed, the troops were withdrawn, and the fort on the St. Francis was dismantled. But the settlements between Lower Louisiana and Illinois still interrupted French communications, and the Chickasaws remained masters of the situation.

Up to this period there had been no attempt made at colonization in the country occupied by the confederacy of the Creeks, or Muskokis. This people, according to their traditions, having immigrated from the West, crossed the Mississippi, the Alabama, the Chattahoochee, and the Appalachicola, whence their country stretched towards the east, north, west, and south. At the earliest period of their settlement in the East, at the kindling of the council-fire, or establishment of a government, they were located on the river Altamaha. There is no doubt that they conquered, and either killed, incorporated with themselves, or ejected, the prior aboriginal inhabitants. Hawkins informs us that they conquered and carried the Uchees as prisoners from the southern part of South Carolina. Oglethorpe, who originated the plan of the Georgia colony in the year 1733, established it in the Creek territory lying between the Savannah and the Altamaha. Like the colonies of the Puritans, the Marylanders, and the followers of Penn, the Georgia colony was designed to be, and became, a refuge for oppressed and needy Europeans. The plan followed was, as had been the case in all previous instances of colonization, to bestow lands upon and afford employment to the colonists, and thus to enable them to improve their condition; always, however, at least in theory, paying a due regard to the rights and condition of the aborigines. The sovereignty and the fee-simple of the territory was held to be vested in the crown, but the right to their usufruct, until settled by presents or by actual purchase, was to be absolutely held by the Indians. The question was reserved as one for settlement by the administration, through the usual medium of treaty, as in all the earlier colonies. All had promised them justice, kindness, fair dealing, and all had urged upon them the benefits to be derived from the promotion of agriculture, arts, letters, temperance, and every other adjunct of civilization. Oglethorpe offered the Indians similar terms to those tendered them by the Pilgrims of New England, by the Duke of York in New York and New Jersey, by Lord Baltimore in Maryland, and by Penn in Pennsylvania. The rewards arising from a life of labor and virtue, and the evils attendant upon error, were, in their estimation, in the hands of the Indians themselves. If the natives preferred idleness, inebriation, and vice, if through neglect they became the victims of disease and death, it must be considered part of that great physical and moral law which entails the punishment as a sequel to the offence. If an Indian would hunt deer instead of guiding the plough, if he preferred alcohol to water as a beverage, and chose to idle away his time instead of improving it, the political economist regretted the fact, without having the power to deter him from pursuing his erroneous course.

For twenty years Oglethorpe persevered in his scheme in the midst of difficulties and discouragements that would have necessitated its abandonment on more than one occasion but for the unswerving fidelity of the Indians. When, in 1752, the province was formed into a royal government, it very soon became the seat of frightful Indian wars. The new authorities neither understood nor kept faith with the Indians, their old friend Oglethorpe had returned to England, and scenes of treachery and massacre ensued.

Each new colony established in America gave to the Indian the same lesson which had been taught him by its predecessors. At the outset civilization had apprised him of its requirements, and, though he learned its lessons slowly, it was hoped that he did learn, and that he made some progress in the right direction. Hope induced perseverance, furnished an apology for ignorance, and forgave repeated injury. The baptism of Manteo, which was performed in Virginia in 1586, may be regarded as indicating the outpouring of light at Cresswicks in 1744.

CHAPTER VI.

THE AQUINOSHIONI, OR IROQUOIS—GOVERNOR SHIRLEY'S WAR—CAPTURE OF LOUISBURG—TREATY OF AIX-LA-CHAPELLE—THE OUTAGAMIES, OR FOXES.

THE close of the seventeenth century appears to be a suitable opportunity for taking further notice of a people whose power had then culminated. There were but two tribes of those that ranged the land east of the Mississippi, north of the Cherokees, and east of the Chippewas of Lake Superior, over whom the Iroquois did not at this early day exercise a primary or a secondary influence; and even of these excepted tribes, one was seated one thousand miles to the northwest and the other one thousand miles to the southwest of their council-fire at Onondaga. The name of Aquinoshioni, signifying a long house or council-lodge, is indicative of their confederate character. Tradition refers the origin of their nationality and advancement to Tarenyawagon, a divinity who in his social state while on earth assumed the name of Hiawatha and imparted to them the knowledge of all things essential to their prosperity. The French, agreeably to their system, gave them the name of Iroquois, a term founded on two Indian radicals, with the Gallic terminal *ois* suffixed.

We are informed by Colden, who wrote the history of the Five Nations, viz., the Mohawks, Senecas, Oneidas, Onondagas, and Cayugas, dwelling near the river and the lakes that bear their names, to the period of the conclusion of the peace of Ryswick (1697), that the tribes composing this confederacy were not originally deemed superior to their neighbors. He commences their history at the epoch of the settlement of Canada (1608), at which time he depicts them as being inferior to the Adirondacks, an Algonkin tribe. They did not equal the Northern group of tribes either in hunting, war, or forest arts, though they possessed an element of subsistence in the cultivation of maize. By ceasing to war against one another, and confederating for their common defence, they laid the corner-stone of their national establishment. They first tried their united strength against the Satanas, a cruel people located on their borders, with a success which so raised their spirits that they at length went to war against the Adirondacks, who had been primarily their tutors in forest arts. After some reverses, they proved themselves an overmatch for the latter in stratagem, and finally obtained decisive victories over them in the St. Lawrence Valley.

Mr. Colden notes in this people a love of liberty and a spirit of independence which particularly mark them, but is at a loss which most to admire, their military ardor, their political policy, or their eloquence in council. The union of the cantons, each possessing equal powers, in one council, was the cause of their triumph among hunters in the east, west, and north, who acknowledged no government but that of opinion, and followed no policy but that actuated by revenge or indefinable impulse. All the weighty concerns of the Iroquois were the subject of full deliberation in open council, and their diplomatic negotiations were managed with consummate skill. When the question of peace or war was decided, the counsellors united in chanting hymns of praise or warlike choruses, which at the same time gave expression to the public feeling and imparted a kind of sanctity to the act. The majority of those who have given their attention to Iroquois history have recognized in their public acts the germs of a national policy which was suited to concentrate in their hands an imperial sway which would have been characterized by greater strength than that of the Aztecs under Montezuma, or of the Peruvians under Atahualpa.

Their tribal relations being conducted according to fixed principles, so also were their commercial affairs placed under a system equally stable. A short time subsequently to the arrival of Hudson and the building of Fort Orange, they formed a close alliance with the Dutch, who regarded the gains of commerce as the most decided advantage to be derived from their colony. They furnished the Indian warriors with guns, powder, flints, strouds, blankets, hatchets, knives, pipes, and all other articles necessary for the successful prosecution of the fur-trade, which was conducted on a basis so advantageous to both that the mutual friendship then contracted was never broken. With the river Indians of the Algonkin type, who lived in the same state of discord and anarchy as the other tribes, there occurred several, and some very serious, quarrels, but the union of the Iroquois and Dutch was intimate, and never more so than when the province was surrendered to the Duke of York, in 1664. By the terms of this surrender the good will of the Iroquois was secured to the English. The trade with the Indians was wholly in the hands of Dutch merchants and traders, and their interpreters, who continued to conduct it. They had extended this traffic through Western New York to the so-called "Far Indians," at Detroit, Saginaw, and Michilimackinac, where there are still some of their descendants.[1] As the Iroquois had for a long period held the balance of aboriginal power in this part of America, this influence became very important to the English, and was analogous to the Algonkin alliance with the French, which, after the fall of Quebec, was also transferred to the English.

The attachment of the Iroquois to the English alone saved Western New York from becoming a French colony. From the time of the action with Champlain, that commander having supplied his Indian allies with guns, the Iroquois had been prejudiced against the French nation. At sundry periods they repelled the invasions of De la Barre, Denonville, and Frontenac, and they also resisted the establishment of missions at Oneida, Onondaga, and Ontario. Their delegates frequently stood in the presence of the Governor-General at Quebec, with wily dexterity counteracting plot by counter-plot. In truth, they defended the territory till the English colonies

---

[1] In these distant localities we still hear of such names as Hance, Riley, Truax, Ten Eyck, Graverod, Fisher, Wamp, Yon, and Wiser.

became strong enough to protect it themselves. In the year 1726, by skilful management, the French succeeded in establishing a permanent military post at Niagara, within the limits of the confederacy.

The French had found themselves so severely taxed to resist the Iroquois that the conclusion of the peace of Ryswick was most welcome news at the castle of St. Louis. Colden observes that the French commissioners who conveyed the intelligence of this peace to the Onondaga country, and by negotiation secured their assent to it, likewise esteemed it a blessing. To the French, heaven could not have sent a greater. "For nothing," it is remarked, "could be more terrible to Canada than the last war with the Five Nations. While this war lasted, the inhabitants ate their bread with fear and trembling. No man was sure, when out of his house, of ever returning to it again. While they labored in the fields they were under perpetual apprehensions of being seized or killed, or carried to the Indian country, there to end their days in cruel torments. They many times were forced to neglect both seed-time and harvest. The landlord often saw all his land plundered, his houses burned, and the whole country ruined, while the French thought their persons not safe in their fortifications. In short, all trade and business was often at an entire stand, while fear, despair, and misery appeared on the face of the poor inhabitants."

Governor Clinton calls the Iroquois the Romans of the West. Charlevoix, who visited the shores of Lake Ontario in 1721, fancied that he perceived a Greek element in their language. While forming some Iroquois vocabularies in Western New York in 1845, Mr. Schoolcraft found it to possess a dual number.

The war of the Austrian succession, known to New England annals as Governor Shirley's war, was declared by France against England March 15, 1744–45. The news reached Canada a month earlier than it did New England, and the French and Indians promptly began the work of destruction. Shirley at once raised five hundred men for frontier service, three hundred of them on the eastern border, and two hundred for the protection of the upper valley of the Connecticut. The General Court of Massachusetts Bay ordered the erection of a line of forts from the Connecticut River to the boundary of New York, and a supply of powder was sent to the exposed settlements.

In 1731 the French had, with great foresight, built Fort St. Frederick at Crown Point, the key to the English settlements bordering on Canada. Fort Oswego had been built by Governor Burnet in 1727, at his own expense, to offset the erection by the French of Fort Niagara, at the entrance of the Niagara River into Lake Ontario. As has been previously stated, the French had in their intercourse with the Indians been far more politic than the English, and therefore easily drew them into their wars against the latter.

A conference between the Six Nations and the Commissioner for Indian Affairs was held June 18, 1744, at Albany, agreeably to the request of the Governor of New York, at which the Indians pledged themselves to stand by their English friends in case they were attacked. Except by a few of the Mohawks, this agreement was faithfully kept.

On the 13th of May the fort of Causo was surprised by M. Duvivier, with a French party, and its garrison of eighty were carried captive to Louisburg. On the 30th the priest La Loutre, with about six hundred Marechite and Micmac Indians, invested Annapolis Royal. Though in no condition to stand a siege, it was successfully defended by Governor Mascarene until relieved by Captain Edward Tyng with a force from Massachusetts, when it was immediately put in repair.

Louisburg, the strongest fortress of North America, was captured June 17, 1745, by the New England forces under General William Pepperell, aided by a British fleet under Commodore Warren, after a siege of seven weeks. Hostilities with the Penobscot tribe began near Fort George (Thomaston) on July 19, when a man was killed, a garrison-house and saw-mill burnt, and forty cattle slaughtered. One man was taken prisoner, and a woman wounded. This was the beginning of a long catalogue of horrors.

Another conference was held at Albany with the Six Nations October 5, 1745, at which were present commissioners from New York, Pennsylvania, and New England, the Indians renewing their covenant to take up the hatchet against the French and Indian enemy whenever called upon to do so by the Governor of New York. On November 16, three hundred French and two hundred Indians, commanded by M. Marin, destroyed the Dutch settlement at Saratoga. Thirty persons were killed, and about sixty captured. Many of the latter sickened and died in the prison at Quebec. A large extent of country was ravaged by this party, houses and mills were burnt, and all the cattle killed. On April 22, 1746, the little garrison of eight men at New Hopkinton was surprised and captured. Next day an unsuccessful attack was made by about one hundred Indians upon the garrison of Upper Ashuelot (Keene), New Hampshire. Six houses and a barn were burned, and two persons killed.

Fort "Number Four" (Charlestown, New Hampshire) was by its situation a point of great importance, and was frequently attacked by the Indians, as it stood in the way of their incursions upon the settlements below. On June 19 a large body of them posted themselves in ambush about it. Its commander, Captain Phinehas Stevens, while out with fifty men, became aware of their presence, and after a sharp conflict routed them with loss. On July 10, a party of Captain Rouse's men, while on shore at Prince Edward's Island, were surprised by two hundred Micmac Indians, and twenty-eight of them killed or captured. August 20, Fort Massachusetts, on the Hoosic River, near the northwest corner of the State, was invested by seven or eight hundred Indians and French under Rigaud de Vaudreuil. Its garrison of twenty-two men surrendered next day, and were taken to Canada. Three women and five children, also in the fort, shared their captivity. Rev. John Norton, chaplain of the fort, on his return from a year's captivity, published an account of the affair, entitled "The Redeemed Captive."

In November, 1746, a party of Mohawks, among whom was "King" Hendrick, made a successful raid into Canada. Colonel Arthur Noble, with seven hundred men, undertook, in January, 1747, to drive the French and Indians out of Nova

Scotia. While on his way, he was surprised in his camp by a superior force, and he, with four of his principal officers and seventy men, was killed, the remainder being taken prisoners. Early in April "Number Four" was again successfully defended by Captain Stevens against a large force of French and Indians, who for three days invested it, and tried, by shooting fire-arrows and by other methods, to compel its brave little garrison of thirty men to surrender.

On June 15 the fort at Saratoga was attacked by two thousand French and Indians, who killed sixty of the garrison. The place was soon after relieved by Colonel Schuyler. June 26, 1748, a severe conflict occurred near "Number Four," between a party of forty men under Captain Hobbs, and a more numerous Indian force who had waylaid them. Notwithstanding the disparity of numbers, Hobbs stood his ground, fighting bravely for four hours, when he fortunately got a shot at the Indian leader, whom he either killed or badly wounded, as the Indians thereupon drew off. In this well-contested fight the Indian loss exceeded that of the whites. The news of the peace of Aix-la-Chapelle was not known in Boston until six months after its conclusion, Indian hostilities meantime continuing, but early in 1749 overtures of peace were sent to the New England authorities, commissioners met the Indian deputies at Falmouth (Portland, Maine) October 14, and on the 16th articles of peace were drawn up and signed.

The Yamassees and the Tuscaroras in the South were not the only tribes who, about the beginning of the seventeenth century, evinced a spirit of hostility and commenced a series of massacres and a war of extermination against the whites. Partial as the Indians were to the French, there were two nations whom the latter could not control. These were the Iroquois, and the Outagamies or Foxes.

Who the Outagamies were is not known, and their early history is a blank. It has been inferred from their language that they were Algonkins, who used the Lenni Lenape pronunciation, in which an l is substituted for n, giving to their speech a more liquid flow. They appear at an early day to have been ejected from or forsaken by the Algonkin family and political organizations. Their traditions refer to a primitive residence at the site of Cataraqui, where it may be supposed they formed an intimacy with the Iroquois; and, if so, they were probably one of the tribes who built those immense ossuaries spread over the interior of Upper Canada.

In 1712, this tribe, swayed probably by the Iroquois influence, attempted to destroy Detroit, and, as in all similar cases, their movements were secret and the attack sudden. There were then but twenty soldiers in the fort. Under various pretexts the Indians gathered in that vicinity, but the plot was revealed in time to save the fort. The assault was made on the 13th of May, but on the same day the commandant was greeted by the voices of a numerous party of friendly Wyandots, Ottawas, and Pottawatomies, who routed the assailants. The Outagamies then retreated to an entrenched camp near at hand, but, becoming finally straitened for food and water, they were forced to sally out and take possession of a house nearer the fort, whence they discharged a destructive volley of lighted arrows, which set fire to the houses within the works. Eventually defeated, they retired to a peninsula jutting out into Lake St. Clair, where they repelled a furious assault of the French and their savage allies. After several days' preparation, during which artillery was brought from the fort, their position was stormed, many were killed, and the rest were forced to flee to the upper lakes, where they located themselves on Fox River, flowing into Green Bay. Here the sequel of their history fully accords with the account given by the French of their cunning and perfidy. They harassed traders at all the portages leading to the Mississippi River, and spread war and alarm in all directions as far as Lake Superior. Being at length besieged by the French commander, De Louvigney, with a competent force, at a selected position, since called on account of this event Butte des Morts, or Hill of the Dead, they were overcome, and suffered immense slaughter, after which the survivors fled to the banks of the Wisconsin. They were nearly destroyed, and received no further notice in our Indian history until within the present century.

In 1712, at the time of the Fox assault on the fort of Detroit, the Iroquois nation comprised five tribes or cantons, namely, the Mohawks, Oneidas, Onondagas, Cayugas, and Senecas. The same year they were joined by the Tuscaroras from North Carolina, making the sixth canton. The latter, once a powerful tribe, had been nearly annihilated by the North Carolina forces, assisted by a body of men under Colonel Barnwell, of South Carolina. The accession of the Tuscaroras, however it might have pleased the cantonal government, could have added but little to the efficiency of a people who had from the earliest times been the terror of other Indian tribes. Colden informs us that the Iroquois cantons had first attained power by their confederation, their wisdom in council, their policy in the adoption of conquered tribes, and their superior bravery in war. Governor Clinton tells us that their acquisition of power was much facilitated by their advantageous location in Western New York, in a region abounding in game, of unsurpassed fertility of soil, and situated at the head of many large and leading streams, down which they could suddenly make their forays, after the successful execution of which they might return by land.

All the tribes in an east-and-west line between Lake Champlain, the Connecticut, and the Illinois, acknowledged the supremacy of the Iroquois. North and south their sway extended from the mouths of the Hudson, the Delaware, and the Susquehanna, to the great lakes; thence northwardly to the Ontawis, or Grand River, of Canada, to Michilimackinac, and to the entrance of Lake Superior. In 1608, under the name of Massawomacks, they were the terror of the Powhatanic tribe of Virginia; as Mingoes, they spread their dominion over Ohio; and as Nadowassies, they were the foes of all the Algonkin or Adirondack races. At periods anterior to the arrival of the colonists they had prevailed over the once proud and powerful Lenni Lenape, and placed them *sub jugo*. They threatened the very existence of Canada. Tribes whom they could not subject to their stern policy were exterminated by the club and the tomahawk.

It became a part of the policy of all the colonies to conciliate such a people; consequently they were in fact parties to all important Indian treaties formed during the period of our early history, and until the colonies finally achieved their independence. In every negotiation involving the question of boundaries, or the termination of a war, the first demand was, What will the Iroquois do? They still in reality held the balance of power.

The war of races was not ended by the treaty of Aix-la-Chapelle. The red man still cherished the hope of repossessing himself of his old hunting-grounds and the graves of his fathers, but that hope grew fainter and fainter as time rolled on and as year by year he saw the constantly increasing tide of white settlers advancing and pushing him still farther towards the setting sun. Pontiac and Tecumseh were yet to attempt the patriotic but useless struggle, and to prove by their heroism that they belonged to a race whose savage virtues afford a sure basis upon which a higher civilization may yet be engrafted.

PERIOD IV.

FRANCE AND ENGLAND CONTEND FOR THE POSSESSION OF THE OHIO VALLEY.

CHAPTER I.

POLICY OF FRANCE—HER INDIAN ALLIES—POLICY OF ENGLAND—THE IROQUOIS—SIR WILLIAM JOHNSON—THE OHIO COMPANY—WASHINGTON.

THE close of the seventeenth century was marked by events which excite in us a more than usual degree of interest. The settlements made at Biloxi, and on other parts of the open shores of the Gulf of Mexico, during the latter years of this century, were followed by the location of others in the Mississippi Valley. New Orleans was founded in 1719. La Salle by his exploration of the Mississippi River had developed important facts in North American geography. Such a river, with such a valley, could be paralleled in the Old World only by the Nile, the Ganges, and the Niger, and in the New only by the Amazon, the La Plata, and the Orinoco of South America. But those streams, although flowing through regions possessing an equally fertile soil, are excelled by the Mississippi in the climate and sanitary advantages of the country in its vicinage.

The foundation of the city of New Orleans furnished a depôt for the products of a region whose extent and resources could scarcely be estimated. This entire territory, extending to the sources of the Arkansas, the Ohio, and the Missouri, as well as to the great chain of lakes, was filled with Indians of various names and families, who roved in wild independence over its plains and through its forests, contributing to a new and attractive branch of commerce,—the fur-trade. To wield political influence among them was, in fact, to secure the most direct means of promoting colonial success. The fine sylvan country of the Illinois had from the period of its first discovery been the universal theme of admiration. At an early day the French were not only established at Kaskaskia and Cahokia, but their settlements, having become the head-quarters of ecclesiastical and commercial functionaries, were continued up the Wabash, the Ohio, the Illinois, and the Wisconsin, where they were met by similar establishments diverging from Quebec and Montreal. From this period may be dated the renewed prosperity of New France.

Fort Niagara, which commanded the Iroquois borders, had been founded as early as 1679; Michilimackinac, on the upper lakes, was erected in 1686; Fort Oswego, the ancient Glinna, was built in 1727, Detroit in 1701, Vincennes in 1710, and a short time subsequently a series of minor posts extending along the lake shores from Green Bay and St. Joseph's to the Miami (Maumee) of the Lakes, and the Sandusky, and thence to Presque Isle, on Lake Erie. Among all the Indian tribes inhabiting these regions the French king, French power and liberality, and French manners were spoken of with praise and regarded with admiration.

The social teachings and manners of the French, so opposite to those of the English, furnish a true means of estimating the relative positions held by the two leading races of Europe, who were so long opposed to each other on this continent, in the estimation of the Indians. The French peasantry, who were in constant intercourse with them, did not themselves profess or practise a very high standard of morality, and were therefore the more acceptable to the natives, whose customs, manners, and opinions they at once adopted. They never ridiculed their religious rites, and freely selected their wives from the tribes among whom they pursued their vocations as boatmen, " merchant voyageurs," and runners to collect credits in the fur-trade. The *coureur des bois* and the Indian resembled each other in a thousand little notions regarding tastes, food, and dress. The Frenchman did not think the wigwam a dirty or disgusting place, and he went to gaze with complacency at the Indians' wabeno and medicine dances. He was not sure that necromancy and spirit-worship were altogether wrong, readily learned the Indian language, fabricated canoes of the finest pattern, and soon acquired a reputation superior even to that of the Indians for navigating these light and beautiful vessels. He smoked the Indian's sacred weed as they socially travelled together, and the native, under the guidance of his white friend, chanted the Frenchman's gay songs with the liveliest emotion. In his social chats the Frenchman represented the "Grand Monarque" as superior to all other sovereigns, and contrasted the relative power of the kings of England and France with a partiality that placed the latter above all comparison. To interest the Indian, conversation must be plain, simple, and adapted to his comprehension, and in these characteristics no class of persons have ever equalled the French.

Such was the progress made by her new ecclesiastical establishments that a commissioner of high standing was deputed by the court of France to visit the Western posts and tribes. Charlevoix, who performed this task, and whose journal and history furnish proofs of the zeal and learning he displayed, journeyed from Quebec through the chain of lakes to the Mississippi, which, in 1721, he descended to New Orleans. He made a thorough investigation into the history and condition of the tribes, the results of which he reported to his government. In his era the worship of an eternal fire was still found to exist among the Natchez, or Chigantualga Indians, who accompanied its rites with imposing ceremonies.

The possession of the Mississippi Valley was in reality the prize for which all these exertions were made, and the British colonies soon became aware that a chain of military posts, extending from New Orleans to Quebec, was about to environ them.

Under the rule of Frontenac, the ablest of Canadian statesmen, occurred the first serious collision of the rival powers, marking the opening of the grand scheme of military occupation by which France strove to secure pre-eminence in the New World. One of Frontenac's first measures was the erection on Lake Ontario of the fort bearing his name. He had remarkable tact in dealing with the Indians, conforming to their ways, borrowing their rhetoric, flattering them adroitly, and yet constantly maintaining towards them an attitude of paternal superiority. His plans would probably have succeeded, but for the miserable colonial policy of France. This was restrictive in spirit, favored monopolies, and taught the colonists to look to the home government upon all occasions instead of relying upon themselves. This lesson they might have learned from their neighbors, the English colonists, whose planting and growth afforded a striking exemplification of the opposite policy.

In 1687 the Canadian authorities with great formality repossessed themselves of the Straits of Detroit, commemorating the event by the issue of a protocol. In 1749 the Governor-General of Canada caused leaden plates, bearing suitable inscriptions, to be nailed to trees, and others to be buried beneath the earth, in the Ohio Valley, as a testimony of the reoccupation of that valley by the French. They aimed at least to make the record strong. But a fraction over fifty years had elapsed when these posts were extended up the Ohio to its source at the junction of the Monongahela and the Alleghany, where Fort Du Quesne was built in 1753. The comprehensive and vigorous movements of the French secured the influence of the tribes, whom they supplied with goods, wares, and merchandise at all the posts. Virginia, the Carolinas, Pennsylvania, and Maryland were the first to take the alarm. The French assumed the sovereignty of the country by right of its discovery by La Salle, and in a short time the Western tribes attacked the Southern and Western frontiers with a vigor which threatened the annihilation of the colonies.

In 1728 the Shawnees and Delawares, pressed by the Iroquois, and feeling the encroachments of the advancing settlements, fled across the Alleghanies to the Ohio Valley. The Iroquois power had long previously driven a part of the Lenni Lenape in the same direction.

It is estimated that in 1736, when at the height of their power in America, the French exercised a control over one hundred and three tribes, comprising a total of sixteen thousand four hundred and three warriors, and a population of eighty-two thousand souls. It no longer admitted of a doubt that the object of the French was, by drawing this line around the colonies, to prevent them from extending their possessions to the westward beyond the summits of the Alleghany Mountains. Such, indeed, was the boast of some of the leading Indian chiefs, who regarded the English as the nation which designed to infringe on their forest domains, to impose upon them the yoke of labor and letters, and to tread out their very existence. The sanguinary inroads of the French and their savage allies on the frontiers first brought the youthful Washington into the field. He was but sixteen years of age, when, in 1748, he made his first exploratory trip in that direction. Five years subsequently he undertook his perilous official journey to the French post on Lake Erie, thus obtaining his first knowledge of the habits of a subtle foe, whose instability of purpose and cruelty of character required perpetual vigilance.

With respect to the great lake basins, they were at an early date in possession of the French. Lake Ontario was commanded by Forts Cataraqui, Niagara, and Oswego, Erie was secured by the location of Fort Le Nou on the Straits of Detroit, and Lake Huron by Fort St. Joseph (the site of the modern Gratiot), situated at the head of the river St. Clair, as also by the old insular fort of Michilimackinac. Lake Superior was overlooked by the fort of St. Mary's, on the Straits of St. Mary, and by that of Madeline, at Chegoimegon; Michigan by a fort on Green Bay, by another at the mouth of the St. Joseph's River, and by the post at Chicago. Small vessels transported arms and supplies to the various posts, and the heavy bateaux of the French, or the light Algonkin canoes, kept up a constant intercourse between the posts and missions both by night and day. The English colonial governors, accustomed to the dilatory movements of their own regular soldiers and sailors, could scarcely conceive of the celerity with which intelligence was communicated.

The jealousy and hatred existing between the tribes prevented extensive hostile combinations against the English, and proved the salvation of the colonies. Every large tribe, from the era of the settlement of Virginia to that of Georgia, deemed itself superior to all others, boasted of its prowess, and despised its enemies. The continent had been overrun by predatory bands long before its discovery by the Europeans, and at that period the tribes were living in a state of intestine anarchy and outward war. When the colonists landed and began to hold intercourse with them, every little tribe exercised an independent sovereignty, sold lands, and prosecuted wars. Of the several stocks who claimed to live in a state of association or confederation, the Iroquois alone possessed anything like a fixed system. The Muskokis, or Creeks, assumed to be a confederacy of seven tribes, but their association was so loosely organized, so destitute of governmental power, that it could not make levies, procure volunteers, mete out punishments, or grant rewards. The Algonkins assimilated in their tribal character and peculiar customs, but every tribe acted as it pleased, without respect to any governmental rule. The seven tribes of the Dakotas styled themselves a united people; the Pokanokets went to war single-handed against all New England; the Tuscaroras determined to destroy North Carolina at a blow; the Yamassees undertook to brave, if not to cope with, South Carolina; and the tribe of the Foxes imprudently resolved, without any auxiliaries but the Sauks, or original occupants of Saginaw,[1] to drive the French out of Michigan.

The refractory tribes of New England, who had either submitted to the colonists or had been conquered by them and fled, derived sympathy and efficient aid from the Canadian authorities. The Pequot refugees, who had found shelter from the Mohawks and been permitted to settle on a tributary of the North River under the name of Schagticokes, finally fled to Lower Canada. The entire canton of St. Regis

---

[1] The modern Saginaws are renegades and refugees from the Chippewa stock, who fled to and reoccupied the original town abandoned by the Sauks.

originally comprised refugees of the Iroquois, who had refused to submit either to the religious teachings or to the political influence of the English.

The tribal and international movements throughout the entire country were controlled, with the sole exception of those of the important cantons of the Iroquois, by the general policy and influence of the French, and tended to the furtherance of the French colonial interests. It was observed at an early day by the English governors, and by the commanders on the frontiers, that a cordon of tribes friendly to the French occupied the whole of the immense line extending from Quebec to New Orleans, and every decade of the existence of the British colonies appeared to increase the apprehensions of evil impending from this quarter. This policy of the French was not a recent one, but can be traced back to the earliest times. From the period when Donnaconna was taken to France, and Agahonna was greeted as the forest monarch of Hochelaga, it had been a primary policy of the Gallic authorities to secure the influence of the Indian tribes. Two great stocks of tribes constituted the leading executors of the French policy.

Along the north shore of the St. Lawrence, from the Three Rivers as far as the entrance of the Ottawa River, the coast was occupied by tribes of the generic stock to whom was given the name of Algonkins. Both shores of the St. Lawrence, below the point denoted, as far down as Gaspé Bay, including Tadousac and the island of Orleans, were covered by parties of the Iroquois of the Wyandot branch. The governmental seat and council-fire of this tribe were located on the mountain-island of Hochelaga, to which Cartier gave the name of Montreal. A close alliance was formed with the Algonkin tribes, and also with the Wyandots, or Hurons. The Wyandots affirm themselves to have been the parent tribe of the Iroquois, and, although they do not appear to have been a member of the confederacy of the Five Nations, they were then on the most amicable terms with them. Their offence against the Five Nations was that they had offered their aid not only to the French, but also to the Algonkins, their enemies. As soon as this alliance with the French was understood, the Five Nations, at first moderately, but afterwards peremptorily and violently, ordered them to leave the island of Hochelaga and remove to New York. The Wyandots having refused to obey this mandate, the Iroquois made war upon them, and so harassed them that they were compelled to seek shelter under the guns of Quebec, in which place, even, they were not safe, but were finally expelled from the valley of the St. Lawrence. The French themselves were fiercely attacked, and at one time became seriously afraid that they would be driven from the country.

The flight of the Wyandots from the St. Lawrence Valley, in 1659, led to a great displacement of tribes. They passed up the great Ottawa River, and across Lake Nipissing to the Manitoulin chain of islands in Odawa Lake, which hence received the appellation of Huron, their French *nom de guerre*. But, the New York Iroquois having pursued them thither, they fled to the rocky island of Tiedonderoga, called Michilimackinac by the Algonkins, with whom they were in close alliance, as they had originally been in Lower Canada. Remarkable evidences of their residence in the interior of this island, and also of their agricultural habits, may still be traced in the large spaces which were cultivated, and which are yet very conspicuous. Of these, the area called by the French Le Grand Jardin, and the ground about Sugar-Loaf and Arched Rocks, will amply repay a visit from the curious. Pursued hither by the Iroquois, they took shelter on Lake Superior. Being followed to that retreat, the Iroquois were defeated by the Algics at Point Iroquois, in the Chippewa country. A sanguinary battle, followed by a massacre, was fought on the cape at the left-hand entrance into that lake, which has since been called Point Iroquois.

Prior to the flight of the Wyandots from the St. Lawrence, a nation of Algonkin lineage called by old writers Utawawas and Atawawas, and by modern ones Odawas and Ottawas, resided on the chain of islands in Lake Huron called Manitoulins, or Islands of the Great Spirit. Portions of this nation participated in the early wars in Lower Canada, and were taught the truths of the Christian religion by the missionaries. The parent tribe had for a long period dwelt on the islands of the Great Spirit, and the lake itself was in consequence called Odawa Lake. At the same period another leading tribe, of diverse lineage, called the Assegun or Bone Indians, resided on the upper parts of the lake. Their council-fire and tribal seat were established on the island of Michilimackinac. They occupied Point St. Ignace, and also the northern shores of the lake as low down as the influx of the St. Mary's River, and likewise extended their possessions westward and northward along the shores and islands of Lake Michigan.

To their position on the Manitoulins the Ottawas refer as the oldest traditional point in their history. Personal bravery, united with the power of performing miraculous or extraordinary feats through the influence of necromancy, was their great object of attainment, and formed a theme for boasting among their heroes. The origin of the tribe they attribute to a renowned personage whom they called Sagima. Sagima had been celebrated during his prime for deeds of prowess and wisdom, and for his great magic powers. But he was now tottering under the weight of accumulated years; his brethren had classed him as an Akiwazi, or one long above ground, and he was soon destined to take his long-anticipated journey to the land of the departed, or Indian paradise. Sagima resided with his wife, and had four sons,—namely, Wau-be-nace, Wauba, Gitchie Wedau, and the youngest, named after himself, Sagima. It is of the feats of the latter, who was the favorite son, that tradition speaks, for he was not only the pride of his parents, but was also endowed with all the intrepidity, wisdom, and magical power of his father. In his youth he was noted for his eccentricities and foolhardy exploits; when he reached the period of manhood he evinced great powers of endurance, frequently fasting ten days, and, after tasting a little food, renewing his fast; and when his future guardian spirit was revealed to him it was the Great Serpent, or Gitchie Kinabik, who lives under the ground and water.

At this time the Asseguns began to trespass on the territory of the Manitoulins, and killed some of their people. A war with this tribe was the result. Accompanying the warriors, at first as a young volunteer, and concealing the great powers he felt conscious of possessing, Sagima performed feats which drew all eyes upon him. He soon became an efficient warrior, and in the end the deliverer of his country. In this contest the Manitoulins were aided by the Ojibwas, or Chippewas. The first great battle with the Bone Indians was fought on the peninsula called by the French Détour. Sagima then pursued his enemies westward to their intrenchments on the northern shore, near some mounds and bivouacs the remains of which are still to be seen northward of St. Ignace. From this position he dislodged them, and took possession of the territory up to Point St. Ignace, where the war terminated, and the Asseguns, crossing the strait to the headland called Piqutinong, the locality where old Fort Michilimackinac was subsequently built by the French, there formed a village. Having conquered the country of the Bone Indians, the Ottawas gradually withdrew from the Manitoulins and located their tribal seat at St. Ignace. The following spring the Asseguns crossed over and killed an Ottawa woman who was planting corn. Sagima raised a war-party and crossed the strait to the Assegun village, which was found to contain only old men, women, and children, the warriors having gone up the Cheboygan, a river ten miles to the eastward. Sagima followed their trail, discovered their canoes hidden in the overhanging bushes, and waylaid them in a shallow, sandy bay. The returning Asseguns were attacked at a disadvantage, and a dreadful massacre followed.

After this event the Asseguns fled to the eastern shores of Lake Michigan, but they were finally pursued south to the banks of the Washtenaw, called by the French Grand River. This formed the limit of the conquests of the Ottawas, and thence they returned to their tribal seat at St. Ignace. The Chippewas, who had been their confederates in this war, settled on Grand Traverse Bay, and at some other locations to the westward, where relics of the two tribes still reside in villages.

During the prosecution of this war on the shores of Lake Michigan the Ottawas and Chippewas became involved in a quarrel with a tribe called by early writers Mascoutins, a term apparently derived from the phrase Mush-co-dains-ug, or Little Prairie Indians. These Indians appear to have allied themselves with the Bone Indians. Clusco, an aged Ottawa, conversant with their traditions, attributes to them the old cleared fields and the mounds on the Michigan coast, particularly those on Grand River. From this period the Asseguns and Mascoutins were confederates. The Ottawas and Chippewas, as soon as practicable, pursued them beyond Washtenaw River to Chicago, whence they fled towards the south and west; and from this point no further trace of them can be found in the Indian traditions.

In an official report of the Indian tribes made to the government of Canada in 1736, the Mascoutins are designated as occupying the locality south of Green Bay, and are rated at eighty warriors, which would indicate a population of four hundred souls. Bouquet and Hutchins, in their tables, formed in 1764, report them as occupying the same locality, and state their numbers at five hundred. Modern estimates make no mention of the tribe. In traits and habits the Mascoutins closely resembled the Kickapoos, and they possibly have been absorbed in that very nomadic, prairie-loving tribe.

Regarding the Asseguns, referred to in their traditions as the predecessors of the Algonkins on the upper waters of Lake Huron, it would be hazardous to offer any conjecture except one founded on philology, their name appearing to assimilate with the French term Osages, and they were very probably of the Dakota or Iroquois stock.

To the events preceding the Assegun wars we can add no chronology. It seems certain that they occurred prior to the flight of the Wyandots to the lakes, in 1649; for when, in this year, the latter reached the Manitoulin group, they found it vacated by the Ottawas, and located their residence on it; hence, as before mentioned, the lake received the name of Huron. Having been allies of the Ottawas and other Algonkins in the St. Lawrence Valley, they were welcomed as friends. Their residence on the island of Michilimackinac under Adario, in 1688, is mentioned by early writers, and, although they were obliged for a time to take shelter among the Chippewas of Lake Superior, the growth of the French colony of Detroit enabled the latter to invite them to locate themselves in that vicinity, where for so long a period they occupied a conspicuous place as the umpire tribe.

By this transfer of the Wyandots to the lakes the Algonkin tribes were in reality strengthened, for they came thither as friends. By the prior expulsion of the Asseguns and Mascoutins, the wide lake-basins had been cleared of all tribes who were adverse to their rule, and they had secured the free use of their lakes as well as of their hunting-grounds. They now began fearlessly to cross the broad waters in their canoes, and soon felt themselves established in the magnificent geographical empire of the great lakes. From the northern limits of Lake Huron, through the Straits of St. Mary to Lake Superior, and from Michilimackinac, around the far-spreading shores of Lakes Huron and Michigan, thence eastwardly to Detroit, and southwardly to the Ohio, there were no languages spoken but those which were derived, more or less recently, from the Algonkin. This generic language was of mild and easy utterance, and possessed a full vocabulary, containing but few sounds not readily enunciated by either the French or the English. The members of these tribes were people of good stature and pleasing manners, who readily adopted European modes of conducting their traffic and of transacting business. They borrowed from the French the complimentary term *bon jour* on meeting, having in their own language no equivalent for that of good-day. If we examine the Algonkin people which extended south from the site of Chicago to Kaskaskia and the mouth of the Ohio, and north to the Crees, near the Lake of the Woods, we shall find a singular agreement of character. There was no tribe in all the broad expanse of country named which did not recognize the French standard as the most desirable one in matters of civilization and religion.

The French now attempted, by taking formal possession of the Ohio Valley, to unite the extreme boundaries of New France and thus prevent the extension of the English colonies.

The expulsion of the Asseguns, or Bone Indians, and of the Mascoutins, from the lake region, in all probability occurred before the close of the sixteenth century, or prior, at least, to the first landing of Europeans. No notice of it can be found in the works of the earliest writers; the Wasashas,[1] a bold, turbulent tribe, who may be thought to correspond in character with that people, having been at a primeval period located in the North, but after their flight to the South always on an affluent of the Missouri. Their traditions furnish nothing but an allegory representing that their origin was derived from a beaver and a shell. If these are symbols, they denote that they lived in a region abounding in trees (the bark of which was their food) and fish, and that their state of life was fortuitous from natural and not from historical causes.

It is uncertain at how early a period the French visited Lake Huron and the upper lakes, but their first journey thither probably occurred between the year 1608 and Champlain's surrender of Quebec to Kirk, in 1629. Whatever the period was, the Algonkins seem to have then exercised dominion in the country. The Mascoutins, who by the name appear to have been of Algonkin lineage, were then located in that territory. The Illinese occupied the valley of the Illinois, and also the left banks of the Mississippi from its outlet to the influx of the Ohio. The Miamis were seated in the St. Joseph's and Grand River valleys of Michigan, and the various bands called Michigamies on the shores of Lake Michigan. The Menomonies occupied the northern shores of Green Bay, and even as early as 1636 the Mascoutins had been driven to the country lying south of the banks of Fox River. The only acknowledged trans-Mississippian Indian tribe residing on Green Bay was that of the Winnebagoes, which, although of Dakota origin, had an Algonkin name and lived in amity with the Algonkins.

That the French succeeded in arraying the numerous and scattered tribes of the Algonkins against the English colonies, is well known to every reader of Americo-Indian history. Intercourse and habits made them one in feeling and policy. Although it has been suggested that the Indian tribes appeared to feel a sense of their ability to crush the primitive English colonies, yet they lacked the power of combination to make any general movement for that purpose. At every phase of their history they felt the necessity of having a European basis of power upon which to lean. In other words, they sought to be allies, and not principals, in the great contests with the colonies, and were in reality the flankers, and rarely or never the main body of fighting-men. From this preference for the French the Algonkin family of the Lenni Lenape may be excepted, for they were friends of the English prior to 1742. In a public council held at Lancaster during this year they were ordered by the Iroquois, in a very harsh manner, to remove from the lands they occupied, because they had sold them to Penn, or to other persons, without having received authority. They were directed to take up their residence in the West, and from this date the Delawares were regarded as being under French influence. Such suspicions gathered strength from year to year, and this influence followed them

---

[1] It may be that Osages is a term derivative from Wasashas: if so, little stress can be laid on the supposed recognition.

westward, until they became residents of the Muskingum Valley, where the Christian Delawares were at length massacred.

It was the early-developed policy of the French to employ against the frontier settlements the Indian forces at their command, a power eminently calculated to annoy and harass, and without which it does not seem probable that the French could have so long maintained their ground against the British colonies. Indian warfare is conducted by a species of guerilla force, which in efficacy exceeds all other kinds of irregular warfare, not only on account of its sanguinary character, but also because of the suddenness of its attacks, its entire freedom from the annoyances of baggage, and the alacrity with which the warriors charge and disperse. There is no regular military arm which can at all cope with, or successfully check, these guerilla parties, as it is their policy never to risk an open battle; consequently, when the clumsy infantry and dragoon soldier is sent into the woods to cope with such a supple and nearly invisible enemy, he appears to be little more than a target for a ball or an arrow.

A review of the colonial policy of the French, from the days of Champlain to those of Montcalm, develops the fact that the Indian power was always one of their most effective means of offence. The great conflicts on land and ocean did not produce great results; but during all this period, extending over one hundred and fifty years, it was the Indian war-parties and marauding expeditions, which infested the frontiers from Virginia to New England, that committed deeds of the most atrocious violence. Men, women, and children sent unheralded into eternity at midnight by the war-club and the scalping-knife, blazing tenements, cruel and prolonged captivities, death at the stake, and murder in its most horrid forms, constituted the main incidents of this epoch.

An Indian considers one hundred miles but a short distance, and one thousand miles as not a long one to march, when the purpose he has in view is to glut his vengeance or gratify himself. He is not a man who pines for the enjoyments of home; there is not much to attach him to it; to camp in the woods is his delight, and the wilderness is his dwelling. Time passes lightly with him, and anything which cheats him of the very idea of its passage is pleasant. He is always at leisure, and death itself receives a rather friendly welcome. To journey to Fort Du Quesne, Erie, Oswego, Niagara, or Quebec for the trifling present of a gun, a blanket, a kettle, a pound of powder, a gorget, or a flag, was in point of enterprise considered as nothing for an Indian chief. To him, to whom time was nothing and wandering a pleasure, the toil was ten times overpaid by the reward. The Indian naturally esteems gifts, and habitually loves the giver. The Frenchman was to the Indian the *beau idéal* of all that was admirable in a foreign race, combining generosity with amiable friendliness and kindness of demeanor.

The French most surely extended their influence by multiplying forts on the frontiers. They had from an early period occupied positions on every important Western river or lake, and by taking formal possession of the Ohio Valley, in 1753, they consummated a long-cherished scheme, and environed the Western colonies with a cincture as of scorpions. Western Virginia and Pennsylvania groaned under new inflictions of savage vengeance; and from this time the Indian forays on the Western frontiers became incessant, being unexampled in our history for their frequency, and for the barbarous inhumanity which characterized them,—murders, ambuscades, and tortures becoming the terror of the settlers. Not the least important feature in the policy which directed these Indian wars was the countenance they received from the French officials at Vincennes, Kaskaskia, Fort Chartres, Detroit, Miami, Sandusky, and other minor posts. It was these depredations, and the policy which directed them, that first brought Washington into the field.

The Gallic and Anglo-Saxon powers were now fairly pitted against each other, and it was evident that this new aspect of French aggression must soon lead to a general conflict. France or England must rule America. The British ministry had in some measure prepared for this struggle. The local commerce had necessitated the erection of Fort Loudon, in the Valley of Virginia. Fort Cumberland had been previously built on Wills Creek, Fort Stanwix at the head of the Mohawk, and Fort Anne on the sources of the Hudson. Fort Edward, also on the Hudson, and Fort William Henry, on Lake George, were soon afterwards constructed. These formed the chief defences in the middle of the eighteenth century, and after the close of Queen Anne's war the colonists were supported by occasional detachments of veteran troops who had served under the Duke of Marlborough and other distinguished officers. These forts served as defences to the frontiers, enabling the colonies to preserve their existence, but they were not sufficiently powerful to roll back the tide of aggression.

At this period, as already stated, France had seized and guarded by a series of skilfully-distributed posts the lakes and streams—those thoroughfares of the wilderness—between her settlements in the valley of the St. Lawrence and the mouth of the Mississippi. A fort at Niagara commanded the interior country, at Detroit the passage from Lake Erie to the north was guarded, and at St. Mary's hostile access to Lake Superior was barred. Michilimackinac secured the mouth of Lake Michigan; posts at Green Bay and St. Joseph protected the two routes to the Mississippi by the rivers Wisconsin and Illinois, while those on the Wabash and the Maumee gave France control of the trade from Lake Erie to the Ohio. French settlements were found at Kaskaskia and Cahokia, in Illinois, and a few small stockades were seen on the Mississippi.

To counteract this policy the English found it necessary to call in the aid of the Iroquois cantons. The Indian is more gratified with a present of ten dollars' worth of merchandise than if he were to receive twenty times the value in money as a permanent annuity. Early partakers of the benefits resulting from Anglo-Saxon proximity of settlement and commerce, the Iroquois became firm friends to all who belonged to that race. The warlike Mohawks were the most prominent tribe in the confederacy at the time of the discovery of the Hudson. They found a very good market for their furs, which rendered them affluent in every comfort of Indian life, and they adhered to their early relations with unchanging steadiness. After being furnished with guns, the Mohawks revisited Lake Champlain, where they encountered the renewed energies of Canada, and in a short time induced all the cantons to join them. Another great advantage accrued to them at this period in the employment of fire-arms against their enemies at the South and West. The introduction of gunpowder into America revolutionized the entire Indian mode of life. Their expeditions not only became more lengthy, but were also characterized by greater frequency, and in a short time no tribe could withstand them. Ambition stimulated every canton, and before the surrender of the province to the English, in 1664, the council-fire at Onondaga burned still more brightly and fiercely. Unaided by this influence, New York, as well as the Northern and Central British colonies, could not have protected so wide a frontier without any extraneous aid. They frustrated the plan for establishing a mission at the old French fields, in Madison County, as also at Onondaga, in Western New York. They likewise defeated the armies of Frontenac and of Denonville.

An agency was also established in the Iroquois country, which, from little beginnings, at length systematically controlled this power for the protection and furtherance of the interests of the English colonies. This was the one which became so celebrated under the management of Sir William Johnson. Johnson emigrated to America in 1734, and, having undertaken the management of an estate in the Mohawk Valley for Sir Peter Warren, embarked in the fur-trade and learned the Indian language. He frequently accompanied the Iroquois delegates who went to Albany to transact business with the government, and therein evinced so much tact, and so intimate a knowledge of the Indian dialects, that in a few years the superintendency of this department of government in the British colonies was committed to his care. The Iroquois had been constantly gaining in power during the previous century, and the authority which they now exercised over the tribes in the North, South, and West enabled Johnson, through their means, to exert a controlling influence. He combined within himself the faculties of close observation, great prudence, judgment, decision, energy, and courage. By his judicious management of affairs, and of a large private estate, he at once acquired a just appreciation of Indian character, and great popularity with the Iroquois. His Indian policy imitated and even surpassed in efficiency that of the French. He paid the utmost deference to their ancient ceremonial, not to say Oriental, mode of transacting public business. He received their delegates and foreign ambassadors with great ceremony, listened to them patiently, answered them carefully, made them liberal and judicious presents, and ordered every attention to be paid to their personal wants. No Indian who came to him ever went away hungry or in want from his agency, and no one ever complained that he had not received an audience. The Indian is always greatly influenced by the respect with which he is received; no European can be more so. He has a high opinion of himself, of his position, and of his destiny; he does not know that he is a savage; he does not feel the want of our knowledge, our letters, our religion; he is a patient, courteous, dignified listener; he watches the features and expression of his interlocutor with great attention, and is a good judge of general character; he is prone to approbativeness, values approval, appreciates kindness, and is altogether reliable as a personal friend.

Such were the materials of the power which Johnson undertook to control. He regarded the proud, noble, but untutored Mohawk, Oneida, Onondaga, Cayuga, and Seneca sachems, with their principle of cantonal representation and confederate unity, as in some measure a reproduction of the Amphictyonic Council. He sent formal messages to them requesting their attendance whenever occasion required it. This careful attention greatly pleased them. Meeting together in council, they transmitted the message to the most distant places. Under the honored title of Mingoes, portions of the Iroquois stock resided in the Ohio Valley, and served as diplomatic agents to communicate intelligence. The most distant valleys of the West, and the remotest lakes of the North, were thus made accessible; and the affairs of the Illinois, and of the tribes of Michilimackinac, Detroit, Niagara, and Oswego, were as well understood at his nominal seat on Tribes Hill, in the Mohawk Valley, as were those of Genesee, Albany, and the Cahoatatea. The high rank which Johnson held in the New York militia caused him to be employed on some of the most important services, and he achieved several momentous victories in the war with the French. No one can peruse the history of New York, Pennsylvania, Maryland, or Virginia, or even of the States farther South, from the beginning of the eighteenth century to the era of the Revolutionary War, without observing how intimately the Indian policy of these colonies was connected with the Iroquois supremacy, and how completely Sir William controlled it through a well-established system of subordinates. Governors of colonies thought it no derogation from their dignity to meet the delegated Iroquois sachems in general council, and the Iroquois sanction was deemed essential to all purchases of land and questions of boundary, even to the utmost limits of Virginia and Kentucky.

The struggle which was at this period impending on the Western frontiers was not only for the possession of supremacy on the Ohio, but in fact, as became apparent in a few years, for the control of the entire Mississippi Valley. It was a contest which would decide whether France or England should govern in North America. The Indians were so far a party to the contest that it was necessary for each nation to pay its court to them, and there was no surer method of acquiring their good will than by respecting their ancient mode of holding councils and paying due reverence to their ceremonial rites and customs. To smoke a national pipe, to deliver a belt of wampum beads, to present a chief with a medal or a flag, were in their eyes acts of the most momentous importance. To do nothing in a hurry, to deliberate slowly, to measure, as it were, the importance of events by the time devoted to the performance of their ceremonies, were to the Indians very pleasing evidences of capacity for negotiation. When an Indian orator arose and pointed to the zenith, to the nadir, to the place of the sun and moon, and to the cardinal points, he fancied himself to be surrounded by a pantheon of supernal and spiritual influences. He loved this pomp of ceremonies, and he felt complimented to see a European official respect them. Trifles lead to success.

It has been mentioned that the inroads of the Indians, which either preceded or succeeded the occupation of the Ohio Valley by the French, had the effect of bringing Washington into that field of adventurous action. He was but sixteen when he first began his explorations on the Alleghany chain. Five years of manly exercise and experience in the life of woodcraft, surveying, and exploration had given him a shrewd insight into Indian character, and prepared him for further and more important trusts in a department of service requiring, above all others, perpetual vigilance and precaution ; and if, in the estimation of the Indians and the pioneers, he surpassed the others engaged with him, it was doubtless owing to the Indians' appreciation of the solidity of his character. Tanacharisson, who was the head sachem of the Mingo-Iroquois of the Ohio Valley, was the presiding chief in the first council or consultation in which Washington took part. In fact, Tanacharisson was well known among the tribes, and performed at the place of his residence the duties of a kind of *chargé-d'affaires*, just as the half-king, Scarooyadi, did on the Juniata, and Skilelamo on the Susquehanna. Favorably impressed from the first, the Indian chief remained a firm friend of the enterprising Virginian to the day of his death.

The double interest created by the fine soil and climate of Ohio, and by apprehension of the hostility of its native tribes, strongly directed the minds of Virginians to that quarter, and at sundry times they despatched agents to visit the country and report its position, its resources, and the feelings of the Indians. Among these reconnoissances, those of Croghan, Gist, and Trent constitute marked epochs in the history of Indian policy and sentiments. The result of these missions, which extended to the Wabash and the Scioto, denoted that French influence was predominant, and that the Algonkin tribes generally were in close alliance with that power, while the Mingoes expressed friendly opinions of the English. From a remark made by a Delaware sachem to one of their agents, it appeared to be a question, not whether the Indians possessed or wished to occupy any part of the country, but simply whether the French or the English should have possession of it. A year or two passed in rather fruitless efforts to obtain a better knowledge of Indian affairs in Ohio, and in endeavors to adjust matters on a firmer footing.

In 1749 a royal grant of six hundred thousand acres, on the Ohio River, was made to a number of English merchants and Virginia planters, who, under the name of the Ohio Company, had associated for the ostensible purpose of trade. The establishment of this company was the first intimation to the French of the intention of the English to prosecute their claims. They viewed it as a step towards wresting the Indian trade from them and breaking the connection between New France and Louisiana. They at once resolved on defensive measures, and seized some English traders near the present site of Pittsburg, whom they conveyed to Presque Isle, now Erie. In retaliation for this outrage, the Twightwees, a friendly tribe, seized some French traders and sent them to Pennsylvania." Finally, the French began the erection of posts on the south side of Lake Erie, sending troops across the lakes with munitions of war, and forwarding bodies of armed men from

New Orleans. One fort was built at Presque Isle, another at Le Bœuf (now Waterford, Pennsylvania), and a third at Venango (now Franklin, Pennsylvania), at the junction of French Creek with the Alleghany River.

The Ohio Company having complained of these aggressions, Governor Dinwiddie deemed it proper to send an agent to the French authorities at the post of Presque Isle, on Lake Erie, and committed the trust to Washington, whose experience on that frontier, together with his judgment and discretion, well qualified him for the task. Accompanied by a French interpreter, Washington left Williamsburg, the seat of government, on the 30th of October, 1753. He rode on horseback across the Alleghanies. At Cumberland Mr. Gist joined him as Indian interpreter, and at another point a second interpreter and four experienced woodsmen were added to his cavalcade. All the rivers were so swollen that he was compelled to swim the horses across. He reached the junction of the Monongahela and Alleghany Rivers (now the site of Pittsburg) without accident, and pointed out that spot as a suitable and desirable location for a fort. In that vicinity he found a Delaware sachem, named Shingiss, who gave him directions for finding Logstown, the residence of Tanacharisson, the half-king. He reached that place after sunset, but the chief was absent. He immediately sent runners to invite him to an interview, and the chief arrived at his lodge the next day. He discovered him to be intelligent, patriotic, and tenacious of his territorial rights. Washington received him with courtesy, and despatched messengers to some of the other chiefs to invite them to a council. They arrived the following day, when he laid before them the purport of his instructions from the Governor of Virginia, and requested guides to conduct him to the French posts, and a safe-conduct on the way. A pause then ensued. The council having deliberated formally on the matter, the half-king arose, assumed an oratorical attitude, and gave his assent, declaring that the English and themselves were one people, and that he intended to return the French belts; thus, in the usual form of Indian diplomacy, rejecting the French overtures. Three days were occupied in summoning the Indians from their camps and securing their compliance, after which Washington was furnished with the required guides and aids. He was accompanied also by the half-king, by Jeskakake, a Shawnee, and by another chief, named the Belt-Keeper, or White Thunder. They reached the post of Venango, a distance of seventy miles, in four days. This was but an outpost of the fortress near Presque Isle. After witnessing some of the peculiar manœuvrings and intrigues of both French and Indian diplomacy, Washington proceeded to Presque Isle, where he was received with ceremonious politeness by the commandant, St. Pierre. The purport of these details is merely to demonstrate how the Indian character fluctuated under the operation of two diverse sets of counsels. Tanacharisson, the Mingo sachem, remained faithful to his professions, and informed Washington of the result of a secret council with St. Pierre, in which it was decided that a present of goods should be sent to secure the good will of his village at Logstown. The entire journey was fraught with unusual peril and hardship, being performed amid the severity of winter; and its results furnish us with a good view of Indian

character, swayed as it then was by the alternating emotions of hope and fear, and well illustrate the operation of motives of self-interest on the Indian mind. The mission was, however, unsuccessful. Early in the spring of 1754 the French under Contrecœur took possession of the point at the junction of the Alleghany and Monongahela Rivers, dislodging a party of men engaged in the same work under Captain Trent of the Virginia militia, and erected Fort Du Quesne. The English had been outgeneralled, and a fixed point established whence to control Indian action. The spirits of the Indian allies of the French had been raised to the highest pitch, and the power of the English colonists defied. This first overt act of hostility was the beginning of the Seven Years' French and Indian War, which terminated with the conquest of Canada.

CHAPTER II.

BRADDOCK'S DEFEAT.

CIVILIZED communities regard military success as, in most cases, the result of superior judgment, but with the Indians it is the effect of an impulsive, irresistible movement, under the operation of which judgment gives place to passion and they are incited to such infuriate action as to produce confusion in the ranks of the enemy. Fort Du Quesne had no sooner been established than it became a centre for the direction of Indian movements in the West. From far and near the Indians resorted to it. Feasts, dances, and the distribution of presents were the order of the day, and the vicinity resounded with shouts and songs. The frontiers of the English colonies were speedily subjected to Indian inroads. Dinwiddie, by his tardy movements, had lost his vantage-ground, and Virginia enterprise, though directed by its best men, failed to recover its former position. The year 1754 was characterized by alarms, murders, apprehension, the formation of plans, and their failure. There was no security on the frontiers from Carolina to Pennsylvania, nor in Western New York. The Catawbas and Cherokees had not been employed to counteract the movements of the Western Indians; this measure was not thought of in the zeal of the Ohio Company to effect settlements, or in the efforts of the local military forces to dislodge the French.

The Virginia Assembly voted ten thousand pounds sterling towards supporting the expeditions to the Ohio. The Carolinas voted twelve thousand pounds sterling. Three hundred men were to be raised, to be commanded by Colonel Joshua Fry, with Washington as his lieutenant. Arriving at Wills Creek April 20, Washington, learning that Trent's force had been dislodged, pushed forward with one hundred and fifty men to attempt to retrieve this loss, confident that Fry with a large force would speedily follow. Ascertaining from the half-king that a French force was about to attack him, he threw up an intrenchment near the Great Meadows, which he called Fort Necessity. On the 27th he surprised a French detachment of fifty men, and defeated them, De Jumonville, their commander, being killed. By the death of Colonel Fry at Wills Creek, the chief command of the expedition now devolved upon Washington, who, with only four hundred men, was marching to attack Fort Du Quesne, when, learning that the French had been reinforced and were marching towards him, he retreated to Fort Necessity, which he reached July 1, and which he at once proceeded to enlarge and strengthen. Two days later the French, seven hundred strong, under De Villiers, attacked the fort. After a brief defence, it was surrendered upon honorable terms. At the close of the year 1754, in the whole valley of the Mississippi there floated no other standard than that of France.

The year 1755 afforded but a gloomy prospect for the cause of the colonies. Never before, perhaps, had they been so boldly threatened by the combined power of the Indians and the French. The Alleghanies were the natural barriers between the East and the West. To retrieve their position in the West, and to open the way for future emigration beyond the Alleghanies, the British cabinet sent out two regiments of veteran troops, under the command of General Edward Braddock, a proud, highly disciplined soldier, who despised the Indians and deemed them incapable of making any impression on the solid columns of a regular army. He had learned the art of war on the battle-fields of Europe, and disdained all skulking and dodging, which form an essential element of success in Indian warfare. He underrated the colonial troops and frontiersmen, not only because they were not highly disciplined, but also because they had to some extent adopted the hunter mode of warfare. His landing at Alexandria (February 20), the glitter and parade of war which pervaded his movements, his councils with the colonial governors, and the fame of the expedition which was designed to cross the Alleghanies, filled the entire country. Braddock was clothed with the fullest powers by the king. Colonial governors waited upon him, and expectation had reached the highest pitch of excitement. Among those who were present at Alexandria was General William Johnson, charged by the New York colonial government with the control of Indian affairs in the Mohawk Valley and among the Iroquois. Braddock appointed him Superintendent-General of Indian affairs in America, clothed him with ample powers, and provided him with funds. Filling up his regiments with the best recruits, having an ample military chest, a well-arranged quartermaster's department, the most experienced guides and pioneers, and Washington himself as an aide in his personal staff, Braddock conquered every delay, and surmounted difficulties of a remarkable and novel character in conveying his troops and cannon over the intricate passes of the Alleghany range, and in reaching the dark and turbid waters of the Monongahela. But it is wonderful that, after this long and laborious march, during which a passage for his platoons had been cut through forests of thick trees, tangled with brushwood, and the artillery had been sometimes lowered over steep precipices by sailors with ropes, he should not have proposed to meet his savage foemen in the manner best calculated to defeat them, and that he turned a deaf ear to all the counsels of experience.

To Franklin, who told Braddock at Fredericksburg that the Indians were dexterous in planning and executing ambuscades, he replied, "The savages may be formidable to your raw American militia; upon the king's regulars and disciplined troops it is impossible they should make any impression. After taking Fort Du Quesne, I am to proceed to Niagara, and, having taken that, to Frontenac. Du Quesne can hardly detain me above three or four days, and then I see nothing that can obstruct my march to Niagara." Franklin's exertions, backed by his great influence in Pennsylvania, supplied the army with horses and carriages, for want of which it had halted at Fredericksburg, unable to move,—a feat that extorted praise from Braddock, and for which Franklin received the unanimous thanks of the

Assembly of Pennsylvania. Among the wagoners employed on this occasion was Daniel Morgan, the future hero of the Cowpens, who, by saving his wages as a day-laborer, had become the owner of a team.

Up to the fatal 9th of July, the army, in a slender line nearly four miles in length, marched through a narrow passage, twelve feet wide, cut through a dense forest into which the eye could scarcely penetrate.

Braddock's force consisted of about two thousand men, one thousand of whom were provincials, among them two companies from New York under Captain Horatio Gates. The advanced division, led by the general in person, consisted of twelve hundred men; the other, under Colonel Dunbar, remained in the rear. Braddock reached the junction of the Youghiogheny and Monongahela Rivers, within fifteen miles of Fort Du Quesne, July 8; at noon of the 9th they were but seven miles from the fort. A detachment of three hundred and fifty men, led by Lieutenant-Colonel Thomas Gage, attended by a working party of two hundred and fifty, was advancing cautiously with guides and flanking parties towards the fort, followed by the general with the artillery, baggage, and the main body of the army, when a very heavy and rapid firing was heard at the front.

Contrecœur, the French commander, informed of the approach of Braddock, and doubtful of his ability to maintain his post, had contemplated its abandonment, when Captain De Beaujeu proposed to head a detachment of French and Indians and meet the English while on their march. This plan was adopted, and on the morning of July 9, with less than nine hundred French and Indians, Beaujeu set out, intending to make the attack at the second crossing of the river. Arriving too late at this point, they posted themselves in the woods and ravines on the line of march towards the fort.

It was one o'clock when, under the rays of a July sun, the British reached the north side of the Monongahela. A level plain extended nearly half a mile northward to a rise, beyond which were higher elevations, thickly wooded, and furrowed by narrow ravines. Just as Gage with the advance was ascending this slope, a heavy volley from the unseen foe was poured into his ranks from the dark woods in his front. Gage's failure promptly to support his flanking parties lost the day. The British fired at random, while the concealed enemy, from behind trees and rocks and bushes, kept up his rapid and destructive volleys. Beaujeu, the French leader, was killed at the first return fire, and M. Dumas took his place. Braddock made all possible haste to relieve his advanced guard, but the panic-stricken soldiers fell back in confusion upon the artillery, and communicated their fright to the whole army. The general tried in vain to rally his troops. He and his officers were in the thickest of the fight, and exhibited indomitable courage. Washington ventured to suggest the propriety of adopting the Indian mode of warfare, each firing for himself without orders, but Braddock would not listen to him. For three hours he tried to form his men into regular columns and platoons, while his concealed enemy with sure aim was slaying his brave soldiers by scores. At length he received a wound which disabled him and terminated his life three days afterwards. Every mounted officer except Washington was slain before Braddock fell, and the whole duty of distributing orders devolved upon him, while from recent illness he was scarcely fit to be in the saddle. Two horses were shot under him, and four bullets perforated his clothing. His Virginians, adopting, contrary to orders, the Indian mode of fighting, did more execution than all the others, and saved the remnant of the army. "That proud army which had that morning crossed the Monongahela in such gallant array, with drums beating and colors flying, fled like sheep before wolves, abandoning their cannon, their arms and ammunition, and even their wounded, to their savage foes." Of three companies, scarcely thirty men were left alive. Secretary Shirley and Sir Peter Halket were killed. Among the wounded were Colonels Burton, St. Clair, and Orne, Lieutenant-Colonel Gage, Major Sparks, and Brigade-Major Halket. Five captains were killed, and five wounded. Out of eighty-six officers, sixty-three were killed or wounded. The loss of privates was seven hundred and fourteen, one-half of whom were killed. Of the enemy, only three officers and thirty men were killed, and about the same number wounded.

This defeat was effected by the Western and Northern Indians, who were chiefly of Algonkin lineage. The French Indians from the lakes were present in great force, and it has been surmised that Pontiac himself was their leader. The Iroquois were not on the field in their tribal character, although some Mingoes and Senecas were present. Johnson had urged the necessity of sending the warriors with Braddock, but they declined. The utmost result of his efforts was that they promised not to oppose him.

It is an error to suppose that Braddock was the only one who placed no faith in the efficiency of Indian guerilla warfare. Educated military men in all ages of our history have been prone to undervalue the Indian system, and these opinions are held by some officers at the present day. While the battle is not always to the strong, it cannot be expected that David, with his sling, will always kill Goliath; but well-drilled armies must be efficiently protected on their flanks, and an accurate adaptation of means to ends must ever be preserved in the tangled forest, which cannot be penetrated, as well as on the level plain, where the view is uninterrupted. The heavy, camp-fed, clumsy-footed soldier is never a match in the forest for the light, active Indian warrior. A review of our Indian history from Braddock's day to the present era proves that a small Indian force in ambuscade will overmatch ten times its number of regular troops who adhere to the system of fighting in platoons. The regulars are either thrown into confusion, become panic-struck, are slaughtered in large numbers, or are totally defeated. Such was the result of Colonel Harmar's attempt to ford the Miami, and of St. Clair's to penetrate the Wabash woods. General Wayne, who was like a lion where there was an opportunity to fight, as at Stony Point, was obliged to abandon the ground on which Fort Recovery was subsequently built. During two entire years he contended against tribes of active warriors, whose fathers, nay, some of whom themselves, had fought against Braddock. It was not until caution had made him wise, and he had attained a true knowledge of Indian woodcraft, that he finally prevailed against them on the Miami of the Lakes.

It was there that he met the Miamis, Piankeshaws, and Weas, under Little Turtle, and the same leaders who had opposed Harmar and St. Clair. They were leagued with the Chippewas, Ottawas, Pottawatomies, Delawares, Shawnees, and other Algonkin tribes, who, with the Wyandots, had overthrown Braddock. It is, however, by no means certain that if the ambuscade so successfully and warily constructed in a wide field of heavy grass at the Miami Rapids had been laid in a dense forest, where horses would have been useless, the result would not have been very different.

It has been asserted that there were but six hundred and thirty-seven Indians engaged in the action which resulted in Braddock's defeat. These consisted principally of Ottawas, Ojibwas, and Pottawatomies, from Michigan; Shawnees, from Grave Creek and the river Muskingum; Delawares, from the Susquehanna; Abenakis and Caughnawagas, from Canada; and Hurons, or Wyandots, from the mission of Lorette and the Montreal Falls, under Athanase, a Canadian. This force, including the recreant Abenakis, was, as may be seen, entirely of the Algonkin family, with the exception of the Hurons, a segregated Iroquois tribe who had always sided with the French, and a few "scattered warriors from the Six Nations." To this force were added one hundred and forty-six Canadian militia and seventy-two regular troops, who fought according to the Indian mode. It is impossible that such a defeat could have occurred under ordinary circumstances; and the fact conclusively attests the efficacy of an Indian auxiliary force as a vanguard to regular troops in a wild forest country, where they can screen themselves from observation and bid defiance to the death-dealing artillery or the attacks of dragoons.

CHAPTER III.

KITTANNING DESTROYED—BATTLE OF LAKE GEORGE—CAPTURE OF OSWEGO AND FORT WILLIAM HENRY.

THE sachem commissioner, Tanacharisson, and his successor, Scarooyadi, had evinced a firm friendship for the English on the Ohio border, in conformity with the general policy of the New York Iroquois tribes, while they at the same time freely condemned the English for their tardy movements and their non-adoption of the Indian mode of warfare.

The consequences of the defeat on the Monongahela were most disastrous. Rumor rapidly disseminated the news in every direction, and all the colonies felt the effects of the blow. The dread of Indian massacres disturbed the quiet of every hamlet; nor was their alarm without due foundation. A band of one hundred and fifty savages crossed the Alleghanies and ravaged the frontiers of Virginia and Maryland. Foremost in these forays were the Delawares, under Shingiss, whose ire appeared to have received an additional stimulus from the recent triumph of the Gallic-Indian forces. The Delawares had long felt the wrong which they suffered in being driven from the banks of the Delaware and the Susquehanna, although it was primarily owing to their ancient enemies and conquerors the Iroquois, whose policy had ever been a word and a blow.

In 1756, the Delawares, after ravaging the Pennsylvania border, returned to their village at Kittanning, within thirty-five miles of Fort Du Quesne. Three hundred Pennsylvanians, under Colonel John Armstrong, of Cumberland, of Scotch Presbyterian descent, marched across the Alleghanies to destroy them. The brave Hugh Mercer, who at twenty-three had shared in the defeat of the Pretender at Culloden, and who afterwards fell at Princeton, commanded one of the companies. At daybreak of October 8, while the Delawares were reposing in fancied security, the attack was made. Jacobs, their chief, raised the war-whoop. The wigwams having been set on fire, some of the warriors, disdaining captivity, sung their death-song in the flames. Jacobs and others were shot down while seeking to escape, and the town was utterly destroyed. Mercer, severely wounded, and separated from his companions, tracked his way by the stars to Fort Cumberland. For this exploit Colonel Armstrong was presented by the corporation of Philadelphia with a vote of thanks, a medal, and a piece of plate.

The Shawnees, friends and relatives of the Delawares, had been from the first a revengeful, warlike, roving people. Originating in the extreme South, they had flitted over half the continent, fighting with every tribe they encountered, until they reached the extreme shores of Lake Erie, where, under the ominous name of

Satanas,[1] they were defeated by the Iroquois, and thence fled to the Delaware, and subsequently to the Ohio Valley. From an early period they were avowed enemies of the colonies, and this enmity never ceased until after the overthrow, in 1814, of the wide-spread conspiracy of Tecumseh. Both tribes, in lineage as well as in language, were Algoukins, and adopted their policy, from first to last being cruel enemies in war, in peace treacherous friends.

While the gloom caused by the defeat of Braddock, and the evidences of Indian hostility, which assumed a tangible shape during the autumn and winter of 1753, still hung like a cloud on the Western frontier, an auspicious sign appeared in the East. The Iroquois threw the weight of their influence into the English scale. It having been a part of the original plan of the campaign to take Crown Point, on Lake Champlain, this enterprise was intrusted to General William Johnson, an officer of the New York militia, whose settlement in the Mohawk Valley, and influence with the Indians, have been previously mentioned. Johnson was placed in command of five or six thousand New York and New England militia, and a chosen body of Mohawk warriors under Soiengarahta, locally called King Hendrick.

Soiengarahta was a chief of high standing among the Mohawks, of approved wisdom, undoubted intrepidity, and a firm friend of the English. He had visited England, where the annexed portrait of him was taken, and had been presented at court. He united great amenity of manners, dignity of bearing, and mild features to the most determined courage and energy. He led two hundred Mohawks, who are described by the gazettes of the day as having on this occasion (the battle of Lake George) "fought like lions."

After laying the foundations of Fort Edward, Johnson proceeded to the southern shores of Lake Sacrament, which he re-named Lake George, in compliment to the reigning house of Hanover. He there located his camp in such a manner as to have the lake in his rear, and some impassable low grounds, or swamps, on his flanks. The Baron Dieskau, who opposed him, was a brave, dashing officer, possessing great spirit and strength of purpose, and, had he led men of similar mettle, would have readily taken the English camp. He had left Crown Point to attack the new Fort Edward with fifteen hundred men, of whom two hundred were drilled grenadiers and six hundred Canadians, the remainder being Algonkin Indians of various tribes.

The Canadians and Indians were so afraid of cannon that when within two miles of the fort they urged him to change his course and attack Johnson in his camp at Lake George. Ascertaining that Johnson was rather carelessly encamped, and probably unsuspicious of danger, Dieskau acceded to the request.

On being apprised of his approach, Johnson called a council of war on the morning of September 8, 1755. It was proposed to send out a party to meet the French. Hendrick's opinion was asked. "If they are to fight," said he, "they are

---

[1] Colden. This war must not be confounded with that waged against the Eries, which took place a century earlier.

too few; if they are to be killed, they are too many." To the plan of separating the force into three divisions, his objections were equally forcible and shrewd. Taking three sticks, he remarked, "Put them together, and you can't break them; take them one by one, and you can break them easily." Twelve hundred men were sent out, under Colonel Ephraim Williams, to meet the enemy. Williams College, in Massachusetts, owes its origin to a bequest in this officer's will, made just before he left home. Before marching, Hendrick mounted a gun-carriage and harangued his warriors in a strain of eloquence which had a powerful effect upon them. He was then about sixty-five years old. His head was covered with long white locks, and he was regarded by his warriors with the deepest veneration. Colonel Seth Pomeroy, who listened to this speech, said that, although he did not understand a word of the language, the animation of Hendrick, the fire of his eyes, the force of his gestures, the strength of his emphasis, the apparent propriety of the inflections of his voice, and his naturalness of manner, were such that he himself was more deeply affected by this speech than by any other he had ever heard.

The French, advised by scouts of the march of the English, approached through a thick wood to Rocky Brook, four miles from the lake, with their line in the form of a half-moon. Into this perilous circle Colonel Williams unsuspectingly led his detachment, when a heavy fire poured upon its front and flanks at the same moment caused a terrible slaughter. Williams was killed, and Hendrick fell mortally wounded. Lieutenant-Colonel Whiting, who succeeded to the command, skilfully withdrew the survivors of the force. The firing being heard at Lake George, three hundred men were sent to reinforce the retreating column, and the pursuit was checked.

Johnson's camp was still without intrenchments. When the firing was heard, two or three cannon were hastily brought up from the margin of the lake, and some trees were felled for a breastwork, affording a slight protection to the militia, whose arms were fowling-pieces, not a bayonet among them. Dieskau's plan had been to rush on and enter the camp with the fugitives, but the Indians and Canadians halted and scattered wherever a shelter appeared. When within one hundred rods of Johnson, Dieskau halted, and placed the Indians and Canadians upon his flanks. The regulars, under his immediate command, attacked the centre at long range, but, having only small-arms, the effect was trifling. The Indians, under the fire of grape-shot from Johnson's field-pieces, soon broke and fled. Johnson, slightly wounded, left the field early in the action, and the battle was continued for five hours by Lyman, the second in command. The French held their ground steadily during all this time, but finally, abandoned by their allies and terribly galled by the English fire, they gave way, and were pursued in all directions. Dieskau, wounded and helpless, was found leaning against the stump of a tree. As the provincial soldier who discovered him approached, he put his hand in his pocket to draw out his watch as a bribe to allow him to escape. Supposing that he was drawing a pistol, the soldier gave him a severe wound in the hip with a musket-ball. Dieskau was afterwards exchanged, and died in Paris in 1767.

This victory revived the spirits of the colonies, and occasioned a feeling of joy far above its real merits or importance. Johnson was created a knight baronet, and voted five thousand pounds sterling by the English Parliament. He was, however, censured for not pursuing the enemy and capturing Crown Point, having simply contented himself with building Fort William Henry, on the site of his camp.

In August, 1756, Field-Marshal the Marquis de Montcalm, who had recently arrived at Quebec, and who had rapidly familiarized himself with the posture of affairs, with great celerity and secrecy concerted measures for the capture of Oswego. The fort, a large stone building surrounded by a wall, flanked by four small bastions, was commanded from adjacent heights. An outpost on the opposite bank was attacked, and its garrison were speedily driven into the fort, having first spiked their cannon. Occupying this height, Montcalm turned his guns upon the fort, soon breaching its walls, and killing Mercer, its commander. On the second day of the siege, just as he was preparing to storm the intrenchments, its garrison, about sixteen hundred in number, capitulated, and one hundred and twenty cannon, six vessels of war, and three hundred boats, besides abundant stores, fell into his hands. The works were immediately razed to the ground.

The colonists struggled on through periods of terror which followed in close succession. The defeat of Braddock was still fresh in the memory of all, when the announcement of the disastrous capture of Fort William Henry rang through the colonies with startling effect. In 1757, Montcalm, the active Governor-General of Canada, crossed Lake Champlain to its attack, with a force of six thousand French and Canadians, and about seventeen hundred Indians, collected from the Great Lakes and from the valley of the St. Lawrence. A person present on the 2d of August, when this force approached the fort, represents Lake George to have been covered with bateaux and canoes, which, combined with their banners and music, formed a scene of military display and magnificence, heightened by the wild and picturesque brilliance of the Indian costume, that has seldom been equalled.

The soldiers anxiously gazed over the walls of the fort at the approaching force as at a panorama. Montcalm disembarked about a mile and a half below the fort without interruption, and advanced in three columns. The Indians burned the English barracks, and scalped their stragglers. The Canadians, under Lacorne, occupied the road leading to the Hudson, and cut off the communication. De Levi, with regulars and Canadians, was at the north, while Montcalm, with the main body, occupied the skirt of the woods on the west side of the lake. On the 4th, Montcalm sent proposals to Munro for surrender, which the latter refused. He then brought up his artillery, and soon the first battery of nine cannon and two mortars opened upon the fort. Two days later a second battery was established, and by means of zigzags the Indians could stand within gunshot of the works.

During five days the fort was defended with intrepidity by Colonel Munro, who had a garrison of five hundred regular troops, supported by a body of provincials. It was closely besieged, while the Indians, encamped on the surrounding fields, made the forest ring with their shouts and war-songs, and illuminated the obscurity of night with their numerous camp-fires. About seventeen hundred provincials, who were encamped outside the fort, took refuge within the works as soon as the enemy arrived. The defence was stoutly maintained, a hope being entertained that reinforcements, which had been demanded, would arrive from Fort Edward. Expresses were repeatedly sent to General Webb imploring aid, but he remained inactive and indifferent in his camp at Fort Edward, where he had four thousand men.

General Johnson was at last allowed to march with Putnam and his rangers to the relief of the beleaguered garrison, but when about three miles from Fort Edward Webb recalled them, and sent a letter to Munro saying that he could render him no assistance, and advising him to surrender. This letter unfortunately fell into Montcalm's hands just as he was about to suspend the operations of the siege preparatory to a retreat, his Indians having informed him of the movement of Johnson and Putnam and represented the English reinforcements to be as numerous as the leaves on the trees. This letter he at once sent to Munro, proposing an immediate surrender. Seeing the hopelessness of the case, half of his cannon having burst, and his ammunition and stores being nearly exhausted, the brave old soldier capitulated on the 9th. The fort was entirely demolished by Montcalm, and was never rebuilt.

One of the terms of the capitulation was that the army should be allowed to march out with their arms, but without ammunition, and, with all the camp-followers, should have a safe-conduct to Fort Edward. No sooner, however, had the English columns marched out of the gates and reached the plain than the Indians began to plunder them of their effects, and finally to strip both officers and men of their clothing. Resistance was followed by blows, and many, stark naked, were glad to escape with their lives. In vain did the troops, destitute of ammunition, claim protection from this outrage. Colonel Munro, after the pillage commenced, took shelter in the fort, and demanded that the terms of the capitulation should be enforced. The French have been blamed, perhaps justly, for not efficiently performing their engagements; but it is no easy matter to restrain marauding Indians. It has been asserted, but not proved, that a large number of the force which surrendered on this occasion perished subsequently,[1] but it is probable that the fears of an officer who narrowly escaped from this scene of pillage far exceeded his capacity for cool judgment. His statements of the carnage are certainly not sustained by any historical authority to which we have had access.

Lieutenant-Governor De Lancey, in a letter written August 24, 1757, observes, "Montcalm, under his own eyes, and in the face of about three thousand regular troops, suffered the Indians to rob and strip them, officers as well as men, of all they had, and left most of them naked." The nation that employs Indians in war places itself in the position of a person who taps a broad lake, leading the waters by a little stream through a sand-bank. When the current swells, he cannot control it, and the augmented flood sweeps everything before it.

---

[1] Carver, p. 211.

CHAPTER IV.

CAMPAIGNS OF 1758-59 — GRANT'S DEFEAT — BOUQUET'S BATTLE — REDUCTION OF FORT DU QUESNE — CONFERENCE WITH THE IROQUOIS — CONQUEST OF CANADA—ITS INFLUENCE UPON THE HOSTILE TRIBES.

AFTER the defeat of Braddock the British interest with the Indians rapidly declined. As Indians judge from appearances alone, it was not an easy task to convince them that the English power had not permanently failed. Johnson, who in the spring of 1755 had been appointed by Braddock the Superintendent-General of British Indian affairs, began his new duties as soon as he reached New York, and labored earnestly to restore confidence among the Iroquois and Algonkin tribes. He was thoroughly acquainted with the geography of the country, as also with the Indian power and resources in America, from North to South, and as thoroughly conversant with the true character of the aborigines. In his speeches he stripped them of their guises, laid bare their secret impulses, and pointed out to them their interests in clear and bold terms. During sixty years, beginning with the foundation of New Orleans, in 1699, the French influence among the Indians had been on the increase. The noble enterprise of La Salle and his followers, who passed through the Great Lakes and down the Mississippi, singing as they went, the gay and sprightly manners of the French, their ready adaptiveness to a nomadic course of life, replete with novelty and breathing the spirit of personal independence, together with their entire political and religious policy, impressed the Indians with almost inexplicable emotions of pleasure and approbation. The French required no cessions of land, built no factories, traded with them in a free and easy way, and did not fill the Indian mind with the idea of the coming of a people who, by the progressive inroads of labor and letters, would eventually sweep them from the earth. Whatever was the cause, certainly no other European nation ever acquired so ample and wide-spread an influence over them.[1]

Immediately after returning from Alexandria, Sir William Johnson assembled a very large number of Indians—some accounts say twelve hundred—at his place on the Mohawk, and communicated to them the fact of his new appointment. He made them offers in this assembly for the purpose of restoring their lost confidence in the English and detaching them from the French interests, to inspire them with a just estimation of the power of Britain, and to interest them in the British cause,— objects in which he by perseverance succeeded. He eloquently pleaded for their

---

[1] One of the Jesuit priests remarks that "the French did not convert the Indians, but turned Indians themselves."—*Halket*.

assent to his proposal to send a body of warriors with General Braddock, but in this he was unsuccessful. Good diplomatists at all times, they met him by a declaration that the Governor of Virginia, who was not a favorite, had, as in the case of the Ohio Company, intruded on their lands in the Ohio Valley, where their sachem, Tanacharisson, resided; also that it was a suddenly originated proposal, which required deliberation. They likewise, for reasons stated, declined accompanying General Shirley to Oswego, but agreed to assist him in the contemplated attack on Crown Point, to the command of the forces detailed for which purpose he had been appointed. The latter promise was promptly fulfilled, and at the defeat of Dieskau on the banks of Lake George, the Mohawks, under Hendrick, acquitted themselves in such a manner as to gain a high reputation.[1]

The victory at Lake George was the turning-point in the ascendency of the British influence with the Iroquois and their allies, which had been at a very low ebb at the beginning of the French war, in 1744. The fame which followed this victory aided greatly in raising Johnson in the estimation of the Indians, and from this date the Indian political horizon began to brighten. In a letter to the Lords of Trade, dated September 28, 1757, Johnson points out their true policy, while he warns them of the deep-rooted dislike which the Indians entertained towards the colonial patentees, who had made the encroachments on their lands, of which the Indians complain. "By presents and management we may be able to keep some little interest yet alive, and induce some nations to a course of neutrality; but I am apprehensive that more expense, speeches, and promises (so often repeated and so little regarded) will never be able to effect a favorable revolution in our Indian interests and deprive the French of the advantages they have over us by their Indian alliances. I would be understood, my Lords, that there is no alternative by which we may possibly avail ourselves so as to keep an even hand with the Indians; but reducing the French to our terms would enable us to give law to the Indians."

This became the British policy. Belts and speeches were inadequate to the result; it was a contest between England and France which must be settled, and the nation that gained it would control the Indians. The triumph at Lake George, in which action Soiengarahta lost his life, seemed to presage events which were soon to take place. The taking of Fort William Henry and the outrages perpetrated upon the prisoners only gave a new impulse to the vigor with which England prepared to contest the supremacy.

No one understood better than Johnson the position of the two parties contending for supremacy; and in a general council convened at his Hall on the Mohawk, April 19, 1767, at which the Shawnees and other Algonkin tribes, as well as the Iroquois, were present, he presented the case in the following forcible manner:

"Brethren, listen, and I will tell you the difference between the English and the

---

[1] Had it not been for the jealousy of General Shirley, and his counteracting counsels with the Six Nations, the force in this battle would have been much greater.—*N. Y. Hist. Col. Doc.*, vol. vii. p. 21.

French. The English desire and labor to unite all Indians into one general bond of brotherly love and national interest. The French endeavor to divide the Indians and stir up war and contention among them. Those who intend to destroy or enslave any people or nation will first endeavor to divide them. This you and all the Indians upon this continent know has always been, and continues to be, the endeavor of the French. But though this is a fact which I think all the Indians must certainly see, yet the French have found means, somehow or other, so to bewitch their understandings as to make many of them believe they love the Indians and mean well towards them. 'Tis very strange, brethren, that any one man, much more any number of men, who are not either mad or drunk, can believe that stirring up brethren to spill each other's blood, dividing them from one another, and making parties among them, are proofs of love and marks of friendly design towards them. Not less unaccountable is it, brethren, that the French should be able to persuade the Indians that building forts in the middle of their country and hunting-grounds is for their interest and protection. I tell you, brethren, and I warn you, that whatever good words the French may give you, how much soever they may now smile upon you, whatever presents they may now make you, your chains are in their pockets, and when their designs are ripe for execution they will take the axe out of their bosom and strike it into your heads. But this they know they cannot do until you have broken the Covenant Chain with your brethren the English and taken up the axe against them. 'Tis for this reason the French are always endeavoring, by lies, by presents, by promises, to stir up all Indians to fall upon the English settlements and destroy their best friends and faithful brethren; and many Indians have been so wicked and so foolish as, in spite of treaties and ancient friendship, to become the dogs of the French, and come and go as they command them.

"Brethren, if the Indians do not return to their senses they will see and feel, when it is too late, that they have ruined themselves, enslaved their posterity, and lost their country. They will find their country fortified by the French, not against the English, but against the Indians themselves.

"Brethren, what I have said, and am going to say, I say not to you only, but to all Indians; and I desire you will with this belt make it known among all the nations you have any acquaintance or connection with.

"Tell them, from me, to look at the French forts built and building through the middle of their country and on their best hunting-lands. Let them look at the French flags flying in their forts at all the great lakes and along the great rivers, in order to oblige them to trade with the French only, sell their skins, and take goods for them at what prices the French please to put on them. And it is a thing well known to all Indians that the French cannot sell them goods nearly so cheap as the English can, nor in such assortments and plenty."

To renew the attempt of Braddock had been the original plan of General Shirley, but the following year passed in merely concerting measures. The plan of the campaign of 1758 contemplated the reduction of Crown Point, on Lake Champlain, and of Fort Du Quesne, on the Ohio. General Abercrombie, who undertook the former, aided by a large army, suffered a repulse. Lord Howe fell while leading an attack, and when, in a few days, it was renewed against an impregnable breastwork of horizontal trees, they were compelled to retreat to Fort Edward. The Mohawks, who were present at this assault, looked on with amazement at this exhibition of heroic but injudicious bravery. As an episode to this siege, Colonel Bradstreet proceeded by a sudden march to Oswego, with the Iroquois in his train, and, crossing Lake Ontario in bateaux, on the 25th of August surprised and took Fort Frontenac, capturing a large amount of supplies, as well as arms.

The reduction of Fort Du Quesne was intrusted to General Forbes. He marched from Philadelphia with an army of five thousand eight hundred regulars and provincials, and a commissary and quartermaster's force of one thousand wagoners. Washington joined him at Fort Cumberland with his regiment of Virginians. At Raystown, Forbes sent Colonel Bouquet forward with two thousand men, but in a spirit of confidence Bouquet despatched eight hundred of this force, under Major James Grant, to make observations in advance. On September 14 the latter commander was surprised on hills overlooking the fort by M. Aubrey, with seven or eight hundred Frenchmen and an unnumbered force of Indians, his troops defeated with dreadful slaughter, and himself and nineteen other officers made prisoners and sent to Montreal. The retreat of the survivors was effected by the skill and energy of Captain Bullit, who with fifty men had been left in charge of the baggage. The loss in Grant's defeat was numerically greater, in proportion to those engaged, than that sustained in Braddock's. Thirty-five officers were killed or wounded. The prisoners taken by the Indians served, as it were, to surfeit their barbarity and cruelty and to disincline them towards proceeding farther, for after reaching Du Quesne they soon dispersed, and deserted the fort. Twelve hundred French and Indians, under De Vetrie, attacked Bouquet's camp with great fury and obstinacy on October 12. The battle lasted four hours, when by a skilful ruse the enemy were repulsed after severe fighting. Colonel Bouquet's loss was sixty-seven killed and wounded. On the arrival of General Forbes the combined English force moved on with regularity, and on the 24th of November encamped at Turtle Creek, within twelve miles of the fort.

No Indians were descried by the scouts, and the night passed away without alarm. On the 25th, at an early hour, the army was put in motion, and as the advance-guard approached the location of the fort they observed large columns of smoke, and at intervals heard heavy explosions. The indications could not be mistaken. The fort had been abandoned, after being set on fire, its artillery being embarked for the Illinois and its infantry for Lake Erie. The defeat of Grant, and the prisoners captured, had proved an escape-valve for Indian barbarity. After practising the most inhuman tortures upon the prisoners, whose bleached skeletons lined the approach to the fort, and after rioting in debauch, they had, with their usual impatience, returned to their forest homes, leaving General Forbes to advance unmolested, and abandoning De Legneris, the French commander. On the 25th the column advanced in force, and the British flag was triumphantly planted on the fort by General Forbes, who bestowed upon it the name of the celebrated British minister Pitt. The western line of the colonial frontiers was thus advanced to the river Ohio.[1] From this period Indian warfare found its principal field of development west of and beyond that border, well named the River Beautiful by the Indian tribes.

At the victory obtained on Lake George in 1755, a year so disastrous to the British army, the Mohawks alone, of the six Iroquois cantons, were present, with Johnson, their beloved Warraghiyagay, and two hundred warriors, headed by the great Soiengarahta. A far greater force had been expected from and promised by the Oneidas, Onondagas, Cayugas, Tuscaroras, and Senecas, but, owing to the influence of General Shirley, whose act appears to have been dictated by no higher motive than personal envy of Johnson's rising power with that people, these tribes withheld their respective quotas of warriors. A vacillating and indecisive policy had been pursued by them for some years, and while they were, to use symbolic language, in the chain of friendship with the English, and held the other tribes in check, in conformity with their own and the British interests, they were lukewarm in taking the field as the auxiliaries of the English armies. Johnson had endeavored, soon after his return from his conference with Braddock, to induce a body of the confederates to cross the Alleghanies with that officer, but they evaded the proposal. Cherishing from ancient times an ill feeling towards Assaragon, their name for the Governor of Virginia, they regarded Braddock's advance as a Virginia movement. They deemed the Virginians land-robbers who coveted the Ohio Valley, and they were sufficiently good diplomatists to bring forward several weighty considerations on the subject. It happened while this negotiation was pending that they furnished Johnson with messengers to the authorities at Fort Cumberland. These Indian runners were there informed that a party of six of the warriors sent out by the Mohawks against the Catawbas had all been killed. This news exercised such a bad effect on the council that they neither promised nor furnished aid to Braddock, although they did not join the Indian forces on the Ohio to oppose him. Not a man of their people who bore the honored title of Mingoes was in the battle of the Monongahela. Tanacharisson, called the Half-King, and Scarooyadi, his successor, evinced throughout a firm friendship for the English, first pledged to Washington during his perilous journey in 1753.

The Iroquois had from the remotest antiquity enjoyed the reputation of eloquent orators and expert diplomatists. But Johnson was not a man to be dazzled by words and speeches while the weightier matter of action was in abeyance. In a general conference with the Onondagas and more westerly tribes, held June 16, 1757, nearly two years subsequent to his victory on Lake George, in which the Mohawks had so nobly supported him, he alluded to this matter, and proceeded to dispose of some of their diplomatic subterfuges.

---

[1] The elements of this word are the Iroquois exclamation *oh*, and *io*, a substantive termination of the exclamation for the beautiful in scenery. It is the same term as that heard in the Wyandot word Ontar-io.

"Brethren," said he, "you tell me the reason you did not make use of the hatchet I sharpened for you last summer, when I was at Onondaga, and at which time I also painted and feathered your warriors for action, was because you found yourselves in danger from the Mississagies, and therefore were obliged to let my hatchet lie by you, and take care of yourselves.

"Brethren, this is the first time I have heard the Misssisagies were your enemies, and I am surprised how it came about. It is but two years ago, at the great meeting here, that you brought down the chief man among the Mississagies, and introduced him to me as your great friend and ally, and told me that he and his people were determined to follow the example of the Five Nations. You then desired I would treat and consider him accordingly, which I did, and gave him presents to his satisfaction, and he took belts from me to his people. For what reason, therefore, you think yourselves in danger from the Mississagies I cannot comprehend, unless it is from some misunderstanding which I hear happened in the woods some few days ago between some of your people and them.

"Brethren, another reason you give me for your inactivity is that you are few in number and you daily hear yourselves threatened by your enemies. As to your numbers, had you taken my advice, given you many years ago, and often repeated, you might now have been a strong people. I should be glad to know who these enemies are, and what grounds you have for these fears.

"Brethren, you say that the English would first make a trial against their enemies, and that if we found we could not do without you, then we would call on you for your assistance. I have looked over the records, where all public speeches and business with the Nations are faithfully written down, and I find no such thing there, and I am very positive you must be mistaken; for from the first meeting I had with the Six Nations, after my return from Virginia, to this day, I have been constantly calling and exhorting them, as children of the Great King of England, as brothers and allies to the English, to join and assist His Majesty's arms against our common enemy, the French; and the Six Nations have as frequently assured me they would act with us and for us; and you must know you have a great number of belts from me on this subject now in your possession. You tell me, though you don't know from what quarter, that you expect in a few months to be attacked by some enemy, and that therefore you think your own preservation requires you to stay at home and be on your guard. What foundation you have for all these fears, so lately come upon you, you have not thought proper to inform me; and therefore I am at a loss about it, especially as I understand several parties of your young men are gone a fighting to the southward. Formerly you told me that if you had forts built at your towns, and some men to garrison them, you might then go to war with your brethren the English, and not be afraid for your old men, your wives and children, during your absence. These forts, though very expensive to the King your Father, were accordingly built for you, and if you had applied you might have had men to garrison them. Brethren, your conduct will, in my opinion, appear very ungrateful, and your reasonings very inconsistent, to the King your Father, and to all your brethren, the English, when they come to their knowledge, as they soon will do; wherefore I would advise you to reconsider the matter and take it into your most serious consideration.

"Brethren, you say Captain Montour and Captain Butler brought you a message in my name, that I expected you would use the hatchet I had put in your hands against the French; that the message was laid before the council of Onondaga, who said they did not expect such a message from you, as the Covenant Chain was for the common safety both of us and you, and that if you were to leave your country unguarded it might end in your destruction.

"Brethren, it is certain the Covenant Chain was made for our common good and safety, and it is well known to you all that it speaks in this manner: *That the English and the Six Nations shall consider themselves as one flesh and blood, and that whenever any enemy shall hurt the one, the other is to feel it and avenge it as if done to himself.* Have not the French hurt us? Is not their axe in our heads? Are they not daily killing and taking our people away? Have not some of your nations, both to the southward and northward, joined the French against us? Nay, some of you, by your own confession, have gone out by yourselves and struck the English. Have you not now several of our people prisoners among you whom you conceal from me? Have you not, lastly, suffered the Swegachie Indians to come through your habitations and take one of our people from the German Flats? Let me ask you now if all this is behaving like brethren, and whether you ought not to be ashamed when you put us in mind of the Covenant Chain. Surely you dream, or think I have forgotten the old agreement between us, when you talk in this manner. I take you by the head, and rouse you from your lethargy, and bring you to your senses.

"Brethren, you say you must take care of yourselves, and not leave your country unguarded. When our brother's house is on fire, will another brother look quietly on, smoke his pipe at his own door, and say he can't help him because perhaps his own house may take fire? Does the Covenant Chain speak this language? Did your forefathers talk after this manner? Did I talk so to you when the Onondagas, Oneidas, and Tuscaroras sent me word last year that they expected the enemy were coming upon them? Did not I and your brethren run through the ice and snow, at two or three different times, to their assistance? Where and who are those enemies you so much dread? Let us know, do you want our assistance? if you are in danger, we know the Covenant Chain, and will be ready to defend or die with you. We won't tell you to make one trial by yourselves, and that we must stay at home and take care of our own preservation.

"You always tell me 'tis for our mutual interest you go so often to Canada: I am apt to think you have brought these alarms and these fears with you from thence.

"Brethren, I must tell you that my orders from the King your Father are to take care of and supply with necessaries such good and faithful Indians as will go out and fight for him and his people; and that such and their families only has he empowered me to arm, clothe, and provide for, which I shall continue to do to all such as will go out upon service; and those I dare say will in the end find they have acted more for their honor and interest than those who stay at home and smoke their pipes.

"Brethren, you have assured me that it is the unanimous resolution of the Five Nations to hold fast the ancient Covenant Chain made by our forefathers and yours. Brethren, our end of this chain is bright and strong, and we shall not be the first to let it go; but it seems to me that your end is grown very rusty, and without great care will be in danger of being eaten through, which I should be very sorry to see, as it would be the means, also, of extinguishing the fire here, and oversetting the Tree of Shelter."

It was the policy of the British colonial government, in establishing a general and central superintendency at Fort Johnson, on the Mohawk River, not only to attach the Six Nations strongly to its interests, but also to govern the entire Indian country through their extensive influence over the other groups of tribes. This general policy had been understood and carried out by the colonial governors of New York from the beginning of the century, and indeed dates back to the Dutch, as it was pursued by them in 1664. Trade was principally conducted at the central point, Albany, but traders were allowed to visit remote places. The French traders from Canada obtained their best supplies from Albany, and the intercourse thus established upon and cemented by a triple interest—that of the tribes, the merchants, and the governing power—became a firm bond of union, and one that gained strength by the lapse of time. The metals, woollens, and other articles of real value which they received in exchange for their furs were so much superior to the products of the rude arts Hudson found in their possession in 1609, that it is doubtful even whether at this period many remembered that the Iroquois had ever used stone knives, axes, and pipes, or made fish-hooks of bones, awls of deer's horns, and cooking-pots out of clay.

But, although a trade so mutually beneficial established a firm friendship, and the growth of every decade of the colonies added to its strength, it was not, in fact, until the abolition of the power of the Indian commissioners at Albany, who were frequently traders themselves, and the transfer of the superintendency of Indian affairs to the hands of Johnson, that an elevated and true national tone was given to the system. When Johnson was placed in the possession of power, he visited their remotest villages and castles, and built stockades in each of their towns to serve as places of refuge if suddenly attacked. In his anxiety to control the Algonkins and the Dionondades, or Quaghtagies, he had visited Detroit, and his agents had scoured the Illinois, the Miami, the Wabash, and the Ohio, before the French built Fort Du Quesne. When he could send them messages by the power of the king, or speak to them in his council-room with the voice of a king, he had also, as we may readily perceive from the records published at this late day, the judgment, firmness, and prudence of a king. No one, it would seem, could be better adapted to give solid advice to the Indians of all the tribes.

Johnson did not limit his attentions to the Six Nations. After the defeat of Braddock the entire frontier line of Pennsylvania, Maryland, and Virginia was left unprotected. Invasion, rapine, and murder were the common inflictions under which groaned the entire interior country from the Ohio to the Susquehanna, and not a farm could be settled or a team driven on the road without incurring the risk of death or captivity. These murders having been chiefly attributed to the Shawnees and Delawares, who were still located on the sources of the Susquehanna, Johnson employed the Iroquois, who from an early period exacted allegiance from them as a conquered people, to summon their chiefs before him. A delegation of the principal men of these tribes attended in his council early in the spring of 1758, to whom he gave a detail of the acts complained of, placing them before them in their just light, and forewarning them of the inevitable consequences which would result from a repetition of such nefarious acts, and that not only Pennsylvania and Maryland but all the neighboring colonies would be aroused against them. At this council a delegation of Nanticokes, Conoys, and Mohikanders attended, who informed him that they lived at Otsiningo,[1] on the Susquehanna, where his messengers would always find them.

Addressing these nomadic members of the disintegrated and fast-decaying Algonkin group, as he did the Iroquois in the full strength of their confederacy, Johnson adopted a line of argument and diplomacy founded on high principles of national polity and guided by a true estimate of the Indian character. He frequently moved their sympathy by an Indian symbol where an argument would have failed. All causes of disaffection, whether arising from questions of trade, the encroachments of settlers, inhuman murders, or any other of the irregularities so common in the Indian country, were handled by him with calm judgment; and good counsels, and the most efficient practical remedies, through the means of agents, presents, and money, were judiciously dispensed.

The year 1759 was a brilliant period for the British arms. Braddock, Loudoun, Shirley, and Abercrombie had respectively exercised their brief authority as commanders of the British forces in America, and passed from the stage of action, leaving a clear field for the induction of a new military policy. Amherst, if not surpassing his predecessors in talent and energy, was at least more fortunate in the disposition of his forces, more successful in the execution of his plans, and especially so in the selection of his generals. The military spirit of the British nation was roused, its means were ample, and its commanders men of the highest capacity. France was about to be subjected to a combined attack on all her strongholds which would surpass anything previously attempted. The colonial struggle, which had been protracted through a century and a half, was about to terminate. Fort Niagara, where La Salle had first erected a palisade, and where Denonville had constructed a fortress, stood on the narrow promontory round which the Niagara pours its waters into the lower lake. It commanded the portage between Ontario and Erie, and controlled the fur-trade of the West. Here the first successful onset was made on July 1, when it was regularly besieged by General Prideaux, who was killed in one of the trenches while encouraging his men to more active exertions. Through this casualty Sir

---

[1] Now Binghamton, New York.

William Johnson succeeded to the chief command, and vigorously prosecuted the plans of his predecessor. Learning that reinforcements, accompanied by a body of Indians from the lakes, had entered the Niagara Valley and were marching to the relief of the fort, he sent against them a detachment of troops, together with a large force of Iroquois, who valiantly met and defeated the enemy. He then summoned the garrison to surrender, which opened the gates of the fort on the 25th of July. Within a week from this time, Louisburg, which had been invested by Admiral Boscawen, succumbed to the military prowess and heroism of General Wolfe, who, having been promoted for his gallantry in this siege, ascended the St. Lawrence, and by a series of masterly movements, conducted with great intrepidity, captured Quebec, losing his own life on the Plains of Abraham, where also ebbed out that of his brave and able foe, Montcalm. The city surrendered on the 18th of September. De Levi, from the opposite point of the river, vainly attempted its recovery. In the spring of 1760, General Murray followed De Levi up the valley of the St. Lawrence to Montreal, and effected a landing at the lower part of the island, while General Amherst and a large regular force, together with Sir William Johnson and his Iroquois, disembarked at Lachine. The troops on the island made no resistance, and with its capture, on the 8th of September, the conquest of Canada was completed. The retention of the colony by the English was one of the chief results of the treaty of peace soon after concluded between France and England. The terms of the capitulation included the smaller posts of Le Bœuf, Detroit, and Michilimackinac, which were surrendered in the year 1761.

By the treaty of Paris, concluded February 10, 1763, France renounced all pretensions to the possessions she had claimed east of the Mississippi, and made over the same to Great Britain. Spain about the same time ceded Florida to England.

The ensuing fifteen years of Indian history are crowded with the records of interesting events. The great question among the Indian tribes had been, "Is England or France to rule?" In a memorial to the States-General of Holland, dated October 12, 1649, it is quaintly said, "The Indians are of little consequence." Whichever power prevailed was destined to rule them, and the controversy was now drawing to a close.

"Be not any longer wheedled, and blindfolded, and imposed on," said Sir William Johnson to the Iroquois, " by the artful speeches of the French, for their tongues are full of deceit. Do not imagine the fine clothes, etc., they give you are out of love or regard for you; no, they are only as a bait to catch a fish; they mean to enslave you thereby, and entail that curse upon you; and your children after you will have reason to repent the day you begot them. Be assured they are your inveterate and implacable enemies, and only wish for a difference to arise between you and us that they might put you all out of their way by cutting you from the face of the earth."

Champlain founded the city of Quebec in 1608, adopting the Algonkin catchword *kebik*, "take care of the rock,"[1] as the appellative for the nucleus of the future

---

[1] The waters of the St. Lawrence at ebb tide run swiftly against part of the rocky shore.

empire of the French. One hundred and fifty-two years, marked by continual strife and negotiations, plots and counterplots, battles and massacres, all having for their object supremacy over the Indian tribes, had now passed away. Wolfe and Montcalm were both dead. The empire of New France, reaching from the St. Lawrence to the Gulf of Mexico, would thenceforth have a place only on the page of history. But had the Indians derived any advantage from the contest? Had they, in fact, struggled for any definite position, or had they only fought on the strongest side, anticipating better usage, more lucrative trade, greater kindness, or more even-handed justice from one party than was to be obtained from the other? Was this hope well defined and permanent, or did it fluctuate with every change of fortune, with the prowess of every warlike, or with the tact of every civic, character who trod the field? Did they not vacillate with every wind, being steady only in the preservation of their chameleon-like character, true when faithfulness was their only or supposed interest, and false or treacherous when, as frequently happened, the current of success changed?

Two prominent races of Indian tribes existed in the North and West from the earliest settlement of the colonies,—namely, the Algonkins and the Iroquois. The Algonkins trusted to the French to enable them to prevent the English from occupying their lands. The Iroquois looked to the English for aid to keep the French off their possessions. When the long struggle was over, and the English finally prevailed, the Indian allies of the French could hardly realize the fact. They did not think the King of France would give up the contest after having built so many forts and fought so many battles to maintain his position. They discovered, however, that the French had been defeated, and they at length became aware that with their overthrow the Indian power in America had departed. The tribes of the far West and North were required to give their assent to what was done, which they did grudgingly. The name of Saganosh had been so long scouted by them that it appeared to be a great hardship to succumb to the English. Nadowa, the Algonkin name for Iroquois, had also from the earliest times been a word of fearful import to the Western Indians, and their shout was sufficient to make the warriors of the strongest villages fly to arms, while their families hid in swamps and fastnesses. Both the English and the Iroquois were now in the ascendant.

In a review of the history of this period it will be found that nine-tenths of the Western Indians were in the French interest. The Shawnees, ever, during their nomadic state, a vengeful, restless, perfidious, and cruel people, had left central Pennsylvania as early as 1755-59, in company with or preceding the Delawares. After the defeat of Braddock, and down to the close of Wayne's campaign of 1795, their tracks in the Ohio Valley had been marked with blood. The Delawares, during the year 1744 and subsequently, were in truth driven from central Pennsylvania, not by the Quakers and Germans, but by the fierce and indomitable Scotch-Irish and English settlers. Unfortunately for this people, they had the reputation of siding with the French. After the massacre of Conestoga, the Iroquois, who had once held sway over the whole course of the Susquehanna, fled back to Oneida and other kindred

cantons. That portion of the Western Iroquois who bore the name of Mingoes, and were once under the rule of Tanacharisson, the half-king, and subsequently of Scarooyadi, were charged with unfriendliness after the stand taken by Logan. The numerous Miamis, Piankeshaws, and Weas of the Wabash were from the first friendly to the French. The Wyandots, or Hurons, of Sandusky and Detroit, who had been driven out by the Iroquois with great fury, and who took shelter among the French and the French Indians, had always been hostile to the English colonies. The numerous and wide-spread family of the Chippewas, Ottawas, and Pottawatomies had exerted a very varied influence on the English frontiers.

Turning our inquiries to the Illinois tribes, had they not from the remotest times found their worst foes in the Iroquois? For an answer consult La Salle and Marquette. The Peorias, the Cahokias, and the Kaskaskias had from the first discovery of the country dealt with French traders, and were thought to be imbued with French sympathies. The Winnebagoes of Green Bay, representing the bold prairie tribes of the Dakota stock west of the Mississippi, at all periods were the friends of the French. Intimate relations had been maintained with the Kickapoos, and with the wandering tribes of the Maskigoes, by the French missionaries and traders. Among all the Algonkin tribes, the Foxes and the Sauks, who had in 1712 assailed the French fort at Detroit, were the only enemies of the French, and they previous to the conquest of Canada had been driven to the Fox River of Wisconsin. On the west the French were in alliance with the Osages, Missouris, Kansas, Quappas, and Caddoes; and on the south with the Cherokees, Choctaws, and Muskokis.

All the necessary arrangements for taking possession of the military posts lately occupied by the French were promptly and efficiently made by General Amherst. Niagara having been garrisoned from the time of the conquest, Major Robert Rogers was sent thence to Detroit in September, 1760. This detachment was followed by Sir William Johnson, the Superintendent-General of Indian affairs, who placed the intercourse with the Indians on a proper footing. Rogers afterwards proceeded to Michilimackinac, where his proceedings subjected him to severe censure. Forts Chartres, Vincennes, Presque Isle, and the other minor posts were garrisoned by English troops. The Indians were still numerous, although they had suffered greatly in the war. The Indian trade yet required arrangement, and the commanding officers of these isolated Western posts at all times had far more need of the counsels of wisdom than of military strength, and required more skill in the arts of Indian diplomacy than in the active duties of the field.

The country was at that time one vast forest, its Indian population so thinly scattered that one might travel whole weeks without seeing a human form. Here and there in some rich meadow the Indian squaws, with their rude implements of husbandry, sowed their scanty stores of maize and beans. The condition of the Indians had not been improved by contact with civilization. The Six Nations of Western New York had already begun to decline. Many of the Delawares were on the Muskingum, in numerous scattered towns and villages. Along the Scioto were the lodges of the Shawnees. To the westward, along the banks of the Wabash and the Maumee, dwelt the Miamis. The Illinois, ruined by their love of fire-water, were scattered and degraded. The Wyandot villages along the Detroit and in the vicinity of Sandusky were the abodes of industry, and had a neat and thrifty appearance.

Scattered along the eastern seaboard were the English settlements, of which Albany, New York, was far the largest frontier town. This was the point of departure of the traders to the Lake region or bound on the hazardous journey to the Western wilderness. Their route lay up the Mohawk to Fort Stanwix, the head of river navigation, thence overland to Wood Creek, carrying their canoes. Embarking here, they followed its devious course until, at the Royal Block-house, they entered the Oneida, which they crossed at its western extremity, and, descending the Oswego, finally emerged upon Lake Ontario. From the middle colonies the principal trail to the Indian country was from Philadelphia westward over the Alleghanies and descending to the valley of the Ohio. No sooner had peace been proclaimed than scores of adventurous fur-traders, transporting their merchandise on the backs of horses, plunged into the forests, crossing mountains and fording streams in pursuit of gain. Their outfit consisted of blankets and red cloth, guns and hatchets, liquor, tobacco, paint, beads, and hawks' bills. In the southern portion of the present State of Illinois were to be seen the old French outposts Kaskaskia, Cahokia, and Vincennes. Farther up on the Wabash stood the little village of Ouantenon, whence a trail through the forest led to Fort Miami, on the Maumee, the site of the modern Fort Wayne. From this point the river was the road to Lake Erie. Here Sandusky lay to the right, and farther north, through the Strait of Detroit, was the fort of that name. Farther east, beyond the Alleghany, were Forts Presque Isle, Le Bœuf, and Venango.

CHAPTER V.

WAR WITH THE CHEROKEES.

WHILE these fundamental changes were taking place in the relations and prospects of the tribes of the North, those of the South remained quiescent, relying for security on the power of the French. Either instigated by hostile counsels, or indulging their natural proclivities for rapine and murder, the Cherokees of South Carolina had committed several outrages on the frontier settlements. The folly and arrogance of Governor Lyttleton precipitated an unnecessary conflict. At the close of the year 1759, having obtained from the legislature authority to raise a large body of men with which to bring the tribe to terms, he promptly marched into the Cherokee country at the head of eight hundred provincials and three hundred regular troops. This incursion, following as it did upon a long period of inactivity and supineness, so much intimidated and surprised the tribe that, being then entirely unprepared for open war, they did not hesitate to sue for peace, which was granted them in too much haste, without understanding the true nature of the Indian character and policy.

It has been remarked by Major Mante that "the Indians are of such a disposition that unless they really feel the rod of chastisement they cannot be prevailed on to believe that we have the power to inflict it; and, accordingly, whenever they happened to be attacked by us, unprepared, they had recourse to a treaty of peace as a subterfuge, which gave them time to collect themselves. Then, without the least regard to the bonds of public faith, they, on the first opportunity, renewed their depredations. Negotiations and treaties of peace they despised, so that the only hopes to bring to reason their intractable minds, and of making them acknowledge our superiority and live in friendship with us, must arise from the severity of chastisement."[1]

At this time the territory of the Cherokees extended from Fort Ninety-Six, on the Carolina frontiers, and Fort Prince George, on the Keowee branch of the Savannah, to the main sources of that river, and across the Appalachian chain to and down the Cherokee or Tennessee River and its southern branches,—a country replete with all the resources requisite in Indian life, possessing a delightful climate, and abounding in fertile sylvan valleys. The tribe was accused of operating against the Southern frontier under the influence of the French, who supplied them with arms and ammunition.

The treaty concluded with Governor Lyttleton refers to certain articles of amity

---

[1] Mante's History of the Late War in North America, p. 289: London, 1772.

and commerce entered into with these people at Whitehall, September 7, 1730, as well as to another pacification of November 19, 1758, and then proceeds with the precision of phraseology of the old black-letter lawyers to rehearse grievances of a later date, for all of which transgressions the tribe stipulate to make amends, and promise future good conduct. They actually delivered up two Cherokees who had committed murders, promised the surrender of twenty others, and gave twenty of their principal chiefs as hostages for the due performance of the terms of the treaty. To this formal document the great chief of the nation, Attakullakulla, and five other principal chiefs, subsequently affixed their assent and guarantee.

Although these hostages were envoys whose persons were by the laws of savage and civilized men sacred, they had been arrested and imprisoned by Lyttleton till twenty-four men should be delivered up to condign punishment for the murders. This was an outrageous violation of plighted faith, and was felt by the chiefs to be a deep disgrace, and one of their number resolved to effect their rescue. This treaty, moreover, was not made by chiefs duly authorized, nor had it been ratified in council, nor could Indian usage give effect to its conditions.

Lyttleton had scarcely returned home, when the Cherokees renewed their ravages. They attacked with great fury the settlement of Long Cane, sparing neither planter, cattle, buildings, women, nor children. They were particularly severe on English traders. This attack was repeated by a party of two hundred warriors, who extended their depredations to the forks of the Broad River, where they surprised and killed forty men. Inspirited by their success, they made an attack on Ninety-Six, but, the fort proving too strong, they proceeded to the Congaree, spreading devastation by fire and sword. Lyttleton, on the receipt of the earliest news of these irruptions, sent an express to General Amherst asking for reinforcements.

On the 18th of February, 1760, the Cherokees assembled around Fort Prince George, on the Keowee, and attempted to surprise it. While the garrison was gazing at the force from the ramparts, a noted chief, called Oconostata, approached, and desired to speak to Lieutenant Coytmore, the commandant, who agreed to meet him on the banks of the Keowee River, whither he was accompanied by Ensign Bell and Mr. Coharty, the interpreter. Oconostata said he wished to go down and see the governor, and requested that a white man might be allowed to accompany him. This request being assented to, he said to an Indian, "Go and catch a horse for me." This was objected to, whereupon the chief carelessly swung a bridle which he held three times around his head. This being a secret signal to men lying concealed, a volley was instantly poured in, which mortally wounded Coytmore, who received a ball in his breast, and inflicted deep flesh-wounds on the others.

This treachery aroused the indignation of Ensign Milu, commanding the garrison of the fort, who determined to put the twenty Cherokee hostages, and also the two murderers, in irons. But the first attempt to seize the assassins was instantly resisted; the soldier who was deputed to effect it was tomahawked and killed, and another was wounded. This so exasperated those within the fort that all the hostages were immediately put to death. The enraged savages at once devastated the Carolina frontier. Men, women, and children were butchered, and the war-belt was sent to the Catawbas and other tribes, inviting them to their aid in exterminating the English. In the evening the Indians fired two signal-guns before the fort, and, being ignorant of the manner in which the hostages had been disposed of, shouted to them, "Fight strong, and you shall be aided." The works were then invested, and an irregular fire maintained all night, with but little effect, however. On searching the room which had been occupied by the hostages, several tomahawks were found buried in the ground, which had been stealthily conveyed to the prisoners by their visiting friends.

Meantime, Amherst, immediately on the receipt of Governor Lyttleton's express, had despatched to his relief six hundred Highlanders, and an equal number of English soldiers, under Colonel Montgomery, afterwards Earl of Eglinton. On reaching Charleston, Montgomery immediately took the field. The celerity of his movements against the Cherokees took them completely by surprise. On the 26th of May he reached Fort Ninety-Six, and on June 1 passed the Twelve-Mile Branch of the Keowee with his baggage and stores, and, conveying them up amazingly rocky steeps, he pushed on night and day, marching eighty-four miles before taking a night's rest. Having progressed forty miles farther, he constructed a camp on an eligible site, and, leaving his wagons and cattle, with his tents standing, under a suitable guard of provincials and rangers, he took the rest of his troops lightly armed and directed his course towards the Cherokee towns. Thus far his scouts had discovered no enemy and his rapid advance had been unheralded. His first object was to attack Estatoe, a town some twenty-five miles in advance, and for this purpose he set out at eight o'clock in the evening. After marching sixteen miles, he heard a dog bark on the left, at the town of Little Keowee, about a quarter of a mile from the road, of the location of which his guides had not informed him. He immediately detached a force with orders to surround it and to bayonet every man, but to spare the women and children. This order was strictly executed; the men being found encamped outside the houses were killed, and their families captured unharmed. In the mean time the main force marched forward to Estatoe, in which they found but ten or twelve men, who were killed. This town comprised about two hundred houses, which were well supplied with provisions and ammunition. Montgomery, determining to make the nation feel the power of the colonies, immediately attacked the other towns in succession, until every one in the lower nation had been visited and destroyed. About seventy Cherokees were killed, and, including the women and children, forty were taken prisoners. Only four English soldiers were killed, and two officers wounded. Montgomery then returned to Fort Prince George, on the Keowee, where he awaited proposals of peace from the Cherokees, but, hearing nothing from them, he resolved to make a second incursion into the middle settlements of the nation. He marched his army from the fort on the 24th of June, and, using the same despatch as on the previous occasion, in three days he reached the town of Etchowee. The scouts discovered three Indians as they approached this place, and took one of them prisoner, who attempted to amuse the colonel with the tale of their being ready to sue for peace; but he, not crediting the story, marched cautiously forward for a mile, when his advanced guard was fired on from a thicket, and in the *mêlée* its captain was killed. Montgomery, hearing the firing, ordered the grenadiers and light infantry to advance, who steadily pushed forward through an ambuscade of five hundred Indians, rousing them from their coverts. As they reached more elevated and clearer ground, the troops drove the Indians before them at the point of the bayonet. Placing himself at the head of his force, he proceeded towards the town, following a narrow path, where it was necessary to march in Indian file, the surrounding country being well reconnoitred in advance by his scouts. On reaching Etchowee it was found to have been abandoned. After encamping on the open plain, Montgomery ordered out detachments in several directions, who performed gallant services, driving the enemy across a river, killing some, and taking several prisoners, after which, scattering their forces, they inflicted upon the Indians a severe chastisement. He then returned to Charleston by way of the fort on the Keowee, and rejoined Amherst in the North.

The Cherokees being disposed to retaliate these severe irruptions of Colonel Montgomery, the month of August had not elapsed before they began to give unmistakable proofs of unabated hostility. Fort Prince George they had found too strong for them, but the garrison of Fort Loudoun, on the confines of Virginia, being reduced in numbers and in great want of provisions, was immediately besieged. After sustaining the siege until reduced to extremity, the commanding officer, Demere, with the concurrence of all his subordinates, very unwisely surrendered the fortification to his savage foe, August 6, 1760. The result of this ill-advised capitulation soon became apparent, the garrison and men being ruthlessly attacked before they had proceeded any distance from the fort, and both officers and privates cruelly massacred. Captain Stuart was the only officer who escaped, his salvation being due to the intervention of Attakullakulla himself, the leader of the attacking party.

Notwithstanding the reduction of Canada, the Indians in remote districts still continued their opposition to the English power. This was particularly the case with the Cherokees, whom French emissaries kept in constant excitement, and who continued their hostilities. Carolina raised twelve hundred men, under Colonel Henry Middleton, his subordinates including Henry Laurens, Francis Marion, William Moultrie, Andrew Pickens, and Isaac Huger, all destined to become distinguished for patriotic service in the coming Revolution. Lieutenant-Colonel James Grant joining them with two regiments, and some Chickasaw and Catawba Indians as allies, made a force of two thousand six hundred men. They reached Fort Prince George May 29, 1761. On the 10th of June, at Etchowee, where Montgomery had fought them, the Cherokees were gathered, well supplied with arms, and presenting a formidable front. They had the advantage of a superior position, and for three hours the contest was severe and bloody. Finally the bayonet was employed, and so effectually that they gave way, falling back inch by inch, until, completely overpowered, they fled, hotly pursued by their conquerors. A large number were slain. The English loss was fifty. Following up his victory, Grant laid Etchowee in ashes;

corn-fields and granaries were destroyed, and the people were driven to the barren mountains. The spirit of the nation was broken, and, through the venerable Attakullakulla, the chiefs humbly sued for peace. A treaty of amity was concluded, and the Cherokees remained peaceful until the Revolution.

The unnecessary cruelty shown by the white man on this and many similar occasions is evident when we consider that these barbarities exposed to the worst privations of famine only those portions of the savage population who had never offended, or who were least guilty,—the women and children, the sick and the aged. The warrior and hunter could easily appease his hunger by procuring game from the contiguous forests, or he could wander off to remoter tribes, resources not available to the weak, the helpless, and the old.

In October, 1763, the French surrendered the post of Mobile. A congress of the Southern tribes—the Catawbas, Cherokees, Creeks, Chickasaws, and Choctaws—was held at Augusta, Georgia, November 10, 1763, and peace with the Indians of the South and Southwest was ratified.

CHAPTER VI.

CONSPIRACY OF PONTIAC—DETROIT BESIEGED—FRONTIER POSTS CAPTURED—DALZELL'S DEFEAT—BATTLE OF BUSHY RUN—RELIEF OF FORT PITT—SIEGE OF DETROIT RAISED.

OTHER tribes besides the Cherokees at this time manifested dissatisfaction or broke out into open hostility. The Shawnees and Delawares of the Ohio Valley had been inimical to the colonies ever since their expulsion from Pennsylvania in 1759. The entire mass of the Algonkin tribes of the upper lakes and to the west of the Ohio deeply sympathized with the French in the loss of Canada. They hoped that the French flag would be once more unfurled on the Western forts, and this feeling, we are assured by Mante,—a judicious historian of that period,—had been fostered by the French, whose mode of treatment of the Indians he at the same time commends. "For," he continues, "it soon appeared that at the very time we were representing the Indians to ourselves completely subdued and perfectly obedient to our power, they were busy in planning the destruction not only of our most insignificant and remote forts, but our most important and central settlements."[1] Under this impression, General Amherst had ordered to the West, to keep the Indians in check, the regular forces which had been employed against Niagara, Quebec, and Montreal. Little more was done in 1761 than to supply garrisons to the forts at Presque Isle, Detroit, and Michilimackinac, by which, though the country was occupied, its native inhabitants were not overawed.

These log forts, with picketed enclosures, situated at points widely remote from one another, were often left dependent on the Indians for supplies, and served only to notify the red man of the design to occupy the country which for ages had been his own. The small garrisons consisted only of an ensign, a sergeant, and a dozen men. To the affable and temperate Frenchman had succeeded the arrogant Englishman, driving away their Catholic priests, and introducing the hitherto prohibited traffic in rum.

Fort Pitt, the most important post west of the Alleghanies, had been occupied from the period of its capture in 1758, but, its garrison having been reduced by the Indian wars in the West, it was on May 27, 1763, invested by the Shawnees and Delawares and their confederates. The defection of the Western tribes was found to be very great, extending from the Ohio Valley to the whole series of lakes and throughout the valleys of the Illinois, Miami, and Wabash.

The plot was discovered in March by the officer in command at Miami. Amherst,

---

[1] Mante's History of the Late War, pp. 479-81.

who held the Indians in supreme contempt, and who had contributed to their alienation by his arbitrary conduct towards them, while preparing reinforcements, hoped the Indians would be too sensible of their own interests to conspire against the English, and wished them to know that in his eyes they would make "a contemptible figure;" "yes," he repeated, "a contemptible figure." It was Amherst's inhuman suggestion that for the reduction of the disaffected tribes the smallpox should be sent among them.[1]

At this time there was living in the vicinity of Detroit an Ottawa chief possessing more than ordinary intelligence, ambition, eloquence, decision of character, power of combination, and great personal energy, named Pontiac. In subtlety and craft he was unsurpassed.[2] Pontiac was of middle height, with a figure of remarkable symmetry. His complexion was unusually dark, and his features, though void of regularity, were expressive of boldness and vigor, which, united with an habitually imperious and peremptory manner, were indicative of unusual strength of will. Major Rogers speaks of him in terms of high praise. "He puts on," he says, "an air of majesty and princely grandeur, and is greatly honored and revered by his subjects." His conspiracy was an heroic attempt to avert the swift decline which the conquest of Canada by England clearly foreshadowed for his race. He appears to have been the originator of this scheme of a Western confederation against the English, for on November 7, 1760, on the first advance of the relief of the French garrison, when Major Rogers, who led the troops, had reached the entrance to the Straits of Detroit, Pontiac visited his encampment, and, employing one of those bold metaphors which the Indians use to express much in a few words, assuming an air of supremacy, he exclaimed, "I stand in the path." "To form a just estimate of his character, we must judge him by the circumstances in which he was placed; by the profound ignorance and barbarism of his people; by his own destitution of all education and information; and by the jealous, fierce, and intractable spirit of his compeers. When measured by this standard, we shall find few of the men whose names are familiar to us more remarkable for all things proposed and achieved than Pontiac." To him the conduct of the plot had been left. It had been secretly discussed in their councils for about two years, during which time he brought the principal tribes of the region into the scheme. While the treaty of peace between France, England, and Spain was being signed at Paris, February 10, 1763, the Indian tribes were preparing for immediate action. The tribes which formed the nucleus of this plot were the Ottawas, Chippewas, Pottawatomies, and the two bands of Hurons residing on the river Detroit. From facts gleaned after the submission of the tribes to General Bradstreet, in 1764, it appears that this combination was more extensive than had been supposed, and that the Miamis, Piankeshaws, Weas, Senecas, and several tribes of the Lower Mississippi had also been compromitted. The remaining tribes of the Iroquois were kept quiet by the strenuous

---

[1] Amherst to Bouquet: Parkman's Conspiracy of Pontiac, ii. 29.
[2] Parkman's Conspiracy of Pontiac, i. 202.

efforts of Sir William Johnson. The time appointed for a general rising having arrived, the whole line of posts on that frontier, comprising twelve in number, extending from Forts Pitt and Niagara to Green Bay, were simultaneously attacked, and, either by open force or by *finesse*, nine of them taken. The most singular mode of attack among the whole was that practised at Fort Michilimackinac. The fortress at that period occupied the apex of the peninsula of Michigan, where it juts out into the strait in a headland (called Piqutinong). It consisted of a square area, having bastions built of stone, surrounded with pickets, which were closed by gates, and was capable of being defended by its garrison of thirty-five men against any attack. But stratagem was resorted to. The king's birthday (June 4) having arrived, the Ojibwas and their confederates engaged in a game of ball, the most exciting sport of the red man, on the level boulevard which led from the landing up by the fort into the village. The gates were open, and the discipline of the garrison was relaxed. The squaws had entered the fort and remained there. Etherington, the commandant, with one of his lieutenants, stood unsuspectingly outside the gate, watching the game. It had lasted some hours, when, throwing the ball close to the gate, they seized the two officers and carried them into the woods, while the rest rushed into the fort, grasped their hatchets which their squaws had hidden under their blankets, and in a moment killed an officer, a trader, and fifteen men. The rest of the garrison and all the English traders were made prisoners, and robbed of all they possessed. The tomahawk was applied so rapidly that not a drum was beaten or a rank formed, and the place became the scene of one of the most startling massacres; but of three hundred Canadians in the fort not one was molested.

Detroit was selected by Pontiac for the display of his own arts of siege and attack. The fort was under the command of Major Gladwyn, who had a garrison of two complete companies of infantry, numbering one hundred and twenty-two privates and eight officers. There were also within its walls forty French traders and *engagées*. The fort was a large stockade, about twenty feet high and twelve hundred yards in circumference, standing within the limits of the present city, on the riverbank, commanding an extensive prospect above and below. Its three pieces of artillery and three mortars were of small calibre, and so badly mounted as to be useless. Two armed vessels lay in the river. Detroit was the largest of the inland settlements, its climate and fertility attracting alike the white man and the savage. Both banks of the river were occupied by a numerous French population, dwelling upon productive farms, "indolent in the midst of plenty, graziers as well as tillers of the soil, and enriched by Indian traffic."[1] The Pottawatomies dwelt about a mile below the fort, the Wyandots a little lower down on the east side of the strait, and five miles higher up, on the same side, the Ottawas. Pontiac invested the place May 9, 1763, with a total force of four hundred and fifty warriors, who had been instructed at the councils, drilled under his own eye, and painted and feathered for battle. But an attack was not his first move; he aimed to take the fort by a deeply-laid plot,

---

[1] Parkman.

RUINS OF OLD FORT MACKINAC, 1763.

which was in effect to visit the commandant at his quarters, accompanied by a limited number of warriors bearing concealed weapons, to smoke with him the pipe of peace, and to present him with a formal address, which was to be accompanied by a belt of wampum, the most solemn and honored custom in Indian diplomacy. This belt was worked on one side with white and on the other with green beads. Having finished his speech with the white side turned towards his auditor, the reversal of it in his hands to the green side was to be the signal of attack. The plan was well devised, and must have succeeded had it not been revealed to the commandant on the previous evening.

On the day appointed, Pontiac appeared at the gates with his three hundred aboriginal fellow-conspirators, demanding an audience. He was freely admitted, but in passing the esplanade observed an unusual display of the military. The garrison was under arms, and the sentinels doubled, a circumstance which aroused Pontiac's fears, but his covert inquiries were met by a ready answer that "it was to keep the young men[1] to their duty, and prevent idleness." The language employed by one who has collated the local traditions on the subject while they were still within reach may here be quoted. "The business of the council then commenced, and Pontiac proceeded to address Major Gladwyn. His speech was bold and menacing, and his manner and gesticulations vehement, and they became still more so as he approached the critical moment. When he was on the point of presenting the belt to Major Gladwyn (and turning it in his hands), and all was breathless expectation, the drums at the door of the council suddenly rolled the charge, the guards levelled their pieces, and the officers drew their swords from their scabbards. Pontiac was a brave man, constitutionally and habitually. He had fought in many a battle, and often led his warriors to victory. But this unexpected and decisive proof that his treachery was discovered and prevented, entirely disconcerted him. Tradition says he trembled. At all events, he delivered his belt in the usual manner, and thus failed to give his warriors the concerted signal of attack. Major Gladwyn immediately approached the chief, and, drawing aside his blanket, discovered the shortened rifle, and then, after stating his knowledge of the plan, turned him out of the fort, and, unwisely perhaps, permitted him to make his escape."

Foiled in his attempt to take the garrison by stratagem, Pontiac commenced an open attack, and his followers began to assail the scattered English settlers in its vicinity, while on every side could be heard the startling sassaquon, or war-whoop. A widow and her two sons were immediately murdered on the common. A discharged sergeant and his family, cultivating lands on Hog Island, were the next victims. Taking shelter behind buildings contiguous to the fort, an incessant fire was maintained against it, which was continued for several days, blazing arrows being discharged by the Indians, which set fire to some buildings within the walls. Determination of purpose marked every act, while the savage yells of the natives, and the continual reports of murders and outrages, filled the garrison with apprehensions.

---

[1] "Young men," with the Indians, is an equivalent phrase for warriors, when speaking on such topics.

The abandonment of the fort and embarkation of the troops for Niagara was contemplated, but the plan was opposed by the prominent French inhabitants, who were better acquainted with the true character of Indian demonstration and bluster, and particularly with the real dangers of such a voyage. A small vessel was, however, despatched to Niagara on the 21st of May, soliciting aid both in provisions and men through a country entirely occupied by Indians. The Indians unabatedly continued their attacks, absolutely confining the garrison within the walls, and preventing them from obtaining supplies of wood and water. Pontiac meantime conceived the idea of decoying Major Campbell into his camp under the pretence of renewing pacific negotiations. This gentleman was favorably known to the Indians as the immediate predecessor of Major Gladwyn, who had but recently relieved him in the command of the fort. By the advice of those most conversant with the Indian character, Pontiac's request was acceded to, and Major Campbell went to his camp, accompanied by Lieutenant McDougal. But all the projects of Pontiac were set at naught by an unforeseen occurrence. In one of the sorties from the fort an Ottawa of distinction from Michilimackinac had been killed, and his nephew, who was present, determined to avenge his death. Meeting Major Campbell one day, as he was walking in the road near the camp of Pontiac, the savage immediately felled him to the earth with his war-club, and killed him. This act was regretted and disavowed by Pontiac, who, by the detention of Major Campbell, sought only to secure ulterior advantages through the person of his hostage.

On the 16th of May some Hurons and Ottawas presented themselves at the gate of the fort at Sandusky. Ensign Paulli, the commander, ordered seven of them, as old acquaintances and friends, to be admitted. At a given signal, as they sat smoking, Paulli was seized and bound. As he was borne from the room he saw the dead bodies of his massacred garrison lying wherever they had happened to fall. The traders were also killed, their stores plundered, and the fort burned. Paulli was taken to Detroit, whence he afterwards escaped.

At the mouth of the St. Joseph's, accessible only to boats around the promontory of Michigan, a Jesuit mission had, at the conquest of Canada, given place to an English ensign, with a garrison of fourteen soldiers and some traders. On the morning of May 25, a party of Pottawatomies approached the fort and were admitted. Suddenly a cry was heard in the barracks, Schlosser, the commanding officer, was seized, and the garrison—excepting three men—were massacred. The survivors were taken to Detroit and exchanged.

In the forest near Fort Wayne stood Fort Miami, garrisoned also by an ensign and a few soldiers. On May 27, Holmes, its commander, was informed that Detroit had been attacked, and communicated the intelligence to his men. An Indian woman pretending that a squaw in a neighboring cabin was ill and required to be bled, he went on the errand of mercy, and was shot. The sergeant following was taken prisoner, and the soldiers—nine in number—surrendered.

Fort Ouantanon, just below Lafayette, Indiana, fell on the 1st of June. Its commander having been lured into an Indian cabin and bound, his men surrendered.

The prisoners were received into the houses of the French, who had procured the favor by gifts of wampum to the victors.

The fort at Presque Isle, now Erie, was the point of communication between Pittsburg and Niagara and Detroit. It was garrisoned by twenty-four men, was quite tenable, and could easily have been relieved. Nevertheless, Ensign Christy, after two days' defence, overcome with terror, surrendered on June 22.

Le Bœuf, attacked on the 18th, kept the foe at bay until midnight, when the block-house was set on fire. The brave commander escaped with his garrison to the woods. On their way to Fort Pitt the fugitives passed the ruins of Venango. No living soul had escaped to tell its fate.

The fury of the savages was not limited to the attack of stockades. They massacred and scalped more than one hundred traders, murdered husbandmen and laborers in the field, and did not spare even the children in the cradle. They menaced Fort Ligonier, and, passing the Alleghanies, carried devastation as far as Bedford. For hundreds of miles from north to south, houses, cattle, and other property were destroyed, and a thrifty population was suddenly reduced to beggary and despair. Two thousand persons were killed or carried off, and nearly as many families were driven from their homes.

Anticipating succors to be on their way to Detroit, the Indians kept vigilant watch at the mouth of the river. This duty appears to have been committed to the Wyandots. Towards the end of May a detachment of troops from Niagara, having charge of twenty-three bateaux laden with provisions and supplies, encamped at Point Pelée, on the north shore, near the head of Lake Erie, wholly unconscious that any danger awaited them. Their movements had, however, been closely reconnoitred by the Indians, who, having formed an ambuscade at this place, furiously attacked them near daybreak. During the resulting panic, the officer in command leaped into a boat, and, accompanied by thirty men, crossed the lake to Sandusky. The rest of the detachment were killed or taken prisoners, and all the stores fell into the enemy's hands. The prisoners were reserved to row the boats. On the 30th of May the first of the long line of bateaux was seen from the fort as it rounded Point Huron, on the Canada shore. The garrison crowded the ramparts to view the welcome sight, and a gun was fired as a signal to their supposed approaching friends. But the only response was the gloomy war-cry. As the first boat came opposite to the little vessel anchored off the fort, the soldiers rowing it determined to recapture it. While the steersman headed the boat across, another soldier threw overboard the Indian who sat on the bow. In the struggle both were drowned, but the boat was rowed under the guns of the fort. Lest the other captive rowers should imitate this example, they were landed by the Indians on Hog Island, and immediately massacred.

News of the treaty of peace concluded at Versailles February 10, 1763, between France and England, reached Detroit on the 3d of June, while these events were in progress. From the French who were assembled on this occasion the intelligence received a full and prompt acquiescence, as a conclusive sovereign act, but the

Indians continued the siege. Pontiac, finding he could not take the fort, proposed to the French inhabitants to aid him, but they refused. About this time the vessel which had been despatched to Niagara by Major Gladwyn arrived at the mouth of the river with supplies and some sixty men. The winds being light and baffling, the Indians determined to capture her, and a large force left the siege and proceeded to Fighting Island for that purpose. While the vessel was lying at the mouth of the river the Indians had endeavored to annoy her by means of their canoes, but the wind had forced her to shift her anchorage to this spot. The captain had ordered his men below decks, to keep the Indians in ignorance of his strength, having apprised them that a loud stroke of a hammer on the mast would be a signal for them to come up. As soon as night fell, the Indians came off in their canoes in great force, and attempted to board her, but a sudden discharge of her guns disconcerted them. The following day the vessel dropped down to the mouth of the straits, where she was detained six days by calms. Meantime, Pontiac, determining to destroy her, floated down burning rafts, constructed of the timbers from barns destroyed by the Indians, dry pine, and a quantity of pitch added to make the whole more combustible. Notwithstanding two such rafts were sent down the river, the vessel and boats escaped them. A breeze springing up on the 30th of June, the vessel was enabled to hoist sail, and reached the fort in safety.

General Amherst, the commander-in-chief, was fully sensible of the perilous position of the Western posts in consequence of the Indian hostility, and, though weakened by the force withdrawn for the Indian war in the West, prepared to send at the earliest period reinforcements to Forts Pitt, Niagara, and Detroit. The relief destined for the latter post was placed under the orders of his secretary, Captain Dalzell, who, after relieving Niagara, proceeded to Detroit in armed bateaux, at the head of a force of three hundred men. To the joy of all concerned, this reinforcement arrived at Detroit on the 29th of July, when the place had been besieged upwards of fifty days. Captain Dalzell, who brought this timely accession to the garrison, proposed a night assault on Pontiac's camp, which the commandant assented to, although with some misgivings. Two hundred and fifty men were selected for this duty, and with this force Captain Dalzell left the fort as secretly as possible at half-past two o'clock on the morning of the 31st. At the same time two boats were despatched to keep pace with the party and, if necessary, take off the wounded. The darkness of the night rendered it somewhat difficult to discern the way, and made it impossible to keep the proper distance between the platoons. After marching about two miles, when the vanguard had reached the bridge over the stream which has since been known as Bloody Run, a sudden fire was poured in by the Indians, creating a temporary panic among the troops, from which, however, they soon recovered. The intense darkness completely obscuring the enemy, a retreat was ordered, when it appeared that there was a heavy force in the rear, through which the column had been allowed to pass. The English were, in fact, in the midst of a well-planned ambuscade. Dalzell displayed the utmost bravery and spirit in this emergency, but was soon shot down and killed. Grant, on whom the command devolved, was severely wounded. The Indians were concealed behind the wooden picketing which lined the fields and sheltered the buildings of the *habitans;* but as the day began to dawn the troops were enabled to discern their perilous position. They then embarked some of their wounded in the boats which had accompanied them, and, concentrating their forces, retreated towards the gates of the fort, which they entered in compact order. The loss in this attack was fifty-nine killed and wounded, being nearly one-fourth of the sallying party. It was a decided triumph for the Indians, who thenceforth pressed the siege with renewed vigor.

As the season for hunting approached, the Indians gradually dispersed, the siege languished, and was finally abandoned. There is no previous record in Indian history of so large a force of Indians having been kept in the field for so long a period; and this effort of the Algonkin chief to roll back the tide of European emigration was the most formidable that was ever made by any member of the Indian race. Rogers styles Pontiac an emperor. He certainly possessed an energy of mind and powers of combination equalling those of any other chief of his race. Opechancanough possessed great firmness, and was a bitter enemy of the white race, Sassacus fought for tribal rights and supremacy, the course of Uncas was that of a politician, Pometakom battled to repel the people whose education, industry, and religion foredoomed his own; but Pontiac took a more enlarged and comprehensive view, not only of the field of contest, but also of the means necessary for the retention and preservation of the aboriginal dominion. At a later period, Brant merely fought for and under the direction of a powerful ally, and Tecumseh but re-enacted the deeds of Pontiac after the lapse of fifty years, when the scheme of repelling the whites was preposterous.

The struggle of the Indians, in conjunction with the French, for supremacy in America, may be said to have commenced in 1753, when Washington first originated the idea among the Western tribes that the Virginians were taking preliminary steps to cross the Alleghanies, the limit of the English settlements, and open the route for the influx of the entire European race. This notion may be perceived in the addresses of Pontiac. "Why," he exclaimed, repeating, as he alleged, the words of the Master of Life, "why do you suffer these dogs in red clothing to take the land I gave you? Drive them from it, and when you are in distress I will help you." The policy of driving back the English accorded well with the views of the French, who carefully encouraged it, and first developed it at the repulse of Washington before Fort Necessity, and gave to it a new impetus the following year at Braddock's defeat, an event which had the effect of arousing the passions of the Indians. From this date they became determined opponents of the spread of British power, and always formed a part of the French forces in the field. Such was their position under Montcalm, at Lake George, in 1757, and also at the sanguinary defeat of Major Grant in 1758. The epoch for making this struggle could not have been better chosen had they even been perfectly conversant with the French and English policy, and the result was ten years of the most troublesome Indian wars with which the colonies were ever afflicted. As time progressed, it became evident that the long colonial struggle between the two crowns must terminate. If the English were defeated, not only the French but the Indians would triumph, while it was equally true that if the French failed the Indian power must succumb. Pontiac perfectly understood this, and so informed his confederates. This question was settled by the peace of Versailles; but the Indians did not feel disposed to drop the contest. Detroit was still closely invested; Fort Pitt, built by General Stanwix, in 1759, upon the ruins of Fort Du Quesne, was also beleaguered, and the only road by which relief could reach it passed through dreary tracts of wilderness and over high mountains. It was likewise located on a frontier, the inhabitants of which lived in continual dread of the Indians. Its garrison consisted of three hundred and thirty soldiers, traders, and backwoodsmen. On the night of July 27 the fort, which had been besieged since the 27th of May, was fiercely attacked, and for five days and nights a constant fire was kept up from all sides, though with slight result. Fire-arrows were frequently shot at it, in the hope of setting it on fire. The guns of the fort were effectively used until the approach of succor caused the Indians to decamp.

General Amherst ordered Colonel Bouquet to relieve this post with the remnants of two regiments which had returned in a feeble and shattered condition from the siege of Havana. The route lay through Pennsylvania, by way of Carlisle and Fort Bedford, and many discouragements were in the way. Troops and supplies came forward slowly. He reached Fort Bedford on the 25th of July, and thence pushed on to Fort Ligonier, relieving that post from a threatened siege. As soon as the Indians who were besieging Fort Pitt heard of his approach, they left that place and prepared to oppose his march. Bouquet had disencumbered himself of his wagons, as also of much heavy baggage, at Fort Ligonier, and moved on with alacrity, conveying his provisions on horses. On entering the defile of Turtle Creek, on August 5, his advance had proceeded but a short distance when it was briskly attacked on both flanks. A severe and desperate battle ensued, which admitted of several manœuvres and gave occasion for the display of Bouquet's gallantry. Captains Graham and McIntosh, of the regulars, were killed, and five officers wounded. As the day closed, an elevation was gained, on which the troops bivouacked. At daybreak the following morning the Indians surrounded the camp and commenced a lively fusillade, making frequent charges, and alternately attacking and retreating. This became very annoying to the troops, who were greatly fatigued and destitute of water. They fought in an extended circle. At length the colonel resorted to the ruse of withdrawing two companies from the outer line and making a feint of retreating. By this movement he decoyed the Indians into a position where they were promptly charged with the bayonet and repelled. Their retreat soon became a rout, which involved a part of the Indian forces hitherto unengaged.

This was one of the best-contested actions ever fought between the white man and the Indian. The savages displayed the utmost intrepidity, and the English would have been defeated had it not been for their coolness and the skilful conduct of their officers.

Bouquet then advanced to Bushy Run, where there was an abundance of water; but he had hardly posted his troops when the Indians again commenced an attack, which was, however, speedily repulsed. The loss in these actions amounted to fifty men killed and sixty wounded, almost one-fourth of his command.

After these battles the Indians did not renew the siege of Fort Pitt, but withdrew beyond the Ohio, and four days subsequent to the action at Bushy Run Bouquet entered Fort Pitt.

Meantime, the Indians were still closely besieging Detroit, and the garrison began to suffer from fatigue and want of provisions. A vessel, manned by twelve men and in charge of two masters, was despatched from Fort Niagara during the latter part of August with stores for its relief. It reached the entrance to Detroit River on the 3d of September, when, the wind being adverse, the crew dropped the anchor. About nine o'clock in the evening the boatswain discovered a fleet of canoes approaching, containing about three hundred and fifty Indians. The bow gun was fired, but too late, as the canoes had by this time surrounded the vessel. The Indians immediately cut the cable and began to board her, notwithstanding the fire from the small arms and also from a swivel. The crew then seized their pikes, a new weapon of defence with which they were provided, and, fighting with great bravery and determination, killed and wounded more than twice their own number of the foe, who were already leaping over her bulwarks. Some of them had gained her deck, when Jacobs, the mate, called out to blow up the schooner. Catching the meaning of his words, the Indians leaped overboard, panic-stricken, to escape the threatened explosion. The ship at the same time swinging around enabled the crew to use their guns effectively. The master and one man were killed, and four men wounded; but, a breeze springing up, the other seamen hoisted sail, and brought the vessel safely to Detroit. For this brave act each of the crew was presented with a silver medal.

The garrison being thus provided with supplies, the further efforts of the Indians proved of no great consequence. As the season for hunting approached, the savages mostly dispersed, except some small parties who watched the fort and prevented any egress from it. Open war never being carried on by the Indians during the winter, Major Gladwyn made such a judicious disposition of his means as prevented any surprise during that season.

Fort Niagara had not been attacked, although its garrison was weak; but its precincts were continually infested by hostile Indians, which made it necessary to send out large escorts with every train despatched from it. To rid the Niagara Valley of this annoyance and open the route to Schlosser, a detachment of ninety men was directed to scour the surrounding country. Owing to the inconsiderate ardor of the officer in command, and also to his ignorance of Indian subtlety in time of war, the detachment was decoyed into an ambuscade, in which he and all his men, with the exception of three or four, were killed.

CHAPTER VII.

EXPEDITIONS OF BOUQUET AND BRADSTREET—PACIFICATION OF THE TRIBES—
DEATH OF PONTIAC.

THE campaign of 1763 had the effect rather to inspire than to depress the hopes of the Indians. The English forces had been withdrawn to further projects of conquest in the West Indies, thus leaving but few troops on the frontiers. Forts Pitt and Detroit had for many months been closely invested by the tribes, who completely debarred ingress and egress. The determination evinced by the forces of Pontiac at Detroit, his attacks on the shipping sent to its relief, the sanguinary encounter at Bloody Run, in which Dalzell was slain, and that at Bushy Run, where Colonel Bouquet was so actively opposed, together with the utter destruction of a detachment of ninety men and its officers on the Niagara portage, afforded an additional stimulus to the efforts of the Indians. These successes not only served to inflate the Indian pride, but likewise denoted a feeble military administration on the part of the British commander.

General Amherst was of opinion that more vigorous action and a more comprehensive and definite plan were required for the campaign of 1764, while at the same time the ministry had crippled his powers by withdrawing nearly all his regular troops. Under these circumstances he called for aid from the colonies, determining to send Colonel Bouquet with an efficient army against the Western tribes, who were beleaguering Fort Pitt and overawing the valleys of the Ohio, Miami, Scioto, and Wabash, and at the same time to direct Colonel Bradstreet to proceed with a large force in boats against the Northwestern tribes at Detroit. To enable him to carry out his plans, he appealed earnestly to the respective colonial legislatures for troops, which were cheerfully supplied. Sir William Johnson determined to hold a general convention of the tribes at Fort Niagara, in connection with the Bradstreet movement, and to endeavor to induce as many Indians as possible to accompany that officer on his expedition to the vicinage of the upper lakes. Having made these arrangements, Lord Amherst, who had zealously and efficiently prosecuted the war against Canada, solicited leave to return to England, and was succeeded in the command by General Gage, an officer of very moderate abilities, who, a few years later, as commander-in-chief of Massachusetts, inaugurated the hostile movements which brought on the Revolutionary War.

It being necessary to conduct the operations of Bradstreet's detachment by water, that officer superintended the work of constructing a flotilla of bateaux at Schenectady, on a plan of his own invention, each boat having forty-six feet keel and being sufficiently capacious to contain twenty-seven men and six weeks' provisions. As soon as this immense flotilla was ready, it was ordered to Oswego, where Sir William Johnson had directed the Indians to assemble. Bradstreet's force of all descriptions, on reaching Oswego, numbered about twelve hundred. These vessels were employed to transport the heavy stores to the mouth of the Niagara, and the Indians in their canoes followed the extended train of bateaux along the Ontario coasts, making the usual landings at the Bay of Sodus[1] and Irondequoit. They arrived at Fort Niagara in the beginning of July. This concourse of boats and men was, however, in reality the smallest part of the display.

A large number of the Indian tribes had been summoned to a council by Sir William Johnson, who had collected seventeen hundred Indians at Niagara. Never before had such a body of Indians been congregated under his auspices. The council was held in Fort Niagara. He had brought with him the preliminary articles of a treaty of peace, amity, and alliance which had been prepared by him at Johnson Hall, where it had received the signatures of several of the leading chiefs. Major Gladwyn had sent Indian deputies from Detroit, and various causes had combined to swell the attendance at this great convention. Henry relates that one of Sir William's messages reached Sault Ste. Marie, at the foot of Lake Superior, and induced the tribe there located to send a deputation of twenty persons. The Senecas, however, whose conduct had been equivocal during the war, did not make their appearance, although their deputies had signed the preliminary articles at Johnson Hall. Sir William sent to their villages on the Genesee repeated messages for them, which were uniformly answered by promises. But promises would not serve, and, consequently, Colonel Bradstreet authorized the baronet to send a final message announcing that if they did not present themselves in five days he would send a force against them and destroy their villages. This brought them to terms; they immediately attended the convention, and at the same time surrendered their prisoners. A formal treaty of peace was then concluded.

Colonel Bradstreet desired to depart immediately, but Sir William begged him to postpone his march until he had finished with the tribes and given them their presents, for although he had just concluded a treaty of peace with them he had no faith in their fidelity, and feared that if the troops were withdrawn they would attack the fort. With this request Bradstreet complied. He at length departed, taking with him three hundred Indian warriors as auxiliaries, although he was conscious they accompanied him rather in the character of spies. Sir William, having accomplished this important pacification, returned home, and on the 6th of August Colonel Bradstreet proceeded on his protracted expedition along the southern coasts of Lake Erie. His intentions, as publicly announced, were to conclude peace with such tribes as solicited it, and to chastise all who continued in arms. Being detained by contrary winds at l'Anse aux Feuilles, he there received a deputation from the Wyandots of Sandusky, the Shawnees and Delawares of the Ohio, and the bands of the Six

---

[1] In a manuscript journal of this expedition, written by John McKenny, an orderly in the 44th, or Royal Scots, and in our possession, this bay is called Onosodus, which appears to be the aboriginal term.

Nations residing on the Scioto Plains. The sachems deputed by these tribes presented four belts of wampum as an earnest of their desire for peace, and in their speeches to Bradstreet excused their respective nations for the murders and outrages committed, on the usual pretext of not being able to restrain their young warriors, or of not being aware of the real state of facts, at the same time soliciting forgiveness for the past and promising fidelity for the future. Variable weather delayed Bradstreet for some days, but he was at length enabled to proceed, and on the 23d of August reached Point Petite Isle, where intelligence reached him that the Indians collected on the Maumee were resolved to oppose his progress. He immediately determined to attack them in that position, whither Pontiac had then retired; but while yet on Lake Erie, pursuing his course to the mouth of the Maumee, he received a deputation from the Indians of that stream, who requested a conference at Detroit. Visiting the Bay of Maumee, and finding the Indian camp abandoned, he returned to Point Petite Isle, and from this position detached Captain Morris, at the head of a body of men, with directions to march across the country and take possession of the territory of the Illinois, which had been ceded to England by the treaty concluded at Versailles in 1763.[1] Bradstreet then proceeded to the head of Lake Erie, and, entering the Straits of Detroit, reached the town and fort on the 26th of August. Never previously had so large a force, accompanied by so much military display, been seen in that vicinity. The long lines of bateaux and barges, filled with their complement of military, with their glittering arms, their colors flying, drums beating, and bugles sounding, were followed by those containing the attachés of the quartermaster's and commissary's departments, and by the fleet of canoes containing the three hundred auxiliary Mohawks and Senecas, together with the deputies of the surrounding tribes. Indians always judge from appearances, and every attendant circumstance indicated that the British government, which could send so numerous and well-appointed a force to so distant a point, must in itself be strong. Bradstreet determined to land his army on the plain extending from the fort along the banks of the river, and as detachment after detachment filed past with military exactitude to its position in the extended camp, the gazing multitudes of red men realized the peril of their past position and trembled for the future. The commander did not take up his quarters in the fort, but directed his marquee, on which the red cross of England was displayed, to be pitched in the centre of this vast encampment. The 7th of September was appointed for the meeting of the council, when the aboriginal deputies were received, decked out with all their Oriental taste, and bearing their ornamented pipes of peace. The first tribes on the ground were the Ottawas and Chippewas, who had been the head and front of Pontiac's offending. They were represented by Wassong, attended by five other chiefs, whose respective names were Attowatomig, Shamindawa, Ottawany, Apokess, and Abetto. Wassong made his submission in terms that would not have been discreditable to a philosopher or a diplomatist. He excused his nation for their participation

---

[1] It appears from Parkman's "Conspiracy of Pontiac" that this duty was ill performed.

in the war, laid the blame where it properly belonged, and then, appealing to the theology which recognizes God as the great ruler of events, who orders them in wisdom and mercy, promised obedience to the British crown. While speaking, he held in his hand a belt of wampum having a blue and white ground, interspersed with devices in white, green, and blue, which, at the close of his speech, he deposited as a testimonial of the truth of his words. He then, holding forth a purple and mixed belt, in the name of his people tendered their submission, depositing this belt also as their memorial. Shamindawa then addressed the council in the name of Pontiac, saying that he regretted what had happened, and asked that it should be forgiven, adding that it would give him pleasure to co-operate with the English. He concluded by praying for the success of the Illinois mission, as though he considered it a perilous undertaking. The Hurons, who had been actively engaged in the war, next presented their submission, and affixed to the treaty the emblematic signature of a deer and a cross. A Miami chief, whose signature was a turtle, next presented himself in the name of his nation, to concur in the terms acceded to by the Ottawas and Chippewas. The Pottawatomies and Foxes then affixed their signatures by the pictograph of a fox, an eel, and a bear. The Mississagies were represented by Wapacomagot, and signified their acquiescence by tracing the figure of an eagle with a medal round its neck. The entire number of Indians present at the conclusion of the treaty with Colonel Bradstreet has been estimated at nineteen hundred and thirty.[1]

Bradstreet, having closed his negotiations with the Indians, reorganized the militia, and established the civil government in the French settlements on a firm basis, prepared to return to Sandusky, with the view of complying with his instructions from General Gage, directing him to bring the Shawnees and Delawares to terms. On reaching Sandusky he received letters from General Gage censuring him for offering terms of peace to the Shawnee and Delaware delegates, and for his general course in concluding treaties of peace with the Indians without consulting Sir William

---

[1] Mante, p. 526. The warriors present, and their numerical force, were as follows:

Ottawas	220	
Chippewas	300	
Saukies	50	
Hurons	80	
		650
Saginaws, including those of St. Joseph.		
Chippewas	150	
Pottawatomies	450	
		600
Of Sandusky.		
Hurons	200	
Miamis	250	
Weas	230	
		680
Total		1930

Johnson, who was the Superintendent of Indian Affairs, and with whom he was directed to put himself in communication. This is the first instance of that collision of authority between the officers of the military and Indian service of which the entire subsequent history of our Indian affairs affords abundant examples down to the present day. Prior to this period, Bradstreet had left a relief of seven companies in the fort at Detroit, under the command of Lieutenant-Colonel Campbell. Two companies under Captain Howard, together with a detachment of artillery and two companies of the recently-organized militia, were at the same time ordered to reoccupy Michilimackinac. To supply that post effectually, a vessel, under command of Lieutenant Sinclair of the Fifteenth Regular Infantry, was directed to enter Lake Huron. This, it is declared, was the first English vessel that ever attempted the passage,[1] and the voyage appears to have been considered an intrepid feat, from which we may reasonably infer that the name of the lake and river Sinclair (St. Clair) was derived.[2] Sinclair, tradition asserts, was the commandant of Michilimackinac prior to the arrival of Captain Robinson, who held the command on the island in 1783, when a façade of its mural precipices fell down.

The post of Michilimackinac was in 1764 situated on a northern headland of the peninsula of Michigan, jutting into the straits, opposite to and in sight of the island, and also of Point St. Ignace. This was the point which had been selected by Marquette as the site of a mission, and in its simple graveyard his remains were interred after his decease at the little river bearing his name on the east shores of Lake Michigan.[3] By order of General Amherst, the French garrison was relieved after the capture of Montreal, and the troops sent for that purpose were led by Major Rogers, the partisan, who had been succeeded by Major Etherington at the time of the massacre in 1763. At the date of the massacre the Indians did not burn the fort, which, as the traders lived within it, would have destroyed their goods, and it was, therefore, reoccupied in 1764, the walls, bastions, and gates remaining entire. Tradition asserts that this fort was visited and supplied by vessels for seven years subsequently. The alarm produced by the American Revolution appears to have caused the transfer of the fortification to the island, which, tradition affirms, was made about the year 1780. The Michilimackinac of the French was, therefore, located on the apex of the peninsula, that of the English on the island.

Michilimackinac had from an unknown period been regarded by the aborigines as a sacred island, consecrated both by their mythology and their history. It was believed to be the local residence of important spirits of their pantheon, and its caverns as well as its cliffs were calculated to favor this idea. They landed on it with awe, and its precincts were preserved from the intrusion of European feet. The bones found

---

[1] It was originally made by the "Griffin," under La Salle, in 1678.
[2] The entire river from Huron to Erie was called Detroit by the early French writers.
[3] After their removal to the island, his bones were interred in the Catholic church-yard, but a question of title springing up many years subsequently caused them to be again disturbed, after which they were reinterred at La Crosse, Michigan.

BOSTON PUBLIC LIBRARY.

in its caves, its deep subterranean passages, the regular heaps of superimposed boulders, and the evidences of cultivation still to be seen in many isolated spots, surrounded with impenetrable foliage, denote that it had not only been occupied from very early times, but that its occupancy was connected with their earliest history, superstitions, and mythology.

Traditions which have been carefully sought out mention that the English were the first nation who were permitted to occupy its sacred shores with troops, by whom a fort, in the form of a talus, owing to the shape of the cliff, was placed on its edge. A village was laid out on the narrow gravel plain below. The harbor, though small, possesses a good anchorage, and is sheltered from all winds except those from the east. Merchants who supplied the traders to a wide extent of country east, west, and north located their places of business on the island. The traders fitted out annually by these merchants held intercourse with the tribes of Lake Superior, Michigan, Green Bay, the Mississippi, and the Illinois. British capital and enterprise established this trade on a new footing, and from this time forth it became a trade-centre for a vast country, the Indians travelling thither a distance of one thousand miles in their canoes, bearing with them their weapons and the tokens of their bravery and decorated with all their feathers and finery. Detroit, Vincennes, Kaskaskia, Cahokia, St. Louis, Prairie du Chien, St. Peters, Chegoimegon, the vicinity of the Lake of the Woods, and Lake Winnipeg, as well as the valley of the Saskatchewan, became mere dependencies of the new metropolis of Indian trade, Michilimackinac.

The great object of the campaign of 1764 was, however, not yet accomplished. The North was safe, but in order to establish a permanent and general peace with the Indians it was requisite that the war should be vigorously and successfully prosecuted in the South and West. Both the British commanders intrusted with the pacification must be triumphant. They must prove to the Indians the ability of the English not only to take but also to hold Canada. Pontiac was not the only aboriginal chief who had doubted this ability.

The plan of Sir Jeffrey Amherst to bring the Western Indians to terms after the final conquest of Canada was well devised. Had he directed but a single operation against them, both the Southwestern and Northwestern tribes would have united to oppose it, but by sending a controlling force, under Bradstreet, to the Northwest, through the great lakes, to Detroit, and at the same time another under Bouquet from the present site of Pittsburg to the Tuscarawas and the Muskingum, against the tribes of the Southwest, he effectually divided their force, and demonstrated to them the power and energy of the government claiming their submission, whose military prowess had caused the time-honored French flag to be struck at Quebec, Montreal, Niagara, and Du Quesne. His successor, General Gage, merely carried out this plan, though, if we may credit the testimony of a contemporary officer, without much appreciation of the necessary details.

The offer of terms of peace to the Shawnees and other Southwestern tribes dubiously represented in the month of August, 1764, as made by Colonel Bradstreet while on his way to Detroit, was deemed by the other officers in the field to be a vainglorious assumption of power and an unnecessary interference with the civic duties of Sir William Johnson. But Bradstreet's ardor and promptitude as a commander created a very favorable impression on the Indians in the region of the lakes, and his expedition to that then remote point inaugurated one of the soundest features of the British Indian policy.

Bradstreet did not leave Detroit until the 14th of September, and on the 18th he reached Sandusky Bay, where he detached a party with orders to destroy a settlement of Mohicans in that vicinity under Mohigan John; but the Indians eluded them. Single delegates from the Delawares, Shawnees, and Scioto-Iroquois, accompanied by a Tuscarora Indian, here met him, and made statements which, it is conceived, were not entitled to any weight, but were dictated by the spirit of Indian subtlety which anticipated coming evil. He then proceeded with his army to Upper Sandusky, where a Wyandot village had been destroyed the previous year by Captain Dalzell. Here he received letters from General Gage disapproving of his offers of peace to the Delawares and Shawnees. He had been directed to attack the Wyandots of Sandusky, and also the Delawares and Shawnees, then residing on the Muskingum and Scioto. The route to the former river, he was correctly informed, was up the Cuyahoga, and to the latter up the Sandusky. Both the carrying-places were stated to be short, and the choice of either was left to him. But on making trial of the Sandusky the water appeared to be too low, and his guides led him to think that from the shortness of the portage his provisions could be transported on men's shoulders. The portage between the Cuyahoga and the Tuscarawas fork of the Muskingum was found to be at that season equally impracticable. In this dilemma, and to enable him to act as a check on the Delawares and Shawnees, against whom Bouquet was marching, Bradstreet determined to encamp on the Sandusky portage. He opened a communication with Colonel Bouquet, who was advancing from Pittsburg at the head of his army; and by occupying this position he likewise exerted a favorable influence towards concluding a general peace with the Western Indians, which effect resulted from that movement. From Indians who visited his camp he learned that the Delawares and Shawnees were already tired of the war and sought to make a peace on the best terms they could obtain. They were the more anxious on this point because of the threat of the Six Nations, who were strongly in the English interest, to make war on them. To them such a war was far more to be dreaded than the English armies, for they trembled at the very mention of the Iroquois. Everything, indeed, pointed to a favorable termination of the war.

During the autumn and winter of 1763-64 Bouquet had remained in garrison at Fort Pitt, where the Indians did not molest him. But experience had demonstrated that the subtlety and agility of the savages, and their superior knowledge of the topographical features of the wilderness, required a degree of caution on the march beyond what would have been necessary in opposing civilized troops. The force destined for Bouquet reached Fort Pitt on the 17th of September, while Bradstreet was on his way from Detroit to Sandusky, but the former did not leave Fort Pitt until the 3d of October. He had under his command fifteen hundred men, furnished with every needful supply. Having become an adept in the use of field-maps, guides, and forest arts, he marched slowly and surely, his army covering a large space in the forest, and indicating great strength of purpose as well as confidence of success. All this was observed and duly reported by Indian spies. The Indians, moreover, were aware that Bradstreet was on the Sandusky at the head of even a larger force. To employ an Indian simile, these armies appeared like two converging clouds, which must soon overwhelm them.

On the 6th of October the army reached Beaver River, where they found a white man who had escaped from the Indians. He stated that the latter were in great alarm, and that those located along Bouquet's line of march had concealed themselves. On the 8th the troops crossed the Little Beaver River, and on the 14th encamped on the Tuscarawas. A competent observer, who visited the country in 1748, reported the number of Indian warriors then in the Ohio Valley at seven hundred and eighty-nine. Of these there were Senecas, one hundred and sixty-three; Shawnees, one hundred and sixty-two; Wyandots, one hundred and forty; Mohawks, seventy-four; Mohicans, fifteen; Onondagas, thirty-five; Cayugas, twenty; Oneidas, fifteen; and Delawares, one hundred and sixty-five. These figures would indicate an aggregate population of a fraction under four thousand, and it is not probable that the number had varied much in sixteen years. While encamped on the Tuscarawas, two men arrived who had been sent by Bouquet from Fort Pitt as messengers to Colonel Bradstreet. On their return they had been captured by the Delawares and conveyed to an Indian village sixteen miles distant, where they were detained until the news arrived of Bouquet's advance with an army. From information subsequently received through Major Smallwood, one of the captives was finally surrendered by the Indians, a report being circulated that Bouquet was advancing to extirpate them. The effect of this news on the Indians implicated was to determine them, with the connivance of a low-minded French trader, to massacre all the prisoners in their hands. The two messengers, however, were liberated, and commissioned to tell Colonel Bouquet that the Shawnees and Delawares would visit him for the purpose of proposing terms of peace. Accordingly, their deputies arrived two days subsequently, and brought information that all their chiefs were assembled at the distance of about eight miles. The following day was appointed for a conference at Colonel Bouquet's tent. The first delegation which advanced comprised twenty Senecas, under the direction of their chief, Kigaschuta; next came twenty Delawares, marshalled by Custaloga and Amik; and then six Shawnees, led by Keissnautchta, who appeared as the representative of several tribes. Each chief tendered a belt of wampum, accompanying its presentation by a speech which embraced the usual subjects of Indian diplomacy, excusing what had been done during the war, placing all the censure on the rashness of their young men, promising to deliver up all their captives, soliciting a cessation of hostilities, and pledging future fidelity to their agreements.

Bouquet realized the advantage of his position, and a day was appointed for his answer, which, when given, embraced all the points in question. He spoke to them as one having full authority, accused them of perfidy, upbraided them for having pillaged and murdered English traders, and charged them with killing four English messengers who carried a commission from the king. He also spoke to them of the audacity of their course in besieging the king's troops at Fort Pitt. The whole tone of his address was elevated, truthful, and manly. He concluded by informing them that if they would deliver up to him all the prisoners, men, women, and children, then in their possession, not even excepting those who had married into the tribes, furnish them with clothing, horses, and provisions, and convey them to Fort Pitt, he would grant them peace, but on no other terms.

He then broke up the conference and put his army in motion for the Muskingum, it being a more central position, and one from which, if the Indians faltered in carrying out their engagements, he could the more readily direct his operations against them. While the army was encamped on the Tuscarawas, the Delawares brought in eighteen white prisoners, and also eighty small sticks, indicating the number still in their possession. The army broke ground on the Muskingum on the 25th of October, and on the 28th Caughnawaga Peter arrived with letters from Colonel Bradstreet. During the ensuing week the camp was a scene of continual arrivals and excitement. During the month of November the Indians of the various tribes delivered up their captives. Such a scene was perhaps never before witnessed, and certainly nothing like it ever afterwards took place. They surrendered of Virginians thirty-two men and fifty-eight women and children, and of Pennsylvanians forty-nine men and sixty-seven women and children. Major Smallwood, an officer who had been captured the previous year near Detroit by the Wyandots, was likewise restored to his friends. These comprised all who had escaped the war-club, the scalping-knife, and the stake; old and young were indiscriminately mingled together in the area. A solemn council ensued, at which Custaloga represented the Delawares, and Kigaschuta the Senecas. The latter began:

"With this belt" (opening the wampum) "I wipe the tears from your eyes. We deliver you these prisoners, the last of your flesh and blood with us. By this token we assemble and bury the bones of those who have been killed in this unhappy war, which the evil spirit excited us to kindle. We bury these bones deep, never more to be looked or thought on. We cover the place of burial with leaves, that it may not be seen. The Indians have been a long time standing with arms in their hands. The clouds have hung in black above us. The path between us has been shut up. But with this sacred emblem we open the road clear, that we may travel on as our fathers did. We let in light from above to guide our steps. We hold in our hands a silver chain, which we put into yours, and which will ever remain bright and preserve our friendship."

Similar sentiments were expressed by the other speakers, and a general cessation of hostilities resulted; the terms of pacification were agreed on, hostages were demanded and furnished, and six deputies were appointed to visit Sir William Johnson. Bouquet set out on his return to Fort Pitt, which he reached on the 28th of November. From this point the rescued captives were sent to their respective homes. Bradstreet also returned, by way of Lake Erie, to Fort Niagara and Albany, a part of his army having marched thither by land. An effectual termination was thus put to the hostilities of the Indians against the British government consequent upon the conquest of Canada.

The subsequent career of Pontiac may here be briefly noticed. After abandoning the siege of Detroit, he withdrew, in November, to the Maumee, whence, during the following year, he made numerous journeys westward, visiting different tribes to obtain their co-operation in his plans, stirring them by his eloquence and imbuing them with his own fierce spirit. With four hundred warriors at his back, he sought St. Ange, the French commandant of Fort Chartres, and demanded arms, ammunition, and troops, a request which that officer was forced to decline. He even sent an embassy to D'Abadie, Governor of Louisiana, with the same object, but with no other result than the good advice to make his peace with the English.

Recognizing at length the fact that his cause was lost, Pontiac wisely concluded to accept the counsel, and with his chiefs journeyed to Oswego to meet Sir William Johnson, and sealed his submission by a treaty concluded with him July 30, 1766. This "champion of his race" was assassinated in April, 1769, while carousing at Cahokia, Illinois, by an Illinois Indian, who is said to have been bribed to commit the act by an English trader for a barrel of whiskey. The body was buried with the honors of war by his friend St. Ange, commandant of St. Louis.

CHAPTER VIII.

LOGAN—DUNMORE'S EXPEDITION—BATTLE OF POINT PLEASANT—PEACE CONCLUDED—INDIAN TRADE—CAPTAIN JONATHAN CARVER—CENSUS OF THE TRIBES.

THE peace concluded with the Indians, influenced as they were by the presence of large armies, and compelled thereto by the force of circumstances, was not consonant to their feelings, and exercised only a temporary restraint upon their actions. Canada having submitted to the British arms, they had no longer their ancient ally to rest on, and they had finally submitted, in 1764, to a power which they could not continue to oppose, assuming the garb of peace and breathing words of submission while their hearts still glowed with desire for war and plunder. The fire was merely smothered. This state of quasi amity and friendship continued for several years subsequent to the expeditions of Bradstreet and Bouquet. These expeditions had, however, been the means of making geographical explorations which had developed districts of country inviting in all their natural characteristics, and which possessed a deep and fertile soil, and in consequence the desire for their acquisition by an agricultural people became ardent and absorbing. The Indians were very soon regarded as a mere incumbrance on the land, and life was freely ventured in its acquisition.

The project for the settlement of Kentucky originated in 1773. A resolution was formed to make the attempt early in the following spring, notwithstanding the fact that the country was occupied by Indians who had committed some mischief and were suspected of hostile intentions. The mouth of the Little Kanawha was selected as the place of rendezvous. Reports of a very alarming nature deterred several persons from joining in the attempt. About eighty or ninety fearless and enterprising men met at the rendezvous, among whom was George Rogers Clarke, the future conqueror of Illinois. The explorers remained encamped at this point for several days, during which time a small party of hunters, who had gone out to obtain supplies of meat for the camp, were fired on at a point on the Ohio below their camp. This act betokened a state of hostile feeling among the Indians. It being deemed necessary to select a commander, Captain Michael Cresap was chosen, who had acquired a wide reputation as a warrior during the previous year, and who was known to be then on the Ohio above with a party. They had purposed attacking a Shawnee town located on the Scioto River at a place called Horsehead Bottom, but Cresap opposed it, on the ground that, although appearances on the part of the Indians were very suspicious, there was no open war, and that, being yet early in the spring, it was most prudent to await further developments. This advice was followed, and the whole party accompanied him up the river to Wheeling,[1] at which place they established their headquarters. The numbers of the armed explorers were quickly augmented by the surrounding settlers, a fort was erected, and, after some negotiations with the commander at Pittsburg, acting under the authority of Lord Dunmore, the existence of a state of war was publicly announced.

This period of Indian history requires a moment's further attention, as a war with the Shawnees, Delawares, and Mingoes was on the point of commencing. A foul deed was committed a few days subsequently by some reckless and unprincipled traders, or vandal scouts, who, according to Colonel Sparks, unknown to Cresap, stole on Logan's lodge and cruelly murdered his family. This crime introduced on the scene of action the celebrated chieftain Logan, whose misfortunes have excited wide-spread sympathy, and whose simple eloquence has electrified the world.

Logan was born at Shamokin, on the Susquehanna, a spot whose precincts have been hallowed by the good deeds of the benevolent Count Zinzendorf and his followers, who there founded the mission of Bethlehem.[2] Logan's father, whose name was Shikelimo, was an Iroquois, of the Cayuga tribe. Logan himself was a tall, active man, of noble appearance and humane sentiments, and was kind and peaceful in disposition and character. The murder of his family and his relations on the Ohio, in 1774, was not the result of the expedition from Virginia which has just been described, but was attributable to the inordinate desire for acquisition on the one hand, and the feeling of exasperation on the other, which have so long characterized the remote sections of the frontiers. The event occurred two days after the final decision at Wheeling, and at a time when uncommonly great excitement existed. Two canoes from the west bank of the Ohio stopped at a trader's station at the mouth of Yellow River, some twenty miles below Wheeling. There is no evidence that the armed frontiersmen at the station knew that either Logan's wife or sister, or any relative of his, was among the number of these trading visitors, and the atrocious act must be regarded as a result of the then prevalent and rancorous hatred of the Indian race. The victims were shot down in their canoes while crossing the Ohio, not because they were obnoxious as individuals, not because they were of the family of Logan, but simply because they were Indians. Such is the generally acknowledged version of this base transaction. But Colonel Sparks, while exonerating Cresap from complicity in this foul deed, either personally or through any orders or permission given to his men, reveals an entirely new feature in the case. No member of Logan's family was in the two canoes which stopped at Baker's Bottom, but they were killed in Logan's own lodge, on Mingo Bottom, during his absence on a hunting excursion. The cowardly deed was done by some of Cresap's men who had stolen away from his camp contrary to his wishes while he was journeying from Wheeling to Pittsburg, and against his express orders, which were to

---

[1] This Indian (Delaware) name is a derivative from *weel*, a human head, and *ing*, a place,—there being a tradition that the Indians had fixed a human head on a pole at this place.

[2] Logan had married a Shawnee wife, spoke that language, lived with the tribe, and was frequently regarded as a Shawnee.

respect Logan's residence and not to attack it. Not only was this so, but when Cresap heard the firing he immediately ran in the direction whence the sounds proceeded, and interposed his authority to stop the massacre. There is another misstatement which requires correction. The pusillanimous attack on the canoes at Yellow Creek was not committed by the men of Cresap's command, then on the Ohio, far less by Cresap himself, or by his orders. On the contrary, not only was Cresap a brave and worthy man, distinguished for his services in the Indian wars of that period, as well as during the Revolution, which succeeded it, but he was also a friend of Logan, and, according to George Rogers Clarke, opposed an attack on Logan's house at Mingo Bottom.

The force congregated at Wheeling soon became engaged in a struggle with the Indians. A day or two after their arrival at that place, some canoes containing Indians were discovered descending the river under shelter of the island. They were pursued for fifteen miles, when a battle ensued, in which a few men were killed and wounded on each side. Hostilities having thus commenced, the entire country soon swarmed with armed Indians, and the settlers, to insure their own safety, were compelled to huddle together in block-houses.

An express was despatched to Governor Dunmore, at Williamsburg, with information as to the position of affairs on the frontiers. The legislature being then in session, measures were at once adopted for repelling the Indians. Early in the month of June a force of four hundred men, collected in Eastern Virginia, reached Wheeling, whence they descended the river to the Indian town of Wappatomica, but without effecting anything, as the town was deserted and the Indians had fled. In this expedition the men suffered much for want of food. After various manœuvrings and much countermarching, during which several Indian towns were burned and a few men killed, Indian subtlety proving more than a match for English discipline and rash confidence, the army returned to Wheeling and was disbanded.

A more formidable expedition, however, was organized at the seat of the Virginia government, of which Governor Dunmore announced his determination to assume the command. By the 1st of September, 1774, a force numbering from one thousand to twelve hundred men was organized, under the immediate command of Colonel Andrew Lewis. After marching nineteen days through the wilderness, Lewis reached Point Pleasant, at the mouth of the Great Kanawha, where he was to have been joined by Dunmore, but instead thereof he received despatches from him changing the plan of operations and directing him to proceed to the Scioto River. At daybreak on the 10th of October, while preparing to comply with this order, his camp was suddenly attacked by a body of one thousand Shawnees and their allies, led on by the Shawnee chief Monusk, or Cornstalk, and a fiercely-contested battle ensued. The Indians exhibited great daring, rushing to the encounter with a boldness and fury which have seldom been equalled, and, as usual, accompanying their onslaught with tremendous noise and shouting.

The battle continued with unabated fury until one o'clock in the afternoon, the Indians slowly retreating from tree to tree, while the gigantic Cornstalk encouraged them with the words, "Be strong! be strong!" The peculiarity of the ground—it being the point of junction of two rivers—made each retreat of the enemy advantageous to the Virginians, because, as the Indian line extended from river to river, forming the base of an equilateral triangle, it was lengthened, and consequently weakened. The belligerents rested within rifle-shot of each other, and kept up a desultory fire till sunset.

Colonels Charles Lewis and Fleming were killed, and the troops were obliged to give ground for a time, but, a reinforcement being ordered up, the Indians were in turn compelled to fall back, and under cover of darkness fled across the river. The Indians engaged were Shawnees, Delawares, Wyandots, and Mingoes.[1] Among the leaders of the latter was Tah-ga-yu-ta, or Logan. The Virginians acknowledge a loss of one hundred and fifty men, and the Indians are estimated to have lost two hundred warriors. Indian history nowhere records a more obstinately contested battle. Neither party could fairly claim the victory. The loss of the Virginians would have been much greater had they not adopted the tactics of the natives, darting from tree to tree with the spring of a cougar, and taking aim with the precision of woodsmen.

Having properly interred the dead, and erected and garrisoned a temporary fort, Lewis moved forward to the Scioto, but in the mean time Lord Dunmore had reached that stream by way of Pittsburg, and had established a camp about seven miles southeast of Circleville, which he called Charlotte, at the mouth of a small stream known as the Sippi.[2] At this camp the Indians were collected, and a treaty of amity was concluded, by which the Shawnees agreed to deliver up their prisoners without reserve, to restore all horses and other property which they had carried off, to hunt no more on the Kentucky side of the Ohio, to molest no boats passing on the river, to regulate their trade by the king's instructions, and to deliver up hostages. Colonel Lewis was greatly irritated because Dunmore would not allow him to crush the enemy within his grasp, and the Virginians, eager for revenge, almost mutinied.

In the council Cornstalk spoke with a manly tone and demeanor which excited remark, adroitly charging upon the whites the outbreak of the war, especially citing the murder of the family of Logan. All the tribes which had been engaged in the battle were there represented, except the Mingoes. The latter being under the influence of Logan, who had entered into this war with the most revengeful feelings, were restrained by him from coming forward. Lord Dunmore sent for the chief, but he declined attending, and transmitted to him this speech, which has given to his name a literary immortality:

"I appeal to any white man to say if ever he entered Logan's cabin hungry, and I gave him not meat; if ever he came cold or naked, and I gave him not clothing. During the course of the last long and bloody war, Logan remained in his tent, an advocate for peace; nay, such was my love for the whites, that those of my own

---

[1] The Iroquois of the Ohio were thus named.   [2] *Sippi* is the Shawnee name for a creek.

country pointed at me as they passed by, and said, 'Logan is the friend of white men!' I had even thought to live with you, but for the injuries of one man. Colonel Cresap, the last spring, in cold blood and unprovoked, cut off all the relations of Logan, not even sparing my women and children. There runs not a drop of my blood in the veins of any human creature. This called on me for revenge. I have sought it—I have killed many—I have fully glutted my vengeance. For my country, I rejoice at the beams of peace; but do not harbor the thought that mine is the joy of fear. Logan never felt fear. He will not turn on his heel to save his life. Who is there to mourn for Logan? Not one."

Logan had ever been the friend of the white man, but on the perpetration of the cruel deed the spirits of his kindred clamored for vengeance. He went upon the war-path with a few followers, and added scalp to scalp until the number was thirteen,—equalling that of the Indian victims. "Now," said the chief, "I am satisfied for the loss of my relations, and will sit still."

The subjugation of the Indians being at length effected, from this period we may trace the progress of the British towards a monopoly of the Indian trade, which tremendous engine of power was destined ultimately to operate in elevating or depressing the tribes, in accordance with the will of those who directed its movements. The trade with the Indians was a boon at which commerce clutched with an eager hand. To secure the coveted prize no hardship was considered too severe, no labor too onerous; dangers and difficulties were laughed at, and life itself was regarded as of little value. The Indians were incited to new exertions in pursuing the chase, little heeding that they were destroying their main resource for the sustenance of life, for when the fur-bearing animals were annihilated their lands became in a great measure valueless to them. In the hands of the English, Quebec, Montreal, Detroit, Michilimackinac, and the Mississippi towns not only equalled their progress under the French, but became still greater centres of trade. Though New York, Philadelphia, and Charleston contributed their capital to the extension of this trade, the above-named original interior towns of the traders still held their prominent position. The tribes scattered over the continent felt severely the effects of this ever-extending empire of trade; they were literally driven from the face of the earth by the rabid and uncontrolled pursuit of wealth through the medium of the fur-trade, which so long promised riches to those who engaged in it.

Sir William Johnson, who had been during forty years the Mæcenas of the Indians, and who knew the disastrous effects which unlicensed trade would have on Indian society, early saw the importance of so systematizing and controlling it that it might become an element not only of power but of prosperity to the colonies and to the Indians. His letters and memoirs on this subject furnish abundant proof of his comprehensive views and of his integrity of character. Indeed, his activity during his entire management of Indian affairs gave evidence that he shrank from no duty. In 1761 he visited Detroit for the purpose of placing matters there on a proper basis, and his agents had for years traversed the Ohio, the Scioto, the Maumee, and other districts of the West, collecting information, and transmitting to him the details of every occurrence. To him the British government owed a heavy debt of gratitude.

Nothing was more important in the readjustment of Indian affairs, and for securing their good will, than a proper organization of the fur-trade. Prior to the conquest of Canada, the English traders had been principally confined to the sources of the streams flowing into the Atlantic, but after this era their operations were extended indefinitely west and north. Under the French authority a variety of regulations and limitations had been enforced, extraordinary privileges and monopolies of particular districts having been specially granted. Something of the same kind was attempted at the commencement of the English domination after the fall of Canada, the power of granting licenses to trade on the frontiers having been at first exercised by the commanding officers of posts. From the time of the capture of Quebec the Indian trade had been in a state of confusion, and before the final surrender of the remote districts the Indians had been prevented from obtaining their regular supplies of goods, wares, and merchandise, which had now become necessary to their comfort. They had long previously lost their old arts, and had become familiarized to the use of metallic cooking-vessels, woollens, arms, and ammunition.

The several memoirs and letters which Sir William Johnson, the Superintendent of Indian Affairs, addressed to the Lords of Trade on the subject before referred to, are good indications of the importance he attached to the correction of irregularities in the fur-trade, of his care in placing before the government the elements on which an equable system could be established, and of his solicitude for its early formation. When the Canadas were added to the area of his jurisdiction it required some time to establish on a proper footing the new relations with all the distant tribes which the occasion required. His great object was to secure political influence with the tribes, and for this purpose he had personally visited Detroit, Oswego, and Niagara. He kept in pay three deputies, who traversed a great part of the West, reporting to him the result of their observations and inquiries; and in the New York publications now before us there is abundant evidence that he omitted no occasion of keeping the government advised concerning the true position of Indian affairs. It was not until after the return of the successful armies of Bradstreet and Bouquet, in the autumn of 1764, that an Englishman could with any safety carry goods into the newly-conquered districts. The very appellation "English trader" was detested by the Northern tribes, and instances occurred where Englishmen were obliged to conduct their operations in the names of the Canadian guides and interpreters in their employ. Even the mere uniform of an English officer or soldier was loathed by them. "Why," said Pontiac, in 1763, "do you suffer those dogs in red clothing to remain on your land?"

We are told that trade at Michilimackinac began in 1766. In 1765, Alexander Henry, who had escaped the massacre at Michilimackinac, obtained a license granting him the monopoly of the trade on Lake Superior, and after one year's sojourn there returned, bringing with him one hundred and fifty packs of beaver, each weighing one hundred pounds, besides other furs. Captain Jonathan Carver,[1] on his arrival there in 1766, found this place to be the great centre of the English trade. At first it was limited to Chegoimegon and Comenistequoia, on Lake Superior, until Thomas Curry, obtaining guides and interpreters, penetrated as far as Fort Bourbon, on the Saskatchewan, and returned the following year with his canoes so amply filled with fine furs that he was enabled to retire from the business. James Finley followed his track the next year to Nipawee, reaping equal profits, and was succeeded in the enterprise by Joseph Frobisher. The way being thus opened, others braved the attendant dangers and hardships, and ardently pursued the business. Thus was inaugurated the Northwest fur-trade, which during half a century proved of more real value than any gold-mines. It is no marvel that every toil was encountered in its pursuit, and health, and often life itself, freely sacrificed to it.

The fur-trade in the West also vigorously commenced about this period. It had been carried on, by means of pack-horses, across the Alleghanies, from Philadelphia and Baltimore to Fort Pitt, from the period of its capture; but until after the return of the expedition of Bouquet, in 1764, the territory beyond the Ohio could not be penetrated without incurring the greatest risks. At length, under the treaty of Versailles, British authority was established on the Mississippi, and in September, 1765, Captain Sterling left Fort Pitt for the Illinois, with one hundred men of the Forty-Second Regiment, in boats, and relieved the French garrison of Fort Chartres. The trading-posts of Kaskaskia, Cahokia, Vincennes, and Peoria were thus brought within the defined limits for trading operations. The following year Matthew Clarkson opened a trading station at Fort Chartres under the auspices of a mercantile house in Philadelphia.

A line of British posts at this period extended from Fort Chartres, in Illinois, by way of Pittsburg, to Niagara, Oswego, and Fort Stanwix, and thence, pursuing the line of trade, up the lake to Detroit and Michilimackinac. The tribes, being thus restrained, made no further efforts to originate hostile combinations. They had lost many men in the war which began in 1755; they had been foiled in all their schemes, from South Carolina to the Straits of Michigan; and, although they had evinced great energy and activity under the direction of Pontiac, their efforts invariably

---

[1] Captain Jonathan Carver, of Connecticut, who had commanded a company of provincials in the French war in 1763, undertook the exploration of the territory on the borders of Lake Superior and the country of the Sioux beyond it. Up to the time of his return to Boston, in October, 1768, during which period he had travelled nearly seven thousand miles, he had explored the bays and rivers opening into the great lake, and had also obtained accounts of the great river Oregon, which flows into the Pacific. To make these discoveries known, as well as the richness of the copper-mines of the Northwest, and to claim a reward for his services, also to recommend English settlements on the Western shores of the continent, and to propose opening by aid of lakes and rivers a passage across the continent as the best route for communicating with China and the East Indies,—a feat accomplished a century later by opening the Pacific Railroad,—Carver went to England, where, disappointed in his efforts for compensation, and reduced to extreme destitution, he ended his days in 1780. His travels were published in 1778, and the commiseration awakened by the story of his sufferings, made known to the public by Dr. Lettsom, led to the establishment in London of the "Literary Fund," a benevolent institution for the relief of poor authors.

resulted in defeat. Such evidences of the possession of power on the part of the British were also developed as to prove to them that the latter, though slow in action and sometimes erring in their movements, had perseverance, energy, and ability sufficient to baffle all their efforts. The Indians had likewise suffered greatly within a few years in the cessation of trade, which had been necessarily interrupted.

Having conquered Canada, one of the first things necessary for the management of Indian affairs by Great Britain was to ascertain the names and numerical strength of the Indian tribes that had been transferred to her jurisdiction, which task was undertaken by Sir William Johnson, the British Superintendent of Indian Affairs. As a central point he began with the population of the Iroquois, who were then, and had long been, the objects of his special care. In a census table prepared by him in 1763 for the Lords of Trade, he represents the number of men capable of bearing arms among the Mohawks at 160, the Oneidas at 250, the Onondagas at 150, the Cayugas at 200, the Senecas at 1050, and the Tuscaroras at 140. He places the outlying band of Oswegatchies (Ogdensburg) at 80, and the Caughnawagas (St. Regis) at 300; making a total of 2330 warriors, who (according to the usual rules of computation) would represent an aggregate population of 11,650 souls. He computes that of Conoys, Tuteloes, Saponeys, Nanticokes, and other conquered and dismembered tribes then living in the Iroquois country, there were 200 men, or 1000 souls.

After leaving the area of New York, there is less reliance to be placed on the census, which was made up, not from actual enumeration, but from the reports of persons journeying among or trading with the tribes, and from the statements of parties supposed to be best informed on the subject. Sir William Johnson estimates the Adirondacks at 150 men, or 750 souls; the Abenakis at 100 men, or 500 souls; and the various tribes of Hurons, or Wyandots, of Canada, at 240 men, representing a population of 1200 souls. This enumeration would allow to the Indians of Canada below Lake Ontario, and to the Iroquois of New York, including the nations conquered by them and residing among them, 2820 fighting-men, or 14,100 souls, a total which is believed to be a little above the actual numbers.

But if the population of the region with which Sir William was least acquainted, namely, the lower St. Lawrence Valley, was sometimes overestimated by his informants, that of the Great West, beyond the Alleghanies and along the upper lakes, if we except errors of synonymes, is believed to have been returned with excellent judgment.

The attempt to estimate the numerical force of the Pontiac confederacy during that year must be considered to have been made under great disadvantages. Johnson had himself visited Detroit, the seat of this confederacy, in 1761, and gathered the elements of his estimates from persons resident there.

The Wyandots, or Hurons, of Michigan, are rated at 250 men, or 1250 souls; the Ottawas, dispersed in various localities, at 700 men, or 3500 souls; the Chippewas, among whom are included the Mississagies of the region of Detroit, at 320 men; and those of Michilimackinac at 400 men, together making an aggregate of

8350. The Pottawatomies of Detroit are set down as comprising 150 warriors, and those of St. Joseph 200, both conjoined representing a population of 1750 persons.

In the valley of the Ohio, and the region of country immediately west of it, the means for making an enumeration were more ample and reliable.

The Shawnees are estimated, with apparently good judgment, at 300 men, or 1500 souls; and the Delawares, with nearly the same probable accuracy, at 3000 persons, which would give them 600 fighting-men.

The Miamis of the Wabash Valley, under their Iroquois name of Twightwees, are numbered at 230 men, the Piankeshaws at 100 men, and the Weas at 200 men, making 2650 souls. In the same general district there are enumerated 180 Kickapoos and 90 Mascoutins, a tribe of prairie Indians who appear in all the earliest estimates, but who have since lost that designation. The name would indicate that they were Algonkins. These add to the estimate 1350 persons.

In the region of Green Bay, comprising the present area of Wisconsin, the Menomonies are computed at 110 men, or 550 souls. This estimate is duplicated under their French synonyme of Folsavoins. But, irrespective of this mistake, the number of Menomonies at that time would not seem to be overrated at 1100 souls. The Winnebagoes, called by the French Puans, are rated at 360 men, or an aggregate of 1750 individuals, which is not excessive. The Sauks are enumerated as having 300 fighting-men, or a population of 1500 souls, a probable excess; and the Outagamies, or Foxes, 320 warriors, or 1600 souls. These two tribes had united their fortunes after their unsuccessful attack, in 1712, on the fort of Detroit, which act procured them the hatred of the French.

The aggregate of these enumerations and estimates of the Western and Northern tribes reaches 24,050 individuals. Add to this the 14,100 of the Eastern or home table of Sir William's superintendency, and there is presented a gross population of 38,150 souls. This does not include the Southern tribes, and those residing on the west banks of the Mississippi, both of which groups of tribes were beyond his jurisdiction, and also outside of the limits of the territory ceded by the treaty of Versailles, concluded February 10, 1763.

Means for testing this estimate were furnished by the respective expeditions of Bradstreet and Bouquet in 1764. The estimate of the former, as given by Major Mante, related only to the tribes assembled at, or living within, a circle of five or six days' march from his camp. This computation furnished data for an aboriginal population of some 9500 persons, of which number 1930 are set down as warriors.

The statistics of the Indian population collected by Colonel Bouquet, and published at Philadelphia in 1766, proceed to the other extreme. Instead of confining the enumeration to tribes which were visited, contiguous, or known, Bouquet not only extended it to tribes residing beyond the region and outside of the limits of the British territory, but also frequently, under various synonymes, duplicated or triplicated the same tribes.

After discarding these redundancies, limiting the estimate of the tribes to the ratio of that of Sir William, and correcting the evident confusion existing between the number of fighting-men and the gross population of the tribes, as in the note,[1] the table of Bouquet does not exhibit, on the same area, a great variance from the corresponding parts of the superintendent's list. He does not show that the entire Indian force in the West residing east of the Mississippi River numbered over 30,950 souls, or 6210 fighting-men. To these he has added 11,350 Southern Indians, comprising the Cherokees, Chickasaws, Choctaws, and the small tribes of the Catawbas and Natchez, who are estimated at 2250 warriors. As if to evidence the peril from which he had escaped, or to show the force that could be brought against the British frontiers, the Sioux, Kansas, and wild prairie tribes of Upper Louisiana, west of the Mississippi, are introduced into the estimates. Thus, the entire number of fighting-men in his estimates is set down at 56,500, which, by the data he furnishes, would indicate a gross population of 283,000 souls,—not a very extravagant computation.

---

[1] Table of comparisons between Colonel Bouquet and Sir William Johnson.

	Bouquet.	Johnson. Warriors.	Men, etc.
Nipissing	400	300	1500
Algonkins	300		
Wyandots	300	300	1500
Chippewas	5000	1000	5000
Ottawas	900	900	4500
Mississagies	2000	400	2000
Pottawatomies	350 men.	350	1750
Puans	750	150	750
Mascoutins	500	100	500
Sauks	400	150	750
Miamis	350 men.	350	1750
Delawares	600 "	600	3000
Shawnees	500 "	500	2500
Kickapoos	300 "	300	1500
Weas	400	400	2000
Piankeshaws	250	250	1250
Kuskaskias	600	120	600
Catawbas	150	100	500
Cherokees	2500 souls.	500	2500
Chickasaws	750 men.	750	3750
Natchez	150 "	100	500
Choctaws	4500 souls.	900	4500

PERIOD V.

THE AMERICAN REVOLUTION.

CHAPTER I.

STATE OF THE INDIAN TRIBES—BRANT—ACTION OF CONGRESS—INVASION OF CANADA, AND DEFEAT AT THE CEDARS.

OHIO was the first of those talismanic names which, dating back as early as 1750, in the days of Franklin and Washington, influenced the spread of the American population over the entire West. But the country so attractive to a civilized people was in possession of fierce, savage tribes, who flitted through the wilderness like the genii of Arabic fable, acknowledging neither the laws of God nor those of man. England was the first to teach to such of these Western tribes as hovered around her colonies the principles of industry, arts, and letters, and the incalculable advantages of the habits of civilization over barbarism. She was the first, also, by the aid of her fleets and armies, to bring these savage hordes to effectual terms, and to make them aware that the plough was superior to the tomahawk. She exercised supervision over a wide and exposed frontier through the medium of lines of forts and agencies, and re-established on better principles the fur-trade, that powerful stimulus to energetic action among the Indians. But after effecting this object by a lavish expenditure of blood and treasure, and after having compelled the savages to acknowledge the British sway, this power would seem to have been acquired by Britain only that it might be wielded against the Americans; for, after controlling this Indian influence during the brief period of fifteen years, it was directed against the colonies by the mother-country, and proved, if not one of the most potent, at least one of the most inhuman auxiliaries of a despotic government in its efforts to coerce and crush a brave and liberty-loving people.

To ascertain the precise strength of this Indian force had been an object with the British government after the conquest of Canada, and it also became a point of much moment to the colonies on the breaking out of the Revolution. The results of the efforts made by the British authorities to determine their numbers have just been stated. The first reliable estimates obtained by the colonies were made under the auspices of the War Department while the government was located at Philadelphia. The elements of the following schedule are extant in the handwriting of Mr. Madison:

FORCE OF THE INDIAN NATIONS ON THE OCCURRENCE OF THE AMERICAN REVOLUTION.

I. IROQUOIS.

Tribes.	Warriors.	Gross Pop.	Locality.
Mohawks	100	500	Mohawk Valley.
Oneidas and Tuscaroras	400	2000	Oneida County, New York.
Onondagas	230	1150	Onondaga Castle, etc., New York.
Cayugas	220	1100	Cayuga Lake, etc., " "
Senecas	650	3250	Seneca Lake to Niagara, " "
	1600	8000	

II. IROQUOIS OF THE WEST.

Wyandots	180	900	Detroit and Sandusky.

III. ALGONKINS.

Ottawas	450	2,250	Miami River to Michilimackinac.
Chippewas	5,000	25,000	Lakes Huron, Michigan, and Superior.
Mississagies	250	1,250	North of the lakes.
Pottawatomies	450	2,250	Detroit, St. Joseph's, and Wabash.
Miamis	300	1,500	St. Joseph's of Miami, etc.
Piankeshaws, Weas, under the name of Musketoons, etc.	800	4,000	Wabash River, etc.
Menomonies	2,000	10,000	West of Lake Michigan, etc.
Shawnees	300	1,500	Ohio, etc., have been exceedingly active.
Delawares, Munsees	600	3,000	Muskingum, etc.
	10,150	50,750	

IV. DAKOTAS.

Sioux	500	2500	Upper Mississippi.

V. APPALACHIANS.

			Authorities.		
Cherokees	500	2,500	Hutchins, vol. iii. p. 555.		
Chickasaws	150	750	"	"	"
Choctaws	900	4,500	Smith,	"	"
Catawbas	150	750	Hutchins,	"	"
Natchez	150	750	"	"	"
Muscogees { Alabamas	600	3,000	"	"	"
{ Cowetas	700	3,500	"	"	"
	3150	15,750			

RECAPITULATION.

	Warriors.	Gross Population.
1. Iroquois of New York	1,600	8,000
2. Iroquois of the West	180	900
3. Algonkins	10,150	50,750
4. Dakotas	500	2,500
5. Appalachians, Southern tribes	3,150	15,750
	15,580	77,900

It is evident from scanning these details that access had been obtained to persons conversant with the locations and population of the Indian tribes. Compared with the more general estimates of Bouquet, made in 1764, they present a commendable approach to accuracy. If the strength of some tribes is overrated, that of others is correspondingly underrated, leaving the average of the Indian force that could by any probability be brought into the field very near the true standard. The Sioux, for instance, might with a much nearer approach to accuracy have been rated at 10,000, but there was no probability that more than 500 warriors could, under the most favorable circumstances, be brought into action. In fact, it is believed that in those days not a man of that stock had ever drawn a bow against the whites, unless it be possible that stray warriors of their ethnological connection the Winnebagoes had wandered to Wyoming or Stanwix. The Iroquois Six Nations are enumerated as having 350 warriors less than they are rated in the estimate of Sir William Johnson, made in 1763; but the later estimate probably a little underrates their actual decline in thirteen years under the combined influence of trade and alcohol. The Chippewas are overestimated at 5000 men, for the report covers only a limited area of their lands, without tracing their scattered bands over a very wide and remote field. The enumeration of the Menomonies, who occupied the present area of Wisconsin, is also, under any circumstances, in excess; but this very nomadic people were in the habit of hunting over an extended territory on the upper Mississippi, where they were accompanied by their intimate associates the Sauks, who have no place in the estimate. The Foxes, the Kickapoos, and their allies the Mascoutins, the aggregate population of which three tribes is computed at 2950 in Johnson's tables, are also entirely left out in this estimate, so that what was overrated on the one hand was, with a considerable approach to accuracy, counterbalanced on the other. Nor is it probable, as Mr. Madison has stated in a note attached to the estimate, that his aggregate of 12,430 warriors was above the truth, or that this number of Indians was employed in the contest. It has been estimated that the number of fighting Indians employed by Great Britain during the Revolutionary War was 770.

Congress, after its primary organization, placed the subject of the Indian intercourse in the hands of commissioners, under the direction of the Secretary of War. The trust was an arduous one, perpetually fluctuating in its aspects, and requiring great knowledge of the Indian character, as well as an accurate conception of the geographical features and natural resources of the country. It was evident from the first that the Six Nations would side with the mother-country, from whom it was earnestly desired to detach them, and to persuade them to remain neuter in the contest. This was the policy prescribed by Washington, and was urged upon them by Rev. Samuel Kirkland, who resided among the Oneidas. He was charged personally by the President to impress upon them the importance of pursuing a neutral line of policy; for then, no matter which party proved triumphant, the Indian interests would not receive injury; but if they were involved in the struggle, their interests would be likely to suffer. This reasoning prevailed with the Oneidas and

Christian Indians under the energetic and popular chief Skenandoah. A portion of the Tuscaroras also sided with the Americans.

The ancient tribe of Mohicans of the Housatonic, whose history has been impressed upon popular memory by their long residence at Stockbridge, Massachusetts, had been for a long period classed among the followers of the gospel, but, as the martial spirit of the era aroused all their warrior feelings, they enlisted themselves on the side of the colonies, and furnished an efficient company of spies and flankers for the American army. About fifty of them were encamped at Watertown during the siege of Boston.

Directing the view to the West, there was but little encouragement in the prospect. The Delawares, who had finally abandoned Central Pennsylvania in 1749, influenced thereto partly by annoyance at the continued encroachments of the settlers, but more by fear of the Iroquois tomahawk, were arrayed in opposition to the colonies.

The Shawnees, who claim a remote Southern origin, appear to have divided in their primary emigration to the North, a part of the tribe pursuing the route within the range of the Alleghanies to the territory of the Lenni Lenape, or Delawares, directly north, and a part descending the Kanawha to the Ohio Valley, whence they ascended the Scioto River to Chillicothe, which became their Western centre. Others located themselves a little below the influx of the Wabash, at a spot now called Shawneetown, Illinois.

There is a circumstance of much interest connected with the history of this tribe. According to the account of the Mohican chief Metoxon, that tribe was originally connected with the Delawares, but, being a restless and quarrelsome people, had involved themselves in inextricable troubles while in the South, and, in the chief's language, had returned to sit again between the feet of their grandfather.

Those of the tribe who had reached their ethnological affiliated relatives the Delawares had either preceded the latter, or accompanied them, across the Alleghanies.

That portion of the Senecas, and of other tribes of the Iroquois, who had emigrated West, or who possibly held a footing there from remote times, were called Mingoes.[1] They were regarded as generally taking part with the Western Indians in their hostilities. When Washington visited their chief Tanacharisson, at Logstown, in 1753, this sachem expressed himself as being friendly to the Virginians, and it is believed that this particular branch of them were not included among those who formed the ambuscade against General Braddock three years subsequently.

Of the Chippewas, Ottawas, Mississagies, and other Algonkin nations embraced in the preceding estimate, it is not known or believed that any of them were friendly to the American cause. They had been firm friends of the French, but after the offence which has been mentioned they transferred their allegiance to the British. It requires to be noticed, however, that being more remote from the scene of conflict

---

[1] Mr. Heckewelder informs us that this term is derived from Mengwe, the Delaware name for the Six Nations, and that the Dutch term Maaqua is derived from the same source.—Phil. Trans., vol. i., Hist. Ind.

than any other tribe, if we except the Mississagies of Canada, there was only one point from which they could have been employed against the Americans, viz., from the central location of Fort Niagara, which was officially visited by the Western tribes, even from Michilimackinac and Lake Superior. Sir William Johnson died in 1774, about the time of the occurrence of the tea riot in Boston. The title and office descended to his son John, whose mansion at Johnstown having been taken in January, 1776, by a body of New York militia under Generals Schuyler and Herkimer, and himself placed on his parole, he fled to Canada, carrying with him the Mohawk tribe. Subsequently Fort Niagara became the seat of the royal influence, where marauding, plundering, and scalping parties were organized, to use the expressive epithet of Sir John's father, "painted and feathered" for war.

The seven hundred and seventy tomahawks and the like number of scalping-knives which the British Indians could wield in this war with the colonies were actively employed on the frontier settlers of New York, Pennsylvania, and Virginia. The savages were incited to greater activity in their bloody deeds by rewards paid for the scalps of the unfortunate victims. For a handful of energetic but undisciplined militia to oppose a powerful nation on the seaboard, possessing as she did every means of offence that ships and armies could furnish, was a great and hazardous undertaking, but to encounter the Indians at the same time on the frontiers required a skilful policy. There was a twofold enemy to cope with. It had occupied England, with all her influence and political tact, backed by all her means, a period of fifteen years to wean the affections of the tribes from the French and to attach them to the British crown. All this the colonies now attempted to undo. The Indians were told that the colonies had taken up the mace, and had begun to wield the sovereignty against the mother country; that it was a contest of son against father. By the British party it was represented that the Americans were weak in numbers, as well as impoverished in finances, and that their generals and leaders were destined to pay the forfeit of their rebellion on the gallows. The Indian, being no casuist, no statesman, no judge of the justice or of the rights of nations, thought that the oldest, the strongest, and the wisest should prevail, and therefore he resolved to fight on the side of Britain. Fifteen years had elapsed after the fall of Canada before the English were enabled to secure the friendship of the Indians and to cement their interests; it was consequently impossible to effect a sudden rupture between them. They neither understood nor appreciated the principles involved in the contest, which was represented to them, by those whose interest it was to do so, as a family quarrel between a father and a son; and, so far as we can collate their expressed opinions, they contended that the father was in the right. But, whether in the right or in the wrong, they believed the British to be the stronger, the wealthier, and the most willing and able to benefit them. The Americans, it was urged, would be very likely to trench upon their rights by locating themselves upon their lands, though the Indians had need of but little for the purpose of cultivation, which they regarded as one of the heresies of civilization. They merely required the domain that on it might be raised deer, bears, and beaver, which animals the migrations from the

Atlantic shores, already beginning to cross the Alleghanies, would drive away. They lived on the flesh of these animals, and by the sale of the skins and furs they procured all else that was necessary to their subsistence. This was a popular strain, on which their speakers could dilate. They had frequently spoken to Warrahiagey on the subject, and opposed the concessions of lands on the banks of the rivers flowing into the Atlantic, made to the colonists by the British governors. They asserted that these patented lands were theirs, and had never been sold. It was an old theme, which had now been invested with renewed vitality.

To conciliate the tribes, therefore, became the cherished policy of the revolted colonies. The Americans represented to them that they were not parties to the contest, and that no matter who succeeded they could only be subordinates. They were, therefore, counselled to neutrality, which, however, required a stretch of ratiocination beyond their ability. The Indian character is formed by war, war is the high-road to honor and renown, and even those tribes which had professed their belief in the truths of Christianity could not be wholly restrained from taking up the tomahawk.

The Mohicans of Stockbridge, as we have said, ranged themselves on the side of the Americans, and performed good service as scouts throughout the contest. The Oneidas did the same. The voice of the popular chief Skenandoah was heard in favor of the rising colonies, and the watchful attention and quick eye of Attatea, known as Colonel Louis, carefully noted the approach of hostile footsteps during the great struggle of 1777, and gave every day the most reliable information of the march and position of the enemy. The residue of the Six Nations acted the part of fierce foes along the frontiers. The Shawnees and Delawares were also cruel enemies. Their fealty to the British cause, it was asserted, was further cemented by a promise that their allies would stand by them and would never consent to a peace which did not make the Ohio River the boundary of the colonies.

Fortunately for the cause of humanity, the great battles of the Revolution were fought on the open plains and cultivated parts of the country, which, being denuded of forests, were unfavorable to the employment of Indian auxiliaries. The battles of Concord and Bunker Hill, Guilford, Long Island, White Plains, Saratoga, Monmouth, Trenton, Camden, King's Mountain, the Cowpens, Brandywine, Germantown, and Yorktown, were the great features of the conflict. But wherever a detached column was marched through forests, or occupied an isolated fort, the war-cry resounded, and the details of the war give evidence that there were other and more dreaded enemies to be encountered than the sword and the bayonet, the cannon and the bomb.

The superior military skill and success of the Iroquois gave them a prominent position in Indian warfare. At the period of the Revolution, circumstances had placed them under the sway of the noted and energetic chief Thayendanagea, more familiarly known as Joseph Brant. We have the speculations of an ingenious and ready writer, who labors to prove that Brant was by the regular line of descent a Mohawk chieftain. It is, however, certain that he was not the son of a chief, and by the Iroquois laws of descent he could not be a chief if the son of a chief, the right of inheritance being exclusively vested in the female line. Brant was, in fact, a self-made man, owing his position to his native energy, talents, and education. The Mohawks had lost their last and greatest sachem, Soiengarahta, called King Hendrick, in 1755, at the battle of Lake George. Little Abraham, who succeeded him in authority, was a man of excellent sense and fine talents, but possessed no reputation as a warrior. The institutions of the Iroquois were guarded by many rules and regulations prescribed by their councils and customs, but they were, nevertheless, of a democratic character, and under the sway of popular opinion recognized and rewarded great talent and bravery. In 1776 no one could compete with Brant in these qualifications. In addition to his natural physical and mental energy, he had been well educated in early life, could read fluently, and was a ready writer. Raised under the eye and the influence of Sir William Johnson, he never dreamed of questioning the fact that Great Britain was beyond all other nations powerful, strong, and wise, and must prevail. He crossed the ocean in February, 1776, and offered to the British Secretary, Germaine, the support of the Six Nations "to chastise the New England people."

In June, 1775, a petition was laid before the Continental Congress from settlers in Western Virginia, who, "fearing a rupture" with the Indians, desired that commissioners might attend a meeting of the Indians at Pittsburg on behalf of the colonies of Virginia and Pennsylvania. Congress at the same time made provision for the appointment of boards of commissioners to superintend Indian affairs in behalf of the colonies. It designated three Indian departments,—the Northern, Southern, and Middle; the first to embrace all the Six Nations and all the Indians northward of them; the second to include the Cherokees and all to the south of them; and the third to include all between the other two departments. These commissioners were empowered to treat with the Indians in the name and on behalf of the colonies, with the object of preserving peace and friendship with them, to seize and confine any of the agents of Great Britain found inciting them to acts of hostility, and also to expend moneys appropriated for their benefit. In the following year Congress passed resolutions to import suitable Indian goods to the amount of forty thousand pounds sterling, to regulate all details of trade with them, and that the Commissioners of Indian Affairs be directed to consider of proper plans in their respective departments for the residence of ministers and school-masters for the propagation of the gospel and the cultivation of the civil arts among the Indians.

In March, 1778, Congress resolved that General Washington be empowered, "if he thinks it prudent and proper," to employ four hundred Indians in the service of the United States, and at the same time Brigadier-General McIntosh was directed to assemble at Fort Pitt fifteen hundred Continental troops and militia, and "proceed without delay to destroy such towns of the hostile tribes as he in his discretion shall think will most effectually tend to chastise and terrify the savages, and to check their ravages on the frontiers." This latter resolution was prompted by the incursion into

Wyoming by "Senecas, Tories, and other banditti," and rumors that other similar expeditions were in contemplation.

During the invasion of Canada, in the spring of 1776, a body of three hundred and ninety Americans, under Colonel Bedell, of New Hampshire, occupied a small post at the "Cedars," a village on the north side of the St. Lawrence, fifteen miles above Montreal. Early in May a detachment from Detroit, under Captain Forster, of one hundred and forty Canadians and regulars, and five hundred Indians, under Brant, appeared before it, and in the absence of Bedell summoned Major Butterfield, its commander, to surrender. The fort and garrison were at once given up by the cowardly major. Meanwhile, Major Henry Sherburne, who had been sent to its relief, ignorant of its surrender, while approaching the fort fell into an ambuscade, and the entire party was either killed or captured.

As soon as General Arnold, upon whom the command in Canada devolved on the fall of Montgomery, heard of these disasters, he marched with seven hundred men to chastise the enemy and release the prisoners. Arriving at St. Annis, he received positive assurances from the British commander that if he persisted in his design of attacking him it would be out of his power to prevent the savages from putting their prisoners, four hundred and seventy-four in number, to death. Major Sherburne confirmed the statement that a massacre had already been agreed on. A cartel for an exchange of prisoners was signed. Congress refused to ratify this agreement coercing its officers by suspending the bloody Indian hatchet over their heads, except upon such terms as the British government would never assent to. The waters of oblivion were, however, allowed to flow over the transaction. The prisoners were finally released by General Carleton, and the hostages at Quebec were sent home on parole.

CHAPTER II.

THE JOHNSONS—ST. LEGER INVADES NEW YORK—FORT STANWIX—BATTLE OF ORISKANY.

Sir William Johnson died suddenly, from the effects of an attack of apoplexy, in the year 1774, at a time when reflecting minds deemed a speedy rupture between the colonies and the British crown inevitable. This gentleman had been forty years in rising to that position in Indian affairs which left him no rival or peer in America. During about twenty years of this period he had been the official head of the Indian department in America, being commissioned by the crown and acknowledged by all the commanding generals. Intimately acquainted with the mental characteristics, the wants, the wishes, and the fears of the Indians, he had, as it were, with one hand wielded the power of government in keeping them in subjection to the laws, and with the other exercised the duties of a Mentor in teaching them how to promote their own best interests. No man in the whole scope of our colonial history can be compared to him. He had a presentiment of his death, which occurred at a most critical period. Great Britain had lavished on him high honors, and he was held in the highest respect by the Indians.

Those who have investigated the proceedings and the character of Sir John Johnson, his son and successor, of Guy Johnson, his deputy, of Colonel Claus, and of the various subordinates who thenceforth controlled the direction of Indian affairs, have arrived at the conclusion that this important interest was managed in a bad way if their object was to serve the crown. The encouragement of murders and massacres was well calculated to arouse the deepest hostility of the colonists and to cement them in the closest bonds of unity against the oppressions of the British. Numbers of persons previously lukewarm in the cause were driven to take an active part in the contest by deeds of blood and Indian atrocity. The several conferences held in the office of the British Indian Department during the years 1775 and 1776 proved the incapacity of Sir William's successors to control great events. The Six Nations were as a body the friends of the British, and did not like to see their officials, in public councils, and by public letters to committees and corporations, palliating or denying acts which they had secretly approved and had stimulated them to perform. Guy Johnson, the Deputy Superintendent, and his subordinates, tampered with the authorities, and became involved in inextricable difficulties, evincing little discretion or devotion to the best interests of the Mohawks. The jarring elements of that period could not be pacified by duplicity, and Sir John fled with the Indians, first to Fort Stanwix, then to Oswego, and finally to Niagara, which became the active head-quarters of the Indian superintendency, and the rendezvous for their marauding and scalping parties.

The colonial public was at this time in a furor of excitement, the people impelling their local governments to vigorous action. The error of the British government, from first to last, was its rigid adherence to its ideal rights of sovereignty, conceding nothing itself, but demanding from the colonies the most unqualified submission. It was ready to forgive and pardon, but never to redress grievances while possessing the power to coerce. The policy adopted at St. James's palace was carried out at Johnson Hall and at every intermediate point, the British maxim being that the weak must submit to the strong, and that might makes right. No sooner had the Mohawks, Tuscaroras, Onondagas, and Cayugas migrated with the fugitive Indian Department, and rallied with the powerful Senecas around their superintendent in Fort Niagara, than efforts were made to induce the Iroquois to attack the border settlements. During a conference with the Indians at Oswego, Guy Johnson had excited them to take up the hatchet against the Americans by inviting them to come and drink the blood of an American and feast on his roasted body. This expression, although but an Indian figure of speech for an invitation to a feast of an ordinary character, furnished a formidable weapon to the Revolutionists, who construed its meaning literally, and represented the deputy superintendent as a monster of cruelty in thus rousing these savages to action.

The first incursion of this kind was the expedition of Colonel Barry St. Leger against the inhabitants of the Mohawk Valley.

The year 1777 has been made ever memorable by the expedition of General Burgoyne, whose coming was heralded by a threat to march through the country and crush it at a blow. A fine and well-appointed army of ten thousand men, indeed, appeared to be sufficient of itself to make the people quail; but it was accompanied by hordes of the long-separated, but now reconciled, Algonkins and Iroquois, who ranged over the country not as auxiliaries on the field of battle, but to destroy the quiet of domestic life by their devastations, and to chill the heart's blood of the colonists by their atrocities. The fate of Miss Jane McCrea may serve as an incident to illustrate the singular barbarity of this warfare, and its effects on the popular mind. Burgoyne was proud of his management of the Indians, of whom he had detachments from seventeen tribes. On the 3d of August they brought in twenty scalps, and as many captives, and Burgoyne praised their activity. The Ottawas wished to return home, but on the 5th of August he took a pledge from all the warriors to stay through the campaign.

Simultaneously with the invasion of the northeastern borders of New York by Burgoyne, St. Leger, accompanied by a compact body of regulars, a park of artillery, and a large number of Indians under Sir John Johnson, entered it from the west. In addition to these, Lieutenant-Governor Hamilton, of Detroit, in obedience to orders from the British Secretary of State, Germaine, sent out at different times fifteen several parties, aggregating two hundred and fifty-nine warriors, with thirty white officers and rangers, to desolate the frontiers of Pennsylvania and Virginia.

St. Leger left Oswego with a total force of seventeen hundred men, including one thousand Indians, the latter consisting chiefly of Senecas, Tuscaroras, Mississagies, —an Algonkin tribe nearly identical with the Chippewas, from the northern end of Lake Ontario,—and fugitive Mohawks, from the Mohawk Valley, under Thayendanagea, or Brant, who now began to take a more active part in the contest. In his youth he had been a pupil at Dr. Wheelock's school, was employed as an interpreter and translator at the missionary station at Fort Hunter, and also as an under secretary at Johnson Hall. As the active and influential brother of the Indian wife of Sir William, he had been constantly rising in the esteem of his people, until he assumed the position of popular leader, when he became the hero of the Iroquois. He combined with great personal activity and a fine manly figure a good common education, undoubted bravery, and an intimate acquaintance with the manners and customs of civilization, and, what was of still more importance to his success, he possessed a thorough knowledge of the geographical features and population of the Mohawk Valley and its environs, together with a good idea of their power, disposition, and resources. He was thus by no means a feeble enemy. Although lacking that comprehensive judgment which was necessary to form an estimate of the true character of the contest, and the unflinching nerve and decision requisite for the control of events, yet he was, after the death of Sir William, fully equal in these particulars to Sir John Johnson and the other managers of British Indian affairs. But he possessed in perfection all the subtlety, subterfuge, and art, and, when he grasped the tomahawk in active war, all the cruelty, of the forest savage.

St. Leger, who was to sweep the valley of the Mohawk and then join Burgoyne at Albany, pursued his route up the Oswego River to the junction of the Seneca and Oneida, at Three River Point; thence up the Oneida River, through the lake of that name, along Wood Creek and across the portage to Fort Stanwix, on the Mohawk. As he progressed, his forces were augmented by the Cayugas and the Onondagas. Fort Stanwix, built in 1759, was the only point at which there was any probability that this invading force would be stopped, and this fortification, though well constructed and protected by earthworks against artillery, was not only in a dilapidated condition, but was garrisoned by only four hundred State troops, under Lieutenant-Colonel Gansevoort, subsequently increased, however, to some seven hundred. The enemy entertained no doubt that the fort would surrender at discretion, and, as the army deployed before the eyes of the garrison, column after column, with banners flashing in the sun, followed by battalions of light artillery and hordes of Indians, the Americans experienced a feeling similar to that which moved David when he laid aside his armor and stepped down into the valley to meet Goliath.

"The 3d of August was a day of deep interest, and revealed a military pageant which made a striking impression. It was a calm and beautiful morning when the enemy took up their line of march from Wood Creek. The intervening ground was an open plain of wide extent, most elevated towards its central and southern edge. Gansevoort's men were paraded on the ramparts, looking in the direction whence the Oneida sachem had told them the enemy would appear. Music soon was heard, and the scarlet color of their uniforms next showed itself. They had taken their standards from their cases that morning, and as color after color came into view, and they unfurled them to the breeze, an intense degree of interest was felt, but scarcely a word was uttered. To many of the men who had newly enlisted the scene was novel. Some of them had served the year before under Montgomery, others in the movements at Ticonderoga and Crown Point under St. Clair. Some veterans dated their service in prior wars under Sir William Johnson, Prideaux, and Bradstreet; there were others who were mere lads of seventeen. The Indians, spreading out on the flanks, gave the scene an air of terror, for their loud yells were heard above the British drum and bugle. The whole display, the exactitude of the order of march, the glitter of banners, the numbers present, and the impending danger of the contest were designed for effect upon the American garrison. Not a gun was, however, fired; the panorama was gazed at in silence."

Never was an investment more complete. The artillery deployed on the south, and took up their position within cannon-shot. The Royal Greens and Loyalists, under Sir John, lined one bank of the Mohawk, the shores and woods being occupied by Brant and his myrmidons. Every avenue was watched by the Indians. Death was the penalty of every attempt to venture a distance of over two hundred yards from the works. Many atrocities were committed by the Indians on officers, men, and even on children, who were captured outside the pickets. The sentinels soon became expert in watching for every cannon fired, and by a warning cry announced the coming of shot or shell. It became evident that the calibre of the enemy's guns was too light to make an impression on the fort, and the garrison made up in diligence what they lacked in power. Sometimes a shell exploded in the hospital, scattering destruction around, and occasionally a man was shot down on the ramparts or on the esplanade. The garrison had not sufficient ammunition to return a brisk fire, but there was one thing they never lacked,—a heroic determination to defend the work at all hazards. The striped flag, which had been hastily made partly out of a camlet cloak, was duly hoisted and lowered every morning and evening, with the firing of the gun that marked the beginning and the close of day. There was not a heart that quailed; they well knew that in addition to the ordinary casualties of war, if the garrison was taken, the Indians would perpetrate the most inhuman massacre. The fort was bravely defended by its garrison, whose intrepidity, firmness, and military endurance had been previously tested.

The siege of Fort Stanwix had continued but three or four days, when an American scout entered it with the intelligence that General Herkimer, at the head of an army of militia, was on his way to relieve it. The same intelligence from Brant's sister to the besiegers caused them to plan an ambush for the relieving force.

Consternation had paralyzed the inhabitants of the Mohawk Valley while the danger was yet distant, but the peril seemed to diminish the moment it came near. A desire for security compelled men to take up arms. If Fort Stanwix fell, the Mohawk Valley would be swept with fire and sword, and General Nicholas Herkimer, who commanded the militia, issued his proclamation summoning them to arms.

Three regiments, numbering eight hundred men, the entire strength of the valley, promptly responding, rendezvoused at Fort Dayton, whence they marched to Oriskany, which was distant but a few miles from the fort.

Brant, who figured as the leader of the Iroquois, had called into requisition all his local knowledge of the route, and all the peculiar art of the Indians in war, that he might decoy General Herkimer and his army into an ambuscade. The system of tactics pursued by the Indians is not to engage in a battle in compact ranks, but to screen themselves, either under the darkness of night or through the intervention of forests, and if in this way a good assault can be made their courage sometimes becomes equal to a contest in very open order, or even to a charge on the field of battle. But in this instance the chief evidently only sought to serve on the flanks, and to fall on the Americans unawares or at a disadvantage. Such is the Indian idea of military triumph. On the evening of the 5th the savages filled the woods with yells. Next morning, divesting themselves of their blankets and fur robes, they went forth, supported by Sir John Johnson and some of his royal Yorkers, by Colonel Butler and his rangers, by Claus and his Canadians, and by Lieutenant Bird and a party of regulars. General Herkimer reached the valley of the Oriskany August 6, at ten o'clock in the morning. The crossing at this stream was surrounded by low grounds, traversed by a causeway, and beyond it were elevated plateaus, covered with forests, which overlooked it. The Americans saw nothing to excite suspicion. Herkimer had entered this pass, which was within six miles of the fort, about an hour before noon, and two regiments had descended into the valley, but before his vanguard had reached the opposite elevation a heavy fire was suddenly poured in from all sides, accompanied by horrid yells, and the pass in his rear was immediately closed by the enemy. At the same moment that he was surprised in front by Johnson, the Indians fell upon his flanks, rushing in with their tomahawks after using their guns. The Americans were completely entrapped in an ambuscade, and for a few moments there was nothing but confusion and panic; the men fell thickly, and the army was threatened with utter annihilation; but they flew to the encounter like tigers; patriot and Tory grappled with each other in deadly struggle. The dark eye of the Indian flashed with delight at the prospect of revelling in human blood, and the Tory sought to immolate his late neighbor who had espoused the hated cause of the Revolution. Falling back without confusion to better ground, the Americans resumed the fight against superior numbers. General Herkimer was wounded and fell from his horse early in the action; a ball had pierced his leg below the knee, and killed his horse under him. His men were falling thickly around him; Colonel Cox was killed, and the yells of the savages resounded in every direction; but the firmness and composure of the general were undisturbed. His saddle was placed near a tree, and he was seated on it, his back being supported by the tree. Here he issued his orders, and drawing from his pocket his tobacco-box, and lighting his pipe, he smoked calmly while the battle raged around. After some forty-five minutes had elapsed, the men began to fight in small circles,—a movement worthy of notice, since it was the only mode of contending successfully with the surrounding enemy, who outnumbered them two to one. From this time the Americans gained ground. A slight cessation in the firing was taken advantage of by the enemy, who ordered a charge. Bayonets were crossed, and a desperate struggle ensued, which was arrested by a sudden and heavy shower of rain, which fell in a massive sheet during one entire hour. The combatants were thus separated. Herkimer's men then, under his direction, chose a more advantageous position, and formed in a large circle. They were from the first as expert as the Indians in firing from behind trees, but the latter, as soon as they saw the smoke of a discharge, would run up and tomahawk the soldier before he could reload. The Americans then placed two men behind each tree, and after one fired the other was ready to shoot down the advancing savage. The fire of the militia becoming more effective, the enemy began to give way, when Major Watts came on the ground with another detachment of the Royal Greens, chiefly composed of fugitive Tories, and the fight was renewed with greater vigor than before. The contending parties sprang at each other from the lines with the fury of enraged tigers, charging with bayonets, and striking at each other with clubbed muskets.

A diversion was now made which became the turning-point in the contest. One of Herkimer's scouts having reached the fort with the news of his position, its commander immediately resolved to make a sally for the relief of the army, detaching for that purpose Lieutenant-Colonel Marinus Willett. The troops were paraded in a square, and the intelligence communicated to them. Colonel Willett then descended to the esplanade and addressed the men in a patriotic manner, concluding with the words, "As many of you as feel willing to follow me in an attack, and are not afraid to die for liberty, will shoulder your arms, and step out one pace in front."[1] Two hundred men volunteered almost at the same moment, and fifty more, with a three-pounder, were soon after added to the force. The rain-storm, which came up suddenly, hindered their immediate march, but as soon as it ceased they issued from the sally-port at a brisk pace, and, rushing down upon the camp of Sir John, carried it at the point of the bayonet, drove the enemy through the Mohawk, and captured all their camp-equipage and public stores, together with five British flags. Colonel Willett then turned his arms against the Mohawk camp, and swept through it, returning to the fort with twenty-one wagon-loads of spoils. The sound of this rapid and severe firing arrested the attention of the belligerents after the cessation of the rain. By a change of caps with a company of men, whose dress in this respect resembled that of the Americans, Major Watts attempted to palm off on the patriots a detachment of his troops as an American reinforcement, but the subterfuge was quickly discovered, and the fight was resumed with bitter enmity. The Indian exclamation of *Oonah!* was at length heard, and the enemy retired, leaving Herkimer in possession of the field. Those who have most minutely described this battle relate instances of personal heroism which would not disgrace the Iliad.

The Indians, who had suffered severely, fought with great desperation. One

---

[1] Verbal account of the late Colonel Lawrence Schoolcraft, one of this number.

hundred of their number lay dead, thirty-six of whom, comprising several chiefs, were Senecas, who had been present in the greatest numbers. When they returned to their lodges and told the story of the slaughter of their chiefs, their villages rang with the howls of mourners and yells of rage. The fighting had become desultory, when suddenly the Senecas, who feared the arrival of American reinforcements, shouted their word for retreat, and commenced to move off, followed by the Loyalists; while the reviving shouts and more spirited firing of Herkimer's men resounded in every direction. Thus ended one of the most severely contested battles of the Revolution. Though not a victory for the Americans, neither was it a defeat, as it has been usually called, for they were left in undisputed possession of the field, which was not visited again by the enemy, either white or red. They constructed forty or fifty litters, on which they conveyed the wounded to their homes. Their loss was about one hundred and sixty killed, besides the wounded and prisoners. Among the number was General Herkimer, who reached in safety his own house, where he died about ten days after the battle from the result of an unskilful amputation of his leg. A monument was decreed by Congress to Herkimer, who, in the opinion of Washington, "first reversed the gloomy scene" of the Northern campaign. Gansevoort was rewarded by a vote of thanks and a command; Willett by public praise and "an elegant sword."

The siege of Fort Stanwix was prosecuted during sixteen days after the battle of Oriskany. There appearing to be no further prospect of relief from the militia, it was resolved to send information of the condition of the fortress to the commandant of the army at Saratoga. Colonel Willett volunteered with a single companion, Lieutenant Stockwell, to undertake this perilous duty. Creeping through the closely-guarded Indian lines at night, he picked his way through woods and unfrequented paths to Fort Dayton (now Herkimer), whence he proceeded to Saratoga. General Schuyler immediately ordered Arnold, with a detachment of nine hundred men and two pieces of artillery, to march to its relief. But before this force reached its destination an apparently trivial circumstance caused St. Leger to break up his encampment and suddenly retreat. Among a company of Tories who had been captured one night in an unlawful assembly at Little Falls was one Hon Yost, a Mohawk half-breed, who had with others, including the noted Butler, been condemned to death by a court-martial. When Arnold arrived at Fort Dayton, the mother of this man, who was a simpleton, but on this account regarded with more favor by the Indians, besought him with piteous supplications to avert his doom. Arnold was at first inexorable, but eventually said that if Hon Yost would, in glowing terms, announce his approach in St. Leger's camp before Fort Stanwix, he would grant him a reprieve from the gallows. The event proved Arnold's sagacity. Hon Yost represented to St. Leger that he had narrowly escaped, and had been hotly pursued; in proof of which assertion he exhibited his coat that he had hung up, fired at, and perforated with bullet-holes. He exaggerated the force of Arnold's detachment in every particular, and, as he spoke Mohawk fluently, he advised the whole Indian force to fly instantly. A perfect panic prevailed. Deaf to the entreaties of St. Leger and of their superintendents, the Indians robbed the British officers of their clothes, plundered the boats, and made off with the booty. The morning after his arrival, which was the 22d of August, the men on the ramparts of the fort beheld with surprise a sudden movement in the enemy's camp. Not only were the Indians in full retreat, but also St. Leger, Sir John Johnson, and Brant, with all their host of Indians and Tories, though Arnold was not within forty miles of them. The tents were left standing, and the whole train of artillery, including the mortars, was abandoned. The following day General Arnold marched into the fort, with General Larned of the Massachusetts line, and was received with salutes and huzzas. During twenty-one days the siege had been closely maintained, and as closely contested. The firmness and endurance of the garrison excited admiration throughout the country, and imparted new spirits to the friends of the Revolution, who had been so recently depressed by Burgoyne's invasion. It was the first of a series of victories, beginning in the most gloomy period of the contest, the year 1777. When the smoke of the Revolution cleared away, and memory reverted to the times that tried men's souls, the site of this fort, afterwards rechristened Fort Schuyler, was named, and has since been called, Rome,[1] in allusion to the bravery of its defence.

This triumph was followed in October by the surrender of Burgoyne. The employment of Indian allies had failed. They had melted away continually after the battle of September 19, while, through the zeal of Schuyler, and contrary to the policy of Gates, a small band, chiefly Oneidas, joined the American camp. Early the following year, on the 6th of February, France joined the colonies, entering into a treaty of amity, commerce, and alliance with them, and from that moment the success of the patriots ceased to be problematical.

[1] Oneida County, New York.

CHAPTER III.

EMPLOYMENT OF INDIANS IN WAR—ADDRESS OF CONGRESS TO THE TRIBES—
MASSACRES OF WYOMING, CHERRY VALLEY, AND ULSTER.

No contest which occurred during the struggle of the Revolution was of so much importance to a wide extent of country as that of Fort Stanwix, in which the Indians were relied on by the British as auxiliaries, and possessed in reality so much power to control the result. It is doubtful if of the seventeen hundred men announced at Oswego as composing the besieging force, more than seven hundred were regular troops. Of these the royalists, commanded by Sir John Johnson, formed one regiment; while the Senecas, the Mississagies, the fugitive Mohawks, and the Cayugas and Onondagas, should not be estimated at less than one thousand warriors. A patriot present at that siege, who was likewise a close observer on the frontiers throughout the war, has asserted that in rancor and cruelty a rabid royalist was equal to two ordinary Indians, for while he was actuated by the same general spirit of revenge, he possessed an intimate knowledge of neighborhoods and families, which he attacked in the assumed guise of a savage.

The policy of employing savages at all in war admits of no defence. The scalping and the indiscriminate slaughter of both sexes are the most horrid traits of savage life. None but a weak and bigoted prince, counselled by a short-sighted and narrow-minded premier, would have adopted this system as a part of the extraneous means of reducing the colonies to subjection. The Indians could never be relied on by British generals, or employed for any other purpose than that of covering their flanks and imparting to the contest a more bitter and vindictive character. If the latter was the object sought, the end was fully answered. The men of the present generation have not forgotten the acts of fiendish cruelty perpetrated by the Revolutionary Tories and their Indian allies.

From the beginning of the contest Congress had made strenuous efforts to persuade the Indian tribes to remain neutral. Commissioners were intrusted with the management of Indian affairs in the North and South. Active and influential men were delegated to visit the savages in their own country, and instructed to reason with them on the subject. These visits were repeated in the years 1775, 1776, and 1777, with what partial effects has been seen; the Oneidas, and their guests and allies, the Tuscaroras and Mohicans, who had long previously acknowledged the good results of Christian teaching, being the only tribes which acquiesced. There was some reason to expect that the Shawnees and Delawares would preserve a neutral position; the object was not one to be relinquished so long as a hope of success remained. The defeat the Indians had suffered at Fort Stanwix appeared to open the way for another formal conciliatory effort. With this view, on the 3d of December, 1777, the Committee on Indian Affairs reported the following address, which, while couched in terms suited to the comprehension of the Indians, at the same time appeals to their ancient pride and best interests, reviewing the grounds of controversy between the two powers, and presenting in a proper light the principles by which they should be guided:

"BROTHERS OF THE SIX NATIONS: The great council of the United States now call for your attention. Open your ears, that you may hear, and your hearts, that you may understand.

"When the people on the other side of the great water, without any cause, sought our destruction, and sent over their ships and their warriors to fight against us and to take away our possessions, you might reasonably have expected us to ask for your assistance. If we are enslaved, you cannot be free. For our strength is greater than yours. If they would not spare their brothers of the same flesh and blood, would they spare you? If they burn our houses and ravage our lands, could yours be secure?

"But we acted on very different principles. Far from desiring you to hazard your lives in our quarrel, we advised you to remain still, in case and at peace. We even entreated you to remain neuter, and under the shade of your trees and by the side of your streams to smoke your pipe in safety and contentment. Though pressed by our enemies, and when their ships obstructed our supplies of arms and powder and clothing, we were not unmindful of your wants. Of what was necessary for our own use we cheerfully spared you a part. More we should have done had it been in our power.

"CAYUGAS, SENECAS, TUSCARORAS, AND MOHAWKS: Open your ears and hear our complaints. Why have you listened to the voice of our enemies? Why have you suffered Sir John Johnson and Butler to mislead you? Why have you assisted General St. Leger and his warriors from the other side of the great water by giving them a free passage through your country to annoy us, which both you and we solemnly promised should not be defiled with blood? Why have you suffered so many of your nations to join them in their cruel purpose? Is this a suitable return for our love and kindness? or did you suspect that we were too weak or too cowardly to defend our country, and join our enemies that you might come in for a share of the plunder? What has been gained by this unprovoked treachery? what but shame and disgrace? Your foolish warriors and their new allies have been defeated and driven back in every quarter, and many of them justly paid the price of their rashness with their lives. Sorry are we to find that our ancient chain of union, heretofore so strong and bright, should be broken by such poor and weak instruments as Sir John Johnson and Butler, who dare not show their faces among their countrymen; and by St. Leger, a stranger, whom you never knew! What has become of the spirit, the wisdom, and the justice of your nations? Is it possible that you should barter away your ancient glory and break through the most solemn treaties for a few blankets or a little rum or powder? That trifles such as these should prove any temptation to you to cut down the strong tree of friendship, by our common ancestors planted in the deep bowels of the earth, at Onondaga, your central council-fire!—that tree which has been watered and nourished by their children until the branches had almost reached the skies! As well might we have expected that the mole should overturn the vast mountains of the Alleghany, or that the birds of the air should drink up the waters of Ontario!

"CAYUGAS, SENECAS, ONONDAGAS, AND MOHAWKS: Look into your hearts, and be attentive. Much are you to blame, and greatly have you wronged us. Be wise in time. Be sorry, and mend your faults. The great council, though the blood of our friends who fell by your tomahawks at the German Flats cries aloud against you, will yet be patient. We do not desire to destroy you. Long have we been at peace, and it is still our wish to bury the hatchet and wipe away the blood which some of you have so unjustly shed. Till time shall be no more, we wish to smoke with you the calumet of friendship around your central fire at Onondaga. But, brothers, mark well what we now tell you. Let it sink deep as the bottom of the sea, and never be forgotten by you or your children. If ever again you take up the hatchet to strike us, if you join our enemies in battle or council, if you give them intelligence, or encourage or permit them to pass through your country to molest or hurt any of our people, we shall look on you as our enemies, and treat you as the worst of enemies, who cover your bad designs under a cloak of friendship, and, like the concealed adder, only wait for an opportunity to wound us when we are most unprepared.

"BROTHERS: Believe us, who never deceive. If, after all our good counsel, and all our care to prevent it, we must take up the hatchet, the blood to be shed will lie heavy on your heads. The hand of the thirteen United States is not short; it will reach to the farthest extent of the country of the Six Nations; and, while we have right on our side, the Good Spirit, whom we serve, will enable us to punish you, and put it out of your power to do us further mischief.

"ONEIDAS AND TUSCARORAS: Hearken to what we have to say to you in particular. It rejoices our hearts that we have no reason to reproach you in common with the rest of the Six Nations. We have experienced your love, strong as the oak, and your fidelity, unchangeable as truth. You have kept fast hold of the ancient covenant chain, and preserved it free from rust and decay, and bright as silver. Like brave men, for glory you despised danger; you stood forth in the cause of your friends, and ventured your lives in our battles. While the sun and moon continue to give light to the world we shall love and respect you. As our trusty friends, we shall protect you, and shall at all times consider your welfare as our own.

"BROTHERS OF THE SIX NATIONS: Open your ears, and listen attentively. It is long ago that we explained to you our quarrel with the people on the other side of the great water. Remember that our cause is just. You and your forefathers have long seen us allied to those people in friendship. By our labor and industry they flourished like the trees of the forest, and became exceedingly rich and proud. At length nothing would satisfy them unless, like slaves, we would give them the power over our whole substance. Because we would not yield to such shameful bondage, they took up the hatchet. You have seen them covering our coasts with their ships, and a part of our country with their warriors; but you have not seen us dismayed: on the contrary, you know that we have stood firm like rocks, and fought like men who deserved to be free. You know that we have defeated St. Leger and conquered Burgoyne and all their warriors. Our chief men and our warriors are now fighting against the rest of our enemies, and we trust that the Great Spirit will soon put them in our power, or enable us to drive them all far beyond the great waters.

"BROTHERS: Believe us that they feel their own weakness, and that they are unable to subdue the thirteen United States. Else why have they not left our Indian brethren in peace, as they first promised and we wished to have done? Why have they endeavored, by cunning speeches, by falsehood and misrepresentations, by strong drink and presents, to embitter the minds and darken the understandings of all our Indian friends on this great continent, from the North to the South, and to engage them to take up the hatchet against us without any provocation? The Cherokees, like some of you, were prevailed upon to strike our people. We carried the war into their country, and fought them. They saw their error, they repented, and we forgave them. The United States are kind and merciful, and wish for peace with all the world. We have, therefore, renewed our ancient covenant chain with their nation.

"BROTHERS: The Shawanese and Delawares give us daily proofs of their good disposition and their attachment to us, and are ready to assist us against all our enemies. The Chickasaws are among the number of our faithful friends. And the Choctaws, though remote from us, have refused to listen to the persuasions of our enemies, rejected all their offers of corruption, and continue peaceable. The Creeks are also our steady friends. Oboylaco, their great chief, and the rest of their sachems and warriors, as the strongest mark of their sincere friendship, have presented the great council with an emblem of peace. They have desired that these tokens might be shown to the Six Nations and their allies, to convince them that the Creeks are at peace with the United States. We have therefore directed our commissioners to deliver them into your hands. Let them be seen by all the nations in your alliance, and preserved in your central council-house at Onondaga.

"BROTHERS OF THE SIX NATIONS: Hearken to our counsel. Let us who are born on the same great continent love one another. Our interest is the same, and we ought to be one people, always ready to assist and serve each other. What are the people who belong to the other side of the great waters to either of us? They never come here for our sakes, but to gratify their own pride and avarice. Their business now is to kill and destroy our inhabitants, to lay waste our houses and farms. The day, we trust, will soon arrive when we shall be rid of them forever. Now is the time to hasten and secure this happy event. Let us, then, from this moment join hand and heart in the defence of our common country. Let us rise as one man and drive away our cruel oppressors. Henceforward let none be able to separate us. If any of our people injure you, acquaint us of it, and you may depend upon full satisfaction. If any of yours hurt us, be you ready to repair the wrong or punish the aggressor. Above all, shut your ears against liars and deceivers, who, like false meteors, strive to lead you astray and to set us at variance. Believe no evil of us till you have taken pains to discover the truth. Our council-fire always burns clear and bright in Pennsylvania.[1] Our commissioners and agents are near your country. We shall not be blinded by false reports or false appearances."[2]

This overture produced no change in the policy of the Indians: in public councils as well as in private their ears were filled with reasonings and persuasions of a very different character. Ever judging from appearances, and from what was tangible and visible, they were impressed with the power, means, and ability of the British government to subdue the colonies. They contrasted its resources with those of the thirteen States, struggling, as it were, in the grasp of a giant, and from that comparison drew the conclusion that, however courageous and resolute the colonists were in battle, they were few in numbers and lacking in means. It being a cardinal principle with the Indians to adhere to the strongest party, they remained unmoved by all the arguments addressed to them.

It would be foreign to the plan of the present work to describe in detail the scenes of Indian outrage and massacre which marked the Revolutionary contest, the object being to present prominent facts. The character of the Indians did not appear in any new light; as the war advanced, they swept over the country like a pestilence, frequently like infuriated tigers springing across the borders and spreading death and devastation where domestic happiness had previously reigned. Any hope that might have been entertained of mollifying their hatred proved to be a delusion. The Iroquois, who were the principal actors in this murderous warfare, were in nearly every instance led on by their chieftain Brant. Sometimes, however, parties of the various tribes of Algonkin lineage from the West were in the practice of visiting the head-quarters of the British Indian Department at Fort Niagara. At this place most of the war-parties were formed, supplied, and equipped. Thither they also returned to report their success, bringing their prisoners with them to pass through the terrible ordeal of the gauntlet, and there likewise they received rewards for the scalps they had taken.

In the early summer of 1778 the movements of Brant and his warriors upon the upper waters of the Susquehanna, and of the Tories in the valley of Wyoming, had aroused the people of that region to a sense of the perils incident to their exposed situation. Apprehension was felt that some of the Loyalists who had left the valley and joined the forces of Colonel John Butler would return and wreak their vengeance on the inhabitants. Atrocities had been perpetrated in the neighborhood of Tioga, and the Indians at Conewawah (now Elmira, New York) were in constant communication with the Tory settlers. The attention of Congress had been often called to their danger, weakened as they had been by drafts upon their able-bodied men for the Continental army, nearly all of whom were absent in service. The remaining

---

[1] Then the seat of government.   [2] Journal of Congress.

population, in dread of the savages, were voluntarily building six forts, or stockades, requiring great labor. Aged men, exempt by law from military duty, were formed into companies to garrison these forts, while the whole of the militia were in constant requisition as scouts and guides. Such was the condition of Wyoming when the Tory and Indian expedition was prepared for its destruction.

It was at Niagara that the plan of the incursion into the valley of Wyoming originated. Towards the close of June, 1778, Colonel John Butler, the commanding officer of that post, ordered three hundred men, principally Loyalists, to set out on an expedition to the Susquehanna, accompanied by a body of Indians, eleven hundred in all, of diverse tribes, under Gi-en-gwa-tah, a Seneca chief. Arriving at Tioga Point, they embarked in floats, or on rafts, and reached the scene of conflict on the first day of July.

Landing on the west side of the river, about twenty miles above Wyoming, they entered the valley through a notch from the west, not far from the famous Dial Rock, and killed three men near Fort Jenkins. Butler made his head-quarters at Wintermoots Fort, whence he sent out scouts and foragers. All the preparation in their power had been made by the people to withstand the foe. A company of forty or fifty regulars and a few militia, under Captain Hewett, composed the military force with which to oppose the enemy. Old men, boys, and even women seized such weapons as were at hand. Colonel Zebulon Butler, an officer of the Continental army, who happened to be at home, was made commander-in-chief. Forty Fort (so called from the first forty Yankee pioneers of Wyoming) was made the place of rendezvous, and thither the women and children fled for safety.

On the morning of July 3 a council of war was held here. The odds were fearful, and there was no alternative but to fight or submit to the tender mercies of the Indians and the more savage Tories. Colonels Butler and Denison, and Lieutenant-Colonel Dorrance, were in favor of delay, hoping for the arrival of reinforcements. Others, having little hope of succor, advised meeting the enemy at once. Already Fort Jenkins had been captured, and the other stockades would doubtless share its fate. The surrender of Forty Fort and the valley had been demanded by Colonel John Butler, and the uplifted hatchet was ready to descend upon the heads of those families that had not succeeded in reaching the fort. Prompt action seemed necessary, and the majority bravely but rashly decided to march out and give battle to the invaders.

The plucky little American force, numbering between three hundred and four hundred, approached the enemy's lines, eleven hundred strong, about four o'clock, the afternoon being intensely hot, and gave battle, advancing a step at each fire. Soon the enemy's left, where John Butler was posted, began to give way, but it was at once supported by a flanking party of Indians, who, from their concealment, kept up a galling fire. For half an hour the Americans maintained the conflict against vastly superior numbers, when the Indians on their left flanked Colonel Denison, and he was thus exposed to a murderous cross-fire. His order to his men to fall back to a more favorable position was mistaken for an order to retreat, and they fell back in confusion. Every effort to rally the fugitives was ineffectual. Riding along the line, exposed to the fire of the contending parties, and seemingly unconscious of danger, Colonel Zebulon Butler besought his troops to remain firm. "Don't leave me, my children," he exclaimed, "and the victory is ours." All that bravery and devotion could do was done by Butler and Denison, but it was too late. Every captain had been killed, and the line broke and fled, some to the fort, and some to Monocacy Island, nearly a mile off. A scene of horror ensued. Only sixty escaped the rifle, the tomahawk, and the scalping-knife. The prisoners were either tortured or butchered in cold blood. Colonel Butler escaped to Wilkesbarre Fort, and Colonel Denison to Forty Fort, where he prepared to defend the fugitive women and children. He surrendered next day, however, there being no hope of a successful defence, the other stockades having fallen, and the people of the valley having generally fled from the scene. The terms of capitulation were soon violated, the Indians before night having spread through the valley, plundering the few people that were left, and burning the abandoned dwellings. The Tory commander endeavored to restrain them, but his orders were utterly disregarded. The village of Wilkesbarre was also burned, and the terrified inhabitants fled to the mountains. Except the few who gathered about the fort at Wilkesbarre, the settlement, which presented one wide scene of conflagration, massacre, and ruin, was wholly abandoned by its former inhabitants, and remained so for months. Terribly as the valley had suffered, it continued to be harassed and devastated by the savage foe until peace was proclaimed.

It was then believed, and it has since been frequently asserted, that Brant led the Indians on this occasion; but it is doubtful whether he was actually present, though he probably approved of the movement, if he was not the instigator of it. This chief was known to cherish such a deadly hatred of the Revolutionists, and had been so frequently connected with the incursions and midnight massacres perpetrated on the frontiers, that in the popular estimation no injustice has been done to his bad reputation in the use which has been made of his name by the poet Campbell. A melancholy catalogue, indeed, would be a detail of the enterprises in which Brant was the leader and principal actor. Though the voice of contemporary history might be stifled regarding his conduct as the leader of the massacre in Cherry Valley, his sanguinary attacks upon Saratoga, German Flats, Unadilla, and Scholarie, as well as the murder of the wounded Colonel Wisner and the inhuman butchery of the wounded at Ulster, will during all future time illustrate the way in which he hovered around the frontiers of New York and Pennsylvania, like the genius of evil, with the enraged Aquinoshioni in his train. If the responsibility for acts committed depends upon the cultivated moral perceptions of the individual, then the great partisan Mohawk will have much more to answer for than his kindred generally, as he not only received a scholastic and religious education, but was for a long time domiciliated in the family of Sir William Johnson, in which he officiated as an assistant secretary, and where he became familiar with the maxims and usages of refined society.

The recovery of the Mohawk Valley was of such importance to the Johnsons, Butlers, and other refugees who accompanied them to Canada as to incite them to extraordinary efforts for the accomplishment of that object. The exposed condition of Cherry Valley and the settlement upon Schoharie Creek had caused the erection of three fortifications,—stone houses surrounded with an embankment of earth and stockaded, affording protection to the women and children. Each of these was manned by a company of soldiers, with a small brass field-piece. A fort was erected in the Oneida country, Forts Schuyler and Dayton were strengthened, and Fort Plain was afterwards enlarged and more strongly fortified. In May, 1778, the village of Springfield, ten miles west of Cherry Valley, had been destroyed by Brant. Cobleskill, in the Schoharie Valley, met the same fate on July 2, after the defeat of a small party of Americans under Captain Brunk, and on the day following Wyoming was devastated. The settlement at Genesee Flats was destroyed towards the close of the summer. Scalping-parties continued to infest the Schoharie and neighboring settlements until late in September, when their depredations were checked for a time by the presence of troops from the main army.

Walter, the son of Colonel John Butler, who after a year's imprisonment had escaped from Albany, thirsting for revenge, obtained from his father the command of a detachment of his rangers, and permission to employ them, in conjunction with Brant, against the settlements in Tryon County. Their united forces amounted to about seven hundred men. Information of the movement was sent to Cherry Valley and the Schoharie forts, but the presence of the Pennsylvania troops had lulled the people into fancied security, and the warning was disregarded.

Cherry Valley, the most important settlement near the head-waters of the East Branch of the Susquehanna, was garrisoned by two hundred and fifty Massachusetts troops, under Colonel Ichabod Alden. On November 8 he received a despatch from Fort Schuyler, informing him that he was to be attacked by a large force of Indians and Tories, then assembled upon the Tioga River. Treating the matter with unconcern, Alden refused to permit the alarmed inhabitants to move into the fort, but on the 9th sent out scouting-parties in various directions. Early on the following morning his quarters, which were outside the fort, were surrounded by the enemy, and he was tomahawked and scalped while attempting to escape. Sixteen soldiers and thirty-two of the inhabitants, mostly women and children, were killed. Every house was plundered and burned. The captured women and children, being found cumbersome, were sent back next day. The inhuman conduct of Walter Butler, the leader of this foray, condemned even by the savage Brant, has consigned his name to eternal infamy. His after-career was cruel but brief, and when in 1781 he was slain by the Oneidas on the banks of the West Canada Creek, his body was left to decay, while his fallen companions were buried with respect.

CHAPTER IV.

HOSTILITIES WITH THE WESTERN INDIANS—THE SHAWNEES—CORNSTALK—FORT HENRY—CONQUEST OF SOUTHERN ILLINOIS—FORT LAURENS.

ALTHOUGH the Iroquois formed, as it were, the "Tenth Legion" of the hostile Indians employed in the war, yet the Western savages had from the beginning evinced their hostility to the colonies, and were implicated to a greater or less extent in the contest against them. This was, as we have seen, the position of the important tribes of the Delawares and Shawnees, then occupying the present area of the State of Ohio. These tribes had originally emigrated west of the Alleghanies with embittered feelings against the English colonists generally. They had accepted the treaty of peace offered them in rather a vaunting spirit by Colonel Bradstreet on Lake Erie in 1764, but subsequently renewed their hostile inroads, and in the autumn of the same year, on the banks of the Muskingum, again submitted to the army under Colonel Bouquet, delivering up, as a test of their sincerity, a large number of prisoners, men, women, and children.

The Delawares had not held a definite tribal position for a long period, even from the middle of the eighteenth century. They were supposed to be in league with the French, and it was an erroneous policy in Count Zinzendorf and the Moravian Brethren not to set the colonies right on this subject, laboring as they did from their advent in 1740 for the benefit of the Delawares, and knowing that there was a suspicion resting on them of being favorable to the French interests. This was the cause of the expulsion of this tribe from Chicomico, in Southern New York, in 1744, and of their removal to the Susquehanna. It was likewise the occasion of their ultimate flight westward to the banks of the Muskingum, and of the unfortunate massacre of their people at Gnadenhütten. But though the proclivities of the Delawares were long uncertain, those of the Shawnees were not; they assumed an openly hostile attitude. The latter tribe had at an early period been inimical to the English colonies, but, being vanquished, they had transferred their hatred to the Americans the moment the Revolutionary contest commenced. In 1755 they were the most bitter assailants of Braddock; in 1758[1] they massacred the garrison of Sybert's Fort, on the Potomac; they had from the year 1763 most strenuously opposed the settlement of Kentucky; they had in 1774 taken the most prominent part in resisting the expedition of Lord Dunmore; and, according to the best local authorities,[2] between the years 1770 and 1779 the activity and bitter hostility of this celebrated tribe converted the left banks of the Ohio, along the borders of

---

[1] De Hass's History of Western Virginia, 1851, p. 208. [2] Doddridge, Withers, De Hass.

Pennsylvania and Virginia, into an aceldama. Brave and dauntless, but vacillating, their ruling passion was a love of war, blood, and plunder. Tradition affirms that in ancient times they had fought their way from Florida to Lake Erie; and desperately did they oppose the advance of the Anglo-Saxon race into the Ohio Valley. Their central location was at Chillicothe, on the Scioto River, which appears to have been from a period long antecedent a metropolis of Indian power. Their influence controlled the entire valley, and they lived on strict terms of amity with the Delawares, the Mingoes, or Ohio Iroquois, the Hurons, Ottawas, Chippewas, and Miamis.

The Shawnee chief Cornstalk was friendly to the colonists, and his voice and influence were for peace, and his efforts in that behalf were very valuable. He was a man of great energy, courage, and good sense, and very reliable. The trouble and confusion then existing about him led him to cross the Ohio River in 1777 to talk matters over with the commander of a post at the mouth of the Big Kanawha. The Americans, believing that the Shawnees were inclined to unite with the British, determined to retain him and Red Hawk, a subordinate chief, who was with him. Cornstalk spoke freely of the condition of affairs, and said to Captain Arbuckle, the commander, that unless he and his friends could have assurances of protection from the "Long-Knives" they might be compelled "to go with the stream." This friendly visit worked differently from what he expected. He was not permitted to depart. Next day an Indian on the opposite shore hailed the fort. He was brought over, and proved to be the son of Cornstalk, who was anxious for his father's safety. The son was also secured as a hostage. A few days later a white hunter was killed by unknown Indians. The cry was instantly raised, "Kill the red dogs in the fort!" Arbuckle attempted, it is said, to prevent this, but his life was threatened. The mob rushed to the place where the captives were confined. Cornstalk met them at the door, and was pierced by seven bullets. His son and Red Hawk were also slain.• "From that hour," says Doddridge, "peace was not to be hoped for."

The Ohio Valley, with its beautiful scenery, its genial climate, and its exuberant fertility, had been from its earliest discovery a subject of contention between the Indians and the white race. Red men had fought for it among themselves for many years, as is proved by its antiquities, and the whites succeeded to the controversy. The feet of Washington trod its soil as early as 1753, when the charter of George II. was granted for its occupancy. Although the primary object of its exploration, and of the commissioners and armies which crossed the Alleghanies and entered its borders, was the furtherance of governmental policy, it is very evident that there were aboriginal minds of sufficient penetration to foresee that the acquisition of the territory, and the spread of the arts and commerce of civilized life, were the ultimate ends in view. This may readily be perceived in the harangues of Pontiac to the tribes of the Northwest in the year 1763, as well as in those of Tenuskund at Wyoming and of Buckongahecla at Kaskaskia. Every movement of the whites towards the West was regarded by thinking Indian minds as having the same object in view.

Prior to the expedition of McIntosh, a friendly Delaware chief, Koquathahecelon, or White Eyes, had used his influence to prevent the tribes from raising the hatchet, but an opposite influence was exercised by Captain Pipe, and the nation became divided. Such was the state of affairs among the Delawares in the spring of 1778. About this time three noted Loyalists, McKee, Elliot, and Girty, fled from Fort Pitt to the Delawares and used their utmost efforts against the American cause. Captain Pipe was so much influenced by their counsel that in a large assemblage of warriors he concluded a harangue by declaring "every one an enemy who refused to fight the Americans, and that all such ought to be put to death." Koquathaheelon boldly opposed him, denounced the policy, and sent a formal message to the Scioto, warning the Indians against the counsels of the fugitives Girty and McKee. This for a while had the effect of keeping the Delawares neutral; but the tribe finally decided to raise the hatchet against the struggling colonies.

Both the Delawares and Shawnees were greatly influenced in their councils by the Wyandots of Sandusky, a reflective, clear-minded people, who had once been at the head of the Iroquois while that nation resided on the Kanawaga, and who still held a kind of umpirage in Western Indian councils. It was against the local residence of this tribe at Sandusky that General Lachlan McIntosh was directed by Congress to proceed. He had during the spring, with a small force of regulars and militia, descended the Ohio from Fort Pitt to the Beaver River, where he erected on a commanding position a fort called McIntosh. It intercepted Indians ascending or descending the Ohio, as well as interior marauding parties who reached the river at this point. The force assigned him for the expedition against Sandusky was one thousand men. But such were the delays in organizing it and in marching through a wilderness to the Tuscarawas, that after reaching its banks he there constructed a fort called Laurens, and, garrisoning it, returned to Fort Pitt.

In the summer of 1777, Simon Girty, who, with two other Tory emissaries, Elliot and McKee, had been confined by the patriots at Pittsburg, and who was inflamed with the spirit of revenge, collected about four hundred Indian warriors at Sandusky, and marched towards Limestone, now Maysville, on the Kentucky frontier. Fort Henry, a small work near the mouth of Wheeling Creek (now Wheeling), was garrisoned by about forty men under Colonel Sheppard. Girty, undiscovered by Sheppard's scouts, appeared before the fort with his followers early on the morning of September 26. Fortunately for the settlers around the fort, they had scented danger on the previous evening, and taken refuge within its walls.

The first onset was upon a reconnoitring party under Captain Mason, who was drawn into an ambuscade, losing half his men. Of Captain Ogle's party of twelve who sallied out to the assistance of Mason, only four escaped, and the little garrison was reduced to only twelve men and youths, among whom Colonel Sheppard and Ebenezer and Silas Zane were the most prominent. Ebenezer Zane, twenty years later, founded Zanesville, Ohio. Girty demanded the unconditional surrender of the fort. Although outnumbered forty-fold, Colonel Sheppard told the scoundrel that it should never be surrendered to him or to any other man while there was an American left to defend it. To the fire of the Indians, kept up for six hours, the sharp-shooters from within replied with fatal effect. At noon they fell back, and the firing ceased. To replenish their almost exhausted stock of ammunition, the daring feat of bringing a keg of powder to the fort was successfully accomplished by an intrepid young woman, a sister of the Zanes. While returning at full speed with the keg in her arms, the Indians sent a volley of bullets after her, but not a ball touched her person.

At half-past two o'clock the attack was renewed. An attempt to force the gate was abandoned after six of their number had been shot down. Approaching darkness did not end the conflict. The Indians converted a hollow maple log into a field-piece, and after dark conveyed it within sixty yards of the fort. It was bound with chains, filled to the muzzle with stones, pieces of iron, and other missiles, and discharged against the gate of the fort. The log burst into a thousand fragments, scattering its projectiles in all directions. Several Indians were killed, but not a picket of the fort was injured. This failure discouraged the assailants, and the conflict ceased for the night. Early next morning Captain Swearingen and fourteen men arrived and fought their way into the fort, and soon after Major McCulloch arrived with forty mounted men. His followers entered the fort in safety, but he, becoming separated from them, was obliged to fly in the opposite direction, and narrowly escaped.

Hopeless of success after this augmentation of the garrison, Girty and his savage band, setting fire to the houses and fences, and killing three hundred head of cattle belonging to the settlers, raised the siege and departed. Not a man of the garrison was lost during the siege, while the loss of the enemy was between sixty and one hundred. The courageous defence of Fort Henry was one of the most remarkable incidents in the long and brilliant record of our border warfare, but it has been unaccountably overlooked by most of our historians.

The erection of Forts McIntosh and Laurens, on the banks of the Beaver and Tuscarawas Rivers, demonstrated to the Indians that they would be held accountable for their actions. But a more important military movement, one which has had a permanent and predominant influence on the history of the West, was originated in the year 1778. Western Virginia having suffered dreadfully from the inroads of the Shawnees, Delawares, and Mingoes, General George Rogers Clarke was commissioned by the State authorities to invade the country of the Illinois. His enterprise, courage, and tact were strongly exemplified in this expedition. He descended the western slope of the Alleghanies by the river Kanawha, the mouth of which was his point of rendezvous, with a force not exceeding two hundred men. The fort at this point was then invested by Indians, whom he successfully routed with the loss of only one man. His next object of attack was Kaskaskia, Illinois, from which he was separated by a wilderness one thousand miles in extent. But he had a force of picked men whom no lack of means could discourage, and whose heroic ardor no opposition of natural impediments could dampen. Descending the Ohio to its falls, he erected a small fort on Corn Island, in their vicinity, which he garrisoned with a few men, and then continued his course down the river to within sixty miles of its mouth, where he landed his men, and with only four days' provisions commenced his march across the wilderness to the Illinois country. He was six days in reaching Kaskaskia, during two of which his little army was destitute of provisions. Reaching the town at midnight, and finding the garrison and inhabitants asleep, he carried it by surprise, taking the commandant, Rocheblave, prisoner, whom he immediately sent under guard to Richmond, together with important letters and papers implicating persons in power. The fort was found to be sufficiently strong to have been defended against a force of one thousand men. The following day, finding horses in the vicinity, General Clarke mounted about thirty of his men, under Captain Bowman, and sent them against the upper towns on the banks of the Mississippi. They took possession of the French towns and villages as high up as Cahokia, and in the course of three days thereafter no less than three hundred of the French inhabitants took the oath of allegiance to the American government. Leaving a garrison at Kaskaskia, General Clarke then proceeded across the country to Vincennes, on the Wabash, which he also surprised and captured. The march was long, the season inclement; the track lay through an unbroken wilderness and overflowed bottoms. His stock of provisions was scanty, and had to be carried on the backs of his men. He could muster only one hundred and thirty men, but he succeeded in inspiring this handful with his own heroic spirit. The difficulties were much greater than he anticipated. For days his route led through the drowned lands of Illinois, his stock of provisions became exhausted, his guides lost their way, and the most intrepid of his followers at times gave way to despair. Emerging at length from these difficulties, Vincennes was completely surprised, the governor and garrison became prisoners of war, and, like their compatriots at Kaskaskia, were sent on to Virginia. This post was in the heart of the Miami country, which had been the seat of French trade, and had been established as a mission in 1710. Its importance was so much felt by Governor Hamilton, of Detroit, that he suddenly mustered a force and recaptured the place. General Clarke, who was at Point Pleasant (West Virginia), on hearing of this, although it was then winter, determined to retake the post, and, with a resolute party of men, who during their march frequently waded through water breast-high, executed his purpose, also making Hamilton prisoner. This man was a rough, bad-tempered, and cruel officer, who had excited the ire of the Indians by his malignancy.

The effect of these movements on the mass of the Indians was more important in a political view than it appeared to be. Kaskaskia and Vincennes had been mere outposts to Detroit, which was a depot for the prisoners taken by the Indians, and where they received the rewards for the scalps they brought in.

The effect upon the Delaware nation of the operations during this year, of which Fort Pitt was the centre, was to promote the conclusion of a treaty of peace, which was signed on the 17th of September, 1778, by the chiefs Koquathaheelon, or White Eyes, Pipe, and Killbuck, before Generals Andrew and Thomas Lewis. This was the first of a long list of treaties with the Indian tribes, in which the nations, when pressed by war, sometimes made a virtue of necessity, and conceded points which on some occasions the want of popular support, and again the lack of power in their governments, did not enable them to comply with, although the aboriginal delegates who gave their assent to them did so with full integrity of purpose. It is certain that the Delaware nation was soon afterwards engaged in hostilities against the United States, for besides the recognition of this fact by the treaty of Fort McIntosh, dated June 21, 1785, a supplementary article to that treaty provided that the chiefs Kelelamand, White Eyes, and one or two other persons of note, who took up the hatchet for the United States, should be received back into the Delaware nation, and reinstated in all their original rights without any prejudice.

Fort Laurens, erected on the Tuscarawas in 1778 by General McIntosh, at the terminus of his march against Sandusky, was left in command of Colonel Gibson, with a garrison of one hundred and fifty men. It was the custom of the garrison to put bells on their horses and send them out to graze in the vicinity, where they were visited and looked after. This being observed by the Indians who infested the surrounding forests, they stole all the animals, first removing the bells from their necks. Selecting a spot suitable for an ambuscade, the bells were tied to the stalks of stout weeds or flexible twigs, and the Indians, lying down on the ground, carefully shook them, so as to simulate the noise they would make while the horses were cropping grass. The stratagem succeeded. Of a party of sixteen men sent to catch the animals, which were supposed to have strayed, fourteen were shot dead, and the other two were taken prisoners: one of the latter returned after the termination of the war, but his comrade was never more heard of. Flushed with the success of this manœuvre, the entire body of Indians towards evening marched across the prairie in full view of the garrison, but at a safe distance. Eight hundred and forty warriors were counted from one of the bastions, painted and feathered for war, and appearing to make this display as a challenge to combat. They then crossed the Tuscarawas, and encamped on an elevated site within view of the fort, where they remained for several weeks watching the garrison. While located at this spot they affected to keep up a good understanding with the officers of the fort through one of those speaking go-betweens who have been so fruitful of mischief in our military history. At length, their resources failing, they sent word that if a barrel of flour was supplied to them they would on the following day submit proposals of peace. The flour being duly delivered, the whole gang immediately decamped, removing to some part of the forest where so considerable a body could more readily obtain subsistence.

It has ever been a fatal mistake to put trust in Indian fidelity under such circumstances. A party of spies were left by the Indians in the woods. As the supplies of the garrison began to diminish, the invalids, amounting to ten or a dozen men, were sent to Fort McIntosh under an escort of fifteen men, commanded by Colonel Clark, of the line. This party had proceeded but two miles when they were suddenly surrounded by the Indians, and all killed except four, one of whom, a captain, succeeded in effecting his escape to the fort.

The garrison now experienced severe suffering from hunger, the fort being in a remote position, so that it could be supplied only by means of trains of pack-horses, convoyed through the wilderness by expensive escorts. Fortunately, General

McIntosh arrived with supplies and seven hundred men; but the joy produced by his arrival wellnigh proved a fatal misfortune, as the salute of musketry fired from the ramparts caused a stampede among the horses of the pack-trains, which, running affrighted through the forest, scattered their burdens of provisions and flour on the ground. When McIntosh departed from the fort he left Major Vernon in command, who, being finally reduced to great straits, and finding himself surrounded by a powerful and treacherous enemy, abandoned the fort, and returned with his command to Fort McIntosh. These transactions furnish material for a good commentary on the treaty of Fort Pitt, concluded on the 17th of the preceding September. The Delawares, who signed this treaty, occupied the entire valley of the Muskingum, of which the Tuscarawas is a branch, and, being generally under the sway of the Wyandots of Sandusky, had in fact no power to carry out, even if they possessed the authority to conclude, such a treaty.

The erection of Fort Laurens was, in truth, a monument of the failure of the military expedition against Detroit, projected with so much confidence at that time, and its abandonment may be regarded as an admission of the uselessness of the position as a check upon the Indians.

While these movements were going forward on the Tuscarawas and in the forests surrounding Fort Laurens, the Indians perpetrated a series of heart-rending murders along the river Monongahela.[1] A recital of these atrocities would only serve to prove that no trust could be placed in any public avowal of friendship by the savages, whether professed in conferences or by formal treaties.

---

[1] De Hass's History of Western Virginia, p. 208; Wheeling, 1851. Chronicles of Border Warfare, Clarksburg, Virginia, 1831. It appears from this author that fifteen persons in Western Virginia of the name of Schoolcraft (connections of the writer) were killed or carried into captivity by the Shawnees during this period.

CHAPTER V.

BATTLE OF MINNISINK—SULLIVAN RAVAGES THE IROQUOIS TERRITORY—INDIAN AND TORY RAIDS IN WESTERN NEW YORK—CHEROKEE HOSTILITIES—MASSACRE OF THE MORAVIAN DELAWARES.

The frequency and severity of the attacks made by the Iroquois on the frontiers of New York and Pennsylvania induced the Americans to make a sudden descent during this year on the Onondagas. The execution of this enterprise was committed to Colonel Van Schaick by General James Clinton, the commanding officer in that district. Five hundred and fifty-eight men, accompanied by Lieutenant-Colonel Willett, and furnished with every necessary supply, embarked in thirty bateaux on Wood Creek, west of the Fort Stanwix summit, and, passing rapidly through Oneida Lake and River, landed during the night at the site of old Fort Brewerton, whence they pressed swiftly forward, using every precaution to prevent an alarm. The surprise would have been complete but for the capture of a warrior near the castle. As it was, however, thirty-three warriors were killed, and the rest fled in the utmost consternation, leaving behind them all their stores, arms, and provisions. The castle and village were burned, and the country devastated within a circuit of ten miles. The army then returned to Fort Stanwix, or Schuyler, without the loss of a man.

It is doubtful whether such retributive measures are attended by any advantages. The Onondagas determining to retaliate, Brant placed himself at the head of three hundred warriors of that and other tribes, who attacked Schoharie and its environs, which had so frequently, since the commencement of the Revolution, been the scene of every species of Indian outrage,—the property of the inhabitants plundered, their houses burned, and themselves murdered and scalped. It appeared as if the Mohawk Indians, and their beau-ideal, Brant, could never forgive the sturdy patriotism of the people of that valley.

Palatine, in the Mohawk Valley, was at the same time attacked by parties of Indians from the Canada border, and many persons killed; but no event which occurred during this year made so deep an impression on the public mind as the battle and massacre at Minnisink, a fertile island in the Delaware River, which had long been the camping- and council-ground of the Lenape and of the Southern Indians in their progress to the Hudson Valley by way of the Wallkill. Few places have better claims to antiquarian interest than the town of Minnisink, or "The Place of the Island."

Having reached the vicinity of this town on the night of July 19, with sixty warriors and twenty-seven Tories disguised as Indians, Brant attacked it while the inhabitants were asleep, burned two dwelling-houses, twelve barns, a small stockade fort, and two mills, killed several of the inhabitants, took others prisoners, and then ravaged the surrounding farms, driving off the cattle and horses to the place where he had left the main body of his warriors. When intelligence of this outrage reached Goshen, the excitement became intense. A militia force of one hundred and forty-nine men instantly marched from Orange County in pursuit, and overtook the enemy on the second day.

Their leader, Colonel Tusten, well acquainted with the craftiness and skill of Brant, opposed the measure, as too hazardous with their small force. He was overruled, and Colonel Hathorne, of the Warwick militia, Tusten's senior, joining them with a small reinforcement just before the battle, took command. At Half-Way Brook they came upon the Indian encampment of the previous night, its numerous watch-fires still smoking, indicating a large force. The two colonels, with the more cautious of the company, were for discontinuing the pursuit, but they were opposed by a large majority, and all pressed eagerly forward. At nine o'clock on the morning of the 22d the enemy were in sight, moving towards a fording-place. Hathorne so disposed his men as to intercept them, but Brant, perceiving his design, wheeled his forces, and, gaining a deep ravine which the whites had crossed, took up an advantageous position in their rear, and then formed an ambuscade.

Disappointed in not finding the enemy, the Americans were marching back, when they were fired upon. A desperate contest ensued, lasting from eleven in the morning until sunset, when the ammunition of the Orange County men failed. The Indians were greatly superior in numbers, and one-third of Hathorne's troops became separated from the rest at the commencement of the action. A final attack broke the hollow square of the Americans, who retreated. One hundred and two had fallen, and seventeen, who were wounded, were placed under Dr. Tusten's care behind a rocky point. The Indians rushed upon them furiously and tomahawked them all, notwithstanding their appeals for mercy. Brant himself sunk his tomahawk in the head of Colonel Wisner, one of the wounded, and his savage cruelty on this occasion remains one of the darkest stains upon his memory.

It is probable that this atrocity was one of the immediate causes of the expedition under General Sullivan, which marched against the Iroquois cantons during the following year.

While these events were occurring in New York, a body of two hundred Indians and one hundred refugee Royalists, under the command of McDonald, appeared on the borders of Northampton County, Pennsylvania, where they burned many houses and committed several murders. A few days subsequently they invested Freeland's Fort, on the Susquehanna, the garrison of which was too weak to defend the works, which had served principally as a shelter for women and children while the men were attending to the duties which they owed their country. Captain Hawkins Boon, who with thirty men was stationed in the vicinity, marched to the relief of the fort, and, upon finding that it had been surrendered, valiantly attacked the besiegers, and was killed, together with eighteen of his men. This affair happened about the same time as the tragic events of Minnisink.

The war had now continued nearly five years, and the operations of the British army during that period, north, south, east, and west, had proved a severe tax on the military resources and strength of the country. But these sacrifices to patriotism and high principles were considered as nothing compared to the sufferings caused by the savage auxiliaries of the British armies, who were utter strangers to the laws of humanity. The Americans bitterly reproached their foes for paying their Indian allies a price for the scalps they took, and it cannot be doubted that the censure was justly deserved.

It was the opinion of Washington that the cheapest and most effectual mode of opposing the Indians was to carry the war into their country. These tribes, nurtured in the secret recesses of the forest, were thoroughly acquainted with every avenue through their depths, and thence pounced upon the unguarded settlements when least expected, flying back to their lairs in the wilderness before an effective military force could be concentrated to pursue them. By these inroads, Washington observes, the Indians had everything to gain, and very little to lose, whereas the very reverse would be the case if their towns and retreats were visited with the calamities of war.

Conformably to these views, the year 1779 witnessed the march of the well-organized army of General Sullivan into the heart of the country occupied by the Iroquois confederacy at a season when their orchards and fields were fully laden with grain and fruits. It was a part of the plan of the expedition to penetrate the country to Niagara, and break up "the nest of vipers" there. Sullivan had gallantly aided Washington in the capture of Trenton, and was selected for this service after mature consideration.[1] His entire force consisted of two divisions, one of which, under General James Clinton, marched from Central New York northwardly through the Mohawk Valley, and the other, from Pennsylvania, ascended the Susquhanna. Clinton, with five brigades, proceeded with great rapidity across the country from Canajoharie, his *point d'appui* on the Mohawk, to Otsego Lake, carrying with him two hundred and twenty bateaux, all his stores, artillery, and a full supply of provisions. From this point he followed the outlet of the lake into the Susquehanna, joining General Sullivan and the Pennsylvania troops at Tioga Point. Their total force amounted to five thousand men. It included the brigades of Clinton, Hand, Maxwell, and Poor, together with Proctor's artillery and a corps of riflemen. After the delays incident to the collection and regulation of such a body of troops, the army proceeded up the river late in August, and ascended the Chemung branch to Newtown, at present called Elmira. The enemy, anticipating the movement, had prepared to oppose the army by erecting a breastwork across a peninsula in front of the place of landing, thus occupying a formidable position. Brant commanded the Iroquois, mustering fifteen hundred warriors, who were supported by two hundred regular British troops and rangers, under Colonel John Butler, Sir John Johnson, and some of the other noted Royalist commanders of that period. This force was so

---

[1] Gates had been at first proposed.

disposed among the adjoining hills, and screened by brush, thickets, and logs, as to be entirely concealed, and it was so covered by a bend in the river that only the front and one flank were exposed to the fire of the assailants. That flank rested upon a steep hill or ridge running nearly parallel with the river. Farther to the left was another ridge, running in the same direction, and passing in the rear of the Americans. Detachments of the enemy were stationed on both hills, having a line of communication, and they were so disposed that they might fall upon the assailants' flank and rear as soon as the action should commence. Their connecting fortification was so disposed that both flanks of the army would be exposed to an enfilading fire. The army landed on the 29th of August, and the enemy's position was discovered by the advance guard, under Major Parr, at eleven o'clock in the morning. General Hand immediately formed the light infantry in a wood within four hundred yards of the Indian breastwork, where he remained until the rest of the troops came up. While these movements were in progress, small parties of Indians sallied from their intrenchments and began a desultory firing, as suddenly retreating when attacked, and making the woods resound with their savage yells. Their intention evidently was to induce the belief that they were present in very great numbers, and were the only force to be encountered. Judging truly that the hill on his right was occupied by the Indians, Sullivan ordered Poor with his brigade to attempt its ascent, and to endeavor to turn the enemy's left flank, while the artillery, supported by the main body of the army, attacked them in front. Both orders were promptly executed. The ascent being gained, the Americans poured in their fire, while the enemy for two hours withstood a heavy fire directly in front. Both the Indians and their allies fought manfully, but the Americans pressed on with great determination. Every tree, rock, and thicket sheltered an enemy, who sent forth his deadly messengers. The Indians yielded slowly, and, as it were, inch by inch, being frequently driven from their shelter at the point of the bayonet. Such obstinacy had not been paralleled since the battle of Oriskany. Brant, the moving and animating spirit of the Indians, urged on the warriors with his voice, and their incessant yells almost drowned the noise of the conflict, until the quickly succeeding and regular reverberations of the artillery overpowered all other sounds. It was remarked by an officer who was present that the roar of this cannonade was most commanding and "elegant." The Indians still maintained their ground in front, though the tremendous fire from Poor's brigade had so thinned their flank that a reinforcement of a battalion of rangers was ordered up to sustain it. In vain did the enemy contest the ground from point to point, endeavoring to maintain a position. This officer at length ascended the hill and attacked them in flank, a move which decided the fortunes of the day. Observing that they were in danger of being surrounded, the yell of retreat was sounded by the Indians, and red and white men, impelled by one impulse, precipitately fled across the Chemung River, abandoning their works, their packs, provisions, and a quantity of arms. The action had been protracted and sanguinary. Contrary to the Indian custom, some of their warriors who had fallen were left on the battle-field, and others were found hastily buried by the way. The American loss was but six killed and fifty wounded. A large part of Sullivan's force was not brought into action at all.

This battle, as subsequent events proved, decided the result of the campaign. It vindicated the opinion of Washington that the Indians must be encountered in their own country, and it effectually destroyed the Iroquois confederacy.

The results of the campaign may be easily demonstrated. The Indians, having fled in a panic, never stopped until they reached the head of Seneca Lake, whence they scattered to their respective villages. They did not rally, as they might have done, and oppose Sullivan's forces at defiles on the route. The Americans pursued them vigorously, with four brass three-pounders and the entire disposable force. The army encamped at Catherine's Town on the 2d of September, and began to destroy villages, corn-fields, and orchards in the surrounding country, continuing the work of devastation through the Genesee country and the Genesee Valley. On the 7th of the month the army crossed the outlet of Seneca Lake, and moved forward to the capital of the Seneca tribe, Kanadasaegea, now Geneva. This place contained about sixty houses, surrounded with gardens, orchards of apple- and peach-trees, and luxuriant corn-fields. Butler, the commandant of the defeated rangers, had endeavored to induce the Senecas to rally here, but in vain. They fled, abandoning everything, and the torch and axe of their foes were employed to level every tenement and living fruit-tree to the ground.

From this point the army proceeded to Canandaigua, where were found twenty-three large and "elegant" houses, mostly frame, together with very extensive fields of corn, all of which were destroyed. The next point of note in the march was Honeoye, a village containing ten houses, which were burned. Here a small post was established as a depot. As General Sullivan advanced towards the valley of the Genesee, the Indians determined again to oppose him, and, having organized their forces, presented themselves in battle-array between Honeoye and Conesus Lake. They attacked the advance-guard in mistake, supposing it to be the entire force, but, having seen it fall back on the main army, they did not await the approach of the latter. In this affray they captured a friendly Oneida, who was inhumanly butchered by a malignant chief named Little Beard. At this time, also, Lieutenant Boyd, who had been sent out with twenty-six men to reconnoitre Little Beard's town, was captured, and most inhumanly tortured, notwithstanding his appeal to Brant as a Masonic brother.

The army moved forward to the flats of the Genesee, where the Indians made a show of resistance. General Clinton immediately prepared to attack and surround them by extending his flanks, but, observing the object of his movement, they retreated. The army then crossed the Genesee to the principal town of the Indians, containing one hundred and twenty-eight houses, which were burned, and the surrounding fields destroyed. It was these fertile fields which had furnished the savages with the means of carrying on their predatory and murderous expeditions. General Sullivan had been instructed to make them feel the strength of the American arms with the bitterness of domestic desolation, for which purpose detachments were sent out at every suitable point to lay waste their fields, cut down their orchards, destroy their villages, and cripple them in their means. In carrying out these orders not less than forty Indian towns were burned, and the tourist who after the lapse of a hundred years visits the ruins caused by these acts of military vengeance is forcibly reminded of the spirit of destruction which descended upon the Indian villages and orchards. Having accomplished one of the objects of the expedition, the army recrossed the Genesee on the 16th of September, passed the outlet of Seneca Lake on the 20th, reached the original rendezvous at Tioga on the 30th, and within a fortnight returned to their respective points of departure. Why Sullivan did not extend his victorious march to Niagara, the head-quarters of the Tories and Indians, the breaking up of which would have secured a period of repose to the white settlements, is not clearly understood. The terrible chastisement inflicted by him, while it awed the Indians, did not crush them. It strengthened their hatred for the white man, and extended it through the tribes upon the Lakes and in the valley of the Ohio. Washington was named by them An-na-ta-kaw-see, taker of towns, or town-destroyer.

Towards the close of this year a detachment of seventy men from the Kentucky district of Virginia, under Major Rodgers, was surprised by the Shawnees while ascending the Ohio River. On approaching the mouth of the Licking River they discovered a few hostile Indians standing on a sand-bar, whilst a canoe was being propelled towards them, as if its occupants desired to hold friendly intercourse. Rodgers, who was on the alert, immediately made his boat fast to the shore, and went in pursuit of the Indians he had seen. They proved to be only a decoy to lead him into an ambuscade. The moment he landed and commenced an assault on the small party, an overwhelming number of the enemy issued from their concealment, poured in a heavy and deadly fire, and then rushed forward with their tomahawks, instantly killing Rodgers and forty-five of his men. The remainder fled towards the boat, but the Indians had anticipated them by its capture. Retreat being thus cut off, they faced the foe, and fought desperately as long as daylight lasted, when a small number succeeded in escaping, and finally reached Harrisburg. The details of the escape of Benham, who was shot through the hips on this occasion, possess a thrilling interest.

The expedition of Sullivan against the Iroquois proved so destructive to them that they were compelled to seek food and shelter from the British authorities at Niagara. The adherence to the American cause of the Oneidas and Tuscaroras, living on their lands, had occasioned ill feelings to be entertained by the other Iroquois against them. Every persuasion had been used in vain to induce them to join the royal standard. Their conduct at Oriskany, and their hospitality to the missionary Kirkland, had been the subject of sharp remonstrances by Guy Johnson, who peremptorily ordered Kirkland to leave the country. Although but few of these tribes joined General Clinton's division in the Genesee campaign, and those only as guides, yet when the Senecas captured the faithful guide, Honyerry, at Boyd's defeat, in their rage they literally hewed him in pieces. General Haldimand, of

Canada, had in a special written message threatened vengeance on the Oneida tribes for deserting, as he termed it, the British cause, and thus forgetting the wise counsels of their old and respected but deceased friend Sir William Johnson. This purpose, notwithstanding the severity of the winter, he executed, with the assistance of Brant and a force of Tories. Suddenly attacking the village of Oneida Castle, they drove the Indians from this ancient seat, burned their dwellings, their church, and their school-house, and destroyed their corn, as well as every other means of subsistence. The Oneidas fled to the Lower Mohawk, where they were protected and supported during the rest of the war.

In the month of May Sir John Johnson entered Johnstown with five hundred regulars, a detachment of his own regiment of Royal Greens, and about two hundred Indians and Tories. Marching from the direction of Crown Point through the woods to the Sacondaga, they entered the valley of the Mohawk at midnight entirely unheralded. This foray was one of the most shocking transactions of the whole war. The Indians roved from house to house, murdering the inhabitants, and plundering, destroying, and burning their property. Among the number of those slain by the savages were four octogenarians, whose locks were silvered by age, including the patriot Fonda, of the Mohawk Valley. Cattle and sheep were driven off, and horses stolen from their stalls. Sir John recovered the plate which had been buried in his cellars in 1776, and then retraced his steps to Canada, after having left a lasting mark of his vengeance on the home and familiar scenes of his childhood and the country of his youth, notwithstanding his father had there risen to power and greatness from an obscure original, and that his bones were there buried. The Mohawk Valley had been subjected to the twofold vengeance of the Indians and the Tories, who rivalled one another in their deeds of cruelty and vandalism, until it presented as denuded an appearance as a swept threshing-floor. The flail of warfare had beaten out everything except that sturdy patriotism which increased in strength in proportion to the magnitude of its trials. This attack was conducted in a stealthy and silent manner. No patriotic drum had sounded the call to arms. The enemy advanced with the noiseless tread of the tiger, and returned to their haunts with the tiger's reward,—blood and plunder.

Some allowance must be made for the complicity of the aborigines in this predatory warfare, on account of their ignorance and their natural lack of humane feelings. This will not, however, apply to men educated in the principles of civilization. Even Thayendanagea, the Typhon of the Revolution, found apologists for the greatest of his enormities, and we have certainly high authority for the palliation of crime in those who know not what they do. But nothing can excuse the conduct of those who perpetrate crimes with a clear moral perception of the enormity of their deeds.

Scarcely had Sir John Johnson and his myrmidons returned in safety to Canada when the nefarious business of plunder, murder, and arson was resumed in the Schoharie Valley, which had ever been deemed one of the richest agricultural regions in the vicinity of the Mohawk. From the year 1712, the period of its first settlement by Europeans, it had been celebrated for the beauty and fertility of its lands, and for the rich abundance of its cereals, the crops of which during the year 1780 had been more than ordinarily profuse.

The troops designed for this foray, and collected at La Chine, were landed at Oswego, and marched across the country to the Susquehanna. They consisted of three companies of Royal Greens, two hundred rangers, a company of yagers, armed with short rifles, and the effective force of the Mohawks. They were joined at Tioga by the Senecas under Cornplanter. The whole force has been estimated at from eight hundred to fifteen hundred men, with three pieces of artillery; each man was supplied with eighty rounds of ammunition. Sir John commanded the regulars, and Brant the Iroquois. Their appearance in the Schoharie Valley was heralded by the smoke of burning dwellings, barns, and hay-stacks, and by the wild tumult of savage warfare. Three small stockaded forts were erected in the valley, which were but feebly garrisoned, and ill supplied with ammunition. The principal attack was made on the central fort, but the resolution of its garrison, weak though it was, supplied the place of military skill. A flag of truce sent forward by the enemy with a summons to surrender was fired upon, which act appeared to be conclusive evidence to the marauders that every preparation had been made to give them a warm reception. The enemy ravaged the entire valley with fire and sword. Families were murdered, the houses, barns, and church burned, and cattle and horses[1] driven off, while the air resounded with the war-whoops of the savages. Of wheat alone eighty thousand bushels were estimated to have been destroyed. One hundred persons were killed, some of them in the most cruel manner, and many were carried into captivity. The enemy, after committing all the devastation possible, sped on to the Mohawk Valley, where their operations embraced a still wider range. On reaching their destination the forces of Sir John were augmented by trained parties of Loyalists; and the march through the valley became a scene of rapine and plunder, the forces being divided, one portion taking the north and the other the south side of the river, thus leaving no part of the doomed section unvisited, or free from the ruthless inroads of the Indians.

While the Northern Indians were thus plundering and destroying the frontier settlements, those at the South also broke out into open hostility.

Tory emissaries had been among the Cherokees, one of the most active and influential of whom was John Stuart, His Majesty's Indian Agent for South Carolina. When, early in 1776, the British attacked Charleston, the Overhill Cherokees began a series of massacres upon the Western frontier. The common peril caused a general rising of the people of Eastern Tennessee and Southwestern Virginia and the Carolinas. The Indians received a check on July 20 at Island Flats,

---

[1] While these devastations were in progress, Lawrence Schoolcraft, a young minute-man in the fort, having a fine horse in a neighboring field, went out to look after him. He observed an Indian, mounted on the animal, riding towards him. Crouching behind a clump of bushes, he fired at the savage, who fell from the horse, which the young man then rode back to the fort in triumph.

losing forty warriors. Next day a party was repulsed from Fort Watauga by James Robertson and his garrison. Colonel Christian, with the Virginia and North Carolina levies, soon recovered the upper settlements on the Tellico and the Tennessee, and the Cherokees sued for peace, which was granted. Towns like Tuskega, where a captive had lately been burned alive, were reduced to ashes. The warriors of the lower settlements poured down upon the South Carolina frontier on July 1, killing and scalping all who fell into their power, without distinction of age or sex. The terrified inhabitants fled to the few stockades for protection. Colonel Williamson, commanding the district of Ninety-Six, with about five hundred men, in a skirmish with the Indians discovered thirteen white men—Tories disguised as savages—wielding the tomahawk and scalping-knife. This was the beginning of the fierce hatred between Whig and Tory which soon produced such bitter results of domestic feud in South Carolina.

While marching to attack a force of Indians and Tories at Oconoree Creek, Williamson fell into an ambuscade. His men were thrown into disorder, but were soon rallied through the skill and coolness of Major Hammond, and were finally victorious. Again ambushed by his wily enemy near the present town of Franklin, Williamson repulsed the foe and destroyed the towns and crops. So severe was the punishment that five hundred Cherokee warriors fled to Florida. At the same time General Rutherford, of North Carolina, with a large force, crossed the Blue Ridge at Swannanoa Gap and laid waste the fertile valley of the Tennessee, joining Williamson September 14. The Cherokees were compelled to submit to the most abject humiliation, and to cede to South Carolina all their lands beyond the mountains of Unacaya, now the fertile counties of Greenville, Anderson, and Pickens, watered by the tributaries of the Savannah, the Saluda, and the Ennoree.

In 1781 the Cherokees again became restive, and made incursions into South Carolina. With a large number of disguised white men, they fell upon Ninety-Six, spreading desolation. General Andrew Pickens, at the head of four hundred mounted militia, rapidly penetrated their country and burned thirteen of their villages, killing a large number, and taking nearly seventy prisoners. Even the speed and decision of Montgomery were excelled. The Indians could not withstand the terrible onset of the cavalry, but fled in consternation, and immediately sued for peace. They promised never to listen to the British again, and for a long time afterwards they remained quiet.

The years 1780 and 1781 were characterized by these inroads, which could always be traced to the machinations of the Tories, whose chief object was to make the patriots of the Revolution suffer not only all the evils of civilized but also all the horrors of savage warfare. But the Revolution could not be suppressed by acts of savage vengeance, to which the barbarian allies of British despotism were impelled by the Indian prophet at his midnight orgies, by unwise counsels in high places, or by the desire of winning the price offered for deeds of blood and cruelty.

Before the close of the year 1780 it became evident to every one except the Indians, who neither understood nor studied cause and effect, that the chances of ultimate success preponderated in favor of the colonies; and after the surrender of Cornwallis this surmise became an absolute certainty. To every one but this infatuated race it was apparent that the struggle had been maintained at the cost of national exertions which even the British crown could not maintain, and the words of Lord Chatham were regarded in England as but little less than the words of inspiration.

While the negotiations preliminary to the formation of a treaty of peace were in progress, there existed a state of Indian excitement on the frontiers which made it the duty of every settler to deem his log cabin a castle and constitute his wife and children the custodians of an armory. The Lowlands of Scotland were never more completely devastated by the raids of their fierce neighbors the Celts, than were the unfortunate frontiers of Virginia by the Indians. These details are, however, the appropriate theme of local history: our attention is required by another topic.

The Mohicans, and their relatives the Delawares, were at an early period benefited by the benevolent labors of the Moravian Brethren. Unfortunately, as we have previously mentioned, this excellent society, even for twenty years before the conquest of Canada, had held the reputation of being politically identified with the French; and, still more unfortunately for the peace of the Delawares, this preference was alleged to have been transferred to the British crown after the conquest. There does not appear to be a particle of reliable evidence of either the former or the latter preference; but the populace had formed this opinion while the Delawares lived east of the Alleghanies, and the impression became still stronger after they migrated to the Ohio Valley. Although these Delaware converts resided permanently in towns located on the Muskingum, they were peremptorily ordered, by the Indians in the British interest, encouraged thereto by the local authorities, to abandon their habitations and remove to Sandusky and Detroit, under the evident apprehension that these converts would imbibe American sentiments. It was very manifest that they neither engaged in war nor were ever encouraged thereto by their teachers, but expressly the contrary. The Munsees, a Delaware tribe, however, took refuge on the river Thames, in Canada, and the so-called "Christian Indians," pure Delawares, of the Moravian persuasion, did the same. This appears to have been the result of political necessity, and, if originally at the solicitation or through the counsel of men in authority, that motive soon ceased to have much effect. In 1735 the "Christian Indians" migrated through the Straits of Michilimackinac to rejoin their parental tribe in the West. Some of the Munsees had previously united with the Stockbridges at Green Bay, in Wisconsin, and others followed them. The majority of the Delawares in the West were enemies to the Americans, which made it the more easy to convey the impression that the Muskingum Delawares were also inimical.

But, however the question of political preference of the Moravian Delawares may be decided, it is certain that in 1782 the common opinion among the people of Western Virginia and Pennsylvania was that they were strongly in the British interest. Nothing short of this could have justified—if anything could be alleged, even at that excited period, in palliation of that action—the expedition of Williamson against the Muskingum towns. It was to no purpose that the hardy forester was told that these Christian Delawares were taught and professed the doctrine of nonresistance and peace towards all men. A majority of the frontiersmen not only had no faith in such a doctrine, but could not realize the fact that an Indian, whose natural element was war, whose very nature was subterfuge, subtlety, and duplicity, could subscribe to the doctrines of peace and good-will without danger of relapsing into his original condition at the sight of blood or the sound of a rifle.

It happened that some hostile Indians from Sandusky made an incursion into the settlements on the Monongahela, committing a series of shocking murders. Infuriated at these outrages, a body of one hundred or two hundred men, all mounted and equipped, set out from the Monongahela, under command of Colonel D. Williamson, in quest of the murderers. They directed their march to the settlements of Salem and Gnadenhütten, on the Muskingum. The vicinity of the latter place was reached after two days' march, and on the morning of the following day the party divided into three sections, entering the town simultaneously at different points. They found the Indians laboring peaceably and unsuspiciously in the fields, gathering up their bundles preparatory to their return to Sandusky. A message from the commander at Pittsburg had apprised them of the march of Williamson's force and warned them to be on their guard, but, conscious of their innocence, no alarm had been excited by this intelligence. Williamson approached the settlement with friendly professions, proposed to the Indians a plan of deliverance from their oppressors the Wyandots of Sandusky, and induced them to deliver up their arms, axes, and working implements, as well as to collect at a place of rendezvous, preparatory to a proposed march to Pittsburg. At this rendezvous they found themselves completely in the power of their enemies, who began to treat them roughly; but neither resistance nor flight was now possible. They were next accused of horse-stealing and other acts of which they were entirely guiltless. It was then determined in a council composed of Williamson's followers to decide their fate. He paraded his men in line, and then put the question, whether they should be sent to Pittsburg or shot, requesting those who were in favor of their removal to step in front. The majority condemned them to death; sixteen or eighteen were in favor of mercy. The Delawares, whose fate had thus been summarily decided, knelt down, prayed, and sung a hymn, whilst a consultation was being held as to the mode of putting them to death. Not an imploring word was uttered, not a tear shed. They submitted silently to their fate, and were successively struck down with a mallet. Ninety-six unarmed Indians were thus slain. Sixty-two of the number were adults, one of them a woman, and the remaining thirty-four children. The demoniacal troop then returned to their homes, giving plausible but false reasons for the atrocities committed, which were published in the newspapers.

CHAPTER VI.

BORDER WARS OF KENTUCKY—BOONESBOROUGH ATTACKED—BOWMAN'S EXPEDITION—ESTILL'S DEFEAT—BATTLE OF THE BLUE LICKS—THE CREEKS ATTACK GENERAL WAYNE.

ON the 1st day of April, 1775, the stockade fort of Boonesborough, on the west bank of the Kentucky River, near the mouth of Otter Creek, was begun. In 1774, James Harrod, a resolute backwoodsman, and a skilful hunter, had led a party of forty-one to Harrodsburg, and during the summer built there the first log cabin in Kentucky. Seventeen delegates from the four settlements—Boonesborough, Harrodsburg, Boiling Springs, and St. Asaph's—met together at the first-named place, and formed the colony of Transylvania, now the Commonwealth of Kentucky, on the 23d of May, 1775, a treaty having been made the previous winter with the Cherokees for the land between the Ohio, the Cumberland Mountains, and the Cumberland and Kentucky Rivers. Before this time it was the common Indian hunting-ground, lying between the Cherokees, Creeks, and Catawbas of the South and the Shawnees, Delawares, and Wyandots of the North, and it was also the scene of occasional bloody encounters between these warlike and hostile tribes. No permanent settlement existed within its borders when first occupied by the white men, but reports of the inexhaustible fertility of its soil had reached Virginia and North Carolina, and very soon parties of emigrants were on their way thither.

No name is better known in the pioneer annals of America than that of Daniel Boone. As a hunter and surveyor he had more than once explored "the dark and bloody ground," as Kentucky afterwards came to be called, and had passed entire seasons alone in its solitary recesses. At this period he was in the prime of life, having attained the age of forty, and his fame as a hunter and explorer, as well as his reputation for sagacity, judgment, and intrepidity, was unsurpassed. Boone was five feet ten inches in height, robust and athletic, fitted by habit and temperament for endurance, his bright eye and calm determination of manner inspiring confidence, while such was the kindliness of his nature that he is said never to have wronged a human being, not even an Indian.

The fort at Boonesborough was the special object of Indian hatred. It was the first fortification built in that region, and it at once excited their jealous fears. The settlement was incessantly harassed by flying parties of Indians, who waylaid and shot at the men working in the fields or while hunting. Few ventured beyond the protection of the fort. In December, 1775, a party of Indians assailed it, but were repulsed. On the 7th of July following, one of Boone's little daughters and two other girls who were amusing themselves near the fort, were seized and carried away by the Indians, but were speedily rescued by Boone and his companions.

An attack made on April 15, 1777, was easily repulsed. Another and fiercer assault by two hundred Indians was made July 4, with a similar result. Logan's Fort, built early in 1776 near the present town of Stanford, and Harrodsburg, were at the same time attacked.

February 7, 1778, Boone, with twenty-seven men, was captured while making salt, and taken to Detroit, where the British commander, Colonel Hamilton, vainly offered his captors a ransom of one hundred pounds sterling. He was then taken to Chillicothe, and adopted into the tribe, and soon succeeded in thoroughly ingratiating himself with the Indians. Learning that an expedition was preparing against Boonesborough, he made his escape, travelled one hundred and sixty miles in less than five days, and appeared before the garrison at Boonesborough like one risen from the dead. The fort was at once repaired and strengthened, and in ten days was ready for a siege. Distant settlements were abandoned, and the forts were put in fighting order; but the escape of Boone disconcerted the Indians, and delayed their enterprise for several weeks.

On the 8th of August five hundred Indians and Canadians, under Captain Duquesne and the Indian chief Blackfish,—the most formidable expedition of the war,—appeared before the fort, then garrisoned by sixty-five men. Harrod's and Logan's forts, menaced at the same time by strong detachments, could afford them no assistance. Summoned to surrender, a truce of two days was granted the garrison by Duquesne in which to consider the matter. The time thus gained was well employed in collecting the horses and cattle within the fort. At its expiration, Boone returned this answer: "We are determined to defend our fort while a man is living. We laugh at your formidable preparations, but thank you for giving us notice, and time to provide for our defence." Duquesne next proposed to the garrison to send out nine chosen men to make a treaty. This was agreed to, and a conference was held sixty yards in front of the fort. At its close, Boone and each of his eight companions, under the pretext of a friendly handshaking, were grasped by two or three stalwart Indians. But they had mistaken their men, and were easily shaken off by the sturdy backwoodsmen, who succeeded in regaining the fort under the protecting rifles of the garrison, who had from the first suspected treachery on the part of the Indians. For nine days and nights the savages persevered in their attack, employing all means known to them to effect its capture, setting it on fire, and even attempting to undermine it. One hundred and twenty-five pounds of bullets were picked up around the fort after their departure, besides what stuck in the logs of the fort,— "certainly a great proof of their industry," as Boone himself says. This memorable siege was the last sustained by Boonesborough, and it saved the Kentucky frontier from depopulation. The enemy decamped on the tenth day, having lost thirty men killed, and a much larger number wounded. The garrison had two killed and four wounded. The capture of the British forts at Kaskaskia and Vincennes soon followed. This blow, striking at the root of the evil, cut off the supplies of arms and ammunition constantly being furnished the Indians, and checked their annual predatory incursions.

In 1779, Colonel Bowman led an expedition consisting of the flower of Kentucky against Chillicothe. Colonel Benjamin Logan was second in command, and Harrod, Bulger, Bedinger, and other brave officers held subordinate positions. The surprise was complete, and the plan of attack well concerted. Logan's division, taking the position assigned to it, awaited the signal for attack, which was to proceed from Bowman. Hour after hour passed, and the opportunity for a decisive victory, that would have spread consternation throughout the Indian tribes and repressed their incursions for a long time, was lost through the imbecility or fears of the commander-in-chief. Logan's division, left unsupported by Bowman, at length retreated in disorder, and the rout quickly became general. Some of the subordinate officers, with daring bravery, charged the enemy on horseback, and covered the retreat, but the failure was as complete as it was unexpected and disgraceful.

A formidable expedition, consisting of English and Indians, under Colonel Bird, was organized in 1780. Cannon were employed for the first time in Kentucky, and Ruddle's and Martin's Stations were destroyed, and their garrisons taken. This was retaliated by Colonel Clarke, who, in the autumn of that year, invaded the Indian country in Ohio, defeated the Shawnees in a pitched battle at Pickaway, laid waste their villages, and destroyed their corn-fields with ruthless severity.

Indian hostility was unusually active in Kentucky in 1782. A party of Wyandots committed shocking depredations near Estill's Station in May of that year. Captain Estill, with an equal force, pursued and overtook them at Hinckstone's Fork of Licking, near Mount Stirling, and here occurred one of the best-fought battles of the war. The creek ran between the two parties, who, behind trees and logs, maintained for hours a close and deadly conflict. One-third of the combatants had fallen, when Lieutenant Miller, with a few men, undertook, by making a détour, to gain the enemy's flank and close the battle. The Indian leader, perceiving the movement, with the rapid decision that marks the great commander, and wholly contrary to the usual Indian tactics, crossed the creek in his front, and throwing his whole force upon Estill, now weakened by the absence of Miller, overpowered him and forced him from the ground. He and nearly all his men were killed, and it was poor consolation that an equal loss had been inflicted on the enemy. This bloody little fight, memorable for the military skill of the Indian commander, created a sensation at the time far beyond its real importance, and was followed by stunning blows from the same quarter in rapid succession.

The disastrous battle of the Blue Licks, which occurred August 19, 1782, spread mourning throughout the Kentucky border. A large force of Indians and a few Canadians, having been repulsed from Bryant's Station, were pursued across the Licking River by one hundred and sixty Kentuckians, under Colonels Todd, Trigg, and Boone, the latter of whom advised waiting for Colonel Logan, then on his way to join them. Had the advice been taken, the result would have been very different. The enemy was before them, and a rapid retreat or a battle against fearful odds was inevitable. Further deliberation was ended by Major McGary, who spurred his horse into the stream, waved his hat over his head, and shouted, "Let all who are not cowards follow me!" Dashing into the deep ford, the gallant band crossed the stream and pressed forward to close with the concealed enemy. Suddenly a withering and murderous fire was poured upon them by the unseen foe, by which the right wing was broken, the enemy rushing up and gaining their rear, and in spite of the heroism of the survivors they were overpowered and compelled to seek safety in flight. The river was difficult to cross; many were killed just entering it, some in the water, others after crossing and while ascending the cliffs. Some escaped on horseback, a few on foot. Seventy-seven were killed, among them Colonels Todd and Trigg and Major Harlan, and a few wounded. Some of the fugitives reached Bryant's Station the night after the battle, and were there met by Colonel Logan at the head of four hundred and fifty men. This terrible blow, the last that was struck by the Indians for the recovery of their Kentucky hunting-grounds, only brought sure and speedy retribution upon their heads. General Clarke's expedition, in September, 1782, was exterminating in its character; the Chillicothe towns on the Scioto were destroyed, their plantations were laid waste, and peace was secured to Kentucky, no formidable war-party ever afterwards invading it.

The last blow which the Indians inflicted upon the regular troops of the colonies was dealt by the Creeks of Georgia. As the contest was drawing to its close, the troops of both parties moved towards the South. During the occupation of Savannah, General Wayne was encamped with an army about five miles from that city, engaged in watching the motions of the enemy. Guristersigo, a distinguished Creek leader of Western Georgia, projected a secret expedition against the resolute hero of Stony Point, who anticipated no danger from an Indian foe distant from him nearly the entire breadth of Georgia. The Indian chief, undiscovered, reached a point near the object of attack before daybreak on the 24th of June, with three hundred warriors.

Wayne, who was a cautious and watchful officer, had been on the alert against the enemy from Savannah, whence he expected an attack; and his men, who had been harassed by severe duty, slept on their arms on the night of the 23d, so as to be ready for action. They were suddenly aroused at midnight by the war-whoop, and the warriors of Guristersigo attacked them with such fury and in such numbers that the troops seemed to be unable to withstand their onset. They intended to fall upon the American pickets, but ignorantly attacked the main body. The infantry at once seized their arms, and the artillery hastened to their guns. General Wayne and Colonel Posey, who had lain down in the general's tent, instantly arose, and proceeded to the scene, the latter leading his regiment of infantry to the charge, thereby restoring confidence and order in the line. At that moment Wayne's horse was shot dead under him, and he saw his cannon seized by the savages. They were soon recaptured, and a fierce hand-to-hand struggle ensued, in which the tomahawk and rifle proved no match for the bayonet. General Wayne at the same time charged at the head of the cavalry, who cut down the naked warriors with their broadswords, and by turning their flank put them to flight. The Creeks fought with desperation, and none with greater courage than Guristersigo, who, by his voice and example, gave animation to his men, seventeen of whom fell around him. He continued to fight with heroic desperation, until he finally fell, pierced with two bayonet-wounds and one from the thrust of a spontoon. Upon his fall the Indians fled, and were pursued far into the forest, many being killed with the bayonet. Wayne's loss was slight. In September Colonels Pickens and Clarke completed their subjugation. Weary of the conflict, the Indians ceded all their lands south of the Savannah and east of the Chattahoochee to the State of Georgia as the price of peace.

PERIOD VI.

POST-REVOLUTIONARY.

CHAPTER I.

INDIAN POLICY OF THE UNITED STATES—TREATIES WITH THE TRIBES.

A DEFINITIVE treaty of peace was signed at Versailles January 14, 1783. As the Indians had fought for no national object, they received no consideration in this instrument. It contained no provision for their welfare,—a fact of which they had been forewarned by the Americans,—as it would have contravened the policy of Europe to recognize the national character of a people whom they had so long regarded as mere savages. The Americans, who succeeded to their guardianship, treated them as quasi nationalities, devoid of sovereignty, but having an absolute possessory right to the soil and to its usufruct, with power to cede this right, to make peace, and to regulate the boundaries to their lands, by which the aboriginal hunting-grounds were so defined that they could readily be distinguished from the districts ceded. Thus was at once laid the foundation of that long list of Indian treaties which record our later Indian history and accurately mark the progress of our settlements between the Atlantic and the Pacific. Under this policy commenced that system of annuities by which, as their exhausted hunting-grounds were ceded, they were supplied with the means of subsistence,—a system designed to promote their gradual advance in agriculture and arts, as well as their improvement in manners, morals, education, and civilization.

The proper management of Indian affairs had been an object of deep and constant concern to Congress, and North and South the duty was for many years intrusted to a board of commissioners composed of men of the highest experience, judgment, and wisdom. Nor were the means of the provisional government lightly taxed for the accomplishment of this object. By reference to the records of the Treasury Department during this time we have ascertained that between the period of the Declaration of Independence and the 4th of March, 1789, embracing the era of the Revolution, the sum of $580,103.41 was disbursed on account of the expenses of treaties with, and of presents to, the Indian tribes, and this was done while, during part of the time, the army had neither shoes nor clothing. There was then no means of obtaining an accurate account of their numbers, but an estimate prepared by Mr.

Madison rates their total force during the contest at twelve thousand four hundred and thirty fighting-men, a very large part of whom were under British influence. This estimate may, as the author says, have been above the truth, but it was far more reliable than the exaggerated enumeration published only ten or eleven years previous by Colonel Bouquet, who reported the number of warriors at fifty-six thousand five hundred.

The question as to the policy to be pursued with tribes who contemned all the maxims and principles of civilized life was one presenting many difficulties. History had demonstrated the instability, cruelty, and treachery of their character. Ever subject to be influenced by those whose interest it was to mislead them, inclined to mistake their rights and true position, and to be turned aside from the pursuit of noble and permanent objects to those that were temporary and illusive, civilization itself appeared to them as one of the most intolerable of evils, and they were as much opposed to the labors of the plough and the loom as they were to the science of letters and the doctrines of Christianity.

Although the task of reclamation was difficult, it was neither hopeless nor discouraging, and, whether pleasant or otherwise, it became one of the earliest subjects for the exercise of governmental powers. To acknowledge sovereignty of the Indians in the vast territories over which they roamed would have been simply ridiculous, but the recognition of their right to the soil replaced in their hands the means of advancing to prosperity and happiness. As this would be a gradual process, supplying from decade to decade the loss suffered from the depreciation in value of their hunting-grounds, by the resources arising from their voluntary cession, the system seemed well suited to their wants, and well adapted to secure permanent peace on the frontiers. The only real difficulty encountered was in the adjustment of its details, and this difficulty was complicated by the removals of the tribes, by infelicity of situation owing to advancing settlements, and by the temptations to indulgence in idleness, dissipation, and savage customs. Frequently the very accumulation of their annuities became the means of their depression, and of accumulated perplexities. It will be seen by scanning the statistics of the tribes in the West that the members of many of those tribes which possessed the largest funds in government securities, and particularly of those small tribes which received per capita the largest annuities in coin, were the most idle, intemperate, and demoralized.

The treaty of Versailles having ignored the national existence of the Indians, they were compelled to negotiate directly with the Republic. The Iroquois, or Six Nations, who had been the most determined enemies of the Americans, made the first treaty in which the question of territory was mooted, which was concluded and signed at Fort Stanwix October 22, 1784, in presence of the commissioners, Oliver Wolcott, Richard Butler, and Arthur Lee. By the terms of this instrument they ceded a strip of land beginning at the mouth of Oyonwaye Creek, on Lake Ontario, four miles south of the Niagara portage path, and running southerly to the mouth of the Tehosaroro or Buffalo Creek, thence to the Pennsylvania line, and along its north and south boundary to the Ohio River. They relinquished any claim by right of conquest to the Indian country west of that boundary. Their right of property in the territory situate in the State of New York eastward of the Oyonwaye line, embracing the fertile region of Western New York, remained unaffected, and the territory of the Oneidas was guaranteed to them. By this treaty the tribes who had fought against the colonies covenanted to deliver up all prisoners, white and black, taken during the war, and as a guarantee that this should be done six chiefs were held as hostages. This treaty was finally confirmed by all the Iroquois sachems in a council held by General St. Clair at Fort Harmar, on the Ohio, January 9, 1789.

New York had been the principal arena of the Iroquois development. According to the earliest traditions, they originally entered it by way of the Oswego River, and assumed separate names and tribal distinctions after their geographical dispersion over it. Their confederation, under the title of Aquinoshioni, is by far the most interesting example of political development among the North American tribes.

The Revolutionary War, having in effect dissolved the confederation, left the sovereignty of the individual States intact, and therefore to New York alone could cessions of territory be rightfully made. These cessions began shortly after the negotiation of the initial national treaty at Fort Stanwix in 1784. On the 28th of June, 1785, at a convocation of the chiefs and sachems held at Herkimer, the Oneidas and Tuscaroras, in consideration of the payment in hand of a sum of money and goods, ceded a tract of land on the New York side of the Susquehanna River, including Unadilla.

At a council held with the Onondaga sachems by George Clinton, Esq., and his associate commissioners, September 12, 1788, the Onondaga tribe ceded all their lands within the State, making such reservations as covered their castle and residences. By a separate article of this treaty they ceded to the State the salt spring tract. Large payments were made in coin and goods, and a perpetual annuity of five hundred dollars in silver was granted.

By the terms of a treaty concluded with the Oneida sachems at Fort Stanwix, before the same commissioner, September 22, 1788, the Oneidas ceded all their lands within the State, with the exception of ample reservations for their own use, and the right to lease part of the same. Five thousand dollars in money, goods, and provisions were then paid to them, and a perpetual annuity of six hundred dollars was granted.

This treaty with the Oneidas contained an important provision sanctioning the arrangements previously made by them in behalf of the expatriated Indians of New England, and others of the Algonkin group, who had been allowed to settle on their lands. The title to a tract of land two miles in breadth and three in length in the Oriskany Valley was confirmed to the tribes that assumed the name of Brothertons and were under the care of Rev. Samson Occum. Another tract, six miles square, located in the Oneida Creek Valley, was confirmed to the Mohicans of the Housatonic, bearing the name of Stockbridges, who were under the charge of the Rev. Mr. Sergeant.

On the 25th of February, 1789, the Cayuga sachems assembled at Albany, and ceded all their lands within the State, with the exception of one hundred square miles, exclusive of the area of Cayuga Lake, a reserve of a fishing site at Scayes, and one mile square at Cayuga Ferry. One mile square was granted to the Cayuga chief Oojaugenta, or Fish-Carrier. Two limited annuities, amounting to five hundred dollars and six hundred and twenty-five dollars respectively, and a permanent annuity of five hundred dollars, were granted by the State.

These agreements to pay the tribes in coin, goods, and provisions were scrupulously complied with, and have been continued to the present day, every attention and respect having been manifested by New York for the habits and wants of the Indians, who have likewise received special gratuities. These transactions constituted the first practical lesson in civil polity and the details of public business which the Iroquois received. The respect paid to their sachems, the care and accuracy with which the titles of the respective tribes to their lands were inquired into, and the good faith with which the State at all times fulfilled its engagement, rendering and requiring even-handed justice, formed an example which was not lost on a people celebrated from early days for their political position and influence. Civilized life was regarded by them with greater respect than heretofore, and a newly-felt influence caused them to act with a stricter sense of responsibility than they had done in past times.

Hitherto their chiefs and sachems had, as independent representatives of free and proud tribes, visited the districts of Eastern and Southern New York, either for political or commercial purposes, without paying much regard to a state of society which did not suit their preconceived ideas. But from this period the aspect of things changed. They resided exclusively on small reservations, which were soon surrounded by farmers, merchants, manufacturers, mechanics, and professional men, who presented to them daily and hourly an example of the beneficial effects of thrift, and demonstrated that only the idle and vicious lagged behind in the general race to the goal of prosperity. Private rights were strictly protected, and those over whom the ægis of the law was extended were taxed for its support. The debtor had his choice either to meet his obligations or be placed in durance until his creditor was satisfied. There was but one rule and one law for all. Little attention was given to the Indians. Wise in their own conceit, regarding proficiency and excellence in the arts of war and hunting as the limit of all attainments, they hated education, deemed voluntary labor equivalent to slavery, and despised morality, as well as the teachings of the gospel. If such a people rapidly disappeared, the magistrates felt little or no sympathy for their fate; the merchants merely sold them what they could pay for, and the majority of the citizens, who remembered their cruel and treacherous conduct during the Revolution, were glad to see them pass away and give place to a superior race.

The public functionaries of the State government, however, regarded their condition from a higher point of view. They were deemed an unfortunate yet not criminal people, who had been misled, but who could not be condemned for lacking political or moral wisdom. Their title to the territories was undisputed, and was

freely acknowledged and respected by all. Another aspect of the position of the Iroquois after the Revolution might likewise be presented. That contest had produced a disastrous effect on them, having by means of its continual alarms and excitements diverted their attention for an extended period from their usual pursuits. They had so long waylaid the farmer at his plough, and the planter in his field, that their corn-fields were in retaliation devastated, their orchards felled to the ground, their villages burned, and themselves often reduced to extreme poverty and destitution. The State authorities, however, interfered in their behalf, and under the treaties just mentioned rescued them from want by the payment to them of annuities in money and goods.

The General Government also took this view, and a commissioner of high standing[1] was appointed to meet the tribes during the autumn of 1794 at Canandaigua, in Western New York. This convocation was numerously attended by all the tribes who had been actors in the war (except the Mohawks), including the Stockbridges. The noted Oneida chief Skenandoah attended, with a delegation of his people. The war chief Little Beard, or Sequidongquee, marked for his cruelties during Sullivan's campaign, represented the Genesee Senecas.[2] The celebrated orator Sagoyewatha, or Red Jacket, first distinguished himself at this council. Honayawus, or Farmer's Brother, represented the central Niagara Indians, and Kiantwauka, or the Cornplanter, those of the upper Alleghany. The Tuscaroras sent the Indian annalist, Cusic; the Housatonics, Hendrik Aupumut.

The treaty was concluded November 11, and recognized the principles of all prior treaties. It provided for the payment of a gratuity of ten thousand dollars in money and goods, which were to be delivered on the ground. A permanent annuity of four thousand five hundred dollars, payable in coin, clothes, cattle, implements of husbandry, and the services of artificers, was likewise stipulated for. All the attendant circumstances of this convocation were imposing, and its results auspicious, being marked by the development of a kindly feeling for the Union by the Indians.

---

[1] Timothy Pickering, Esq.

[2] The word Seneka, or Seneca, has been a puzzle to inquirers. How a Roman proper name should have become the distinctive cognomen for a tribe of American Indians it is not easy to say. The French, who first encountered them in Western New York, termed them, agreeably to their system of bestowing nicknames, Tsonontowans; that is, Rattlesnakes. Being one of the members of the Five Nations, they, like all the others, bore the generic name of Iroquois. The Dutch, who recognized them in the trade established on the site of Albany as early as 1614, appear to have introduced the term as the catchword of trade, from which the word is derived. This numerous and warlike tribe appears to have had a partiality for the use of vermilion as a war-paint. This article is called by the Dutch cinnabar (vide "Niew Zak Woorden Book," Dordrecht, 1831). From some notices of the early times we learn that the pronunciation of the letter b in this word was changed to that of k or g, from which it may be inferred that they were named *Sin-ne-kars*. In one of the oldest maps, published at Amsterdam, the word is written *Sen-ne-caas*. The double a in the Dutch language assumes the sound of a in *make;* which is precisely the sound still retained. All the early New England writers consulted adopted this sound, with little variation.

In Lawson's "Travels in the Carolinas in 1700" he calls them *Sinnegars*, and sometimes *Janitos*, and identifies them as a tribe of the Iroquois. The Senecas call themselves Nundowa, or "People of the Hill," from an eminence at the head of Canandaigua Lake.

The organization of a territorial government northwest of the Ohio exercised a favorable influence on Indian affairs. The majority of the tribes on that border were tired of war, having lost as many warriors by disease as by casualties in battle. The marching of armies had frightened away the large game, and disorganized the Indian trade. They had been fighting, also, as they now began to see, for a phantom; for, granting that they imagined themselves to have been engaged in preventing the colonies from progressing beyond the Ohio (as they had been taught by foreign traders, whose interests in the West would have suffered by the extension of the settlements), they could not fail to understand that it had never constituted an object with the British government, as it received no consideration in the treaty concluded at Versailles. The Wyandots, Delawares, Chippewas, and Ottawas were the first of the Western tribes to express a desire for peace. They united in a treaty concluded with the commissioners, George Rogers Clarke, Richard Butler, and Arthur Lee, at Fort McIntosh, on the Ohio, January 21, 1785. This treaty was important principally as inaugurating a system of dealing with the tribes by written contracts. It evinced the disposition of the government to treat them with friendly consideration, at the same time demonstrating that it possessed the means of enforcing its mandates. Boundaries were established between the Wyandots and the Delawares, who agreed upon the Cuyahoga and the Tuscarawas as the division-line, the treaty thus giving them an idea of the necessity of establishing and respecting geographical limitations.

None of the Southern tribes had been so much involved in hostile proceedings as the Cherokees, who resided nearest the scene of conflict, and had participated in some of the forays and outrages committed on the Ohio. They also at an early period expressed a desire for peace.

On the 25th of November, 1785, a treaty was concluded with them at Hopewell, on the Keowee fork of the Savannah. The commissioners were Benjamin Hawkins, Andrew Pickens, and Joseph Martin. By this treaty a firm friendship was declared to be established, the surrender of prisoners and negroes was stipulated for, and a definite boundary-line was fixed within which the fur-trade should be conducted exclusively under an American system of license or authority. A similar policy controlled the Choctaws and Chickasaws. The former tribe entered into negotiations with the same commissioners on the 3d of January, 1786, and the latter on the 10th of the same month. The Southwestern frontiers were thus placed in a condition of security by the proceedings of a commission composed of energetic men well acquainted with the character of the Indians, by whom they were held in great respect.

There was still another tribe which had been a scourge of the frontiers, no one organization having evinced such unmitigated hatred and unrelenting cruelty as the Shawnees. Bearing a name indicating a Southern origin, they had from the first resisted with desperate fury all attempts of the frontiersmen of North Carolina and Virginia to extend their settlements beyond the Ohio River. With the agility and subtlety of the panther, they crept stealthily through the forests and sprang suddenly on their victims. They fought at the battle of Kanawha with an intrepidity unsurpassed in Indian warfare. Virginia had in every decade of her existence as a colony been obliged to repel their incursions. After the lapse of twelve years from the conclusion of their treaty with Lord Dunmore, on the Scioto, in 1774, their chiefs assembled at the mouth of the Great Miami, signified their submission, and on January 31, 1786, signed a treaty of peace. By its terms they agreed to surrender all the prisoners in their possession, and were assigned a territorial position south of the line fixed for the Wyandots and Delawares by the treaty of Fort McIntosh of January 21, 1785.

Various disturbing elements exercised an influence on the powerful Creek nation during the entire Revolutionary contest; and, after pursuing a fluctuating policy, which called for perpetual vigilance on the part of the authorities of Georgia and South Carolina, their hostility was clearly evinced by the formidable night-attack made under Guristersigo on the camp of General Wayne, near Savannah, in 1782. But when the issue of the Revolutionary contest became a fixed fact, the Creeks expressed a wish to enter into friendly relations with the Union. For this purpose, in the year 1790, a delegation, comprising twenty-four of their most distinguished chiefs, visited the seat of government, then located at the city of New York. This delegation represented all the principal towns and septs from the Coosawhatchie and Chattahoochee to the sources of the Altamaha; it also embraced a delegation of the Seminoles, and was headed by Alexander McGillivray, who had during many years exercised a controlling influence over this nation. The distinctions of Upper, Middle, and Lower Creeks were insisted on, they being regarded as so many septs. General Washington received the delegates with comity, and deputed General Knox, Secretary of War, to treat with them. After a full discussion of all the questions involved, the terms were agreed on, and the treaty was signed August 7, 1790. The most important of its provisions was the establishment of boundaries. It contained the usual professions of amity, and stipulated for the surrender of prisoners taken during the war, whites and negroes, many of the latter being refugees. These refugees in the Indian territories furnished the nucleus of slavery among the Creeks, Seminoles, Choctaws, Chickasaws, and Cherokees. The Africans were not adopted as members of the tribes, but held as persons in servitude, and by performing the field-labor enabled these tribes to pursue agriculture without being themselves compelled to engage in manual labor. To induce the Creeks to make greater advances towards civilization, a clause was inserted providing that they should be furnished from time to time with cattle and agricultural implements. This wise provision has had the effect of rendering the nation wealthy in animals and stock, thus enabling them to make further progress in the social scale.

After all the negotiations were concluded, the government appointed a special agent to accompany the delegates to their homes and report on their condition. This agent, Major Caleb Swan, performed his task skilfully, being a cautious and shrewd observer; and, after his return, he communicated to General Knox a valuable report, accompanied by a map of the country, a detailed account of their principal places of residence, and a carefully prepared and comprehensive view of their manners and customs. He gave the names and designated the locations of fifty-two towns, which were estimated to contain from twenty-five thousand to thirty thousand souls. Of these, between five thousand and six thousand were reported to be gun-men, or warriors. It may be remarked, *en passant*, that the confederacy of the Creeks is well deserving of study as an illustration of Indian political and social order.

By some of the older writers the Creeks are called Muscogulgees, a term which has apparently been shortened to Muskokis. The English appellation of Creeks was derived from a geographical feature of the country originally occupied by them, which is remarkable for its numerous streams. The appellations of Alabama and Okechoyatte were borne by them at an early period. Their language is one of the most musical of the Indian tongues, but agrees with the other languages in its principles of synthesis, its coalescence of the pronoun with the noun, and its agglutinative quality.

Politically speaking, the Creeks possess a standing and influence second to none of the other tribes, being one of the most strongly characterized families of the aboriginal race, and one from whom we may expect great development.

CHAPTER II.

ESTABLISHMENT OF THE NORTHWESTERN TERRITORY—WAR WITH THE WESTERN TRIBES—HARMAR'S DEFEAT—SCOTT'S EXPEDITION—ST. CLAIR'S DEFEAT—CONFERENCE WITH BRANT—WAYNE'S CAMPAIGN—VICTORY OF THE MAUMEE RAPIDS—PACIFICATION OF GREENVILLE.

ONE of the earliest objects of attention on the part of the government, under the old Articles of Confederation, had been the incorporation of the Indian territory northwest of the Ohio. No sooner had the war terminated than all eyes began to be directed to that quarter as the future land of promise to the Union, which expectations have been most amply fulfilled, for it has been emphatically the Mother of States, the most prominent among them being the stalwart commonwealths of Ohio, Indiana, and Illinois. General Arthur St. Clair was appointed by Washington the first governor of the territory. The most important topic which called for his attention was the state of the Indian tribes, which question he found to be surrounded with peculiar difficulties. None of the tribes had suffered so little by the war as the Miamis, Weas, and Piankeshaws of the Wabash. For several years the Indians exceeded in numbers the settlers, who were located at various prominent points; and, consequently, the frontier settlements were entirely at the mercy of the savages. It was therefore necessary to strengthen the bonds of amity with the Indians by treaty stipulations. When the treaty system was introduced in negotiations with the Indian tribes, who could neither read nor write, an expectation of security and advantage from such instruments was indulged far beyond what the moral character of the aborigines and their actual appreciation of the advantages secured to them ever justified. Still, this system promised the surest means of attaining success. From the earliest traditionary times it had been the custom of the Indians to hold formal meetings of their chiefs for the purpose of adjusting their affairs, to which the greatest ceremony and solemnity were given by smoking the sacred weed and by the exchange of wampum-belts. The like ceremony and solemnity were used by the commissioners and commanders to whom these negotiations were intrusted on concluding the treaties, by exchanging the *muzziniegnns*[1] on which the verbal agreements had been written. To renew and extend these obligations was, according to Indian phraseology, to tighten the chain of friendship.

On the 9th of January, 1789, nearly three months before the adoption of the present Constitution, General St. Clair concluded a treaty with a large delegation of the Six Nations assembled at Fort Harmar, at the mouth of the Muskingum. The

---

[1] Meaning treaties or graphic papers.

chief object of this treaty was to renew and confirm that entered into at Fort Stanwix in 1784. To secure order, a body of United States troops was encamped there, under Colonel Harmar, and the treaty of Fort McIntosh of January 21, 1785, was reconfirmed by the original parties to it, to whom was added a delegation from the Pottawatomies and Sacs.

From an explanatory article appended to this treaty it appears that the Wyandots accused the Shawnees of having laid claim to lands that did not belong to them, these lands being a part of the Wyandot domain. The respected Wyandot chief Tarhe was present at the negotiation of this treaty. It was affirmed by the Wyandots that the Shawnees, who signed the treaty of peace concluded at the Miami, had been guilty of injustice; and they further averred that "the Shawnees have been so restless, and caused so much trouble, both to them and to the United States, that if they will not now be at peace, they (the Wyandots) will dispossess them, and take the country into their own hands; for the country is theirs of right, and the Shawnees are only living upon it by their permission."

In 1789, General St. Clair also negotiated a treaty with the Wyandots, Delawares, Ottawas, Chippewas, Sacs, and Pottawatomies, through the chiefs assembled at Fort Harmar. This treaty has been called "a piece of Indian diplomacy which the Indians never intended to abide by any longer than suited their convenience." These assemblages, however, were convened in pursuance of the pacific policy of Washington, and had their effect. This last treaty of the confederated nations of the lake, the Ojibwas, Ottawas, Kickapoos, Weas, Piankeshaws, Pottawatomies, Eel River Indians, Kaskaskias, and Miamis, refused to acknowledge as binding. They wished the Ohio to be the perpetual western boundary of civilization, and would not sell an acre north of it.

Our Indian relations were at this time in a very critical state. By the terms of the treaty of peace, Great Britain was to evacuate all the posts and forts held by her without delay. From complications not then anticipated, she retained possession of the frontier posts for a number of years. This fact gave the impression to the Indians that the controversy was not yet closed, and their minds were poisoned by those about the posts. The British purposely aided and abetted them in their hostility to the United States. Brant, their leader, formed them into a confederacy, and visited England to obtain the support of the British government in case of war. Emigration flowed over the Alleghanies with great rapidity, and the lands to which the Indian title had been extinguished were daily filling up. The nucleus of the future State of Ohio had been established at Marietta in 1788. Collision could not be avoided between two races so antagonistic in habits and feelings as the Anglo-Saxon and the Indian. Murders were committed, which were retaliated by similar outrages. It became evident that an open Indian war must speedily ensue. The Delawares, the Shawnees, and the Wyandots having measured swords, to their cost, with the British, as also with the colonies, it was clear that the issue would not be with either of these tribes. Hostile demonstrations were apprehended from the Miamis and their co-tribes, the Weas and Piankeshaws. The residence of these tribes was located in the Wabash Valley, one of the most genial regions in the West. Possessing an extraordinarily fertile soil, which yielded large quantities of corn, grain, and fruit, with exuberant forests abounding in deer, bears, and other animals, their population was remarkably vigorous, while their insolence knew no bounds. In September, 1790, Colonel Josiah Harmar was directed to advance into their country and endeavor to bring them to terms. Such a march, encumbered with stores and supplies, through a wilderness destitute of roads, was in itself an arduous undertaking. The pioneer work of an army has always been one of the severest duties of a Western campaign : it is the toil and the triumph of the quartermaster's department. Roads must be made, bridges built, provisions packed, arms and ammunition carried; every delay must be endured, every difficulty overcome. On October 19, with a force of thirty regulars and four hundred and eighty militia, Colonel Harmar, who had reached the elevated grounds forming the present site of Fort Wayne, which are washed by the river Maumee, whose swift but shallow rapids are easily forded, engaged the Indians and was defeated. Observations made on the rising grounds beyond the stream on the 22d disclosed the presence of the enemy, whose demonstrations were intended to convey the idea that they were in force in that quarter. But this proved to be only a decoy: they had crouched down in the thick undergrowth and weeds, and were concealed along the western shore. The army was directed to cross the stream at this rapid, but had not proceeded far when a heavy fire of musketry was poured in, accompanied by the most frightful cries. The men were rallied by spirited officers, Major Wyllis and other brave officers being killed in this effort. The fire of the Indians was continued and well sustained, they being plentifully supplied with guns and ammunition. The line having faltered and fallen back, the retreating columns were marched to an elevated position, where they were reorganized. The loss in the two engagements amounted to one hundred and eighty-three killed and thirty-one wounded.[1] On the side of the Indians the loss was fifteen or twenty. So severe a defeat could not be repaired without a reinforcement, and Harmar determined to return to the banks of the Ohio, which he did without further molestation from the Indians.

Washington expressed doubts as to the justice of an offensive war upon the tribes of the Wabash and Maumee. Instead of assuming the offensive in 1790 and 1791, government should have sent commissioners of high character to the Lake tribes, and in the presence of the British ascertained their causes of complaint and offered fair terms of compromise. That such a step would have been wise and just is acknowledged by its subsequent action, and it was surely more likely to be effective before the savages had twice defeated the army than afterwards.

Only three tribes aided the colonies to any extent in the Revolutionary contest, —the Oneidas, the Tuscaroras, and the Mohicans. Thus far, treaties of peace had been concluded with the recreant Onondagas, Cayugas, and Senecas in the North, with the Creeks, Chickasaws, Choctaws, and Cherokees in the South, and with the

---

[1] Metcalf's Collection of Narratives of Indian Warfare in the West, p. 109.

298   THE INDIAN TRIBES OF THE UNITED STATES.

Wyandots, Delawares, Shawnees, Chippewas, Ottawas, Pottawatomies, and Sacs in the West; but the seven latter, who bore a very questionable character, could not be relied on, while the Miamis, Weas, and Piankeshaws of the Wabash were in open hostility. They had during the previous year defeated Harmar at the joint sources of the Great Miami of the Ohio and the Miami of the Lakes. The river Maumee formed the grand medium of Northern Indian communication with the Ottawas of the lower part of that valley, the Wyandots of Sandusky and Eastern Michigan, and the Chippewas of Detroit, as well as other Lake tribes, who were in the practice of joining the Wyandots, Delawares, and Shawnees in their inroads on the Ohio frontiers.

The Miamis were an active, bold, and numerous race, who, under the name of Twightwees, had been the objects of special attack by the Iroquois ever since the era of the French occupancy. They had been driven by them to more southerly and westerly locations than those which they had formerly inhabited, and were now the undisputed masters of the Wabash Valley. During the fierce and sanguinary warfare of 1782, when so many expeditions were sent against the Shawnees, Wyandots, and Delawares, the Miamis received no specific notice, but appear to have been included in the widely-diffused Ottawa and Chippewa race, whom they resemble in features, manners, customs, and language. General James Clinton, during the campaign against the Six Nations, in 1779, observed that the sympathy existing between the races, even where they were placed in antagonistic positions, was so great that but little reliance could be placed on them in exigencies. When war broke out, it required close observation to discriminate very particularly between the grades of hostility, if indeed there was any at all, existing among the different members of affiliated tribes. Nor did the Indians make any distinction between the various races of the whites. It was, in truth, a war of races; an attempt, if we may so term it, of the descendants of Japhet to shackle the wild sons of Shem and to "dwell in his tents."

The earliest movement of any note in the campaign of 1791 against the Wabash Indians and their allies was made by the expedition intrusted to General Charles Scott, of Kentucky. On the 23d of May in that year, General Scott set out from the banks of the Ohio with a total force of eight hundred and fifty men, a part of whom were regulars, under command of Colonel James Wilkinson, but by far the largest part of his army consisted of brave and experienced mounted volunteers. The month of June was passed in traversing the vast extent of forest-land watered by the tributaries of the Wabash River. On the 1st of August he reached the vicinity of Ouiattonon, the largest of the Miami towns. This place was promptly attacked, several warriors were killed, and the Indians, under a severe fire from the riflemen, were driven across the Wabash, their landing being covered by the warriors belonging to a village of Kickapoos, who maintained a constant fire. A detachment under Colonel Hardin having been ordered to cross the river at a point lower down, did so unobserved by the Indians, and stormed the Kickapoo town, killing six warriors and taking fifty-two prisoners. The following morning five hundred men were directed to capture and destroy the important town of Kithlipecamuk, located on the west bank of the Wabash, at the mouth of Eel River, a distance of eighteen miles from the camp. After demolishing the Indian towns and villages, devastating their corn-fields and gardens, and killing thirty-two warriors, besides taking fifty-eight prisoners, General Scott returned to the Ohio, which he reached on August 14 without the loss of one man, and with but five wounded.

This detail is but a necessary preface to what follows. The Indians, being a people of imperturbable character, are but slightly affected by those lessons of military warfare which are not fraught with calamities of a continuous character. They dexterously avoid the danger they cannot resist, and when no longer threatened they at once return to their former acts of pillage and atrocity. Some more formidable and permanent efforts were evidently necessary to bring the tribes to terms, and "to secure the great object of the campaign, the establishment of a strong military post at the Miami village at the junction of the St. Mary's and St. Joseph's Rivers." In this connection it is well to remember that by the terms of St. Clair's treaty, three years before, this territory was confirmed to the Indian nations "forever," "the said Indian nations to punish all intruders as they see fit." For the purpose above mentioned, Arthur St. Clair was commissioned a major-general in the army of the United States early in March, 1791.[1] Washington was very anxious on the subject, and urged on the general the importance of proceeding with all practicable promptitude.

St. Clair was a disciplined soldier, who, having served under Wolfe, Monckton, and Murray, and through all the campaigns of the Revolutionary war, enjoyed the confidence of Washington as a man of undoubted bravery and prudence. On the 15th of May he reached Fort Washington, now the site of Cincinnati. The delays attending the arrival of troops and supplies and the organization of the army gave rise to complaints, the whole summer being passed away in this manner. Fort Hamilton, the point of support on the Great Miami, was not completed until the 13th of September, and the month of October had arrived before the different corps of troops and levies were all mustered into service. On the 13th of October the army had advanced forty-four miles from Fort Hamilton, and encamped on an eligible spot, where St. Clair built Fort Jefferson. Then advancing with caution and order, on the 3d of November he arrived at a stream twelve yards in width, which he supposed to be the St. Mary's, one of the principal sources of the Maumee, but which was in reality a branch of the Wabash. It being four o'clock in the afternoon when the army reached this stream, St. Clair proceeded up its banks nine miles, and encamped on an eligible piece of ground in military order. He had designed constructing a breastwork at this place for the security of his baggage, but before he could effect this purpose the Indians, half an hour before sunrise the following morning (the 4th), made a furious attack on his lines. They were in great force, the slowness of St.

---

[1] See "A Narrative of a Campaign against the Indians, under the Command of Major-General St. Clair," Philadelphia, 1812, p. 1.

Clair's march up the stream having allowed them an opportunity to concentrate all the forces of their allies.

St. Clair was governor of the Northwest Territory. Old and infirm, he suffered so severely from gout as to have to be carried about on a litter. The proximity of the foe was communicated to General Richard Butler, second in command, but not to St. Clair. The latter was particularly unpopular in Kentucky, and, as none would volunteer under him, one thousand men were drafted, who were compelled to serve "under a gouty old disciplinarian" whom they disliked, and in conjunction with a regular force which they regarded as doomed to destruction in Indian warfare. Many in consequence deserted, an entire regiment leaving him on May 1, and at the time of the battle only two hundred and fifty Kentuckians remained in camp.

Unfortunately, the Indians, who were led into action by the valiant Wapacomegat,[1] a Mississagie, first encountered the militia and raw troops, who immediately fled through the line, pursued by the Indians, thus producing irremediable confusion. The Indians were checked, however, by a spirited fire from the front line, but in a few moments that and the second line were vigorously attacked, and the soldiers of the artillery corps, who formed the centre, were shot down at their guns. The slaughter was terrific on every side, and the confusion extended to the centre. At this moment St. Clair ordered the front line to charge, which they did very gallantly, under the command of Colonel Darke. The Indians fled several hundred yards, but again rallied when the troops returned to their position. At this time the second line also charged with effect, but the fire of the Indians was very galling, and produced greater confusion because of the large number of officers killed and wounded. The artillery were silenced, all the officers being killed but one, and he was wounded. The Indians simultaneously attacked front, flanks, and rear. General Butler was killed, as also Colonel Oldham, and Majors Hart, Ferguson, and Clarke. More than one-half the rank and file of the army had fallen, and the extermination of the rest seemed inevitable. The combat had lasted from about six o'clock to nine A.M.,[2] when General St. Clair led a charge through the Indian line in the rear, under cover of which the remains of the army retreated in disorder until they reached Fort Jefferson. The camp and the artillery were precipitately abandoned, and the men threw away their arms and ammunition. The army had originally consisted of about fourteen hundred men, of whom six hundred and thirty-two were killed and two hundred and sixty-four wounded, including sixty-four officers, a loss equal to that experienced at Braddock's defeat.

The effects of this defeat were most disastrous to the Western settlements. Immigration was checked, and dismay prevailed along the entire frontier. After a thorough investigation, a committee appointed by Congress completely vindicated General St. Clair from the charges made against him.

---

[1] This chief had attended the general peace convention and submitted to the British under General Bradstreet in 1764. See Mante.

[2] At this period of the year the sun rises in this latitude at thirty-two minutes past six.

Before St. Clair's army set out on its ill-fated expedition, a "talk" was held at Niagara between Brant, the Mohawk chief, with some fifty other Indian deputies, and General Benjamin Lincoln, Beverly Randolph, and Colonel Timothy Pickering, United States Commissioners, with the object of running a new boundary-line to take in Indian lands north of the Ohio.

The reader will bear in mind that the treaty of Fort McIntosh, made January 21, 1785, was with the Wyandot, Delaware, Chippewa, and Ottawa nations only, and that St. Clair's treaty of 1789 was with the above-named and the Pottawatomie and Sac nations only. Other Northwestern tribes had no part in either. In the ordinance of 1787 establishing the Northwestern Territory, the following provision is found: "The utmost good faith shall always be observed towards the Indians; their lands and property shall never be taken from them without their consent; and in their property rights and liberty they shall never be invaded or disturbed unless in just and lawful wars, authorized by Congress; but laws founded in justice and humanity shall from time to time be made for preventing wrongs being done to them, and for preserving peace and friendship with them."

The final reply to the talk of the commissioners at Niagara was adopted in a general council of the confederate Indian nations held at the Maumee Rapids, August 13, 1793. Among other things, they said, "Governor St. Clair, your commissioner in the beginning of the year 1789, after having been informed by the general council of the preceding fall that no bargain or sale for any part of their Indian lands would be considered binding unless agreed to by a general council, nevertheless persisted in collecting together a few chiefs of two or three nations only, and with them held a treaty for the cession of an immense country, in which they were no more interested than as a branch of the general confederacy, and who were in no manner authorized to make any grant or concession whatever. That part of these lands which the United States now wish us to relinquish, and which you say is settled, has been sold by the United States since that time."

In answer to the proposal to give the Indians a large sum of money for their lands, they replied that money was of no value to them, and to most of them was unknown, and that no consideration would induce them to sell. They also pointed out a very simple mode by which the settlers might be removed and peace secured. "Divide," said they, "this large sum of money which you have offered us among these people. Give to each, also, a proportion of what you say you would give to us annually over and above this large sum of money. They would most readily accept of it in lieu of the land you sold them. If you add, also, the great sums you must expend in raising and paying armies, you will certainly have more than sufficient for the purpose of repaying these settlers for all their labor and all their improvements. We want peace. Restore to us our country, and we shall be enemies no longer. Let the Ohio be the boundary-line between us."

To this document, signed by the deputies of the principal Western tribes, the commissioners made no reply: indeed, they could make none; and the only alternative was a resort to arms. It cannot be denied that the invasion and occupation of the territory northwest of the Ohio River was made anterior to any arrangement with the natives for that purpose. The arguments and facts presented by them to our commissioners could be answered only by the military power, and, unable to contend successfully with this, the red men were ultimately compelled to yield the required boundary.

The effect produced in Philadelphia, then the capital, by the intelligence of St. Clair's defeat was electric. Washington had never counselled half-way measures with the Indians, and this result had disappointed his expectations. Knox, his Secretary of War, had no personal experience in Indian warfare. It was of the utmost moment to make another effort, as early the following spring as possible, to gain the ascendency in the West, where the plan of establishing a chain of forts between Cincinnati and the Miami villages had been thus overthrown. An examination of the list of officers experienced in savage military manœuvres resulted in the choice of General Anthony Wayne, whose decision of character was well known. He had in 1782 led a successful cavalry charge against a night-attack of the Creeks near Savannah. Firm and cautious, but of chivalrous daring, nature had bestowed on him the talents and energy necessary to cope with the Western Indians.

Prior to the march of General Wayne, Washington resolved to make another attempt to bring the hostile Indians of the West to terms by negotiation. For this purpose Colonel Hardin and Major Trueman, two experienced men, were appointed commissioners, and directed to visit the towns on the Scioto. But these officers were both waylaid and killed while descending the Ohio, and thus the overture failed. Various peace-makers were sent into the Indian country, but their overtures were rejected one after another by the victorious savages. General Wayne's movements were also delayed by another object of pressing moment, which was to intercept a threatened invasion of Louisiana from Kentucky. For this purpose he was detained at Fort Massac during a portion of the year 1793, after which he contented himself with ascending the Miami Valley, six miles above Fort Jefferson, where he established himself in a fortified camp called Greenville.

It is unnecessary to detail here the process of organizing the new army, or the difficulties and delays it encountered. Wayne was determined not to be defeated; and defeat, when operating against an enemy so subtle as the Indians and so intimately acquainted with the peculiar geographical features of the surrounding country, could be guarded against only by the most untiring vigilance, prudence, and caution. The season for active operations was spent in collecting the forces on a remote frontier and bringing them into the field. It was necessary to proceed slowly, as roads must be opened, bridges built, and block-houses erected to serve as points of supply and communication. A large corps of pioneers was required to be constantly employed, which it was necessary to protect by a strong force of cavalry and riflemen. The delays arising from these causes were the subject of unjust complaint in the newspaper press of that period. Two armies had been defeated in endeavors to penetrate the great wilderness to the Wabash,—a country well suited to the operations of a savage foe, but abounding in obstacles to the progress of a civilized army, encumbered with baggage, cannon, and stores, who must have a passable road, and could not cross a stream of even the third magnitude without a bridge. The army was systematically employed in this difficult and laborious service, ever distasteful to volunteers, who composed a part of the forces. This labor, however, was the forerunner of success. Every day devoted to these toils, and to the discipline of the army, rendered it more active, efficient, and fit for the purpose in view. Wayne then took possession of the grounds where St. Clair had been defeated in 1791, and, having built Fort Recovery, wintered his army there.

On the 30th of the following June this fort was invested by a large body of Indians under Little Turtle, the successful commander in the battle with St. Clair, whose spies had closely reconnoitred it, while the main force lay near by under cover. They had noticed that at certain times the horses of the officers were admitted into the fort through the sally-port, and on one of these occasions they followed them with a desperate onset, knowing that the outer gates would be opened. The troops, however, being well disciplined, repelled this assault of a prodigious force of the hitherto concealed Indians. The following day they made the forest echo with their whoops, renewing the attack in greater force and with greater violence, but they were again repulsed with loss.

Fort Recovery was located near the head of the Maumee, and formed the key of the route to the Northwest, this valley being at that time the great thoroughfare of the Northwestern Indians from Detroit and the upper lakes, through which, with great vindictiveness, they had so long poured their infuriated hordes over the fertile regions of the Ohio Valley and the settlements west of the Alleghany chain. The area of their attacks embraced not only the present limits of Ohio, Indiana, and Illinois, but all Western Pennsylvania, Virginia, Kentucky, and part of Tennessee. It was from these States that Wayne drew all his levies and volunteers, who were imbued with such hatred of the savages, consequent upon a vivid remembrance of Indian cruelties, that it required a man like Wayne to restrain them. Rash courage and vindictiveness are but poor qualifications for an encounter with Indians in a forest, as many a partisan commander has realized to his cost.

A fortnight after the last Indian attack, Wayne continued his march down the Miami Valley. An impenetrable forest lay before him, through which nothing but an Indian footpath or a trader's trail could be discerned. But every company of his men was in itself a phalanx, and the order of march was such as to set surprise at defiance. In four days he reached the junction of the river Au Glaize with the Maumee, where he built Fort Defiance. Crossing the Maumee at this point to its west banks, he continued his march to the head of the first rapids, called Roche du Bout, or the Standing Rock. At this place a temporary work was constructed wherein to deposit the heavy stores and baggage, and he then pushed forward in the same order, and with like vigilance, for the principal Indian towns at the lower rapids.

Using the figurative language of the Indians, General Wayne's army resembled a dark cloud moving steadily and slowly forward. He had driven them one hundred and fifty miles from their fighting-ground on the river St. Mary's, and the sources of the Wabash, and it appeared impossible for them to oppose him in battle. At every point of attack they had found him prepared. They said of him that he was a man who never slept, and they named him the Strong Wind. They had found it impossible to stay the impetuosity of his march, and it was doubted in their councils whether a general battle should be hazarded, but, after much discussion, this measure was resolved on. The place selected was Presque Isle, a thickly-wooded oasis, such as is common to prairie districts in the West, encompassed by low and grassy meadow-lands, the upper part of which was encumbered by old, fallen timbers, where horses could not be employed, and here was fought the battle of the Maumee Rapids. On the 20th of August the Indians arranged their forces in three lines, within supporting distance, and at right angles with the river. Wayne knew not whether they would fight or negotiate, as offers of peace had been made to them. His army marched in compact columns, in the usual order, preceded by a battalion of volunteers so far in advance that timely notice could be given to the troops to form in case of an attack. This corps had progressed about five miles when they received a heavy fire from the concealed enemy, compelling them to fall back on the main army, which immediately formed in two lines. General Charles Scott, with his mounted volunteers, was directed to turn the right flank of the enemy by a circuitous movement, while Captain Campbell, with the legionary cavalry, effected the same object on the left flank by following an open way close to the banks of the river and between it and the cliffs of Presque Isle. The first line of infantry was ordered to advance with trailed arms, rouse the Indians from their coverts in the grass at the point of the bayonet, and then deliver a close, well-directed fire. These troops were promptly followed by the second line, the martial music of drums and trumpets giving animation to the scene. The whole of these movements were executed with alacrity and entire success. The Indians fled precipitately, and could not be rallied by their leaders. The army pursued them for two miles through the woods, and the victory obtained was complete. Wayne had about two thousand men under his command in this contest, not one-half of whom were engaged. His loss in killed and wounded was one hundred and thirty-three men. Captain Campbell was killed at the head of his legion, and Captain Van Rensselaer was shot through the body, but recovered. For a distance of two miles the forest was strewed with the dead bodies of the enemy, among which were recognized some of their white allies. The red men were denied entrance into the British fort at Maumee, the officers of which were compelled to witness the burning of the towns and the destruction of the Indian settlements. in the valley. The houses, stores, and property of the British Indian agent McKee, a principal stimulator of the Indian war, were also destroyed. General Wayne was highly incensed against the garrison of Fort Maumee, and sought to give them cause for open hostilities. There being a fine spring near the fort, the conversations at which could be overheard on the ramparts, the general rode around the fort to it with his staff, dismounted, took off his hat, and drank of the water, at the same time using expressions of indignation against the allies of the Indians, who had first incited them to attack him, and had then closed their gates against them. Those who are aware of the general's enthusiastic character need not be told that he expressed himself energetically. At the junction of the St. Joseph and St. Mary he built Fort Wayne, completed October 22, 1794, which was well fortified and strongly garrisoned. The savages made no further effort to oppose the course of the victorious army, which finally, after laying waste the corn-fields and villages for fifty miles on each side of the Maumee, returned to Greenville, where it went into winter quarters.

The object for which the Indians had fought had proved to be illusory, and their defeat on the Maumee terminated their struggle for the possession of the country northwest of the Ohio. They appear to have learned the truth of this from their late reverses, and in a short time thereafter they determined to bury the hatchet and smoke the pipe of peace.

It had been the policy of Washington's administration to employ force against the Indians only when absolute necessity required it, and compulsory measures were never adopted until after every other means of accommodating existing differences had failed. The Indians were to a certain extent regarded as public wards. The assassination of Hardin and Trueman on the Ohio, with the olive-branch in their hands, after the defeat of St. Clair and previous to the expedition of Wayne, is evidence of the insufficiency of this conciliatory policy. Even after Wayne had reached Roche du Bout, and but a day or two before the decisive battle, he tendered overtures of peace to the Indians, of which, however, it is affirmed that they were kept in ignorance by foreign agents.

In response to the renewal of these overtures the Indians crowded to Wayne's camp, at Greenville, during the summer of 1795. Their necessities during the preceding winter had been very great, in consequence of the total destruction of their crops, and, as the English, on whom they were dependent, had not supplied their wants, they were in a starving condition. The entire area embraced between the banks of the Ohio and Lake Erie, luxuriant with indigenous vegetation, had been the scene of the marching and countermarching of war-parties and armies from the period of the conclusion of the sham treaty made with Lord Dunmore in 1774, and the no less unreliable one signed at Fort McIntosh in 1785, but during the five years which had just closed it had been almost constantly trodden by hostile feet. The bitter chalice which they had so long held to the lips of the people of Kentucky, Pennsylvania, and Virginia was now being drained by themselves. After the demonstration at the Maumee Rapids they fled to their wintering-grounds in the extensive forests of Lake Erie, Michigan, and Canada. The local foreign traders of these precincts, the commandants of posts, who had counselled them to war, could no longer be regarded by them as oracles. The Indians had been unable to keep the whites east of the Ohio; nay, it began to be perceived by these subtle sons of the forest that the white race could not be confined within the limits fixed by the treaty of Versailles. During the winter and spring they exchanged prisoners and prepared to treat upon preliminaries, which were agreed upon in January. Before the month of July arrived, the savage, with altered feelings, entered on the forest-paths that led to Greenville, where the American chief was seated, surrounded by all the panoply of war, with the emblems of peace intermingled.

Foremost among the tribes who turned their steps to his camp were the proud and influential Wyandots, who had so long been regarded as wise men and umpires among the tribes of the West. Driven from the St. Lawrence Valley in 1659 by the Iroquois, they had for a century and a half held a high position in the West, sustained a part of the time by France, their earliest and most constant friend, and, after the conquest of Canada, by the English. They were astute, reflective, and capable of pursuing a steady line of policy, which had been, with some lapses, the stay of those Western tribes who were willing to tread in their footsteps. This tribe was the last to assent to the scheme of Pontiac, and when the confederation was broken up by Great Britain they adhered to that power with extraordinary devotion.

In their train followed the Delawares, who had been, since the time they first fled from Pennsylvania and crossed the Alleghanies, bitter enemies of the settlers in the West. Thither also came the Shawnees, the most vengeful and subtle of all the Western tribes. Every day witnessed the arrival in the surrounding forests of delegates, decked with all their peculiar ornaments of feathers, paint, silver gorgets, trinkets, and medals. The Chippewas, Ottawas, Pottawatomies, Miamis, Weas, Kickapoos, Piankeshaws, and Kaskaskias were all present. The entire official power of the Algonkins was on the ground. Each delegation carried the pipe of peace and expressed pacific desires. The whole camp presented a gorgeous display of savage magnificence, and for the number and variety of costumes the scene has probably never since been equalled in America. All came bending to Wayne, who on the 16th of June met them in council.

A treaty was signed on the 3d of August, which constitutes the first example of a thoroughly reliable treaty-stipulation of any great importance in the history of the Indians. The draft of this treaty, perhaps the most important ever made between the red men and the Americans, sent to General Wayne from the War Department, was drawn up under the supervision of Washington, and appears to have been full and elaborate. It established the system of boundaries and reservations and introduced the fundamental regulations as to trade and intercourse with the tribes which have been embodied in all subsequent treaties. A donation of twenty thousand dollars in goods, and a permanent annuity of nine thousand dollars, payable in merchandise at invoice prices, to be divided *pro rata* among the different nations, were granted to the Indians.

Having traced the negotiation of treaties from their first inception under the American government to this important period, when the Indians buried the hatchet, it will not be necessary to pursue the subject further. Subsequent negotiations with the tribes are connected with a lengthy detail of dates, names, and figures, which are readily accessible in the volumes containing the treaties between the United States and the Indians. The treaty of Greenville forms a definite era in the Indian history from which the tribes may be viewed. Both parties regarded this peace as a final conclusion of the aboriginal war which, following the close of the Revolution, had spread, as it were, a bloody mantle not only over the Ohio Valley, but over the entire region to the northwest of it. The position attained by the United States through this treaty had been the result of at least a decade of years, characterized by wars and negotiations, in which the sword and the olive-branch had either failed of effect or produced only temporary results; and the length of time the treaty was observed by the aborigines is in part attributable to the full assent it received from the united judgment of the principal chiefs of all the leading tribes who were parties to it. On the part of the Wyandots it received the signature of the venerated Tarhe, or the Crane; on that of the Delawares, it was subscribed to by the gifted Bukongehelas; the Shawnees assented to it through the venerable Cutthewekasaw, or Black Hoof, and Weyapiersenwaw, or Blue Jacket; Topinabi, or Thupenebu, signed it for the Pottawatomies, and for the Miamis it was signed by Meshekunnoghquoh, or the celebrated Little Turtle,—the latter of whom, with the Shawnee chief Blue Jacket, had been the marshal or leader of the Indians at the final battle on the Maumee. As long as these chiefs, the last of the forest-kings, lived, this peace was observed.

The lake posts were surrendered by the British in 1796, and American garrisons replaced those of the English at Niagara, Presque Isle, Maumee, Detroit, Michilimackinac, and Green Bay. The Indians, who are quick at recognizing the nationality of a flag, began to accommodate their visits and addresses to this new state of affairs. The government also sought as much as possible to divert the Indian trade from foreign hands into those of the Americans; but this was a difficult matter, and it required time to effect it. Along the Georgia and Carolina borders this trade had been concentrated in the hands of, and continued to be carried on principally by, enterprising and talented Scotchmen, who intermarried with the Indians. The most noted of these were McIntosh, McGillivray, Ross, and Weatherford, the latter somewhat better known as the Black Warrior of 1814. Throughout Louisiana, in all its amplitude of extension north and west, the French exercised the controlling influence; and this was especially the case in the territory now constituting the States of Arkansas, Tennessee, Missouri, Illinois, Indiana, Michigan, Wisconsin, and Iowa. In the basins of the upper lakes, and at the sources of the Mississippi River, British and Scotch factors for many years controlled the trade and influenced the tribes.

CHAPTER III.

EXPLORATIONS OF LEWIS AND CLARKE—LIEUTENANT PIKE—ELEMENTS OF DISCORD—TECUMSEH AND THE PROPHET ORGANIZE THE TRIBES FOR A CONFLICT WITH THE UNITED STATES—BATTLE OF TIPPECANOE.

Mr. JEFFERSON, on being called to occupy the Presidential chair in 1801, felt the importance of the claim which the existing state of the Indian tribes had upon his attention, and his views were of the most comprehensive character. To him we owe the passage of the fundamental act to preserve peace on the frontiers and regulate intercourse with the Indian tribes. By this act the boundaries of the Indian country and the operations of the laws in it are clearly defined. Regulations are established for the government of the Indian trade. The territory of the tribes is protected from depredations by the whites, who are permitted to visit it for no other purpose than trade or mere transit through it. The jurisdiction of courts is established, and the methods of proceeding are particularly pointed out. In fine, a system of policy is laid down calculated to advance the prosperity of the Indians and at the same time to secure the speedy settlement of the Western lands.

The act establishing the Northwest Territory was the first step towards the induction of this practical mode of teaching among the Indians,—teaching by example. However slight the effect of its lessons may have been on the remote tribes and bands, they were not wholly inoperative even there, while at points within the civil jurisdiction they carried with them a monition which caused them to be obeyed.

The commonwealth of Ohio was the first organization of the kind in the West, and the extension of State sovereignty west of the Ohio River insured to that area an expansion which has had few parallels in history. While Ohio heralded to the Western tribes the rule of government and law, Louisiana, by a wise forecast of executive policy, came in at this critical time to confirm and greatly extend the system. In fifty years the limits of the Union had reached the shores of the Pacific Ocean. Neither men nor States practise what is not conceived to be best suited to promote their prosperity. By offering to the Indians the protection of the laws and the benefits of intercourse with civilized society, the highest assurances were given that we were sincere and sought only to advance them in the scale of knowledge and happiness. But, as the Indian is an extraordinarily suspicious being, the good faith of this offer has ever been doubted by him, and some sinister purpose has been supposed to be concealed.

To ascertain the character and extent of Louisiana, and the numbers of the Indian tribes within its area, Mr. Jefferson despatched expeditions up the Missouri and Mississippi. The first was led by Merriwether Lewis and William Clarke, cap-

tains in the army, both of whom were commissioned for that purpose. They left St. Louis May 14, 1804, and ascended the Missouri through the territories of the Osages, Kansas, Otoes, and Sioux to that of the Mandans, where they wintered. The following year they continued their route through the countries of the Teton Sioux, Crows, and Blackfeet to the source of the Missouri, in the Rocky Mountains, and, crossing this range, they followed the course of the Columbia to the point where it flows into the Pacific. Retracing their steps from this remote position, they descended the Missouri to St. Louis, where they landed September 23, 1806. This was the first important exploratory expedition sent out by the government, and its results, while they evinced the great personal intrepidity of the explorers, were suited to convey an exalted opinion of the value and resources of this newly-acquired section of the Union. It was found to be a difficult task to enumerate the Indian population of the Columbia Valley, owing to the confusion of synonymes and other causes; consequently overestimates were inevitable. The aboriginal population was rated at eighty thousand, and the distance travelled, from the mouth of the Missouri to that of the Columbia, on the Pacific, is estimated at three thousand five hundred and fifty-five miles. The observations made by Mr. Lewis on the Indian trade disclosed gross irregularities, which were directly traceable to the era of Spanish rule, and such modifications were suggested as would tend to place the natives in a better position. The amount of information obtained by the officers of this expedition constituted a valuable addition to our knowledge of the Indians and their country; and the observations of General William Clarke, joined to his acquired experience, admirably qualified him for the duties of the office to which he was in after-time appointed,—that of Superintendent of Indian Affairs at St. Louis, on this frontier.

At the same period Lieutenant Z. M. Pike, U.S.A., was commissioned to explore the sources of the Mississippi. He started from St. Louis with his expedition on August 5, 1805, and, according to his own estimate, reached a point two hundred and thirty-three miles above the Falls of St. Anthony, where the accumulated snow and ice prevented his farther progress by water. He then proceeded on snow-shoes to Sandy Lake, and was thence drawn by teams of dogs to Leech Lake, the largest southerly source of the Mississippi River. Commerce with the Indians was found to be entirely in the hands of the British traders, who wielded an influence adverse to the institutions of the United States. Early in the spring of 1806, Lieutenant Pike descended the Mississippi River, arriving at his point of departure on the 30th of April. His estimates of the Indian population of the Upper Mississippi give a total of eleven thousand one hundred and seventy-seven souls, including Chippewas, Sacs, Foxes, Iowas, Winnebagoes, Menomonies, and the various scattered bands of Dakotas, called Yanktons, Sissetons, and Tetons.

A considerable addition was thus made to our knowledge of the character and habits of the extreme Western and Northern Indians, and the duties of the Indian Department were thereby greatly increased. The State of Ohio was admitted into the Union in 1803, at which period the Territory of Indiana was organized, and General William Henry Harrison appointed its Governor, as well as, *ex officio,* Superintendent of Indian Affairs. Harrison had served as an aide to General Wayne in his Indian campaigns, and entered upon the duties of his office with the additional experience acquired under this redoubtable chief, his skill in military tactics being fully equalled by his knowledge of the aboriginal character, which, combined with his address and activity, soon made him respected as a plenipotentiary at their council-fires. For many years he shared with General Clarke, of St. Louis, the onerous and responsible duty of preserving peace on the frontiers.

Two or three elements of discord had existed in the Indian communities located along the frontiers from the outbreak of the Revolution, which were not extinguished by its successful termination, and still smouldered after the close of the Indian war in 1795. Among these was the preference of the Western tribes for the British nation, arising, perhaps, from the conquest of Canada, but kept up by political fallacies. England had secured the good will of the French residents, in whose hands the important commerce with the Indians was concentrated and still remained. The possession of the Indian trade has ever exercised a controlling influence on the policy of the Indians, which is wielded not by ministers plenipotentiary or high secretaries of state, but by the little local traders on the frontiers, petty clerks, interpreters employed by commercial houses, and *coureurs du bois*, who never fail to make their principles square with their interests; and it is a matter of little moment to the limited ambition of this class who influence the destinies of courts or of nations, provided they be permitted to control the traffic in beaver-skins.

While the French held Louisiana, no counter-interests disturbed the harmony of their intercourse with the natives; but when the government was vested in the Spanish crown the rival interests of the Spanish and French merchants had produced discord between their subordinates, which extended also to the Indians. The cession of Louisiana to the United States calmed these troubles, all differences were forgotten, and the contending parties readily accommodated themselves to the American system. But in Florida there was never the least abatement in this strife for commercial supremacy, the thirst for gain acknowledging no nationality. On the contrary, during the short period when Florida was held by the British crown, a new feature was developed in the character of the Indian trade, which imparted to it additional vigor and system. We have in a preceding page alluded to this fact, which was the introduction of the Scottish element among the aboriginal population. One of its most important results was the intermarriage of the Scotch traders with the native females, which gave a permanent character to their influence and had a beneficial ethnological effect on the chiefs and ruling families of the native race. While the Galphins, the Millidges, and their compeers reaped the harvest of trade, the McIntoshes, the McGillivrays, and other chiefs of their race, by infusing their blood into the aboriginal current, gave to the Creeks, Cherokees, Chickasaws, Choctaws, and Seminoles a higher social and national character. The fact that this intermixture of the races was coincident with the employment of African slave labor by the higher Indian class was merely incidental. The negroes fled into the Indian territory to escape servitude in the Southern States, and voluntarily assumed the performance of labor as an equivalent for the shelter, support, and comparative ease and enjoyment Indian life afforded them.

Along the entire northern borders, southward to the line of demarcation designated by the treaty of Versailles, and throughout Michigan, Indiana, and Illinois, as well as the present areas of Wisconsin, Iowa, and Minnesota, British capital and enterprise were the great basis and stimulus of the Indian traffic. The limits of this trade had receded very far to the northwest after the victories of Wayne: Maumee, Vincennes, Kaskaskia, Detroit, and Michilimackinac no longer formed centres for the trade. There had been, up to the commencement of Mr. Madison's administration, no public effort made to prevent foreigners from pursuing their traffic with the Indians north of the shores of Lakes Huron and Michigan. One of the peculiar characteristics of the Indians is that they are wont to give their attention to the lowest order of counsellors, not because of any preference they have for an inferior grade of intellect, but from a natural suspicion that persons in higher positions are always governed by sinister motives; and suggestions from these subordinate sources would appear sometimes to be invested with importance in the precise ratio that they are removed from plausibility or truth. Whoever has, either as a plenipotentiary or a commissioner, passed through the ordeal of an Indian council controlled by the diverse interests of the trade and of the half-breed relations and *protégés* of the tribes will appreciate the force of this remark.

For years after the treaty of Greenville, few difficulties occurred with the Indians. But as settlements extended and encroached upon their domain, it was deemed necessary to renew our treaty relations with them. Between 1803 and 1809 six treaties, all of them for cessions of land, were made, and Wayne's treaty of 1795, with all its excellent provisions for the government and protection of the Indian, was substantially obliterated, vast bodies of the land assured by it to the Indian nations being transferred to the white man and the original proprietors dispossessed. As cession after cession of land was obtained from the Indians by this almost constant process of treaty-making, Tecumseh and his brother, the Prophet, as well as other leading Indians, became alarmed, and set about reviving the confederacy and forming a union of the tribes to prevent further cessions as well as settlements on their lands. Tecumseh protested strenuously against the cession of the Wabash lands at Fort Wayne in 1809, justly insisting upon the recognition of the principle that no cession could be valid unless sanctioned by a council representing all the tribes which were parties to the Wayne treaty of 1795 as one nation. Though the Shawnees were specially interested in these Wabash lands, not a Shawnee signed the treaty. While disclaiming any intention of making war on the United States, he declared it to be his unalterable resolution to oppose any further incursions of the whites upon the territory of the Indians.

Conspicuous among the heroic names of the century stands that of the Indian chief Tecumseh. For years he labored with enthusiasm upon a grand, arduous, and unselfish project, enlisting in it by his personal magnetism great multitudes of various tribes, contending for it with unflinching valor long after there had ceased to be a hope of success, and finally dying fighting for it to the last, falling with his face to the enemy and covered with wounds. His parents had emigrated from the Tallapoosa region in Alabama about the middle of the last century to the valley of the Miami, and there Tecumseh was born, near Springfield, Ohio, about the year 1770. He gave evidences of the possession of a superior nature when, at the age of sixteen, he first saw a prisoner burnt. He expressed his detestation of the act in such powerful terms that the party resolved never to burn another prisoner. In a fight with some Kentuckians on Mad River, when he was twenty, he is said to have run at the first fire; yet in the wars ending with Wayne's victory, in 1795, he had certainly won distinction. He surpassed his tribe in the arts and feats which Indians honor, winning renown as orator, hunter, and ball-player. His skill in hunting is attested by the story that in a contest with the best hunters of the tribe he returned at the end of three days with thirty deer-skins, while none of his competitors brought in more than twelve. He was well educated, could read and write, and had a confidential secretary and adviser named Billy Caldwell, a half-breed, who was afterwards head chief of the Pottawatomies. It was the sale of the favorite hunting-ground on the Wabash that gave Tecumseh such deep offence and led to the conception of his great design. He proclaimed the great principle that no single tribe could rightfully sell any portion of the lands which, as he claimed, belonged to the red men as a common possession. "The Great Spirit," said he to General Harrison, "gave this great island to his red children. He placed the whites on the other side of the big water; they were not contented with their own, but came to take ours from us. They have driven us from the sea to the lakes; we can go no farther. They have taken upon them to say this tract belongs to the Miamis, this to the Delawares, and so on; but the Great Spirit intended it as the common property of all. Our father tells us that we have no business on the Wabash, that the land belongs to other tribes; but the Great Spirit ordered us to come here, and here we will stay."

General Harrison could not recede, Tecumseh would not. The utmost the general could do was to refer the dispute to the President. "Well," said Tecumseh, "as the Great Chief is to determine the matter, I hope the Great Spirit will put sense enough into his head to induce him to give up this land; it is true he is so far off he will not be injured by the war; he may sit still in his town and drink his wine, while you and I will have to fight it out!" His words were prophetic.

For four years Tecumseh devoted himself to the task of preparing the tribes for a general war. In this work, while displaying eloquence of the highest character in descanting upon the Indian's wrongs and the white man's encroachments, he acquired an astonishing ascendency over the savage mind. General Harrison, who was long his adviser and ultimately was his conqueror, spoke of him as "one of those uncommon geniuses who, but for the proximity of the United States, might have founded an empire that would have rivalled in glory Mexico or Peru. He is constantly in motion. You see him to-day on the Wabash, and in a short time hear of him on the shores of Lake Erie or Michigan, or on the banks of the Mississippi, and wherever he goes he makes an impression favorable to his purpose." His plan was to surprise and capture Forts Detroit, Wayne, Chicago, St. Louis, Vincennes, and the adjacent American posts, and to unite all the tribes east of the Mississippi.

In the spring of 1811, Tecumseh, leaving his affairs in the hands of his brother the Prophet, went to the South, preaching his crusade and sowing the seeds of future wars in Florida among the Seminoles, in Georgia and Alabama, among the powerful Creeks and Cherokees, and in Missouri among the tribes of the Des Moines, holding the war-council and delivering his impassioned "talk." He returned in November, 1811, only to learn that his brother, disregarding his own prudent counsels, and puffed up with self-importance, had rashly attacked Harrison's army and met with the disastrous defeat of Tippecanoe.

The prestige of the Prophet, who had promised certain victory, was gone forever among the Northern Indians. Tecumseh's chosen warriors, the nucleus of the great army he had hoped to lead, were killed or dispersed. An opening was, however, unexpectedly afforded him by the breaking out of the war between Great Britain and the United States. In a few days he was in the field. His scheme of uniting the tribes was at once adopted as a part of the system of carrying on the war by the British generals, who took him into high favor, and who testify in strong language to his quick intelligence, his military abilities, and his high courage. A commission as brigadier-general was given him in the British army. The first blood shed in the war was shed through him, and the first advantage gained by the British was due to his assistance. Such were his zeal and activity, and such his knowledge of Indian nature, that the news of our disasters in Canada was whispered among the Creeks in Alabama before they had been heard of by the white settlers. He was present at the siege of Fort Meigs, and at the second assault he headed two thousand warriors. The fall of 1812 again found Tecumseh, accompanied by the Prophet and a retinue of thirty warriors, haranguing the Creeks in the midnight council, and this time with prodigious effect. Now he could point to the successes of the British in the North, now he could give certain promises of assistance from the English and from the Spanish in Florida, and now he spoke with the authority of a British agent and officer.

As we have already seen, considerable influence had been at this period attained by the Shawnee prophet Elkswattawa over the entire body of tribes. This person, though belonging to the reservation of his tribe at Wappecanotta, had located his residence principally on the Wabash, in the vicinity of the mouth of the Tippecanoe River, which became the centre of his power, and whence emanated his oracular revelations. By the recital and interpretation of dreams, by fasting, and by an assumed indifference to all worldly considerations and rewards, he had attained a high position and influence. Elkswattawa had lost one eye, which defect he concealed by wearing a black veil or handkerchief over the disfigured organ. He affected great sanctity, did not engage in the secular duties of war or hunting, was seldom seen in public, devoted most of his time to fasting, the interpretation of dreams, and offering sacrifices to spiritual powers, pretended to see into futurity and to foretell events, and announced himself to be the mouth-piece of God. The Indians flocked to him from every quarter; there was no name that carried such weight as his. They never ceased talking of his power or expatiating on the miracles he wrought; and the more extraordinary the revelations he made, the more readily were they believed and confided in. He combined a remarkably clear conception of the Indian character with great shrewdness and astuteness. It being essential to his purposes that he who was the concentrated wisdom of the Indian race should have no rival, the minor priests and powwows became but the retailers of his words and prophecies; and when one was found who disputed his authority or resisted his power he did not proceed against him in a direct manner, but insidiously operated upon the superstitions of the Indian mind. In this way he disposed of Tarhe, the venerable sachem of the Wyandots, who, being accused of witchcraft, was condemned to be burned at the stake. The very knowledge that he possessed such an indomitable will increased the fear and respect entertained for him by the Indians,—a respect which was, however, based on an implicit belief in his miraculous gifts. It has been mentioned that the Prophet was not a warrior; his whole object was to employ his power in furtherance of the projects of his brother Tecumseh. As early as 1807 the Shawnee chieftain and his brother were actively engaged in sending their deputies with large presents and bloody war-belts to the most distant nations to persuade them to come into the league, and when the comet appeared in 1811 the Prophet artfully turned it to account by practising on the superstitions of the savages.

There was a higher purpose concealed under these manifestations of Elkswattawa. He told the Indians that their pristine state, antecedent to the arrival of the Europeans, was most agreeable to the Great Spirit, and that they had adopted too many of the manners and customs of the whites. He counselled them to return to their primeval simple condition, to throw away their flints and steels, and to resort to their original mode of obtaining fire by percussion. He denounced woollen stuffs as not equal to skins for clothing; he commended the use of the bow and arrow. Above all, they should discard the white man's whiskey. These maxims he enforced by various ingenious tales. He said, for example, that he himself had formerly been a great drunkard, but on visiting, as prophets may do, the abode of the devil, he observed that those who died drunkards were all there, with flames of fire issuing from their mouths, and that, alarmed at the sight, he had reformed, and now called on all Indians to follow his example. To a surprising extent the Indians obeyed his directions. Like Pontiac, who, however, had made no pretensions to priestly power, he professed a profound respect for the ancient manners and customs of the Indians. Perhaps he was influenced thereto by his knowledge, derived from tradition, of the potency of this argument as made use of by that renowned chief, though it is very likely that the idea originated with himself. Fifty years only had passed since the era of Pontiac, and young men who had been engaged in that bold attempt to resist British power might yet be on the stage of action. Now, however, the real purpose was not to resist the British power, but to invite its co-operation. This was the secret of his actions. This was the argument used by the subordinate emissaries of the Indian trading agencies located in Canada who visited the Wabash, the Scioto, the Illinois, and the Upper Mississippi. In the course of a few years the doctrines of Elkswattawa had spread among the tribes in the valley of the Missouri, over those located on the most distant shores of Lake Superior, and throughout all the Appalachian tribes of the South. They were as current on the Ocmulgee, the Chattahoochee, and the Alabama as they were on the Wabash and the Miami. Elkswattawa was himself a half-Creek.

The speeches of the Indians in their assemblages had for some time savored of these counsels, and the name of the Shawnee prophet was known and the influence of his teaching disseminated throughout the country. In 1811 the congregation of large masses of Indians around the residence of this oracular personage, on the banks of the upper part of the Wabash, created considerable alarm, and General Harrison, who had closely watched this secret movement, reported it to the government, by which he was authorized to march a military force from Vincennes up the Wabash. This army, comprising one regiment of regular infantry, an auxiliary body of mounted Kentucky volunteers, and also volunteer militia from other Western States, left Vincennes in October, 1811, and on November 6 reached the Indian villages located on eligible open grounds near the confluence of the Tippecanoe. A preliminary conference was immediately held with the Indians, who recommended a locality at a moderate distance inland as a suitable one for an encampment. General Harrison had no reason to suspect Indian treachery, nor is it quite clear that any was originally intended. But that night the Prophet was observed practising his secret rites of divination, and he reported that the omens were favorable for an immediate attack. The army was encamped with the skill and precaution indicated by the teachings of Wayne, and, agreeably to his rigid rules, General Harrison had arisen to order the reveille, and was in his tent engaged in drawing on his boots, when the chief musician stepped in to ask whether he should commence the beat. "Not yet; but presently," was his reply.[1] The expression had scarcely passed his lips when the Indian war-cry was heard. One of the sentinels on post had observed an arrow fall on the grass, which did not, it seems, reach its destination; and, his curiosity being aroused, he was endeavoring to peer through the intense darkness in the direction whence the arrow came, when the Indians made a sudden onslaught. A thousand wolves could not have produced a more horrific howl. The lines were driven in, the horses of the officers, fastened to stakes in the square, broke loose, confusion everywhere prevailed, and the army was assailed from all points. General Harrison gallantly mounted his horse, and endeavored to restore order at the principal points of attack. The mounted volunteers from Kentucky and Indiana charged as well as they could through the darkness. The Fourth Regiment of United States Infantry, which was in a high state of discipline, restored confidence to the foot, and as soon as the dawn of day permitted them to act they repulsed the Indians. At the same time the volunteer cavalry drove the enemy across the prairie to their coverts. There had been, however, a most severe and lamentable slaughter.

---

[1] Narrative of Adam Walker, a musician in the Fourth Regiment.

Daylight rendered visible the dead bodies of the chivalric Colonel Daviess, of Kentucky, and Colonel Owens, of Indiana, a Senator in Congress. Our loss was thirty-seven killed and one hundred and fifty-one wounded. The army was saved from destruction only by the rising of the sun, which rendered the enemy visible. It was, however, a decisive victory for the United States, and a death-blow to the plans of the Prophet and his brother Tecumseh, and for some time afterwards the frontiers enjoyed peace. Numbers of the Indians had been slain by the broadsword in their retreat. This battle was not, however, fought by Tecumseh, who, as has been said, was then absent on a mission to the Creeks, his relatives by his mother's side.

CHAPTER IV.

WAR OF 1812—DISASTERS ON THE CANADIAN FRONTIER—DETROIT SURRENDERED —DEFEAT AT THE RIVER RAISIN—DUDLEY'S DEFEAT—VICTORY OF THE THAMES, AND DEATH OF TECUMSEH.

On the 18th of the June following the battle of Tippecanoe, Congress declared war against Great Britain. This war, according to the newly-announced oracular view, appeared to the Indians as the manifestation of the power of the Great Spirit, and was regarded as the means employed to disenthrall them from the hated rule of the white race. Their great Shawnee prophet had announced to the tribes from his oracular *jesukean*, or prophet's lodge, on the banks of the Wabash, the approaching epoch of their deliverance, and the news had been diffused far and wide. The intimate political relations of his brother Tecumseh with the British authorities of Canada formed the nucleus of their power, and hence they could depend on the British for arms, provisions, and clothing. Was it any wonder that they flocked to the British standard as soon as it was displayed? Twenty-seven days after the declaration of this war by Congress the Indians were in possession of Michilimackinac, and on the same day their tomahawks were red with the gore of the slaughtered garrison of Chicago, who had abandoned the fort and sought safety on the sandy shores of Lake Michigan. The war resulted mainly from long-pending disputes concerning maritime rights and national injustice. The concurrent Indian hostilities on the frontiers were but a small part of the original cause of complaint. Yet the assumption that they were originated by British emissaries was clearly deducible from the events which took place on the frontiers, and it derived additional confirmation in a short time from the fact that these Indian tribes were engaged to "fight by the side of white men" and to serve as auxiliaries to the British army in the West. In the war of 1812 Great Britain made the same unjustifiable use of the Indians as she had previously done in that of 1776,—they were her cruel and bloody satellites. Thayendanagea had gone to the hunting-grounds of the spirit-land, but his place was more than filled by Tecumseh, who possessed greater energy of purpose, with equal bravery, and had more deeply enlisted the warmest sympathies of the Indians. The former, it is believed, had ere his death overcome his violent prejudices against the Americans; the latter fell in defence of rights and of a cause which he felt to be just, while his dishonest adviser and auxiliary in command, General Proctor, fled ingloriously from the field.

The Indians believed that in the war of 1812 they had an opportunity of regaining possession of the Western country, perhaps to the line of the Illinois, while the British hoped to secure a more southerly line of boundary than that prescribed by the treaty of 1783,—a motive which, in the minds of sober, thinking people, hardly redounded to their credit. Their conduct in this war, as in that of the Revolution, served only to add to its horrors, and by acts of cruelty incited the Americans to greater exertions. That the Indians had been told that they would be able to recover their territory northwest of the Ohio is evident from the speech of Tecumseh made to General Proctor at Amherstburg in 1813. "When the war was declared," said the great Indian captain, "our father stood up, and gave us the tomahawk, and told us that he was now ready to strike the Americans; that he wanted our assistance; and that he would certainly get us our lands back which the Americans had taken from us."

After reciting the long course of maritime injustice and wrong, the Congressional Committee on Foreign Affairs emphatically say, "Forbearance has ceased to be a virtue. . . . Whether the British government has contributed by active measures to excite against us the hostility of the savage tribes on our frontiers your committee are not disposed to occupy much time in investigating. Certain indications of general notoriety may supply the place of authentic documents, though these have not been wanting to establish the fact in some instances. It is known that symptoms of British hostility towards the United States have never failed to produce corresponding symptoms among those tribes. It is also well known that on all such occasions abundant supplies of the ordinary munitions of war have been afforded by the British commercial companies, and even from British garrisons, wherewith they were enabled to commence that system of savage warfare on our frontiers which has been at all times indiscriminate in its effect on all ages, sexes, and conditions, and so revolting to humanity."

"Summer before last" (*i.e.*, 1810), says Tecumseh, "when I came forward with my red brethren, and was ready to take up the hatchet in favor of our British father, we were told not to be in a hurry; that he had not *yet* determined to fight the Americans." This impatience on the part of the Indians was so great that they took the initiative at the battle of Tippecanoe. That action thrilled through the nerves of the Americans like an electric shock, and was the first intimation that the frontiers were about to become the scene of another desperate contest with the bloodthirsty and infuriated savages. But though the impatient Indians chafed at the delay, it served to give a degree of unanimity to their hostility which even the war of the Revolution had not witnessed. From the termination of the Appalachian chain to the great lake-basins of Erie, Huron, Michigan, and Superior, onward to the Falls of St. Anthony, and southward to the gulf, the Indians assumed an attitude of determined hostility; and as soon as the key-note was sounded in Canada by the British bugle, an answering yell of discord resounded through the land which electrified the people on the frontiers, made the mother quake with dread in her nursery, and summoned the patriotic militiaman to arms.

During the winter following the action on the Wabash, Elkswattawa continued his incantations, delivering his oracular responses with more and more authority, while his distinguished brother continued those negotiations with the tribes which were necessary to prepare them for conflict, and we should not have known that they were ready to take up the hatchet two years previously had not Tecumseh stated it in his celebrated speech.

Early in the spring of 1812, the forests surrounding every military post in the West were at nearly the same time filled with armed warriors, who watched the gates with the keen eyes of a panther ready to spring upon its prey. Their central rendezvous, and the depot whence they drew their supplies, was Fort Malden, at Amherstburg, near the mouth of the Detroit River. They had watched the movements of Hull in Michigan with the accuracy of a vulture, or of an eagle on its perch; and, with the same rapacious vigilance, they had permitted no one to escape who ventured from the gates of a fort or of any guarded enclosure. When the apprehensions of Hull had reached their climax, and the British flag was hoisted on the ramparts of Fort Shelby, their exultation was extreme. The Chippewas and Ottawas, with delegations of the Menomonies, Winnebagoes, and Sioux, had, on the 17th of July preceding, enabled Captain Roberts, with a trifling force,[1] to surprise and capture Michilimackinac. On the 4th of August a large body of Wyandots and other Indians, lying in ambuscade at Brownstown, defeated Major Van Horn, with a force of two hundred riflemen, driving him back to Detroit with great loss. On the 9th of August, after Hull had recrossed Detroit River, Colonel Miller also encountered at Brownstown the same force of Indians, led by Tecumseh, and supported by a large body of British regulars, located behind temporary breastworks, whom he gallantly charged with the bayonet and defeated. On the 16th of the same month Detroit was surrendered to an inconsiderable army hastily mustered by General Brock, who officially intimated that the Indians could not be restrained. General Hull observes that "the history of barbarians in the north of Europe does not furnish examples of more greedy violence than these savages have exhibited," and thus consoles himself by an historical truism for a surrender which is a lasting stigma on the military history of the Union.

On the 15th of August the garrison of Chicago (where Fort Dearborn had been erected in 1804), under Captain Heald, was surrounded by Pottawatomies while on its march to Detroit along the open shores of Lake Michigan, and all but about fifteen massacred, including the women and children who followed the camp. The stock of stores and baggage was captured.

On the 8th of September the Wabash Indians invested Fort Harrison, on the Wabash, about sixty-five miles above Vincennes, and a short distance above the present city of Terre Haute, then garrisoned by a few men under command of Captain Zachary Taylor.[2] They killed several persons outside of the fort, and invested it closely for two days. Finding they could not force an entry, they fired one of the block-houses, the lower part of which contained the provisions of the garrison. At-

---

[1] According to Lieutenant Hanks, there were but forty-six regular British troops, with three hundred and sixty Canadian militia and seven hundred and fifteen Indians.—*Official Letters*, p. 36.

[2] Thirty-seven years afterwards, this officer was elected President of the United States.

tempts to save it proving unsuccessful, it was burned down, leaving an opening about eighteen feet in width. With great self-possession and cool courage, Captain Taylor caused the breach to be repaired, though subjected to an incessant fire from the enemy, and finally beat them off.

On the 5th of the month the savages laid siege to Fort Madison, on the Upper Mississippi, commencing their operations by shooting and scalping a soldier near the gate. They then opened a brisk attack with ball and buckshot, killed the cattle in an outer enclosure, fired at the flag-staff, and cut the rope which held the flag, causing it to fall, and also made several bold and dexterous attempts to set the works on fire.

Early in October, Governor Edwards, of Illinois, marched against the Indian town of Peoria and the savages in its vicinity. He was attacked by the Indians in their usual manner, but succeeded in burning their towns and destroying their corn, losing only a few men. In the month of November the hostilities of the Wabash Indians became so troublesome that a force of about twelve hundred and fifty volunteers, under General Hopkins, was marched from Vincennes against them. On the 20th, 21st, and 22d he applied the torch to several of their villages, utterly destroyed the Prophet's town, and drove the enemy from their strongholds, who, however, avoided any decisive battle. On the 12th of December two or three hundred Indians assaulted the camp of Colonel Campbell, on the Mississinewa branch of the Wabash, killing eight men and wounding thirty-five or forty. General Harrison commended the intrepidity with which this attack was repulsed.

The year 1812 closed very inauspiciously. In wars with his own race the Indian never continues hostile operations during the winter season. The trees have then lost their foliage, and do not hide his movements; the snows at that season present a complete map of his track; the cold is too intense for him to dispense with fire, the light of which would reveal the position of his encampment. But when an Indian is quartered among civilized troops he is protected in the use of camp-fires, he builds huts to ward off storms, draws his provisions from a commissary, and clothes himself in woollens which are not paid for by beaver-skins. Under these circumstances a winter campaign can be endured, and does not become distasteful.

The river Detroit had been from the earliest period the principal entrance to the Indian territory in the Northwest, and the area of lower or eastern Michigan consequently became the meeting-place of Indian councils, and the grand rendezvous of war-parties. The surrender by Hull of this territory appeared to have abandoned it to them under the protection of their allies. It was renowned in their mythology as having been trodden by the fabled heroes and demi-gods Inigorio, Manabozho, and Hiawatha, and celebrated in their traditional history by the deeds of a Pontiac and a Minnavivina. The great object of the manoeuvres of the United States troops was to regain possession of Michigan. Tecumseh, whose head-quarters were located near Amherstburg, separated from it only by the river Detroit, had, as has been already mentioned, defeated Major Van Horn at Brownstown on the 4th of August, 1812, and likewise had aided in the determined resistance made to Colonel Miller at the same place on the 9th.

On January 18, 1813, Lieutenant-Colonel William Lewis, with six hundred Kentucky volunteers from General James Winchester's division, which had just marched through the snow from the Miami, made a forced march from the rapids to the river Raisin, where he attacked a force of five hundred British and Indians under Major Reynolds, who were driven from their defences. The night of the 21st was intensely cold, and no pickets were posted upon the road by which the enemy at Malden, only eighteen miles distant, might be expected. At daybreak on the morning of the 22d, Winchester's camp was suddenly attacked by about one thousand British and Indians, commanded respectively by Colonel Proctor and Tecumseh, with artillery. They were kept at bay by the detachment of Colonel Lewis, which was protected by picketing, but Colonel Wells's regiment, encamped on the open ground, and attacked from the cover of the houses and enclosures upon its flanks, soon gave way and fled panic-stricken. They were pursued and slaughtered without mercy by the Indians, scarcely a man escaping death or captivity. The Kentuckians gallantly held their position, though subjected to the fire of six field-pieces, until their ammunition was expended, when they surrendered upon honorable conditions. These conditions, as respected the wounded, were inhumanly violated. They, having been left without a guard, were all murdered by the Indians under circumstances of shocking barbarity. This terrible disaster resulted in a loss to the Americans in killed, wounded, and prisoners of about one thousand.

The Northern Indians assembled under British colors around Fort Meigs, on the Maumee, aided materially in effecting the defeat, on the 5th of May, of twelve hundred volunteers under General Green Clay and Colonel Dudley. Clay, who on May 4 had reached Fort Defiance, was ordered by General Harrison to land eight hundred men on the north shore, opposite Fort Meigs, to carry the British batteries, spike the cannon, and destroy the carriages, and then to cross over to the fort. Colonel William Dudley, who was charged with the execution of this order, after finishing his work, instead of withdrawing as ordered, pursued the enemy nearly two miles, his men being scattered in the woods in all directions. In this situation the enemy intercepted their retreat, and the whole detachment, with the exception of about one hundred and fifty men, were killed or captured, many being shot down and scalped after becoming prisoners. The siege of Fort Meigs by about three thousand British and Indians under General Proctor, which had lasted eleven days, was raised on the 9th of May.

The Northwestern Indians, who were under the influence of Tecumseh, and of the Shawnee prophet, his brother, had manifested considerable restlessness and dissatisfaction at the course pursued by the British generals during the spring, summer, and autumn of 1813. Their decided and unexpected defeat by Croghan in the sharp action at Upper Sandusky, their abandonment of the siege of Fort Meigs and withdrawal from the American shores of Lake Erie, and, above all, the capture of the British fleet by Perry, had appeared to the Indians to be presages of evil. As early as the 18th of August, only eight days after Perry's victory, Tecumseh had protested against these retrograde movements. He was then in ignorance of the result of the naval battle, which had been concealed from him, but he feared the worst. "We have heard the guns," he said, "but know nothing of what has happened to our father with one arm.[1] Our ships have gone one way, and we are very much astonished to see our father tying up everything and preparing to run away another, without letting his red children know what his intentions are. You always told us to remain here and take care of our lands; it made our hearts glad to hear that was your wish. Our great father, the King of England, is the head, and you represent him. You always told us that you would never draw your foot off British ground. But now, father, we see you are drawing back, and we are sorry for our father doing so without seeing the enemy."

The victory obtained by Perry was the turning-point in the campaign. A fleet being now at the command of General Harrison, he could at once transport his entire army, with its artillery and baggage, across the lake, thus avoiding long and perilous marches, through almost impassable bogs, such as that of the Black Swamp, and the peril of ambuscades in the forests. General Harrison landed his army on the shores of the lake, a few miles below Amherstburg, on the 23d of September, and in less than one hour he marched into the town, where not a single British soldier was to be found. General Proctor, the commandant, had fled, with all his troops and the Indian auxiliaries, after burning the fort, barracks, navy-yard, and public stores. He was pursued the following day, and on the 5th of October was overtaken at the Moravian town on the river Thames, when a general action ensued, in which he was utterly defeated.

The ground occupied by the British was the river-bottom, about three hundred yards wide, and thickly set with beech-trees. Their left rested upon the river, and their right upon a swamp which ran parallel to the river and covered their right flank. Beyond this swamp their line was prolonged by their Indian allies, who occupied low grounds behind a dense forest of beeches, impenetrable by horsemen. The position was well chosen, and evinced the judgment of their great captain, Tecumseh, who commanded the Indians and by word and example animated them to a vigorous resistance. Proctor's force consisted of eight hundred regulars and twelve hundred Indians. Harrison's army numbered twenty-five hundred, chiefly Kentucky volunteers. His line of battle was formed by the two divisions of Henry and Desha, including the brigades of Trotter, King, Chiles, Allen, and Caldwell. Henry's division confronted the British regulars, while that of Desha was formed at a right angle with it, facing the swamp, the Indian stronghold. The venerable Isaac Shelby, of King's Mountain fame, took his station at the point where the lines intersected. Colonel R. M. Johnson's regiment of mounted gunmen had originally been intended to turn the Indian flank and operate in the rear, as in Wayne's battle, but, learning that the British regulars were deployed as skirmishers in loose order, he directed them to charge Proctor in front. Johnson, finding that the whole of his regiment could not act with effect upon the narrow front of the British line, ordered

---

[1] Commodore Barclay.

his brother to charge them with one battalion, while he charged the Indians with the other. The charge upon the British was completely successful. Proctor fled, and the whole right wing threw down their arms and surrendered. The charge upon the Indians, from the nature of the ground and their more vigorous resistance, proved unsuccessful. The horsemen recoiled in disorder, and, dismounting, commenced an irregular skirmish with the Indians. Colonel Johnson, who had gallantly led a forlorn hope of twenty men, was desperately wounded, and borne off before the close of the action. The defeat of Proctor in front, however, left Tecumseh unprotected, and he would have been compelled to retreat had not the action in this quarter terminated in the death of the great chief.

With the fall of Tecumseh the Indian league was virtually broken. The Indians generally abandoned the contest and dispersed. A strong party of them, however, accompanied by the British troops, crossed the Niagara before daybreak on the 30th of December and laid the village of Buffalo in ruins. On the 16th of October, General Harrison issued a proclamation granting an armistice to the Miamis, Pottawatomies, Weas, Eel River Indians, Chippewas, Ottawas, and Wyandots, each of these tribes having delivered into his custody hostages for the faithful performance of their agreement. The same tribes, together with the Kickapoos, had previously sent delegates to Generals McArthur and Cass, commanding at Detroit, offering to conclude a peace.

CHAPTER V.

HOSTILITIES WITH THE CREEKS—MASSACRE AT FORT MIMS—BATTLES OF TUL-
LUSHATCHES, TALLADEGA, HILLABEE, ATTASEE, EMUCKFAU, ENOTOCHOPCO,
AND TOHOPEKA—SURRENDER OF WEATHERFORD—CAPTURE OF PENSACOLA
—THE WAR ENDED.

WE must now turn our attention to the Southern tribes. The fallacy of concluding treaties with an ignorant, wild, and nomadic people, destitute of sound moral principles, was never more fully demonstrated than in the case of the Appalachian group of tribes. The Creeks, a full delegation of whom, with McGillivray at its head, visited New York in 1790, and, amid great ceremony, entered into solemn compacts with General Washington, renewing the same in 1796, and again in 1802, as well as in 1805, were, all the while, only carrying out a diplomatic scheme. They hated the Americans, and the more so, it seems, because they had as colonies prevailed over the British. This great tribe had in early days subdued the once proud Uchees and Natchez and the Florida tribes, and in truth wielded the power of a confederacy, which they averred to consist of seven tribes or elements. But in a confederacy of savages it was necessary to keep the tomahawk ever lifted. Destitute of political compactness, and its leaders lacking the power of combination as well as moral steadiness, this league was powerful only against savages like themselves, and proved to be an utter failure when opposed to the policy of a civilized nation.

Tecumseh had harangued in their councils early in his career. His mother having been a Creek, they listened to his words with peculiar favor, more especially as he was fresh from the banks of the Wabash, where he had heard the voice of inspiration. In common with the Western tribes, the Creeks believed that they were on the eve of a great revolution, through which the Indians would once more regain their ascendency in America.

So long had the Creeks been at peace with the settlers, and such progress had many of them made in civilization, and so attached to the whites had the more intelligent of the chiefs become, that the process of fomenting a civil war was a long and doubtful one. To his public addresses from time to time Tecumseh added private persuasion. Prophets howled, danced, and performed miracles at his bidding. His utmost efforts were employed in gaining over the leaders, among the first of whom was Weatherford, a half-breed, possessing a genius similar to his own, handsome, sagacious, eloquent, and brave. Returning northward, Tecumseh's injunctions to secrecy were so well observed that for six months afterwards, while the war question was agitating thirty thousand souls, the whites knew nothing of it, and as late as midsummer, 1813, they were still in doubt whether the Creeks intended hostilities.

Thoroughly alarmed at last, the planters along the Alabama River, few in number and defenceless, left their houses and crops and took refuge in the block-houses and stockades, of which there were twenty in a line of seventy miles. The neighbors of Samuel Mims resorted to his enclosure of upright logs, pierced for musketry, on the shores of Lake Tensaw, each family hastening to construct within it a rough cabin for its own accommodation. Major Daniel Beasley, with one hundred and seventy-five volunteers, had command of the fort, which, on the fatal morning of August 30, contained no less than five hundred and fifty-three souls, of whom more than one hundred were women and children. Days passed: the first panic subsided, the danger was made light of, discipline was relaxed, and the inmates gave themselves up to fun and frolic. At noon, August 30, Weatherford and one thousand Creek Indians, who, armed to the teeth and hideous with war-paint, had all the morning lain hidden in a ravine only four hundred yards distant, leaped from their lair, and were only one hundred and fifty yards from the gate when first seen. For three hours the garrison maintained a destructive fire through the port-holes and from the houses. But at length, by means of burning arrows, the buildings were fired, and a scene of slaughter ensued. Weatherford tried to stop the carnage, but the Indians, delirious with blood, could not be controlled. At sundown four hundred mangled corpses strewed the ground. Not a white woman or child escaped. A few half-breeds were made prisoners, and a number of negroes were spared and kept as slaves. Major Beasley was one of the first that fell. Of the Indians, four hundred were killed and wounded. The news of the massacre flew upon the wings of the wind. In the country of the Alabama River and its branches every soul fled in terror to the stockades or towards Mobile. Property of all kinds was abandoned. Parties of Indians roved about the country rioting in plunder, and for weeks it seemed as if the white settlers of Alabama were about to be exterminated.

The Northern tribes were to a considerable extent controlled by climatic influences. They could not continue together in large bodies without being furnished with regular supplies of food and some of the requisites of a military camp. When, therefore, their white allies and supporters were defeated they were dismayed, but when their own great leaders and captains were killed they were placed entirely *hors du combat*. There were no reserves from which to recruit defeated Indian armies; there was, in truth, no recuperative power in the Indian character. To some extent the tribes south of latitude 40° north were an exception to this rule. From 40° to 46° north the snow falls to a greater or less depth between the months of November and March. North of 46°, corn, on which the Indian relies for his supply of vegetable food, must be purchased from the Indian traders who visit his villages during the winter; but a war with Europeans, whose armies can operate either in winter or in summer, is adverse to hunting and destructive of his means, as the Northern Indian can neither raise corn in summer nor hunt deer or search the streams for beaver in winter. It is far otherwise with the tribes located between the latitudes of the capes of Florida and the Appalachian Mountains. A large part of this territory, lying between the longitudes of the Atlantic coasts of Georgia and Florida and the banks of the Mississippi, have an almost tropical climate, and produce sub-tropical vegetation. Here are grown the indigo-plant, cotton, rice, and sugar, also the orange, banana, and other far Southern fruits. The forests are redolent with the aromatic odors of groves of illicium, myrtle, laurel, and bignonia. The Indian spreads his simple mantle here, and lies down on the ground without a tent or a fire. The forests are filled with the deer and wild turkey. The soil yields the arrow-root and wild potatoes, and the sea-coasts, as well as the lakes, abound with shell-fish and the various species of water-fowl. These tribes had not yet been circumscribed in their movements by the onward progress of the emigrant; and no such idea had mingled in their dreams as that the fertile and extensive territories on the Chattahoochee, the Alabama, and the Tuscaloosa were designed for nobler pursuits than the mere hunting of deer. Antiquity of opinion, manners, and arts is what the native unsophisticated Indian loves; novelty is distasteful, progress is unrelished, agriculture is regarded as servitude, letters and religion are detested.

The laying down of the war-club by the Northern tribes, who had been led on by Tecumseh in their crusade against civilization, had little or no effect on the Southern tribes. Within one month after the decisive battle of the Thames, in the North, the Creeks assumed such an attitude of hostility at Tullushatches, on the Coosa River, that General John Coffee marched against them with a brigade of cavalry and mounted riflemen. The Indian town was reached at sunrise, November 3, when the beating of the drums of the savages indicated that they were prepared to meet them. A sham attack and retreat by a single company effectually succeeded in decoying them from their houses in close pursuit. This sally was checked by their encountering the main body of Coffee's command, which charged them and drove them back to their shelter, where they were in a very short time surrounded by superior numbers. They fought with great desperation, without "shrinking or complaining; no one asked to be spared, but all fought as long as they could stand or sit." One hundred and eighty-six dead bodies were counted on the field, and eighty prisoners were taken, chiefly women and children. General Coffee's brigade lost five killed and forty-one wounded.

Only a few days elapsed when the Creeks appeared in great force at Talladega, surrounding a small fort into which one hundred and fifty-four friendly Creeks had fled for safety, and investing it so completely that not a man could escape. With only a small quantity of corn and scarcely any water, outnumbered seven to one, and unable to send intelligence of their situation, the inmates of the fort seemed doomed to massacre. The assailants, sure of their prey, whooped and sported around it, waiting for terror or starvation to save them the trouble of conquest. Days passed, and the sufferings of the beleaguered Indians from thirst began to be intolerable. At length a noted chief, enveloped in the skin of a hog, left the fort, and, rooting and grunting about, succeeded in gradually working his way through the enemy's line, and next day reached the camp of General Jackson, thirty miles distant. That energetic officer, to whom the command had been assigned, promptly advanced to their relief, and by great exertions and night-marches reached the vicinity of the fort on the 9th of November. At sunrise he attacked the Indians and gained a decisive victory, two hundred and ninety of them being left dead on the field. The joy of the rescued Creeks was affecting in the extreme, and they thronged around their deliverer, testifying their delight and gratitude. Jackson had seventeen killed and eighty-three wounded.

The Hillabee warriors who had been defeated at Talladega at once sent a messenger to Fort Strother to sue for peace. Jackson's reply was prompt and characteristic. His government, he said, had taken up arms to avenge the most gross injuries, and to bring back to a sense of duty a people to whom it had shown the utmost kindness. When these objects were attained the war would cease, but not till then. "Upon those," he continued, "who are disposed to become friendly I neither wish nor intend to make war, but they must afford evidences of the sincerity of their professions; the prisoners and property they have taken from us and the friendly Creeks must be restored; the instigators of the war and the murderers of our citizens must be surrendered; the latter must and will be made to feel the force of our resentment. Long shall they remember Fort Mims in bitterness and tears." Before this message reached the Hillabees, an event occurred which banished from their minds all thoughts of peace, changing them from suppliants for pardon to deadly enemies. Totally unaware of the state of feeling among them, nay, supposing them to be inveterately hostile, Brigadier-General James White marched against their towns on the Tallapoosa, about one hundred miles from Fort Armstrong, on November 11, without Jackson's knowledge.

He captured five Creeks on the Little Oakfuskee, and burned a town comprising thirty houses. The town of Genalgo, consisting of ninety-three houses, shared the same fate. Having arrived at a point within five or six miles of the principal Hillabee town, where he was informed the Indians would make a stand, he dismounted part of his forces and prepared to make a night-attack. This was the town from which the messenger had been sent to Jackson asking peace, and to which that messenger was that day to return. It was daylight on the 18th before the troops reached the town, which they succeeded in surrounding and surprising. Sixty were killed on the spot, and two hundred and fifty-six persons taken prisoners. The Indians naturally supposed this to be Jackson's answer to their friendly overtures, and from that hour fought with desperation, asking no quarter.

On the 29th of November, Brigadier-General John Floyd fought a general battle with the Creeks at Attasee, some eighteen miles from the Hickory Ground, on the waters of the Tallapoosa. His force was composed of nine hundred and fifty Georgia militia, between three and four hundred friendly Cowetas, under McIntosh, and the Tookabatchees, under their chief, Mad Dog. These fought with intrepidity when incorporated with the line of the troops. After some changes of plan, caused by ignorance of the local geography, the army approached the upper town, where the action became general. "The Indians presented themselves at every point, and fought with the desperate bravery of real fanatics." By the use of artillery and the bayonet the enemy were obliged to retreat and take shelter in houses, thickets, and caves in a high bluff on the river. The action terminated at nine o'clock in the morning, when the town was burned. The loss of the enemy was about two hundred killed, and four hundred buildings are estimated to have been consumed. Floyd's loss was twenty-eight killed and eighty-five wounded.

On the 23d of December, General F. L. Claiborne, with a brigade of volunteers and a part of the Third Regiment of United States troops, attacked the Creek town of Eccanachaca, on the Alabama, about eighty miles above the mouth of the Cahawba. Being advised of his approach, the Indians were prepared for him, and immediately commenced an attack, but they were quickly repulsed, with the loss of thirty warriors killed.

On the night of the 27th of January a large body of Creeks stealthily seized the sentinels, and then attacked the army of General John Floyd, some forty miles west of the Chattahoochee River. They were perfectly wild with fury, and rushed to within fifty yards of the artillery, evincing a rash courage similar to that which the Indians had previously displayed in the action against St. Clair. They were encountered with firmness, and as soon as day dawned were successfully charged with the bayonet and the broadsword. General Floyd gained a complete victory; thirty-seven dead bodies were found on the field, of which fifteen had been sabred. Floyd's loss was twenty killed and one hundred and twenty-five wounded.

The determination with which the Creeks had entered into this war has hardly a precedent in Indian contests. They had been five times defeated in battle; they had lost several hundred men on the battle-field; and upwards of forty of their towns, some of them comprising ninety houses, had been consigned to the flames. The Choctaws and Chickasaws did not assist them, and the Cherokees, being remote, either stood entirely aloof, or only sent out small parties of friendly scouts and spies. A limited number of the Creeks themselves, the tribes of the Cowetas and Tookabatchees, were friendly to the whites; but the main body of the nation fought as if their salvation depended on defeating the Americans. If, as may naturally be conjectured, they opposed Narvaez and De Soto in 1628 and 1641 with this determined spirit, no wonder need be expressed that the former proceeded no farther than the mouth of the Appalachicola, or that the troops of the latter were driven out of the Mississippi Valley. The numerous population of the tribe, located in a genial climate, in which all the productions necessary for the subsistence of Indians grew spontaneously, constituted them a powerful enemy. Their intellectual development and stability of character had also been promoted by intermixture with the Scotch race. It is not improbable, when we consider their heavy losses in battle, that we have never possessed anything like an accurate enumeration of their strength. Major Swan, who visited the country as an official agent in 1791, enumerates fifty-two towns; and, with our knowledge of their fecundity and means of subsistence, they could not well be estimated at less than two hundred souls to each town, which would give an aggregate population of ten thousand four hundred. There could not have been less than three thousand Creek warriors in the field during the greater portion of the years 1812 and 1813 and a part of 1814. The tribe appears to have possessed an active military element, and the spirit to conquer other tribes. According to Bartram, they had been involved in wars and contests before they crossed the Mississippi on their route to the present area of Florida; and, having progressed to the Altamaha, still fighting their way, they first "sat down," to use their metaphor, at the "old fields" on that river. While their council-fire was located at this place, they subdued the Savannas, Ogeechees, Wapoos, Santees, Yamassees, Utinas, Icosans, Paticas, and various other tribes, always making it a rule to incorporate the remnants with themselves, and within the period of our own history they had thus absorbed the Uchees and Natchez.

By a scrutiny of the official documents of that period we are led to infer that the Creek war had been carried on by spirited and gallant leaders, who were, however, deficient in an accurate knowledge of the geography of the country. Military expeditions were led into the interior under the guidance of ignorant men, who frequently misled the officers, and the latter were occasionally content to escape from perilous positions with the *éclat* of a victory which neither secured the possession of the country nor humbled the tribe. Tennessee, however, presented an officer of a very different character in Andrew Jackson, a general of her State militia. He despised fair-weather soldiers and mouthing patriots. His observations of Indian life had given him better defined views of their character, and he saw at a glance that half-measures would not do. The Indian is not a sensitive man, but a stoic by nature as well as by education, and quickly recovers from calamities which are not of long continuance. The Indian's alertness and quickness at the adoption of expedients must be opposed by a similar course of policy. The general who operates against them must be willing and ready to fight by night as well as by day, should not encumber himself with baggage, must occasionally run the risk of losing all his camp equipage for the purpose of defeating his enemy, and must endure hardships and fatigue like an Indian. Jackson's first march to and victory at Talladega taught him all this. The system of rapid movements and impetuous charges introduced by Napoleon, which overthrew the old military tactics of Europe, also gave success to Jackson's operations against the Indians. His attacks were quick and terribly effective.

Notwithstanding the severity of their punishment, the Creeks inhabiting the valley of the Tallapoosa maintained a resolute mien, and even those of the town of Talladega were unintimidated. Very early in January (1814), General Jackson, having been authorized to march against the hostile bands, designated the 10th of that month for the assembling of his new levies of volunteers, including cavalry and infantry, who amounted in the aggregate to nineteen hundred and fifty men. They were not, however, finally mustered until the 17th. On the 18th Jackson reached Talladega fort, where he was joined by between two and three hundred friendly Indians, of whom sixty-five were Cherokees and the remainder Creeks. Learning that the entire force of warriors of the Oakfuskee, New Yaucau, and Eufaula towns was concentrated at a place called Emuckfau, in a bend of the Tallapoosa, he determined to proceed thither. The march was a hazardous one, being over a varied surface and through many defiles, which presented great difficulties to raw and undisciplined troops. On the 20th he encamped at Enotochopco, a Hillabee village, twelve miles from Emuckfau, where he was much chagrined at ascertaining the geographical ignorance of his guides, as well as by discovering the insubordination and want of skill which became apparent in his troops. They were, however, spirited and courageous men, and the following day he pushed on with them to the banks of the Tallapoosa, where he struck a new and well-beaten trail, which disclosed his proximity to the enemy. Late in the day he encamped his troops in a square, doubled his pickets, and made preparations to reconnoitre the enemy's camp the same night. At eleven o'clock his spies returned with the information that the Indians were encamped in great force at the distance of three miles, and either preparing for a march or an attack before daylight. At six o'clock the following morning the Indians commenced a desperate onslaught on Jackson's left, both in front and in rear, which was vigorously met. The contest raged with great violence for half an hour, and was participated in by the most efficient of the field and staff officers, as well as by a reinforcement of infantry which immediately marched to the relief of the troops attacked. As soon as it was sufficiently light to discern surrounding objects, a charge was ordered, which was led by General Coffee; and the enemy, being routed at every point, were pursued with great slaughter for two miles. Jackson then ordered their town to be burned, if practicable, but General Coffee, after marching thither, deemed it unadvisable, and returned. The Indians here evinced some skill in manœuvring, for after Coffee's return they attacked Jackson's right, thinking to draw to that point reinforcements from the left, which had been weakened by the battle in the morning; having made this feint, they immediately prepared to renew their onslaught on the left. This movement had been anticipated by Jackson, who prepared for it by ordering a cavalry charge on the Indians' left, and by strengthening his own left with a body of infantry. The entire line met the enemy with great intrepidity, and after discharging a few rounds made a general charge, the effect of which was immediate: the enemy fled with precipitation, and were pursued by the troops, who poured upon them a galling and destructive fire. In the mean time, Coffee, who had charged the left of the Indians, was placed in considerable jeopardy, some of his force not having joined him, and a part, comprising the friendly Creeks, having left their position. As soon as the front was relieved, the Creeks, who had taken part in the first charge, rejoined Coffee, and enabled him to make another charge, which accomplished his purpose. The enemy fled in confusion, and the field was left in possession of the Americans.

Jackson passed the night in a fortified camp, and on the 23d, at ten o'clock in the morning, commenced his return march to Camp Strother, whence he set out. He encamped on the Enotochopco before dark, having been unmolested on his route, which lay through a dangerous defile. Having a deep creek and another dangerous defile before him, he decided to avoid it by making a détour; but the next morning, while in the act of crossing the creek, the enemy, who from signs observed during the night had been expected, began a furious attack. The vanguard, and a part of the flank columns, as well as all the wounded, had passed over, and the artillery were about to follow, when the alarm-gun was fired. He refaced his whole line for a backward movement, but while the columns were manœuvring to gain a position, a part of the rear of both the right and left columns gave way, causing a great deal of confusion. There then remained but a part of the rear-guard, the artillery, and the company of spies, with which the rout was checked and the attack repulsed. It was on this occasion that Lieutenant Armstrong (the late General Armstrong) performed a deed of heroic valor by ascending an eminence with his gun, under a hot fire, and driving back the enemy with volleys of grape-shot. This battle was fought on the 24th of January. In these actions the loss on each side was very great, and several brave officers fell. There were twenty-four Americans killed and seventy-five wounded, and the bodies of one hundred and eighty-nine Indian warriors were found on the field.

The Indians of the Tallapoosa did not, however, drop the tomahawk, but, having determined to make a more effective stand, they assembled on a peninsula of the Tallapoosa River, called by them Tohopeka, and the Horse-Shoe by the whites. On this point, surrounded on all sides but one by the deep current of the river, one thousand warriors assembled. Across the connecting neck of land, three hundred and fifty yards in width, they had erected a solid breastwork of earth from six to eight feet high, which afforded a perfect covert. This breastwork was so sinuous in its form that it could not be raked even by a cannon placed at one angle, and was so drawn that an approaching enemy would be exposed to both a direct and a raking fire. Behind it was a mass of logs and brushwood. At the bottom of the peninsula, near the river, was a village of huts. The banks of the river were fringed with the canoes of the garrison, so that no retreat was practicable. The Indian force was too small to defend so extensive a line, but they felt confident of their ability to hold it.

General Jackson, who approached it with his army on the 27th of March, thought the position had been admirably selected for defence, and well fortified. He began his approaches by directing General Coffee so to occupy the opposite sides of the river with his mounted men as to prevent the Indians from crossing in canoes. He then proceeded slowly and in complete order to move towards the breastwork in front, at the same time opening a cannonade, at the distance of one hundred and fifty to two hundred yards, with one six- and one three-pounder, using muskets and rifles where an opportunity offered. Meanwhile, General Coffee sent some of his best swimmers across the river, who cut loose and brought away the canoes of the enemy. In these he sent over a party under Colonel Morgan with orders to set fire to the cluster of huts at the bottom of the bend, and then to rush forward and attack the Indians behind the breastwork. This was gallantly done, but proved ineffective. Jackson then ordered his troops to storm the breastwork. Major L. P. Montgomery, the first man to spring upon the breastwork, fell dead. His men soon followed, driving the Indians before them. No quarter was asked for, nor was any accepted when offered. They fought for hours with desperation from behind trees and logs, and from the bluffs on the river-bank. Night put an end to the carnage. Five hundred and fifty-seven Indians were found dead, besides many more who found a grave at the bottom of the river. Jackson's loss was fifty-five killed and one hundred and forty-six wounded. This was the finishing blow. In a few days fourteen of the leading chiefs had submitted. Those of the conquered tribe who despaired of making terms, and those whose spirit was not yet completely crushed, fled to Florida, and there sowed the seed of future wars.

One of the striking scenes in Indian history was the surrender of the Creek chief Weatherford. His father, a white trader who married a Seminole woman, owned a plantation and negroes, became noted as a breeder of fine horses, and won prizes on the Alabama turf. In his son William were united the features of the white man and the frame and complexion of the Indian. His eyes were dark and piercing, and few could withstand the glance of his fiery anger. The white men who were in after-days his neighbors speak of him as an honorable and humane man, a patriot who had endeavored to preserve the independence of his tribe. He was a skilful hunter, and identified himself with the Indians in all respects.

At the time when Tecumseh came from the North to stir up the Southern tribes to war, he was the most influential of the Creek chiefs, but, though in sympathy with him, was not an adherent. But when the news came of the American disasters at the beginning of the war of 1812, when the British cruisers were seen in the Gulf of Mexico, and Spanish Florida was acting in the British interest, then Weatherford joined heart and hand with Tecumseh, and became chief of the war party in Southern Alabama. His surprise and capture of Fort Mims, where he tried in vain to stop the massacre, his battle with Claiborne in December following, when his celebrated exploit, known far and wide as "Weatherford's leap," occurred, the chief escaping his pursuers by spurring his horse headlong over the bluff into the Alabama, and his attack upon General Floyd's camp upon Calabee Creek,—all but a victory,—these exploits sufficiently exhibit the calibre of the man, and rank him with Philip, Pontiac, and Tecumseh. But the battle of the Horse-Shoe annihilated the Creeks as a sovereign power, and Weatherford's force melted away, leaving him alone with a multitude of women and children whom the war had made orphans and widows, and who were perishing for want of food.

Then the chief formed a resolve worthy of his high renown. Mounting his horse, the same that had safely carried him over the Alabama, he rode to Jackson's camp. "How dare you," exclaimed the general, in a furious tone, "ride up to my tent after having murdered the women and children at Fort Mims?"

"General Jackson," replied Weatherford, "I am not afraid of you. I fear no man, for I am a Creek warrior. I have nothing to request in behalf of myself. You can kill me if you desire. But I came to beg you to send for the women and children who are now starving in the woods. Their fields and cribs have been destroyed by your people, who have driven them to the woods without an ear of corn. I tried in vain to prevent the massacre of the women and children at Fort Mims. I am now done fighting. If I could fight you any longer I would most heartily do so. Send for the women and children. They never did you any harm. But kill me if the white people want it done."

A crowd had gathered about the tent. "Kill him! kill him!" cried out some of the soldiers, to whom the hated name of Weatherford was associated only with the horrors of Fort Mims. The general commanded silence, and added, with great energy, "Any man who would kill as brave a man as this would rob the dead." He then invited Weatherford to alight and enter his tent. The chief did so, at the same time presenting him with a deer which he had killed on the way. A friendly conversation ensued, in which were mentioned the terms upon which the nation could be saved. "If you wish to continue the war," Jackson added, "you are at liberty to depart unharmed; but if you desire peace you may remain, and you shall be protected." At the close of the interview, Weatherford retired to his plantation upon Little River. His life being there in constant danger from the relatives of those who had perished at Fort Mims, he withdrew from the State. When the war ended, Weatherford resumed farming in Monroe County, Alabama, and lived many years in peace with the white man, greatly respected for his many good qualities. He died in 1826 from the fatigue caused by a "desperate bear-hunt."[1]

The war with the Creeks was now drawing rapidly to a close, the entire extent of the valleys of the Coosa and Tallapoosa, their strongholds, having been scoured, and their ablest chiefs defeated. Weatherford, the indomitable Black Warrior, on whose head a price had been fixed, had been allowed to return to his nation unharmed, the object of the war being to convince them that the counsels of their prophets were only evil, and destructive to their best interests. Reason having failed to make them acquainted with this fact, the sword was the only resort left. Fortunately for the country, this duty was intrusted to a man noted for his decision, and who also possessed a just conception of the Indian character, capacity, and resources. Had it been otherwise, the war would have been protracted in the same manner as the subsequent contest with the Seminoles of Florida, and, like that war, would possibly have cost the treasury millions of dollars.

One of the most atrocious acts committed by the Creeks was the massacre at Fort Mims, and many of the negroes taken at that time, as also a woman and her children, were now liberated. Tustahatchee, king of the Hickory-Ground band, followed the example of Black Warrior by delivering himself up, and Hillishagee, their prophet, absconded. During the month of April the army swept like a resistless whirlwind over the Creek country, and by the early part of May all its operations were closed except so far as concerned the retention of garrisoned posts.

As the American armies acquired better discipline and greater experience, the assistance of Indian auxiliaries on the flanks of the enemy became less a subject of interest or apprehension, the most important tribes in the South, West, and North having also suffered such defeats as caused them to keep aloof from the contest. Still, though defeated whenever they fought without the aid of their British allies,

---

[1] Pickett's History of Alabama.

they were, as a mass, unfriendly, and ill concealed their secret hostility under the guise of neutrality. They did not, however, fail to rally in their strength whenever the presence of a detachment of regular troops promised them protection. In the sharp action fought by Major A. H. Holmes on the 4th of March, 1814, within twenty miles of the river Thames, and near Detroit, the Indians formed a part of the forces which he had to encounter. Also, in the attempt to retake the fort at Michilimackinac, in the month of August of the same year, the Chippewa, Ottawa, Menomonie, Winnebago, Sac, and Sioux Indians occasioned the defeat of the army under the orders of Colonel Croghan. The troops employed on this service comprised a regiment of infantry and a detachment of artillery, with a supply of ordnance and ammunition adequate to the reduction of the place, had not the plan of attack been ill advised. Instead of sailing directly for the harbor and post located on this cliff-crowned Gibraltar of the Lakes, time was wasted in making an excursion up the St. Mary's Strait and River for the purpose of burning the empty fort on St. Joseph's Island and detaching a party to plunder the Northwest Factory. This force likewise pillaged some private property, and committed other acts of questionable morality. When the fleet of Commodore St. Clair, with the army on board, made the white cliffs of the island, it manœuvred and sailed around it, thus expending some days uselessly, instead of promptly entering the harbor and assaulting the town, which, being but feebly garrisoned, would have been easily captured. On first descrying the fleet the populace were in the wildest confusion. Meantime, the Indians thronged on to the island from the contiguous shores, filling the woods which extended back of the fort. On the margin of this dark forest the attack was made. Major Holmes, who had recently displayed such intrepidity in the engagement on the river Thames, landed with the infantry and artillery, and led them successfully through the paths which wound among the thick foliage of the undergrowth on that part of the island, deploying his men on the open ground of Dousman's farm.

Meantime, Colonel McDowell, who had but sixty regulars in the fort, recruited as many of the Canadian militia as he could muster and equip, marched out to Dousman's, and commenced firing with a six-pounder from an eminence which overlooked the battle-field. Not less than five hundred warriors were on the island, who opposed the landing from their coverts, entirely surrounding the field, and crouching behind clumps of trees on the plain, from which they poured an effective fire. Major Holmes, as soon as his men were formed, pushed forward with great gallantry, waving his sword, and had advanced some hundred yards, when he was shot by an Indian who was concealed behind a bush. When this officer fell the troops faltered, and then retreated to the landing-place. Mr. Madison, in his message of September 20, 1814, observes of Major Holmes, in speaking of this expedition, that "he was an officer justly distinguished for his gallant exploits."

The general battles of the Thames and the Horse-Shoe having in reality broken up the Indian combination in the North and South, they played only a secondary part in those events of the war which occurred subsequently. A few of the friendly Iroquois valiantly aided General P. B. Porter's regulars and militia in the triumphant sortie made from Fort Erie against the British camp on the 17th of September. There were also parties of friendly Creeks, of the Cowetas, under McIntosh, and of the Cherokees and Chickasaws, who performed good service on the side of the Americans. The hostile Creeks, who had been expelled from the Southern plains, having taken shelter at Pensacola, in Florida, General Jackson deemed it essential to the preservation of peace on the frontiers that the governor of that town, and the commander of the fort located there, should have an opportunity of making an explanation of his policy in furnishing protection and supplies to the Indians. With this view he appeared in that vicinity on the 6th of November at the head of the army which had traversed the Creek country, and forthwith dispatched a field-officer to the town with a flag, desiring a conference. The flag being fired on by the cannon of the fort, Jackson immediately determined upon storming the town, and, having made some preliminary reconnoissances, he attacked it with his entire force on the 7th. He was assailed by a fire of musketry from the houses and surrounding gardens, and a battery of two guns opened on his front. This battery was immediately stormed by Captain Laval's company, and, after sustaining a heavy and continuous fire of musketry, the garrison of the fort submitted unconditionally. The Choctaws were highly commended by Jackson for their bravery on this occasion. The following day the Barrancas fort was abandoned and blown up by the enemy, and Colonel Nichols, the governor, retreated to the vessels of the British squadron lying in the bay, which then put to sea.

This action was the closing event of the Indian war in that quarter. "It has convinced the Red Sticks,"[1] remarks the general, "that they have no stronghold or protection except in the friendship of the United States."

---

[1] This term is used in a figurative sense, to denote the Southern hostile Indians.

CHAPTER VI.

TREATIES WITH THE NORTHWESTERN TRIBES, AND EXPLORATIONS OF THEIR TERRITORIES—THE CHIPPEWAS—THE SIOUX—CESSION OF INDIAN LANDS—CHIPPEWA AGENCY ESTABLISHED AT SAULT STE. MARIE.

THE ninth article of the treaty of Ghent, signed December 24, 1814, left the Indian tribes to make their own terms with the United States. They had fought in vain, and had received so little consideration from their late ally at the close of the contest that they were not even accorded a national position in the treaty of peace concluded between the belligerent powers. The year 1815 was the commencement of a new period in their history. Misled by the false theories of their prophets, and defeated in numerous battles, they had yet believed that they were fighting to preserve intact their ancient territorial limits. They had lost great numbers of their warriors in battle the Creeks alone, in their contests with Generals Coffee and Jackson, having suffered to the extent of not less than one thousand men. The losses experienced in battle, by all the tribes, however, were small compared with those they suffered from diseases engendered in camps, superinduced by unsuitable, bad, or scanty supplies of food, as well as by the toils and accidents incident to forced marches. Fevers, colds, and consumptions, to which they are specially liable, had been fearfully prevalent, and the smallpox had nearly decimated them. In addition to this, their families had been left in a starving condition at home. In 1812 the numbers summoned by the voice of the Shawnee prophet to the banks of the Wabash were immense. They abandoned everything for the purpose of participating in this new revolution, and many who left their Western and Northern homes on this errand never returned. The writer has walked over the sites of entire villages thus desolated, which had been in a few years covered by weeds and a young forest growth.

This was not, however, the worst of their misfortunes. Their hunting-grounds had been rendered valueless by the operations of the contending armies. The deer, elk, and bear always precede the Indians to more dense forests; the cunning beaver immediately abandons a stream into which he cannot by gnawing make the trees fall, on the bark of which he subsists; the otter, which lives on fish, remains for a longer period. But all the species of furred animals, whose skins form the staple of the Indian trade, were greatly diminished, and the vast region of country extending from 38° to 44° north, between the Ohio and Mississippi Rivers, had been rendered useless as a hunting-ground. Another result of the passage of troops through remote parts of the Indian country was the discovery of tracts of arable land of great value to the agriculturist, as well as of water-powers, mines, and resources, offering tempting inducements to the mill-wright, manufacturer, and miner. Coal, iron, and lead were found in abundance, and, subsequently, copper and gold. War, bad seasons, and the depreciation of a very extended and inflated paper currency, with a resulting decline in the prices of all merchantable articles, had alarmed thousands of persons in the Atlantic States, who sought to repair their fortunes, or find a field for the exercise of their ingenuity and talents, by emigrating to the West; so that when the Indians began to part freely with their exhausted hunting-grounds by sales to the government, the emigrant masses clamored for new and ample farms on these ceded tracts, where both they and their children might lay the foundations of happy homes. This movement was the germ of new States.

The close of the war of 1812 not only ended the Indian hostilities, but also initiated a thorough geographical exploration of the Mississippi Valley, the extent, fertility, and resources of which were then fully ascertained. Noble rivers, the names of which had been for years known only by their connection with romantic tales and the narratives of adventurous exploits, now attracted attention by the facilities they afforded for navigation. The entire valley seemed to be one vast series of plains, reticulated by streams which poured their resistless currents into the Mexican Gulf. These plains, once the haunts of uncounted herds of deer, elk, and buffalo, were now deserted by them, and elicited interest only by their fertility, and by their adaptiveness to the purposes of agriculture.

We have placed the commencement of this era of emigration in the year 1816, which was as early, indeed, as the full cessation of Indian hostilities rendered it safe for the emigrant to enter remote districts. The Creeks had signed the treaty of Fort Jackson as early as August 9, 1814, and they were followed by other tribes in both the North and the South. On the 8th of September, 1815, an important treaty was concluded with the Wyandots, Senecas, Shawnees, Miamis, Chippewas, Ottawas, and Pottawatomies, by which these tribes were restored to all the immunities accorded them by the treaty entered into at Greenville in 1795, and the three latter tribes reinvested with all the territorial rights which they possessed at the outbreak of Tecumseh's war in 1811. Treaties were also concluded during this year with the Kickapoos, Weas, Winnebagoes, Sacs and Foxes, Sioux, Osages, Chickasaws, Choctaws, and other tribes. These treaties were negotiated by commissioners appointed by the United States, who were well acquainted with the territories, character, resources, local history, and feelings of the tribes. Some of these commissioners had been military commanders, or had occupied high civil stations on the frontiers. No one of them was so celebrated for his knowledge, experience, and standing as General William Clarke, of St. Louis, the companion of the intrepid Lewis in his adventurous journeys to the mouth of the river Columbia in 1804, 1805, and 1806. He had succeeded Lewis as governor of the Missouri Territory in 1806, and had acquired the respect and confidence of the Southwestern and Western tribes who were located on the banks of the Mississippi and Missouri Rivers. He was a man possessed of great sagacity, amenity of manners, and a comprehensive knowledge of the geography of the country. In many respects he was comparable to Sir William Johnson, who so long exercised a similar power in the North. Indian disputes were frequently referred to him for settlement by the tribes themselves, and the number of Indian treaties he negotiated in the course of his long administration of Indian affairs on the frontiers is a proof of his abilities in this department.

The war of 1812 on the Northwestern frontiers had brought into notice another man who was destined to exercise for many years an important influence on our Indian relations. Lewis Cass was a brigadier-general in the United States army, and had served in the war of 1812 with great credit to himself. A lawyer by profession, marshal of the State of Ohio at the commencement of the war, he united civil with military talent, and on the conclusion of peace held the commission of commandant of Detroit, succeeding to the executive chair of Michigan after the overthrow of Governor William Hull and the subsequent interregnum. Great energy was required to revive and reinstate on their former basis its civil and social institutions. Six years of wild wars and turmoils had left the Territory without either civil or military organization. It was a work of time to restore the Indian relations to a permanent footing, to induce the inhabitants to return to their old locations, to apply the civil code to an almost anarchical condition of society, and, above all, to ascertain and develop the resources of the Territory.

Michigan had been a very strong rallying-point for the Indians from the days of Denonville. It was visited by La Salle in 1679, and formal possession was taken of the straits between Lakes Erie and Huron in the month of June, 1687, but Detroit was not occupied by an authorized agent of the French government at Quebec until the year 1701.[1] One hundred and twenty years had served to spread its fame and importance in Indian wars, Indian trade, and Indian affairs. But the hand of time had still left it a remote outpost, surrounded by the original French settlements, among which might here and there be found an adventurous American. The houses of the French *habitans* were surrounded with cedar palings, as if to resist an attack, and in their orchards they raised apple-trees the parent stocks of which were originally brought from Normandy. In their dress, manners, suavity, nonchalance, gayety, and loyalty to the governing power, the French of Michigan presented a striking similitude to the peasantry under Francis I. and Louis XIII. It was at this ancient seat of French dominion on the lakes that Pontiac formed his confederacy in 1760 and Tecumseh convened the natives in 1810–11. The failure of the latter, stoutly backed as he was by the British army and navy, convinced the Indians that their efforts to resist the onward march of civilization were vain, and that education, arts, and labor must triumph. This was the language of Ningwégon in 1812.

In 1814 General Lewis Cass was appointed governor of this Territory, the condition of which has been shown to have been one of extreme prostration. Desolated

---

[1] M. Cadillac arrived at this spot on the 24th of July, 1701, and immediately commenced clearing the ground and preparing to fortify it.

by wars, its inhabitants decimated by appalling murders and massacres, with but few resources, and neither enterprise nor capital, another such forlorn district could not have been pointed out in America. It had neither roads nor bridges, and its very soil was considered so worthless that it was deemed unfit to be given in bounty-lands to the surviving soldiers of the war of 1812. The Indian tribes who had rallied under Proctor and Tecumseh were still unfriendly and vindictive. By the interposition of a friendly hand, Cass's life was once saved from a rifle-ball aimed by an Indian from behind a tree, and many of the red men hovered around Detroit, destitute of everything, daily besieging the doors of the Territorial executive. The tide of emigration had not at that period set strongly in that direction, and the business of the Superintendent of Indian Affairs on that frontier was for some years the most important function of the gubernatorial office. Cass commenced his negotiations with the sons of the forest at the rapids of the Maumee on the 29th of September, 1817. This event was followed in 1818 by an important assemblage of various Algonkin tribes at St. Mary's, near the sources of the Maumee, and in 1819 by the conclusion of an important treaty with the Chippewas of Saginaw, in Michigan, which gave an impetus to settlements in that Territory. The wide area over which the Chippewa tribe extended, its multiplicity of bands or tribal communities, each of which professed to be independent, and the imperfect knowledge of their location and statistics, as well as of the geographical features and resources of their territory, induced Governor Cass to call the attention of the War Department to their examination. The cherished policy of Mr. Calhoun being to keep the military posts in the West in advance of the settlements, that they might cover the progress of the new emigrants and shield them from Indian depredations, the Secretary cordially approved of this measure; to carry out the objects of which an expedition composed of a corps of scientific observers, under the escort of a small detachment of infantry, was organized at and despatched from Detroit in the spring of 1820. This enterprise first brought Mr. Schoolcraft into the new field of observation on Indian life and manners. Being appointed geologist to the expedition, he became its historiographer, and during the following year published a journal of its progress. The extent of Indian hunting-grounds traversed was nearly four thousand miles, and at only one point, namely, St. Mary's Falls, at the lower end of Lake Superior, was there any demonstration of hostile feelings. The effect of this extensive exploratory tour was to convince the Indians that a wise government sought to ascertain the extent of their territory and its resources, as well as to bring the tribes into friendly communication with it. The Chippewas were found, with some slight change of name, to occupy the entire borders of Lakes Huron and Superior, together with the eastern side of the valley of the Upper Mississippi, above lat. 44° 53' 20" north. On the west banks, in about lat. 46°, the frames of Sioux lodges were still standing which had evidently been but recently occupied. On the 30th of July they reached the Falls of St. Anthony, between which and Prairie du Chien, but nearer to the latter, the Sioux inhabited both banks of the river. The Sacs and Foxes occupied the Mississippi Valley between Prairie du Chien and Rock Island, at the entrance to the river Des Moines. The Winnebagoes were in possession of the Wisconsin and Rock River Valleys. The Menomonies were scattered along the Fox River to Buttes des Morts and Winnebago Lake, thence quite to Green Bay, and, with interchanges of location with the Winnebagoes, to Milwaukee on Lake Michigan. Some Pottawatomies, Chippewas, and Ottawas were located at Chicago, as also in Northern Illinois and Southern Michigan. Ottawas also lived in Grand River Valley, as well as on Little Traverse Bay, and the Chippewas on the peninsula and shores of Grand Traverse Bay. An escort of infantry having accompanied this expedition, the flag of the Union was thus displayed in regions where previously it had seldom or never been seen.

The effect of this expedition was not only to attract the attention of the Indians to the power and vigilance of the government, but also to direct popular enterprise to this hitherto unceded part of the Union, the value and importance of which can already be attested by an examination of Upper Michigan, Wisconsin, Iowa, and Minnesota.

During the exploration several instances were observed of the Indian mode of communicating ideas by pictographic inscriptions on scrolls of bark. Statistics of their population and trade were obtained, and knowledge was acquired of their manners and customs, feelings and disposition. One of the peculiar customs observed while in the Dakota country was that of offering the first ears of the green corn to the Great Spirit, of which ceremony the party were, by permission of the chiefs, allowed to be spectators.

In the Chippewa territories, extending from the precincts of Rock Island to the sources of the Mississippi, the ruling power was found to be exercised by certain totemic families, who claimed the right by descent. This right, however, was ascertained to be nugatory when not supported by the popular voice of the clans, which voice virtually bestowed upon this rude government all the force of a representative system. The ancient seat of the Chippewas, at Sault Ste. Marie, at the lower end of Lake Superior, had for its ruling chief Shingabawassin, a tall, well-made, grave man, who possessed an easy, dignified, and pleasing manner. The Indians residing on the upper shores of the lake were ruled by a chief called Pezhikee, or Buffalo, and Sappa. At Sandy Lake, on the Upper Mississippi, Katawabeda, Babisikundabi, and Gueule Plat were the presiding chiefs. The Mendawakantons, or Dakotas of the River, acknowledged the government of the younger Wabasha. The Winnebagoes were ruled by De Corrie and Tshoop, the *quatre jambes*, or "Four Legs," of the French. The Pottawatomies acknowledged the sway of Topinabee, an aged man, who had signed the treaty of peace concluded at Greenville by General Wayne in 1795. At Grand River presided the Ottawa chief Nawagizhi, or Noon-Day; at Grand Traverse Bay, Aishquagonabi, or the Feather of Honor; and at the Ottawa towns of L'Arbre Croche, the very old chief Nishcaudjinine, or the Angry Man, and Pauskooziegun, or the Smoker.

The Indian government, though founded on certain established customs and prescriptions, was largely controlled by popular opinion, which changed with the passage of time and the occurrence of events. Although the totemic sovereignty was hereditary, yet among most of the tribes the tribal succession could be set aside at any time when it was thought necessary to reward with the chieftaincy bravery on the war-path, great energy of character, talent as a speaker, or skill as a magician, and the tribes were thenceforth ruled by the newly-installed chief.

Treaties were concluded with the Indians at L'Arbre Croche and at Sault Ste. Marie. An incident occurred at the latter place which for a time threatened serious difficulty. The negotiations for this treaty were begun about the middle of June, at which period of the year, the hunting season being ended, the Indians crowd to the towns nearest the frontiers, to enjoy themselves in dancing, feasting, and the celebration of ceremonies. Only four or five years having elapsed since the conclusion of the war, there was still a vivid feeling of hostility existing among them towards the Americans. It chanced that among the large number assembled was a war-captain who had led the Chippewas into action,—an ambitious chief called Sassaba, of the reigning totem of the Crane, whose brother had been killed fighting beside Tecumseh at the battle of the Thames. An attempt was made to deter Cass's party from carrying the American flag through the Chippewa country. Sassaba, having broken up a public council, raised the British flag on a brow of the height where the Indians were encamped, and it was observed that at the same moment women and children were precipitately sent from the lodges across the river to the Canada shore. Strong apprehensions were entertained of a hostile encounter: the party grasped their rifles and stood ready for conflict. General Cass, by his knowledge of the Indian character, and his self-possession and decision, disconcerted their plans and averted the danger. Unarmed, and accompanied only by an interpreter, he ascended the elevated plain on which the Indians were encamped, and, proceeding to the lodge of Sassaba, pulled down the flag, and addressed the Indians in terms of just reproof for this act of bravado. This rebuke was received without any demonstration of hostility. On the following day negotiations were renewed, and a treaty was concluded, which renewed an old grant originally made to the French by a cession of territory four miles square.

When the French traders and missionaries first visited the head of Lake Superior, which event may be placed as early as the year 1620, the Chippewas and Sioux were at war. The most ancient local traditions, both of the red and the white men, represent the Chippewas to have migrated from the east towards the west, and to have conquered certain Indian tribes, from whom they wrested the territories lying west of Lake Superior. Traditional evidence attesting the early existence of hostility between these two prominent tribes was obtained in 1820 during the expedition through their territory to the sources of the Mississippi. The history of the contest, as well as its origin and cause, was investigated as a preliminary step towards effecting a pacification between the contending tribes. In an official communication to the government, Governor Cass makes the following observations regarding this hereditary war, which are worthy of notice, not only as embodying the views of aged and respectable chiefs then living, with whom he conversed, but also because they reveal the existence of a means of communication between the Indians through the interchange of ideographic notes by devices inscribed on slips of the inner bark of the paper-birch:

"The Chippewas and Sioux are hereditary enemies, and Charlevoix says they were at war when the French first reached the Mississippi. I endeavored when among them to learn the cause which first excited them to war, and the time when it commenced. But they can give no rational account. An intelligent Chippewa chief informed me that the disputed boundary between them was a subject of little importance, and that the question respecting it could be easily adjusted. He appeared to think that they fought because their fathers fought before them. This war has been waged with various success, and in its prosecution instances of courage and self-devotion have occurred within a few years which would not have disgraced the pages of Grecian or of Roman history. Some years since, mutually weary of hostilities, the chiefs of both nations met and agreed upon a truce. But the Sioux, disregarding the solemn compact which they had formed, and actuated by some sudden impulse, attacked the Chippewas, and murdered a number of them. Babisikundabi, the old Chippewa chief, who descended the Mississippi with us, was present upon this occasion, and his life was saved by the intrepidity and generous self-devotion of a Sioux chief. This man entreated, remonstrated, and threatened. He urged his countrymen, by every motive, to abstain from any violation of their faith, and, when he found his remonstrances useless, he attached himself to this Chippewa chief and avowed his determination of saving or perishing with him. Awed by his intrepidity, the Sioux finally agreed that he should ransom the Chippewa, and he accordingly applied to this object all the property he owned. He then accompanied the Chippewa on his journey until he considered him safe from any parties of the Sioux who might be disposed to follow him.

"The Sioux are much more numerous than the Chippewas, and would have overpowered them long since had the operations of the former been consentaneous. But they are divided into so many different bands, and are scattered over such an extensive country, that their efforts have no regular combination.

"Believing it equally consistent with humanity and sound policy that these border contests should not be suffered to continue, satisfied that you would approve of any plan of pacification which might be adopted, and feeling that the Indians have a full portion of moral and physical evils without adding to them the calamities of a war which had no definite object and no probable termination, on our arrival at Sandy Lake I proposed to the Chippewa chiefs that a deputation should accompany us to the mouth of the St. Peter's with a view to establish a permanent peace between them and the Sioux. The Chippewas readily acceded to this proposition, and ten of their principal men descended the Mississippi with us.

"As we approached St. Peter's, our Chippewa friends became cautious and observing. The flag of the United States was flying upon all our canoes, and, thanks to the character which our nation acquired by the events of the last war, I found in our progress through the whole Indian country, after we had once left the great lines of communication, that this flag was a passport which rendered our journey safe.

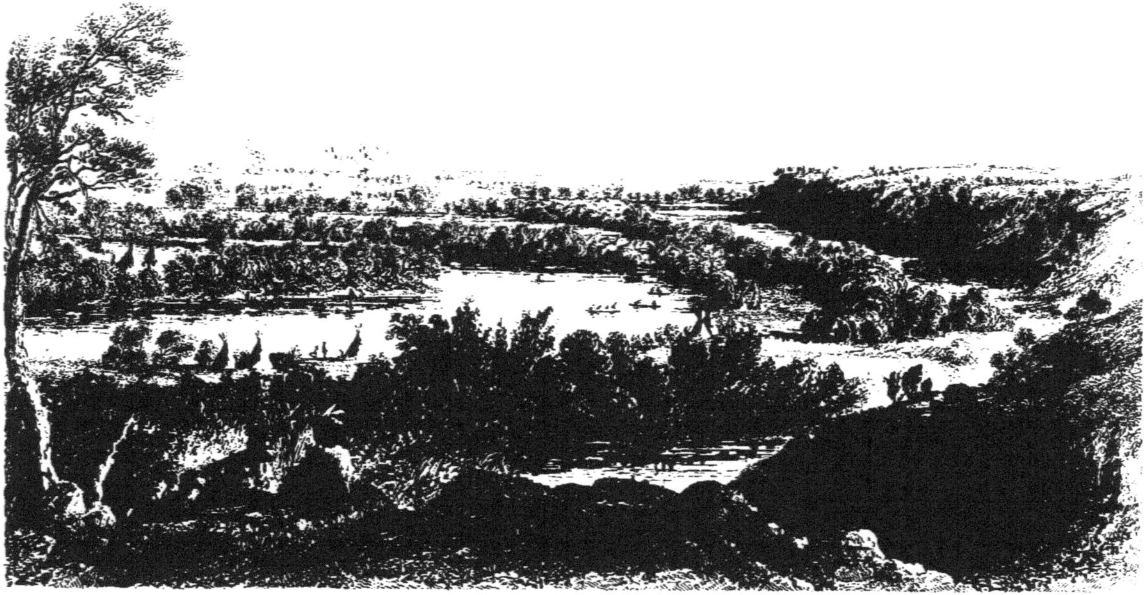

We consequently felt assured that no wandering party of the Sioux would attack even their enemies while under our protection. But the Chippewas could not appreciate the influence which the American flag would have upon other nations; nor is it probable that they estimated with much accuracy the motives which induced us to assume the character of an umpire.

"The Chippewas landed occasionally, to examine whether any of the Sioux had recently visited that quarter. In one of these excursions a Chippewa found in a conspicuous place a piece of birch bark, made flat by being fastened between two sticks at each end, and about eighteen inches long by fifteen broad. This bark contained the answer of the Sioux nation to the proposition which had been made by the Chippewas for the termination of hostilities. So sanguinary has been the contest between these tribes that no personal communication could take place. Neither the sanctity of the office nor the importance of the message could protect the ambassadors of either party from the vengeance of the other. Some time preceding, the Chippewas, anxious for the restoration of peace, had sent a number of their young men into these plains with a similar piece of bark, upon which they had represented their desire. The scroll of bark had been left hanging to a tree in an exposed situation, and had been found and taken away by a party of the Sioux.

"The propositions had been examined and discussed in the Sioux villages, and the bark which we found contained their answer. The Chippewa who had prepared the bark for his tribe was with us, and on our arrival at St. Peter's, finding it was lost, I requested him to make another. He did so, and produced what I have no doubt was a perfect *fac-simile*.

"The Chippewas explained to us with great facility the intention of the Sioux, and apparently with as much readiness as if some common character had been established between them.

"The junction of the St. Peter's with the Mississippi, where a principal part of the Sioux reside, was represented, and also the American fort, with a sentinel on duty, and the flag flying. The principal Sioux chief is named the Six, alluding, I believe, to the bands or villages under his influence. To show that he was not present at the deliberations upon the subject of peace, he was represented upon a smaller piece of bark, which was attached to the other. To identify him, he was drawn with six heads and a large medal. Another Sioux chief stood in the foreground, holding the pipe of peace in his right hand and his weapons in his left. Even we could not misunderstand that. Like our own eagle, with the olive-branch and arrows, he was desirous of peace but prepared for war.

"The Sioux party contained fifty-nine warriors, and this number was indicated by fifty-nine guns, which were drawn upon one corner of the bark. The only subject which occasioned any difficulty in the interpretation of the Chippewas was owing to an incident of which they were ignorant. The encampment of our troops had been removed from the low grounds upon the St. Peter's to a high hill upon the Mississippi: two forts were therefore drawn upon the bark; and the solution of this enigma could not be discovered till our arrival at St. Peter's.

"The effect of the discovery of this bark upon the minds of the Chippewas was visible and immediate. Their doubts and apprehensions appeared to be removed, and during the residue of the journey their conduct and feelings were completely changed.

"The Chippewa bark was drawn in the same general manner, and Sandy Lake, the principal place of their residence, was represented with much accuracy. To remove any doubt respecting it, a view was given of the old Northwest establishment, situated upon its shore, and now in the possession of the American Fur Company. No proportion was preserved in their attempt at delineation. One mile of the Mississippi, including the mouth of the St. Peter's, occupied as much space as the whole distance to Sandy Lake, nor was there anything to show that one part was nearer to the spectator than another; yet the object of each party was completely obtained. Speaking languages radically different from each other (for the Sioux constitute one of three grand divisions into which the early French writers have arranged the aborigines of our country, while the Chippewas are a branch of what they call Algonkins), and without any conventional character established between them, these tribes thus opened a communication upon the most important subject which could occupy their attention. Propositions leading to a peace were made and accepted, and the simplicity of the mode could only be equalled by the distinctness of the representations and by the ease with which they were understood.

"The Sioux language is probably one of the most barren which is spoken by any of our aboriginal tribes. Colonel Leavenworth, who made considerable proficiency in it, calculated, I believe, that the number of words did not exceed one thousand. They use more gestures in their conversation than any Indians I have seen, and this is a necessary result of the poverty of their language."

Reference has been already made to the immigration which commenced after the close of the war of 1814. Such a transfer of population had never then been known to have occurred. In all other countries, prior to this era, civilization had proceeded with slow and measured steps, but here it moved forward with such rapid strides that the expedition of the Argonauts and the march of the Huns into Europe sink into insignificance when contrasted with it. Unlike those efforts, it was not a hostile inroad backed by the spear and the sword, but a peaceful movement of agriculturists, artisans, and artists. The plough, the hammer, the sickle, and the hoe were the means of extending this vast empire, which was conquered in a very short period. Ohio, Kentucky, Tennessee, and Louisiana were occupied, and entered the Union at an early day, though not without some little delay; but Indiana, Mississippi, Illinois, Alabama, and Missouri seemed to spring into existence as if by magic, and were admitted into the confederacy within six years after the conclusion of the treaty of Ghent. Owing to this cause, the demands made on the Indians for new territory were continuous, and the circle of civilization was constantly expanding, while that of the hunter was proportionally contracting. It would be anything but a light task to trace the resulting sequence of treaties, cessions, annuities, and stipulations for the payment of coin, merchandise, seeds, implements, and cattle to the savage in return for his land, but while any section of their territories abounded in game the Indians elected to retire thither, and bestowed but little attention on either grazing or agriculture. There was, therefore, a singular concurrence in the desire of the emigrants to buy and in the willingness of the Indians to sell their lands.

Some of these treaties merit notice on account of the wide-spread and beneficial influence they exercised. In the month of August, 1821, the Pottawatomies, Chippewas, and Ottawas, of Illinois and Western Michigan, having been summoned to attend a council at Chicago, about three thousand persons assembled at that place. On the 17th of that month the public conferences were opened with the chiefs, when the commissioners laid before them the business for the transaction of which the council had been convened. The venerable chief Topinabee, who had been present at Greenville in 1795, where he signed the treaty then concluded, and who had also appended his name to that formed at the rapids of the Maumee in 1817, was the principal personage among the sachems and counsellors. The most conspicuous speaker was Metea, a Pottawatomie, from the Wabash, whose tall and slender person was disfigured by a withered arm, and whose sullen dignity of manners was relieved by sparkling black eyes, a good voice, and ready utterance. He was the popular speaker on this occasion, and, as he possessed considerable reflective powers, his opinions and sentiments may perhaps be regarded as fairly representing those of the Algonkin tribes of his day. "My father," he said, addressing the delegated authority of the government, "you know that we first came to this country a long time ago, and when we sat ourselves down upon it we met with a great many hardships and difficulties. Our country was then very large, but now it is dwindled to a small spot, and you wish to purchase that. This has caused us much reflection, and we bring all our chiefs and warriors and families to hear you.

"Since you first came among us we have listened with an attentive ear to your words, we have hearkened to your counsels. Whenever you have had a favor to ask of us our answer has been invariably yes!

"A long time has passed since we came upon these lands. Our old people have all sunk into their graves; they had sense. We are all young and foolish, and would not do anything they could not approve if living. We are fearful to offend their spirits if we sell our lands. We are fearful to offend you if we do not. We do not know how we can part with the land.

"Our country was given to us by the Great Spirit to hunt upon, to make cornfields to live on, and, when life is over, to spread down our beds upon and lie down. That Spirit would never forgive us if we sold it. When you first spoke to us at St. Mary's we said we had a little land, and sold you a piece. But we told you we could spare no more. Now you ask us again. You are never satisfied. . . .

"Take notice, it is a small piece of land where we now live. It has been wasting away ever since the white people became our neighbors. We have now hardly enough to cover the bones of our tribe."

The discussions of the conference were principally sustained by Topinabee, Metea, Metawa, and Keewaygooshkum, with more spirit, freedom, and justice of reasoning than the Indians generally evince. Full two weeks were devoted to the discussion of the treaty, which was finally signed on the 20th of the month. By it these nations ceded five millions of acres lying within the southern boundaries of Michigan, but from this tract four hundred and eighty-four square miles were reserved for the Indians. A permanent annuity of one thousand dollars in coin was granted, as also a limited annuity of fifteen hundred dollars per annum, which was designed to be used for the promotion of agriculture and the advancement of the useful arts.

The exploratory expedition through the Great Lakes to the sources of the Mississippi in a few years led to the introduction of an agency among the widely-dispersed Chippewa nation on that frontier. Owing to the rapid establishment of settlements in the valley of the Wabash, the Indian tribes inhabiting it found the middle and lower parts of it, which they had reserved for hunting-grounds, of little or no value. As early as the year 1820 the Kickapoo and Wea tribes entered into treaty stipulations with the agent at Vincennes by which they ceded their reservations and transferred their interests in consideration of annuities to be paid to them at locations farther south and west. The Miamis residing on the head-waters of the Wabash had for many years reported themselves to and received their annuities from the superintendent of the agency at Fort Wayne. The old Vincennes agency being no longer necessary, the President, by virtue of the power vested in him to remove such agencies to new fields of duty, in the spring of 1822 transferred it to Sault Ste. Marie, at the outlet of Lake Superior, and appointed Mr. Schoolcraft as agent, with directions to establish an intercourse with the Chippewa nation. This officer accompanied a detachment, comprising a full battalion of the Second Regiment of Infantry, to that remote position, arriving there on the 6th of July. Fort Brady was erected at this point. Sault Ste. Marie, an ancient seat of the Chippewas, had been occupied by the French as early as 1644, and became the site of one of the earliest Jesuit missions. It was from this point that D'Ablon and Marquette had at successive periods explored the country around Lake Superior, and the latter returned from the shores of the Great Lake to this place prior to the establishment of the mission at Point St. Ignace and Michilimackinac. At the period of the capture of Quebec and of the occupation of Canada by the British, in 1760, the missionary operations had been transferred to another locality, but from the narrative of Alexander Henry's visit thither in 1760 we learn that a military post was still maintained there, to protect the operations of the Indian traders and to preserve general friendly relations with this branch of the Algonkin family of tribes. The accession of the United States to the sovereign power in this part of the Union was greatly retarded. When the Lake posts were surrendered in 1796, after Wayne's campaign, the American flag replaced that of St. George at Michilimackinac, but the authority of the republic was not acknowledged at Sault Ste. Marie, and in 1806 Pike found the entire Indian trade in the hands of British factors. The St. Mary's River and Lake Superior, indeed, formed the line of demarcation between the British colonies and the United States, agreeably to the original treaty of 1783, which was reaffirmed by that of Ghent in 1814, but the line remained unsurveyed, and consequently many portions were disputed. Major Holmes, who visited the place in August, 1814, finding that the Northwest Company, whose factory was situated at the foot of the falls, on the north shore, was exerting an influence adverse to the United States, destroyed the establishment. The large private trading establishment of John Johnston, Esq., a gentleman from the north of Ireland, located on the opposite or American shore of the falls, suffered severely at the same time,—an impression prevailing that it was either connected with the Northwest Factory, or that an unfriendly feeling was generated against the Union among the Chippewas, over whom Mr. Johnston had much influence. It was not until 1816 that Congress perceived that it was necessary to the preservation of peace on the frontiers to pass an act placing this trade exclusively under the control of Americans, and forbidding its being carried on by British subjects, or the employment of British capital therein. The purpose contemplated by this measure was one which required time to accomplish. The Indians, being attached to the British rule, were slow to give their confidence to Americans.

The first important enterprise in connection with this trade was that of John Jacob Astor, of New York, who visited Montreal in 1816, and purchased all the property, consisting of trading-houses, boats, etc., belonging to the Northwest Company, located between St. Joseph's Island and the parallel of 49° north latitude. He organized the American Fur Company, which established its central depot and place of outfit at Michilimackinac. An important feature in the inauguration of this new commercial enterprise was that the Canadian boatmen, interpreters, clerks, and subordinates employed by the company were precisely the same persons who had previously served the Northwest Company. The feelings of the Indians were not easily changed, and they were deeply prejudiced against the American character. As an illustration of this feeling, we may mention that when Generals Brown and Macomb came to this place to reconnoitre it, in 1818, and were gratifying their taste by a short exploratory trip on Lake Superior, their boat was fired on by Indians above the falls. So late as the year 1820, as we have seen, the Chippewas, from their ancient camping-ground on the American side of the river, attempted to resist the passage of the exploring expedition into their country.

It was not, therefore, an ordinary task to induce this important tribe to acknowledge fealty to the American government. Firmness of purpose, combined with mildness of manner, was eminently necessary. The establishment of an agency, a smithy, and an armorer's shop, the supply of food to them in their necessity, and the bestowal of presents, were important means. The display of so considerable a force on the frontier as the garrison of Fort Brady enabled the agent to act efficiently. By acting in concurrence with the military, an effective controlling power was established. Murderers of white men were demanded from the Indians, the country was cleared of freed men, or discharged boatmen, who had taken up a permanent residence among the Indians, and none but licensed traders, with their boatmen, were permitted to pass into the country. Ardent spirits were excluded. The remote chiefs soon began to visit the agency. The Indians are very fond of making visits to distant parts of the country, and are always gratified with the comity and ceremony of diplomatic attention. The pacific results of this intercourse soon began to appear.

The principal chief at Sault Ste. Marie was a tall and dignified man, called Shingabawassin, a term used to designate a species of abraded stones found on the lake shores, which assume various imitative forms and are connected in their minds with magical influences. His armorial badge was the Crane totem, the distinguishing mark of the reigning clan. Shingabawassin had in his youth been on the war-path, but he was at this period principally respected for his prudence and wisdom in council. He was about six feet three inches in height, straight in form, having a Roman cast of countenance, and mild manners; he was a good speaker, but prone to repetition. He had three brothers, likewise chiefs, and a large retinue of cousins-german and other relatives, who generally followed him. The attainment of his good will insured the friendship of the tribe, through whom an extensive influence was established with the interior bands.

CHAPTER VII.

EMIGRATION OF THE EASTERN CHEROKEES SANCTIONED—TREATIES WITH THE SOUTHERN TRIBES—INDIAN BUREAU ORGANIZED.

A GENERAL peace was concluded with the Cherokee nation on the 14th of September, 1816.

As early as the year 1808 the project of drawing a dividing line between the upper and lower bands of the Cherokees was broached in this nation. The idea promulgated was to erect lines of demarcation between the hunter bands and those who wished to pursue agriculture and adopt a more regular form of government. A deputation of both parties was sent to Washington to obtain an interview with the President, and, as they clearly foresaw the impracticability of effecting their object while they remained in their existing location, to procure his sanction to a proposal on the part of the hunter portion to emigrate to some part of the territory of the United States west of the Mississippi, where they would be able to find game in greater abundance.

On the 9th of January, 1809, Mr. Jefferson, who was then in the Presidential chair, returned the deputation an answer, and gave his sanction to this plan, in these words:

"The United States, my children, are the friends of both parties, and, as far as can be reasonably asked, they are willing to satisfy the wishes of both. Those who remain may be assured of our patronage, our aid and good neighborhood; those who wish to remove are permitted to send an exploring party to reconnoitre the country on the waters of the Arkansas and White Rivers, and the higher up the better, as they will be the longer unapproached by our settlements which will begin at the mouths of those rivers. The regular districts of the government of St. Louis are already laid off to the St. Francis.

"When this party shall have found a tract of country suiting the emigrants, and not claimed by other Indians, we will arrange with them and you for an exchange of that for a just portion of the country they leave, and to a part of which, proportioned to their numbers, they have a right. Every aid towards their removal, and what will be necessary for them there, will then be freely administered to them, and when established in their new settlements we shall still consider them as our children, give them the benefit of exchanging their peltries for what they will want at our factories,[1] and always hold them firmly by the hand."

This sanction to the emigration of a part of the Cherokees may be considered as

---

[1] The factory system was not abolished by Congress till 1822.

the initiatory step in the plan of a general removal of the tribes from the old States to the westward of the Mississippi,—one, however, which required the national experience of sixteen years to guarantee and fully adopt.

At the Cherokee Agency, on the 8th of July, 1817, this measure received the sanction of the commissioners[1] appointed to treat with the nation. This treaty made provision for the proper distribution of the annuities of the tribes between the East and West Cherokees, and also for taking a full and perfect census of the whole nation during the following year. Other stipulations and agreements were entered into, discordant opinions respecting the faithful and prompt execution of which have been the occasion of the internal dissensions which have distracted that nation. From the treaty concluded by Mr. Calhoun with the nation at Washington on the 27th of February, 1819, we learn that the census prescribed for the year 1818 was not taken. New boundary-lines were designated for the Cherokee territories lying east of the Mississippi, a fund was set apart for the use of schools, and a division of the national annuities made, it being agreed that one-third of the amount should be paid to the Cherokees west of the Mississippi, and the other two-thirds to those residing east of that river. The stipulation that white emigrants should be prevented from settling on the lands situate along the Arkansas and White Rivers was renewed.[2]

The Creeks had been after a hard struggle subdued rather than conquered in the war of 1814, but their disastrous defeat on the Tallapoosa, at the battle of the Horse-Shoe, March 27, was so discouraging that they did not again venture to assume a warlike attitude. On the 9th of August, 1814, they signed a treaty of peace with a feeling of humiliation and disappointment. This treaty was in the first instance subscribed by Tustannuggee Thlucco and thirty-six of the leading miccos and chiefs of both the upper and the lower division of the nation. During the entire continuance of the war considerable feeling had existed among the Americans against the Spanish and British authorities in Florida, and particularly against the traders who had furnished the Creeks with supplies of arms and ammunition. Those members of the Creek nation who fled to Pensacola after their final defeat on the Tallapoosa did not present themselves in the council which formed this treaty, or signify their submission by sending delegates to it. On the 6th of the following November, the southern coasts being then strictly blockaded by the enemy, the American army, as previously stated, appeared before the gates of Pensacola, and succeeded in taking that fortress. No further aid being furnished to the tribes from foreign sources, a general peace resulted. The stipulations of this treaty were subsequently carried out and extended by another formed March 28, 1818, and by that concluded January 8, 1821.

The Chickasaws and Choctaws had maintained a position of neutrality during the war, but a few individuals of each tribe were present in the American camp during the Creek war, which circumstance furnishes a reason for the recital of the

---

[1] Andrew Jackson, Joseph McMinn, and D. Meriwether.

[2] Mr. Schoolcraft passed through that tract in 1818, and found the country occupied by white hunters and trappers, who were bitterly opposed to the coming of the Cherokees.

names of these two tribes in the treaty of pacification with the Creek nation, signed August 8, 1814. These tribes, as mentioned in preceding pages, lay claim to high antiquity in the country, to which they migrated from the West at an early period. The Chickasaw nation possesses a tradition which evidently refers to the landing of De Soto on the Chickasaw bluffs.

The treaty entered into October 10, 1821, with the Choctaws may be said to have inaugurated a new and important feature in the policy of the Indian removals. Heretofore treaties had been made for temporary purposes only, the Indians consuming the principal of their annuities, and establishing no fund which would be beyond the reach of agrarian distribution, paying also but little regard to their permanent welfare or their intellectual advancement. This treaty would seem to indicate their apprehension that the pressure of the surrounding white population would render it impossible for them to reside permanently east of the Mississippi River. They stipulated that the same quantity of land which they held east of that river should be given to them west of it, and its possession guaranteed. This was exclusive of a tract in the East to be temporarily retained by them and divided into farms, on which they were to remain until they had attained a state of civilization and advancement in industrial arts which would qualify them for beginning their Western emigration. They were also to receive temporary aid while in their present location and after removing to the West. The most striking feature in this treaty was the appropriation of the proceeds of fifty-four sections, each one mile square, of the ceded lands, to constitute a school fund. In the same treaty provision was made for the support of the deaf, dumb, blind, and distressed of the tribe, and for the payment of an annuity to a superannuated chief of their nation called Mushulatubbee. Power was granted to the United States agents to seize and destroy all ardent spirits introduced into their country, and a police force, under the name of lighthorse, was authorized to act as a *posse comitatus* in maintaining order and enforcing obedience to the laws.

The increase in the number of treaties, and of the Indian business generally, began to press so heavily on the Secretary of War that in 1824 he placed this department under the charge of Thomas L. McKenney, Esq., as chief of the clerical staff, an office for the establishment of which Congress subsequently passed an act. A regular system of accountability was established in all departments of the bureau, affecting all officers, from the lowest to the highest.

From early times a close connection had existed between the civil and military departments of Indian affairs, and while the tribes stood in their normal hunter state it was difficult to manage the one without reference to the other. Sir William Johnson, as early as 1757, only two years subsequent to his appointment as General Superintendent, had endeavored to relieve himself from the onerous duties of his office by the employment of a secretary, a man of talents and learning, who was in the habit of preparing the reports transmitted to the Lords of Plantations. During the war of the Revolution, and subsequent thereto, Congress managed the government of Indian affairs by intrusting it to commissioners for the North and South, who were usually men of sound practical experience and judgment. The executive documents abound in details of their acts. On the organization of the present government, in 1789, General Knox negotiated one or more treaties. The same system prevailed from Washington's administration through the administrations of Adams the elder, Jefferson, Madison, and Monroe, and when the bureau was organized by Congress it was continued under the administrations of the younger Adams, Jackson, Van Buren, Harrison, and Polk, at the close of whose term of office, by an act of Congress, the duty was transferred from the War Department to that of the Interior.

Among the men who rendered long and valuable services in this department, General Harrison and General William Clarke deserve especial mention. As *ex-officio* Superintendents of Indian Affairs, while performing the duties appertaining to the office of Governor of the Indian Territories, they negotiated a very large proportion of the treaties made between the years 1804 and 1812 with the tribes residing east and west of the Mississippi. After the close of the war, in 1815, their talent in this department appears to have been inherited by General Lewis Cass.

These men took the most prominent part in the negotiations with the Indians, and to them we are indebted for the permanency of our Indian relations, and for making the aborigines acquainted with the peculiar features, practices, and institutions of our government. From the time of the return of General Clarke from the exploration of the Columbia River, in 1806, to the day of his death, in 1838, he was the Mæcenas of the tribes west of the Mississippi. The Indians located on the Missouri, Platte, Kansas, Osage, and Arkansas Rivers, as well as those residing among the distant peaks of the Rocky Mountains, were frequent and welcome visitors at the government council-house in St. Louis. The official records of his proceedings with the Indians have been carefully examined, and are found to contain a mass of speeches and traditions, constituting a valuable collection of material, whence the historian may derive much information regarding the sons of the forest.

PERIOD VII.

REMOVAL OF THE TRIBES WEST OF THE MISSISSIPPI.

CHAPTER I.

PLAN OF REMOVAL—STATISTICS OF THE TRIBES.

THE plan of a concentration of the tribes and fragments of tribes as colonial communities, on territory specially appropriated to their use, where, under the operation of their own laws and institutions, their better qualities might develop themselves, was first suggested by Mr. Monroe, the fifth President of the United States, who, in a message communicated by him to Congress on the 27th of January, 1825, thus invites the attention of that body to the topic:

"Being deeply impressed with the opinion that the removal of the Indian tribes from the lands which they now occupy within the limits of the several States and Territories to the country lying westward and northward thereof, within our acknowledged boundaries, is of very high importance to our Union, and may be accomplished on conditions and in a manner to promote the interest and happiness of those tribes, the attention of the government has been long drawn, with great solicitude, to the object. For the removal of the tribes within the limits of the State of Georgia the motive has been peculiarly strong, arising from the compact with that State whereby the United States are bound to extinguish the Indian title to the lands within it whenever it may be done peaceably and on reasonable conditions. In the fulfilment of this compact I have thought that the United States should act with a generous spirit, that they should omit nothing which should comport with a liberal construction of the instrument and likewise be in accordance with the just rights of those tribes. . . . Experience has clearly demonstrated that in their present state it is impossible to incorporate them in such masses in any form whatever into our system. It has also demonstrated with equal certainty that without a timely anticipation of and provision against the dangers to which they are exposed, under causes which it will be difficult if not impossible to control, their degradation and extermination will be inevitable.

"The great object to be accomplished is the removal of those tribes to the territory designated on conditions which shall be satisfactory to themselves and honorable to the United States. This can be done only by conveying to each tribe a good title to an adequate portion of land to which it may consent to remove, and by providing for it there a system of internal government which shall protect their property from invasion, and by the regular progress of improvement and civilization prevent that degeneracy which has generally marked the transition from the one to the other state.

"The digest of a government, with the consent of the Indians, which should be endowed with sufficient power to meet all the objects contemplated, to connect the several tribes together in a bond of amity, and preserve order in each, to prevent intrusions on their property, to teach them, by regular instructions, the arts of civilized life, and make them a civilized people, is an object of very high importance. It is the powerful consideration which we have to offer to these tribes as an inducement to relinquish the lands on which they now reside, and to remove to those which are designated. It is not doubted that this arrangement will present considerations of sufficient force to surmount all their prejudices in favor of the soil of their nativity, however strong they may be. Their elders have sufficient intelligence to discern the certain progress of events in the present train, and sufficient virtue, by yielding to momentary sacrifices, to protect their families and posterity from inevitable destruction. They will also perceive that they may thus attain an elevation to which as communities they could not otherwise aspire.

"To the United States the proposed arrangement offers many important advantages in addition to those which have been already enumerated. By the establishment of such a government over these tribes, with their consent, we become in reality their benefactors. The relation of conflicting interests which has heretofore existed between them and our frontier settlements will cease. There will be no more wars between them and the United States. Adopting such a government, their movement will be in harmony with us, and its good effect be felt throughout the whole extent of our territory to the Pacific. It may fairly be presumed that through the agency of such a government the condition of all the tribes inhabiting that vast region may be essentially improved, that permanent peace may be preserved with them, and our commerce be much extended.

"With a view to this important object, I recommend it to Congress to adopt, by solemn declaration, certain fundamental principles in accord with those above suggested, as the basis of such arrangements as may be entered into with the several tribes, to the strict observance of which the faith of the nation shall be pledged. I recommend it also to Congress to provide by law for the appointment of a suitable number of commissioners who shall, under the direction of the President, be authorized to visit and explain to the several tribes the objects of the government, and to make with them, according to their instructions, such arrangements as shall be best calculated to carry these objects into effect.

"A negotiation is now pending with the Creek nation for the cession of lands held by it within the limits of Georgia, and with a reasonable prospect of success. It is presumed, however, that the result will not be known during the present session of Congress. To give effect to this negotiation, and to the negotiations which it is proposed to hold with all the other tribes within the limits of the several States and Territories, on the principles and for the purposes stated, it is recommended that an adequate appropriation be now made by Congress."

It is hardly necessary to remind the reader that the event has most signally failed to justify the pleasing anticipations of Mr. Monroe of the success of the plan for placing the tribes upon reservations.

One of the first measures necessary in carrying this plan into effect was to ascertain the names, positions, and numbers of the Indian tribes to be removed. Mr. Calhoun, Secretary of War, in communicating the subjoined information from the newly-organized Bureau of Indian Affairs, thus expresses his views of the entire feasibility of the plan:

"It appears by the report enclosed that there are in the several States and Territories (not including a portion of Michigan Territory, west of Lake Michigan, and north of the State of Illinois) about 97,000 Indians, and that they occupy about 77,000,000 acres of land.

"The arrangement for the removal, it is presumed, is not intended to comprehend the small remnants of tribes in Maine, Massachusetts, Connecticut, Rhode Island, Virginia, and South Carolina, amounting to 3023. To these also may be added the remnants of tribes remaining in Louisiana, amounting to 1313, as they are each of them so few in number that it is believed very little expense or difficulty will be found in their removal, making together 4336, which, subtracted from the 97,000, the entire number in the States and Territories, will leave 92,664 to be removed. Of these there are residing in the northern part of the States of Indiana, Illinois, in the peninsula of Michigan, and New York, including the Ottawas in Ohio, about 13,150, which I would respectfully suggest might be removed with advantage to the country west of Lake Michigan and north of the State of Illinois. The climate and nature of the country are much more favorable to their habits than that west of the Mississippi, to which may be added that the Indians in New York have already commenced a settlement at Green Bay, and exhibit some disposition to make it a permanent one, and that the Indians referred to in Indiana, Illinois, and in the peninsula of Michigan, will find in the country designated kindred tribes, with whom they may be readily associated. These considerations, with the greater facility with which they could be collected in that portion of the country compared with that of collecting them west of the Mississippi, form a strong inducement to give it the preference. Should the proposition be adopted, the Indians in question might be gradually collected, as it became necessary from time to time to extinguish the Indian title in Indiana, Illinois, and Michigan, without incurring any additional expense other than what is usually incidental to such extinguishment. Deducting, then, the Indians residing in the northwestern parts of Indiana, Illinois, in Michigan, and New York, with the Ottawas in Ohio, amounting to 13,150, from 92,664, will leave but 79,514. It is proper to add that a late treaty with the Quapaws stipulates and provides for their removal, and that they may also be deducted from the number for whose removal provision ought to be made. They are estimated at 700, which, deducted from 79,514, will leave 78,814 to be removed west of the State of Missouri and Territory of Arkansas, should the views of the department be adopted.

"Of these, there are estimated to reside in the States of Virginia, North Carolina, Tennessee, Alabama, and Mississippi, 53,625, consisting of Cherokees, Creeks, Choctaws, and Chickasaws, and claiming about 33,573,176 acres, including the claim of the Cherokees in North Carolina; 3082 in Ohio, and in the southern and middle parts of Indiana and Illinois, consisting of Wyandots, Shawnees, Senecas, Delawares, Kaskaskias, and Miamis and Eel Rivers; 5000 in Florida, consisting of Seminoles and remnants of other tribes; and the remainder in Missouri and Arkansas, consisting of Delawares, Kickapoos, Shawnees, Weas, Iowas, Piankeshaws, Cherokees, Quapaws, and Osages.

"The next subject of consideration will be to acquire a sufficient tract of country west of the State of Missouri and Territory of Arkansas in order to establish permanent settlements in that quarter of the tribes which are proposed to be removed. The country between the Red River and the Arkansas has already been allotted to the Choctaws under the treaty of the 18th October, 1820. The country north of the river Arkansas and immediately west of the State of Missouri is held almost entirely by the Osages and the Kansas, the principal settlement of the former being on the Osage River not far west of the western boundary of Missouri, and the latter on the Missouri River near Cow Island. There is a band of the Osages situated on the Verdigris, a branch of the Arkansas. Governor Clarke has been already instructed to take measures to remove them from the Verdigris to join the other bands on the Osage River. To carry this object into effect, and to extinguish the title of the Osages upon the Arkansas and in the State of Missouri, and also to extinguish the title of the Kansas to whatever tract of country may be necessary to effect the views of the government, will be the first object of expenditure, and would require an appropriation, it is believed, of not less than $30,000. After this is effected, the next will be to allot a portion of the country to each of the tribes, and to commence the work of removal. The former could be effected by vesting in the President discretionary power to make the location, and the latter by commencing with the removal of the Cherokees, Piankeshaws, Weas, Shawnees, Kickapoos, and Delawares, who now occupy different tracts of country lying in the northwestern portion of the Arkansas Territory and the southwestern portion of the State of Missouri. It is believed that the Cherokees, to whom has been allotted a country lying between the Arkansas and White Rivers, will very readily agree to removing their eastern boundary farther west on the consideration that for the lands thereby ceded they may have assigned to them an equal quantity farther west, as they have evinced a strong disposition to prevent the settlement of the whites to the west of them. It is probable that this arrangement could be effected by an appropriation of a few thousand dollars, say five thousand, for the expense of holding the treaty. Nor is it believed that there will be any difficulty in inducing the Piankeshaws, Weas, Shawnees, Kickapoos, and Delawares to occupy a position that may be assigned to them west of the State of Missouri, or that the operation will be attended with any great expense. The kindred tribes in the States of Ohio and Indiana, including the Wyandots, the Senecas, and the Miamis and Eel Rivers in those States, and the Kaskaskias in Illinois, it is believed might be induced without much difficulty to join them after those now residing in Missouri are fixed in their new position west of that State. Of the sum that will be necessary for this purpose it is difficult to form an estimate. These tribes amount to 3082. The expense of extinguishing their title to the lands occupied by them will probably be high in comparison with the price which has been usually given for lands in that quarter, as they, particularly the Indians in Ohio, have made some advances in civilization and considerable improvements on their lands. The better course would be to remove them gradually, commencing with those tribes which are most disposed to leave their present settlements, and, if this arrangement should be adopted, an appropriation of $20,000 would be sufficient to commence with.

"It may, however, be proper to remark that these tribes, together with those in New York, have indicated a disposition to join the Cherokees on the Arkansas, and that a deputation from the former, with a deputation from those Cherokees, are now on their way to the seat of government in order to make some arrangements to carry the proposed union into effect. Should it be accomplished, it would vary the arrangement which has been suggested in relation to them, but will not probably materially vary the expense.

"It only remains now to consider the removal of the Indians in Florida, and the four Southern tribes residing in North Carolina, Georgia, Tennessee, Alabama, and Mississippi.

"It is believed that immediate measures need not be taken with regard to the Indians in Florida. By the treaty of the 18th September, 1823, they ceded the whole of the northern portion of Florida, with the exception of a few small reservations, and have had allotted to them the southern part of the peninsula; and it is probable that no inconvenience will be felt for many years, either by the inhabitants of Florida or the Indians, under the present arrangement.

"Of the four Southern tribes, two of them, the Cherokees and Choctaws, have already allotted to them a tract of country west of the Mississippi. That which has been allotted to the latter is believed to be sufficiently ample for the whole nation should they emigrate, and if an arrangement, which is believed not to be impracticable, could be made between them and the Chickasaws, who are their neighbors, and of similar habits and dispositions, it would be sufficient for the accommodation of both. A sufficient country should be reserved to the west of the Cherokees, on the Arkansas, as a means of exchange with those who remain on the east. To the Creeks might be allotted a country between the Arkansas and Canadian Rivers, which limits the northern boundary of the Choctaw possessions in that quarter. There is now pending with the Creeks a negotiation, under the appropriation of the last session, with a prospect that the portion of that nation which resides within the limits of Georgia may be induced, with the consent of the nation, to cede the country which they occupy for a portion of the one which it is proposed to allot for the Creek nation on the west of the Mississippi. Should the treaty prove successful, its stipulations will provide for the means of carrying it into effect, which will render any additional provision at present unnecessary. It will be proper to open new communications with the Cherokees, Choctaws, and Chickasaws for the purpose of explaining to them the views of the government, and inducing them to remove beyond the Mississippi, on the principles and conditions which may be proposed to the other tribes. It is known that there are many individuals of each of the tribes who are desirous of settling west of the Mississippi, and, should it be thought advisable, there can be no doubt that if by an adequate appropriation the means were afforded the government of bearing their expense they would emigrate. Should it be thought that the encouragement of such emigration is desirable, the sum of $40,000, at least, would be required to be appropriated for this object, to be applied under the discretion of the President of the United States. The several sums which have been recommended to be appropriated, if the proposed arrangements should be adopted, amount to $95,000. The appropriation may be made either general or specific, as may be deemed most advisable.

"I cannot, however, conclude without remarking that no arrangement ought to be made which does not regard the interests of the Indians as well as our own, and that to protect the interests of the former decisive measures ought to be adopted to prevent the hostility which must almost necessarily take place if left to themselves, among tribes hastily brought together, of discordant character, and many of which are actuated by feelings far from being friendly towards each other. But the preservation of peace between them will not alone be sufficient to render their condition as eligible in their new situation as it is in their present. Almost all of the tribes proposed to be affected by the arrangement are more or less advanced in the arts of civilized life, and there is scarcely one of them which have not benefited by the establishment of schools in the nation, affording at once the means of moral, religious, and intellectual improvement. These schools have been established, for the most part, by religious societies, with the countenance and aid of the government, and on every principle of humanity the continuance of similar advantages of education ought to be extended to them in their new residence. There is another point which appears to be indispensable to be guarded in order to render the condition of this race less afflicting. One of the greatest evils to which they are subject is that incessant pressure of our population which forces them from seat to seat without allowing time for that moral and intellectual improvement for which they appear to be naturally eminently susceptible. To guard against this evil, so fatal to the race, there ought to be the strongest and the most solemn assurance that the country given them should be theirs as a permanent home for themselves and their posterity, without being disturbed by the encroachments of our citizens. To such assurance, if there should be added a system by which the government, without destroying their independence, would gradually unite the several tribes under a simple but enlightened system of government and laws, formed on the principles of our own, and for which, as their own people would partake in it, they would, under the influence of the contemplated improvement, at no distant day become prepared, the arrangements which have been proposed would prove to the Indians and their posterity a permanent blessing. It is believed that if they could be assured that peace and friendship would be maintained among the several tribes, that the advantages of education which they now enjoy would be extended to them, that they should have a permanent and solemn guarantee for their possessions, and receive the countenance and aid of the government for the gradual extension of its privileges to them, there would be among all the tribes a disposition to accord with the views of the government. There are now in most of the tribes well-educated, sober, and reflecting individuals who are afflicted at the present condition of the Indians, and despondent at their future prospects. Under the operation of existing causes they behold the certain degradation, misery, and even the final annihilation of their race, and no doubt would gladly embrace any arrangement which would promise to elevate them in the scale of civilization and arrest the destruction which now awaits them. It is conceived that one of the most cheap, certain, and desirable modes of effecting the object in view would be for Congress to establish fixed principles, such as have been suggested, as the basis of the proposed arrangement, and to authorize the President to convene at some suitable point all of the well-informed, intelligent, and influential individuals of the tribes to be affected by it, in order to explain to them the views of the government and to pledge the faith of the nation to the arrangements that might be adopted. Should such principles be established by Congress, and the President be vested with suitable authority to convene the individuals as proposed, and suitable provision be made to meet the expense, great confidence is felt that a basis of a system might be laid which in a few years would entirely effect the object in view, to the mutual benefit of the government and the Indians, and which, in its operations, would effectually arrest the calamitous course of events to which they must be subject without a radical change in the present system. Should it be thought advisable to call such a convention, as one of the means of effecting the object in view an additional appropriation of $30,000 will be required, making in the whole $125,000 to be appropriated."

The following additional details were presented by the newly-created Bureau of Indian Affairs:

"There are now remaining within the limits of the different States and Territories, as is shown by the table, sixty-four tribes and remnants of tribes of Indians, whose 'names' and 'numbers' are given, who number in the aggregate 129,266 souls, and who claim 77,402,318 acres of land.

"It will be seen by adverting to the table that the Indians residing north of the State of Illinois, east of the Mississippi, and west of the lakes, are comprehended in the estimate of the number in Michigan Territory, although in estimating the quantity of land held by Indians in that Territory the portion only so held in the peninsula of Michigan is estimated. It was found impossible from any documents in possession of this office to distinguish the number of Chippewas and Ottawas residing in the peninsula of Michigan from those residing on the west side of Lake

Michigan. It is, however, believed that the whole number residing in the peninsula does not exceed 3500, and these, as has been stated, are principally of the Chippewa and Ottawa tribes.

"It may be proper also to remark that of the 6400 Sacs and Foxes who are included in the estimate as part of the 129,266, and who occupy lands on both sides the Mississippi, not more than one-third of that number are supposed to reside on the east side, and of the 5200 Osages who by the table are assigned to Missouri and Arkansas it is believed not more than one-third of that number reside within the State of Missouri and Territory of Arkansas. If, therefore, the number assumed for the peninsula of Michigan be correct, and two-thirds of the Sacs and Foxes, as is believed to be the fact, reside on the west of the Mississippi, and two-thirds of the Osages west of Missouri and north of Arkansas, there will remain 'within the limits of the different States and Territories'—confining the Michigan Territory to the peninsula—97,384 Indians, possessing (if the 200,000 acres claimed by the Cherokees in North Carolina be added) 77,602,318 acres of land."

CHAPTER II.

REMOVAL BEGUN—CREEK DIFFICULTIES—DEATH OF THE CHIEF McINTOSH—TREATY FOR THE FINAL SETTLEMENT—BOUNDARY TREATIES WITH THE NORTHWESTERN TRIBES.

THE treaties concluded respectively with the Cherokees July 8, 1817, with the Choctaws October 18, 1820, and with the Creeks January 8, 1821, constituted the primary steps towards the removal of the aborigines to the lands west of the Mississippi. Under these treaties the hunter portions of these tribes voluntarily assumed the initiative, and made preparations for their migration to the Arkansas Territory. The hunter bands, as contradistinguished from the agricultural bands of the Southern or Appalachian group of tribes, were the first to perceive that this land must be their national refuge. Hence the provision in the first article of the Choctaw treaty stipulates that they should be furnished with a Western tract, "where all who live by hunting and will not work may be collected and settled together." This proviso was the natural suggestion of the Indian mind: oxen, ploughs, and implements of handicraft were not attractive objects to the aborigines, who delighted in the pursuits of the chase, which were hallowed in their memories by reminiscences of their fathers. The whites did not so readily perceive that the stock of wild animals must soon decline and the chase prove unreliable in the regions east of the Mississippi, or if they did foresee this result they did not at first propose a general removal. But the executive power favored such migrations as originated with the Indians themselves, and insensibly, perhaps, the system of removal became the policy of the government. When the question was discussed on its merits, and the removal began to be put in operation, it became evident not only that the West was an outlet to the hunter population, but that all the means necessary for their improvement in arts, and for their progress in education also, in order to be permanently beneficial, must be applied in that quarter. Driven from their original residences, or from reservations in the States, their attainments in civilization would be shared by those tribes originally resident in the West, and all the tribes would thus in a measure become assimilated in manners and arts.

The question of removal became one of much interest, and was freely discussed in all parts of the Union, the ardent friends of the Indians maintaining that it would have a tendency to make them retrograde towards barbarism, while the advocates for removal contended that it would be accompanied by the beneficial effects referred to. Another question of a grave character arose at the same time,—viz., the claim to sovereignty asserted by some of the most advanced tribes over the districts they inhabited. This claim was, however, principally confined to the Creeks, who had received a powerful national impulse during the occupancy of Florida by Great Britain. Their prominent chiefs had become wealthy planters through the medium of the labor of fugitive African slaves from the contiguous States, who cultivated for them crops of cotton and corn. The result was that they not only amassed riches, but also attained to that kind of social elevation which is characterized by the introduction of castes or classes, and thus became averse to transferring their lands and emigrating westward.

The people of Georgia, feeling the expansive force of their population, clamored for the Creek lands, the Indian title to which the United States had promised to give them as soon as it could be obtained "peaceably and on reasonable conditions." The Creeks, when they began to appreciate the benefits of civilization through their experience of the agricultural and school systems, declined to listen to any proposal looking towards a cession of their territory. A law was eventually passed by their council, enacting that if any one of the chiefs or rulers should sign a treaty ceding lands, he should incur the penalty of death.

General William McIntosh, the presiding chief of the Coweta tribe of the Lower Creeks, subjected himself to this penalty by signing the treaty of February 12, 1825. The penalty was enforced by the dissenting part of the tribes in a peculiar manner. They did not arraign and try the guilty party, but a large number of armed warriors surrounded his house and poured into it an indiscriminate fire, so that the onus of the murder might not rest on any one individual. Fifty other chiefs, warriors, and head men had signed the same treaty, but they were not held accountable, doubtless on the Indian principle that the punishment of a crime should fall on the real instigator of it, whether he or another committed the act.

The United States made no attempt to carry this treaty into effect. Mr. Monroe, in a message previously quoted, mentions the difficulty which surrounded the subject, and expresses a hope that the negotiations with the tribe then in progress would result favorably. A treaty was concluded at Indian Springs, in the Creek Nation, March 7, 1825, three days after the expiration of Mr. Monroe's Presidential term. This instrument was designed to enable the government to comply with its contract of April 24, 1802, to transfer the Indian title to Georgia, as well as to remove the existing dissatisfaction with the treaty of February 12, 1825. But neither object was attained. All efforts thus far proved unsuccessful, and the Creek controversy was left unadjusted.

The Creek question attained its highest point of interest about this time. Public opinion was much divided, some siding with the Indians in their assertion of the right of sovereignty within the territorial area of Georgia, and others as decidedly opposing it as a new and inadmissible claim. Mr. Adams, who succeeded to the Presidency, directed the attention of the War Department to the subject, and authorized Mr. Barbour, the Secretary of War, to confer with the Creek chiefs. By the treaty concluded at Hopewell in 1785 the United States had undertaken to extinguish the Creek title and transfer it to the State of Georgia at the earliest practicable moment. But the lapse of time only made the Indians cling more closely to the land. The period for the chase had passed away, and the plough began to be appreciated. The experience of forty years had so operated as to give them a more definite and just idea of its value, and they now undertook to ignore the laws of Georgia, and to dispute her sovereignty over the country. The political aspects of the controversy had been communicated to Congress during the last few months of Mr. Monroe's second term. He had given much thought to the subject, and recommended the only plan which appeared to meet the question, insisting on the certain decadence and speedy extinction of the tribe if they remained in the State, in view of which fact it seemed just and right to urge their removal as a means to their ultimate welfare and prosperity.

Mr. Adams exerted himself to bring this vexed question to an equitable close, the Creek nation and the people of the Union being much agitated by its discussion, and the friends of the Indians being apprehensive that some great injustice was about to be done them. Georgia having demanded their expulsion, the Creeks appealed to the government, and early in the year 1826 sent a large and respectable delegation to Washington to represent their cause. Negotiations were renewed, and resulted in the formation of the important treaty, signed January 24, 1826, the first article of which abrogates the prior treaty of February 12, 1825, and declares every clause thereof "null and void to every intent and purpose whatsoever." By this treaty the Creeks ceded large tracts of their lands in Georgia, and agreed to remove to the West. The McIntosh party, and all who signed the objectionable treaty, were reinstated in their rights, indemnified for the damages sustained by them, and permitted to send a delegation to locate lands for their party in the West. A perpetual additional annuity of twenty thousand dollars was granted, and the Creeks agreed to remove within one year. Other stipulations were included in the treaty, which was by its friends pronounced to be "in the highest degree liberal."

Under the authority of the treaty-making power, the President continued to receive such cessions of the exhausted and surplus tracts of all the tribes situated east of the Mississippi as they felt inclined to make in view of the final relinquishment of their possessions and transfer to the West.

The treaty of January 24, 1826, was the first effective step taken towards the transference of the Indian tribes to the West. This treaty, negotiated by Mr. Barbour, Secretary of War, made very extensive cessions of territory, retaining, however, important reserves for the Indians, who were confined to their particular localities.

It is impossible to conceive, unless from a perusal of the numerous public documents printed at that period, how numerous and complicated were the difficulties surrounding this subject. Some of the tribes, more advanced in civilization than the rest, regarded the whole movement as an endeavor to drive them back into barbarism, and the best people of the whole country sympathized with this view. The newspaper press very generally asserted that the Indian question had reached a point where it had become necessary to pause and ponder on the duties which the nation owed to the tribes, who, even when acting under delusive impulses, should be regarded with deep sympathy, not only as our predecessors in the country, but also as individuals entitled to the benefits of Christian civilization.

At the same time it appeared to many people that nothing but the removal of the tribes from the jurisdiction of the several States to a separate territory, where they would be free from molestation, could avert their entire annihilation at no very distant period. Portions of the Cherokees seem to have realized their true condition as early as the year 1809, when they obtained Mr. Jefferson's sanction to their proposal, which was subsequently embodied in the treaty negotiated in 1816. From a clause of the treaty with the Shawnees, negotiated by General Clarke in 1825, we learn that a small fragment of that tribe had crossed the Mississippi into Upper Louisiana, and there located themselves on a tract of land twenty-five miles square, granted to them by Governor Carondelet as early as 1795. This movement, which was at first merely precautionary and intended to furnish an outlet for their restless population, was imitated by several other tribes at a later date, and at various epochs a similar course was adopted by a part of the Choctaws and the Chickasaws, the majority of the Cherokees, and, finally, of the Creeks. Yet the dispersed hunter tribes, living on large reservations in the Western and Northern States, east of the Mississippi, regarded the measure with deep-rooted aversion. They clung with tenacity to the land of their forefathers, and to those latitudes where the varying climate, and the happy alternation of spring, summer, autumn, and winter, gave a piquancy to the enjoyment of life. The chase was the poetry of their existence, war the true path to honor, and the traditions and reminiscences of their forefathers the proper food of the Indian mind. Books were for scholars, and labor for slaves. This was Indian philosophy.

But while the Indian indulged in his day-dreams, the race which labored at the plough, the anvil, and the loom, and chained the rippling and murmuring streamlet to the revolving wheel of the saw- and grist-mill, was rapidly encompassing him with the bonds of civilized life. There were then no railroads, but the steady and rapid advance of civilization foreshadowed their approach. The plan of removing and concentrating the Indian population was no sooner announced than it was warmly advocated as the proper mode of arresting their decline and averting their final extinction. The result of careful scrutiny into their condition and future prospects by the President, whom they regarded as their great political father, was a provision, while yet the means were at hand, for their future prosperity and permanent welfare. As such, the plan was detailed to the tribes by the officers charged with the care of Indian affairs; not, however, with a view of forcing it upon them, but of submitting it to their calm consideration and decision.

The Indians, ignorant alike of history and of the progress of society, required time to consider any new propositions advanced, and to realize their own position. All the Northern tribes expressed fears as to the healthfulness of the Southern latitudes, being accustomed only to the bracing Northern seasons and to the customs of Northern hunters. Their very mythology, singular as it may seem, warned them of the seductive manners and habits of the South. It was a difficult matter for them to exchange their established customs for others entirely at variance with them.

The intestine wars and feuds of the Indians had been one of the principal causes of their decline, and in some cases of the utter destruction of tribes. These wars, which had no limits to their fury, and were often waged without any clearly-defined object, began before America was discovered, and continued throughout every period of aboriginal history. The Indian wars have in fact exercised a more baneful influence on the prosperity of the race than all other causes combined, with the single exception of their passionate craving for ardent spirits. Efforts were frequently made to put a stop to these intestine wars, and as frequently defeated, but after the close of the war of 1812 the efforts were again vigorously resumed. Mr. Monroe made strenuous endeavors to enforce this policy throughout the eight years of his administration. The several expeditions of Long, Cass, and Schoolcraft to the sources of the Mississippi, to the mouth of the Yellowstone, to the sources of the Arkansas and Red Rivers, to those of other principal streams, and to the central portions of the Mississippi Valley, in 1820, 1821, and 1822, had promoted this purpose by accumulating accurate geographical statistics of the Indian territory, its inhabitants, and its resources. The visit of the venerable Dr. Jedediah Morse to the Lake tribes, in 1820, to learn their dispositions, feelings, and social and moral condition, had the same tendency.[1] This period witnessed a practical renewal of the explorations originated by Mr. Jefferson in 1804. A more intimate acquaintance with the Indians afforded that knowledge of their peculiar habits which was necessary to their proper management, and to induce them to abandon their hunter mode of life and adopt the more elevating pursuits of civilization.

As internal tribal wars were continually distracting the Indians, one tribe trespassing on the lands of another, and as the civilized population was at the same time pressing into the ceded districts, it was thought by the government that one of the most practical methods of allaying their territorial disputes would be to establish definite boundary-lines between their possessions, a method of settling their difficulties which had never occurred to the Indians.

A series of conventions held with the Indian chiefs of the Western and Northwestern tribes marked the early part of Mr. Adams's administration, the first and most important of which assembled at Prairie du Chien, on the Upper Mississippi, during the summer of 1825, under the auspices of General William Clarke, then General Superintendent at St. Louis, and of Governor Lewis Cass, of Michigan, *ex-officio* Superintendent of the Northern Department. This convention was attended by the Mendawacanton and Yankton Dakotas, or Sioux, of the St. Peter's and the Plains, the Chippewas and Pillagers, from the sources of the Mississippi, and the Sacs, Foxes, Iowas, Winnebagoes, Menomonies, Chippewas, Ottawas, and Pottawatomies, of the lakes and the Illinois River. Maps drawn on birch bark, giving the outlines of their hunting-grounds, were exhibited by the several tribes, and, after a

---

[1] Morse's Report to the Secretary of War, 1 vol. 8vo, 400 pp.: New Haven, 1822.

full discussion with each of their respective agents, a treaty of peace and limitation was signed by them on the 29th of August, 1825. The same plan was further carried out by a convention which assembled at Fond du Lac, at the head of Lake Superior, in 1826, and was attended by the chiefs of that region. A treaty was signed by these representatives of the Northern tribes which established peaceful relations among the Indians and definitely settled the boundary-lines of their territories up to the forty-ninth parallel of north latitude. A convention of a similar character was held at Butte des Morts, on Fox River, for the purpose of settling the boundary between the Menomonies and Chippewas, and certain bands of the Oneidas and Stockbridges, better known by the designation of New York Indians, which resulted in the signing of a treaty at this place, August 11, 1827.

These treaties with the hunter tribes of the North secured for them accurate boundaries, and the acknowledgment by the United States, as well as by the other tribes, of their claims to territory. They were likewise of the greatest advantage to them in their subsequent history, and gave them the benefits of a system under which they began to exchange their surplus lands for annuities in goods and coin.

While the treaty of Butte des Morts was under consideration, the Winnebagoes committed some hostile acts at Prairie du Chien, on the Mississippi. They there fired into a boat, plundered several individuals, and endeavored practically to enforce an obsolete idea that they had a right to interdict merchandise from passing the portage of the Wisconsin without receiving some acknowledgment therefor in the nature of toll. General Cass, who, as one of the commissioners, was then in the vicinity, immediately embarked in his light canoe, manned by skilful Canadians, crossed the portage, and, entering the Mississippi River, journeyed night and day until he reached St. Louis, whence he returned with a body of troops, whose sudden appearance prevented any further trouble from this source.

The primary arrangements for the expatriation of the Cherokees and Choctaws had been commenced by the Indians themselves in 1817 and 1820. Their transference to the West was, however, a tedious operation, and undertaken only after a thorough exploration of their new territory had been made. The Indian exercises great caution, and is never in a hurry in the transaction of business: he must have time to think. One after another, the tribes residing in the southern and middle, and, finally, to a considerable extent, those in the northern latitudes, adopted the plan of removal, and accepted locations west of the Mississippi in exchange for those surrendered on the east of that river. It was an object to preserve pacific relations with those indigenous tribes in the West on whose territories the Eastern tribes were to be concentrated, and who yet possessed the title to the soil. Those stern lords of the wilderness, the Osages, the Quapaws, the Kansas, and their compeers, required to be kept at peace not only with the United States, but also with each other, and with the tribes from the east of the Mississippi. Parties of the migrating Indians required from time to time to be directed to the places on which they were to reside, and to be furnished with the means of beginning life there. It was likewise necessary that their annuities, derived from former cessions of country, should be apportioned between the Eastern and Western divisions of the tribes in accordance with their respective numbers. Sometimes the tribes settled in positions whence their restless spirit induced them to remove and locate elsewhere. Murders not unfrequently occurred, and frontier wars were prevented only by judicious negotiations, military watchfulness, and a system of compensation for all losses. The onerous official duties incident to the removal of the red men were ably performed by the veteran Superintendent of Indian Affairs at St. Louis. The most important tribes of Ohio, Indiana, and Illinois had so far entered into arrangements for their removal as to have sent out either pioneers or emigrant parties. Early in the month of April, 1827, Elkswattawa, the Shawnee Prophet, arrived at St. Louis from Wahpakoneta, with the Shawnee tribe on their route to the West. This was the celebrated man who, assuming the prophetic office, had in 1811 incited the aborigines to wage war against the United States, in which the Indian hosts were led to battle by Tecumseh. After the defeat and death of his brother Tecumseh, the Prophet had fled to Canada, where he lived for some years, until the long continuance of peace removed all apprehension of mischief from his oracular voice, when General Cass permitted him to return to his tribe at Wahpakoneta, where his people, having directed their attention to farming and to the raising of horses and cattle, had made considerable advance in arts, industry, and civilization. He was a man of original ideas, strong purpose, and much natural shrewdness, and was well adapted by his manners, and by habits of extreme abstemiousness, as well as by his total lack of selfishness, to win the favor of the Indians. In stature he was considerably above the average height, his body was very spare, and his countenance always wore an austere aspect, which, with the loss of one eye, over which he constantly wore a patch or blind, tended more deeply to impress the Indians with an idea of his sanctity of character. His revelations were promulgated with all that careful attention to manner, circumstance, time, and place necessary to insure them full credit, and but few men of his race, possessing such marked peculiarities, have figured in Indian history. Bowed down with the accumulated weight of years, he was now the leader of his tribe in their journey to a land of refuge, and as such was received by the superintendent and officials at the West with friendship, respect, and kindness.

Assuming an oratorical attitude, he said in effect that he had come in obedience to the desire of the President, whose wishes had been communicated by the agent. His Great Father at Washington had seen that the Shawnees owned but a small piece of land, and that the whites were pressing upon them so much that they could not long remain on it in prosperity. Therefore, to insure their preservation and enable them again to become a great nation, he would give them a new location in the West, where the sun shone as brightly, and the soil was as rich, on which they might live forever under their own laws. He had advised them to send a party to view it and judge of its fitness. He had promised to sustain them on the way, and to pay them for their improvements, orchards, and agricultural implements left behind. They received this voice as the voice of wisdom and kindness. They regarded it as one with the voice of the Great Spirit, which he had himself heard. It came over the Alleghanies as the pleasing sound of many waters. The old men at first objected to the plan. At last the young men reviewed the subject, and said, "Let us go and look at the land." He got up and came with his people. There were two hundred persons with him. There were some left behind who would also come. They did not come of their own motion. It was the Great Ruler of the land who sent them. It was his promises that he came to test. He now asked that they should be carried out. They were hungry, and had worn out most of their clothes. Their horses were lean and poor. They must rest to gain strength.

The removal of all the Indians to the west of the Mississippi went forward, partly of their own volition, and partly under the influence of the government officials. The movement was founded on the strength of treaty stipulations alone. The more closely the plan was examined by both white and red men, the more favor it received. Congress was much interested in the project, and several acts were presented to the consideration of both Houses which had for their object to facilitate and give the force of legal security to the plan. On February 1, 1825, the Senate passed a bill "for the preservation and civilization of the Indian tribes within the United States," but it failed to receive the sanction of the House of Representatives. On December 27 of the same year the House instructed their Committee on Indian Affairs to devise a plan for allotting to each tribe a sufficiency of land, "with the sovereignty, or right of soil, in the same manner that the right of domain is secured to the respective States of the Union." In January, 1826, the bill brought forward in the House at the previous session was referred to the Secretary of War, with the view of obtaining such information as the subject demanded. Mr. Barbour made a very elaborate report, but no final action was taken in the matter. The principles then discussed were, however, incorporated in the treaty formed May 8, 1828, with the Cherokees, which secured to that nation a permanent home in the West, under the most solemn guarantee of the United States, by which this territory was granted to them forever, with an appended stipulation that they should be provided with plain laws, and that the individuality of the right to the land should be acknowledged whenever it should be desired.

CHAPTER III.

CONGRESS AUTHORIZES THE COLONIZING OF THE INDIANS IN THE WEST—THE TRIBES GENERALLY CONCUR IN THE PLAN.

EVERY year increased the pressure of civilization on the Indian tribes: the tide of white emigration rolled westward with ever-increasing volume. For the Indians the era of the chase had passed away forever, and they had now the alternative of employing themselves manfully in the pursuits of agriculture and the arts, or of perishing from indolence and want: to remain where they then were, within the jurisdiction of the States, was impossible. In his first message to Congress, delivered at the close of the year 1829, General Jackson introduced the subject in a very forcible manner.

In the month of May, 1830, Congress passed an act authorizing the necessary exchanges and purchases of lands from the indigenous tribes west of the Mississippi. This act legalizes the removal of the Indians, guarantees them the possession of their new lands, agrees to defend them in their sovereignty, grants compensation for improvements made on their late possessions, and appropriates five hundred thousand dollars with which to commence the removal of the tribes.[1]

---

[1] AN ACT to provide for an exchange of lands with the Indians residing in any of the States or Territories, and for their removal west of the river Mississippi.

SECTION 1. *Be it enacted by the Senate and House of Representatives of the United States of America in Congress assembled,* That it shall and may be lawful for the President of the United States to cause so much of any territory belonging to the United States, west of the river Mississippi, not included in any State or organized Territory, and to which the Indian title has been extinguished, as he may judge necessary, to be divided into a suitable number of districts, for the reception of such tribes or nations of Indians as may choose to exchange the lands where they now reside, and remove there; and to cause each of said districts to be so described by natural or artificial marks as to be easily distinguished from every other.

SEC. 2. *And be it further enacted,* That it shall and may be lawful for the President to exchange any or all of such districts, so to be laid off and described, with any tribe or nation of Indians now residing within the limits of any of the States or Territories, and with which the United States have existing treaties, for the whole or any part or portion of the territory claimed and occupied by such tribe or nation, within the bounds of any one or more of the States or Territories, where the land claimed and occupied by the Indians is owned by the United States, or the United States are bound to the State within which it lies to extinguish the Indian claim thereto.

SEC. 3. *And be it further enacted,* That in the making of any such exchange or exchanges, it shall and may be lawful for the President solemnly to assure the tribe or nation with which the exchange is made, that the United States will forever secure and guarantee to them, and their heirs or successors, the country so exchanged with them; and, if they prefer it, that the United States will cause a patent or grant to be made and executed to them for the same: *Provided always,* That such lands shall revert to the United States if the Indians become extinct or abandon the same.

SEC. 4. *And be it further enacted,* That if, upon any of the lands now occupied by the Indians, and to

In his message to Congress, sent to that body on the 4th of December, 1830, President Jackson again presented this topic to their notice, and solicited for it their mature consideration. "It gives me pleasure," said he, "to announce to Congress that the benevolent policy of the government, steadily pursued for nearly thirty years, in relation to the removal of the Indians beyond the white settlements, is approaching to a happy consummation. Two important tribes, the Choctaws and the Chickasaws, have accepted the provision made for their removal at the last session of Congress, and it is believed that their example will induce the remaining tribes, also, to seek the same obvious advantages."

Obvious as these advantages seemed to men familiar with history and the civil polity of nations, the Indians were slow to comprehend and loath to admit them. Meantime, Georgia and Alabama sedulously pressed the subject on the notice of the government, which at length made provision for the settlement of the question as a necessary measure for preserving the quiet and promoting the prosperity of the States. Time was, however, required to adjust the controversy, the discussions meantime being continued with vigor. One year later the Executive again presented the subject to Congress, and acquainted them with the progress of the experiment, at the same time expressing his decided conviction that colonization was the only feasible method of relieving both the States and the Indian tribes from their constantly accumulating embarrassments.

"Time and experience have proved," said the President, "that the abode of the native Indian within State limits is dangerous to their peace, and injurious to him-

---

be exchanged for, there should be such improvements as add value to the land claimed by any individual or individuals of such tribes or nations, it shall and may be lawful for the President to cause such value to be ascertained by appraisement or otherwise, and to cause such ascertained value to be paid to the person or persons rightfully claiming such improvements. And upon the payment of such valuation the improvements so valued and paid for shall pass to the United States, and possession shall not afterwards be permitted to any of the same tribe.

SEC. 5. *And be it further enacted*, That upon the making of any such exchange as is contemplated by this act, it shall and may be lawful for the President to cause such aid and assistance to be furnished to the emigrants as may be necessary and proper to enable them to remove to and settle in the country for which they may have exchanged; and also to give them such aid and assistance as may be necessary for their support and subsistence for the first year after their removal.

SEC. 6. *And be it further enacted*, That it shall and may be lawful for the President to cause such tribe or nation to be protected at their new residence against all interruption or disturbance from any other tribe or nation of Indians, or from any other person or persons whatever.

SEC. 7. *And be it further enacted*, That it shall and may be lawful for the President to have the same superintendence and care over any tribe or nation in the country to which they may remove, as contemplated by this act, that he is now authorized to have over them at their present places of residence : *Provided*, That nothing in this act contained shall be construed as authorizing or directing the violation of any existing treaty between the United States and any of the Indian tribes.

SEC. 8. *And be it further enacted*, That for the purpose of giving effect to the provisions of this act the sum of five hundred thousand dollars is hereby appropriated, to be paid out of any money in the Treasury not otherwise appropriated.

APPROVED May 28, 1830.

self. In accordance with my recommendation at a former session of Congress, an appropriation of five hundred thousand dollars was made to aid the voluntary removal of the various tribes beyond the limits of the States. At the last session I had the happiness to announce that the Chickasaws and Choctaws had accepted the generous offer of the government and agreed to remove beyond the Mississippi River, by which the whole of the State of Mississippi and the western part of Alabama will be freed from Indian occupancy and opened to a civilized population. The treaties with these tribes are in course of execution, and their removal, it is hoped, will be completed in the course of 1832.

"At the request of the authorities of Georgia, the registration of Cherokee Indians for emigration has been resumed, and it is confidently expected that one-half, if not two-thirds, of that tribe will follow the wise example of their more westerly brethren. Those who prefer remaining at their present homes will hereafter be governed by the laws of Georgia as all her citizens are, and cease to be the objects of peculiar care on the part of the general government.

"During the present year the attention of the government has been particularly directed to those tribes in the powerful and growing State of Ohio, where considerable tracts of the finest lands were still occupied by the aboriginal proprietors. Treaties, either absolute or conditional, have been made, extinguishing the whole Indian title to the reservations in that State, and the time is not distant, it is hoped, when Ohio will be no longer embarrassed with the Indian population. The same measure will be extended to Indiana as soon as there is reason to anticipate success.

"It is confidently believed that perseverance for a few years in the present policy of the government will extinguish the Indian title to all lands lying within the States comprising our Federal Union, and remove beyond their limits every Indian who is not willing to submit to their laws. Thus will all conflicting claims to jurisdiction between the States and the Indian tribes be put to rest. It is pleasing to reflect that results so beneficial, not only to the States immediately concerned, but to the harmony of the Union, will have been accomplished by measures equally advantageous to the Indians. What the native savages become when surrounded by a dense population, and by mixing with the whites, may be seen in the miserable remnants of a few Eastern tribes, deprived of political and civil rights, forbidden to make contracts, and subjected to guardians, dragging out a wretched existence, without excitement, without hope, and almost without thought."

Petitions were presented to Congress in favor of the rights of the Indians, and also remonstrances against their removal, some of which were the elaborate productions of benevolent societies, while others emanated from distinguished individuals. The citizens of Massachusetts and Pennsylvania took a prominent part in these efforts. In the autumn of this year the Secretary of War, to whom was intrusted the execution of the act of March 28, 1830, presented a comprehensive report to Congress, in which the subject is viewed in all its aspects, speculative and practical, theoretical and demonstrative. In it he made the following excellent suggestions:

"1. A solemn declaration, similar to that already inserted in some of the treaties, that the country assigned to the Indians shall be theirs as long as they or their descendants may occupy it, and a corresponding determination that our settlements shall not spread over it; and every effort should be used to satisfy the Indians of our sincerity and of their security. Without this indispensable preliminary, and without full confidence on their part in our intentions, and in our abilities to give these effect, their change of position would bring no change of circumstances.

"2. A determination to exclude all ardent spirits from their new country. This will no doubt be difficult; but a system of surveillance upon the borders, and of proper police and penalties, will do much towards the extermination of an evil which, where it exists to any considerable extent, is equally destructive of their present comfort and their future happiness.

"3. The employment of an adequate force in their immediate vicinity, and a fixed determination to suppress, at all hazards, the slightest attempt at hostilities among themselves.

"So long as a passion for war, fostered and encouraged as it is by their opinions and habits, is allowed free scope for exercise, it will prove the master-spirit, controlling if not absorbing all other considerations. And if in checking this evil some examples should become necessary, they would be sacrifices to humanity, and not to severity.

"4. Encouragement to the severalty of property, and such provision for its security as their own regulations do not afford and as may be necessary for its enjoyment.

"5. Assistance to all who may require it in the opening of farms and in procuring domestic animals and instruments of agriculture.

"6. Leaving them in the enjoyment of their peculiar institutions as far as may be compatible with their own safety and ours, and with the great objects of their prosperity and improvement.

"7. The eventual employment of persons competent to instruct them as far and as fast as their progress may require, and in such manner as may be most useful to them."

The Indian, although slow to investigate and decide, began to regard the plan with favor, and the better he understood it the more did he approve of it. From this period increased activity and efficiency were imparted to the colonization project.

On the 4th of April, 1832, the Creeks entered into a treaty with the Secretary of War by which they ceded all their lands east of the Mississippi to the United States government in consideration of a grant of seven million acres in the Indian Territory west of that river, to which they agreed to remove at the earliest practicable period.

At Payne's Landing, on the Ocklawaha River, May 9, 1832, the Seminoles ceded their lands in Florida, and agreed to migrate to the country of the Creeks, west of the Mississippi, there to reunite themselves with this cognate tribe. This treaty provided for the immediate payment of fifteen thousand dollars in cash, and the sum of seven thousand dollars was agreed to be paid as a reimbursement to owners of fugitive slaves. This, and other features of the treaty, the Seminoles did not, on reflection, deem satisfactory, and it has been referred to as one of the original causes of the Florida war. They claimed that their assent was obtained through the influence of intoxicating liquors and bribery, denied its validity, and refused to remove from the reservations assigned them in former treaties.

October 11, 1832, the Appalachicolas renewed a prior agreement to remove to the west of the Mississippi, and to surrender the tract on which they lived at the mouth of the Appalachicola River. The Chickasaws, finding themselves surrounded by adverse circumstances, followed these examples by ceding, October 20, 1832, their entire territories east of the Mississippi River. This convention, known as the treaty of Pontitock Creek, is remarkable for the introduction of a stipulation of a new character. The Chickasaws direct that the lands ceded be subdivided and sold for their benefit in the Land Office of the United States, which provision manifests more forecast than the tribes have generally evinced, and in effect has secured their future prosperity and independence.

October 24, 1832, the Kickapoos, by the treaty of Castor Hill, in Missouri, acceded to the plan of removal. On the 26th of October the Pottawatomies ceded their lands in Indiana, taking in payment annuities in money, and agreed to accept a location in the Indian Territory, west of the Mississippi. On the 26th of the same month, the Shawnees and Delawares, near Cape Girardeau, ceded their old Spanish location in that quarter, with the view of removing West, and on the same day the Piankeshaws and Peorias also accepted a location in that region. On the 29th the Weas gave their assent to the project. On the same day the Senecas and Shawnees of the Neosho relinquished the title to their lands, the more perfectly to accommodate themselves to the new plan of settlement.

Without these details it is impossible to form an adequate idea of the class of duties which originated from this scheme of colonization. The labor was incessant, and required to be renewed year after year. It was difficult to satisfy the Indians, as they were ignorant of all the primary elements of knowledge, and very suspicious of the white man's arts. Knowing nothing of the first principles of geometry, space and quantity were estimated in gross. To reduce miles to acres, roods, chains, and links was an art requiring arithmetical accuracy. They had likewise no correct or scientific standard of value for coins. They required to be located and re-located, informed and re-informed, paid and re-paid. This was especially the case with the hunter tribes, whose standard of value had not long previously been a beaver-skin, and whose land-measure had been a day's or a half-day's walk.

CHAPTER IV.

THE BLACK-HAWK WAR.

WHILE the removal of the tribes from the Southwest to their new location in the West was proceeding prosperously, a sudden and unexpected difficulty arose with some tribes residing along the banks of the Upper Mississippi.

The remote key-note of the war-song had been sounded by the Wyandot, Shawnee, and Delaware prophets in 1783, by Elkswattawa in 1812, and by the Creek prophets in 1814. The government of the Union had in various ways been apprised of the dissatisfaction and threatened hostility of the Sacs and the Foxes. The Sac chief Black Hawk, or Muccodakakake, was born in 1767 at the Sac village on Rock River, Wisconsin. His grandfather had lived near Montreal, whence his father, Pyesa, had emigrated to the boundless and attractive field of the great West. He was not a chief's son, but rose to that station through his own ability, having attained great distinction by his successes in war-parties. Black Hawk was one of those dreamers and fasters of the aboriginal race who mistake the impressions of dreams for revelations of the Great Spirit. In his own person he united judgment with courage, and he had acquired much influence in the Indian councils. Pyesa having emigrated to the West while Great Britain exercised sway over it, his preference for that power was very decided. His son, holding the same views, kept up the bias by annual visits to Malden, where presents were distributed by the British Indian Department to the tribes, whether residents of the United States or not. Tales of the generous policy of the British towards the Indians, and of the grasping spirit of the Americans, had been circulated for years by every foreign subordinate in the Indian Territory, who had selfish aims to promote thereby, and who was at the same time indebted to the clemency of the American system for permission to remain in the country the policy of which he traduced. Black Hawk had brooded over the early history of his tribe, and to his view, as he looked down the vista of years, the former times appeared much better than the present, and the vision so wrought upon his susceptible imagination that he began to look upon the past as a veritable golden age. He had some remembrance of a treaty made by General Harrison in 1804, to which his people had not given their assent; and his feelings were with difficulty controlled when he was desired to leave the Rock River Valley in compliance with a treaty made with General Scott at Prairie du Chien, July 15, 1830, by Keokuk, a friendly chief. That valley, however, he peacefully abandoned with his tribe on being notified, and in 1831 went to the west of the Mississippi; but he had spent his youth in that locality, and the more he thought of it the more determined he was to return thither. He readily enlisted the sympathies of the Indians, who are ever prone to ponder on their real or imaginary wrongs; and it may be readily conjectured that what Indian counsel could not accomplish, Indian prophecy would. Without doubt he was encouraged in his course by some tribes, who finally deserted him and denied their complicity when he took up arms and began to experience reverses. Black Hawk claimed to have close relations with the Foxes, Winnebagoes, Sioux, Kickapoos, and others. Early in 1831 he sent a symbolical miniature tomahawk, made of wood, and smeared with vermilion, to the principal war-chief of the Chippewas. This warlike invitation was received at the Chippewa agency, Sault Ste. Marie, at the lower end of Lake Superior, and a report of the effort to enlist the Chippewas in this conspiracy was communicated to the government at Washington. Mr. Schoolcraft was directed to visit the suspected district. He accordingly passed through the Indian country lying between the south shore of Lake Superior and the Mississippi, traversing the lakes and rivers in light canoes manned by Canadian voyageurs, and under a small escort of infantry,—devoting the season to that expedition. He did not discover that any of the tribes were committed to open hostility, but there appeared to be a great familiarity with Black Hawk's plans, and the tribes in league with him were named. In consequence of these disclosures of the existing state of affairs, the spring and summer of the following year (1832) were by direction of the government devoted to a further inspection of the Sioux and Chippewa tribes towards the north.[1]

The Rock River Valley and the adjacent country was ceded to the United States, November 3, 1804, by the Sac and Fox tribes, with a proviso permitting the Indians to continue to reside and hunt on the lands until they were required for settlement. The Sac chief Black Hawk (as we have seen), after an undisturbed occupancy of the lands for twenty-seven years subsequent to the negotiation of this treaty, affected to believe that the chiefs who ceded it, and who were then dead, had not been duly authorized to do so, or that after such a lapse of time his tribe was unjustly required to comply with the terms of the treaty by crossing the Mississippi to its opposite banks. At all events, this plea furnished an excuse for giving vent to the hostility which he had long felt against the Americans.

Black Hawk was one of those aborigines who dwell so long on a single idea that it appears to assume at last sufficient importance to engage the attention of the entire Indian race. The theme of Black Hawk's delusion was the Americans, the hated Americans, who had unjustly supplanted the English in the country, and who were treating the Indians with injustice. He had been a regular attendant at the annual convocations of the aboriginal tribes in Canada, which has been the source whence so much evil political counsel has been transmitted to the Indians residing on the contiguous territory of the United States. It was there that presents were

---

[1] These visits to the distant Northern tribes were the immediate occasion of the discovery of the remote source of the Mississippi. The depth of water on the vast and elevated summits being favorable, the occasion was embraced to trace the Mississippi to its actual source, which was ascertained to be a considerable body of water called Itasca Lake.—See *Discovery of the Sources of the Mississippi*, 1 vol., New York, 1834.

distributed to them in acknowledgment of the services they had formerly rendered to the British armies, and as a means of securing their aid in future contingencies. Hither had Tecumseh come for the benefit of British counsels prior to and during the war of 1812. The Indian tribes regarded Malden as the metropolitan centre, which Detroit had been before the days of General Wayne. The aboriginal chiefs, from Detroit to the Mississippi, as high up as the Falls of St. Anthony, and to the head of Lake Superior, never ceased boasting of the profuse liberality, the wealth, and the power of their British Father. So far as these demonstrations were confined to the limits of the British provinces, no objection certainly could be made to the policy, but on the tribes of the United States, who constituted generally by far the largest part of the assemblages, the effect was to disturb and distract their minds, and to fan the flames of an enmity which, if left to itself, would have died away. Meantime, the few blankets, kettles, and guns which the United States tribes received were no equivalent for the time lost in long journeys, the occasional losses suffered on the road, and the moral degradation to which their families were exposed.

In an evil hour the chief determined to renew the experiment of keeping the intrusive feet of emigrants from his native valley and from the flowing line of the Mississippi. Black Hawk was then about sixty-seven years of age. His features showed great firmness of purpose, and his wisdom had acquired him great respect among the united tribes of the Sacs and Foxes, as well as the Winnebagoes, Iowas, and surrounding tribes. He had undertaken to form a confederacy of the tribes, a task much easier to propose than to effect, there being no certainty how far the tribes who hearkened to his messengers and counsels would fulfil their engagements when the trying hour arrived. But little alarm was excited by the details of Black Hawk's proceedings. At the St. Louis superintendency not much importance appears to have been attached to the menaced hostilities, not only because the time was so unsuitable for the Indians to make another attempt to roll back the tide of civilization, but also because there was no reliable information as to how far the other tribes had consented to act in concert with the Sac chief. The officials at the Michigan superintendency, being nearer to the Indian rendezvous at Malden, were more intimately acquainted with the state of Indian feeling, and, consequently, as considerable uneasiness was felt, the agents on the Chicago borders were instructed to watch closely the Indian movements. Everything denoted that there was an active combination forming among the tribes of the Upper Mississippi, extending to the waters of Lake Superior. The expedition directed to that quarter in June, 1831, proceeded through Lake Superior in canoes and boats to Chegoimegon or La Pointe, thence entered and followed the Muskigo or Mauvais River, ascending through difficult rapids to a lake at its source, passing numerous and intricate portages, and rafts of drift-wood, crossing a portage into the Namakagon or south branch of the St. Croix River, and then descending the main stream to Yellow River. At the St. Croix River it was ascertained that the combination of Black Hawk embraced nine tribes. From the Yellow River the expedition proceeded to Lac Court-Oreille, or Ottawa Lake, at the head of Chippewa River, and by a difficult portage to the Red

Cedar fork, whence it descended the latter to the mouth of the Chippewa River, at the foot of Lake Pepin, on the Mississippi. In its course it diverted from their purpose and arrested a war-party of Indians, under Ninaba, who were on their way to the Mississippi to attack the Sioux. The Mississippi River was finally descended to Galena.[1]

Indications of immediate hostilities were apparent in the spring of 1832. Early in April Black Hawk crossed to the eastern side of the Mississippi with all his tribe, including five hundred warriors, took possession of the Rock River Valley, and announced his intention to plant corn. Troops under the command of General Henry Atkinson, U.S.A., were ordered to ascend the Mississippi and preserve the peace of the frontiers; and the utmost excitement existed in the contiguous Illinois settlements. As soon as the troops were known to be on their way, Black Hawk's warriors proceeded to the residence of the agent, Mr. St. Vrain, at Rock Island, whom they regarded as the instigator of this military movement, and immediately murdered him, scalping and mutilating his body. All the neighboring families received like treatment. The Illinois militia were promptly ordered to the frontier, and an action took place on the 14th of May at Sycamore Creek, in which a battalion of militia under Major Stillman were severely handled. Black Hawk, in his narrative, says that they retreated before a determined fire from forty warriors.

In the mean time, before any overt hostile acts were committed, the agent of the Chippewas was instructed to make a reconnoissance of the Indian country extending north and west of the parts visited in 1831, for the purpose of acquiring more perfect information as to the extent of the dissatisfaction.

The agent was furnished with a small military force of but twelve men, under the command of Lieutenant J. Allen. Leaving the agency at St. Mary's early in June, he passed through Lake Superior to its extreme head, at Fond du Lac, ascended the river St. Louis to the Savanne portage, and thence entered Sandy Lake and the Mississippi. The latter was followed through its windings to the extreme point before visited, at Cass Lake, where an encampment was formed and the baggage left. The height of the waters being favorable, Mr. Schoolcraft set forward from this point in Indian canoes with a select party, fully resolved to discover the source of the Mississippi. The search was pursued, with the aid of an Indian guide, up falls, across lakes, around precipices, through defiles, over drifts, and through winding channels, for three days. The result of this toilsome journey was the arrival of the party at Itasca Lake, which is generally accepted as the true source of the Mississippi, although its remotest springs are several miles away.

The information obtained in this journey demonstrated that the Chippewas and Sioux, whatever sympathies they had with Black Hawk and his scheme, were not committed to his project by any overt participation in it. The Indians were vaccinated, as directed by an act of Congress, and their numbers definitely ascertained. While on a visit to the large band at Leech Lake, their leading chief, Gueule Plat,

---

[1] Schoolcraft's Expedition to Itasca Lake.

exhibited to the agent several British medals which were smeared with vermilion, the symbol of blood, but it appeared to be done rather in a spirit of boastful self-importance than as a threat of alliance with Black Hawk. Information obtained in these reconnoissances implicated the Winnebagoes, Iowas, Kickapoos, Pottawatomies, and some Missouri bands. Meantime, while this expedition was pursuing its explorations, the Sac chief had commenced the war, and had been driven by Generals Atkinson and Dodge to the mouth of the Bad Axe River, between the Falls of St. Anthony and Prairie du Chien. Without being apprised of the impending peril, the expedition escaped all danger by ascending the river to the influx of the St. Croix and passing up that river to the waters of Lake Superior.

An Indian war on the frontiers is always appalling, a few hundred hostile Indians having the power of alarming the inhabitants and disturbing the settlements throughout a wide extent of country. Their apparently ubiquitous character, their subtlety, the facility with which they thread the mazes of the forest, the horrid cruelties practised on the defenceless inhabitants, and their wild onset and noisy outcries when driven into open conflict, always make a deep impression. The ordinary militia are not adequate to the task of repelling such inroads. A man suddenly summoned from his plough or his work-bench to the field has not sufficient discipline or knowledge of camp duty to render him of much service in sudden emergencies. Frequently he does not know either the position or the number of his enemies, and rather helps to increase the confusion and panic than to allay it. Such was the case when Black Hawk made his inroad into Illinois and Wisconsin, and before a sufficient force of the regular army could be drawn from remote points, the most that the militia and volunteers could effect was to keep him in check. For a considerable time the head-quarters of the Sac chief were located at or about Lake Koshkonong, near the upper end of Rock River Valley, or near the Four Lakes, now the site of Madison, the State capital of Wisconsin.

One of the appalling incidents of this campaign was the fact that the Asiatic cholera first made its appearance among the United States troops while on their march to the scene of conflict. On the banks of the St. Clair, at Fort Gratiot, at Michilimackinac, at Chicago, and at every harbor for vessels and steamers, the most frightful mortality occurred. A characteristic feature of this disease was the rapidity with which it terminated in a fatal result,—a few hours intervening only between the appearance of the first symptoms and death. The best medical men were at fault, and had to study the features of the disease before they could cope with it.

This calamity added to the delay in reaching the scene of action, and gave the wily chief a little breathing-time. General Scott landed his army at Chicago with all practicable expedition, and instantly sent forward a detachment to reconnoitre the position of Black Hawk and force him to give battle. A general action is, however, one of the very last resorts of an Indian captain. It is contrary to the Indian mode of warfare, which consists of operations in detail, secret and crafty attacks, and sudden movements, which are practicable only for an army unencumbered with baggage. General Scott did not reach the Indian country, however, until the last gun had been fired. General Atkinson pursued the Indians up the Rock River Valley, where their trail gave evidence of their suffering from want of food. In this pursuit, the knowledge of wood-craft, of the Indian mode of warfare, and of the local geography, possessed by Colonel Henry Dodge, enabled the commander to conduct his movements with great precision. Atkinson's force consisted of four hundred regulars and nine hundred volunteers, commanded by Generals Henry, Alexander, and Dodge. After some skirmishing, Black Hawk was traced across the Wisconsin River, and hotly pursued towards the west. After a harassing march, his ill-fed, starving, and worn-down forces were finally overtaken at the junction of the Bad Axe River with the Mississippi, where a steamer (the Warrior) opened her fire on him. While in the act of effecting a crossing, on the 2d of August, the American army arrived, and an immediate action ensued, in which the Indians were defeated and nearly one hundred and fifty of them killed. Some of the Sac warriors, and the women and children of the tribe, had, however, succeeded in crossing. Black Hawk escaped, but soon afterwards voluntarily delivered himself up to the agent at Prairie du Chien.

Black Hawk was carried a prisoner to Washington. Private vengeance clamored for his blood in expiation of the foul murders perpetrated by his warriors, but, to the credit of the President, General Jackson, he firmly resisted these importunities, saying that the chief had surrendered as a prisoner of war, and that he should be treated as such. After his advent at the capital, Black Hawk was taken to see the military works at Fort Monroe by an officer of the army, who was appointed to escort him through the seaboard cities to his own country, that he might form adequate notions of the populousness of the Union. He was safely conducted to his home on the distant Mississippi, where he lived many years, a wiser and a better man. After his death his tribesmen gave to his remains those rites of sepulture which are bestowed only upon their most distinguished men. They buried him in his war-dress, in a sitting posture, on an eminence, and covered him with a mound of earth.

The campaign lasted seventy-nine days. The captives were taken to Rock Island. They informed General Scott that the Winnebagoes, our professed allies, had been operating on both sides; and in the treaty which followed their treachery was punished, and the lands upon which they had lived from time immemorial, and to which they were strongly attached, were taken from them.

CHAPTER V.

SUBDIVISION OF THE INDIAN TERRITORY AMONG THE EMIGRANT TRIBES—
IMPORTANT TREATIES.

The proper adjustment of boundaries between the tribes in the new Territories became a subject of infinite perplexity. As the Indians acquired a better knowledge of arithmetical measures and quantities, they became keen bargainers, and strenuously demanded their full dues. It sometimes happened that boundaries conflicted, and whenever an interest or a right was surrendered to accommodate another tribe, the United States government was ready to grant an equivalent in land, money, or right of occupancy. The volumes of treaties contain an amount of interesting matter on this subject which is creditable alike to the Republic and to the activity of the Indian mind. An acre, an improvement, a salt-spring, or a stream of pure water was held at its just value.

On the 14th of February, 1833, the United States engaged to secure to the Cherokees forever seven millions of acres of land in the Indian Territory, including the smaller tract previously granted them by the Barbour treaty, signed May 6, 1828. By a separate article the Cherokees released the United States from providing "a plain set of laws, suited to their condition."

On the same day a treaty was concluded specifying the boundaries between the United States, the Creeks, and the Cherokees, which also provided that collisions between the tribes should be avoided, and compensation made to them by the United States for the improvements they surrendered, in order to enable the government to furnish the Cherokees with their full quota of lands. By a treaty concluded on the 28th of March, 1833, a definite location was assigned to the Seminoles, who had migrated to the West and settled down among the Creeks. On the 13th of May the Quapaws relinquished their territory to the Caddoes, a cognate tribe on the Red River, in consideration of a tract of one hundred and fifty sections of land granted them by the United States on the Neosho, with liberal donations of cattle, oxen, hogs, sheep, agricultural implements, arms, ammunition, clothing, the services of a blacksmith and farmer, and other advantages.

On the 18th of June, 1833, the Appalachicolas, of Florida, ceded certain lands, with the exception of some reservations, and were admitted, on the principle of a reunion, to share with the Seminoles the benefits of the treaty concluded at Payne's Landing. It was stipulated that they should sell their reservations before leaving Florida and removing West, in which case they engaged to defray the expenses of their removal.

On the 21st of September, the Otoes and Missourias surrendered their lands to the United States for valuable considerations, agreeing to accept another tract in lieu thereof, and to engage in agricultural pursuits.

Under the provisions of the act passed July 14, 1832, three commissioners were appointed to proceed to the Indian Territory, west of the States of Missouri and Arkansas, to make an examination of its character and resources and divide it into suitable districts for the expatriated tribes. These commissioners, after an elaborate examination and survey, occupying nearly two years, made a report on the 10th of February, 1834. They had set apart, and recommended to be allotted to the tribes, the entire district west of the States of Missouri and Arkansas, comprised between the latitude of Red River and that of the Platte or Nebraska River, extending west to the line of Texas, thence north along the 100th degree of longitude to the banks of the Arkansas, and up the latter river to the Rocky Mountains. The Indian Territory originally included Kansas and Nebraska.

Congress having now the requisite data, and being prepared to act definitely on the subject, the Hon. Horace Everett, Chairman of Indian Affairs in the House of Representatives, made an elaborate report reviewing the policy and action of the government from the beginning, and submitting for consideration and approval separate acts for the organization of the Indian Department, for the revision of the original act of 1802 regulating trade and intercourse with the Indian tribes, and for the organization of the Indian Territory. The former of these acts received the sanction of Congress,—the plan of a mixed civil and Indian government, which was prepared, having been abandoned because it was regarded as in some respects incongruous, and, on the whole, rather in advance of their actual necessities. The act of March 28, 1830, laying the legal foundation of the colonization plan, was the organic law, but these acts followed out the general features of that law, to which we may ascribe the completion of the colonization plan originally recommended to Congress by Mr. Monroe nine years previously.

The year 1835 was distinguished by several treaties of an important character. Hitherto the inchoate confederacy of the Pottawatomies, Chippewas, and Ottawas of Northern Illinois had retained its ancient position in the vicinity of Chicago, at the head of Lake Michigan. On the 26th of September, 1833, they ceded to the United States their lands on the western shores of that lake in exchange for a tract comprising 5,000,000 acres in the West, in consideration of very large annuities, to be paid in coin and its equivalents. It was stipulated that $150,000 should be appropriated to the purchase of goods and provisions, $100,000 to satisfy the claims of sundry individuals to certain reservations, $150,000 to liquidate the claims of debtors against the tribes, agreeably to a schedule annexed, $280,000 to the payment of annuities of $14,000 per annum for twenty years, $150,000 for the erection of mills, farm-houses, shops, and the supply of agricultural implements and stock, and for the support of such artisans, smiths, and other mechanics as were necessary to the inauguration of their colonial existence in the West, and $70,000 for educational purposes. This treaty encountered numerous objections in the Senate, and was not ratified until the 21st of February, 1835, and then only with certain exceptions.

The principle of acknowledging the individual debts of the hunter tribes as national obligations had been previously recognized in a treaty with the Quapaws, concluded May 13, 1833, but the amount appropriated for that object in the Chicago treaty, and the extensive personal schedules accompanying it, excited remark in the Senate, and induced that body to question the propriety of nationalizing the debts of the tribes. The experience of the Senate also made it averse to granting large reservations in lands to the tribes, as well as to their blood-relations, especial local friends, and habitual benefactors, out of the tracts ceded; since it was found that such reservations, being in a few years surrounded by a civilized population, acquired such a value as to render their purchase again necessary for the purposes of agriculture. General Jackson, whose knowledge of Indian affairs had been acquired by personal observation, censured this policy decidedly, and deemed it preferable for many reasons to compensate both the tribes and their blood-relations with payments in money.

In order to accommodate the emigrating tribes, it was necessary to procure the cession of large tracts from the aboriginal nations in the West, who roved over immense plains, cultivating nothing, and living principally on the flesh of the buffalo. By the treaty of October 9, 1833, the Pawnees ceded a large district lying south of the Platte, or Nebraska, which afforded locations to several of the Eastern tribes. The Kansas, by the treaty of August 16, 1825, ceded all their lands lying within the boundaries of the State of Missouri, as also the wide tracts lying along the Missouri River, to the west of the western line of the State, comprising the valleys of the Kansas, Nodaway, and Nemaha.

The tract ceded by the Kansas tribe comprehended a large part of the present State of Kansas. It is somewhat remarkable that while a geographical exploration was being made of this Territory, a respected and intelligent agent reported to the Secretary of War, May 12, 1834, that not over one-half the quantity of land lying within this parallel of latitude, north of the Osage Reservation, and extending to the Nebraska, was adapted to the purposes of agriculture. So far from this being the fact, it is precisely this part of Kansas which has been settled most rapidly and is most esteemed for its fertility and admired for its sylvan beauty. Michigan, one of the best regions in the West for the growth of wheat and corn, was at first pronounced unfit to bestow upon the soldiers of the war of 1812 as bounty lands. In 1680, that stout old joker and unfrocked monk, Baron La Hontan, called the area of the upper lakes, now an immense mart of commerce and agriculture, "the fag end of the world." Not only subsequent to the explorations of the several expeditions to the sources of the Mississippi and Red Rivers, in 1820 and 1823, but even so late as 1836, much of the country lying north of Green Bay, and nearly the entire area of Minnesota, at the period when the country of Lake Superior was annexed to the State of Michigan, was considered to be unfavorable, if not wholly unsuitable, for agricultural purposes. A large part of the Indian Territory, located west of

Arkansas, likewise, at the period of the inception of the colonization plan, was reported to be deficient in timber, water, and fertility.

The Chickasaw Indians evidently labored under this impression during some years, for at the original sale of their lands at Pontitock, October 20, 1832, many of them expressed a determination to remain on their old reservations and there cultivate the soil. Two years' experience, however, caused them to change their views. In the preamble to a treaty negotiated at Washington, May 24, 1834, they express a regret that they " are about to abandon their homes, which they have long cherished and loved; and, though hitherto unsuccessful, they still hope to find a country adequate to the wants and support of their people somewhere west of the Mississippi, and within the territorial limits of the United States." By this treaty they ceded their reservations east of the Mississippi, at the same time making some personal, beneficiary, and eleemosynary provisions. They also directed the proceeds to be added to their vested funds, and agreed to send a delegation to the West to seek a location. This delegation visited the West during the year 1835, and selected a location in connection with the Choctaws, a closely-affiliated people, making their own terms, as tribe with tribe.

There now remained but one question of any importance to settle with the Southern tribes,—viz., that with the Cherokees, who had been the first to suggest a Western outlet for their hunter population. The nation had now become politically divided into two parties, the one being favorable to emigration, the other adverse to it. The latter numbered among its leaders the noted chief John Ross, and comprised a majority of the nation. Their policy contemplated the retention of their lands, the continuance of the agricultural labors so successfully commenced, and the fostering of the ample educational facilities they then possessed, as well as of those arts and domestic industrial pursuits which had been developed by their location in a region eminently fruitful, healthful, beautiful to the eye, and hallowed by associations connected both with the living and the dead. The emigration party contended that these superlative advantages could not be permanently maintained, that the right of sovereignty to the country could not be wrested from the States who possessed it, that schools could be established and teachers obtained in the West, and that they were offered an ample and fertile country, beyond the limits of any State or Territory, under the solemn guarantee of Congress, over which they could extend their own laws and form of government, and where the arts, industry, and knowledge they had acquired could not but hasten the development of their character and make them a powerful as well as prosperous people.

A treaty ceding their lands was concluded at New Echota December 29, 1835, with the party favorable to emigration. In consideration of the payment of five million dollars, they ceded all their territory east of the Mississippi River, and agreed to remove to the West and rejoin their brethren already there. Twenty chiefs of high character, and possessed of influence and intelligence, signed this treaty,—Ridge, Rogers, Starr, Gunter, Belt, and Boudinot being of the number. A delegation of influential Cherokees, members of the opposing party, immediately proceeded to

Washington with the view of preventing its ratification by the Senate. The subject excited deep interest, but the validity of the treaty was finally sustained. Some supplementary articles were added to the original instrument, and the Senate, by a resolution, granted to the Cherokees an additional sum of $600,000 to liquidate claims held against them. In this form the treaty was eventually ratified, May 23, 1836.

Other conventional agreements followed. A treaty was concluded with the Caddoes as early as July 1 of this year, though not ratified until 1836. This tribe, in whom we recognize one of the bands descended from the indomitable Kapakas of De Soto's era, ceded all their lands lying within the boundaries of States, and expressed their determination to remove to Texas, which was not then a part of the United States.

The Comanches and Wichitaws, two important tribes then residing in Texas, now first opened a political intercourse with the United States. A treaty with them was signed on August 24, 1835, and ratified on May 19, 1836. In order that it might effectually serve the ends sought, and be the evidence of peace and friendship not only with the United States, but also with the tribes by whom they were surrounded and with whom they associated, it was assented to and signed by large delegations of the Western Cherokees, Choctaws, Osages, Senecas of the Neosho, and Quapaws. The Comanches promised to restrain their marauding parties from encroaching on the territory of the United States, to make restitution for injuries done, to receive Indians and citizens of the United States on terms of amity, and to take the first steps towards progress in civilization.

From early times the Chippewas had, under their generic appellation and the various local names of their several subdivisions, constituted one of the most powerful bodies of Indians in the Northwest. In a region half covered with lakes, to be good canoe-men, expert warriors, keen hunters, active foresters, and eloquent speakers, are most important qualifications in the members of the tribes. Having been friends of the French from the period of their landing in Canada, the Chippewas adhered to the fortunes of that nation until the final surrender of the country to the English, when they transferred their attachment to the latter power. They fought for the French on the bloody field which was the scene of Braddock's defeat, at Michilimackinac, and at Detroit, and aided their new allies, the British, at St. Clair's defeat, and in almost every battle fought during the Revolutionary and post-Revolutionary wars. At length, having been defeated on the Thames, under Tecumseh, by General Harrison, they returned to their haunts, vexed and dissatisfied. In 1820 they opposed the entrance of an official American exploratory expedition into Lake Superior, and hoisted the British flag in defiance. Two years subsequently an American garrison was stationed and an Indian agency located at the foot of that lake, and intercourse opened with them. Some few years later the British withdrew the post from Drummond Island, at the entrance of the Straits of St. Mary, and, retiring to a post on Lake Huron, at Penetanguishene, planted an Indian colony on the large limestone chain of the Manitoulin, where the tribes were invited to settle by Sir Francis

Head, without respect to the political boundaries of their home location. This policy was ill judged. The Indians as a body did not wish to engage in agriculture, and such as did found the soil was poor and that there existed no compensating advantages. Many of the tribes lived in the United States and received annuities, which they must relinquish by permanently migrating to the Manitoulin. Hence the failure of the plan. Having been warriors and hunters during all that period of their history with which we were acquainted, these tribes still continued to pursue the same vocations, with the difference that, the wars in which they had been allies of Europeans having terminated, they were destitute of employment, while at the same time their hunting-grounds were exhausted. War had reduced their numbers, and the decline of the fur-trade had left them in debt. But one general mode of recruiting their affairs remained to them: they were possessed of immense tracts of lands, some of which were of a rich agricultural character, others contained valuable mines and were covered with forests of timber, while on the lake shores were valuable fisheries. Many millions of square miles intervened between their extreme borders. To cede a portion of their lands in consideration of annuities, and to pledge a part for the establishment of schools, arts, and agriculture in their midst, was clearly the proper course to be pursued; and for this purpose a large delegation of the chiefs visited Washington during the autumn and winter of 1835–36, where they were joined by a similar delegation of the Ottawas. With respect to the Manitoulin scheme, it required means, which the British government withheld, and industry, which the Indians did not possess. Besides, if they were inclined to form industrious habits, the most advantageous position for their exercise would be that pointed out by the American government, in the fertile fields of the West.

The Chippewa tribe had always exercised an important influence. These natives were personally a tall, active, and brave race of men, renowned in Indian story for prowess in war, for skill in the chase and diplomacy, and for their excellent oratorical powers. It was observed by the French, at a very early period, that they possessed a body of oral legendary lore which made their lodge-circles attractive, and an ingenious mode of distinguishing family ties and clans by totemic devices or pictographic symbols. A similar system of ideographic signs was used to supply the place of the art of notation, for their songs, and for brief memorials displayed on their cedar grave-posts.

When the delegates of the tribe arrived at Washington, the Secretary of War, to whom the government of Indian affairs at that time pertained, and who, having formerly resided in the West, was aware that the Ottawas and Chippewas held their lands very much in common, directed the Chippewa chiefs to be present at the conferences, and intrusted the negotiation to their agent, Mr. Schoolcraft. The conferences occupied the entire season, delegates having been invited from remote points, and the deliberations were protracted, but on the 28th of March they united in a general cession. The Ottawas and Chippewas of Grand Traverse Bay ceded all their territories, extending from Grand River, on the lower peninsula, to the Straits of Michilimackinac, thence north, along the Straits of St. Mary's, to Lake Superior, and up its southern shores to the influx of Gitche Seebi, or the Great River, thence to the river Menominee of Green Bay, and along a water-line to the place of beginning at Grand River Lake, Michigan.

The cession of 1836 was far the largest ever made by this tribe, including hunting-grounds, homesteads, burial-grounds, and ossuaries which they had possessed and cherished for centuries. Seas were, in fact, comprised within the limits of the territory ceded, for the character and amplitude of the lakes entitle them to be so called. About 16,000,000 acres of these lands were located in the upper peninsula, or the Algoma region, lying along the shores of Lake Superior, in addition to those situate in Lower Michigan. Large reservations of the best tracts were secured to them in different locations; upwards of $3,000,000 were stipulated to be paid them in annuities within twenty years, $300,000 to be expended in liquidation of their debts, $150,000 to be distributed in gratuities to their half-breed descendants, and presents of goods and clothing to the amount of $150,000 to be made them on the ratification of the treaty. Ample provision was made for their education, and for their tuition in agriculture and the arts. Their surplus lands, which had lost their value as hunting-grounds, thus furnished the means not only for their present subsistence, but also for their instruction in arts and letters, and for their advancement in every element of civilized life. The number of persons who participated in these benefits was about four thousand five hundred. In a report of the superintendent made to the government on the 30th of September, 1840, they are returned on the pay-rolls, as organized in their separate bands and villages, at five thousand and twenty souls.

CHAPTER VI.

WAR WITH THE SEMINOLES OF FLORIDA—MASSACRE OF DADE'S COMMAND—
BATTLE OF THE WITHLACOOCHEE—BATTLE OF OKEECHOBEE—OSCEOLA—
GENERAL WORTH BRINGS THE WAR TO A CLOSE.

The Seminoles[1] are connected with the Creeks by ties both of blood and of language. Their sympathies had been with the Creeks in their long controversy with Georgia, but their action during the period of which we are about to speak appears to have arisen from internal dissatisfaction. In an elaborate report, made February 9, 1836, and communicated by the President to Congress, it is asserted that the Seminoles were not satisfied with the terms of the treaty concluded at Payne's Landing, May 9, 1832. For this dissatisfaction they had excellent reasons. Its extent and importance were not then known. The difficulty does not appear to be stated in any of the reports made by the agents, and the government was ignorant of it. On their failure to comply with their treaty agreement to remove to the West, and the expiration of the time granted for that purpose, troops were concentrated in the vicinity of the Seminoles, and the local commander, General Clinch, was directed to organize companies of regulars. In February, 1835, he was authorized to draw from the North six additional companies, four of which were artillery. A spirit of restlessness was evinced by the Indians during the summer and autumn. Several outrages occurred while keeping up the communications between fort and fort, and it was apprehended that the Creeks secretly participated in this feeling of animosity. In November, General Clinch having reported that it would be necessary to call out volunteers for the protection of the frontiers, he was authorized to deliver arms from the public stores for their equipment. The maintenance of the lines of communication between distant posts, separated by a wilderness country, interspersed with deep creeks, and frequently with dense thickets and hammocks, was a difficult and harassing service. The lines were attacked at various points, and the defiles and quagmires offered singular facilities for the prosecution of the Indian mode of warfare. Fort King, the head-quarters of the army, was situated about one hundred miles from Fort Brooke, on Tampa Bay, the Withlacoochee River intervening. The Indians burned down a bridge over a deep stream, within six miles of Fort Brooke,

---

[1] The name Seminole designates their assumption of tribal independence, and was intended to be derogatory in its first application by the Creeks. It may, as more or less censure is intended, be rendered "separatists, refractory men, rebels, or refugees." The period of the separation is uncertain. They withdrew from the parent tribe either while residing on the Altamaha, or at an earlier period, before the Creeks had reached the eastern terminus of their migration. When the Seminoles left the upland valleys of Alabama and Georgia they withdrew to the intricate recesses of the interior lakes, lagoons, hammocks, and everglades of Florida.

but it was rebuilt. At this time there were upwards of six hundred regular troops in the field.

The Seminoles, or Mickosaukies, occupied all the extensive range of country lying between the Cape of Florida on the south, the St. Mary's River on the north, and the Perdido on the west. Including women, children, and negroes, the estimated number of Indians was three thousand, four hundred or five hundred of whom were fighting-men,—an under-estimate, as events proved.

A mail-carrier had been murdered in August within six miles of Tampa Bay, Charles Emathla, a chief friendly to emigration, had been scalped, the Mickosaukies were hostile, and held a strong position on the Withlacoochee River, the Tallassees were accused of holding secret councils, and the Pea Creek band were engaged in continual depredations. The aspect of affairs was extremely threatening.

While matters were in this position, on the 23d of December, Major Francis L. Dade, with a detachment of two companies, one six-pounder, and the usual complement of military stores and supplies, marched from Fort Brooke, on Tampa Bay, for Fort King, distant one hundred and thirty miles, the route lying through an unsettled country. The entire force numbered one hundred muskets. The first day he halted at a stream, distant seven miles from Fort Brooke, called the Little Hillsboro River, the bridge over which had been burned by the hostile Indians and subsequently rebuilt. The following day he progressed six miles, reached the Big Withlacoochee on the 27th, and on the 28th arrived at the defile where he was waylaid by the Indians, distant sixty-five miles from Fort Brooke. He was attacked about ten o'clock on the morning of the 28th. It appeared that the Indians had narrowly watched his march, disturbing his barricades at night, but keeping out of sight on his flanks during the day, until he had proceeded a few miles beyond the Withlacoochee, where one hundred Pea Creek warriors, under the negro Harry, and, as has been estimated, more than double that number of the Mickosaukies, and of the bands of Eufaulas and Alafias, under the chiefs Little Cloud and Alligator, formed an ambuscade on both sides of the road. The column, marching in ordinary open order, was suddenly attacked on all sides with showers of arrows and balls. Major Dade and nearly half his command fell at the first fire. Those who survived took shelter behind trees, while Lieutenant Basinger poured in five or six rounds of canister upon the Indians, which checked them for a time, and they retired behind a small ridge. Under the direction of Captain Gardiner, the soldiers at once began to construct a breastwork of pine-trees. Soon the Indians returned and opened a crossfire upon the work with deadly effect. About two o'clock the last man fell, and the Indians rushed into the defenceless breastwork.

Lieutenant Basinger, after being fatally wounded, had his throat cut by a negro. The most horrid butchery occurred. Several of the wounded, who knew the leaders of the enemy, appealed for their lives in vain: the cry for quarter was answered by the knife or tomahawk. Not an officer nor any of the command escaped, except two soldiers who crept off. After being badly wounded, but yet remaining perfectly conscious, they lay motionless among the dead until an opportunity offered for escape. Some accounts estimate the American loss at one hundred and twelve men. The Indians had three killed and five wounded.

Such was the massacre (for battle it was not) of the Withlacoochee, the news of which operated like an electric shock, and made as deep an impression on the Americans as the massacre at Cabul did, in after-times, on the British in India. An officer writing from Fort Brooke on the 1st of January, four days after the sanguinary event, says, "Such are the Indian combinations that it is not considered practicable to force or keep open a communication with Fort King with less than a well appointed and instructed force of one thousand men. Three out of four bridges are destroyed, and two fords are very difficult, and the country may generally be described as a series of ambuscades and defiles."

On the 31st of December, General Clinch, with two hundred regulars and a large force of militia volunteers, marched to the Withlacoochee, and fought a sharp action on the banks of that stream, near the scene of Dade's defeat, with the same Indians, who manifested as much determined intrepidity as they had previously evinced. The regulars and twenty-seven volunteers had crossed the river when the attack began. The Indians, led by Osceola and Alligator, numbered two hundred and fifty. The latter were protected by a heavy hammock and scrub, and poured a galling fire upon the troops, who, after being twice repulsed, in a final charge succeeded in routing them. The regulars lost four killed and twenty-five wounded. The volunteers had fifteen wounded.

It is difficult to depict the commotion created in Florida by these events. The Indians attacked every defenceless house and plantation, murders and conflagrations devastated the country, and the accounts of the atrocities of the savages, were they collated, would fill a book. "The newspapers," says a writer from St. Mary's, in Georgia, under date of January 16, "have, perhaps, abundantly informed you to what a deplorable situation we are now reduced. The temporizing policy of General Thompson, the Indian Superintendent, and the forbearance of our government, have set the merciless savages upon our plantations, our crops, and our dwellings, and really I do not see what is to become of us and this country if military succors do not immediately arrive. The Indians seem to be fully bent on the most determined resistance, and in the action on the Withlacoochee displayed a firmness and desperation never exceeded in the history of Indian warfare."

A simultaneous outbreak took place throughout Florida. On the 28th of December, the day of Dade's massacre, a party of ten men were dining with Rodgers, the sutler at Fort King, in a dwelling distant not two hundred and fifty yards from the block-house, when they were suddenly beset and fired on by a party of Indians. A hundred shots, it is estimated, were discharged through the open window, by which the host, who was sitting at the head of his table, and four of his guests, were killed. Among the latter were General Thompson, the Indian Agent, Lieutenant Constantine Smith, U.S.A., and two others. Five persons, who fled to the fort, escaped. The officials and attendants sought refuge in a hammock, but were shot down before they reached it. The cook, a negro woman, who hid herself behind a barrel, and succeeded in effecting her escape, witnessed all the barbarities committed. Osceola, who was the leader of the party, entered first, upset a table, gazed sternly round for a moment, and then went out. The body of Thompson, the agent, was found to have been pierced with fifteen bullets, and sixteen entered that of Rodgers. The Indians scalped all the dead to the very ears, and then beat in their skulls.

Between the day of the massacre and the middle of the ensuing January a wide extent of country was made a scene of desolation. Houses were burned, the occupants killed, cattle and stock driven off, the mail-routes interrupted, and a general panic and confusion created.

The causes which originated this war become apparent when attention is directed to the peculiar prejudices and mental reservations of the Indians. By the treaty negotiated at Payne's Landing, on the Ocklawaha, May 9, 1832, the Seminoles ceded their lands, and all claims to lands which they held in Florida, in consideration of the payment to them of a yearly annuity of $15,400. They also agreed to send a delegation of their most respected chiefs to view the territory offered them west of the Mississippi, and to ascertain whether the Western Creeks would allow the Seminoles to rejoin them. It was stipulated in the treaty that the improvements left in Florida should be paid for by the United States, their cattle be estimated and paid for, and the blacksmiths' services, sanctioned by a prior treaty, be continued to them in the West. Provision was made that each person, on reaching the new location, should receive a blanket and a home-spun frock, and an additional annuity of $3000 per year for fifteen years was to be divided among them. Claims having been made on them for runaway slaves from the Southern plantations, $7000 were allowed for the satisfaction of such demands. Under the seventh article of this treaty they agreed to remove within three years, at the expense of the United States, by whom they were to be supplied with one year's subsistence in the new territory. A treaty concluded with the Creeks at Fort Gibson, March 28, 1833, provided for the rebel tribe an ample country. The Seminoles living north of the boundary-line designated by the treaty of Camp Moultrie began to remove to the West, but these removals proceeded slowly, being delayed by embarrassments. At the close of the time stipulated by the treaty of May 9, 1832, it having been decided that the emigrants should proceed by water across the Gulf of Mexico to their Western home, vessels for their transportation arrived at Tampa Bay, and their speedy embarkation was urged. Throughout the year 1835 there appeared to be strong objections to emigration on the part of all the principal Seminole bands, and they finally refused to go.

In a full report made to Congress by the War Department, February 9, 1836, this general dissatisfaction with the treaty of Payne's Landing is the cause assigned for the war. In its prosecution geographical phenomena singularly favored the cause of the Seminoles, and it may be figuratively said that the country itself fought for them; every swamp and hammock was a fortress.

Unquestionably this war was waged on the part of the United States government to obtain possession of the lands of the natives, but it arose primarily from a desire to reduce to slavery the warriors of Florida, and from the determination of South

Carolina and Georgia not to permit the existence so near their borders of an asylum for fugitive slaves.

Nature has rendered the peninsula of Florida peculiarly attractive to the Indians. Its tangled morasses, its dense and impenetrable hammocks, and its serpentine streams form so many natural defences against European enemies; and spontaneous means of subsistence are abundant. The rivers are the haunts of vast numbers of waterfowl, the adjoining seas abound in turtle, and the soil yields a profusion of vegetable nourishment in the coontie-plant, which affords a kind of sago, known locally, but incorrectly, as arrow-root. Cattle, originally introduced by the Spaniards, were found to reproduce on the prairie meadows with great rapidity. The Florida war was a contest waged against geographical and climatic laws. To elude the pursuit of an enemy in these labyrinths was so easy a matter that an Indian hidden in a hammock could not be discovered at the distance of ten feet.

Successive commanders, Generals Gaines, Scott, and Call, having failed to produce any appreciable result in Florida, the task was assigned to General Jesup, who began a vigorous campaign in 1837. A succession of defeats soon convinced the Indians that they could not longer maintain themselves against the United States forces, and by the 23d of June upwards of seven hundred of them, including Micanopy, their head chief, under the terms of capitulation at Fort Dade, March 6, 1837, came in prepared to emigrate, and had camped near Tampa, where twenty-five transports had been stationed to take them to Arkansas. Everything was in readiness, when suddenly Osceola, at the head of two hundred Mickosaukies, appeared upon the scene, and either forced or persuaded the entire number to leave the camp and take refuge in the everglades. Various causes contributed to bring about this result. Many negroes had taken refuge with the Indians, and were liable to be returned to their owners, contrary to the terms of the treaty, if the emigration should take place. The younger chiefs, at the head of whom was Osceola, were anxious to defeat the emigration project, and the latter had the address to make them credit such absurd stories as that once embarked their throats would all be cut.

Volunteers from the neighboring States were now called out, and active hostilities, which had ceased while negotiations were going on at Fort Dade, were resumed. In October Osceola and Coe-Hajo, who had come to Fort Peyton for an interview with General Hernandez, were seized by General Jesup's order, upon the ground of their having capitulated at Fort Dade in March previous, and imprisoned at Fort Augustine. On December 25, Colonel Zachary Taylor, afterwards President of the United States, fought the severe battle of Okeechobee, against about four hundred Indians under Alligator, Halleck-Tustenugge, and Coacoochc, whom he routed and pursued. His loss was twenty-six killed and one hundred and twelve wounded. The Indian loss was comparatively slight. Taylor succeeded Jesup in the chief command May 15, 1838, and after two years of harassing service was succeeded by Colonel Armistead. This officer was in turn relieved, in May, 1841, by Colonel William J. Worth, making the eighth commander sent out to close the war.

Undeniably the master-spirit of this war was As-se-se-ho-lar, or Black Drink, commonly called Osceola, or Powell. He was a half-breed, and when a child had been taken by his mother, who was of the Creek tribe, to Florida, and lived near Fort King. He was about thirty-three years of age when captured, and was of medium size and of resolute and manly bearing, with a clear, frank, and engaging countenance. By his firmness and audacity he forced the nation into a war which a large majority were averse to, and either broke up every attempt at negotiation or prevented its fulfilment. He was to have been one of the leaders at Dade's massacre, but was delayed by his participation in the affair at Fort King, previously narrated, and respecting which we have the following explanation:

While on a visit to Fort King, in company with his wife and a few friends, for the purpose of trading, the wife of Osceola, in the presence of Agent Thompson, was seized as a slave. She was a beautiful woman, the daughter of a chief, but, having negro blood in her veins, the law pronounced her a slave. Osceola became frantic with rage, but was instantly seized and placed in irons, while his wife was hurried away to slave-holding pollution. He remained six days in irons, when, General Thompson says, he became penitent, and was released. From the moment when this outrage was committed, Osceola swore vengeance upon Thompson and those who assisted in the perpetration of this crime, and the Florida war commenced. He or some of his friends kept constant watch on Thompson's movements, and soon found an opportunity for vengeance.

He was in the battle of the Withlacoochee, and led the attack upon Micanopy, where, within sight of the fort, he attacked in an open field upwards of one hundred regulars supported by a field-piece. His capture by General Jesup while under the sanction of a flag of truce was a flagrant violation of the laws and usages of nations. Dignified and courteous in his manners, Osceola showed himself a brave and at the same time cautious leader upon the field. It is said that he instructed his warriors in their predatory incursions to spare the women and children. Upon his removal to Charleston he became dejected, pined away, and in a few weeks died of a broken heart (January 30, 1838). He was buried just outside of the principal gateway of Fort Moultrie, where a monument marks the resting-place of this native patriot and hero.[1]

Okeechobee was the last great fight in which the Indians were engaged. Their policy now was to avoid giving battle, and, moving rapidly by night, to seize every opportunity to wreak their vengeance on the unarmed inhabitants. Murders were committed by them within a few miles of Tallahassee and St. Augustine. This state of things continued with brief intervals of quietness until the spring of 1841, when Worth was assigned to the command. No officer ever entered upon a more unpromising field in which to acquire distinction. All the best officers of the army, many of them experienced in Indian warfare, had failed to conquer the Indians, who were effectually concealed in almost inaccessible everglades and swamps, where their families and crops were secure, and whence they could sally forth upon long expedi-

---

[1] Fairbanks's History of Florida, p. 315.

tions for murder and rapine. Fully comprehending the task before him, the new commander at once organized his force in the most effective manner, establishing his head-quarters at Fort King. Simultaneous movements against the Indians took place in every district, breaking up their camps and destroying their crops and stores. Every swamp and hammock between the Atlantic and Gulf coasts was visited, and the band of Halleck-Tustenuggee was routed out of the Wahoo swamp. The detachments continued scouting the country twenty-five days. Six hundred men were engaged, about one-fourth of whom were obliged to be sent to the hospitals, the mercury averaging 86°. The capture of Coacoochee, June 15, was so well improved by Worth that during the month of August his entire band, two hundred in number, at that chief's persuasion, came in and surrendered. In October a combined land and naval expedition was made through the Everglades and the Big Cypress swamp, the Indian stronghold, where Arpeika and the Prophet held supreme command. Their huts were burned, their fields devastated, and they fled in every direction. The Indians now saw that no hiding-place was secure, and that, with a vigilant and energetic commander like Worth to deal with, they had no further hope. Parties of them sued for peace, came in, and were from time to time forwarded to Arkansas.

Early in 1842, General Worth made a final effort to capture Halleck-Tustenugge and his band. This cunning and vindictive chief had hitherto baffled every detachment sent after him. He was now brought to bay and surrounded in the Pilaklikaha swamp, and here, in April, 1842, the last important action of the war was fought. The troops charged the hammocks with great gallantry, and received the fire of the Indians, who discharged their rifles rapidly but soon broke into small parties and escaped. The band was shortly afterwards captured by Colonel Garland while attending a feast, and a little later its chief was secured by General Worth. This was one of the most important steps yet taken towards bringing the war to a close. The surrender of Tustenugge, Octiarche, and Tiger-Tail had removed nearly all the Indians from the central and northern parts of East Florida, when the capture of Pascoffer, with his entire band, on the Ocklockonnee, by Colonel Hitchcock, entirely relieved Middle and Western Florida. No other Indians now remained in the State except those under Arpeika (Sam Jones), an aged sub-chief, and Bowlegs, who were in the limits assigned them south of Pea Creek; and the credit of finally closing this terrible war was justly attributed to the rare combination of qualifications for the work manifested by the gallant Worth. In a little more than a year, and with great economy of life and treasure, he had solved a problem which had baffled the ablest of his predecessors. The war was closed by official proclamation August 14, 1842, having lasted nearly seven years, at a cost of upwards of nineteen million dollars. Of regular troops, including two hundred and fifteen officers, fourteen hundred and sixty-six had died during the contest. A few Indians still remain in the southerly portion of the State, supporting themselves by hunting and fishing.

CHAPTER VII.

REMOVAL OF THE CHEROKEES—OPPOSED BY THE ROSS PARTY—EFFECTED PEACEABLY BY GENERAL SCOTT.

Two obstacles to the successful execution of the plan of removal had existed for several years, one of which was the difficulties between Georgia and the Creeks. The treaty concluded with the Creeks at Indian Springs on February 12, 1825, had been the source of much discord, having been negotiated without the full consent of all the chiefs who should have participated in it, and ratified only a few days prior to the close of the Presidential term, before the objections to it were made known or fully understood. Mr. Adams, in his first message, expresses his intention to communicate to Congress a special message on the subject, and also respecting the general feeling of the Cherokees. Causes of dissension had been created with two of the principal tribes such as had not before occurred in our Indian history. After the lapse of seven years the Creek question was virtually adjusted by the treaty signed at Washington on March 24, 1832, but the difficulties were not terminated. By this treaty they ceded all their lands east of the Mississippi, making personal reservations for a limited number of years; but the Indians were not disposed to comply with its terms.

The Cherokee nation had been divided in opinion on the subject of emigration since the year 1817, at which period the Western Cherokees removed to the West. The treaty of New Echota, concluded December 29, 1835, together with the policy of emigration, had created two distinct and violently antagonistic parties, one of which favored the removal, and the other opposed it. The leader of the latter was John Ross, the ruling chief, who was supported by many other chiefs, and by the majority of the tribe. Being attached to their residence by historical associations dating back to the era of the discovery of the country, possessing a fertile soil, and enjoying a mild climate, amid a district of hill and dale whose scenic beauty is rarely surpassed, this party, having in their own hands the means of civilization, were averse to exchanging it for territories beyond the Mississippi with the character of which they were imperfectly acquainted and regarding the climate of which they were in doubt. Congress had, by a resolution passed in March, 1835, offered $5,000,000 to the Cherokees for their lands. December 29, 1835, a treaty assenting to the government policy was formed at New Echota with the party favoring exchange and migration, at the head of which was Major Ridge. This treaty threw the nation into a tumult of excitement, and a numerous delegation visited Washington to oppose its ratification by the Senate. While the terms of the treaty were under discussion at Washington, Congress granted $600,000 for the purpose of covering the incidental expenses of their removal, and to meet sundry contingent claims which it was apprehended might arise therefrom. The Western Cherokees also appended their approval of the measure, without claiming any interest in the fiscal provisions of the compact. In this form the treaty was ratified by the Senate on May 23, 1836.

The malcontent party of the Cherokees denied the validity of the treaty, averring that the majority of the nation should not be bound by the terms of a treaty to which they had not given their consent, and which they alleged had been surreptitiously negotiated. The minds of the people were intensely excited, one party contending that the removal policy would be their destruction, and the other that it would prove their salvation. The public press of the United States took part in the discussion, being governed in the expression of their opinions by their adhesion to existing parties, and by the different views they entertained of the true policy to be pursued with respect to the future disposition of the Indian tribes.

It appears that Mr. Ross and his coadjutors had made an agreement with a functionary of the government, long prior to the treaty of 1824, to accept for the Cherokee lands and claims situate east of the Mississippi whatever sum the Senate might award, on the submission of the question to that body. The Senate, to whom the question was eventually submitted, awarded $5,000,000, and on this basis the treaty of New Echota was negotiated, but not with Mr. Ross and his colleagues. During the pendency of the negotiations certain influences were brought to bear upon Mr. Ross, and he became apprised of the fact that there was a large body of the people of the United States who not only concurred with the malcontent party of the Cherokees in their ideas of aboriginal sovereignty within the limits of the United States, but approved of their reluctance and refusal to exchange their lands, and deemed the compensation awarded by the Senate inadequate. Individuals of high moral and legal standing in the North promulgated these views, in which they were supported by a part of the newspaper press of the Northern and Middle States. It was affirmed that an agent of the party in the North opposed to the policy of the administration visited the Cherokees, held interviews with the malcontent chiefs, and encouraged them in their resistance to the government. The opposition to the execution of the treaty of New Echota thus assumed the character of resistance to the legal officers of the government who were charged with the duty of removing the tribe. When, therefore, Commissioners Carrol and Schermerhorn visited the Cherokee country, and offered to conclude a treaty on the five-million basis, the Ross party declined to negotiate. The authority of these commissioners was at one time questioned and denied, and at another time their character was unjustly assailed. Finally, the Ridge party, who regarded the compensation offered as amply sufficient, and believed the removal policy to be one suited to advance their permanent prosperity, concluded the treaty, and thus the Cherokees became divided into Rossites and Ridgeites, a division which produced a state of discord eventually terminating in the shedding of blood.

It has been already stated that a delegation proceeded to Washington to oppose the ratification of the treaty, that the treaty lay before the Senate from December until May, that an increase of $600,000 was granted to cover expenses, and that the full assent of the Western Cherokees was obtained, who were anxious to facilitate the measure and to welcome their brethren to the West. During the attendance of this delegation of the Rossites at Washington, they evinced the morbidly suspicious character of the red man, who doubts when he should decide, and hesitates when he ought to act. It is stated that when it was intimated to the Rossites by a Senator in the confidence of the administration that a new treaty might be entered into with Mr. Ross and his party if he should propose it, true to their native instincts, the Cherokees assumed the position that such a measure if contemplated should be officially and *pro forma* communicated. The influence of the delegation at Washington may be deemed to have procured the appropriation of the sum to defray the expenses of their emigration, but Congress deemed the $5,000,000 an adequate allowance for the territory relinquished. When it is considered that in addition to this sum the nation was gratuitously furnished with an ample domain in the West of a fertile character, and abounding in all the requisites for an agricultural colony, the compensation awarded by this body cannot but be considered as not only liberal, but munificent.

The ordinary method of negotiation through agents, commissioners, and governors having been resorted to without any beneficial result, troops were ordered into the field, under commanders of acknowledged repute. There was no occasion for a war of extermination. Generals Gaines, Jesup, Scott, Taylor, and others, to whom the conduct of the war was intrusted, kept the Indians in check, and evinced their abilities by their conciliatory yet firm mode of operation.

Every year's delay in the removal of the Cherokees and other malcontent tribes only increased the difficulties interposed, and allowed the opponents of the measure time to originate new causes for procrastination.

To overawe the malcontents and give support to the government authorities, four thousand men, nearly the entire disposable force of the army at that time, were kept in the field. Not only was the war with the Seminoles of Florida protracted in an extraordinary manner, but the difficulties with the Cherokees arising out of the treaty of New Echota at this time reached their culminating point. The Rossites refused to remove under the provisions of that treaty, and this party, being a majority of the nation, assumed a position of defiance to the government. The Senate had originally assessed the value of their lands at $5,000,000, and after great deliberation, and the allowance of $600,000 more to cover claims for improvements and for expenses of removal, ratified the instrument. It then became the imperative duty of the Executive to see that these treaty engagements were complied with, and not suffer them to be overslaughed by a system of factious delays and wily subterfuges. No attempt was made to show that the compensation was not adequate or liberal. A territory of greater extent and equal fertility, situated in a fine climate, and abounding in all necessary facilities for an affluent agricultural community, was granted to them, in addition to the award of $5,600,000. This new territory West being under no State or Territorial jurisdiction, their own institutions and laws could be established and enforced, and the Indian mind and character have ample scope for development. No new system of policy was introduced by government; it was merely desired to enforce the old. The course of the preceding administration had been marked by foresight, comprehension, decision, and a regard for the advancement and permanent prosperity of the Cherokee nation. The people of Tennessee, Alabama, and Mississippi having earnestly demanded the removal of the Cherokees, General Scott was ordered to the Cherokee country to enforce the treaty stipulations and preserve order during their transportation,—a delicate and difficult duty, which the excellent judgment of that officer enabled him to perform with decided success.

By the treaty ratified May 23, 1836, the Cherokees had stipulated to remove within two years. Early in the year 1837, several parties of the Ridgeites had successfully emigrated to their new location, and had been received in the most friendly spirit by the Western Cherokees. These parties in the aggregate were estimated to number six thousand, but the mass of the nation still remained. After the arrival of General Scott, and the disposition of his forces at suitable points of observation, it was no longer doubted that the day for decision had arrived.

On the 23d of July, in a general council of the nation, it was resolved to propose to the commanding general that they be allowed to conduct their own migration, and delegates were appointed to communicate this request. To this the general replied approvingly, if certain conditions necessary to insure it were agreed to, the migration to begin on the 1st of September, and the parties to succeed one another at intervals not exceeding three days. These terms being assented to, and the stipulation being repeated that the migration must commence on the 1st of September and be terminated by the 20th of October, reservations being made for the sick and superannuated, General Scott demanded estimates of the expenses attending these removals. The Cherokees furnished details, estimating the removal of each thousand persons at $65,880, and proposed that the Indians employ physicians. To this he assented, although he criticised some of the items, adding that the entire expense of their migration would be paid out of an appropriation of Congress, the surplus of which was directed to be paid over to the Cherokees, thus furnishing them an incentive for their economical expenditure of the sum.

This arrangement being entered into, the removal was made under the personal superintendence of Mr. Ross. On reaching the Mississippi, the parties ascended it to the junction of the Arkansas, and, following the latter, in due time arrived at their new homes in the Indian Territory. No disturbance occurred at any point on the route, and they conducted this exodus of the tribe with order and propriety. In this manner twelve thousand Cherokees were removed, which, added to the six thousand who had migrated during the previous year, coincides with the former estimate of their population at eighteen thousand.

Thus was a measure finally accomplished which had kept the country in turmoil for several years and threatened serious results. The conduct of General Scott was entitled to commendation, but the initiative of this final movement was due to a higher quarter. A delegation of the Cherokees visited Washington in the month of May, and called on the Secretary of War. Mr. Poinsett told them that the most strenuous efforts of the administration would be exerted to prevail on the Southern States interested in their removal to refrain from pressing them inconveniently and from interfering with their migration; that this migration should, if they desired, be conducted by their own agents; that he thought the entire expenses of it should be borne by the United States, and that a military escort should be provided for them while on the route. Mr. Van Buren sanctioned these terms, and received the delegation with great courtesy. He recommended to Congress that an adequate provision should be made to meet the expenses of their removal in such a spirit of liberality and good will as should justly mark all the national dealings with that people. The result was an appropriation of $1,147,067. This was the foundation of success. General Scott, therefore, did not go to the Cherokee country with his hands tied, but was enabled to dispense the liberality of the government in a manner at once just and munificent. The Rossites were conciliated, and they emigrated to the West completely pacified, and entertaining friendly feelings towards the United States.

The removal of the Cherokees and of the Creeks was an act done in violation of treaties made by the United States government, and in opposition to the wishes of the Indians. The State of Georgia determined upon the deed, defied the government, and forced it to adopt and carry out its policy.

CHAPTER VIII.

EMIGRATION OF THE TRIBES, CONTINUED—THEIR CONDITION—RAVAGES OF THE SMALLPOX—DISCORDS BETWEEN THE EASTERN AND WESTERN CHEROKEES—BOUDINOT AND THE RIDGES ASSASSINATED—CLOSE OF THE FIRST DECADE OF COLONIZATION.

The removal of the friendly portion of the Seminoles was intrusted to General Jesup about the middle of February, 1836. The friendly portions of the tribe separated themselves from the hostile, to the number of four hundred and fifty, and fled for protection to the military post at Tampa Bay. On the 10th of April, four hundred and seven persons were enrolled and mustered preparatory to embarking on the transports which were to convey them to the West. Of this number, three hundred and eight arrived at Little Rock, Arkansas, on the 5th of May.

After the commission of hostile acts by the Creeks, their removal was also intrusted to the efficient management of General Jesup. Under contracts which secured them every comfort and the attention of careful emigrant agents, they were located at different points in the Indian colony in bands of twenty-three hundred, of one hundred and sixty-five, and of thirteen hundred, leaving behind seven hundred warriors to operate against the Seminoles.

The removal of the Creeks was commenced through the influence of the chief, Roly McIntosh, under the provisions of the original McIntosh treaty, concluded February 12, 1825, as modified by the treaty signed at Washington January 24, 1826, and finally determined by the treaty entered into at Washington March 24, 1832. During the year the respective emigrant parties arrived in the Territory and were satisfactorily located on their lands. The agent remarks, "They have a rich country, and those that emigrated with McIntosh have been engaged busily in making corn; they usually have a large surplus, as high some years as thirty thousand bushels, besides stock of every description. As there is now a large emigration coming into the country, they will find a sale for all they have to sell."

The number of the Choctaws was then estimated at eighteen thousand in all, a large proportion of whom were in the Territory, or in the process of removal to the fine tract of country they had acquired in it. Immediately on their arrival they turned their attention to labor, in which they evinced striking proficiency. They adopted a form of government which was administered by an elective council and presiding magistrates, and had a written code of laws. They introduced the culture of cotton, erected cotton-gins, planted large fields of corn, raised horses, hogs, and cattle, which were pastured on the prairies, erected smiths' shops, and pursued various mechanical trades. They conducted their own mercantile operations, importing large stocks of goods, for which they exchanged their products.

In 1835 a census of the Cherokees, east of the Mississippi, placed their number at eighteen thousand. The Western Cherokees had segregated themselves from the nation under the provisions of the treaties of July 8, 1817, and February 27, 1819, after which time they had emigrated to the West in parties under their own organization, and settled on the lands which were assigned to them. At the era when the census was taken, these Western Cherokees constituted, to a great extent, a separate nationality. The government agent in his report represents them as gradually progressing in civilization and the cultivation of the soil, and depicts their society as containing many intelligent men. He remarks that they raised corn, beef, pork, sheep, etc., to a considerable extent, and that in travelling through their country one might be quite comfortably entertained. Many of them engaged in trade with their own people. They had some mills erected, and, with a wide extent of country, a portion of it finely watered, they bade fair, with frugality and temperance, to become a leading tribe. In this report the Choctaws, Creeks, and Cherokees are stated to have collectively seventeen churches within their territorial limits,—viz., ten in the Choctaw, four in the Cherokee, and three in the Creek country.

Regarding the other and for the most part minor tribes, the report gives data of which the following is a synopsis. The Seminoles, who had recently arrived, were reported to be in possession of one of the finest sections of the Indian country, and, with their local advantages, could soon prosper. The Osages, an indigenous people, were still addicted to the chase, raised no corn except what their women cultivated, hunted the buffalo, and stored the jerked meat for winter use. They are stated to have little or no stock, all their extra means of support being derived from their annuities. The Quapaws, advantageously located on the banks of the Neosho, were in possession of one hundred and sixty sections in one place, surveyed and marked off, adjacent to the Cherokees and Osages. The Senecas, and the mixed band of Senecas and Shawnees, had 60,000 acres. The Senecas of Sandusky had 67,000 acres. These lands adjoined, and were fertile and well watered. The Senecas cultivated the soil, and had a mill in operation, which was of great service to them.

Nine tribes were located north of the district just mentioned. They were the relics of the Shawnees, Delawares, Kickapoos, Kansas, Weas, Piankeshaws, Peorias, Kaskaskias, and Ottawas. These nine tribes had then an aggregate population of four thousand four hundred and sixty-seven souls. The Shawnees and Delawares, who are agriculturists, were industrious, temperate, and thrifty, possessed a fertile country, and were supplied with schools, shops, mills, and churches. They now successfully cultivate the various cereals, and raise large stocks of horses, cattle, and hogs. The Kickapoos began to turn their attention to agriculture in 1835, and both men and women labor assiduously. The Kansas, like the Osages, are indigenous, and live by the chase. The small bands of the Weas, Piankeshaws, Peorias, and Ottawas are cultivators of the soil. The manners, habits, dress, and deportment of all the agricultural tribes and bands denote a decided advance towards civilization.

The general result of the negotiations with the Indians during eight years prior to January 1, 1837, was the cession of 93,401,637 acres by the tribes, for which the sum of $26,982,068 was paid, together with the grant to them of 32,381,000 acres west of the Mississippi, valued at $40,476,250, the total compensation amounting thus to $67,458,318.

In 1837 the tribes and remnants of tribes still residing east of the Mississippi were greatly disturbed by the discussion of the question of their removal, and the hope of improving their social condition by the acceptance of lands in the West induced them to make frequent treaties. A retrospect of the succession of these is essential to the proper understanding of their history.

The important treaty of cession made at Washington March 28, 1836, by the Ottawas and Chippewas, and the beneficial effects of it on the affairs of those tribes, caused their more westerly brethren and kinsfolk, on the Upper Mississippi, to meditate seriously on pursuing the same course. The Ojibwas[1] comprised an infinity of bands, scattered over an immense surface of territory. A treaty with the Western and Northern bands of these people was concluded by General Henry Dodge at St. Peter's on July 29, 1837. By this treaty, in which the Pillager tribe of Leech Lake is first introduced to notice, the Chippewa nation ceded the country from a point opposite the junction of the Crow Wing River with the Mississippi, to the head of Lake St. Croix, and thence along the ridge dividing the Ochasawa River from a northern tributary of Chippewa River, to a point on the latter twenty miles below the outlet of Lake Flambeau. From this point the cession absorbed the whole Chippewa boundary to the lines of the Menomonies, on the Wisconsin and Sioux Rivers.

This important compact ceded a large part of the present area of Southern Minnesota, with its valuable pineries, fertile prairies, beautiful lakes, and flowing rivers. By this cession the tribes secured an annuity of $38,000 for twenty years, payable in money, goods, and provisions, besides obtaining the services of mechanics and farmers and a supply of agricultural implements. The sum of $70,000 was appropriated to the payment of their debts, and $100,000 to be divided among their half-breed descendants.

This treaty collected into one group families and bands of the same stock who had wandered over hundreds and thousands of miles of country, comprising the far-reaching shores of Lake Superior and the almost illimitable steppes of the Upper Mississippi.

The Chippewas of Saginaw, in Michigan, by a treaty concluded December 20, 1837, ceded their lands in the region of the Flint, Shiawassee, Tittabawassee, and Saginaw Rivers. By this treaty the United States granted them the entire proceeds of the sales of their lands in the public land-office, together with an amount

---

[1] This term has been Anglicized by the term Chippewa; Ojibwa or Otchipwe more nearly expresses the native pronunciation obtaining in the most remote bands. The original term, it is said, refers to the power of virility.

of fertile lands in the West equal to those ceded, and an annual appropriation for schools and agricultural purposes while resident during a limited period in the country. The Saginaws had previously been regarded as refugees from various bands of the Algonkin stock. Their central location had been occupied in former times by the warlike tribe of the Sacs or Sauks; hence the term Sauk-i-nong, from which originated the name Saginaw. About the year 1712 the Sacs united with the Foxes and made an attack on the French at Detroit. The failure of the attempt of these two restless and warlike tribes drove them at first to the banks of the stream since known as the Fox River of Wisconsin, whence they afterwards migrated to the west of the Mississippi.

On the 17th of January, 1837, the Chickasaws and Choctaws entered into a treaty, under the auspices of the United States, which provided that the Chickasaws should be located in a separate district of the Choctaw territory, west of the Mississippi, and should enjoy equal political rights and privileges with them, except only in questions relative to their fiscal affairs. In consideration of this location, and of the rights and privileges granted them, the Chickasaws agreed to pay the Choctaws $530,000; $30,000 of this sum to be paid down, and the remainder to be invested by the United States in stocks for their benefit, under prescribed regulations. This initial step towards the reunion of tribes speaking dialects of the same language is important as foreshadowing a further and final tribal reunion.

The tendency of affiliated tribes to coalesce after long periods of separation, weary wanderings, and disastrous adventures, was first demonstrated in the history of the Iroquois, who, we are informed, in ancient times warred furiously against each other. By the confederation, in the fifteenth century, of the Mohawks, Oneidas, Onondagas, Cayugas, and Senecas, a native power was created which made itself feared and respected by the other tribes; and at the period when the colonies were sent West they held a position among the other savage tribes which fully verified the axiom that in union there is strength. Nothing analogous to this organization existed among the Algonkins, such as the New England tribes and the Illinois. These had no public council or general convocation of tribes where important questions relative to their political affairs were discussed. The Dakota tribe is also composed of discordant materials, there being no controlling organization for the public welfare, each band being the sole judge of what it considers right and politic.

The Sacs and Foxes coalesced on a firmer basis, the tribes being so closely united by the ties of language, intermarriage, customs, and by local influences, that they have preserved the co-tribal relation.

Very similar, and weakened only by their dispersion over the wide country they occupy, is the coalescence, or social league, existing between the Chippewas, Ottawas, and Pottawatomies.

The year 1837 was marked by the migration of separate colonies from the Ridgeite Cherokees, the Creeks of Georgia, and the Choctaws and Chickasaws in the South. From the Northern section of the Union, emigrant parties of the Pottawatomies and Ottawas departed for the West. There were still remaining in this region the Wyandots, of Ohio, the Menomonies, Stockbridges, Munsees, and Oneidas, of Wisconsin, the Iroquois, of New York, the Miamis, of Indiana, and the Chippewas, of Lake Superior.

By the terms of the treaty negotiated by General Scott, September 15, 1832, immediately succeeding the close of the Sac war, the Winnebagoes ceded their lands lying east of the Mississippi, in the State of Wisconsin, and accepted a location west of that river, on a tract designated in the treaty as "the Neutral Ground;" a fine district of country, abounding in game, and possessing a very fertile soil, situated between the territory of the Sioux and that of the Sacs and Foxes. As Wisconsin filled up with a white population, and the position of the Winnebagoes as a hunter tribe became more and more inconvenient, they were urged by the local authorities to remove to the Neutral Ground, which they hesitated to do from a dread of being embroiled in the fierce and sanguinary wars constantly raging between the Sacs and Foxes and the Sioux. Strenuous exertions were made by the government to quell these hostilities, and the removal of the Winnebagoes was finally effected during the year 1837. A treaty was concluded with the Saginaw Chippewas, of Michigan, on the 20th of December of this year, by which the tribe ceded their reservations in that State, and agreed, after a residence of five years on a tract designated, to remove to the west of the Mississippi.

In 1834 the Miamis had ceded their lands on the Wabash for a heavy consideration, and agreed to remove West; but this treaty, which was communicated by the President to the Senate for their approval, was not, owing to certain modifications requiring the concurrence of the Indians, finally confirmed by the Senate until the close of the session of 1837.

In order to protect the emigrant tribes on the South and West, treaties were concluded on the 25th of May with the barbarous tribes of the Kiowas, Katakas, and Takawaros, of the prairies, and friendly relations were established with the Comanches, or Niuñas, of Texas, a powerful and dominant tribe in that quarter.

The removal of the Cherokees in a peaceful and conciliatory manner produced a favorable effect, although the other events of the year 1838 were of equal interest to the public mind. Positions requiring energy of action were taken by several tribes. The Pottawatomies of Indiana ceded their lands in 1833, and agreed to remove West, Indiana and the adjoining State of Illinois having filled up very rapidly with settlers on their northern borders, the rich prairies and fine commercial marts and outlets presenting great attractions to an enterprising people. This tribe, being the recipient of large annuities, was counselled by the traders and other interested persons to remain where it was, that the distribution of these sums might be made in the country. The emigrant agent, finding his operations impeded, and fearing an outbreak and consequent bloodshed, called on the Governor of Indiana for aid, who authorized General John Tipton to raise one hundred volunteers to assist the agent in the removal of the Indians. This duty was promptly performed, and, from the report of that officer, eight hundred and fifty-nine Pottawatomies were delivered to the emigrant agent on the Illinois on the 18th of September; these were sent West, escorted by dragoons to preserve order, and safely conveyed to their location, every attention being paid to their health, comfort, and convenience. Such as were overfatigued by the rapidity of the marches, and were sickly, or invalids, were allowed to ride the horses of the dragoons while the men walked.

There were removed during this year 4106 Creeks, chiefly comprising the families of the warriors of this tribe who had been engaged in the Florida war, 177 Choctaws, 4600 Chickasaws, 151 Chippewas, and 1651 Appalachicolas and Florida Indians, making an aggregate of 29,459. The Winnebago Indians, of Wisconsin, evinced great tardiness and unwillingness to leave the country. The isolated tribes in the settlements became entangled with associations which it is difficult for a people of so little decision of character to abandon. This tribe, by a treaty made at Washington on the 28th of October, renewed the engagements entered into and endorsed by the treaty concluded at Rock Island in 1832, after the close of the Sac war, and agreed to remove to the Neutral Ground in eight months. As this limitation expired in the winter, they solicited permission, and were allowed, to remain in Wisconsin until spring. A treaty was concluded with the Saginaws by the Acting Superintendent of Michigan, guaranteeing them the minimum prices for their lands ceded by the treaty of the 20th December, 1837, a measure necessary to prevent combinations to control the sales, which were designed to be exclusively for their benefit.

The Superintendent of Indian Affairs for Michigan, in his annual report for this year, makes the following allusions to the Saginaws:

"This isolated tribe has lived down to the present time with all the essential traits common to the darkest period of their history. They are heady, bad-tempered, fond of drink, and savage when under its influence. Yet they are a people of strong mental traits, of independent and generous feelings, and warmly attached to their ancient mode of living and superstitions. They speak a well-characterized dialect of the Chippewa language, holding nearly the same relation to the great Algic family of the North that the Seminoles do to the Creeks of the South. Their country appears to have been a place of refuge to the other tribes. They succeeded to the possessions of the Sauks, who were driven from the banks of the Saginaw about the close of the sixteenth or beginning of the seventeenth century. They have been observed for at least a century to have had a ruling chief, who exercised more of the powers of a dictator than is usual with the other tribes. They are known to have indulged their predatory and warlike propensities by participating in the scenes of attack and plunder which marked the early settlements of Western Virginia, Pennsylvania, and Kentucky.

"The country occupied by the Saginaws is fertile, densely wooded, and abounds in streams affording valuable water-power. It is still but sparsely settled, but in proportion as the lands are taken up the natural means of subsistence of the Indians must diminish, although it is stated that portions of the public lands west and north of the Tittabawassee will afford a theatre for hunting for many years. The recent ratification by the Senate of the treaty of January 14, 1837, with this tribe, extinguishes their title to all their possessions in Michigan, saving the right to live for five years on two of the ceded reservations on Saginaw Bay. In 1837 this tribe lost three hundred and fifty-four persons by the smallpox, of whom one hundred and six were men, one hundred and seven women, and one hundred and forty-one children. Their present population, by a census just completed, is nine hundred and ninety-three, two hundred and twenty-one of whom are males, two hundred and ninety-eight females, and four hundred and seventy-four youths and infants. In 1837 their corn-fields were either damaged or wholly destroyed by high water in the Saginaw and its tributaries.

"The department maintains for them a sub-agent, an interpreter, a blacksmith and assistant, and one principal and several subordinate farmers. They appear to have been overlooked by philanthropists, having up to this date neither schools nor teachers of any description."

On the 6th of November a treaty was entered into with the Miamis at the forks of the Wabash, by which this tribe ceded 170,000 acres of reservations in that quarter, for which they received $335,000. They were compensated for all buildings and improvements, and furnished by the United States with a location in the Indian Territory west of the Mississippi, "sufficient in extent, suited to their wants and wishes," and contiguous to that occupied by the tribes which emigrated from the States of Ohio and Indiana. They agreed to send a delegation to explore the country proposed to be given them, their expenses to be defrayed by the government. This treaty and exploration led to the eventual removal of this tribe, once the terror of the West, and so numerous and warlike that during Washington's administration they defeated successive armies under Harmar and St. Clair, and for years prevented the settlement of the Anglo-Saxon race in the West. This tribe finally migrated to the Indian Territory, diminished in numbers, degraded in morals and habits, wanting in industry, and lacking education, but affluent in government funds and annuities. After their final defeat by Wayne, in 1794, they submitted to the authority of the United States, and took up their residence in one of the richest valleys of the West, abounding in game and all the requisites for Indian subsistence. They pursued the usual course of hunters, being satisfied if the exertions of the year afforded them the means of living, little heeding that they would soon be surrounded by an industrious population and finally supplanted by them. In this thoughtless, careless, idle manner they lived in the Wabash Valley until their lands became valuable. They began to cede their territory in 1809, and continued that course in 1814, 1818, 1826, and down to the date of their removal. But the large sums they received through this channel had the effect to destroy their self-reliance and native independence of character, to degrade them in habits and morals, to introduce disease, and to lead in every way to a rapid depopulation. This tribe, which in 1764 was estimated in its divisions at five thousand souls, or one thousand warriors, and at the commencement of the American Revolution at three hundred and fifty warriors, or seventeen hundred and fifty souls, was reduced at the time of its removal to about seven hundred persons, and when a census of the tribe was taken in 1850 it had dwindled to five hundred souls, who were in receipt of an annuity of $44,000.

The summer of 1837 is memorable in Indian history for the visitation of one of those calamities which have so much reduced the Indian population,—viz., the ravages of the smallpox, which then swept through the Missouri Valley. The disease was introduced among them from a steamboat which ascended that river from the city of St. Louis in July. On the 15th of that month the disease made its appearance in the village of the Mandans, great numbers of whom fell victims to it. Thence it spread rapidly over the entire country, and tribe after tribe was decimated by it.

The Mandans, among whom the pestilence commenced, are stated to have been reduced from an estimated population of sixteen hundred souls to one hundred and twenty-five.[1] The Minnetarees, or Gros Ventres, out of a population of one thousand persons, lost one-half their number. The Arickarees, numbering three thousand, were reduced by this pestilence to fifteen hundred. The Crows, or Upsarokas, lost great numbers, and the survivors saved themselves by a rapid retreat to the mountains. The Assiniboins, a people roughly estimated at nine thousand, were swept off by hundreds. The Crees, living in the same region, and numbering three thousand souls, suffered in an equal degree. The disease appears to have at length exhausted its virulence on the Blackfeet and Bloods, a numerous and powerful genus of tribes. One thousand lodges are reported to have been desolated, and left standing, without a solitary inhabitant, on the prairies, once the residence of this proud and warlike race,—a sad memorial of this dreadful scourge.

Visitors to these regions during the year when this dread pestilence was raging there represent the Indian country as being truly desolate. Women and children were met wandering about without protection, or seated near the graves of their husbands and parents, uttering pitiable lamentations. Howling dogs roamed about, seeking their masters. On every side was desolation, and wrecks of mortality everywhere presented themselves to the view. It is reported that some of the Indians, after recovering from the disease, when they saw how it had disfigured their faces, threw themselves into the Missouri River.

The dissensions between the antagonistic parties of the Cherokees, called the Rossites and Ridgeites, originated by the treaty of New Echota, reached their crisis during the year 1839. The smothered dislikes and hatred of four years burst forth with a fierceness which threatened to drench the Territory with blood. The brutal murder of the Ridges, father and son, and of Elias Boudinot, will long remain as foul blots on their tribal escutcheon, for, however ignorant the Eastern Cherokees may have been of moral law and the theory of government, no plea can shield them from censure for the assassination of their fellow-men on account of political dissensions or differences of opinion.

The Western Cherokees, who had emigrated with the sanction of Mr. Jefferson's administration, and fixed their residence in Arkansas, as early as 1817, had established a form of government and adopted written laws. When the treaty party

---

[1] In 1836 this tribe was reported to the Indian Office as having a population of 3200. In 1852 the number returned was 385. Mr. Catlin was mistaken when he reported its extinction.

migrated, under the supervision of Messrs. Ridge and Boudinot, they united with the old settlers, and lived contentedly under the established order of things. But the malcontent party, who migrated with Mr. Ross in 1838, went thither with embittered and revengeful feelings against the treaty party and the old settlers, and refused to submit to the existing government and laws of the Western Cherokees. On reaching the country, the Rossites, finding that they outnumbered the Ridgeites in the proportion of about two to one, at once became sticklers for the democratic doctrine that majorities should rule. It would have been well if in grasping at power they had not forgotten right. But it soon became evident that they were determined not only to ignore the old form of government and laws, but to establish new ones, and to compel the minority to submit to them, right or wrong. The Western Cherokees, however, so stoutly contested the ground that within an incredibly short time a desperate feud was enkindled, and the entire country was plunged into discord. Neither party were as conciliatory in their views and opinions, or in their deportment and manners, as men of twenty years' experience in self-government ought to have been, and neither appear to have duly estimated the importance of compromise and union. The words, though spoken, had no place in their hearts: one party was unyielding, the other was furious and aggressive.

A convention for the adjustment of their difficulties was summoned to meet at Tukatokah on the 20th of June, 1839, which remained in session for eight or nine days. Its discussions were exciting, discordant, and bitter. The Rossites, who were in the majority, resolved to hold their power, and the Ridgeites determined not to succumb. When it became evident that a compromise could not be effected, threats were used, whereupon some of the Ridgeite chiefs withdrew to their homes, and the council adjourned without effecting anything except the manifestation of a deep and settled prejudice on both sides, and of the irreconcilable character of the feud. It is said that on the evening when this council was dissolved a secret conclave of the leaders of the Rossites was held, who selected forty men, to whom was assigned the duty of assassinating the leaders of the Ridgeites, the party who had signed the treaty of New Echota, of the 28th of December, 1825. For fourteen years this grudge had been nourished in the hearts of the malcontent party, until it at last resulted in the commission of a cowardly murder. However true may be the assertion regarding the session of this dark conclave, it is certain that on the following day the inhuman and cruel murders of Boudinot, and of the Ridges, both father and son, were perpetrated. Boudinot was in the act of superintending the erection of a building, when he was accosted by four Indians, who solicited him to visit a house some hundreds of yards distant, and administer some medicines, he being a physician. With his usual promptness he complied, and had proceeded about half the distance, when he was suddenly assassinated. The fiends were not satisfied with killing him, but cut him into pieces in the most shocking manner. The younger Ridge was the next victim of this secret band of executioners. He was dragged from his bed, in the midst of his family, and dispatched. The elder Ridge, who was absent on a visit into the adjoining limits of Arkansas, was waylaid and shot by persons who occupied an eminence beside the road, and his body when discovered by his friends was found to have been pierced by five rifle-balls.

This violence excited great commotion in the nation, and, far from checking the zeal of the Ridge party, it only inflamed it. Discord reigned everywhere, and Mr. John Ross, who was accused of concerting the plot of the assassination, surrounded his house with a guard of five hundred of his adherents. Several chiefs of the opposite party took shelter within the walls of Fort Gibson, where they were protected by General Arbuckle, who also offered a refuge to Mr. Ross, which he declined. In the correspondence which ensued between the commandant of the fort and Mr. Ross, the latter disclosed a subtle, cautious, and evasive policy. Extreme positions were taken by both parties, evincing a bitterly discordant and hostile spirit. The darkest of the ensuing transactions on the part of the Rossites was the calling of a convention, or general council, composed almost exclusively of their own party, which passed a resolution granting an amnesty to the murderers. They also subsequently declared some of the leading Ridgeites outlaws. These proceedings were disapproved by the local military and officers of the department, whose suggestions for effecting a reunion were unheeded. The government at Washington instructed its officers to demand the surrender of the murderers, that they might be brought to trial, and directed them to withhold the Cherokee annuities while this discordant state of society existed.

Mr. Ross, having evaded any direct issue in the correspondence, sought to procure an investigation of the matter at a distant point, where witnesses could not be so readily summoned, and for this purpose sent his brother, Lewis Ross, and two other Cherokees, to Washington. A personal interview with the Secretary of War was obtained, and an appeal made by Lewis Ross in favor of his brother, in which he spoke of the murders as private acts, and of the decree of their general party council extending pardon to the actors therein as being conclusive of the matter. He urged that an investigation should be instituted at the seat of government. This Mr. Poinsett denied, remarking that if John Ross were innocent he would not oppose the arrest of the murderers, or attempt to shield them; that with his known influence over the nation he might have prevented the commission of the savage deeds; but he could now contribute to the ends of justice by surrendering the criminals whose barbarities had been countenanced and themselves exonerated by the national council. The secretary said that the council had no legal right to sanction a violation of all laws, human and divine, and that no investigation was required so long as John Ross, the chief magistrate, refused to deliver up the murderers to justice. He was not charged, it was conceded, with having ordered the murderers to perform the criminal act, but he had permitted it to be done when a word from him would have spared the effusion of innocent blood. He might justify himself by withdrawing his protection from the murderers and giving them up, but the government would continue to regard him as the instigator and abettor of these foul deeds until that was done. Mr. Poinsett concluded by saying that the majority ought to rule while guided by law and principle, but that they had by their cruel, savage, and lawless course forfeited all right to govern the old settlers, who were in a minority; that they had proved themselves tyrants in the worst sense of the term; and that the government would not for a moment uphold or sanction tyranny, least of all brutal, savage tyranny.

The Cherokees were convulsed by political turmoils for some years, during which unmistakable tokens gave evidence that, however dissensions might prevail, the ultimate result would be a union of all the jarring elements, and the institution of a permanent government. Strong wills and clear minds were to be found in their councils. The rivalries and jealousies of the chiefs had been fearfully excited by the transaction of New Echota, which it was hoped the conciliatory measures of the government would have soothed, but, like a violent and stubborn disease, the evil could not be cured by palliatives, and required stronger applications, which, while they relieved, at the same time infuriated the patient. It required time to quell discords which had distracted the Cherokee nation to the centre, and the result has proved that time was the true remedy. No tribe of the same aggregate population had emigrated, and no other tribe which removed to the Territory had been so long and so successfully the subject of instruction. A people who had invented a new alphabet, who had long participated in the school system, who had learned the arts of the loom and spindle, and who had reached a condition of domestic society and manners, the refinement, tastes, and elegance of which may be judged of by the bright example of Catherine Brown, could not lack clearness of conception, or the power of distinguishing between the principles of right and wrong. To deny this, as there was a Scottish element in the nation, would be as absurd as to aver that the mental calibre of the Scottish people at a distinct era of Caledonian history should be judged by the examples of Rob Roy or the actors in the brutal atrocities of Glencoe.

The smaller tribes who yet lingered in the States may be regarded as occupying the relative position of boulders in the geological system. They had been removed from their natal positions, and located in questionable situations. The flood that swept them forward before its resistless waves was the European race, and it seemed doubtful whether they would ever again find a permanent foothold on the soil.

One of these boulder tribes, who of their own accord sought refuge in the colonized territory, was the so-called Stockbridges, comprising remnants of the ancient Mohicans. At the period of the discovery of the river Hudson (Chatemuc, the Mohican of their own vocabulary, and the Cohahatatea of the Iroquois) this people resided on its western banks, opposite to and south of Albany. When the population of the colonies pressed upon them they crossed the Taconic range, and concentrated their people in the valley of the Housatonic, in Massachusetts, where for years they received tuition from the eminent theologian Edwards. They espoused the cause of the colonies during the Revolutionary War, their services as runners, flankers, and gun-men having been highly appreciated. After the close of that contest they removed to the upper waters of the Oneida Creek Valley by virtue of an arrangement with the Oneida canton, then under the government of the benevolent Shenandoah. About the year 1822 they entered into negotiations with the Menomonies, of Wisconsin, and subsequently removed to and settled on Fox River, of Green Bay; but ten or twelve years' residence in this quarter was sufficient to satisfy them that the white population would soon hem them in as closely there as they had done in New York. They entered into frequent negotiations with the government, first accepting a tract on the banks of Lake Winnebago, but subsequently, selling this, they stipulated for a location on the banks of the Mississippi. In 1840 a considerable number of the tribe, located on Lake Winnebago, in Wisconsin, withdrew from the others, and emigrated to the Indian colony west of the Missouri. They were accompanied by the Munsees, whose ancestors had been their neighbors on the west bank of the Hudson in ancient times, and by an emigrating party of Delawares from the river Thaines, in Canada, under command of the chief Thomas T. Hendrick. The entire party, numbering one hundred and seventy-four persons, were received by their tribal relatives, the Delawares, who furnished them with a residence on their large reservation near Fort Leavenworth, on the Kansas River.

The oft-tried temporizing and erroneous policy of removing Indians from one location within the States to another, however remote, also within their limits, has uniformly proved to be a failure. The experience of the Stockbridges, Munsees, and segregated Delawares was now added to prove the evil results arising from this policy. Such removed tribes and bands were speedily surrounded by a white population, with whom they did not coalesce, and naturally wasted away under the influence of adverse manners and customs.

The same attempt to remove a tribe from one State to another was made with the Winnebagoes. Having been implicated in the Sauk war, they agreed in 1832, at Rock Island, where the American army was then encamped, to leave the east banks of the Mississippi, abandoning their favorite Rock River, Wisconsin, and Fox River Valleys, and remove to a position west of the Mississippi denominated the Neutral Ground. For them, however, it was not "neutral ground." It was, in fact, the war-ground of the Sacs and Foxes and Sioux, and they had, under the influence of the presence of a military force, agreed to a proposition which they had neither the ability nor the will to perform. Though ethnologically of the Sioux stock, their affinity was not to be relied on; they possessed a nationality of their own, and could not, after ages of separation, take shelter under the Sioux flag. The plan of the neutral ground was a benevolent theory, which it was hoped and believed would work well, but it eventually proved to be an utter fallacy. It had, however, strong advocates, being favored by many persons who did not wish to see the Winnebagoes removed, with their large means and annuities, beyond the reach of a peripatetic peddler's footsteps, or to lose sight of the distribution of their annual per capita dollars.

In 1837 the Winnebagoes renewed by treaty their engagement to remove to the Neutral Ground, in Iowa, within eight months after the ratification of that instrument. The treaty was not ratified until June, 1838, which would limit the period for their removal to February, 1839. They still lingered in the valleys of their ancient home, until the matter of their removal was placed in the hands of General

Atkinson. When they discovered that the government was in earnest, the mass of them removed across the Mississippi without causing much difficulty, but, though still urged to proceed to the Neutral Ground, they encamped on the western margin of the river, where they were allowed to remain until the following year. Meantime, they were afflicted by considerable sickness, and surrounded by whiskey-shops, together with every temptation that Indians possessing heavy annuities are sure to encounter. Their agent established his buildings and shops on the Neutral Ground, where the tribe was eventually induced to settle by the announcement that there only would they be paid their annuities. It will be seen in the sequel that in a few years it became necessary to remove the Winnebagoes from the limits of Iowa.

A mistake of a similar kind was made with the united Chippewas, Ottawas, and Pottawatomies, who ceded their lands in Illinois by the treaty concluded at Chicago in 1833. A part of the consideration named in it was the grant of 5,000,000 acres of land in the West; in accordance with which they were placed on a tongue of land situate between the western boundary of the State of Missouri and the Missouri River. The progress of the settlements in Missouri made this tract of land so essentially a geographical part of that State, and so necessary to its agricultural and commercial development, that Congress annexed it thereto; which act rendered it imperative for the government to provide these Indians with the stipulated 5,000,000 acres west of the Missouri River.

Other bands of Pottawatomies, residing in Indiana, who had ceded their possessions in that quarter, were removed during this year, under the immediate surveillance of General Brady. There were also some accessions of the Seminoles from Florida, and of fragments of the segregated bands of the Black River and Swan Creek Chippewas, of Michigan. The whole number of Indians removed in 1840 was 5671. The Cherokee difficulties had this year been so far compromised between the two contending parties that Mr. Poinsett, the Secretary of War, directed the annuities to be paid.

Internal dissensions, arising from private jealousies and ambitions, have been the real but secret source of many tribal discords. Questions regarding the disposition of funds, and the regulation of their internal policy, have been discussed and settled in both general and tribal councils. The object for which these bodies are now convened is not, as formerly, during the hunter state of the tribes, to discuss the policy of proclaiming war or concluding peace, and to wrangle with one another respecting trespasses on tribal boundaries, but to adjust their civil affairs. Morals, education, arts, and agriculture respectively occupy a share of attention in these public assemblies, and the progressive improvement in the Indian character has been such that their councils and assemblies have been completely changed in a few years, from arenas for the display of wrangling and disputatious and declamatory elocution, to legislative bodies whose meetings are characterized by calm and sober discussion and dispassionate decision. Reference is had particularly to the five tribes of the Cherokees, Creeks, Chickasaws, Choctaws, and Seminoles. The representative principle has been generally adopted for limited periods and definite objects. The beneficial effects of temperance, a virtuous life, and habits of industry on the manners of society, and on public as well as private prosperity, have been recognized and acknowledged as the true elements of political economy. These leading tribes have, indeed, fairly embarked in their national career, which perseverance, energy, and decision will enable them to pursue triumphantly.

The Cherokee disturbance, once so threatening, entirely subsided in a few years, and it is now evident that the prosperity of the nation was well secured by the treaty of New Echota, although the execution of that instrument by the minority gave the political and personal preponderance to the majority, and took the power from the leading pacific and progressive chiefs. The act was regarded by the malcontent chiefs as a usurpation of authority, and their feelings were more highly excited by the loss of personal power than by that of national wealth.

Events occurring among the Indian tribes are slow in development, and years elapse before discords are forgotten or opinions become nationalized. This may be fully demonstrated by reference to the history of the Cherokees. Years have passed away, and the blood of Boudinot and the Ridges has not, to use an Indian metaphor, been washed from the assassins' hands. The sanguinary deeds which once harrowed the feelings of the nation and aroused the sympathies of the Union have been succeeded by peace, though the atrocities are not forgotten; and the government of the Cherokees, the great bone of internal contention for so many years, remains in the hands of the Rossite party. The true friends of the nation may feel a consolation in reflecting that the wise forecast and decision of character which induced the Cherokees to relinquish their ancient residences east of the Mississippi, and begin a new career of industry in the West, have laid the foundation of the permanent prosperity and civilization of the tribe, and that Elias Boudinot and John Ridge will long be remembered as the great benefactors and moral heroes of their country. Those who stained their hands in the patriotic blood of these men failed thereby to arrest the onward progress of the Cherokees.

At the time when their systematic removal was commenced by the government, there still remained within the States east of the line of the Mississippi and Missouri 110,349 souls. At the close of the year 1836, 45,690 of this number, comprising portions of nineteen tribes, had been transferred to the West. At this time there had been established for these tribes in their new locations fifty-one schools, at which twenty-two hundred and twenty-one pupils were instructed. In addition to this, one hundred and fifty-six pupils of an advanced grade were instructed at the Choctaw Academy, in Kentucky, and four of the graduates were studying the legal profession in New York, Vermont, and elsewhere.

In 1855 the four Southern or Appalachian tribes, namely, the Cherokees, Choctaws, Chickasaws, and Creeks, including the Seminoles, had an aggregate population of 62,176. The twenty small tribes and tribal bands located in the Territory of Kansas numbered 13,481, making a total aggregate population of 75,657.

PERIOD VIII.

INDIAN AFFAIRS SINCE THE ACQUISITION OF NEW MEXICO AND CALIFORNIA.

CHAPTER I.

ORGANIZATION OF THE TERRITORIES OF KANSAS AND NEBRASKA—HOSTILITIES IN CALIFORNIA AND OREGON—SIOUX WAR OF 1862-63 IN MINNESOTA—THE CHEROKEES IN THE REBELLION.

FOLLOWING the acquisition of territory on the Pacific coast, resulting from the Mexican War in 1846-48, numerous emigrant trains began to cross the plains, necessarily passing through the Indian reservations west of the Missouri. Depredations were committed upon the Indians, whose rights were utterly disregarded, and whose lives were often taken. The pledge of the United States to every tribe that they should be protected in the peaceful enjoyment of the country assigned them was derided and held of no avail. The Indians were alarmed, and justly indignant, at these violations of treaty stipulations. In the month of August, 1853, the Commissioner of Indian Affairs, by direction of the President, visited the Indian country to confer with the various tribes with a view to procuring their assent to a Territorial government, and to the extinguishment of their title to the lands owned by them. He found the people on the border discussing the question whether portions of the Indian country were not then open to white settlements, and some of them actually exploring it with that intention. All this had a very unfavorable influence on the Indians, who were apprehensive of being driven from their homes.

The commissioner visited some twenty of these tribes, but did not find them as prosperous or as far advanced in civilization as he had been led to expect. He came to the conclusion that the administration of the affairs of the Indians was not wholly free from abuses, and that such of the Indians as resided near Fort Leavenworth and the Missouri line were more demoralized than those who lived in localities more distant.

In 1854, treaties were made with the Omaha, Otoe and Missouria, Sac and Fox of the Missouri, Iowa, Kickapoo, Delaware, Shawnee, Kaskaskia, Wea, Peoria, Piankeshaw, and Miami Indians, and the Territories of Kansas and Nebraska were organized. All of the Indian lands, except in the aggregate about 1,300,000 acres reserved for their homes, were ceded to the government. Some of the tribes made these cessions in trust, the net proceeds of the lands when sold to be paid to them; others made unconditional cessions. In the summer of this year an association of persons seized upon a piece of land fronting on the Missouri, two miles below Fort Leavenworth, and laid out thereon a town called the city of Leavenworth. This was in direct violation of the treaty with the Delaware Indians, who complained to the Indian Office. Other parties entered the Delaware tract and pre-empted claims. The commissioner requested that all intruders should be expelled by the military force at the fort. They, however, under the influence of city lots, denounced the commissioner and defended the squatters. The executive of the Territory, in disregard of the organic law, established his office within the Shawnee country. The Territorial Legislature held its session at the Shawnee Mission, and embraced some of the Indian reserves within the organized counties. All appeals in favor of the rights of the Indian were in vain. No spot of land within the territory occupied by an Indian tribe appeared to be free from ceaseless intrusion. "In the din and strife," says Commissioner Manypenny,[1] "between the anti-slavery and pro-slavery parties in November, 1856, in which the rights and interests of the red man were completely overlooked and disregarded, the good conduct and patient submission of the latter contrasted favorably with the disorderly and lawless conduct of their white brethren, who, while they quarrelled about the African, united upon the soil of Kansas in wronging the Indian." In 1860 and 1862, treaties were made with the Delawares, by which the valuable tract of 224,000 acres reserved in the treaty of 1854 for their "permanent" home was conveyed to the Leavenworth, Pawnee, and Western Railroad upon payment of $287,000. On July 4, 1866, still another treaty was made with them, by which they agreed to remove to the Indian Territory, and to sell their remaining land in Kansas to the Missouri River Railroad Company.

About 1852 the mountain Indians of California began to manifest distrust towards the white men, and in December, 1855, by which time they had learned to use fire-arms, the Klamaths and adjacent Indians simultaneously began hostilities, murdering seven men in one day. They were severely chastised in several engagements, and through the good judgment and discretion of the agent, S. G. Whipple, peace was restored. He established a reservation on the Klamath River, which was kept up until the winter of 1861–62, when the improvements were washed away by a severe freshet, and the Indians were removed to Smith River. Since 1855 the Klamath Indians, the most numerous and powerful tribe in the northwestern portion of the State, have remained at peace.

In 1856 the Indians on Redwood Creek, Upper Mad River, Grouse Creek, and the head-waters of Eel River began a war that resulted in the loss of many valuable lives and the destruction of an immense amount of property. For want of concert between the regular troops and the settlers, nothing was done towards the suppression of hostilities until, in 1858, Captain Messic, at the head of a volunteer company,

---

[1] "Our Indian Wards."

BOSTON PUBLIC LIBRARY.

induced some nine hundred Indians to come in. Placed upon the Mendocino Reservation, these Indians soon found their way back to their old homes, more embittered and hostile than before. The peace that followed their removal was of short duration, all the tribes of the north participating in the renewal of hostilities except the Klamaths and the Indians on Lower Mad and Eel Rivers. Many white men were killed, and the country was laid waste, the whites retaliating in kind. The proposition to exterminate the Indians, though opposed by the respectable and influential citizens, bore fruit on April 3, 1859, in the brutal massacre, on Indian Island, of about one hundred and fifty Indians, principally women and children. Depredations and disturbances continued from 1859 to 1861, when a regiment under Colonel Lippitt took the field. After more than a year of unsuccessful and expensive operations, he was relieved by a battalion under Lieutenant-Colonel S. G. Whipple. The Hoopa Indians about this time openly joined the hostiles, and were the leading spirits in the bloody warfare that ensued. All the settlers in the mountains were driven in, and their improvements burned. The vast herds of stock that ranged on the grazing-land back from the coast were swept away. The business of the country was prostrate, and the people were in a state of great despondency. The war continued two years longer, with varying results. The Hoopa, Redwood, South Fork, and Grouse Creek Indians were, however, finally induced to treat, and were placed in the Hoopa Valley, where they have ever since maintained peaceful relations with the United States.

On September 10, 1853, a treaty was made with the Rogue River Indians, of Oregon, by the terms of which they were assigned a reservation within their own country, in Southern Oregon, and were to receive from the United States certain annuities. November 18, 1854, a similar treaty was effected with the Chasta-Scotons. They received their annuities until the fall of 1855, when a general Indian war was inaugurated, in which all the tribes of Southern Oregon participated, including the treaty as well as the non-treaty Indians.

After the southern portion of the then Territory of Oregon had become nearly desolate, the government adopted the policy of removing all the Indians from their old homes in the South, and keeping them assembled upon the coast reservation (Siletz), under military surveillance. Twelve bands were removed by military force, and the experiment resulted in the maintenance of a permanent peace. At the time of their removal, in 1856, they numbered about five thousand. They were fierce, warlike, turbulent, and intractable, and averse to labor. It was for several years only possible to retain them upon their reservations by issuing to them full rations of food and considerable quantities of clothing. This was necessarily so, as they had been deprived of their arms and had no means of gaining their own subsistence.

The immediate cause of the Sioux outbreak of 1862 was the failure of the government to make its annual payment to the tribe, followed as it was by the refusal of the traders to give them credit at a time when they were in sore need. The Indians knew that the great civil war was raging with doubtful result, depleting the country of fighting-men, and were told by rebel emissaries that it was uncertain whether the full payment would be made, and that, whatever it was, it would probably be the last. There was no lack of pre-existing causes, such as were only too common in transactions between them and the white men. Prominent among these were the frauds perpetrated upon them growing out of the sale of their lands, the non-fulfilment of treaty stipulations, and the attempt then being made to pay their annuity in goods, instead of in money, as agreed. About $400,000 of the cash payment due the Sioux for their land under the treaties of 1851 and 1852 were paid to the traders on old indebtedness. So intense was the indignation of the Indians at this that a general outbreak was at that time seriously apprehended. For the further cession, in 1858, of all their reservation north of the Minnesota River they were to receive $166,000. Not a penny of this money reached them; but four years afterwards goods to the amount of $15,000 were sent to the Lower Sioux, and the value of these was deducted from what was due them under former treaties.

Those who engaged in the massacre were, with few exceptions, members of the M'dawakanton, Wahpekuta, and Sisseton tribes, of the fierce and warlike Sioux or Dakota nation. They formerly occupied the northeastern portion of Iowa, part of western Wisconsin, the southeastern half of the State of Minnesota, and adjoining possessions in Dakota,—a vast, fertile, and beautiful land, abounding in buffalo and deer, its countless lakes and streams filled with fish and teeming with wild-fowl, and its shores alive with the otter, the mink, and the beaver.

In June, 1862, a number of chiefs and head-men of the Sissetons and Wahpetons visited the Upper Agency and asked about the payment. The agent informed them that he would send them word when the money arrived, and they returned home, but on July 14 they came again, to the number of five thousand, and camped. They were afraid they would not get their money, having again been told so by the whites. Here they remained for some time, all of them pinched for food, and several dying from starvation. They dug up roots to appease their hunger, and, when corn was given them, like famished animals they devoured it uncooked. On the 4th of August some of the young braves, driven by hunger, broke into the government warehouse, but, by persuasion and the issue of a quantity of provisions, the whole body were induced to return to their homes.

The Lower or Redwood Agency was fourteen miles above Fort Ridgely, on the Minnesota River. Here was the reservation of the M'dawakantons and Wahpekutas, and here likewise the excitement was intense for a month before the outbreak. A "Soldiers' Lodge," a secret organization of the young men, designed to stimulate the tribe to hostile action, was formed here about the 1st of July, and succeeded at length in exciting the passions of the Indians to the required pitch. Early in the morning of August 18, a party of one hundred and fifty Sioux, under Little Crow, began an indiscriminate massacre of the whites on both sides of the river. All the buildings at the agency but two were burned. News of the outbreak reached Fort Ridgely before noon, and Captain Marsh, of the Fifth Minnesota Volunteers, started at once for the agency with forty-eight men. They were surrounded by the Indians at the ferry opposite the agency, and one-half of the party were killed, the rest

escaping by flight. Messengers were sent to the Upper Indians at Little Medicine River, and to all the others, many of whom soon joined their brethren in the work of massacre and terror. That night a friendly Indian notified the people at Hazlewood, the Mission Station, six miles above the Upper Agency, of the danger, and forty-two persons, including the missionaries Riggs and Williamson, made their escape, having almost miraculously passed through the numerous scattered bands of Indians on their route. On the very day of the outbreak, $72,000 for the payment of the Indians had reached Fort Ridgely. This fort and New Ulm, a German settlement, almost within a stone's throw of the reservation, were that night filled with terror-stricken fugitives, many of whom were bleeding from ghastly wounds.

For nearly three weeks the Indians were masters of the situation, meeting with no effectual resistance, so many of the able-bodied of the inhabitants being absent in the Union army. Their depredations extended along the whole western frontier of Minnesota, and into Iowa and Dakota. They were repulsed from Forts Ridgely and Abercrombie, and from the towns of New Ulm and Hutchinson. In two weeks fifteen or twenty of the frontier counties were almost depopulated. From Fort Abercrombie to the Iowa line, a frontage of two hundred miles, and extending from Big Stone Lake to Forest City, an area of over twenty thousand square miles, the torch and the tomahawk asserted themselves supreme. More than six hundred victims had fallen, and two hundred persons, mostly women and children, had been carried into captivity.

By the last of August some fourteen hundred men had been collected at Fort Ridgely, under Colonel H. H. Sibley. A force of one hundred and fifty men, under Colonel Joseph R. Brown, was at once sent up to the Lower Agency as a burial-party. After performing this sad service, no signs of Indians being visible, they encamped for the night. At dawn next day their camp at Birch Coolie was attacked, and, as it was in an exceedingly exposed situation, the men fought at a great disadvantage. In three hours nearly one-half the force was *hors du combat*. When relieved by Colonel Sibley they had been thirty-one hours without food or water. Twenty-three were killed or mortally wounded; Major Brown, Captain Anderson, and forty-five of the men were wounded severely.

Late in September the troops moved up the Minnesota Valley, and on the 23d fought the battle of Wood Lake, by which Little Crow's force was put to rout and the contest ended. The camp was attacked by eight hundred Indians early in the morning. After a severe action of an hour and a half, a charge was made, headed by Lieutenant-Colonel Marshall, of the Seventh Minnesota, and the Indians fled in all directions. Little Crow, Little Six, and their followers escaped northward to the British possessions. The Indian camp, left in charge of the friendly Indians, fell, with all its plunder, into the hands of the victors, and the white captives, two hundred in number, regained their liberty. That their lives had been spared was due chiefly to the heroic exertions of Paul, a friendly Indian belonging to the Upper tribe, and to a feud between the Upper and Lower Indians, occasioned by the neglect of the latter to notify their brethren of their hostile intentions before the outbreak, and afterwards by their refusal to give them a share of the plunder. The final catastrophe at Wood Lake may also be attributed to the fact that the Upper Indians withheld their support and openly condemned the hasty acts of Little Crow's band.

Only forty-two Indians were known to have fallen during the entire contest. A large number were subsequently captured and tried by a military commission. Over four hundred were tried, of whom three hundred and three were sentenced to death and eighteen to imprisonment. Most of those acquitted were Upper Indians. Thirty-eight of those condemned were hung at Mankato on February 26, 1863. The remainder were released in April, 1866. Tah-o-ah-doo-ta, or Little Crow, determined to end his days in the land of his fathers, made his way back to Minnesota with a few followers in the ensuing spring, who renewed their depredations. The chief, while engaged in picking berries with his son, six miles north of Hutchinson, was discovered by two white men, and shot. Thus perished one of the foremost hunters and orators of the Sioux. He had been forced into the war against his own better judgment, yet did not shrink from the responsibility, and died like a brave and a warrior of the Dakotas.

On July 20, 1863, an expeditionary force, under General Sibley, left the vicinity of Devil's Lake to chastise the hostile Sioux. In three successive encounters, with some two thousand warriors, mostly Tetons and Yanktonnais, he drove them across the Missouri River, forcing them to abandon all their provisions, vehicles, and skins designed for clothing. The point on the river reached by General Sibley was in latitude 46° 42′, longitude 100° 35′, about forty miles below Fort Clarke, and five hundred and eighty-five miles from Fort Snelling. The object of the expedition was accomplished, and at a trifling sacrifice of life.

At the commencement of the war of the rebellion the Cherokees numbered about 22,000. Of these, some 8500, influenced by rebel emissaries, joined the Confederates and went South, leaving their wives and children in most cases behind them. Many of the remainder of the tribe were disloyal. These, under the lead of their chief, John Ross, assumed a quasi-neutrality. Soon, however, this disguise was thrown off, and two regiments were raised who joined the rebel army. Of those who refused to pursue this course, some joined the Union army, some removed to a more secure place of residence, and others joined Opotheholo, a loyal Creek, who had crossed the Arkansas with a part of his people. The latter, after gaining a victory over a pursuing rebel force, was in a second engagement defeated with great loss, and with his remaining followers fled to Kansas, suffering severely from hunger and cold by the way. The victors plundered the loyal Indians, burned their houses, barns, and fences, and destroyed everything they could not take away with them. The loyalists fled to the mountains, where many died from exposure. In the spring of 1863 large numbers were carried off by the smallpox.

Most of the Cherokees who remained or who had returned from the South entered the Union army as a "Home Guard." In April, 1863, three Indian regiments were stationed with others at Fort Gibson to protect the property and persons of the Cherokee people. This "protection" extended as far as the guns of the fort would reach, and no farther. When a bushwhacking party raided across the Arkansas into the Cherokee country, all the Indians that were out were called in to protect Fort Gibson. They knew the fort was in no danger, but their families were. Thus against their will they were tied hand and foot in the fort while their families were insulted, outraged, plundered, and sometimes murdered or carried into captivity. The close of the war left them destitute of everything except the insufficient supply of clothing, blankets, and provisions furnished by the government. It is estimated that the tribe during its continuance diminished at least 2500. In the matter of civilization, in which the tribe had made especial progress, the four years of war produced much retrogression. Vice and immorality had made rapid strides.

Two-fifths of the Cherokees, more than half of the Creeks, Seminoles, and Uchees, and nine-tenths of the Choctaws and Chickasaws joined the South in the rebellion.

CHAPTER II.

OPERATIONS AGAINST THE INDIANS OF NEW MEXICO AND ARIZONA IN 1862-63-64, IN 1869-72, AND IN 1880—MASSACRE OF FRIENDLY APACHES AT CAMP GRANT—COMANCHES DEFEATED BY COLONEL MACKENZIE—VICTORIA'S BAND OF APACHES DESTROYED.

WHEN the Territory of New Mexico was acquired by the United States, in 1848, its Indian population was composed of the Pueblo, Navajoe, Comanche, and Apache tribes. The Pueblos lived in villages: their form of government was democratic, and they had churches and schools. The Navajoes, whose customs in some respects resembled those of the Pueblos, and who, like them, were partly civilized, relied for support chiefly on their flocks and herds, and on the manufacture of blankets, in which they excelled. The Apaches subsisted chiefly by the chase, and on the mezcal which they stored up for winter use. Frequent collisions took place between these Indians and the Mexicans, the consequence of thieving raids on the one hand and retaliatory expeditions on the other. Troubles between the Comanches and Apaches and citizens of the United States were rife in 1854 and 1855, and they increased with the influx of prospectors and miners. Several military expeditions were sent into the country to punish the savages for not submitting to wrong and injustice. In one of these, Major Van Dorn attacked a large body of Comanches near the Washita Village, October 1, 1858, and killed fifty-six of them. He again struck them successfully on May 13, 1859, in the valley of the Nescatunga.

Finally the rebellion came, and Texan troops invaded the Territory. General James H. Carleton took command of the Department of New Mexico in 1862, and, the Navajoes, Kiowas, Mescalero Apaches, and Comanches having committed depredations, that officer immediately began to discipline those Indians. His subordinates were instructed that no councils or "talks" were to be held with them, and that "the men were to be slain wherever found." An important part of his savage programme seems to have been to secure the development of the rich mines of the Upper Gila, and to do this successfully the Indians were to be exterminated. His field of operations was extended in 1864 to include the Indians in portions of Arizona and Colorado. The renowned Colonel "Kit" Carson, of the First New Mexican Volunteers, took the field against the Navajoes with success. The troops were in constant service, and were engaged in frequent conflicts. Many of the Indians were, despite the sanguinary orders of the general, captured, and many surrendered and were placed on a government reservation at the Bosque Redondo, upon the open plains east of the Rio Grande. Here they were kept for several years.

Colonel Carson's operations against the Kiowas, Comanches, and Apaches were

less successful, owing to the greater difficulty of reaching them and bringing them to action. On November 25, 1864, he attacked a Kiowa village of about one hundred and fifty lodges on the Canadian River, Texas, and after a severe engagement compelled them to retreat, with a loss of sixty killed and wounded. Their village was then destroyed.

The result of military operations in Arizona in 1869 is thus stated by General Ord, the commander of that department. He says in his report, "I have encouraged the troops to capture and root out the Apaches by every means in my power, and to hunt them as they would wild animals. This they have done with unrelenting vigor. Since my last report over two hundred have been killed, generally by parties who have trailed them for days and weeks into mountain-recesses, over snows, among gorges and precipices, lying in wait for them by day and following them by night. Many villages have been burned, large quantities of supplies and arms and ammunition, clothing, and provisions have been destroyed. A large number of horses and mules have been captured, and two men (?), twenty-eight women, and thirty-four children taken prisoners. . . . The Apaches have few friends, and, I believe, no agent. Even the officers, when applied to by them for information, cannot tell them what to do. There seems to be no settled policy but a general idea to kill them wherever found."

This humiliating record of barbarity and outrage lacks the finishing touch, which is supplied by the story of the massacre at Camp Grant, in Arizona, in 1871, of a friendly band of Apaches by citizens of Tucson, aided by Mexicans. The hostile bands of Cochise and others had committed outrages upon the inhabitants of the Territory, and upon travellers passing through. Much fault was found with General Stoneman, the department commander, for his failure properly to protect the citizens. In June, General Crook took command, and proceeded to enlist friendly Indians to operate against the hostiles, securing the aid of a prominent chief named Miguel. This plan he was forbidden to put in execution by Mr. Vincent Collyer, one of the Indian Peace Commissioners. In February, 1871, a young Apache chief, with some of his band, came to Camp Grant and stated that they desired peace,—that he and his people had no home, and could make none, being in constant fear of the troops. Lieutenant Whitman, then in command, told him to bring in his band, and he would aid them. Other small bands also came in, so that early in April some five hundred Indians were encamped near the post, awaiting the action of the department commander. They were fed, and, being very poor and nearly naked, were encouraged by Lieutenant Whitman to cut and bring in hay for his post, and in about two months had brought in about three hundred thousand pounds, carrying it on their backs. Additional bands, with whom these had intermarried, were preparing to come in also.

Lieutenant Whitman became much interested in these Indians, and said officially, "I had come to feel respect for men who, ignorant and naked, were still ashamed to lie or steal, and for women who would work like slaves to clothe themselves and children, but, untaught, held their virtue above price. . . . They frequently expressed anxiety to hear from the general, that they might have confidence to build for themselves better houses, but would always say, 'You know what we want, and, if you cannot see him, you can write.'"

Such was the situation, when, at daybreak of April 29, their camp was surrounded and attacked by a large body of men from Tucson. So sudden and unexpected was the onslaught that no one was awake to give the alarm, and quite a number of the women were shot while asleep beside their bundles of hay, which they had collected to bring in on that morning. The women who were unable to get away had their brains beaten out with clubs or stones. Of the whole number killed and missing— about one hundred and twenty-five—eight only were men. Those who escaped the massacre came into Camp Grant singly and in small parties so changed as hardly to be recognized, having neither eaten nor slept for forty-eight hours. Lieutenant Whitman's denunciation of this murderous and cowardly act, and of those engaged in it, had no other effect than to cause his being relieved from duty at Camp Grant, where the Indians, who knew him to be their friend, had expressed an earnest desire that he might be retained.

A successful expedition under Colonel R. S. Mackenzie, Fourth United States Cavalry, against hostile Indians raiding into Texas, struck, on September 29, 1872, a camp of Qua-ha-du Comanches on McClellan's Creek,—that of Maowi, the most disaffected and dangerous of all the "out" Comanches,—and, after a brisk fight, carried their village, killing twenty-three Indians and taking one hundred and twenty-four prisoners, principally women and children. The command lost two killed and two wounded. This blow was promptly followed by the surrender of the white captives remaining in their hands, and by a large increase in number of the Indians on the reservation.

The Southern Apaches, especially Victoria's band, had long been troublesome, but in 1879 that chief had, with his people, come in to the Mescalero Agency, expressing a desire to remain there permanently. The cause of his hostility was the abolition of the Ojo Caliente Reservation, known as the Southern Apache Agency, and the attempted removal of his band to the San Carlos Agency, with some of whose tribes they were not on friendly terms. Very soon thereafter, however, he had left, and was marauding and murdering citizens ten miles distant from the reservation. Some of his band were, during the winter and spring of 1880, in the mountains, within forty miles of the agency, in constant intercourse with the Indians of the reservation, and successful in evading the military. Nearly two hundred and fifty of the worst Indians of the agency joined him. It was found necessary in January, 1880, soon after active military operations were begun against this band, to cut off all communication between Victoria and the Mescaleros on the reservation, and also to disarm and dismount the latter. The remarkable success of Victoria and his followers in skirmishes with the soldiers during the year 1880, as well as in evading pursuit, sufficiently attests the skill and prowess of that chief. Driven at last into Mexico by our forces, Victoria and nearly all his followers were attacked and destroyed by a body of Mexican troops under General Terrasas.

CHAPTER III.

HOSTILITIES WITH THE CHEYENNES, ARAPAHOES, AND SIOUX—SAND CREEK MASSACRE—POWDER RIVER WAR—MASSACRE OF COLONEL FETTERMAN'S COMMAND—HANCOCK'S EXPEDITION—POWELL'S ENGAGEMENT.

WITH the accession of territory to the United States at the close of the Mexican war, our Indian population, the greater part of which was wholly uncivilized, was largely increased. The discovery of gold in our new possessions induced an immense emigration to California across the plains. The rights of the Indians were overlooked or disregarded, and complications and wars ensued. By a treaty at Fort Laramie, September 17, 1851, with the Sioux, Cheyennes, Arapahoes, Crows, and others, the boundaries of these tribes were settled, and they agreed to abstain from hostilities with one another, and to permit the United States to establish roads and military posts within their limits, the United States agreeing to protect them from white depredations and to pay them annually for fifty years the sum of $50,000. This was the price of the "right of way." The Senate amended the treaty, and limited the annuity to fifteen years. The bad faith as well as the unwisdom of this step soon became apparent. Peace was broken in August, 1854, when an officer with a file of soldiers, in attempting to arrest an Indian belonging to a band of Brulé Sioux near Fort Laramie, was killed with all his men. Then followed General Harney's Sioux expedition, the crowning act of which took place September 22, 1855, in Northwestern Nebraska or Northeastern Wyoming, and was styled by him the "Battle of the Blue Water." At this point a band of Brulé Sioux, of which Little Thunder was the principal chief, was encamped, with his braves, women, and children. They were not a war-party, and had nothing to do with the affair at Fort Laramie. It was a peaceful and unoffending Indian village that General Harney surprised early in the morning, killing eighty-six men, women, and children, and capturing seventy women and children. This is only one of many cases in which our troops have struck the Indians, not caring to know whether they were guilty or innocent. Serious trouble grew out of this campaign, resulting in the loss of many lives of white people. On July 29, 1857, Colonel E. V. Sumner defeated three hundred Cheyennes on Solomon's Fork of the Kansas River, burnt their village to the ground, and destroyed their winter supplies.

The boundaries assigned to the Cheyennes and Arapahoes by the Fort Laramie treaty included a large part of the Territory of Colorado and Western Kansas. Some years later, gold and silver were discovered in the mountains of Colorado, their lands were occupied by miners, who founded cities, established farms, and opened roads, and before 1861 they had been driven down upon the waters of the Arkansas, and were sullen and discontented because of these violations of their rights. The third article of the treaty of 1851 bound the United States to protect the Indians against all depredations after its ratification. This treaty was broken, but not by the savages. It became apparent to them that nothing was left for them to do but to ratify a treaty confirming the act.

This was done February 18, 1861, at Fort Wise, Kansas. The tribes ceded what now constitutes two great States of the Union, retaining only a small reservation on the Arkansas River and including the country around Fort Lyon. "Not being able," say the Peace Commissioners in their report, "to protect them in the larger reservation, the nation re-resolved that it would protect them in the quiet and peaceable possession of the smaller tract." Thirty thousand dollars per annum was to be paid them for fifteen years, houses were to be built, lands were to be broken up and fenced, stock, animals, and agricultural implements were to be provided, mills were to be built, and engineers, farmers, and mechanics were to be sent among them.

From this time until the 12th of April, 1864, notwithstanding the non-fulfilment of these promises and their natural dissatisfaction thereat, the Indians remained peaceful. On that day, Lieutenant Dunn, with forty men from Camp Sanborn, undertook to disarm some Indians who, it was said, had stolen some stock claimed by a man named Ripley. The Indians resisted, and Dunn withdrew discomfited. In May following, Major Downing, of the First Colorado Cavalry, moved against the Indians, and surprised at daylight the Cheyenne village of Cedar Bluffs, in a small cañon, about sixty miles north of the South Platte River. Twenty-six were killed, and thirty wounded. No prisoners were taken. Their lodges and other property were all destroyed. About the same time, Lieutenant Ayres, of the Colorado troops, had a difficulty in which an Indian chief, under a flag of truce, was murdered. During the summer and fall occurrences of this character were frequent.

Black Kettle and other prominent chiefs of the Cheyennes and Arapahoes sent word to the commander at Fort Lyon that the war had been forced upon them, and that they desired peace. They were then on their own reservation. Major Wynkoop, the commander at Fort Lyon, proceeded with them to Denver, and held an interview with the governor, who wished to have nothing to do with them, not believing it to be policy to make peace with them "until they were properly punished." Wynkoop then ordered the Indians to move their villages nearer to the fort and bring their women and children, which was done. In November this officer was removed, and Major Anthony, of the First Colorado Cavalry, took command, assuring the Indians of safety. They numbered about five hundred men, women, and children. Here, while under the pledge of protection, they were slaughtered by the Third Colorado and a battalion of the First Colorado Cavalry, under Colonel Chivington. He marched from Denver to Fort Lyon, and about daylight in the morning of November 29 surrounded the Indian camp and commenced an indiscriminate slaughter. This massacre is scarcely paralleled in the records of Indian barbarity. Fleeing women, holding up their hands and praying for mercy, were brutally shot down, infants were killed and scalped, and men were tortured and mutilated in a manner that would put to shame the utmost ingenuity of the savage. This atrocious affair is known as the Sand Creek massacre. No one will be astonished that a war ensued which cost the government thirty millions of dollars and carried conflagration and distress to the border settlements. During the year 1865 not less than eight thousand troops were obliged to be withdrawn from the forces engaged in suppressing the rebellion to take part in this Indian war. The results of the year's campaign satisfied all sensible men that war with Indians was both useless and expensive. Fifteen or twenty Indians had been killed, at a cost of more than a million dollars apiece, while hundreds of our soldiers had lost their lives, many of our border settlers had been butchered, and much property had been destroyed. This war was something more than useless and expensive: it was dishonorable to the nation, and rendered its originators justly infamous.

When the utter futility of conquering a peace was made manifest to every one, peaceful agencies were employed. Generals Sanborn, Harney, and others were selected as commissioners to hold a council with the hostile tribes, which they succeeded in doing in October, 1865, at the mouth of the Little Arkansas, with the Kiowas, Cheyennes, Arapahoes, Comanches, and Apaches. Agreements were soon made, and no sooner were treaties signed than the war, which had been waged for nearly two years, ceased. Travel on the plains was again secure. What eight thousand troops had failed to secure, this simple agreement, rendered nugatory by the Senate, and requiring nothing but a pledge of friendship, obtained. During the remainder of the year 1866 comparative peace prevailed.

In March, 1865, a joint special committee of both houses of Congress, of which Senator Doolittle was chairman, was appointed to inquire into the condition of the Indian tribes, and especially as to the manner in which they had been treated by the military and civil authorities of the United States. On January 26, 1867, this committee reported that everywhere except in the Indian Territory the tribes were rapidly decreasing in number through disease, intemperance, wars among themselves and with the whites, the steady and resistless tide of white emigration, which, confining the Indians to still narrower limits, destroys their game, and the irrepressible conflict between a superior and an inferior race. The committee found that a large majority of our Indian wars were traceable to the aggressions of lawless whites upon our borders. This was the testimony of old frontiersmen like Colonel Bent and Colonel Carson, whose lives had been spent upon the plains and in intercourse with the natives.

In 1866 the Sioux Indians were disturbed by the emigration over the Powder River route to the gold-fields of Montana. This was Sioux territory, and their especial buffalo-range, and therefore indispensable to them. The treaty of 1851, granting them an annuity for fifty years, had without their consent been amended to fifteen years. This period had expired, and they claimed that the grant to the United States for the location of roads and establishment of posts had ceased also. In March, 1866, General Pope, in command of the Department of the Missouri, ordered the establishment of military posts on that route. When, in the summer, troops were placed in the newly-erected Forts Phil Kearney, C. F. Smith, and Reno, the Indians notified the government that the occupation of the country by troops would be resisted; but the warning was disregarded. A treaty was tried. Some of the Indians voluntarily signed it, but Red Cloud retired from the council, and, placing his hand upon his rifle, said, "In this and in the Great Spirit I trust for the right." Soon war broke out. Emigrant travel ceased, the forts were besieged, and the country was overrun with Indians. On the 21st of December a wood-party from Fort Phil Kearney was attacked, and Colonel W. J. Fetterman went out to its relief. In the fight that ensued, every man of the force was killed. The costly effort to keep open this route continued until the spring of 1868, when, by a treaty with the Sioux, the posts were abandoned, and the Powder River route to Montana was closed.

In April, 1867, an expedition under General Hancock, commander of the department, left Fort Larned with the object of showing the Indians that he was "able to chastise any tribes who may molest people travelling across the plains." He proceeded up the Pawnee Fork of the Arkansas in the direction of a village of one thousand or fifteen hundred Cheyennes and Sioux. When near their camp, the chiefs visited him, as they had already done at Fort Larned, and requested him not to approach the camp with his troops, as otherwise the women and children, having the remembrance of Sand Creek, would abandon the village. On the 14th he resumed his march, and when about ten miles from their village he was again met by the head-men, who stated that they would treat with him there or elsewhere, but that they could not, as requested by him, keep their women and children in camp if he approached with soldiers. He informed them that he would march to within a mile of their village, and treat with them that evening. As he proceeded, the women fled. The chiefs and part of the young men remained. Orders were then given to surround the village and capture the Indians remaining. The order was obeyed, but the chiefs and warriors had departed. The fleeing Indians, hotly pursued by General Custer and his cavalry, destroyed a station at Smoky Hill, and killed several men. When the news reached Hancock, he at once burned the Indian village of three hundred lodges, together with the entire property of the tribe.

The Indians—all on the plains—now became outlaws, and, exasperated by the destruction of their village, waged a determined war. Many soldiers and settlers were killed, valuable trains were captured, stations were destroyed, and operations on the Union Pacific Railroad were seriously retarded. Engineers engaged in surveying the route, and workmen employed upon the road, were frequently waylaid and murdered, and stock and building-materials were destroyed and carried away. Overland immigration and traffic were interrupted, and attended with great danger. Early in August a freight-train in Nebraska was thrown off the track near Plum Creek Station, and all the employees save one were murdered, and the cars and merchandise burned. General Augur promptly sent troops to the scene of the disaster. On the 16th of August he had a battle with five hundred Sioux, sixty of whom were killed. Our troops were aided by a band of friendly Pawnees. The most

important engagement in the region of the Powder and Yellowstone Rivers took place August 2, near Fort Phil Kearney. A party of woodcutters, with an escort of forty soldiers, under Captain James Powell, and about fifty citizens, were set upon by a large body of Cheyennes and Arapahoes, and a desperate fight ensued, lasting for three hours, when they were relieved by two companies of soldiers, with a howitzer, who drove off the Indians, with a loss of fifty or sixty killed and a large number wounded.

CHAPTER IV.

INDIAN PEACE COMMISSION OF 1867-68 — TREATIES WITH THE HOSTILE TRIBES—REPORT OF THE COMMISSIONERS—GENERAL SHERIDAN—RENEWAL OF HOSTILITIES—FORSYTH'S BATTLE—SURPRISE AND SLAUGHTER OF BLACK KETTLE AND HIS BAND—CESSATION OF THE WAR.

MILITARY operations against the hostile tribes having proved wholly ineffectual, Congress, on July 20, 1867, created a commission "to establish peace with certain hostile Indian tribes." The "Peace Commissioners" appointed were N. G. Taylor, Commissioner of Indian Affairs; J. B. Henderson, Chairman of the Indian Committee of the United States Senate; J. B. Sanborn and S. F. Tappan, civilians; and Generals Sherman, Harney, Terry, and Augur, of the army. They were to meet the chiefs and head-men of the hostile bands, and, if advisable, to make treaties with them, with a view,—first, to remove, if possible, the causes of war; secondly, to secure peace to our frontier settlements, and the safe construction of our railroads to the Pacific; and, thirdly, to suggest or inaugurate some plan for the civilization of the Indians. They were "also to examine and select a district or districts of country having sufficient area to receive all the Indian tribes occupying territory east of the Rocky Mountains not then settled upon reservations, which should have sufficient arable or grazing land to enable the tribes placed on them to support themselves, and so located as not to interfere with travelled highways and contemplated railroads to the Pacific."

At this time war existed with several tribes, and great diversity of opinion existed as to the proper method to be pursued, some believing in the efficacy of peaceful negotiations, while others saw no hope except in the entire subjugation of the Indians. With great difficulty the commissioners succeeded in procuring interviews with the leaders of these hostile tribes, through the facilities afforded by the military posts and Indian agencies. On September 12 they met at North Platte, on the Pacific Railroad, a large number of Sioux and Northern Cheyennes, some of whom had recently been engaged in war. At this meeting a full and friendly understanding was arrived at, which, though not reduced to writing, was faithfully kept by the Indians. The commissioners next proceeded to a point about eighty miles south of the Arkansas River, where they met, on Medicine Lodge Creek, the Kiowas, Comanches, Arapahoes, and Apaches. The Cheyennes were at first distrustful of the purpose of the commission, and encamped at a distance. A treaty was in due time made with the other tribes, and finally, on October 28, 1867, with the Cheyennes and Arapahoes. The Sioux, owing to the lateness of the season, and a belief prevalent among them that they were to be exterminated, did not appear at Fort Laramie at the time appointed. Red Cloud, however, sent word that his hostility was with a view to save the Powder River country from intrusion, it being the only hunting-ground left to his people, and that whenever the garrisons of Forts Phil Kearney and C. F. Smith were withdrawn his hostility would cease. He agreed, however, to a truce until he could meet the commissioners in the following spring.

Resuming its duties at that time, the commission, on April 29, 1868, concluded a treaty with the Ogalalla and Brulé Sioux at Fort Laramie, afterwards accepted and ratified by the Blackfeet, Upper and Lower Yanktonnais, Uncpapas, Sans Arc, Two-Kettle, Minneconjou, Lower Brulé, and Santee Sioux, providing that war was to cease forever. Bad men upon either side were to be arrested and punished, and persons injured were to be reimbursed. By the treaty with the Kiowas, Comanches, and Apaches, a district of country in the Indian Territory, between the Red and Wachita Rivers and the 98th and 100th meridians of west longitude, was set apart for their absolute use and occupation, and for such other friendly tribes or individual Indians as from time to time they chose to admit among them; and the United States solemnly agreed that none but properly authorized persons should be permitted "to pass over, settle upon, or reside in the territory described, or in such territory as may be added to this reservation for the use of said Indians."

The same guarantee was given against outside intrusion on their lands in the treaty with the Cheyennes and Arapahoes, whose reservation adjoined theirs on the south, the Indians in both cases relinquishing their right of occupancy to the territory outside their reservations, but reserving the right to hunt on lands south of the Arkansas so long as the buffalo could be successfully chased therein. To the Sioux, with the same guarantee, was assigned the district between the Missouri River and the 104th meridian of west longitude, and between the 46th parallel of north latitude and the State of Nebraska. All these treaties stipulated that no cession of any part of the reservation should be valid unless executed and signed by three-fourths of all the adult males interested therein, and that no cession should deprive such Indians as had selected homesteads of their rights without their consent.

In the Sioux treaty the United States stipulated that the country north of the Platte and east of the summit of the Big Horn Mountains should be held to be unceded Indian territory, upon which no white person should settle without the Indians' consent, and that within ninety days after the conclusion of peace the military posts established in this territory should be abandoned, and the roads to them and by them to the Territory of Montana closed up. While ceding all territory outside of their reservation, they reserved the right to hunt north of the Platte and on the Republican Fork of the Smoky Hill. This treaty was ratified and proclaimed in the latter part of February, 1869.

In their report, made January 7, 1868, the commission recommended the setting apart of two districts for permanent Indian colonization,—one to be bounded north by the 46th parallel, south by the north line of Nebraska, east by the Missouri River, and west by the 104th meridian; the other east by the States of Missouri and Arkansas, west by the 101st meridian, north by Kansas, and south by Texas.

They also recommended that for each district a territorial government should be established, that agriculture and manufactures should be introduced as rapidly as possible, schools established, and courts and other institutions of government suited to their condition organized. Tribal distinctions should be blotted out, and the English language should be substituted for their barbarous dialects.

With reference to removing causes of complaint, the commissioners say, "This would be no easy task. It is now rather late in the day to think of obliterating from the minds of the present generation the remembrance of wrong. Among civilized men war usually springs from a sense of injustice. The best possible way, then, to avoid war is to do no act of injustice. When we learn that the same rule holds with Indians, the chief difficulty is removed. But it is said, 'Our wars with them have been almost constant. Have we been uniformly unjust?' We answer unhesitatingly, Yes!" They say, further, that in every case of complications then, and for several years previously, existing, which they had investigated, the cause of difficulty was traced to the wrong-doing of our own people, both civil and military. Although no treaty had then been made with the Sioux, the commissioners said in their report that "with anything like prudence and good conduct on the part of our own people in future, we believe the Indian war east of the Rocky Mountains is absolutely closed."

From this ably-written and carefully-prepared document we quote still further:

"The treaty stipulations with many of the tribes are altogether inappropriate. They seem to have been made in total ignorance of their numbers and disposition, and in utter disregard of their wants.

"It is useless to go over the history of Indian removals. If it had been done but once, the record would be less revolting. From the Eastern to the Middle States, from thence to Illinois and Wisconsin, thence to Missouri and Iowa, thence to Kansas, Dakota, and the plains; whither next we cannot tell. Surely the policy was not designed to perpetuate barbarism; but such has been its effect. Many of the tribes are now beyond the region of agriculture, where the chase is a necessity. So long as they have to subsist in this way, civilization is out of the question."

The commission recommended, among other things, that the intercourse laws subsisting should be thoroughly revised, that white persons who trespass on Indian reservations should be removed by the military authorities, and that Indian affairs should be committed to an independent bureau or department.

For nearly a year the treaties made by the commission remained unratified,—a delay that worked great injury. The Indians had surrendered their old reservations, upon which the whites had already begun to settle, though by the terms of the treaty three years were to elapse before they should do so. General Sheridan, in taking command of the Department of the Missouri, in April, 1868, found encamped near Fort Dodge, Kansas, a large number of Kiowas, Comanches, Cheyennes, and Arapahoes, but declined the interview they sought in which to make known their needy condition. These Indians were practically without a home, had not received the annuities due them, and no appropriation had been made for fulfilling the provisions of the treaty of 1867. They were destitute. Government failed to respond to the urgent and repeated requests of the Indian Commissioner, their agents, and others, to save them from actual starvation. Their outspoken dissatisfaction at this cruel treatment seems to have inspired General Sheridan with no other idea than that they required to be "soundly whipped, the ringleaders hung, their ponies killed, and such destruction of their property made as will render them very poor." Proceeding upon this theory, and believing that making peace with the Indians was an error of judgment on the part of the Peace Commissioners, it was not long before, in his judgment, the Indians, especially the Cheyennes and Arapahoes, were "hostile," and he began to prepare troops to operate against them. Upon his representations, a majority of the Peace Commissioners met in Chicago in October, 1868, reversed all their previous work, abrogated the hunting privileges outside of reservations, and decided to compel the Indians to go on the reservations assigned them, and that the Indian Bureau should be turned over to the War Department!

In August a new military district had been created, bounded east by the Arkansas River, south by Texas, north by Kansas, and west by the 100th meridian, to which General Hazen was assigned, with the supervision and control of the Cheyennes, Arapahoes, Kiowas, and Comanches. Just previous to this a dissatisfied party of Cheyennes had perpetrated outrages against the whites on the Saline River. Agent Wynkoop demanded of the principal chiefs, Medicine Arrow and Little Rock, that they should deliver up the perpetrators, which they promised should be done, but before sufficient time had elapsed for them to fulfil this promise, the troops were in the field, and the Indians in flight. General Sheridan was then operating with detached squads of troops, who annoyed and harassed the Indians, killing them whenever possible. In turn the Indians retaliated, killing some of Sheridan's scouts. In addition to his regular troops he obtained the services of two hundred Osage Indians, whom he attached to Custer's command. Governor Crawford, of Kansas, raised a regiment of volunteers, which he led in person.

One of the actions of this campaign furnishes a remarkable instance of heroism and endurance. Brevet Lieutenant-Colonel George A. Forsyth, Ninth U.S. Cavalry, was permitted to raise and lead a force of fifty men for a scouting expedition. Following a fresh trail, the morning of September 17 found them in camp on the bank of the Arickaree, in which stream there were but a few inches of running water. A small island in the middle of the stream, directly behind the bivouac, was fringed with willows and bore a few stunted trees. At daybreak the Indians rushed upon them, but were soon driven back. Forsyth, seeing their overwhelming numbers, at once decided to take position on the sand island, which was separated from the mainland by a mere thread of water. The movement was effected, and the men distributed in a circle, ordered to lie down, and as soon as possible dig rifle-pits for themselves in the sand. An annoying fire was kept up by the Indians until about nine o'clock, when a charge was made, with unearthly yells, by three hundred mounted warriors. When within thirty yards of the rifle-pits, a rapid and effective discharge stopped the savages, and caused them to take to flight as rapidly as they had advanced.

The ground was strewed with dead warriors, foremost among them Roman Nose, their principal war-chief. At two o'clock another assault was made and repulsed, and a third and much feebler one at about four o'clock in the afternoon. A September rain set in. Every horse and mule was killed by the enemy's fire. The second in command, Lieutenant Beecher, and five men, had been killed or mortally wounded, and seventeen severely wounded, among them the gallant Forsyth.

Fort Wallace, the nearest point whence succor could arrive, was one hundred miles distant. The men were without food, and surrounded by nine hundred well-armed warriors. A well was dug, the dead animals' flesh was cut into strips for food, the line was strengthened with saddles and dead animals, and at nightfall two men were despatched through the enemy's line to Fort Wallace. Day after day the heroic band sustained the steady fire of the Indians, but by the fifth day the suffering from hunger, as the meat could no longer be eaten, was intense. By this time the Indians began to disappear, and by the seventh day all had left, but the beleaguered force was too weak to move, when, on the morning of the ninth day, succor at length arrived. The Indians encountered were Northern Cheyennes, Brulé and Ogalalla Sioux, and about one hundred and seventy "Dog Soldiers," the banditti of the plains. Their loss is said to have been thirty-five killed and one hundred wounded.

On November 23, 1868, General Custer, with the Seventh Cavalry, proceeded south towards the Antelope Hills from his camp on the North Canadian River in search of hostile Indians. On the morning of the 27th he surprised Black Kettle's camp of Cheyennes on the Wichita, killed that chief and one hundred and three warriors, and captured the camp, including all their winter supply of flour, meat, and other provisions, fifty-three women, and their children. Black Kettle was assisted by the Arapahoes, under Little Raven, and the Kiowas, under Satanta, who were encamped six miles below, and who kept up a fierce attack on the troops from noon until about three P.M. Custer's loss was twenty-nine killed, including Major Elliot, and fourteen wounded. General Sheridan states that this battle took place one hundred miles beyond the reservation, and that it was this band that committed the first depredations upon the Saline and the Solomon. Both statements have been questioned.

In a communication from Colonel Wynkoop to the Indian Office he said that "a few thousand dollars for subsistence for these starving Indians at the proper time would have saved millions to the treasury, saved many white men's lives, saved the necessity of hunting down and destroying innocent Indians for the fault of the guilty, and driving into misery and starvation numbers of women and little children, not one of whom but then mourned some relative brutally murdered at the horrible massacre at Sand Creek, and who still suffer from the loss of their habitations and property wantonly destroyed by General Hancock." After the affair of the Wichita he wrote to the Commissioner of Indian Affairs as follows : "I am perfectly satisfied that the position of Black Kettle at the time of the attack upon his village was not a hostile one. I know that he had proceeded to the point at which he was killed with the understanding that it was the locality where those Indians who were friendly disposed should assemble. I know that such information had been conveyed to Black Kettle as the orders of the military authorities. . . . In regard to the charge that Black Kettle was engaged in the depredations committed on the Saline and Solomon during the summer of 1868, I know the same to be utterly false, as Black Kettle was at that time camped near my agency on the Pawnee Fork." Superintendent Murphy, of the Osage Agency, wrote the commissioner, December 4, 1868, that the party thus attacked and slaughtered by General Custer and his command was Black Kettle's band of Cheyennes,—"Black Kettle, one of the best and truest friends the white man had among the Indians of the plains." The testimony of General Carr, who, July 11, 1869, surprised a camp of Dog Soldiers and Cheyennes near Valley Station, killing fifty-two and capturing a number of women and children, confirms the above statement. "We followed them," says Carr, "for ten days, and found them at a spring east of the South Platte, near Valley Station, then went back towards the head of Frenchman's Fork. . . . The prisoners report this to be the only body of Indians known on the Republican. It is the same that fought Forsyth and all other parties on the Republican last year."

Mo-ka-ta-va-ta, or Black Kettle, the principal Cheyenne chief, at a council held at Fort Ellsworth, Kansas, in the winter of 1866–67, spoke at length, and with earnest natural eloquence entreated that the Great Father would stop the building of the iron road, which would soon drive away the buffalo and leave his children without food. He was described at this time as a fine-looking man, of middle age, with heavy features and frame. He possessed great influence with his tribe, and by his wise counsel had more than once averted war. His dress was simple, with the exception of a massive necklace of crescent-shaped silver plates, from the front of which depended a heavy silver medal bearing the profile in relief of Washington. It had been presented long ago by the President of the United States to one of Black Kettle's ancestors, and was worn with evident pride.

December 22, 1868, General Custer reported that all the Apaches, nearly all the Comanches, and the principal chiefs and bands of the Kiowas had come in and placed themselves in a peaceful attitude. The Cheyennes and Arapahoes were supposed to be concentrated in the mountains forty or fifty miles from Fort Cobb. The Uncpapa Blackfeet, Lower Yanktonnais, Sans Arcs, Upper and Lower Brulé, Two Kettle, Minneconjou, and Ogalallas, were for years prior to 1868 hostile to government, and depredated upon the white settlers. Claiming the ownership of Dakota and of parts of Montana and Wyoming, as well as Western Nebraska, they made every effort to prevent the settlement of that region, their hostility being specially directed against the Union Pacific Railroad. The military operations of 1867–68 convinced the Sioux of the hopelessness of the contest, and disposed them to accept the provision made for them by the treaty of 1868. Except the main portion of the Ogalalla band, and a considerable body from all the bands known as the "hostile Sioux," of whom Sitting Bull and Black Moon were the principal chiefs, their bands were at the close of the year within their reservations.

Lieutenant-Colonel Evans moved from Fort Bascom up the main Canadian, scouting to the head-waters of the Red River, and there discovered a trail of Comanches, followed it up, and on December 25 attacked the party, killing some twenty-five, wounding a large number, capturing and burning their village, and destroying all their property. General Carr operated on the Canadian, west of the Antelope Hills, and forced the Cheyennes and Arapahoes over into the eastern edge of the Staked Plains, where there was no grass, and, being without supplies, they were compelled to surrender, and promised to go upon their reservation. The Arapahoes were faithful, and delivered themselves up; the Cheyennes broke their promise, and did not come in until General Custer came upon them on the head-waters of Red River.

CHAPTER V.

TROUBLES IN MONTANA—PIEGAN MASSACRE—RED CLOUD VISITS WASHINGTON—CHEYENNE, ARAPAHOE, AND WICHITA CHIEFS VISIT NEW YORK AND BOSTON—MODOC WAR—BLACK HILLS EXPEDITION—UNLAWFUL ORDER OF GENERAL SHERIDAN—SIOUX AND CHEYENNE WAR OF 1876—DESTRUCTION OF CRAZY HORSE'S VILLAGE—BATTLE OF THE ROSEBUD—MASSACRE OF GENERAL CUSTER'S COMMAND—AGENCY INDIANS DISARMED AND DISMOUNTED—SITTING BULL SURRENDERS—GENERAL McKENZIE DESTROYS A LARGE CHEYENNE VILLAGE—BANNOCK WAR—FLIGHT OF DULL KNIFE'S BAND OF NORTHERN CHEYENNES.

TROUBLES between the invading horde of miners and the Indian population of Montana culminated in the fall of 1869 in a proclamation of war by Acting-Governor Meagher, who on his own motion called out troops and offered a liberal bounty for Indian scalps. The Bloods and Blackfeet, who had for many years been on friendly terms with the whites, tried to avoid conflicts with Meagher's forces; nevertheless, some of them were plundered and a number were killed.

Mountain Chief's band of Piegans was disposed to retaliate these injuries, but this band had in the winter of 1869-70 gone north, and was wintering in the British possessions. An expedition under Colonel E. M. Baker, Second U.S. Cavalry, was sent against this party by General Sheridan, which on the 19th of January, 1870, moved towards the Maria's River. On the morning of the 23d he surprised the Piegan village of Bear Chief and Red Horn, a band against which no complaint had ever been made, and which at the time was terribly afflicted with smallpox, and, no resistance being offered, killed one hundred and seventy-three Indians, mostly women and children, and took about forty women and children prisoners. The latter were turned loose upon the prairie, to starve or perish otherwise. The report of Lieutenant Pease, Indian Agent for the Blackfeet, and a reliable officer, states that of the Indians killed thirty-three were men, fifteen only being warriors. These sickening details aroused the popular indignation, and the conduct of those engaged in the "Piegan Massacre" was severely condemned.

Two occurrences in 1870 tended to bring about a better understanding between the government and the Indian tribes. One of these was the visit to Washington of two deputations of powerful chiefs, headed by Red Cloud, the Sioux leader. A patient hearing of their grievances tended in some measure to allay their discontent, and after their return to the plains they labored faithfully for the preservation of peace. Their neighbors the Kiowas, angry at the arrest of their chiefs Satanta and Satank, earnestly pressed them to go on the war-path, but they firmly refused.

Finding themselves unsupported, the Kiowas concluded to remain at peace. The other encouraging circumstance was found in the humane policy of President Grant, who appointed commissioners to visit the Indians from the Society of Friends, and called on other denominations of the country to send their best men among the savages as missionaries, and to bring them into accord with the ways of civilized society. The idea that the Indian could not be civilized had begun to be questioned.

Another deputation of chiefs visited Washington early in 1871 to confer with the government respecting their boundaries, and extended their visit to New York and Boston. In New York they were addressed by the venerable Peter Cooper, by Professor B. N. Martin, and others, and in Boston by Vincent Collyer and by Wendell Phillips, who alluded to Mo-ka-ta-va-ta (Black Kettle) as the Philip Sidney of the plains. Among these chiefs were Little Raven, Powder Face, and Bird Chief, of the Arapahoes; Little Robe and Stone Calf, of the Cheyennes; and Buffalo Goad, of the Wichitas. They were dressed partly in their native style, wearing moccasins and ear-rings, and having their long black hair braided. Buffalo Goad, their most eloquent speaker, wore a plain black suit. The prevailing type of face was that of the warlike Sioux,—a coarse, broad lower face, Hebrew nose, and retreating forehead. Powder Face formed a marked exception among them, his profile having all the grandeur of the traditional "noble red man." Stone Calf appeared in all the paraphernalia of a warrior. Speeches were made by several of the chiefs. Little Raven said, "Long ago the Arapahoes had a fine country of their own. The white man came, and the Indians gave him buffalo-meat and a horse to ride on, and told him the country was big enough for the white man and the Arapahoes too. After a while the white man found gold in our country. They took the gold, and pushed the Indian from his home. I am an old man now. I have been waiting many years for Washington to give us our rights. The white man has taken away everything. I hope justice will be done to my children, if not to myself. God gave this country to the Indian, and God sent the white man here; but I don't think God sent the white man to do injustice to the Indians always. I want my people to live like white people, and have the same chance. I hope the Great Spirit will put a good heart into the white people, that they may give us our rights." Buffalo Goad said, "We want houses built for our people to live in, and school-houses for our children, the same as white children have. The white people have done a great deal of wrong to our people, and we want to have it stopped. I want you to stop the white men from killing the Indians after this. I and my brother represent five different tribes who have always been friendly to the whites. But because we do not fight, Washington takes away our lands and gives them to the tribes that are fighting them all the time. When I got to Washington they said they knew all about my people. If they did know it, why didn't they help us and fix it? I would like to see churches and school-houses built in my land, and would like to see my children educated before I die."

A treaty with the Klamath and Modoc tribes, and the Yahooskin band of Snake Indians, of Oregon, ceding all their lands, and accepting a tract known as the Klamath Reservation, was made October 14, 1864. The Modocs went to work with zeal to build cabins and enclose ground for cultivation. In April, 1870, they left the reservation for their camp on Lost River. Captain Jack and his band of Modocs would have remained and settled down to civilization if there had been ordinary encouragement and assistance, and if the Klamaths, their hereditary enemies, who largely outnumbered them, had allowed them to do so. The agent could not protect them from their hostility, the issue of rations was suspended for want of funds, and Captain Jack and his band returned to their old home on Lost River, where collisions soon began with the whites who in the mean time had settled on the ceded lands.

The attempt to remove them in November, 1872, resulted in a conflict between the Modocs and the troops and white settlers. The Indians took refuge in the Lava Beds, an inaccessible region south of Tule Lake, where for weeks they successfully defied all the troops that could be brought against them. To bring about a peaceful settlement of the difficulties, a commission was appointed consisting of A. B. Meacham, L. S. Dyer, and Rev. E. Thomas, who were placed under the direction of General Canby. April 11, 1873, while engaged in a conference with Captain Jack and others under a flag of truce, the two latter were brutally murdered, and Mr. Meacham was severely wounded. After seven months' severe fighting, the Modocs were subdued, and Captain Jack and three of his principal men, who were implicated in the murder of the commissioners, were tried by court-martial and executed, October 3. The remnant of the tribe was captured June 5, 1873, and placed on a reservation in the Indian Territory.

A campaign against the Southern Cheyennes in 1873–74 was successfully and vigorously carried on by General Miles, and on March 6, 1874, the main body surrendered. Thirty-three were selected for punishment, and sent to Fort Marion, St. Augustine, Florida, to be closely confined. A few days after, nearly four hundred of the Cheyennes "stampeded," went north, and joined their relatives in Dakota. In the following year the Cheyennes, Kiowas, and Comanches, on the borders of the Staked Plains, were brought under subjection and disarmed, and an active campaign was carried on against the Indians who had committed outrages on the Mexican border. The campaign against the Cheyennes, Arapahoes, Kiowas, Comanches, and other bands in the Southwest was successfully terminated, the former surrendering themselves as prisoners of war and giving up their captives.

By the treaty of 1868 with the Sioux, the country lying between the northern boundary of Nebraska and the 46th parallel of north latitude, bounded east by the Missouri River and west by the 104th degree of west longitude, together with the reservations then existing on the east side of the Missouri, was set apart for the absolute and undisturbed use and occupation of the Sioux for their permanent home. It also provided that the country north of the North Platte and east of the summit of the Big Horn Mountains should be held and considered unceded Indian territory, upon which no white person should enter without the consent of the Indians first had and obtained. They thus reserved the right north of the North Platte and on the Republican Fork of the Smoky Hill River. The treaty left it to the discretion of the Indian whether he would be a farmer or a nomad, the former living on reservations and receiving a larger annuity. Many naturally preferred to follow the chase. This treaty was the work of the Peace Commission, whose honor as men, as well as the faith of the United States, was pledged to the faithful performance of its stipulations. In less than three months after its ratification came the order of General Sheridan, dated June 29, 1869, declaring all Indians outside the well-defined limits of their reservations to be under the original and exclusive jurisdiction of the military authority, and stating that, as a rule, they would be considered hostile. This unlawful order was executed until December, 1876.

While the Sioux were hunted down and punished from time to time for exercising their right to roam and hunt in the surrendered territory, the whites in large and small bodies passed through and prospected in the forbidden territory, protected by the military. A formidable expedition, in charge of General Custer, left St. Paul in June, 1874, to explore the Black Hills, at which the Sioux were exceedingly incensed. Gold was said to be abundant, and expeditions were soon organized. It was also decided to locate the line of the Northern Pacific Railroad to the south of the Yellowstone. These measures completed the alienation of the Indians, and, depredations upon them having begun, they retaliated. The surveying parties who attempted to run the new line of the railroad were driven off. Early in 1876 there were a large number of trespassers in the Black Hills.

On December 6, 1875, the Commissioner of Indian Affairs, in pursuance of the instructions of the Secretary of the Interior, through the agencies, notified Sitting Bull and other hostile Indians to remove within the bounds of their reservations on or before the 31st of the next month. These Indians were nomads who were hunting in the unceded Indian country under the guarantee of the treaty of 1868. They returned for answer that they were then engaged in hunting buffalo, but that early in the spring they would visit the agency and discuss the points at issue. Although required to repair to the reservations, no food was provided for them had they done so. On the 1st of February, 1876, Sitting Bull and his followers were turned over to the War Department by the Secretary of the Interior, and thus the unjustifiable and impolitic Sioux war of 1876 was inaugurated.

Military operations began in the latter part of February, 1876, General Crook taking the field with about thirteen hundred troops, and sending a part of his command, under General Reynolds, against the band of Crazy Horse. His village was at Bear Buttes, and the Indians were on their way to Red Cloud Agency. They had been delayed here some time by severe weather, as the women and children could not be moved with safety. On the 17th of March Reynolds surprised the village, which he attacked and destroyed. He captured eight hundred ponies, but they were recovered by the Indians next day. The severity of the weather caused the return of the expedition to Fort Fetterman on March 26.

General Crook again marched against the Indians on May 29. On June 17 he encountered the Indians under Sitting Bull. The so-called Battle of the Rosebud ensued, and so skilfully were the Indians handled that General Crook was obliged to retreat. The battle of the Little Big Horn occurred on the 25th, between a portion of the force of General Terry, under General Custer, and the Indians under Sitting Bull. Coming upon a large Indian village, Custer attacked with five companies of the Seventh Cavalry, and his entire command was obliterated. The remaining seven companies, under Major Reno, were nearly surrounded, and fought from two o'clock of the 25th till six o'clock of the 26th. They were relieved by the timely arrival of General Terry's command on the 27th. Our loss was twelve officers and two hundred and fifty-five men killed, two officers and fifty-one men wounded. The Indian force was estimated at from two thousand five hundred to three thousand warriors. They say that their victory was not so much owing to superior numbers as to the exhausted condition of Custer's men and horses, and their advancing into a gorge where they could easily be cut off.

After this disaster various columns of troops visited the Red Cloud, Standing Rock, and Cheyenne River Agencies, and disarmed and dismounted the Agency Indians as a part of the operations supposed to be necessary to settle finally the Sioux difficulties. Colonel Otis, at Glendivi, and Colonel Miles, at Tongue River, had encounters with the Indians, during which over four hundred lodges surrendered. These Indians, who agreed with Colonel Miles to go into the agency, were in fact Agency Indians of the Minneconjou and Sans Arc bands, who had long desired to return home, but were excluded by the order to dismount and disarm them which preceded the expedition of General Crook, and which had caused them to abandon their agencies. They were no part of Sitting Bull's followers. At this time Sitting Bull, in an interview with General Miles, told that officer that he desired peace, but that if troops came out to him he would fight them. He desired to hunt buffalo and to trade, but wanted no rations or annuities, and desired to live as an Indian. He resided peaceably and undisturbed in the queen's dominions until July 10, 1881, when he, with the remainder of his band, surrendered to Major Brotherton, of the Seventh Infantry, at Fort Buford. Sitting Bull was the son of chief Jumping Bull, and was born in 1837, near old Fort George, on Willow Creek, below the mouth of the Cheyenne River. He very early acquired skill and fame both in war and in the chase. The order requiring him to dwell upon an agency was in plain violation of his treaty rights, and the attempt to enforce it was an outrage and a national dishonor. Of a piece with this was the conduct of the government in robbing the peaceable Indians at the agencies of their arms and ponies. Red Cloud was told by the military that it was done by the order of the President. He asked if his Great Father had given such an order, and said, "What have I done, that I should receive such treatment from him whom I thought my friend? My faith in justice being done to the Indians has been destroyed by the course that has been pursued towards these peaceable people."

In November, 1876, General Crook again resumed offensive operations. He sent a column under General McKenzie in pursuit of the Northern Cheyennes, whose village he surprised and attacked on the morning of the 25th. At the first alarm the Indians jumped on their ponies, and were hurrying their squaws and children out of the camp when the troops came upon them. Panic-stricken, they fired a volley and fled, taking refuge among the rocks and ravines, from which they began to fire on the cavalry, then just forming for the attack. Some gained the bluff commanding the camp, while others occupied the upper part of the village, from which they were driven by a cavalry charge. The contest continued all day. Many Indians were killed, and the village, whose population consisted of twelve hundred souls, of whom three hundred were warriors, was burned. Of McKenzie's force eight officers and privates were killed and twenty-five wounded. Eighty thousand pounds of buffalo-meat,—their winter store,—twelve hundred robes, and all their property were burned. Those that escaped were utterly destitute, and the weather was intensely cold.

Let us for a moment examine the status of these Indian wards of the United States. Here was a remote, secluded village, whose inmates had not recently been on the war-path, but who had been engaged in providing their winter stock of food and in preparing for market the hides of the buffalo they had slain. They had no home on any reservation, but had a right to roam and hunt in the country in which they then were. This right was guaranteed to them by the treaty of May 10, 1868. In the agreement of September, 1876, with these and the Sioux Indians, was the pledge that each individual should be "protected in his rights of property, person, and life." The covenants of this agreement were known to Generals Crook and McKenzie and all the military officers in the Sioux country. Such were the circumstances attending this fresh crime against humanity. A portion of the Indians that escaped surrendered to General Miles in the following spring. The chief Hump, their spokesman, handed his belt and gun to the general, and also turned over all his ponies, saying, "Take these: I am no longer chief or warrior." To a newspaper correspondent who asked why he had put himself in hostility to the government, he replied, "I never went to war with the whites. The soldiers began chasing me about, for what cause I do not know to this day. I dodged as long as I could, and hid my village away, but at last they found it, and I had no alternative but to fight or perish."

In May, 1877, Crazy Horse and his band came to Red Cloud Agency. Their wish was to be assigned to some district where they could chase the buffalo and be free. In August, in consequence of some troubles at the agency, the bands of Crazy Horse were dismembered and distributed among other bands, and the chief was arrested and held as a prisoner. He was sent to Camp Robinson September 5, and while being disarmed at the guard-house was stabbed with a bayonet by a soldier, and died in a few hours.

During the year 1878 the services of the army were required against the Bannock Indians, of Oregon, whose acts of violence and final outbreak in June of that year were caused by the insufficiency of food on the reservation. This in turn was owing to the inadequacy of the appropriation made by Congress to the wants of the Indians at a time when they were prevented from supplying the deficiency by hunting. After an arduous pursuit by the United States troops, and several engagements, the hostile Indians were reduced to subjection, and the larger part of them surrendered themselves as prisoners.

The Northern Cheyennes, numbering nine hundred and seventy, were transferred in August, 1877, to the Indian Territory, and turned over to the agent of the Southern Cheyennes and Arapahoes. They were dissatisfied with their new home, refused to affiliate with these Indians, and manifested a repugnance to farming, but strongly desired to return north, where they said they would settle down. Among the disaffected was Dull Knife's band, which had intermarried with the Ogalalla or Red Cloud Sioux and longed to return north and join their friends. On the night of September 9, 1878, this band, more than three hundred in number, left their lodges and started north. There were eighty-seven warriors in the party. They were pursued by the military, and several engagements took place as they passed through Kansas, where they killed settlers, burned houses, and committed other hostile acts. After a journey of six hundred miles, greatly reduced in number, they reached Northern Nebraska, where they surrendered to the troops on condition that they should be taken to Dakota. After two months' imprisonment at Fort Robinson, they were sent back to the Indian Territory, Dull Knife and his warriors protesting that they preferred death to that alternative. It was midwinter, and the cold was intense, and it is stated that as a means of reducing them to submission they were for five days deprived of proper food, clothing, and fuel. Such inhumanity seems incredible. On the evening of January 9, 1879, Dull Knife and his warriors, followed by the women and children, fled from the fort and made for the bluffs, three miles distant. They were hunted down and slain like wild beasts. The surviving women and children, seventy-five in number, were sent to dwell with the Ogalalla Sioux, their relatives, at the Pine Ridge Agency, Dakota.

CHAPTER VI.

ATTEMPT TO REMOVE JOSEPH'S BAND OF NEZ PERCÉS RESISTED—BATTLES OF WHITE BIRD CAÑON AND THE CLEARWATER—PURSUIT OF JOSEPH'S BAND BY GENERAL HOWARD—REPULSE OF GENERAL GIBBON—STAMPEDE OF HOWARD'S PACK-TRAIN—BATTLE OF BEAR-PAW MOUNTAIN, AND SURRENDER OF THE INDIANS TO GENERAL MILES—TROUBLES WITH THE UTES—CESSION OF THEIR LANDS, SEPTEMBER 13, 1873—MURDER OF AGENT MEEKER AT THE WHITE RIVER AGENCY—ATTACK ON MAJOR THORNBURGH'S COMMAND—UTES AGREE TO LEAVE COLORADO AND SETTLE ON A RESERVATION.

In consequence of troubles between the Indians and the white settlers, the government, early in 1877, decided to remove chief Joseph and his band of Nez Percés from their old home in the Wallowa Valley, Oregon,—a strip of country fifty miles broad, following the windings of the Snake River from the Powder River,—to the Lapwai Reservation, in Idaho, where since 1863 the larger part of the tribe, known as "treaty Indians," had resided. Joseph, with about five hundred Indians who had refused to accede to the treaty of 1863 excluding them from their homes, rightfully claimed the valley under the Stevens treaty of 1855, and it had also been conceded to them by President Grant in 1873. Two years later this order was revoked, and "in the interests of peace" General Howard was directed to induce Joseph to remove.

When the commissioners appointed to endeavor to compose the trouble with Joseph's band held a council with them, in 1876, and asked them to abandon their claim to the valley, within which a few whites were settled, that chief said, "I was made of the earth, and grew up upon its bosom. The earth, as my mother and nurse, is too sacred to my affections to be valued by, or sold for, silver and gold. . . . I ask nothing of the President. I am able to take care of myself. I am disposed to live peaceably. I and my band have suffered wrong rather than do wrong. One of our number was wickedly slain by a white man last summer, but I shall not avenge his death. But the voice of that brother's blood, unavenged by me, will call the dust of our fathers back to people the land in protest against this great wrong." At the last moment the chief was thought to be acting in good faith for the removal, when some of the younger Indians opposed to it, and panting for excitement, murdered some white settlers, and he was constrained to go with the current now setting so strongly among his followers in the direction of war.

Hostilities began on June 13. Two companies of cavalry under Captain Perry, sent by General Howard to the scene of disorder, were ambushed and defeated on the 17th at White Bird Cañon, losing one lieutenant and thirty-three men,—one-third of the command. On the 11th of July Howard attacked the Indians in a deep ravine on the Clearwater, near the mouth of Cottonwood Creek, and, renewing the conflict the next day, routed them, capturing their camp and much of their provisions. Twenty-three warriors were killed, a much larger number were wounded, and twenty-three were taken prisoners. Howard's loss was thirteen killed, and two officers and twenty-two men wounded.

On the 17th Joseph began his famous retreat eastward towards the buffalo country, taking the Lolo trail through a pass of the Bitter Root Mountains into Idaho. Followed on the 27th by Howard, the pursuit continued across plains, over mountains, and through forests, most of the way being over a desolate and exceedingly difficult country, for thirteen hundred miles, and lasted seventy-five days. The Indians, accompanied by their women and children, drove along a large herd of ponies, which furnished them with fresh remounts whenever hard pressed. Colonel Gibbon, who with one hundred and fifty men attacked them, August 9, on Wisdom River, Montana, was soon placed on the defensive, and he and his entire command would have been killed or captured but for the approach of Howard. On August 20 Joseph turned upon Howard at Camas Prairie, stampeding and running off his pack-train. On September 13 Colonel Sturgis had a fight with him on the Yellowstone, below the mouth of Clark's Fork. By September 20 the Indians had reached the Missouri River, near Cow Island, and would doubtless have succeeded in their purpose of joining Sitting Bull in the British Dominions had not General Miles been where he could, with his comparatively fresh troops, intercept them. That officer had moved promptly across the country from Tongue River, crossed the Missouri near the mouth of the Mussel-Shell, and on September 30 surprised the Nez Percés in a ravine at Bear-Paw Mountain, near the mouth of Eagle Creek. Making his dispositions to prevent their escape, he fought a bloody and successful battle, winning it before the arrival of Howard. He lost two officers and twenty-one men killed, and four officers and thirty-eight men wounded. The Indians lost six of their leading chiefs and twenty-five warriors, besides forty wounded. On October 5 Joseph and his people, numbering between four hundred and five hundred, surrendered. They were held at Fort Leavenworth until July, 1878, when they were attached to the Ponca Agency, in the Indian Territory.

"Throughout this extended campaign," says General Sherman, "the Indians displayed a courage and skill that elicited universal praise. They abstained from scalping, let captive women go free, did not murder indiscriminately as usual, and fought with almost scientific skill, using advance- and rear-guards, skirmish-lines, and field fortifications." Thus closed one of the most extraordinary Indian wars on record.

Seven different bands of Indians compose the Ute Nation, which formerly roamed over the vast territory embraced in Western Colorado, Eastern Utah, Northern New Mexico and Arizona, and Southern Wyoming. They also followed the buffalo through Eastern Colorado during their periodical hunts, at the risk of war with the Cheyennes and Arapahoes and the Comanche and Kiowa Indians, who claimed as theirs the country over which the great Southern herd of buffalo ranged. The four principal of these bands of Utes are the Uintahs, in Northeastern Utah, estimated at four hundred and thirty souls; the Los Pinos, in the Uncompahgre Valley, two thousand; the Southern Utes, in Southwestern Colorado, nine hundred and thirty-four; and the White River Utes, in Northwestern Colorado, eight hundred. They are among the fiercest and most warlike of the tribes, and occupy a rough and difficult country, whose mineral wealth alone renders it attractive to white settlers. They hunt the bear, elk, and deer of the mountain-region, and will do no work, nor attempt farming. Captain J. Gunnison, U.S.A., while executing a government survey, was murdered by the Utes, with his entire party, on the Sevier River, October 26, 1853.

In March, 1868, N. G. Taylor, Commissioner of Indian Affairs, Alexander C. Hunt, Governor of Colorado Territory, and Colonel Kit Carson, on the part of the United States, concluded a treaty with representative chiefs of these bands, among whom were Ouray, Kinache, and José Maria, by which a large tract of land in Western Colorado was set apart for their "absolute use and occupation," the United States solemnly agreeing that no persons except those authorized by the treaty should ever be "permitted to pass over, settle upon, or reside in the territory described." The Utes agreed to relinquish all claims to any portion of the territory except such as was embraced in the limits defined in the treaty. It was not long before miners began to enter the Ute Reservation and to work the mines. The Utes were uneasy, and in 1871 Ouray asked that a military post be established near the reservation to prevent further intrusion and to expel those unlawfully within it. In July, 1873, a commission consisting of Felix R. Brunot and Nathan Bishop was sent to negotiate with the Utes for the purchase of the reserve. During the conference that ensued, Brunot stated that the intruders could not be kept away. To this Ouray responded with the pertinent question, "Why cannot you stop them? Is not the government strong enough to keep its agreement with us?"

Finally, on September 13, 1873, the commissioners succeeded in making an agreement with the Utes ceding to the United States nearly four million acres of their reservation, comprising the mineral lands. It was, however, stipulated that the Utes should be permitted to hunt on this land as long as the game lasted and the Indians were at peace with the whites, twenty-five thousand dollars per annum to be disbursed or invested, at the discretion of the President, for the use and benefit of the Utes annually forever. It was also stipulated that all the provisions of the treaty of 1868 should remain in force, the prohibitions against unauthorized persons settling upon the reservation being expressly reaffirmed.

With the surrender of this portion of their reservation, the Utes had a right to expect and did expect that they would be relieved from further inroads, and that they would be protected in what was termed the agricultural lands. But it was not so to be, and "ranchmen" soon intruded wherever a good grazing-spot could be found for their stock, and occupied the valleys with their ranches. Early in September, 1879, Mr. Meeker, of the White River Agency, had a difficulty with Chief Johnson about ploughing a piece of land belonging to the Indians, and sent for troops to arrest such

Indian chiefs as were insubordinate, and to afford the agent requisite protection. As soon as the Indians learned that the troops were advancing, they became greatly excited, regarding it as a declaration of war. They requested Major Thornburgh, the commander, to halt his troops, and with five soldiers to come to the agency, where a talk and a better understanding could be had. That officer decided not to comply with this request, and the command entered the Ute Reservation in the afternoon of September 28. On the 29th, Agent Meeker and all his male employees at the White River Agency were killed by the Indians residing there. On the morning of the same day, when about to enter a cañon, and fifteen miles from the agency, Lieutenant Cherry, who had been sent forward with an advance guard to reconnoitre, was fired upon. The fact being communicated to Major Thornburgh, he withdrew his troops and placed them in line of battle, with orders to await the attack of the Indians. The warriors, under Chief Jack, numbering about one hundred, soon delivered a volley, and the battle began. Major Thornburgh, two other officers, eleven citizens, and two soldiers were killed, and forty-one wounded. The Indians admitted a loss of thirty-nine.

A delegation of chiefs and principal men of the Utes visited Washington early in 1880, and by an agreement, dated March 6, and an Act of Congress, approved June 15, consented to remove from the State of Colorado to some other location, on being paid the value of their Colorado lands. George W. Manypenny, Alfred B. Meacham, John B. Bowman, John J. Russell, and Otto Mears were appointed commissioners to secure the ratification and to execute the provisions of the same. Its ratification by three-fourths of the adult males of the tribe having been procured, steps were taken, in September, 1880, to cause the money appropriated to be paid over to the Indians, the portion of the White River Utes to be withheld from that band until the surrender or apprehension of those implicated in the murders at their agency, September 29, 1879.

INDEX.

A.

Abenakis, i. 254, ii. 147, 150.
Acuera's speech, ii. 34.
Adario, a Wyandot chief, i. 401.
Address of Congress to the Six Nations, i. 259.
Agassiz, Professor, i. 28, 132.
Agriculture, ancient Indian, i. 112.
Alabama fort stormed by De Soto, ii. 42.
Alaska tribes, i. 415.
Alden, Colonel Ichabod, killed, i. 263.
Alexander of Pokanoket, ii. 128.
Algonkin language, i. 48.
    tribes, i. 250-338.
Alleghans, i. 275.
Allegory, the hunter's dream, i. 59.
Alligewis, i. 107.
Alvarado, Hernando de, ii. 51.
Amherst, General, i. 201, 212, 222.
Amidas and Barlow explore the American coast, ii. 65.
Andastes, i. 406, ii. 102.
    war with the Senecas, ii. 104.
Annawan, a Pokanoket chief, i. 144.
Antiquities, i. 81-141; garden-beds of Lake Erie, i. 112.
Apaches, i. 416-423; disciplined, ii. 420; massacre of Camp Grant, ii. 421.
Appalachians, i. 86, 337-353.
Aquinoshioni, or Iroquois, i. 382-403, ii. 159-165.
Arapahoes, i. 325.
Arickarees, i. 372, ii. 406.
Armistead, Colonel, in Florida war, ii. 392.
Armstrong, Colonel, destroys Kittanning, ii. 187.
Armstrong, Lieutenant, bravery of, ii. 331.
Arts and industries, i. 64-76, 128-141.
Assegun or Bone Indians, ii. 172.
Assiniboines, i. 369.
Atahentsic, i. 55, 397.
Athabascas, i. 32.
Atkinson, General Henry, ii. 379.
Atotarho, i. 399.
Attakullakulla, ii. 206, 209.
Attasee, battle at, ii. 327.
Atwater, Caleb, theory respecting mounds, i. 98, 107.

B.

Bad Axe, battle of, ii. 379.
Bancroft, H. H., i. 29.
Bannocks, i. 448.
Bartram, William, i. 140.
Bear-Paw Mountain, battle of, ii. 442.
Beaujeu, Captain de, ii. 185.
Beers's defeat, ii. 134.
Bianswah, heroism of, i. 291, 295, 303, 304.
Bienville defeated by the Chickasaws, ii. 157.
Birch Coolie, action at, ii. 417.
Black Duck, i. 312.
Blackfeet, i. 282-284, ii. 406.
Black Hawk's war, ii. 374-379.
Black Hills explored, ii. 437.
Black Hoof, ii. 307.
Black Kettle's camp surprised, ii. 421, 432.
Bloodhounds employed against Indians, i. 35, 130.
Bloody Brook massacre, ii. 134.
Bloody Run, battle of, ii. 216.
Blue Jacket, ii. 307.
Blue Licks, battle of, ii. 284.
Blue Water, battle of, ii. 423.
Boone, Daniel, ii. 282.
Boonesborough attacked, ii. 283.
Boudinot, Elias, assassinated, ii. 407.
Bouquet, Colonel Henry, repulses De Vetrio, ii. 195; at Bushy Run, 219, 420; expedition against Western tribes, 222; makes a treaty with them, 230.
Bowman, Colonel, ii. 284.
Braddock, General Edward, ii. 184.
Bradstreet's expedition against the Northwestern Indians, ii. 222-225.

Brant, Joseph, Mohawk chief, ii. 245, 252, 262, 272, 301.
Brookfield attacked, ii. 134.
Brothertons, i. 322-325.
Brunswick, Maine, burned, ii. 150.
Brush Creek Mound, i. 103.
Buckongehelas, ii. 307.
Buffalo Goad, speech at Boston, ii. 435.
Burgoyne's expedition, ii. 151.
Butler, Colonel John, at Wyoming, ii. 261.
Butler, General Richard, killed, ii. 300.
Butler, Walter, at Cherry Valley, ii. 263.
Butler, Colonel Zebulon, at Wyoming, ii. 261.

C.

Cabeça de Vaca, ii. 20, 30.
Cahokia mound, i. 102.
California tribes, i. 355-360; war with, ii. 414.
Campbell, Major, assassinated, ii. 215.
Canada conquered, ii. 202.
Canassatego, i. 277, 384, 388.
Canby, General E. R. S., assassinated, ii. 436.
Canonchet, capture and death of, ii. 140.
Canonicus's challenge, ii. 89.
Canso surprised, ii. 162.
Captain Jack, Modoc chief, ii. 436.
Captives released by Colonel Bouquet, ii. 230.
Caribs, i. 31.
Carleton, General James H., ii. 420.
Carolina Indians, ii. 111-114.
Curson, Colonel "Kit," ii. 420, 421.
Cartier, Jacques, ii. 21-29.
Carver, Captain Jonathan, ii. 238.
Casa Grande, i. 124.
Cass, Governor Lewis, i. 104, ii. 338.
Castin, Baron de St., ii. 131.
Catawbas, i. 353, 405-409, ii. 111.
Celtic inscriptions, i. 90.
Cession of lands, ii. 382.
Champlain founds Quebec, ii. 87.
Chanco saves Jamestown, ii. 78.
Charles Emathla murdered, ii. 388.
Charlevoix, ii. 168.
Cheraws, i. 409.
Cherokees, language, i. 49; alphabet, 50; nation, 339-341, 407; wars with, ii. 206-210, 278, 279; treaty with, 292, 368, 383; emigration, 349, 400; removal, 383-387, 394; troubles, 406-409, 418, 419.

Cherry Valley devastated, ii. 263.
Cheyennes, i. 325, ii. 424, 430-433.
Chicago massacre, ii. 319.
Chichimecs, i. 36.
Chickasaws, i. 348-350, ii. 41, 157, 292, 373, 402.
Chicora Indians, ii. 58.
Chippewas, i. 34, 284-318; territory explored, 340.
Chippewyans, i. 33, 410.
Chivington, Colonel, at Sand Creek, ii. 424.
Choctaws, i. 347, ii. 292; removal, 399.
Chowan tribe, ii. 70.
Church, Captain Benjamin, ii. 143.
Cibola, seven cities of, ii. 30.
Clarke, General George Rogers, i. 106, ii. 267, 284.
Clarke, General William, ii. 337, 352.
Clay, General Green, ii. 321.
Clinch, General D. L., ii. 387, 389.
Coacoochee captured, ii. 393.
Cocheco burned, ii. 148.
Cochisi, i. 457.
Coe-Hajo, ii. 391.
Coffee, General John, ii. 326, 331.
Colden, Cadwallader, i. 384.
Comanches, i. 434, 451, ii. 384, 420.
Combahees, ii. 11.
Conestogas, ii. 105, 106.
Confederated tribes of the lakes, ii. 296, 301.
Conference with Brant at Niagara, ii. 301.
Congarees, i. 353.
Connecticut tribes, i. 274.
Connewangos, i. 406, 407.
Copper-mining, ancient, i. 116.
Cornplanter, ii. 291.
Corn spirit, legend of, i. 305.
Cornstalk, Shawnee chief, ii. 234, 265.
Coronado, expedition of, ii. 48-56.
Costume, i. 199, 413, 436, 443.
Craven, Governor, defeats the Yamassees, ii. 156.
Crazy Horse, Sioux chief, ii. 437, 439.
Creeks, i. 86, 225, 341-347, ii. 285, 293, 294; war of 1813-14, 324-333, 350; removal of, 362, 399-404; treaties, 350, 362, 372.
Cresap, Captain Michael, i. 39, ii. 233.
Crook, General George, i. 23, ii. 437, 438.
Crow Indians, i. 374.
Cumming, Sir Alexander, ii. 156.
Cunningham's Island antiquities, i. 119.
Cusic, David, Iroquois chronicler, ii. 90.
Custer, General George A., destroys Black Kettle's village, ii. 431; defeated and slain, 438.
Customs. *See* Manners and Customs.

D.

Dade, Major, defeat of, ii. 388.
Dakotas, i. 144, 228-237, 364-382.
Dalzell, Captain, defeated and slain, ii. 217.
Dare, Virginia, ii. 72.
Dartmouth College, origin of, i. 323, 324.
De Ayllon, Lucas Vasquez, ii. 10.
Deerfield burned, ii. 134, 149.
Delawares, i. 276-282, ii. 108-110, 201, 264; reservation invaded, 414.
Deluge, Chippewyan tradition of, i. 411.
Denison, Captain George, ii. 140.
Denonville, i. 402, ii. 147.
De Soto, Hernando, expedition of, ii. 30-47.
Detroit, ii. 153, 164; besieged, 214-217.
Dieskau, Baron, defeated, ii. 189.
Digger Indians, i. 432, 448.
Dighton Rock inscription, i. 88.
Dignefios, i. 358.
Donnacouna, ii. 28, 29.
Doolittle, Senator J. R., i. 23.
Downing, Major, surprises Cheyennes, ii. 424.
Drake, Sir Francis, ii. 69, 71.
Ducoign, Baptiste, i. 107.
Dudley's defeat, ii. 321.
Dull Knife, Cheyenne chief, ii. 440.
Dunmore's expedition, ii. 234, 235.
Dutch and Indian wars, ii. 83, 161.

E.

Eliot, John, i. 253, 261, 268, ii. 91.
Elk-Mountain Utahs, i. 445.
Elkswattawa, the Prophet, i. 54, ii. 313, 367.
Emigration, progress of, ii. 344.
Employment of Indians in war, i. 248, 258, 318.
Enotochopco, battle of, ii. 330.
Erie tribe, i. 118, 403; wars of, 405.
Estevan put to death, ii. 49.
Estill's defeat, ii. 284.
Evans, Lieutenant-Colonel, attacks Comanches, ii. 433.
Evils of our Indian system, i. 23.
Explorations of Indian country, ii. 339.

F.

Fetterman massacre, ii. 426.
Fire Nation, i. 319; origin of, 398.
Five civilized tribes, i. 338.
Flat-Mouth, i. 304, 312.
Florida, i. 9, 16, 30; war, ii. 387-394.
Floyd, General John, ii. 327, 328.
Forbes's expedition, ii. 196.
Forsythe's fight with Cheyennes and Sioux, ii. 430.
Fort Ancient, i. 102; Dade, capitulation of, ii. 391; Duquesne, ii. 182, 196; Harrison attacked, ii. 319; Henry defended, ii. 266; Hill, Elmira, i. 101; Laurens, ii. 269, 270; Loudon, massacre at, ii. 209; Massachusetts captured, ii. 163; Meigs besieged, ii. 321; Michilimackinac taken, i. 216; Mims massacre, ii. 325; Niagara taken, ii. 201; Pitt besieged, ii. 211; Sandusky captured, ii. 213; Stanwix besieged, ii. 252; William Henry taken, ii. 190.
Fortifications, i. 126.
Foster, Professor J. W., i. 20, 132.
Fox tribe, i. 297, 306.
Franklin, Benjamin, ii. 85.
French settlements and posts, ii. 167-177; policy with the tribes, 168.
Frontenac, Count de, ii. 148, 169.

G.

Gage, Colonel Thomas, ii. 185, 222.
Gallatin, Albert, i. 48, 49.
Gansevoort, Colonel, at Fort Stanwix, ii. 252.
Garces, Father Francisco, i. 455.
Garfield, President, policy of, i. 25.
Gaspé Indians, ii. 26.
Gatschet, Albert S., i. 48, 50.
Geological changes, i. 139.
Gibbon, General John, i. 24, ii. 442.
Gila Apaches, i. 419.
Girty, Simon, ii. 266.
Gladwyn, Major, defends Detroit, ii. 213.
Goffe, the regicide, ii. 143.
Gosnold, Bartholomew, ii. 74.
Gourgues, Dominic de, ii. 61.
Granganameo, ii. 65, 70.
Grant, Major James, ii. 196, 209.
Grave Creek Mounds, i. 95, 110.
Greenville, Sir Richard, ii. 66, 69.
Greenville, treaty of, ii. 306.
Gros Ventres, i. 372.
Guess, George, invents Cherokee alphabet, i. 50.
Guristersigo defeated and killed, ii. 285.

450 *INDEX.*

H.

Hadley attacked, ii. 143.
Hagler, king of the Catawbas, i. 409.
Halleck-Tustenugge, ii. 393.
Hancock, General, destroys a Cheyenne and Sioux village, ii. 426.
Hardin and Truman killed, ii. 302.
Harmar, Colonel Josiah, defeated, ii. 296, 297.
Harney, General, surprises a Sioux village, ii. 423.
Harriot, Thomas, his account of the Virginia Indians, ii. 68.
Harrison, General William H., ii. 309, 315, 322.
Hatfield attacked, ii. 135, 143.
Haverhill burned, ii. 149.
Hawkins, Colonel Benjamin, i. 105.
Hayden, Professor, i. 31.
Hendrick, King, ii. 188, 189.
Henry, Dr. Charlton, i. 417.
Herkimer, General Nicholas, ii. 253–256.
Hertel de Rouville, ii. 148, 149.
Hiawatha, ii. 160.
Hildreth, Dr. S. P., i. 101.
Hillabee towns destroyed, ii. 327.
Hirrihigua, ii. 17.
Hobbs's fight at Number Four, ii. 164.
Hochelaga, ii. 29.
Holmes, Major A. H., ii. 334.
Holyoke, Captain, at Turner's Falls, ii. 142
Hou Yost's stratagem, ii. 256.
Hopkins, General, expedition of, ii. 320.
Horseshoe, battle of, ii. 331.
Houghton, Dr. Douglass, i. 135.
Howard, General O. O., ii. 442.
Hualapais, i. 458.
Hudson explores New York, ii. 81–83.
Hull, General William, surrenders Detroit, ii. 320.
Hurons, i. 400.

I.

Illinese tribe, i. 313.
Indian, affinity with Mongolian type, i. 29.
    agriculture, i. 71, 112.
    antiquities, i. 81–141.
    architecture, i. 122.
    arts and industries, i. 64–76, 128–141, 177–182.
    Bureau, i. 24, ii. 351.
    coins, i. 72.
    compared with the Asiatic, i. 44.
    demonology, i. 208.
    doctrine of metempsychosis, i. 42.
    fortifications, i. 126.
    languages, i. 31, 47–50.
    literature, i. 51.
    magic, i. 156–163.
    maize plant, i. 61, 72, 116.
    manitos, i. 43, 139, 207.
    manners and customs, i. 40, 149, 164–237, 449, 450; of the Apaches, 421; Chippewyans, 411–415; Comanches, 435–444; Creeks, 225; Dakotas, 229; Kenistenos, 332–338; Massachusetts tribes, i. 249–253, ii. 93; Navajoes, i. 425–428; Ojibwas, i. 226; Shoshones, i. 432; Virginia tribes, ii. 67.
    medas and jossakeeds, i. 154–163.
    medical knowledge, i. 76–80.
    mental and physical traits, i. 36–38.
    meteorology, i. 43.
    migrations, i. 83–87.
    myths, i. 27, 33, 55.
    oratory, i. 38–53.
    organization and government, i. 248–250.
    origin of, i. 27–36.
    origin of the name, i. 137.
    ossuaries, i. 218.
    pictography, i. 61–63.
    policy of the United States, i. 23, 287–293.
    population, i. 26.
    religion and mythology, i. 142–162.
    songs, i. 51–53.
    sports and pastimes, i. 190–199.
    superstitions and omens, i. 42, 206.
    theology, i. 32, 41.
    totems, i. 178, 245.
    trade, i. 236–238, ii. 308.
    wrongs and abuses, i. 23.
Indian Territory, i. 26, 339, ii. 382.
Iowas, i. 380.
Iroquois, or Aquinoshioni, theology, i. 41; myths and traditions, 55, 56; customs, 218–225; history, 382–390, ii. 160–166, 273–278; treaties, 288–292.

J.

Jackson, General Andrew, subdues the Creek Nation, ii. 326–35.
Jacobs, Delaware chief, killed, ii. 198–200.
Jamestown settled, ii. 75.
Jefferson's Indian policy, ii. 308.
Jesup, General T. L., in Florida war, ii. 391.
Jicarilla Apaches, i. 424.

Johnson, Sir John, ii. 250, 277, 278.
Johnson, Colonel Richard M., ii. 322.
Johnson, Sir William, ii. 178, 184, 188, 189, 193, 198 -200, 202, 223, 236, 250.
Joseph, chief of the Nez Percés, ii. 441.
Jumonville defeated and slain, ii. 183.

K.

Kahquas, or Andustes, i. 406.
Kaskaskias, i. 330, ii. 44.
Kaws, or Kansas Indians, i. 382, ii. 382.
Keene, New Hampshire, attacked, ii. 163.
Kekeewin inscriptions, i. 62.
Kenistenos, i. 286, 331-338.
Kickapoos, treaty of 1832, ii. 373.
Kicking Bird, i. 451.
Kiowas, i. 452, ii. 421.
Kirkland, Rev. Samuel, i. 395.
Kittanning destroyed, ii. 187.
Klamaths, i. 356, 357.
Kondiaronk, i. 401.

L.

Lake George, battle of, ii. 188.
La Loutre invests Annapolis Royal, ii. 163.
Lancaster, Massachusetts, burned, ii. 138.
Lane, Ralph, i. 67; explores Virginia, 70, 71.
Lathrop's defeat, ii. 134.
Laudonnière, René de, ii. 59.
Lawson, John, account of the Congarees, i. 353.
Le Bœuf, Fort, captured, ii. 215.
Lenape, i. 276, ii. 108-110.
Lewis, Colonel Andrew, ii. 234.
Lewis and Clarke's exploring tour, ii. 309.
Lipans, i. 419.
Little Big Horn battle, ii. 438.
Little Crow, Sioux chief, ii. 417, 418.
Little Raven, Arapahoe chief, ii. 435.
Little Turtle, Miami chief, ii. 303, 304.
Logan, Tah-ga-yu-ta, i. 39, ii. 233, 234.
Logan, Colonel Benjamin, ii. 284.
Long Cane, settlement destroyed, ii. 207.
Long Prairie battle, ii. 304.
Louvigny defeats the Outagamies, ii. 165.
Lovewell's fight, ii. 151.
Lyttleton, Governor W. H., ii. 206.

M

Mackenzie, Colonel R. S., ii. 422, 438.
Maine tribes, i. 254.
Manabozho, i. 56, 308.
Mandans, i. 289, 370, ii. 406.
Manhattans, i. 81, 83.
Manners and customs, i. 164-237.
Maricopas, i. 458.
Marietta mounds, i. 95, 101.
Marlborough, Massachusetts, burned, ii. 139.
Maryland Indians, ii. 96.
Mascoutins, i. 319, ii. 173.
Mason and Brent's expedition, ii. 101.
Mason, Captain John, ii. 116.
Massachusetts colonized, i. 88.
  tribes, 251-254.
Massacre at Gnadenhütten, ii. 281.
Massacres in Virginia, ii. 77, 78.
Massasoit, ii. 88.
Maumee Rapids, battle at, ii. 304.
Maury, M. F., i. 36.
Mauvilla, battle at, ii. 39.
McGillivray, General Alexander, i. 346, ii. 293.
McIntosh, General W., ii. 362.
Meadow Indians, i. 321.
Medfield burned, ii. 139.
Menendez, Pedro de, ii. 60.
Menomonies, i. 286, 328.
Mercer, Hugh, ii. 187.
Mescalero Apaches, i. 419, 424.
Metea, Pottawatomie chief, ii. 345.
Miami, Fort, captured, ii. 214.
Miamis, i. 326, ii. 298, 405.
Miantonomo, ii. 89.
Micanopy, Seminole chief, ii. 391.
Michigamies, i. 313.
Michilimackinac captured, ii. 212.
Micmac and Marechite tribes, ii. 163.
Miles, General Nelson A., ii. 436, 442.
Minnetarees, ii. 372.
Minnisink battle and massacre, ii. 271.
Mississagies, i. 286, 390, 404.
Mississippi River discovered, ii. 42.
Missouri Indians, i. 357.
Modocs, i. 330, 361, ii. 436.
Mohaves, i. 457.
Mohawks, i. 400.
Mohicans, i. 274, ii. 115, 245.
Monacans, ii. 80.
Mondamin, feast of, i. 194.

452 INDEX.

Mongolian type, affinity of Indian with, i. 29.
Monroe, President, removal policy of, ii. 353.
Monseys, i. 217.
Montcalm, ii. 190.
Moutezuma, i. 454.
Montgomery, Colonel, attacks the Cherokees, ii. 49.
Moore, Governor James, ii. 154.
Moquis, i. 455.
Moravian Delawares massacred, ii. 281.
Morgan, Daniel, ii. 185.
Morgan, Lewis H., i. 87, 111.
Mormon outrages, i. 448.
Moscoso succeeds De Soto, ii. 45.
Mound-Builders, i. 30, 107-112.
Mounds, i. 41, 95-111.
Munroe, Colonel, surrenders Fort William Henry, ii. 191.
Muscogees. *See* Appalachians.
Muskigoes, i. 286.
Mystic, Fort, destroyed, ii. 118.

N.

Nadowaqua, story of, i. 175.
Nauticokes, ii. 98.
Narragansetts, i. 273; their fort captured by General Winslow, ii. 137.
Narvaez, Panfilo de, ii. 16.
Natchez tribe, i. 148, 351, ii. 45, 160.
Nauset tribe, i. 251.
Navajoes, i. 75, 424-428, 455, ii. 420.
Nemattanow, the invulnerable, ii. 77.
Nepissings, i. 284, 286.
Neuter Nation, i. 405.
New Hopkinton surprised, ii. 152.
New Mexico tribes, i. 416-444.
Newport ruin, i. 92.
Newport's colony in Virginia, ii. 74.
New River, General, i. 409.
New York Indians, i. 399, ii. 84.
Nez Percés war, ii. 441, 442.
Niantics, i. 273.
Ninigret, ii. 140.
Nipmucks, i. 251, 261.
Niza, Marcus de, ii. 48.
Noble, Colonel Arthur, defeated and slain, ii. 163.
Norridgewocks, i. 255; surprised, ii. 152.
Norton, Rev. John, "the redeemed captive," ii. 163.
Nottaways, ii. 79.
"Number Four," Fort defended, ii. 163, 164.

O.

Occum, Rev. Samson, i. 323.
Oconostata, ii. 206.
Odawas, i. 286, 320.
Oglethorpe, Gen. James, i. 345, ii. 158.
Ohio, settlement of, ii. 295, 296.
Ohio Company, ii. 180.
Ojibwas, or Chippewas, i. 237; history of, i. 284-318; cede their lands, ii. 401.
Okeechobee, battle of, ii. 391.
Omahas, i. 380.
Oneidas, i. 390-397, 400, ii. 277, 289.
Oneida stone, i. 93, 390.
Onondagas, i. 397-400.
Onondaga sepulchral stone, i. 110.
Opechancanough, ii. 77.
Opothleholo, Cherokee chief, ii. 418.
Oregon tribes, i. 360-62.
  war with, ii. 415.
Oreybe, i. 454.
Origin of the Indians, i. 27-36.
Oriskany, battle of, ii. 254-256.
Ortez, Juan, i. 33.
Osages, i. 382, ii. 400.
  traditions of, i. 58.
Osceola, Seminole chief, ii. 389-392.
Ossuaries, i. 218.
Otoes and Missourias, i. 329.
Ottawas, i. 329, ii. 172, 385.
Ouantenon, Fort, captured, ii. 216.
Outagamies, or Foxes, i. 306, ii. 164.
Oyster River settlement destroyed, ii. 148.

P.

Pacific coast tribes, i. 355-363.
Pah-Utes, i. 446.
Pah-Vants, i. 445.
Papagos, i. 458.
Parrow-a-kifty, i. 434.
Passaconnaway, i. 261, 264-273, ii. 146.
Paugus, Pequawket chief, slain, ii. 151.
Pawnees, i. 329.
Paxton Boys massacre Conestogas, ii. 106.
Peace Commissioners of 1866, ii. 425, 427, 428.
Penn, William, founds Pennsylvania, ii. 119, 120.
Pennacooks, i. 251, 260-272, ii. 146.
Penobscots, ii. 163.
Pensacola captured, ii. 335.

INDEX.   453

Peorias, i. 330.
Pequawkets, ii. 151.
Pequots, i. 274, ii. 93, 115-121.
Philip, King, war with, ii. 125-145
Piankeshaws, i. 329.
Pickens, General Andrew, ii. 279.
Pictography, i. 61-63.
Piegan massacre, ii. 434.
Pierce, Captain, defeated and slain, ii. 139.
Pike, Z. M., exploring expedition of, ii. 309.
Pilgrims land at Plymouth, ii. 89.
Pillagers, i. 286, 300, 310.
Pimos, i. 458.
Pitt, Fort, besieged, ii. 319, 320.
Pi-Utes, i. 362, 446.
Pocahontas, ii. 76.
Point Pleasant, battle of, ii. 232, 233.
Poisoners, i. 294.
Pokanokets, i. 251.
Poncas, i. 380.
Ponce de Leon, ii. 9.
Pontiac, war with, ii. 210, 229.
Population, Indian, ii. 237-239, 241, 242.
Port Royal (Annapolis) taken, ii. 149.
Pottawatomies, i. 58, 286, 330, ii. 373, 403.
Powell's fight with Red Cloud, ii. 426.
Powhatan, ii. 75.
Presque Isle, fort at, captured, ii. 215.
Proctor, General Henry, ii. 321, 322.
Pueblos, i. 75, 452-457.
Putnam, General Rufus, i. 101.

Q.

Quapaws, i. 329, 382, ii. 44, 400.
Quinnipiacs, i. 274.

R.

Raisin River, defeat at, ii. 321.
Rale, Father Sebastian, i. 255, ii. 149-151.
Raleigh, Sir Walter, ii. 64.
Red Cloud, Sioux chief, i. 367, ii. 426-438.
Red Jacket, i. 389, ii. 291.
Rehoboth burned, ii. 139.
Religion and mythology, i. 142-162.
Removal policy, i. 22, ii. 361, 369, 370.
Report of Indian Commissioners, ii. 428, 429.
Reservations such in name only, i. 22.
Rhode Island Indians, ii. 273, 274.
Ribault, Jean, ii. 57.

Richardville, John B., i. 327
Riggs, Rev. S. R., i. 48.
River Rouge mound, i. 102.
Rogers, Major Robert, ii. 204.
Rogue River Indians, i. 356, 361.
Ross, John, Cherokee chief, ii. 394, 407-409, 418.

S.

Saco tribe, i. 255-260.
Sacrifice of a Sioux girl, i. 211.
Sacs and Foxes, i. 331, 375, ii. 375, 402.
Sagima, Ottawa warrior, ii. 172.
Saginaws, i. 286, ii. 404, 405.
Salmon Falls burned, ii. 148.
Sampitches, i. 445.
Sand Creek massacre, ii. 424.
Saratoga destroyed, ii. 163, 164.
Sassacus, Pequot chief, i. 274, ii. 94, 119, 120.
Satanta, Kiowa chief, i. 451.
Saulteurs, i. 286.
Scalps, Indian, bounty offered for, ii. 150.
Scandinavian explorations, i. 88.
Scarooyadi, the Half-King, ii. 180.
Schenectady burned, ii. 148.
Schoharie Valley devastated, ii. 278.
Schoolcraft, H. R., ii. 35, 346, 375.
Schurtz, Carl, i. 24.
Scott, General Charles, ii. 298, 304.
Seminoles, i. 350, ii. 372, 387-393, 399.
Senecas, i. 400, ii. 147, 291, 400.
Seven Cities, tradition of the, i. 35, ii. 48.
Sewee tribe shipwrecked, i. 353.
Shawnees, i. 33, 221, 222, ii. 187, 245, 264, 292.
Shelby, Colonel Isaac, ii. 322.
Sheridan, General, ii. 430, 437.
Shikellimo, i. 180.
Shingabawassin, ii. 348.
Shirley, Governor, war of, ii. 162-164.
Shorikowani, Mohawk chief, i. 405.
Shoshones, or Snakes, i. 429, 430.
Sibley, General H. H., ii. 417, 418.
Sioux (see Dakotas), i. 85, ii. 415-418, 426.
    war of 1876, ii. 437.
Sitting Bull, Sioux leader, ii. 438.
Skeleton in armor, i. 92.
Skenandoa, i. 392.
Slavery among the Southern Indians, ii. 293.
Smallpox ravages on Western tribes, ii. 406.
Smith, Edmund P., i. 24.
Smith, Captain John, ii. 76.

Waxhaws, i. 408.
Weas, i. 330.
Weatherford, Creek leader, ii. 324–332.
Weber Utes, i. 445.
Westbrooke, Captain, surprises the Norridgewocks, ii. 150.
Wheelock, Rev. Eleazer, i. 323.
Wheelwright, John, Indian deed, i. 265.
Whipple, Lieutenant A. W., i. 358.
White, John, colonizes Virginia, ii. 72.
Wichitas, i. 451.
Williams, Colonel Ephraim, ii. 189.
Willett, Lieutenant-Colonel, sortie of, ii. 255.
Wingina, ii. 67–71.
Winnebagoes, i. 374, 380, ii. 403, 404, 410.
Winslow, General Josiah, attacks the Narragansetts, ii. 136.
Withlacoochee, battle of, ii. 389.
Wood Lake, battle of, ii. 417.

Worth, General William J., closes the Florida war, ii. 392–394.
Wyandot Hurons, i. 400, ii. 171, 266, 292, 296, 306.
Wyoming massacre, ii. 261.

Y.

Yamassee war, i. 355, ii. 154, 155.
Yampa Utahs, i. 445.
Yogowanea, queen of the Eries, i. 404.
Yumas, i. 356, 358, 458.

Z.

Zane, Elizabeth, heroism of, ii. 267.
Zuñi, i. 454.
    captured by Coronado, ii. 50.

THE END.

Song of the Okogis, i. 53.
Soug-uk-um-ig, i. 304, 305.
Sowahageus, i. 269.
Sports and pastimes, i. 194-199.
Spotted Tail, i. 367.
Springfield attacked, ii. 134.
St. Augustine founded, ii. 60.
St. Clair, General Arthur, ii. 295, 299.
St. Leger, Colonel Barry, ii. 251, 252.
St. Pierre, Chevalier de, ii. 181.
St. Regis tribe, ii. 171.
Stevens, Captain Phinehas, ii. 163, 164.
Stockbridge tribe, i. 254, ii. 409.
Striking the post, i. 189.
Sudbury fight, ii. 139.
Sullivan, General John, ii. 273-275.
Sumner, Colonel E. V., defeats the Cheyennes, ii. 423.
Sun-worship, i. 40, 147-150, 191, 352.
Susquehannocks, ii. 96, 98-102, 107.
Swan, Major Caleb, on the Creeks, ii. 344-347.
Sycamore Creek, skirmish at, ii. 377.

T.

Talcott, Major John, ii. 144.
Talladega, battle of, ii. 326.
Tanacharisson, ii. 180, 181.
Tarhe, ii. 307, 314.
Tarratines, i. 255.
Tash Utahs, i. 444.
Taylor, General Zachary, ii. 319, 391.
Tecumseh, ii. 311, 319, 321-324.
Teton fortifications, i. 86.
Thames, battle of the, ii. 322.
Thayendanagea, 245.
Thompson, General, killed, ii. 389.
Thornburgh, Major, killed, ii. 444.
Three Nations make a treaty, ii. 99.
Timpanagos, i. 445.
Tinneh tribe, i. 416.
Tippecanoe, battle of, ii. 315.
Tobacco, i. 40, 83, ii. 68, 71.
Tohopeka, battle of, ii. 331.
Tonkawas, i. 420.
Tonto Apaches, i. 419, 423.
Topinabi, ii. 307.
Totems, i. 178, 245.
Trade, Indian, i. 236-238, ii. 308.
Traditions, i. 31-36, 56-58.

Treaties, Paris, ii. 202; Southern tribes, 210, 292, 319, 361, 363, 368, 372; (Payne's Landing), 372, 390; (New Echota), 383; Fort Stanwix, 288, 289; Fort McIntosh, 292; Fort Harmar, 296; Greenville, 306; Northwestern tribes, 337, 365, 373; with Chippewas (1836), 401; Fort Gibson (1833), 390; Fort Laramie, 423; Fort Wise, 424.
Tullushatches, battle of, ii. 326.
Turner's Falls, battle of, ii. 142.
Tuscaloosa, the Black Warrior, ii. 38.
Tuscarawas, i. 400, ii. 155.

U.

Uchees, ii. 93, 116.
Uinta Utahs, i. 445, 446.
Uncas, ii. 93, 116.
Upsarokas, or Crows, i. 374, ii. 406.
Utahs, i. 444-448.
Ute troubles, ii. 442.

V.

Van Schaick, Colonel, expedition against the Onondagas, ii. 271.
Verazzani, John de, ii. 13.
Victoria, Apache chief, ii. 422.
Vincennes and Kaskaskia captured, ii. 268.
Virginia Indians described, ii. 65.
  exterminated, ii. 78.
Vitachucco, ii. 35.

W.

Wabashaw's speech, i. 54, 55.
Wabenos, i. 161.
Wacoes, i. 420.
Wadsworth, Captain, defeated at Sudbury, ii. 139.
Walker, Utah chief, i. 447.
Wampanoags, ii. 126.
Wampum, i. 72-74, 385.
Wanalancet, i. 267.
Wapaconequet, ii. 300.
War weapons and customs, i. 70, 157, 185, 188, 218.
Warfare, i. 184.
Washington, ii. 169, 180, 181, 183.
Washington Territory tribes, i. 362.
Waub o-jeeg, i. 297, 306.
Wayne, General Anthony, defeats Guristersigo, ii. 285.
  defeats the Western Indians, ii. 302-304.

www.ingramcontent.com/pod-product-compliance
Lightning Source LLC
Chambersburg PA
CBHW021425300426
44114CB00010B/659